MW00985382

THE HANDBOOK OF STUDENT AFFAIRS ADMINISTRATION

THE HANDBOOK OF STUDENT AFFAIRS ADMINISTRATION

FOURTH EDITION

George S. McClellan,
Jeremy Stringer
and Associates

A Wiley Brand

Published by Jossey-Bass
A Wiley Brand
One Montgomery Street, Suite 1000, San Francisco, CA 94104-4594-www.josseybass.com

Jossey-Bass books and products are available through most bookstores. To contact Jossey-Bass directly call our Customer Care Department within the U.S. at 800-956-7739, outside the U.S. at 317-572-3986, or fax 317-572-4002.

Wiley publishes in a variety of print and electronic formats and by print-on-demand. Some material included with standard print versions of this book may not be included in e-books or in print-on-demand. If this book refers to media such as a CD or DVD that is not included in the version you purchased, you may download this material at http://booksupport.wiley.com. For more information about Wiley products, visit www.wiley.com.

Library of Congress Cataloging-in-Publication Data is Available:

ISBN 978-1-118-70732-6 (hardback)
ISBN 978-1-119-10183-3 (ePDF)
ISBN 978-1-119-10189-5 (ePUB)

Cover design by Wiley

Cover Image: © ProVectors/iStockphoto

Printed in the United States of America
FOURTH EDITION
HB Printing   10 9 8 7 6 5 4 3

CONTENTS

LIST OF FIGURES, TABLES, AND EXHIBITS

Figures

Tables

Exhibit

NASPA—STUDENT AFFAIRS ADMINISTRATORS IN HIGHER EDUCATION

NASPA is the leading association for the advancement, health, and sustainability of the student affairs profession. We serve a full range of professionals who provide programs, experiences, and services that cultivate student learning and success in concert with the mission of our colleges and universities. Established in 1918 and founded in 1919, NASPA comprises of fourteen thousand members in all fifty states, twenty-five countries, and eight US territories.

Through high-quality professional development, strong policy advocacy, and substantive research to inform practice, NASPA meets the diverse needs and invests in realizing the potential of all its members under the guiding principles of integrity, innovation, inclusion, and inquiry. NASPA members serve a variety of functions and roles, including the vice president and dean for student life, as well as professionals working within housing and residence life, student unions, student activities, counseling, career development, orientation, enrollment management, racial and ethnic minority support services, and retention and assessment.

For more information about NASPA publications and professional development programs, contact:

NASPA—Student Affairs Administrators in Higher Education
111 K Street NE, 10th Floor
Washington, DC 20002
202-265-7500
office@naspa.org
www.naspa.org

PREFACE

This is the fourth edition of the *Handbook of Student Affairs Administration* (HSAA4). Like its predecessors, HSAA4 is intended to serve as a practical and informative resource for those interested in the student affairs profession. Drawing on both the classic and contemporary literature of the field, and making use of case studies and examples from a diversity of institutional settings, HSAA4 includes information on the administrative environment of student affairs, organizational and administrative models of student affairs, core competencies needed by professionals, professional development models, and current and future issues facing the profession.

The handbook is organized in seven broad constructs, the first six of which mirror those in previous edition. The seven constructs are

1. Contexts of professional practice
2. Frameworks of professional practice
3. Students: the reason for our professional practice
4. Human resources in professional practice
5. Interpersonal dynamics in professional practice
6. Skills and competencies of professional practice
7. Looking back and looking forward in professional practice

Although it shares a similar organizational structure to the previous version, the fourth edition of the *Handbook for Student Affairs Administration* includes a number of changes in content. The chapters on governance, pursuing a doctoral degree, programming, and facilities have been set aside for a number of new chapters. These include chapters on student affairs as teaching and learning; student success; helping students prepare for lives of purpose; intercollegiate athletics, recreation, and student-athletes, friend raising and fund raising; and changing roles and responsibilities in student affairs. In addition, the recurring chapters have been revised and refreshed to include an emphasis on emerging student populations, changes in technology, and contemporary legal and policy issues.

Another tradition of the *Handbook of Student Affairs Administration* is the quality of its contributing authors. The authors in this edition include the profession's most prominent scholars and practitioners as well as some its outstanding emerging voices. The contributors reflect the diversity of student affairs with regard to personal characteristics, professional experience, and institutional setting.

Audience

HSAA4 is written to meet the needs of entry-, mid-, and senior-level student affairs practitioners. It will also be helpful to those entering the profession from the faculty, administrative realignment, and other pathways. Finally, it serves as a resource for graduate students and graduate faculty in college student affairs or higher education programs.

ACKNOWLEDGMENTS

We owe a tremendous debt of gratitude to the authors who have generously contributed their energies and insights to this handbook. You are a truly remarkable group of scholars and practitioners, and working with you has been both an honor and a pleasure.

We are grateful to Erin Null, Alison Knowles, and Shauna Robinson from Jossey-Bass, who have been encouraging, helpful, and supportive travel companions on this journey. We also thank Peggy Barr, Mary Desler, and David Brightman for their contributions to the success of this handbook over the years.

We acknowledge the support we received from NASPA and the NASPA staff, particularly Gwen Dungy and Kevin Kruger, as we planned for our work on this edition. NASPA has been a partner throughout the handbook's history, and we are delighted to continue the tradition of having a portion of the proceeds from sales support the NASPA Foundation.

George McClellan is thankful to his colleagues at Indiana University Purdue University Fort Wayne (IPFW), particularly the incredible Student Affairs and Enrollment Management team, for their dedication to the success of students. Thanks also to Chancellor Vicky Carwein for her support of his professional and scholarly activities and to Danita Davis for her warm smile, encouraging words, and gentle reminders of where to go and when to be there. Jeremy Stringer thanks Seattle University for employing him for more than three decades and allowing him to follow his passions, which sometimes turned out to be different than either party could have predicted thirty years ago. His work on this volume was eased by the approval of a year-long sabbatical, for which he is most grateful.

Jeremy Stringer is deeply appreciative of the opportunity to work in higher education, a circumstance made possible by his loving parents who provided him with the gift of a college education. We can only imagine how our world would be different if everyone could be so fortunate. He is especially thankful for the love and support of his wife, Susan, and his three incredible daughters, Shannon, Kelly, and Courtney. George McClellan is thankful for the friendship and support of Steve Grud, Jason Laker, Peter Lake, Joe Minonne, and the combined Practical Theater/Riffmaster and the Rockme Foundation nation. He is also thankful to the inventors of the Don Dog, the dollar menu, and deep dish pizza.

Finally, we thank both our students and our colleagues in student affairs. Students are the reason we do what we do, and they have taught us both so many wonderful lessons along the way. We are awed and honored that you continue to allow us to be a part of the pursuit of your dreams. As for our professional colleagues, we are grateful that you share our passion for serving students and for the ways in which your work inspires and informs our own. It is our most sincere hope that this handbook will help you serve students and therefore help students to be successful.

George S. McClellan
Jeremy Stringer

THE AUTHORS

Josie Ahlquist is a nationally recognized speaker on digital identity and leadership, and her research explores the intersection of digital communication technologies and leadership. Her blog, which focuses on higher education, social media, and leadership, is available at http://www.josieahlquist.com. Follow her on Twitter at @josieahlquist.

Victor Arcelus is the dean of student life at Connecticut College. He has worked in higher education for more than fifteen years. He has recently contributed to *Contested Issues in Student Affairs: Diverse Perspectives and Respectful Dialogue* and *Campus Housing Management*.

Margaret J. Barr is professor emerita in the School of Education and Social Policy at Northwestern University and is retired vice president for student affairs at that same institution. She is the author, coauthor, editor, or coeditor of numerous chapters and books. Among her most recent works are *Making Change Happen in Student Affairs: Challenges and Strategies* (with George S. McClellan and Arthur Sandeen); *Budgets and Financial Management in Higher Education* (with George S. McClellan), and the *Handbook for Student Affairs Administration* (second edition with Mary Desler). She was named by NASPA as a John T. Blackburn Distinguished Pillar of the Profession.

Stan Carpenter is dean of the College of Education at Texas State University, where he was previously the chair of the Counseling, Leadership, Adult Education, and School Psychology Department. He has served as the executive director of the Association for the Study of Higher Education (ASHE) and as editor/chair of the ACPA Media Board, as well as on the NASPA Board of Directors and the NASPA Foundation Board. He is author or coauthor of more than one hundred articles, chapters, and other works, most recently on professional development in student affairs and on scholarship as an ethos for student affairs.

Linda M. Clement is the vice president for student affairs at the University of Maryland, where since 1974 she has served in a variety of roles. Clement was a Trustee and Chair for The College Board and has authored numerous journal articles and book chapters, as well as her own book, *Effective Leaders in Student Services: Voices from the Field.*

Michael D. Coomes is Associate Professor Emeritus of Higher Education and Student Affairs at Bowling Green State University. He is the editor of three volumes in the Jossey-Bass New Directions for Student Services series, coauthor of numerous national and international higher education journal articles, and codeveloper of the Student Affairs History Project (http://www2.bgsu.edu/colleges/library/cac/sahp/). He is the recipient of the 2013–14 Master Teacher of the Year award from Bowling Green State University.

Anita Crawley is the chief student services officer for the California Community College Online Education Initiative Launch Team. Her book, *Supporting Online Students: A Guide to Planning, Implementing, and Evaluating Services,* was published in 2012.

Pamela C. Crosby is coeditor of the *Journal of College and Character.* A Milken Family National Award Educator, she is a former high school teacher and department chair, past associate editor of the *American Journal of Theology and Philosophy,* and past chief editor of the *Character Clearinghouse.*

Jon C. Dalton is emeritus professor of Higher Education and former vice president for student affairs at Florida State University. He served as president of NASPA and was an ACPA Senior Scholar. He serves as coeditor of the *Journal of College and Character.*

Zebulun R. Davenport serves as the vice chancellor for student life at Indiana University Purdue University Indianapolis. He is coauthor of *First-Generation College Students–Understanding and Improving the Experience from Recruitment to Commencement* (with Lee Ward and Michael Siegel) and has also contributed chapters to other publications.

Tracy L. Davis serves as professor in the Department of Educational and Interdisciplinary Studies at Western Illinois University, where he also coordinates the College Student Personnel Program. In 2011 he began serving as founding director of the Center for the Study of Masculinities and Men's Development. His most recent authored and edited books include *Advancing Social Justice: Tools, Pedagogies, and Strategies to Transform Your Campus* (with Laura Harrison), *Masculinities in Higher Education: Theoretical and Practical Considerations* (with Jason Laker), and the *ASHE Reader: Critical Perspectives on Gender in Higher Education* (with Rebecca Ropers-Huilman, Ana Martínez Alemán, Susan Marine, and Kelly Winters).

Tiffany J. Davis is a teaching assistant professor at North Carolina State University, where she also serves as coordinator of the Higher Education Master's Program. Davis's research reflects her desire to conduct research that helps practitioners do their work in the most effective way possible, and it examines the process we use to prepare student affairs professionals.

David Eberhardt currently serves as the vice president for student development at Birmingham-Southern College. His scholarly interests have focused on the ethical and spiritual development of college students, and he has written for and serves as an editor for the *Journal of College and Character*.

Shannon Ellis is vice president of student services at the University of Nevada, Reno. She served as president of NASPA and has edited and authored numerous publications including *Dreams, Nightmares and Pursuing the Passion: Personal Perspectives on College and University Leadership; Strategic Planning in Student Affairs; The Association of Governing Board's Student Affairs Committee Handbook;* and *Exceptional Leadership: SSAO Strategies and Competencies for Success.*

Nancy J. Evans retired from Iowa State University, where she was professor in the School of Education and coordinator of the masters program in student affairs. She served as president of ACPA-College Student Educators International and has been honored by ACPA with the Contribution to Knowledge Award. She was named an ACPA Annuit Coeptis Senior Professional and Senior Scholar. She is a member of the *Journal of College Student Development* editorial board and past editor of *ACPA Books and Media.*

Joy Gaston Gayles is an associate professor of higher education at North Carolina State University. Her research focuses on the college student experience and how those experiences affect desired outcomes of undergraduate education, most notably for student athletes as well as women and under-represented minorities in STEM fields. She has been published in the *Journal of Higher Education, Research in Higher Education,* and the *Journal of College Student Development.* In addition, she serves on the editorial board for the *Journal of College Student Development.*

Janice Gerda is the director of residence life at Case Western Reserve University and teaches at Kent State University. She has worked in student affairs for more than twenty-five years, previously as a member of the communities of Grinnell College, the University of Virginia, and Bowling Green State University.

Sean Gehrke is a doctoral candidate and researcher in the Pullias Center for Higher Education at the University of Southern California. His research focuses on organizational issues in higher education regarding social networks, leadership, and organizational change, as well as how the college environment and student experiences influence learning and development. His research has been published in the *Journal of College Student Development and Educational Policy,* as well as several book chapters in edited volumes relating to leadership and college student spirituality.

Stephanie A. Gordon is the vice president for professional development at NASPA – Student Affairs Administrators in Higher Education. Her research interests include retention and persistence of first- generation and underrepresented student populations, as well as mental health and wellness within the context of student learning and success.

Kevin R. Guidry is the senior research analyst in the Center for Teaching & Assessment of Learning at the University of Delaware. He has been conducting research in students' and student affairs professionals' use of technology for more than a decade. His blog is available at http:// mistakengoal.com, where you can also find his contact information.

Joan B. Hirt is professor of Higher Education Administration in the Department of Educational Leadership and Policy Studies at Virginia Tech. She has also served as the interim director of the School of Education and Interim Dean of the College of Liberal Arts and Human Sciences at the University.

Mary Howard-Hamilton is a professor of Higher Education in the Department of Educational Leadership at Indiana State University. She has authored or coauthored numerous articles, chapters, and books. Her areas of research are multicultural identity development and diversity issues in higher education.

Andy Howe has more than twenty years of professional experience in private and public universities and community colleges in student affairs, academic affairs, and retention initiatives. His professional interests, research, and experience include strategic planning, assessment and evaluation, student learning and support technologies, diversity and inclusion, and organizational change.

Adrianna Kezar is a professor of higher education and codirector of the Pullias Center for Higher Education at the University of Southern California. Kezar is well published with fourteen books, more than seventy-five journal articles, and more than one hundred book chapters and reports. Her recent books include *How Colleges Change, Enhancing Campus Capacity for Leadership,* and *Recognizing and Serving Low Income Students.*

Jillian Kinzie is the associate director for the Center for Postsecondary Research and the National Survey of Student Engagement (NSSE) Institute at Indiana University Bloomington. She is coauthor of *Student Success in College: Creating Conditions that Matter,* and *One Size Does Not Fit All: Traditional and Innovative Models of Student Affairs Practice.* She is on the editorial board of the *Journal of College Student Development.*

Susan R. Komives is professor emerita in the Student Affairs Program at the University of Maryland after forty-three years in student affairs. She is past president of the Council for the Advancement of Standards in Higher Education (CAS) and of the American College Personnel Association (ACPA). She served as vice president of two colleges and is the author or editor of a dozen books or monographs, including *Student Services: A Handbook for the Profession, Exploring Leadership, Leadership for a Better World,* and the *Handbook for Student Leadership Development.* She is the 2012 recipient of the ACPA Life Time Achievement Award and the 2013 Leadership and Service Award from the Association of Leadership Educators.

Linda Kuk currently serves as the program chair for the Higher Education Leadership Program in the School of Education at Colorado State University and is an associate professor of Education. Prior to her return to the faculty in 2006, she served as the vice president of Student Affairs at Colorado State University, her alma mater. Kuk is the coauthor or coeditor of three books: *Positioning Student Affairs for Sustainable Change, New Realities: Emerging Specialist Roles and Structures in Student Affairs Organizations;* and *The Handbook for Student Affairs in Community Colleges.* She has published more than twenty-seven articles in referred journals, as well as numerous book chapters and presentations.

Jason Laker is a professor of Counselor Education (and former vice president) at San José State University. His scholarly work includes two edited texts regarding gender and men's development, one each in the United States and Canada; and two texts coedited with colleagues in Spain and Croatia focused on the role of postsecondary institutions in fostering citizenship and democratic education, comparing the contexts of Eastern and Western Europe, and North America.

John Wesley Lowery is department chair and professor in the Student Affairs in Higher Education Department at Indiana University of Pennsylvania. He is a frequent speaker and author on topics related to student affairs and higher education, particularly legislative issues and student conduct, on which he is widely regarding as a leading expert.

Marilee Bresciani Ludvik is professor of Postsecondary Educational Leadership at San Diego State University, where she coordinates the certificate in institutional research, planning, and assessment, and the doctorate in community college/postsecondary education leadership. Her research focuses on outcomes-based assessment, program review effectiveness, and the role of intuition in evidence-based decision making.

Peter Magolda is a professor in Miami University's Student Affairs in Higher Education Program. His scholarship focuses on ethnographic studies of college subcultures and critical issues in qualitative research. He is coeditor of *Contested Issues in Student Affairs* and *Job One 2.0: Understanding the Next Generation of Student Affairs Professionals.* Magolda is the author of books, chapters, and journal articles on a variety of topics related to student affairs.

Sherry L. Mallory serves as dean of student affairs of Revelle College at the University of California, San Diego, and is an adjunct faculty member at San Diego State University. She has worked in the field of higher education for nearly twenty years as a faculty member and administrator at the University of Arizona, University of Arkansas, and Western Washington University.

George S. McClellan serves as the vice chancellor for Student Affairs at Indiana University–Purdue University Fort Wayne (IPFW). He is a member of the editorial board for NASPA's *Journal of College and Character* and served in a similar role for a number of years for ACPA's *Journal of College Student Development.* In addition to collaborating on a number of articles and chapters, McClellan is coauthor or coeditor of *Making Change Happen in Student Affairs: Challenges and Strategies* (with Margaret J. Barr and Arthur Sandeen); *The Handbook for College Athletics and Recreation Management* (with Chris King and Don Rockey); *Stepping Up to Stepping Out: Preparing Students for Life after College* (with Jill Parker); *The Handbook for Student Affairs Administration* (third edition, with Jeremy Stringer); *Budgets and Financial Management in Higher Education* (with Margaret Barr); *In Search of Safer Communities: Emerging Practices for Student Affairs in Addressing Campus Violence* (with Peggy Jablonski and colleagues); *Ahead of the Game: Understanding and Addressing Campus Gambling* (with Tom Hardy and Jim Caswell); and *Serving Native American Students in Higher Education* (with Maryjo Tippeconnic Fox and Shelly Lowe).

Michele C. Murray is vice president for student development at Seattle University. Murray serves on several executive boards, including the Jesuit Association of Student Personnel Administrators and the Center for Women. With Robert Nash, she coauthored both *Helping College Students Find Purpose: The Campus Guide to Meaning Making* and *Teaching College Students Communication Strategies for Effective Social Justice Advocacy.*

Robert J. Nash has been a professor in the College of Education and Social Services, University of Vermont, Burlington, for forty-five years. He has published more than 110 refereed articles, fifteen books, and numerous book chapters, monographs, and essay book reviews. He is a member of the editorial board for the *Journal of Religion & Education* and a regular contributor to *About Campus.*

Dale Nienow is executive director of the Center for Ethical Leadership, a nonprofit that builds leadership to advance the common good. He co-led the national Kellogg Leadership for Community Change program on behalf of the W. K. Kellogg Foundation and served on the Seattle University Student Development Master's Degree Program Advisory Board and as senior adjunct instructor.

Anna M. Ortiz is professor and department chair of Educational Leadership at California State Long Beach. She has worked in higher education as an administrator and faculty member for thirty years. Her research interests include ethnic identity, Latino/a college students, professional development of faculty and student affairs administrators, and multicultural understanding. She has authored or edited numerous publications, including *Ethnicity in College.*

Brett Perozzi is the associate vice president for student affairs at Weber State University. He currently serves as the chair of NASPA's International Advisory Board and has written book chapters, articles, and monographs on international education and student affairs.

Enrique Ramos is a former national director for student affairs at the Tecnológico de Monterrey in México. He served as a member of the NASPA board of directors and has written articles on student affairs.

Jessica J. Ranero-Ramirez is the coordinator of the Transition Center at Del Mar College in Corpus Christi, Texas. She has a passion for equity, access, social justice, and student success.

Tony Ribera is the director of program evaluation at Indiana University School of Medicine. In this role, he oversees the statewide evaluation of the medical school curriculum and facilitates the various institutional processes to review and use assessment and evaluation data. His research interests include how student affairs professionals are prepared to collect and use evidence of teaching and learning.

Claire K. Robbins, assistant professor of higher education at Virginia Tech, has published more than ten articles, book chapters, and other publications She has more than ten years of experience in higher education and student affairs administration, research, and teaching at public and private colleges and universities.

Arthur Sandeen served as vice president for student affairs and as professor of educational leadership at the University of Florida. He is the author of numerous articles, chapters, and books. Among his recent books are *Making Change Happen in Student Affairs: Challenges and Strategies* (with Margaret J. Barr and George S. McClellan); *Enhancing Leadership in Colleges and Universities;* and *Enhancing Student Engagement on Campus.* A past president of NASPA, in 2001, he was the recipient of the John L. Blackburn Distinguished Service Award from the NASPA Foundation.

John H. Schuh is director of the School of Education and distinguished professor of educational leadership and policy studies at Iowa State University.

Schuh is the author, coauthor, or editor of more than 235 publications, including 28 books and monographs, 75 book chapters, and more than 110 articles. Among his books are *Assessment Methods for Student Affairs, One Size Does Not Fit All: Traditional and Innovative Models of Student Affairs Practice* (with Kathleen Manning and Jillian Kinzie), and *Student Success in College* (with George D. Kuh, Jillian Kinzie and Elizabeth Whitt).

Terrell L. Strayhorn is professor of higher education at The Ohio State University, where he also serves as director of the Center for Inclusion, Diversity & Academic Success (iDEAS) and chief diversity officer in the College of Education and Human Ecology. He has authored eight books, more than a hundred journal articles and chapters, and presented more than two hundred keynotes, conference papers, and sessions. He is editor of *Spectrum: A Journal on Black Men* as well associate editor of both the *NASAP Journal* and *Journal of Higher Education.*

Jeremy Stringer is professor emeritus of Student Development Administration at Seattle University. He founded the Student Development Administration program at Seattle University, and served as program director for its first two decades. He has been a vice president of student affairs, an associate provost, both an academic and student affairs department chair, led a university-wide strategic planning process, and chaired the NASPA Faculty Fellows. He is coeditor, along with George S. McClellan, of the *Handbook of Student Affairs Administration* (third edition).

Aurélio Manuel Valente serves as dean of students and associate vice president of academic affairs at Governors State University and is the chief student affairs officer (CSAO) for the university. His research interests include student development in the first year of college and institutional efforts to promote student engagement and academic success.

Lori Varlotta serves as president of Hiram College. Prior to being named to that position, she was the senior vice president for planning, enrollment management, and student affairs at California State University, Sacramento. Varlotta has written and presented extensively on issues such as strategic planning and outcomes-based budgeting, transparency and accountability, retention and graduation, and student health and wellness.

Stephanie J. Waterman, Onondaga, Turtle clan, is a faculty member in Leadership, Adult, & Higher Education in the Ontario Institute for Studies of Education at the University of Toronto. She formerly taught at the University of Rochester, Warner School of Education & Human Development. She is a coeditor of *Beyond the Asterisk: Native Students in Higher Education*, with Dr. Heather Shotton and Shelly C. Lowe. She has publications in the *Journal of American Indian Education*, the *Journal of Student Affairs Research and Practice*, the *Journal about Women in Higher Education*, and the *Urban Review*.

Penelope H. Wills serves as president of Yavapai College. Prior to her arrival in Arizona, Wills was the president of Northeast Iowa Community College. Her career includes various leadership positions in higher education at the state, regional, and national levels. She has extensive experience in such fields as economic development, assessment, planning, student development, and quality improvement.

David F. Wolf is vice president for advancement at the University of North Texas. Prior to joining his alma mater, Wolf served as executive director for individual giving at UCLA, vice president for advancement at the University of Southern Mississippi, assistant vice president and director of athletic development at the University of Alabama, vice president for development at Cameron University, and director of development at the University of Texas at Arlington. Wolf also serves as a lecturer and faculty member speaking and conducting research on donor behavior and university advancement organizational leadership

Eugene L. Zdziarski II is vice president of student affairs at DePaul University. He has worked in the field of higher education for more than thirty years. Zdziarski has edited and authored publications including *Crisis Management: Responding from the Heart; Campus Crisis Management: A Comprehensive Guide to Planning, Prevention, Response and Recovery*; and *In Search of Safer Communities: Emerging Practices for Student Affairs in Addressing Campus Violence*.

THE HANDBOOK OF STUDENT AFFAIRS ADMINISTRATION

PART ONE

CONTEXTS OF PROFESSIONAL PRACTICE

Student affairs administration is situated in historical, institutional, environmental, economic, political, and national contexts. These contexts shape and in turn are shaped by our work as professionals. We begin our conversation about student affairs by examining several of these contextual dimensions. In chapter 1, Michael Coomes and Janice Gerda trace the historical development of the student affairs profession from its earliest iterations to the present day. They show how the profession has remained true to the essential goal of helping all students get the most from their college experience by adapting to new students, new institutional forms, and new imperatives. Joan Hirt and Claire Robbins, in chapter 2, focus our attention on the various milieus in which student affairs is practiced. They describe the impact of various institutional types and unique institutional missions on professional practice. In chapter 3, Jillian Kinzie and Victor Arcelus provide an overview of environmental theories applicable to higher education, outline approaches for assessing the conditions for student learning and success, and discuss the importance of assessing the impact of college environments on student success. The ability of students to attend college and to succeed in obtaining a college degree is often strongly influenced by economic conditions. In chapter 4, John Schuh describes the economic implications of demographic and social trends and the impact of legislative initiatives and state support on higher education and its students. In recent years fiscal pressures on higher education have resulted in stronger calls for institutional accountability. Sherry Mallory and Linda Clement discuss the implications of the accountability movement for the practice of student affairs in chapter 5. The final contextual piece in this first part of the handbook is the international perspective offered by Brett Perozzi and Enrique Ramos in chapter 6. They relate how the concepts of globalization and internationalization affect the practice of student affairs and share models of how student affairs is practiced in various international settings.

CHAPTER ONE

"A LONG AND HONORABLE HISTORY"

Student Affairs in the United States

Michael D. Coomes and Janice J. Gerda

Student affairs is a profession with a long and proud history of service. Today's student affairs professionals walk in the footsteps of women and men who, for more than 100 years, have loved learning so much that they dedicated their lives to colleges and universities and to their students. With creativity and grit, they quietly pushed the larger enterprise to adapt to new students and imagined better things in the service of students and the mission of a college or university. At its core, student affairs is the work of helping each and every student get the most out of his or her unique college experience.

It does not stop there, however. The ability of students to thrive and graduate is a short-term goal. As a profession, student affairs strives for nothing less than to change the world for the better. Although most student affairs work is done in the context of the college years, its goal is to be a catalyst for lifelong growth and curiosity, for worldwide citizenship and care for one another, and for a more just and humane society for generations to come. This work is done through seemingly mundane, day-to-day teaching moments and the very down-to-earth sharing of the student experience. All of the college experience is a learning lab for life. It is this paradox of audacious limitless goals and right-now pragmatism of the present that ties together student affairs professionals through its history.

To be sure, all good teachers care deeply about the educational experiences of their students. In that sense, student affairs shares its mission with the faculty. But over time, as higher education expanded, some positions were created that called for someone whose primary purpose was to step back and view both students and the college experience as a whole rather than in the context of a specific course or discipline. So, student affairs professionals are specialists in a larger universe of teachers and helpers. Not all who help students are student affairs professionals, but all student affairs professionals have as their primary purpose helping students.

In this chapter, we lay out some of the stories of those who have contributed to the development of student affairs as a profession. We also tell the story of how the profession has remained committed to its goal of helping all students realize the most from their higher education experience while adjusting to new students, new institutional forms, and new learning imperatives. We encourage readers to dig deeply into student affairs' professional history and values and write their own version of our profession's story.

Time proceeds linearly; however, stories do not. This is especially the case of a story as complex as the development of a profession. Rather than one event leading clearly to another, events occur sequentially, concurrently, and recursively. The image of a tree with many roots helping to develop a trunk and a trunk supporting many branches may be a better metaphor for the story we tell in this chapter than that of a river that flows inexorably from source to sea. Our story does not unfold in strict chronological order because we have focused our attention on how the work of serving students has changed over time—different sources of influence have shaped that work at the same point in time. Rather than leaving one story to join another for the sake of chronological consistency, we have decided to complete the different story lines and present the facts in nonchronological sequence.

The First Student Affairs Professionals

When did student affairs start? This is a natural question, and a deceptively difficult one. Because we have retroactively named and defined this profession, we can not simply look up what those in the past wrote. We must make some judgments about what fits our definition and identify our professional ancestors from the perspective of the present. So, in the past, who on a college campus did the job of helping students to get the most out of their college experiences?

For much of the history of American higher education, colleges and universities were very small communities with student bodies that numbered in the dozens or hundreds. For example, in 1770, 413 students were enrolled at Harvard College and 338 were enrolled at Yale (Thwing, 1906). The small number of faculty members and the president or a few other administrators could easily facilitate the entirety of the whole student experience (Leonard, 1956). More important, their students were very much like younger versions of themselves (that is, male, White, and Christian), and imagining what it might be like to be a student was a fairly easy and intuitive activity.

In 1833, the leaders of Oberlin College started a daring experiment. They decided to admit women and men, and in 1835 they expanded their experiment in equality by admitting African American students. Although today we might imagine that the African American men had unique needs, what stood out then was the new idea of a woman college student. Suddenly, faculty and other leaders could not just rely on their own personal experience to intuit what a student needed. As women students entered more colleges, and some colleges were founded just for them, male leaders were at a loss to decipher the mysteries of what women students needed. To solve this problem, a number of presidents began to create positions largely filled by women who would focus only on women students and their needs. Some of the first titles for these positions were preceptress and lady principal (Gerda, 2007).

At first, the most obvious unmet needs to be addressed by these new women administrators were social, such as how to protect women students from the kinds of social errors that could ruin their reputations for life, or how to maintain the expectations of restrictive and modest clothing with the need to study and live in the college community. But over time these early professionals and their students made it clear that the deeper issues of available career paths, employment opportunities, and mentoring were also factors in whether or not women students got the most out of their college experience (Nidiffer, 2000).

By the 1890s, the women who filled these positions were increasingly well educated and were given roles pertaining to the academic needs of women students so that they could address issues beyond just the social. To reflect this broadening of responsibilities, the title of dean of women was created. In 1892, President William Rainey Harper of the University of Chicago tapped Alice Freeman Palmer (then president of Wellesley College) to be the dean of women, signaling the prestige and importance of the position. Palmer negotiated to begin the job with an associate, Marian

Talbot, who ultimately crafted the position and set a standard for the many deans of women across the country. In a 1910 speech, Gertrude Martin of Cornell University remarked, "I am sure that it was the University of Chicago that really made it fashionable, though her dean of women was by no means the first" (Martin, 1911, p. 66). The position proliferated.

At about the same time that the University of Chicago was implementing the position of dean of women, another prestigious university was redesigning ways to think about the student experience as a whole. Harvard University did not have women students. It did, however, have women graduate students, and they had new and different needs from the men of the college. In 1890, President Charles Eliot decided he could not manage student relations and his burgeoning responsibilities for faculty, finances, and facilities, so he created a position titled dean of the college and appointed the well-respected and beloved faculty member LeBaron Russell Briggs to the position. Briggs's primary responsibilities were to attend to undergraduate student needs (as opposed to focusing on subject matter or teaching) making him unique at Harvard for his focus on students (Findlay, 1938).

The appointment of many deans of women across the country and Briggs's appointment as dean of the college at Harvard prompted a re-examination of the needs of male students (Findlay, 1938). Men could see the advantages that women students gained from having an advocate, and administrators elsewhere wanted to emulate Harvard's model. As the twentieth century began, some institutions tapped a faculty member who already had a student orientation to focus on the student experience as a whole. Thomas Arkle Clark, an English professor at the University of Illinois, had already gladly worked on student life projects. In 1901, President Andrew Sloan Draper began to formalize some of those roles, and Clark would become legendary for his oversight of the men of Illinois. In 1909, he was given the title of Dean of Men (Fley, 1978; Gaytas, 1998; Schwartz, 2010).

The Beginnings of a Profession

These early student affairs pioneers conducted their important work of helping students "face the academic rigors and social freedom of campus life" individually and independently (Schwartz, 2010, p. 3). However, what establishes a profession as a profession is not the work of any single person (regardless of how professionally that work has been conducted), but rather the desire of a group of individuals to work collectively to establish, maintain, and enhance a professional identity. This work includes deciding who is allowed to claim membership, set expectations for members, study the nature of the work, and set long-term goals. In student affairs, the first collective meeting of professionals we can find took place on November 3 and 4, 1903, when eighteen women met on the campuses of the University of Chicago and Northwestern University to talk about their work (Gerda, 2007).

Most of the attendees of this meeting were deans of women, but some were there because their college had not yet appointed a dean and so they were doing the work until that happened. They talked about ideas, concerns, and topics in ways that probably seem very familiar to today's student affairs professionals. A few topics surprise, showing that 100 years does change some things, but the bedrock issues included safe on-campus housing that was conductive to academic work, good health, self-governance and equity among the student community, and building alliances with (and judicious independence from) national sororities and religious organizations that shared a mission of helping students. Just as important, they clearly found support, solace, and renewal in each other's company as they shared their challenges. At the end of the meeting, they voted on a set of resolutions that represented their collective opinion about best practices, and made plans to meet regularly ("Minutes," 1903). Although vastly simpler than the association activity of student affairs today, the basic components of this meeting happen at student affairs conferences today. For inaugurating collective professional activity and for setting a tone of collegiality that carries through student affairs to this day, the 1903 Conference of Deans of Women of the Middle West is remembered as the birth of the profession of student affairs (Gerda, 2007).

A New Approach: Deaning

If the first approach to student affairs work was the pragmatic social tutelage provided by lady principals and preceptresses, then the first big new idea was the concept of *deaning*. The president of Oberlin, when giving advice to the University of Michigan as it explored creating a position of dean of women, said she should be a "wise and pious matron" (Holmes, 1939, p. 6; Nidiffer, 2000, pp. 16–17). The new dean model required a woman who was an academic in her own right. This allowed a dean of women to advocate for students as a scholar and teacher, but more important to act as a peer to faculty and other administrators (Mathews, 1915). Deans of women often reported directly to the president, and they worked closely together to do the politically delicate work of changing higher education to better fit women students in a time when coeducation was still being hotly debated. The Association of Collegiate Alumni (ACA), an organization for women who had graduated from college, pushed colleges and universities not only to create the dean of women position, but also to make sure the job description had the high standards needed for the position to be valued and respected. They withheld valuable membership and "refused to recognize and recommend an institution which did not have a dean of women who qualified under the Association standards" (Iva L. Peters, as cited in Findlay, 1938, p. 28). All together, this set the bar very high for prospective deans, and institutions invested great resources in national searches for candidates. Public universities in the Midwest were among the first to fully invest in this new idea, while others simply appointed a woman faculty member to perform some of the functions. Deans at women's colleges and coordinate colleges had different challenges, but their work was similar enough that they joined to share professional improvements and speak as a group to presidents. From 1903 to 1922, the Conference of Deans of Women refined the idea of deaning, producing scholarship, mentoring and teaching new deans, and spreading best practices with their higher status in the academy (Gerda, 2007).

The proliferation and success of the position of dean of women spurred a slightly later but parallel version of the deaning approach. In the early twentieth century, society (and by extension, higher education) had very different expectations of men than of women. This affected how each was educated. So, although deaning approaches were developed for both women and men students, they took on slightly different flavors. James Findlay (1938) has suggested that the development of the position of dean of men usually came as a direct result of the position of Dean of Women, and at least at its inception was intended to provide parallel services and advocacy for male students.

However, the men who filled these positions held different statuses and therefore did the work differently than did deans of women. By virtue of their gender and because many of them were already faculty members at the institution when they were appointed, they were more able to function as insiders to the core group of administration and faculty. Their work was less about advocating for men as a group and more about advocating for individual men who were struggling because of a lack of funds, a family emergency, youthful indiscretions, or peer pressure. Deans of men worked through force of personality, functioning as wise uncles shepherding older boys into manhood (Schwartz, 2010). They met one on one with students for personal consultations and saw fraternities and athletics as allies in their goals. Presidents and boards needed someone to discipline male students when they misbehaved and charged the dean of men position with taking care of conduct issues. However, for the most part the deans of men resisted the role of disciplinarian as antithetical to the familial mentor personae they wished to project (Schwartz, 2010).

We know about these approaches because in 1919, a group of deans of men founded a professional association (the Conference of Deans and Advisors of Men) to share their challenges and ideas. The first meeting was spurred by their mutual relief that World War I had ended. The Student Army Training Corps (SATC) was finally leaving their campuses, and student life could once again be guided by the principles of deaning. It was a casual and collegial group of carefully selected colleagues who gathered in Madison, Wisconsin, but they kept near-verbatim records that allow us to almost hear their discussions even today. Their organization still exists, much changed, as NASPA: Student Affairs Administrators in Higher Education.

Together, the development of the positions of dean of women and dean of men constitute an approach we call *deaning*, enacted by a collection of professionals others (for example, Rhatigan, 2009) have called *early deans*. From the early deans, the profession retains the goals of advocacy for struggling students, the pragmatic focus on individual student crisis response, and the desire to address all the basic needs of students with little staff and few resources.

A New Approach: Vocationalism

Even as deaning spread and strengthened, a new idea was developing and slowly making an impact on student affairs work. The vocational movement was the effort to use scientific psychological principals to match students with their best possible jobs and career paths. Frank Parsons is considered the founder of vocational psychology in the United States and was the author of the 1909 book *Choosing a Vocation* (Hoff, Kroll, MacKinnon, & Rentz, 2004). Vocational work was an ideal theory base for student affairs, and it translated into the pragmatic administrative work of placement.

The deans of women, in particular, adopted this approach as a large part of their work, perhaps because of the challenges of helping young alumnae to plan and implement careers. Some deans of women became vocationalists, and some vocationalists from outside academe became deans of women. What we might now call "career services" became a significant part of the work of higher education in general, and of the work of student affairs professionals in particular. It did not replace deaning but altered and added to it. The work became more organized and scientific and required more knowledge of the world of work beyond college. Academic expertise and experience in history or chemistry became less useful to a student affairs professional than expertise in psychology, business, sociology, or even teacher placement.

In 1913, this need for different expertise led a small group of deans of women to approach the faculty at Teachers College, Columbia University, to ask about creating a curriculum that would help them draw from new and different disciplines to be better prepared for the new kind of work. This resulted in the first degree program in student affairs targeted at "special training exclusively on a graduate level, designed to train 'deans, and advisors of women'" (Lloyd-Jones, 1950, p. 262). This interdisciplinary program employed faculty members with backgrounds in psychology, home economics, family relations, religious education, and the problems of youth (Lloyd-Jones, 1950). In 1914 a course in vocational guidance was offered, and the Teachers College bulletin listed a course in "Dean of Women in Colleges and Normal Schools" (LaBarre, 1948). In 1928, the academic department changed its name from Deans and Advisors of Women and Girls to Student Personnel Administration. By 1945, fifty-three personnel work graduate degree programs had been developed that offered some courses preparing personnel workers for employment on college campus; five of these (Cornell University, Mount Holyoke College, University of Pittsburgh, Radcliffe College, and Southern Methodist University) offered courses only for those seeking employment in a college or university. In total, 105 universities had personnel preparation programs preparing practitioners for elementary, secondary, or higher education. An additional seventy-seven colleges and universities offered graduate training in personnel work in such noneducation fields as business, government, industry, religious life, rehabilitation, social work, and psychological services (LaBarre, 1948).

In 1916, some of the same women who pushed for the creation of the Teachers College deaning degree began a new professional association, called the National Association of Deans of Women (NADW). From its inception, it was a large, structured organization, which grew rapidly as it brought together a wider constituency. Seeking influence through open membership rather than exclusivity, organization leaders invited as speakers and participants anyone who was doing the work or related work. In contrast to the early deans, the new members of NADW included women deans from two-year colleges and normal schools, high school deans, vocational bureau directors, government officials who worked with career issues and education, and faculty who studied vocational choice. Notably, they actively sought male speakers and experts who could add to the discussion (Gerda, 2004). This openness eventually extended to inclusion of professionals of color such as Lucy Diggs Slowe, Dean of Women at Howard University, whose steadfast challenge to segregation led to some of the profession's earliest self-struggles with social justice and inclusion based on race and ethnicity (Miller & Pruitt-Logan, 2012). More so than the deaning associations and their meetings, the conferences of the NADW resemble the national student affairs conferences and conventions of today. The NADW continued with a strong vocationalism bent, then adopted many of the principles of the next big idea, *student personnel*, and other new approaches after that. It grew, shifted its mission, and changed its name several times, all while playing the role of one of three major student affairs associations throughout the twentieth century. In 2000, as a result of a significantly smaller membership base, brought about to some degree by a confusing and unclear mission and the cooptation of women educators who worked in higher education by other organizations, the organization disbanded (Gangone, 2008).

We have chosen to discuss vocationalism as its own new approach, but it really became a force when a new approach called student personnel came on the scene. Student personnel used all of the core ideas of vocationalism plus a broader approach to higher education (indeed, administration as a whole). Although vocationalism can be seen as a sub-idea of student personnel, it remains in student affairs today as the functional area of career services and as a part of many student affairs administrative units.

A New Approach: Student Personnel

Student personnel is arguably the most powerful and influential idea to have been brought into the student affairs profession. It was more than just an idea or even an approach; it was referred to by its proponents as a Movement (with a capital M) and was part of the larger Personnel Movement that permanently changed the direction of other professions, including business management, military operations, and human resources. The student personnel idea was so influential when it arrived that the whole profession adopted the term as its name from the 1920s until the 1970s. Even today, you will find that publications, graduate degree programs, and job titles have or recently had the term *student personnel* in their official names (ACPA: College Student Educators International, 2012).

To understand student personnel, it is necessary to retrace our steps and examine ideas that were shaping other fields when student affairs was still creating and refining deaning. In the 1890s, Walter Dill Scott was studying in the relatively new field of psychology as it applied to business. He noticed that some men were better salesmen than others, not because of differences in training, but because of their personalities and natures (Wright & Dimsdale, 1974). He developed a set of questions that could help an employer determine which men would be better salesmen even before they were hired, saving an employer money, time, and supervisory effort (Biddix & Schwartz, 2012; Lynch, 1968). Scott was not the only person exploring ways that the science of psychology could make industry more efficient, but he spread his ideas through consulting and recruited a number of other people to spread his ideas. They developed a larger scheme of personnel through the use of scientific psychology, intelligence and personality testing, time studies, and efficiency analyses, which matched the right person with the right job.

During World War I, Scott observed the way that the British military assigned its soldiers to tasks; he thought it was inefficient and could benefit from personnel principles. When the United States entered the war, Scott approached US military leadership and offered his services as a consultant. They were skeptical at first but soon adopted personnel as a philosophy for sorting and assigning soldiers to the work that needed to be done. In retrospect, Scott's more efficient assignment process has been credited with nothing less than American success in World War I (Mathews, 1937).

When the war ended and the soldiers came home, the idea of personnel was very quickly applied to colleges and universities. Former military officers took positions on campuses and began to organize student life in a way that was far more efficient and able to manage the large number of students then flooding higher education. Scott himself aided the movement by accepting an offer to become president of Northwestern University, where he not only implemented student personnel, but also actively promoted it across the nation (Biddix & Schwartz, 2012). Building on commonalities with vocationalism and layered over the basics of deaning, student personnel rapidly became the driving conceptual framework for student affairs.

In 1924, personnel workers under the leadership of May Cheney adopted the constitution of the National Association of Appointment Secretaries. Cheney had started her own commercial venture for teacher placement in California, and was reported to be "the first woman in the country to begin a college appointment service" ACPA: College Students Educators International, 2012, p. 9). In 1929, the name of the organization changed to the National Association of Placement and Personnel Officers to reflect a more contemporary understanding of the work of "placing teachers and other college graduates" and the increasing influence of the Personnel Movement (Sheeley, 1983. p. 180). The organization was to undergo one more name change in 1931 when it became the American College Personnel Association. The goals of ACPA included bringing all those who were involved in personnel work together in a single organization while still maintaining its unique divisions and the development of professional meetings that would bring together personnel workers for the purpose of "the interchange of ideas, … by formulating and maintaining standards; and by cooperative effort in research, experimentation and service" (American College Personnel Association, 1933, p. 87). The association is currently ACPA: College Student Educators International.

After almost two decades of haphazard implementation of student personnel, there was a national effort to encourage the profession to fully adopt the student personnel approach. In 1937, nineteen student personnel workers, faculty members, elementary and secondary school educators, businessmen, and government officials met under the auspices of the American Council on Education to develop a statement on the "philosophy and development of student personnel work" (American Council on Education [ACE], 1937; Gerda, Coomes, & Asimou, 2012). The 1937 *Student Personnel Point of View* (SPPV) (American Council on Education, 1937), grounded in a "long and honorable history," provided the clearest statement of the philosophy of the Student Personnel Movement to date by emphasizing that colleges and universities were obligated to "consider the student as a whole … [with] an emphasis, in brief, upon the development of the student as a person rather than upon his intellectual training alone" (ACE, 1937, p. 1). The document also detailed twenty-three functional responsibilities (for example, academic and career advising, extracurricular activities) that should constitute the student services function and advocated coordination between and among professionals, institutions, and associations (ACE, 1937, p. 9). As

Gerda et al. (2012) argued, this document represented more that just a statement of philosophy. It was the articulation of the history of the Student Personnel Movement; a record of the 1937 ACE-sponsored conference; and, perhaps, an attempt by the American Council on Education to stake out a leadership position in student affairs. Regardless of its intent, the 1937 SPPV has become known as the foundational document that advanced the idea that "*student affairs professionals are educators*" [emphasis in the original] focused on "transformational thinking for the benefit of developing the whole student" (Torres, DeSawal, & Hernandez, 2012). By comparison, deaning and earlier, less structured approaches began to look like "sentimentalized intuition" (Brubacher & Rudy, 1958/1997, p. 335).

As the United States faced entry into another World War, student personnel was a broad and influential conceptual framework for student affairs work. Leaders were still spreading the word to campuses that had not yet converted as the entire country turned its attention to World War II. During the Second World War, college campuses were forced to respond to smaller student enrollments, and professional associations declined to meet so as to save resources that would otherwise have gone to travel. When the war ended, Student Personnel would remain, but it would need to adapt to the postwar world.

Student Personnel, Continued and Deeper

As the war ended and the nation's focus returned to domestic concerns, higher education found itself in a very different world. Among the changes that significantly influenced student affairs were the flood of veterans into higher education; the return of military leaders to student personnel administration; and a re-examination of the nature of student personnel, resulting in a new point of view and a call for refocusing on deeper teaching.

The passage of the Serviceman's Readjustment Act—more commonly known as the G. I. Bill—resulted in one of the most significant periods of growth in the history of higher education. This explosive growth fostered the creation of new student affairs functional areas and the evolution of new administrative forms. Department of Education statistics showed that college enrollments "nearly doubled between the fall of 1945 and the fall of 1946, and by 1947 enrollment was 70 percent higher than its prewar levels" (Stanley, 2003, p. 677). By the time the bill expired, "a total of 1,232,000 veterans utilized their GI Bill" for college (Olson, 1973, p. 602). Like other "outsiders" (Lefkowitz Horowitz, 1987, p. 14), these students demonstrated "maturity, increased initiative, greater sense of purpose and social consciousness and wider experience" than their traditional-age counterparts (Olson, 1973, p. 603). The rules that guided student affairs practice on college campuses were designed for younger, less worldly students, and the veterans found those restrictions constraining and insulting. They were eager to get on with their lives after the interruption of the war. They were attuned to vocational ends and frequently began families before finishing their education. These factors required campuses to expand services such as family health care, build extensive new residence hall systems, and reconsider the student-institution relationship, as more mature veterans were demanding greater autonomy and individual rights.

During the war the primary responsibilities for student support fell to the dean of women (Coomes, Whitt, & Kuh, 1987), but with the return of men to campus, senior administrators determined that these women were ill fitted for the job of directing services for men and placed the dean of women in a subservient relationship to the dean of men or, more frequently, developed the new position of dean of students and almost always filled that position with a man. As Schwartz (1997) noted, "The position of dean of women was an inevitable victim of the pervasive hostility that greeted women in general on campus, while the position of dean of men assumed new administrative importance" (p. 433). The appointment of men to these newly created positions was compatible with the student personnel tenet of efficiency and was probably also a result of acknowledged or unacknowledged sexism (Tuttle, 1996). Although a small number of dean of women titles still exist today, postwar student personnel generally ended the dean of women position.

Finally, student personnel was affected by pressure for change from within. A committee reviewed and reissued the *Student Personnel Point of View* in 1949 and added language to emphasize citizenship and global democracy. Esther Lloyd-Jones, who had been a primary author of the 1937 SPPV and was a protégé of Walter Dill Scott at Northwestern, joined with others to question whether student personnel needed to readjust to account for some of the weaknesses that had become apparent over the decades and especially as a result of World War II. At its extreme, student personnel aimed toward efficiency and organization in a way that glossed over the individual student and his or her unique, qualitative, unclassifiable challenges and identities. As the enrollments at institutions climbed well into the thousands in the 1950s and 1960s, the approach was in danger of missing the trees for the forest. Lloyd-Jones and Smith

(1954) called for keeping the core principles of student personnel while being careful to keep the deeper teaching of the individual student at the center of the work of the profession.

Another New Approach: Student Development

In the late 1960s and early 1970s another new approach emerged: that of the student developmentalist. This approach was similar to previous approaches in that it was still committed to the larger educational goal of educating the whole student. However, like the previous approaches it differed on tactics and sources of insight.

By the late 1960s, previous dominant approaches were viewed as inadequate to meet the rapidly changing face of higher education caused by a significantly different student-institutional relationship (Harvey, 1974), the increasing post–World War II emphasis on science in the academy and the role that emphasis played in shaping the priorities of faculty members (Committee on the Student in Higher Education, 1968; Wilson, 1983), and new sources of insight into the nature of the American college student through formal theories on individual development and the college experience (Chickering, 1969; Feldman & Newcomb, 1969; Perry, 1970, Sanford, 1962). Student affairs practitioners questioned their foundational beliefs as campus events of the 1960s and early 1970s shook long-held cultural, educational, political, and sexual norms. With the civil rights, women's rights, antiwar and anti-draft movements, and the newly recognized status of students as adults, the nature of the student-institution relationship changed, and the role of student affairs professionals became ambiguous (see Appleton, Briggs, & Rhatigan, 1978; Wolf-Wendel, Twombly, Tuttle, Ward, & Gaston-Gayles, 2004).

This professional identity crisis was clearly reflected in the titles of numerous articles published in the period's professional journals and newsletters, including "Identity Crisis—1965" (Kirk, 1965); "Whither Student Personnel Work from 1968 to 2018" (Shaffer, 1968); "Student Personnel Work: A Profession Stillborn" (Penny, 1969); "Student Affairs Administration in Transition" (Chandler, 1973); and "Student Personnel—All Hail and Farewell!" (Crookston, 1976).

Reviews of contemporary documents laying out the developmentalist approach (for example, Brown, 1972) frequently noted that new challenges and an unclear identity could be addressed by focusing the work of student affairs educators on the developmental needs of students. This new approach was heralded as "a promising omen" that included the "increasing summons from within the profession for student personnel workers to view themselves as behavioral scientists and the growing volume of research and thought on what influences and promotes student development" (Brown, 1972, p. 10). The Tomorrow's Higher Education (T.H.E.) Project defined and justified the student development approach:

> Student development in the higher education context, is the application of human development concepts in the post-secondary setting. Human development is a patterned, orderly, lifelong process leading to the growth of self-determination and self-direction, which results in more effective behavior ... The goal of the [T.H.E.] Project is to reconceptualize student affairs work in a way that will provide a measure of creative input from the student affairs profession toward the shaping of post-secondary education for the future. Student development must be the keystone of future programs and ... incorporate student development into and throughout the institution. ("A student development model," 1975, pp. 336, 341)

The student development approach would dominate the 1970s and 1980s. By the early 1990s, it had its detractors (Bloland, 1986a, 1986b; Crookston, 1976; Plato, 1978), but it had become such a pervasive perspective it would eventually be called an "essential ideal" guiding higher education (Strange, 1994).

The fluid nature of student affairs during this period can also be seen in a number of attempts to consolidate or strengthen the collaborative bonds between proliferating student affairs professional organizations. Perhaps the most active collaboration was the Council of Student Personnel Associations (COSPA), which included ACPA, NASPA, NAWDC (the former NADW), the Western Personnel Institute, the Association of College Unions, the Association of College and University Housing Officers, and the National Association of Foreign Student Advisors. COSPA existed from 1963 to 1970 when NASPA departed the organization to "pursue significant relationships with ACPA and NAWDC through joint executive committee meetings" (Bloland, 1972, p. 487). Other examples of collaborative efforts among the three largest student personnel associations during this time period include the publication of the *Joint Statement on Rights and Freedoms of Students* (American Association of University Professors, 1967) and occasional cosponsored professional meetings.

One More New Approach: Student Learning

With the 1980s came increasing criticism that higher education had lost rigor, content knowledge transmission, and its competitive edge in preparing American students for jobs. As an echo of the Cold War, some worried that other countries were producing smarter and more scientifically adept students than was the United States. A series of documents identified by Coomes, Forney, Keim, Kuh, Rodgers, and Stamatakos (1987) trace pressure from government and society for the full spectrum of the American education system to focus on such essentials of education as math, reading, writing, science, and cultural literacy (Hirsch, 1987). The key focus on maturation and individual development advocated by the student development approach was criticized as peripheral by core learning advocates. But student development was still important to student affairs, and as with previous ideas, it was kept in large part even as new approaches were proposed.

While holding fast to the utility of student development approaches to the end goal of helping students, a new document called for a readjustment to bring intellectual development theories closer to the forefront, and for student affairs professionals to work closely with faculty to feature learning theory more prominently in student affairs expertise. *The Student Learning Imperative* (American College Personnel Association, 1994) envisioned pairing an out-of-classroom understanding of learning processes with the formal teaching processes of the university to bring student affairs closer to the learning mission. It called for a review of all student affairs activities to make sure they were in support of this goal, and in a way harkened back to the deaning approach's strong connection to the faculty and curricular decisions.

Approaches for the Twenty-First Century

Inherent in an urgent call for change is the assumption that something is not working. As the twentieth century came to a close and the twenty-first began, many within and outside of higher education were asking whether all the activities of higher education were necessary to the missions of institutions, or whether resources should be allocated to other activities. Too little time has passed yet to put these questions in focus or cluster them into an identifiable new approach to help the profession adapt. These questions are offered as clues to understanding the current era, and how it might look from a future vantage point.

- How do we balance student needs and student wants? Deaning sometimes imposed structure on students for their own good. Vocationalism and student personnel steered students to their best fit, sometimes discouraging unrealistic paths. Student development challenged growth to the next developmental stage, even if it was uncomfortable. How will we resolve the question of balancing student needs and student wants?
- How will new forms of institutions and new students change our work? The entry of new constituent groups into higher education created the profession and changed it over time. Will online education, for-profit start-ups, and job-focused institutions fundamentally change student affairs?
- How will higher education value and fund student affairs' role? Student personnel and student development both benefited in times of increased resources and expanded accordingly. As higher education struggles to justify the levels of student debt, how will student affairs' roles fare?
- How will student affairs respond to shifts in what society expects from higher education? Laws about how universities must treat students changed the profession drastically in the 1960s, and governmental attention is increasing today. Expectations of students and their parents have played a role in each approach. How will student affairs change to adapt?
- Until recently, learning was almost always delivered face to face, from teacher to student, and in place-bound settings. The advent of distance learning and asynchronous mobile technology has forced student affairs practitioners to once again reconsider the nature of how we do our work and with whom we do it. Technological advances force us to ask, How will we build relationships with students on our virtual campuses? How can we assist students who are not there physically but still require our support, encouragement, and direction?

Conclusion

We wonder whether we will keep the term *student affairs* or some future historian will see our current methodology as yet another type of approach on the historical list. But whatever the future holds, we believe that there will always be a need for professionals who dedicate their hearts to helping each and every student to get the most out of her or his college experience. We are excited to do that work, in whatever form it might take. We do it in concert with our colleagues, in honor of our professional ancestors, and for our students, past, present, and future.

The history of student affairs is still being written! If you feel enlightened by what you have read, or curious about something omitted, or want to challenge something we have written, we invite you to contribute to the scholarship of our history by contributing your own stories and visiting and supporting the Student Affairs History Project (Bowling Green State University, 2006).

References

ACPA: College Student Educators International. (2012). *Mary Cheney (1924-1925): First President.* http://www.myacpa.org/mary-l-cheney.

American Association of University Professors. (1967). Joint statement on rights and freedoms of students. *AAUP Bulletin, 53*(4), 365–368.

American College Personnel Association. (1933). *Tenth annual report.* Minneapolis, MN: Author.

American College Personnel Association. (1994). *The student learning imperative: Implications for student affairs.* Washington, DC: ACPA.

American Council on Education. (1937). *The student personnel point of view: A report of a conference on the philosophy and development of student personnel work in college and university* (Series 1, Vol. 1, No. 3). Washington, DC: Author.

Appleton, J. R., Briggs, C. M., & Rhatigan, J. J. (1978). *Pieces of eight: The rites, roles, and styles of the dean by eight who have been there.* Portland, OR: National Association of Student Personnel Administrators.

Biddix, J. P., & Schwartz, R. A. (2012). Walter Dill Scott and the student personnel movement. *Journal of Student Affairs Research and Practice, 49*(30), 285–298.

Bloland, P. A. (1986a). Student development: The new orthodoxy? (Part I). *ACPA Developments, 13*(3), 1, 13.

Bloland, P. A. (1986b). Student development: The new orthodoxy? (Part II). *ACPA Developments, 13*(4), 1, 22.

Bloland, P. A. (1972). Ecumenicalism in college student personnel. *Journal of College Student Personnel, 13*(2), 102–111.

Bowling Green State University. (2006, November). *The student affairs history project.* http://ul2.bgsu.edu/sahp/.

Brown, R. D. (1972). *Student development on tomorrow's higher education—A return to the academy.* Washington, DC: American College Personnel Association.

Brubacher, J. S., & Rudy, W. (1997). *Higher education in transition: An American history, 1636–1956.* New York, NY: Harper. (Original work published 1958)

Chandler, E. M. (1973). Student affairs administration in transition. *Journal of College Student Personnel, 14*(5), 392–398.

Chickering, A. W. (1969). *Education and identity.* San Francisco, CA: Jossey-Bass.

Committee on the Student in Higher Education. (1968). (J. F. Kauffman, Chairman). *The student in higher education.* New Haven, CT: Hazen Foundation.

Coomes, M. D., Forney, D., Keim, M., Kuh, G., Rodgers, R., & Stamatakos, L. (1987, October). *What messages do the national reports on higher education hold for the student affairs profession?* Paper presented at the Midwest Meeting of Graduate Faculty in Student Personnel, East Lansing, MI (October 1987).

Coomes, M. D., Whitt, E. J., & Kuh, G. D. (1987). Kate Hevner Mueller: Woman for a changing world. *Journal of Counseling and Development, 65(*8), 407–415.

Crookston, B. B. (1976). Student personnel—All hail and farewell!" *Personnel and Guidance Journal, 55*(1), 26–29.

Feldman, K. A., & Newcomb, T. M. (1969). *The impact of college on students.* San Francisco, CA: Jossey-Bass.

Findlay, J. F. (1938). *The origin and development of the work of the dean of men in higher education.* Unpublished doctoral dissertation, New York University.

Fley, J. A. (1978). Thomas Arkle Clark: Patriarch and dean from Illinois. *Journal of the NAWDAC, 41*(3), 120–123.

Gangone, L. M. (2008). National Association for Women in Education: An enduring legacy. *Journal About Women in Higher Education, 1*(1), 1–22.

Gatyas, K. (1998). Thomas Arkle Clark and the office of dean of men at the University of Illinois, 1901–1917. *Journal of Educational Administration and History, 30*(2), 129–145.

Gerda, J. J. (2004). *A history of the conferences of deans of women 1903–1922.* Unpublished doctoral dissertation, Bowling Green State University.

Gerda, J. J. (2007). Gathering together: A view of the earliest student affairs professional organizations. *NASPA Journal, 43*(4), 147–163.

Gerda, J. J., Coomes, M. D., & Asimou, H. M. (2012). "A report of a conference": When, who, and questions of philosophy. In K. M. Boyle, J. W. Lowery, & J. A. Mueller (eds.), *Reflections on the 75th Anniversary of The Student Personnel Point of View* (pp. 29–34). Washington, DC: ACPA—College Student Educators International.

Harvey, T. R. (1974). Some future directions for student personnel administration. *Journal of College Student Personnel, 15*(4), 243–247.

Hirsch, E. D. (1987). *Cultural literacy: What every American needs to know.* New York, NY: Vintage Books.

Hoff, K. S., Kroll, J., MacKinnon, F. J. D., & Rentz, A. L. (2004). Career services. In F.J.D. MacKinnon (ed.), *Rentz's student affairs practice in higher education* (pp. 108-143). Springfield, IL: Charles C Thomas.

Holmes, L. A. (1939). *History of the position of dean of women in a selected group of co-educational colleges and universities in the United States.* New York, NY: Teachers College, Columbia University, Bureau of Publications.

Kirk, B. B. Identity crisis—1965. (1965). *Journal of College Student Personnel, 6*(4), 194–199.

LaBarre, C. (1948). *Graduate training for educational personnel work* (Series VI, Vol. *12*, No. 11). Washington, DC: Author.

Lefkowitz Horowitz, H. (1987). Campus life: Undergraduate cultures from the end of the eighteenth century to the present. Chicago, IL: University of Chicago Press.

Leonard, E. A. (1956). *Origins of personnel services in American higher education.* Minneapolis: University of Minnesota Press.

Lloyd-Jones, E. (1950). The beginnings of our profession. In E. G. Williamson (ed.), *Trends in student personnel work* (pp. 260–264). Minneapolis: University of Minnesota Press.

Lloyd-Jones, E., & Smith, M. R. (1954). *Student personnel work as deeper teaching.* New York, NY: Harper.

Lynch, E. C. (1968). Walter Dill Scott: Pioneer industrial psychologist. *Business History Review, 42*(2), 149–170.

Martin, G. S. (1911). The position of dean of women. *Journal of the Association of Collegiate Alumnae, 4,* 65–78.

Mathews, E. J. (1937). The registrar and the dean of men. *Secretarial Notes, Nineteenth Annual Conference of the National Association of Deans and Advisors of Men.* University of Texas, Austin. April 1–3, pp. 77–84.

Mathews, L. K. (1915). *The dean of women.* New York, NY: Houghton Mifflin.

Miller, C. L. L., & Pruitt-Logan, A. S. (2012). *Faithful to the task at hand: The Life of Lucy Diggs Slowe.* Albany: State University of New York Press.

Minutes of the Conference of Deans of Women of the Middle West. (1903). Bowling Green, OH: Bowling Green State University, Center for Archival Collections, National Student Affairs Archives, NAWE MS-218.

Nidiffer, J. (2000.) *Pioneering deans of women: More than wise and pious matrons.* New York, NY: Teachers College Press.

Olson, K. W. (1973). The G.I. Bill and higher education: Success and surprise. *American Quarterly, 25*(5), 596–610.

Penny, J. F. (1969). Student personnel work: A profession stillborn. *Journal of College Student Personnel, 47*(10), 958–962.

Perry, W. G. (1970). *Forms of intellectual and ethical development in the college years: A scheme.* New York, NY: Holt, Rinehart, & Winston.

Plato, K. (1978). The shift to student development: An analysis of the patterns of change. *NASPA Journal, 15*(4), 32–36.

Rhatigan, J. J. (2009). From the people up: A brief history of student affairs. In G. S. McClellan & J. Stringer (eds.), *The handbook of student affairs administration* (3rd ed., pp. 3-18). San Francisco, CA: Jossey-Bass.

Sanford, N. (Ed.) (1962). *The American college: A psychological and social interpretation of the higher learning.* New York, NY: Wiley.

Schwartz, R. (1997). How deans of women became men. *Review of Higher Education, 20*(4), 419–436.

Schwartz, R. (2010). *Deans of men and the shaping of modern college culture.* New York, NY: Palgrave Macmillan.

Shaffer, R. H. (1968). Whither student personnel work from 1968 to 2018. *NASPA Journal, 6*(1), 9–14.

Sheeley, V. L. (1983). NADW and NAAS: Sixty years of organizational relationships (NAWDAD—ACPA: 1923–1983). In B. A. Belson & L. E. Fitzgerald (eds.). *Thus, we spoke ACPA—NAWDAC 1958–1975* (pp. 179-189). Carbondale: Southern Illinois Press.

Stanley, M. (2003). College education and the midcentury GI Bills. *Quarterly Journal of Economics, 118*(2), 671–708.

Strange, C. (1994). Student development: The evolution and status of and essential idea. *Journal of College Student Development, 35*(6), 399–412.

A student development model for student affairs in tomorrow's higher education. (1975). *Journal of College Student Personnel, 16*(4), 334–341.

Thwing, C. F. (1906). *Higher education in America*. London, UK: Sidney Appleton.

Torres, V., DeSawal, D., & Hernandez, E. (2012). The importance of *The Student Personnel Point of View* in honoring the past and acknowledging current perspectives. In K. M. Boyle, J. W. Lowery, & J. A. Mueller (eds.), *Reflections on the 75th Anniversary of The Student Personnel Point of View* (pp. 25–28). Washington, DC: ACPA—College Student Educators International.

Tuttle, K. N. (1996). *What became of the dean of women? Changing roles for women administrators in American higher education, 1940–1980*. Unpublished doctoral dissertation, University of Kansas, Department of Policy and Leadership.

Wilson, J. T. (1983). *Academic science, higher education, and the federal government, 1950–1983*. Chicago, IL: University of Chicago Press.

Wolf-Wendel, L. E., Twombly, S. B., Tuttle, K. N., Ward, K., & Gaston-Gayles, J. L. (2004). *Reflecting back, looking forward: Civil rights and student affairs*. Washington, DC: National Association of Student Personnel Administrators.

Wright, J. S., & Dimsdale, P. B. Jr., (1974). *Pioneers in marketing*. Atlanta, GA: Georgia State University.

CHAPTER TWO

THE IMPORTANCE OF INSTITUTIONAL MISSION

Joan B. Hirt and Claire K. Robbins

The American system of higher education is often described as the
envy of the world, largely because of its rich array of institutional
types (Jaquette, 2013). Some colleges and universities offer vocational
training and workforce development opportunities, while others conduct
groundbreaking research or engage in outreach activities to benefit
citizens at the local, national, or international levels. An assortment of
variables differentiate institutions, including the number of students they
enroll, their type of control (public versus independent campus), and
the number and type of certificates and degrees they offer. Indeed, the
breadth and scope of the higher education enterprise is so complex it can
seem indecipherable at times. Yet there is a mechanism that can assist in
decoding that complexity: institutional mission.

The mission statement of a college or university serves several purposes. First and foremost, it captures the essence and distinctive character
of the organization. A mission statement describes why a college or university was founded, whom it serves, and what it strives to accomplish. In short,
the statement reveals to key external and internal constituents where the
institution came from, where it is heading, and how it plans to get there
(Barr, 2000; Morphew & Hartley, 2006).

To those outside the organization, the mission expresses the goals of
the institution, the span of activities and academic offerings of the college

or university, as well as the types of students it serves (Barr, 2000). Such public proclamations of purpose and intent convey important information to critical external groups. Prospective students may evaluate the mission to see whether an institution would enable them to achieve their educational aspirations. Potential faculty members look to the mission to gain a sense of institutional purpose and the relevance of that purpose to their areas of expertise. Public officials may rely on the mission when identifying criteria by which to assess the organization's effectiveness.

For external groups, the mission statement serves to *inform,* but for those inside the institution the mission statement serves to *conform.* It identifies the role that the college or university plays in the higher education enterprise. This helps academic leaders determine what falls within the scope of the organization and where to allocate resources. The mission statement guides decision makers when they consider adopting, expanding, revising, or eliminating programs and services. In an era of declining resources and increasing demands, the mission statement can serve as a beacon for institutional managers.

Understanding institutional mission is particularly important for student affairs leaders. As Barr (2000) notes, "Failure to understand, appreciate, and translate the mission of the institution into programs and services can rank among the biggest mistakes a student affairs administrator can make" (p. 25). Although other chapters in this volume discuss models of professional performance and the competencies considered fundamental to successful practice, this one focuses on the milieus in which those models are enacted. The chapter opens by describing different frameworks for classifying colleges and universities. Next, we depict the social, economic, and political trends that influenced the emergence and mission of different institutional types. There follows a discussion of how mission influences the work of student affairs administrators at different types of institutions. Finally, we explore the relationship between institutional mission and professional mobility.

Institutional Classification Systems

Unlike other countries, the United States does not have a centrally coordinated national system of postsecondary education. Instead, higher education has always been the domain of the states. As a result, there are literally fifty systems of higher education in the country, not including those in the District of Columbia, Puerto Rico, and other affiliated territories. Although there are some common organizing patterns, the structure of higher education in each state has its own unique qualities and quirks. This uniqueness renders comparisons across state systems somewhat challenging. To address that challenge, experts have developed a number of frameworks to sort colleges and universities into comprehensive (and comprehensible) categories. For example, Barr (2000) identified factors that influence mission, including institutional affiliation, history, and governance system. Nexus of control (public, private, tribal), purpose of charter (not-for-profit, proprietary), size, and athletic league are other ways of categorizing colleges and universities. This chapter is organized around one of the most well-known and frequently used frameworks: the Carnegie Classification of Institutions of Higher Education.

The Carnegie framework identifies categories of like colleges and universities. Originally published in 1973, the system was refined, revised, and reissued in 1976, 1987, 1994, 2000, 2005, and 2010 (Carnegie Foundation for the Advancement of Teaching, 2000; Carnegie Classification, 2010). The first five iterations grouped colleges and universities according to their mission: doctoral and research universities, master's colleges and universities, baccalaureate colleges, associate's colleges, specialized institutions (for example, seminaries, schools of art), and tribal colleges and universities.

Over the years, scholars and administrators have used the system for research and assessment purposes. The framework has also been used in unintended ways, however: as an institutional ranking system or a mechanism for allocating funds, for example. These more pernicious uses of the classification system prompted leaders at the Carnegie Foundation to reconceptualize the typology. In addition to grouping institutions by mission, the 2005 framework classified institutions by the nature of their undergraduate instructional program, graduate instructional program, enrollment profile, undergraduate profile, size and setting, and level of community engagement. These new categories were intended to paint a richer picture of the higher education landscape (Carnegie Classification, 2010).

The 2010 Carnegie framework categorizes a total of 4,634 institutions. Most (3,418) are two- or four-year not-for-profit colleges and universities. The rest (1,216) are for-profit (proprietary) institutions. The remainder of this chapter employs a modified version of the 2010 Carnegie Classification model. We describe missions for baccalaureate colleges (both secular and sectarian), master's colleges and universities, research and doctoral granting universities, and associate's colleges. We also discuss missions of tribally controlled colleges, historically Black colleges and universities, Hispanic-serving institutions, and for-profit organizations.

Institutional Mission Statements

To appreciate fully the profound influence that mission statements have on institutions, one must understand the historical contexts in which different types of colleges and universities emerged. Scholars have produced works on the history of higher education in America (for example, see Brubacher & Rudy, 1997, or Thelin, 2004) that are far richer than what is offered here. Rather, this chapter simply touches upon the conditions under which certain types of colleges and universities developed in the United States so that the discussion of mission statements is placed in some pertinent historical context.

Baccalaureate Colleges

The first type of higher education institution established in America was the baccalaureate college. Baccalaureate colleges were modeled after Cambridge and Oxford universities in England (Brubacher & Rudy, 1997; Thelin, 2004; Urban & Wagoner, 2000). Colonial leaders founded these early institutions in order to educate those who would serve the religious and political interests of the colony. The number of colleges swelled as the country expanded, and over time some baccalaureate institutions moved away from their religious roots and evolved into secular colleges. Others retained their religious affiliations.

The 2010 Carnegie Classification system assigns not-for-profit institutions to various categories. Of those, 19.6 percent are classified as baccalaureate colleges and 8.8 percent are labeled Special Faith Focused Institutions. The latter group includes some baccalaureate colleges as well as seminaries, bible colleges, and other faith-based institutions. The distinction between sectarian and secular colleges is evident in their mission statements.

Liberal Arts Colleges. Secular institutions are hereafter called liberal arts colleges. These institutions tend to be independent (as opposed to public), residential campuses that typically serve eighteen- to twenty-four-year old undergraduates. They are small, on average enrolling between 1,600 and 1,800 students, and offer traditional curricula of general education classes and majors in the arts and sciences.

Mission statements for liberal arts colleges reflect their character. They tend to be brief—only a paragraph or two—and often highlight the campus's historical roots. They articulate a holistic approach to education, referring to the outcomes that their students achieve: intellectual sophistication, the ability to think clearly and communicate effectively, and global citizenship. In general, students are at the center of the mission for liberal arts colleges (Morphew & Hartley, 2006).

Religiously Affiliated Colleges. We refer to baccalaureate colleges that retained their sectarian ties as religiously affiliated colleges. These institutions tend to be independent, small, and enroll primarily traditional-age students. Their mission statements talk about a liberal education that is grounded in the arts and sciences. What sets religiously affiliated colleges apart from secular liberal arts institutions is the clear enunciation of religious ties in their mission statements. Denominational campuses spotlight spiritual development and talk about the role of the institution in glorifying a higher power or encouraging the evangelical spirit. The mission statements of these colleges proudly proclaim their sectarian nature (Estanek, Herdlein, & Harris, 2011).

Master's Colleges and Universities

Although baccalaureate colleges and universities dominated the landscape through the first 250 years of American higher education, other institutional forms eventually emerged (Gonzales, 2013). Master's colleges and universities are one such form. Most of the 651 not-for-profit institutions assigned to this classification in the 2010 Carnegie framework arrived at their current status in one of two ways. Some started out as baccalaureate colleges and thrived through the middle of the twentieth century when the Baby Boomers completed their undergraduate educations. At that time, enrollments threatened to drop precipitously, and some of these tuition-dependent campuses elected to introduce professional (for example, business, teacher education) and graduate programs to survive (Breneman, 1994). This change led to their reassignment in the Carnegie system from baccalaureate to master's colleges and universities.

The bulk of institutions in this category, however, followed an evolutionary path that was closely linked to the development of K–12 education. It may seem surprising, but the current tiered system of elementary, middle, and secondary education was not fully developed in the United States until the 1940s. As these lower forms of education became institutionalized, the need for teachers grew. Teacher training programs, or normal schools, developed to meet this demand (Thelin, 2004). As industrialization gripped the country in the early twentieth century, scores of normal schools expanded their curricula and morphed from normal schools to state colleges, then to state universities. Many ultimately became part of a state university system. During the latter part of the twentieth century, most of these campuses increased their regional span of influence and added master's degrees, and in some instances a limited number of doctoral programs, to their curricula (Lucas, 1994; Urban & Wagoner, 2000).

Most master's institutions are midsized (4,000–8,000 students), though a limited number are quite large, enrolling up to 35,000. About 40 percent are public (Carnegie Classification, 2010); many of those are former baccalaureate campuses. A review of mission statements reveals the transformations these institutions have undertaken. They typically educate students in their region, often serving as pathways to upward mobility for those who might not otherwise have access to higher education. Their graduate programs serve working adults who seek professional advancement. The mission statements characteristically are lengthy and talk about the various roles these campuses fulfill: liberal arts degrees for undergraduates, professional programs for graduate students, and cultural hubs for their regions.

Research and Doctoral Granting Universities

Research and doctoral granting universities emerged in the latter half of the nineteenth century when a confluence of factors catalyzed the development of this sector. First, the Enlightenment produced rapid advancements in science and technology, leading to new curricular offerings. Second, higher education started enrolling students from a broader socioeconomic spectrum to provide trained workers for emerging industries. Additionally, states recovering from the Civil War and capitalizing on postwar industrialization sought to expand higher education. Indeed, the federal government endorsed this expansion through the Morrill Acts (1862 and 1890) that encouraged states to establish public universities. Finally, the introduction of graduate education in the United States occurred during this time (Gonzales, 2013). Collectively, these factors spawned the growth of research and doctoral granting universities (Thelin, 2004; Urban & Wagoner, 2000).

As of 2010, only 6.3 percent of all not-for-profit institutions were research or doctoral granting universities, but they served 27.9 percent of the 20,727,660 students enrolled in higher education; most are large public campuses with average enrollments over 20,000. Their size is often reflective of their complexity. All offer undergraduate, graduate, and professional programs, and most are home to research institutes and cross-disciplinary endeavors that add another layer of density to the organization (Anderson, 2001; Etzkowitz, Webster, & Healey, 1998; Slaughter & Leslie, 1997).

Mission statements of research and doctoral institutions reflect both this density and a sense of elitism. Nearly all discuss their tripartite mission of teaching, research, and service, but research is clearly the crown jewel. References to research are rampant, describing it as the bedrock that enables the university to attract high-quality students, top-notch scholars, and international recognition. These mission statements also proclaim the exclusive status of research and doctoral institutions. Phrases like *world class* and *cutting edge* are sprinkled throughout research university mission statements. In fact, the term, *statement,* does not really capture the nature of these documents; most are several pages long and might better be termed reports.

Associate's Colleges

Associate's or community colleges are the sixth type of postsecondary organization discussed. They represent 34.1 percent of all not-for-profit institutions (Carnegie Classification, 2010). They offer multiple programs and have distinct service (geographic) areas that tie them to their communities. These ties are linked to the historical era in which community colleges materialized. At the start of the twentieth century, there was an emergent educational ladder (elementary, middle, secondary, college levels). Curricular development, however, was not as clear. Colleges sought students who had studied math, science, and languages. Secondary schools were designed to offer terminal education. A debate ensued, and associate's colleges initially served two purposes: vocational training for those who completed high school and did not aspire to obtain a college degree, and transfer education for high school graduates who were ill prepared for the rigors of college. During the twentieth century, they added two more functions: remedial education, particularly for the growing numbers of immigrants in America, and continuing education opportunities for people in their service areas (Cohen & Brawer, 2003; Urban & Wagoner, 2000).

Community colleges educate 39.6 percent of students (Carnegie Classification, 2010) with average enrollments ranging from 1,222 at small, rural-serving campuses to more than 14,000 at multicampus, urban institutions. Indeed, this range reflects the variety among these institutions. The 2010 Carnegie system identifies fourteen forms of community colleges, representing a significant departure from the earliest classifications in which all such campuses were grouped into a single category.

Despite their categorical differences, mission statements of associate's colleges share some commonalties (Abelman & Dalessandro, 2008). They tend to be straightforward; many statements consist of enumerated lists of the programs the institution offers. Almost without exception, however, these public pronouncements identify the four traditional missions of associate's colleges: vocational development, transfer education, remedial or developmental education, and continuing education. Most also acknowledge their role as a community resource and their commitment to serving the interests of their local districts.

Tribally Controlled Colleges

Scholars (Carney, 1999; McClellan, Fox, & Lowe, 2005) have written about the history of Native American higher education far more fully than can be captured here. The first tribally controlled community college was established in 1968 (McClellan et al., 2005) and thirty-two tribally controlled colleges are listed in the 2010 Carnegie Classification, and the American Indian Higher Education Consortium (AIHEC) cites thirty-seven institutions that operate seventy-five campuses (American Indian Higher Education Consortium, 2013). Nearly all of these institutions offer associate's degrees and a handful offer bachelor's or master's degrees (Carney, 1999). Most campuses are small, enrolling on average 615 students (Carnegie Classification, 2010). Those enrollees tend to be older women who often have children, typically come from low-income backgrounds, and are first-generation students (Belgarde, 1996) who see higher education as a means to improve their lives.

The mission statements for tribally controlled colleges are typically short; most are a single paragraph. Without exception they talk about serving Native American students in general, and members of the sponsoring tribe in particular. Nearly all describe their mission as providing vocational training and educational opportunities designed to better individuals, families, and tribal communities. Indeed, a focus on the welfare of the community is a distinguishing characteristic of tribally controlled institutions that play a key role in tribal economic development and preservation of language and culture. Since tribes, not state governments, control them, these colleges are powerful symbols of tribal sovereignty.

Historically Black Colleges and Universities

Historically Black Colleges and Universities (HBCUs) is not a Carnegie Classification, per se. Some HBCUs are baccalaureate colleges, while others are master's or doctoral granting universities (Coaxum, 2001). They constitute a unique type of institution, however, because many were founded to educate a certain segment of the population—the sons and daughters of former slaves. Allen and Jewell (2002) and Brown and Davis (2001) are excellent sources of history on these institutions. For this discussion, some basic statistics serve to illustrate the need for HBCUs. On the eve of the Civil War, there were 4,000,000 people in the United States, but only twenty-nine Black individuals earned bachelor's degrees between 1619 and 1850 (Humphries, 1995). The emancipation of slaves after the Civil War created an urgent need for educational services and religious and secular groups stepped up to fill this gap. Most HBCUs started out offering elementary education to illiterate former slaves and gradually increased their curricular offerings to include secondary, postsecondary, and graduate education.

The number of HBCUs has varied over time. The general consensus is that there are currently 103 such institutions in the United States (Brown, 2013; Brown, Donahoo, & Bertrand, 2001), representing 3 percent of the not-for-profit campuses included in the 2010 Carnegie Classification system. Collectively, they enroll 300,000 students, meaning that most HBCUs are relatively small (3,000 or fewer students) (Brown & Davis, 2001), but they confer 20 percent of all bachelor's (Brown, 2013), 15 percent of all master's, and 10 percent of all doctoral degrees earned by Black individuals in the United States.

The mission statements of most HBCUs are hybridized. On the one hand, they discuss functions reflective of their Carnegie type. Those that are baccalaureate colleges refer to liberal education, while those that are master's institutions talk about serving their regions and offering graduate education. On the other hand, nearly all discuss their commitment to Black students, and many mention their role in educating offspring of former slaves. This is an overriding theme in the mission statements of HBCUs: they are public declarations about the value of educating Black people and of preserving Black culture in the United States.

Hispanic-Serving Institutions

Hispanic-Serving Institutions (HSIs) are also not a category of colleges and universities in the Carnegie Classification system. They may be baccalaureate, master's, research, or associate's colleges. Like their HBCU and tribal counterparts, the students served by HSIs distinguish them. Demographic shifts over the past thirty years have spawned these institutions (Benitez, 1998). Hispanics comprise 13 percent of the US population, a proportion expected to climb to 22 percent by the year 2015 (US Census Bureau, 2002). Federal initiatives in the 1990s, coupled with efforts of Latina/o leaders, led to the recognition of postsecondary institutions that served large numbers of Hispanic students. Inclusion of HSI status in both Title III of the 1992 Higher Education Reauthorization Act and Title V of the same act in 1998 made these institutions eligible for extra funding, further cementing their presence in the higher education hierarchy.

Estimates about the number of HSIs vary from 131 to 738. Puerto Rico accounts for the largest number of HSIs (Laden, 2001). The rest are primarily located in states where large numbers of Hispanics reside. In 2006, 242 institutions met the federal criteria to apply for Title V funding (Contreras, Malcom, & Bensimon, 2008). Although exact numbers are elusive, estimates suggest that enrollments at HSIs have increased by 14 percent over the past decade (US Department of Education, 2002). There is little doubt that HSIs are major providers of higher education to Latina/o students and will play an increasingly critical role as this population proliferates (Gregory, 2003).

Like those of HBCUs, mission statements for HSIs typically parallel those of their Carnegie group. HSIs that are associate's colleges talk about the four traditional missions of community colleges, while statements from HSIs that are baccalaureate colleges focus on a liberal education. In one sense, however, HSIs are unlike their HBCU counterparts: service to Latina/o students is not usually mentioned in HSI missions. The ways in which Hispanic students are served is evident in what institutions do rather than in the ways they talk about themselves in mission statements.

Proprietary Colleges and Universities

Proprietary schools are perhaps the least understood sector of the higher education system in America. Kinser (2006) identifies some common misperceptions about these institutions. First, they are not recent additions to the postsecondary landscape. For-profit education has existed for more than a hundred years (Kinser, 2005). Second, proprietary campuses are not typically distance education providers; most are brick-and-mortar operations. Nor are most for-profit colleges and universities publicly traded corporations; the majority of such institutions are privately owned. Finally, though national attention has focused on mega-organizations like the University of Phoenix or DeVry University, multicampus institutions enrolling tens of thousands of students are not representative of this sector (Davidson, 2008; Kinser, 2006).

Since the 1980s, for-profit education has experienced unprecedented expansion. The number of institutions has grown by 29 percent and enrollment has increased by an astonishing 125 percent (Davidson, 2008; National Center for Educational Statistics, 2005), resulting in a spate of research about this sector of higher education (Breneman, 2005; Kelly, 2001; Kinser, 2005, 2006). The Carnegie Classification system (2010) identifies 1,207 for-profit colleges and universities that span the institutional spectrum, from associate's colleges to doctoral granting universities. These campuses enroll 1,893,777 students (Carnegie Classification, 2010), and one report suggests that in 2010, 10 percent of all college students were enrolled at for-profit campuses (Hanford, 2013). Two taxonomies offer other ways to conceptualize these colleges and universities. The first identifies three types of proprietary institutions: small single-campus organizations, distance education providers, and large multicampus operations (Kelly, 2001). The other (Kinser, 2006) suggests assorting proprietary campuses by their geographic span, level of degree offerings, and type of ownership.

Regardless of which classification system is used, proprietary institutions are just like not-for-profit campuses in many ways. They offer certificates, along with associate's, bachelor's, master's, doctoral, and professional degrees. The proprietary sector differs in one important way, however: it is revenue driven. In one recent report, the average profit margin for publicly traded institutions was 19.7 percent (Hanford, 2013). Kinser (2007) offers a glimpse at the complexity of this difference in his discussion of publicly owned education corporations. In the final analysis, missions for proprietary schools are influenced by a profit motive that distinguishes them from the not-for-profit segment of postsecondary education.

How Mission Informs Student Affairs Professional Practice

Thus far, this discussion has focused on the institutional types in the American schema of higher education. Institutions within these categories, to a large extent, share missions. These shared missions, in turn, influence the work of administrators, the relationships they form with students and others, and the rewards they reap from their jobs. A number of studies (Estanek et al., 2011; Hirt, 2006; Hirt, Amelink, & Schneiter, 2004; Hirt, Strayhorn, Amelink, & Bennett, 2006; Kinser, 2006; Taylor & Morphew, 2010) have examined the nature of professional life for student affairs administrators at different types of colleges and universities and inform the following discussion.

Liberal Arts Colleges

Most liberal arts colleges are small, residential, and committed to educating traditional-age students (Taylor & Morphew, 2010), which influences professional life in a number of ways. First, there are limited numbers of staff so many student affairs administrators have both primary and ancillary job responsibilities (for example, residence hall director and assistant director of student activities) and practitioners tend to work collaboratively—they need to rely on one another if large-scale programs are to succeed. Consequently, they operate much like a family and know one another personally and professionally. The family-like atmosphere fosters institutional loyalty. Professionals find a niche and it is not at all unusual for people to work twenty or more years at the same campus. Job advancement thus occurs either very slowly or through a move to a new college (Hirt, 2006).

The signature element of work at these institutions is the enduring ties that professionals and students sustain. Student affairs administrators at liberal arts colleges know about their students' academic, social, personal, and emotional lives. They frequently deal with parents and families, furthering their insights into their students. Those at liberal arts colleges often refer to seeing students develop over their undergraduate years and describe how their work with students nourishes them (Hirt et al., 2004).

The mission of liberal arts colleges influences the functions that professionals serve. At their core, these are student centered, teaching institutions (Urciuoli, 2003). Hence, faculty members are influential and professionals would be well served to understand the role they play. Engaging faculty in the design of programs and services is important to professional success. The student-centered nature of the campus translates to a need for professionals who are well versed in communication and counseling skills. These skills enable them to engage deeply with students over time to maximize the educational experience for those students.

Religiously Affiliated Colleges

Professional life at religiously affiliated colleges is similar to that at liberal arts colleges. Staff members often have ancillary responsibilities, their numbers are limited so they work closely together, and they often spend their entire career at a single campus. There are two distinctive aspects to working at a sectarian college, however. First, there is an additional layer to campus life—denominational issues. The politics of religious organizations are ever present and must be addressed in professional life (Briel, 2012). Student affairs administrators must be politically savvy to succeed. They often find themselves interpreting denominational issues to students and student issues to both denominational and campus leaders (Hirt, 2006).

The second distinction has to do with matters of personal faith. Professionals at religiously affiliated institutions know the academic, social, emotional, and personal lives of their students, and may also get involved in students' spiritual lives. In doing so, they are able to incorporate their own faith into their work (Stringer & Swezey, 2006). In fact, they often refer to their work as a calling or a mission, and it is the allure of incorporating their religious beliefs into their professional work that draws them to these campuses in the first place and sustains them once they are there.

Student affairs functions at religiously affiliated campuses can be closely linked to the sectarian mission. For instance, although many liberal arts colleges have a chapel on campus (often an artifact of their sectarian roots), most religiously affiliated campuses have large and active campus ministry offices. Religious services are commonplace as are programs with a denominational focus. Service is also fundamental, and service-learning centers are often very active on campus.

Master's Colleges and Universities

Professional life at master's colleges and universities is unique in several ways. First, although student affairs administrators tend to have a single job assignment, they have opportunities to work with professionals in other functional areas. Serving on campus-wide committees is a hallmark of work at master's colleges and universities. Second, because many campuses are members of a statewide system, professionals at these institutions are adept at cross-institutional work, especially strategic planning on a system-wide basis in order to routinize work (Hirt, 2006).

Their exposure to a broad spectrum of functional areas mirrors their exposure to a broad array of students. Master's colleges and universities offer both undergraduate and graduate education and primarily serve students from the region in which they are located (Gonzales, 2013). Student affairs professionals at these campuses value the opportunity to work with both populations of students and are deeply committed to providing opportunities to students whose circumstances might otherwise prevent them from seeking higher education.

Mission influences the functions for student affairs professionals at master's colleges and universities. These institutions typically serve under-represented and/or adult students who live within commuting distance of the campus. Consequently, they may have smaller residence hall systems but offer more programs to assist students in their transition to college, and more academic support and career services. Services for graduate students are also evident at these campuses. Finally, since many of their students are working adults, special services, like child care, are often provided and hours of operation for programs and services frequently extend to evenings and weekends.

Research and Doctoral Granting Universities

Unlike baccalaureate and master's campuses, most research and doctoral granting universities are mammoth, enrolling tens of thousands of students. Student affairs administrators at these institutions specialize in a single functional area (for example, career services, judicial affairs). They work closely with other professionals within that area, and usually with colleagues in one or two other departments on campus, but typically do not know most other student affairs staff members on campus. These universities strive for excellence, creating a politically charged and often competitive environment (Jaquette, 2013). Administrators need to understand and appreciate campus politics. One advantage to working in this large, complex environment is advancement opportunities. Those at research and doctoral granting universities can more easily move up to higher levels of responsibility at the same institution, although their counterparts at baccalaureate campuses may need to relocate to another college to assume higher-level positions.

The nature of relationships between administrators and students is also markedly different. Those at liberal arts and religiously affiliated colleges get to know many of their students personally and talk about seeing their students develop over time. At research and doctoral universities, professionals know most students only in the context of their functional area. For example, fraternity and sorority life professionals deal with students about issues associated with Greek life but not necessarily with personal or emotional issues. Instead of *seeing* students develop, those at doctoral and research campuses *believe* that what they do makes a difference in the lives of students.

The mission of these universities influences the breadth and scope of services for students. At many, for example, auxiliary programs like housing, the student newspaper, or campus radio station operate almost as independent enterprises. Some activities, like career advising, may take place within academic colleges rather than through a central office. Perhaps the most distinctive difference relates to graduate students. In addition to services for master's and doctoral students in the arts and sciences, programs for professional students in law, medicine, nursing, veterinary science, and the like require student affairs professionals with a unique knowledge base and skill set.

Associate's Colleges

Professional life at associate's colleges offers a different set of challenges and rewards. To start, most community colleges are relatively small so student affairs professionals often work closely with and get to know their students personally. They routinely talk about the changes they see in their students. Since community colleges serve a localized population, professionals frequently have contact with family members, adding another dimension to their relationships with students.

The nature of work for professionals at associate's colleges is fast paced (Abelman & Dalessandro, 2008). Staffs tend to be small and get to know one another well. Turnover is usually low, so professionals may work together for many years. Their work is highly bureaucratized and routinized, so professionals must both produce and perform at a high level of quality on a daily basis. Meeting this standard entails strategic planning on the part of administrators. Offsetting this pressure to produce, community college professionals work evenings and weekends very infrequently and are able to balance their work and personal lives in fairly predictable ways.

The mission of community colleges also affects the services they offer. Given their local service districts, for example, very few offer residence halls. Most, however, require students to complete academic assessments prior to enrolling so testing services is often a major component of a student affairs division. On a related note, most community colleges offer the first two years of baccalaureate education and prepare students to transfer to other four-year institutions. Consequently, experts in articulation agreements (policies governing what classes transfer to which four-year institution) are standard at community colleges.

Tribally Controlled Colleges

Information about the nature of work at tribally controlled institutions is sparse, perhaps because a different tribe (and hence, different tribal histories and traditions) controls each college. Nevertheless, Cajete (2005) characterizes tribal college education as "learning about life through participation and relationship to community, including not only people, but plants, animals, and the whole of nature" (p. 70). Students learn through experience, storytelling, ritual and ceremony, dreaming, apprenticeship, and artistic creation.

The work of student affairs professionals needs to be understood in light of tribal epistemologies. Nearly all tribes believe they exist at the center of seven directions: East, West, North, South, Zenith, Nadir, and the Center (Cajete, 2005). Seven foundations guide learning and development, including the environmental, the mythic, the visionary, the artistic, the affective, the communal, and the spiritual (Cajete, 2005). Culturally relevant programming is essential for the well-being and retention of Native American students, and professionals play a critical role in offering such programs (Martin & Thunder, 2013). Parallels appear to exist between student affairs work at tribally controlled colleges and the holistic approach to education that characterizes work at liberal arts, religiously affiliated, and community colleges. Far more information about professional life at tribal institutions is needed, however, to confirm any such assumption.

The mission of tribal colleges suggests some specific functions and skills not found at other types of institutions. For example, knowledge of tribal history and customs is essential and programming to tribal interests is common (Martin & Thunder, 2013). Given the role of tribal colleges in economic development, close ties with the tribal community are necessary (AIHEC, 2013). Finally, the student population at tribal colleges suggests that certain services, like child care, are more important than at some other types of campuses.

Historically Black Colleges and Universities

HBCUs reflect a variety of institutional types—from community colleges to liberal arts colleges, master's, and research universities (Brown, 2013).

Yet there are common threads in administrative life at these campuses. Many student affairs professionals are graduates of HBCUs, often of the college or university for which they work. Administrators view themselves as surrogate family members for students and describe themselves as students' mothers, fathers, siblings, or grandparents. This approach, referred to as "othermothering" (Guiffrida, 2005, p. 715), is an artifact of the damage done to Black families during slavery (see Guiffrida, 2005, for a detailed discussion of this phenomenon). HBCU professionals are irrevocably committed to providing educational opportunities for their students and believe that serving as family surrogates helps students achieve their potential.

Notions of family and commitment to racial uplift translate to other professional arenas of work life. To start, staff turnover at most HBCUs is limited. People tend to stay in the employ of one institution for many years, and staff become like family to one another. Additionally, resources at most HBCUs are very limited. Yet despite the deprivations imposed by limited resources, professionals at HBCUs are profoundly committed not only to their own campus but to HBCUs as an institutional genre. They see themselves as guardians of a species of higher education institutions that is threatened with extinction and they are determined to protect the educational opportunities that HBCUs offer for Black students.

HBCUs' missions can influence the breadth and scope of student affairs functions. Their dedication to racial uplift often extends to the local community and community service offices are common on these campuses. Likewise, events celebrating Black history and culture dominate campus life. In fact, some organizations, like fraternities and sororities, operate very differently than their counterparts at predominately White institutions and experts who understand those differences are indispensable.

Hispanic-Serving Institutions

Like their HBCU counterparts, HSIs include the full range of institutional types—community colleges, master's, and doctoral granting universities, among others. Yet certain aspects of work life for student affairs professionals transcend those institutional differences. To start, their work with students is grounded in the notion of respect. HSI professionals often talk about the respect they have for students and families. Administrators are open about the fact that dealing with a student often means dealing with the student's family.

Some of this respect translates to how HSI professionals view their work with students who might not otherwise participate in higher education. They genuinely marvel at their students. For many, serving students from underrepresented groups is what motivates and sustains them. Their dedication is admirable, particularly since many HSIs face severe resource deficits despite enrollments that are proliferating. As the Hispanic population in the United States continues to expand, HSIs will play an increasingly important role in higher education.

Because HSIs span many institutional types (Gonzales, 2013), it is more difficult to discern how mission influences the scope of student affairs work. Certain offices and functions, however, stand out at HSI campuses. Programs and services for parents and families are particularly evident because of the significance of family in many Hispanic cultures. Likewise, an ability to speak Spanish and an understanding of the many and varied Spanish speaking cultures are much needed skills for professionals at HSIs.

Proprietary Colleges and Universities

Like its HBCU and HSI counterparts, the for-profit sector runs the gamut of institutional types, from associate's colleges to doctoral granting universities. Yet the work of student affairs professionals is narrower and more focused at these campuses. Only a limited number of proprietary colleges offer traditional student services like housing, student activities, or athletics. Nearly all, however, offer programs and services associated with access (admission, financial aid), retention (academic advising, learning assistance), and vocational planning (career services, internships) (Davidson, 2008). Professional work on these campuses consists of getting students in, getting them through, and finding them work.

In large part, students drive the nature of work at for-profit institutions. These campuses serve disproportionately high numbers of racial and ethnic minorities, part-time students, and adult learners. Many students are employed and have families, juggling multiple roles in their lives (Kinser, 2006). Proprietary colleges and universities appeal to these students because they operate on a corporate model. Instruction is offered during evening and weekend hours, typically on a year-round basis, for the convenience of learners. Student services are available when courses are offered, so students can seek assistance when they are on site for classes. These institutions strive to deliver education in an effective and efficient manner.

This service-delivery focus is consistent with the mission of proprietary institutions. They are profit-driven organizations that identify an educational market niche and develop their business model to serve that niche (Yeoman, 2011). Institutional goals typically reflect student demands, and student affairs professionals align their work to achieve institutional goals. This alignment often requires administrators to partner with faculty so that curricular and co-curricular demands are addressed concurrently. In fact, Kinser (2006) argues that managers at not-for-profit colleges and universities might learn something about academic-student affairs partnerships from their for-profit colleagues. Student affairs professionals who seek to work closely with faculty, and who respect and appreciate issues like cost containment and efficiency, might appreciate professional life at these institutions.

Student Affairs Professional Mobility: Individual and Institutional Perspectives

It seems clear that institutional mission shapes professional practice in student affairs. Less clear, however, is whether mission also shapes professional mobility. Any student affairs administrator who has conducted a job search in recent years has probably fallen victim to the myopia that institutional mission can create. Most job announcements include language that refers to mission. Baccalaureate colleges seek individuals who understand and appreciate the value of a liberal education. Associate's colleges often require candidates to have prior experience in a community college setting. Once inculcated into the environment of a particular type of institution, there is an assumption that only others who have experience at a like campus are able to transition successfully to that institution. This is an increasing concern among student affairs professionals. Indeed, some younger professionals are convinced that the first position they assume will dictate the institutional sector in which they will spend their entire careers.

Yet the discussion suggests that there are certain elements of professional life that might translate across institutional types. For instance, student affairs administrators at both liberal arts colleges and community colleges develop relationships with students that are sufficiently close that they can see development in those they serve. Professionals at both types of campuses, along with their counterparts at sectarian colleges and HSIs, deal extensively with families of students. Work for professionals at master's campuses is often highly bureaucratized, requiring strategic planning skills, which is also descriptive of work at community colleges. The ability to work with diverse populations of students is essential at community colleges and master's institutions and would likely be transferrable to all other institutional types. It would seem counterproductive to limit applicant pools to those who have worked in certain settings without examining the skills professionals at other organization types might have garnered. Both employers and candidates need to ensure that individual talents, as opposed to experience at select institutional types, drive professional mobility.

Employers can start by determining whether experience at a particular type of institution is really a necessary prerequisite for a job at their campus. Instead of focusing on where a candidate has worked they might identify what a candidate has done—that is, the skill sets and talents they seek in applicants. Writing job announcements and descriptions accordingly would be a first step in broadening the applicant pool. They might also shape interview processes around those skill sets. Professional development programs can offer candidates with requisite skills insights into the peculiarities of the institutional type.

Student affairs administrators also need to be proactive. If a job announcement calls for experience at a certain type of campus, some applicants may self-select out of the process without further consideration. Instead, professionals would be well served to identify particular talents that would transfer readily from one institutional setting to another. They then need to highlight those talents during the job search process. Addressing the commonalities in the nature of work between the two institutional types is likely to go a long way in convincing employers that a candidate has an understanding of the new work environment.

Conclusion

This chapter has discussed mission and professional life at an array of institutional types, but there are many other kinds of institutions (for example, women's colleges, the emerging sector of Asian/Pacific Islander campuses) that merit further attention. Indeed, the diversity of institutional types in the American higher education enterprise is one of its greatest strengths. The variety of missions these institutions serve is impressive, even daunting. There is little doubt that institutional mission shapes professional practice for student affairs professionals, yet recognizing and appreciating differences in mission provides an avenue of professional mobility within the student affairs profession.

References

Abelman, R., & Dalessandro, A. (2008). The institutional vision of community colleges. *Community College Review, 35*(4), 306–335.

Allen, W. R., & Jewell, J. O. (2002). A backward glance forward: Past, present, and future perspectives on Historically Black Colleges and Universities. *Review of Higher Education, 25*(3), 241–261.

American Indian Higher Education Consortium. (2013). http://www.aihec.org/about/index.cfm .

Anderson, M. S. (2001). The complex relations between the academy and industry: Views from the literature. *Journal of Higher Education, 72*(2), 226–246.

Barr, M. J. (2000). The importance of the institutional mission. In M. J. Barr & M. K. Desler (eds.), *Handbook of student affairs administration* (2nd ed., pp. 25-49). San Francisco, CA: Jossey-Bass.

Belgarde, W. L. (1996). History of American Indian community colleges. In C. Turner, M. Garcia, A. Nora, & L. I. Rendon (eds.), *Racial and ethnic diversity in higher education* (pp.18-27). ASHE Reader Series. Boston, MA: Pearson.

Benitez, M. (1998). Hispanic Serving Institutions: Challenges and opportunities. In J. P. Merisotis & C. T. O'Brien (eds.), *Minority-serving institutions: Distinct purposes, common goals* (pp.57-68). San Francisco, CA: Jossey-Bass.

Breneman, D. (2005). Entrepreneurship in higher education. In B. Pusser (Ed.), *Arenas of entrepreneurship: Where nonprofit and for-profit institutions compete.* New Directions for Higher Education, no. *129.* San Francisco, CA: Jossey-Bass.

Breneman, D. W. (1994). *Liberal arts colleges: Thriving, surviving, or endangered?* Washington, DC: Brookings Institution.

Briel, D. B. (2012).Mission and identity: The role of faculty. *Journal of Catholic Higher Education, 31*(2), 169–179.

Brown, M. C. (2013). The declining significance of Historically Black Colleges and Universities: Relevance, reputation, and reality in Obamamerica. *Journal of Negro Education, 82*(1), 3–19.

Brown, M. C., & Davis, J. E. (2001). The Historically Black College as social contract, social capital, and social equalizer. *Peabody Journal of Education, 76*(1), 31–49.

Brown, M. C., Donahoo, S., & Bertrand, R. D. (2001). The Black college and the quest for educational opportunity. *Urban Education, 36*(5), 553–571.

Brubacher, J. S., & Rudy, W. (1997). *Higher education in transition: A history of colleges and universities* (4th ed.). New Brunswick, NJ: Transaction.

Cajete, G. A. (2005). American Indian epistemologies. In M. J. T. Fox, S. C. Lowe, & G. S. McClellan (Eds.), *Serving Native American students.* New Directions for Student Services, no. *109.* San Francisco, CA: Jossey-Bass.

Carnegie Foundation for the Advancement of Teaching. (2000). *A classification of institutions of higher education.* Princeton, NJ: Carnegie Council for the Advancement of Teaching.

Carnegie Classification of Institutions of Higher Education. (2010). http://
    classifications.carnegiefoundation.org/summary/basic.php.
Carney, C. M. (1999). *Native American higher education in the United States.* New
    Brunswick, NJ: Transaction.
Coaxum, J. (2001). The misalignment between the Carnegie Classifications and Black
    colleges. *Urban Education, 36*(5), 572–584.
Cohen, A. M., & Brawer, F. B. (2003). *The American community college* (4th ed.). San
    Francisco, CA: Jossey-Bass.
Contreras, F. E., Malcom, L. E., & Bensimon, E. M. (2008). Hispanic-serving
    institutions: Closeted Identity and the production of equitable outcomes for
    Latino/a Students. In M. Gasman, B. Baez, & C.S.V. Turner (eds.), *Understanding
    minority-serving institutions* (pp. 71-90). Albany: State University of New York Press.
Davidson, D. L. (2008). *Including all institutional types: Student services at for-profit
    institutions.* Paper presented at the Annual Conference of the American College
    Personnel Association, Atlanta, April 2008.
Estanek, S. M., Herdlein, R., & Harris, J. (2011). Preparation of new professional and
    mission driven hiring practices: A survey of senior student affairs officers at
    Catholic colleges and universities. *College Student Affairs Journal, 29*(2), 151–163.
Etzkowitz, H., Webster, A., & Healey, P. (Eds.). (1998). *Capitalizing knowledge: New
    intersections of industry and academia.* Albany: State University of New York Press.
Gonzales, L. D. (2013). Faculty sensemaking and mission creep: Interrogating
    institutionalized ways of knowing and doing legitimacy. *Review of Higher Education,
    36*(2), 179–209.
Gregory, S. T. (2003). Planning for the increasing number of Latino students.
    Planning for Higher Education, 31(4), 13–19.
Guiffrida, D. (2005). Othermothering as a framework for understanding African
    American students' definitions of student-centered faculty. *Journal of Higher
    Education, 76*(6), 701–723.
Hanford, E. (2013). The case against for-profit colleges and universities. http://
    americanradioworks.publicradio.org/features/tomorrows-college/phoenix/case-
    against-for-profit-schools.html.
Hirt, J. B. (2006). *Where you work matters: Student affairs administration at different types of
    institutions.* Washington, DC: American College Personnel Association.
Hirt, J. B., Amelink, C., & Schneiter, S. (2004). The nature of professional life at
    liberal arts colleges. *NASPA Journal, 42*(1), 94–110.
Hirt, J. B., Strayhorn, T. L., Amelink, C. T., & Bennett, B. R. (2006). The nature of
    student affairs work at Historically Black Colleges and Universities. *Journal of College
    Student Development, 47*(6), 661–676.
Humphries, F. S. (1995). A short history of Blacks in higher education. *Journal of
    Blacks in Higher Education, 6,* 57.
Jaquette, O. (2013). Why do colleges become universities? Mission drift and the
    enrollment economy. *Research in Higher Education, 54*(5), 514–543.
Kelly, K. F. (2001). *Meeting the needs and making profits: The rise of for-profit degree granting
    institutions.* Denver, CO: Education Commission of the States.
Kinser, K. (2005). A profile of regionally accredited for-profit institutions of higher
    education. In B. Pusser (Ed.), *Arenas of entrepreneurship: Where nonprofit and for-profit*

institutions compete. New Directions for Higher Education, no. *129.* San Francisco, CA: Jossey-Bass.

Kinser, K. (2006). Principles of student affairs in for-profit higher education. *NASPA Journal, 43*(2), 466–481.

Kinser, K. (2007). Dimensions of corporate ownership in for-profit education. *Review of Higher Education, 30*(3), 217–245.

Laden, B. V. (2001). Hispanic-serving institutions: Myths and realities. *Peabody Journal of Education, 76*(1), 73–92.

Lucas, C. J. (1994). *American higher education: A history.* New York, NY: St. Martin's Griffin.

McClellan, G. S., Fox, M.J.T., & Lowe, S. C. (2005).Where we have been: A history of Native American higher education. In M.J.T. Fox, S. C. Lowe, & G. S. McClellan (eds.), *Serving Native American students.* New Directions for Student Services, no. *109.* San Francisco, CA: Jossey-Bass.

Martin, S. C., & Thunder, A. L. (2013). Incorporating Native culture into student affairs. In H. J. Shotton, S. C. Lowe, & S. J. Waterman (eds.), *Beyond the asterisk: Understanding Native students in higher education* (pp. 39-52). Sterling, VA: Stylus.

Morphew, C. C., & Hartley, M. (2006). Mission statements: A thematic analysis of rhetoric across institutional type. *Journal of Higher Education, 77*(3), 456–471.

National Center for Education Statistics. (2005). *Digest of education statistics: 2005.* http://nces.ed.gov/programs/digest/d05/tables/dt05_170.asp.

Slaughter, S., & Leslie, L. L. (1997). *Academic capitalism: Politics, policies and the entrepreneurial university.* Baltimore, MD: Johns Hopkins University Press.

Stringer, J., & Swezey, E. (2006). The purpose of a student affairs preparation program within Catholic higher education. *Catholic Education: A Journal of Inquiry and Practice, 10*(2), 181–198.

Taylor, B. J., & Morphew, C. C. (2010). An analysis of baccalaureate college mission statements. *Research in Higher Education, 51*(5), 483–503.

Thelin, J. R. (2004). *A history of American higher education.* Baltimore, MD: Johns Hopkins University Press.

Urban, W., & Wagoner, J. (2000). *American education: A history* (2nd ed.). Boston, MA: McGraw-Hill.

Urciuoli, B. (2003). Excellence, leadership, skills, diversity: Marketing liberal arts education. *Language and Communication, 23*(3–4), 385–408.

US Census Bureau. (2002). *Resident population estimates of the United States by sex, race and Hispanic origin: April 1 to July 1, 1999, with short-term projection to June 1, 2001.* Washington, DC: Author.

US Department of Education, National Center for Education Statistics. (2002). *Hispanic serving institutions: Statistical trends from 1990 to 1999.* NCES 2002–051, by Christina Stearns & Satoshi Watanbe. Project Officer: Thomas D. Snyder. Washington, DC: Author.

Yeoman, B. (2011, May–June). The high price of for-profit colleges. *Academe.* http://www.aaup.org/article/high-price-profit-colleges#.UmMOwiR1GUc.

CHAPTER THREE

UNDERSTANDING CAMPUS ENVIRONMENTS

Jillian Kinzie and Victor Arcelus

Athletic fields, a bell tower, young adults walking with backpacks, and signs directing traffic to the stadium, library, performing arts center, or admissions office are all unmistakable symbols of a traditional collegiate environment. These elements and most basic features of institutions of higher education are recognizably similar, including the configuration of classrooms, laboratories, and studios, the structure of the academic calendar, curriculum, the availability of enriching experiences like speakers and events, and the interaction among students and faculty. Although colleges and universities are commonly distinguished by specific institutional characteristics, including enrollment or size, public or private, two-year or four-year, or religious affiliation, most of the conditions for undergraduate education are similar across institutions. Even the growing sector of distance education and virtual platforms for postsecondary education share common environmental elements. Yet, the collegiate environment, both physical and virtual, is unique; distinct from the setting in which it is located, each institution has its own culture, language, behavior, artifacts, rules, and symbols. In addition, all students bring their own life experiences to the collegiate experience, which then intersects with the campus culture. At this intersection, the campus environment has an effect on the quality of students' experience, influencing how students feel and what they do by presenting complex choices and opportunities, with consequences that may or may not be productive for learning and success. Given the imminent shifts in the college-going population, including more adult and part-time students, greater racial/ethnic and socioeconomic diversity, and the varied ways students participate in college, for example, online or attending multiple institutions concurrently, it is critical for college educators to understand the role of the campus environment, its intersection with the life experiences and personal characteristics students bring to campus, and the elements that optimize the conditions for student learning and success.

Contemporary concerns about expanding access to postsecondary education and increasing student success rates demand collective and immediate action. Among a range of suggested steps for improving college attainment rates is that of focusing on the collegiate environment, namely, enhancing the environment to foster student success and to create a more "student-centered culture" (American Council on Education, 2013, p. 12). Decades of research demonstrate that institutional context and campus environment matter to student learning and success (Astin, 1993a; Kuh, Kinzie, Schuh, Whitt, & Associates, 2010; Kuh, Schuh, Whitt, & Associates, 1991; Pascarella & Terenzini, 1991; 2005; and Strange & Banning, 2001). The institutional context influences who goes to college, what students do when they get there, what they gain from their experience, and their likelihood for completing a degree. As a result, colleges and universities are advised to assess the institutional conditions for educational purposes and amplify aspects of the environment that help increase the number of students who stay enrolled, engaged, and complete their educations.

Another pressing matter that focuses attention on the campus environment are calls to improve the quality of undergraduate education by creating more inclusive, holistic, integrated learning environments (American College Personnel Association, 1996; Association for American Colleges and Universities, 2002, 2007; National Association of Student Personnel Administrators, 2004). The need to be inclusive requires the creation of learning-centered environments in and out of the classroom in which any individual or group can feel welcomed, respected, supported, and valued. This view broadens the setting for learning across the college context and exposes students to multiple opportunities for intentional learning through the academic curriculum, environmental structures, student life experiences, co-curricular programming, community-based instruction, and global experiences. This expanded view requires greater awareness of the institutional conditions and their influence on learning, it and demands the gathering of information through assessment of the environment and action to create environments for maximum educational advantage. This whole-environment view also requires stronger partnerships among campus educators to make sure all are pulling in the same direction.

To ensure greater success rates for all students, higher education must attend to the features of the campus environment that matter to student learning and success. Certain campus environments can be empowering and can facilitate high levels of achievement, while others may be alienating or stress inducing. Student affairs educators must understand how they help students navigate, adjust to, and make the most of the campus environment. These educators must help students connect to the institution, find a sense of belonging, achieve their educational and personal goals, and make the most of their educational opportunities.

This chapter provides an overview of different environmental theories applicable to higher education settings. It introduces the most important contextual conditions that foster student learning and encourages the use of multiple perspectives to more fully appreciate the influence of college and university environments on student learning and success. Following the review of environmental theories, the chapter outlines approaches for assessing the conditions for learning and success. It then moves to a discussion of the impact of the college environment on student success, and highlights two topics important to student affairs—the importance of adopting a holistic, learning-oriented framework for optimizing the impact of the college environment, and bridging the divide between student and academic affairs.

Frameworks for Understanding Campus Environments

College and university environments are dynamic networks of factors and conditions. In the broadest sense, the term *campus environment* denotes the entirety of the college and university surroundings and conditions in which people live or function. The term implies a multiplicity of individuals, forces, and systems interacting, and usually suggests a physical space, or a virtual equivalent, and features connections to other places. Although campus environments are a mix of the deliberate and the accidental, the combination of planned and unanticipated events, student affairs professionals must understand how the environment affects students and know how to modify conditions in ways that induce students to participate fully in the features of the campus environment that matter to learning, development, and student success.

A range of theories addressing the conditions of environments and the design of environments for educational outcomes (for example, Astin, 1993a; Banning & Bartels, 1997; Kuh et al., 1991; and Strange & Banning, 2001) provide student affairs educators useful perspectives for understanding the features of the campus environment and their influence. One well-established theory that broadly frames the interaction between students and their campus environment and the achievement of desirable student outcomes is Astin's (1985, 1993a) conceptual model: input-environment-output (I-E-O). Astin concluded that the growth and change that students experienced in college was attributable to college experiences and that institutions can actively shape the conditions to positively affect important outcomes. Astin's (1993a) findings summarized in *What Matters in College* are vital resources for understanding the powerful influence of hundreds of environmental characteristics of colleges and how these factors shape student outcomes.

Theories of campus environments are further defined by their particular focus. For example, theories that address the physical components of environment (Strange & Banning, 2001) emphasize the physical structure and landscape of the campus. Another category includes human aggregate theories such as Holland's (1997) person–environment interaction models, and conceptions of subcultures as described by Astin (1993b), Clark and Trow (1966), and later, Hendrel and Harrold (2007). Theories focused on constructed environments emphasize models of environmental press (Pace, 1979; Moos, 1979, 1988) and models of campus culture (Kuh & Hall, 1993; Kuh & Whitt, 1988; Moffatt, 1989).

Strange and Banning (2001) offer a comprehensive synthesis of most of the aforementioned models for understanding campus environments and educational design. Their summary associates environmental purposes related to student success, including adjustment and security, involvement, and full membership in the learning community, to four dimensions of campus environments:

1. *Physical*: The design and quality of physical features
2. *Human aggregate*: The collective characteristics of groups of people
3. *Organizational*: The dynamics of campus organizational structures that serve specific goals
4. *Constructed*: The collective meanings constructed by members and attributed to environmental dimensions

These four components are the sources of influence on human behavior on campus and actively shape the achievement of educational purposes. The sections that follow introduce the four components of campus environments and provide fundamental information about the most critical environmental elements and how they can be designed and manipulated to optimize student success.

Physical Environments

The first element of campus environments pertains to the natural and synthetic features of the campus. The physical structure, such as gates welcoming students to an exclusive setting, the sidewalks converging on the entrance to the library from all directions, and the overall landscape and spatial arrangement of campus buildings, creates a powerful influence on students' attraction to a campus and their satisfaction and commitment to the learning environment. The fields of design, art, architecture, landscape, and planning shape the campus environment. Most important to understanding physical components is attending to what the features permit, enable, and inhibit. For example, the library at Indiana University/Purdue University Indianapolis (IUPUI) was redesigned so that that a long wall that once held sixty-eight isolated, stationary study carrels was transformed into a more contemporary environment for individual and group study and to encourage more collaboration and active participation. The flexible workspaces were designed to accommodate differences in individual learning styles and to reflect the study habits and methods of today's students.

Physical features of a campus environment can also discourage behaviors and inhibit belonging. For example, a lack of seating near classrooms discourages students from arriving early or meeting with classmates and faculty for informal discussions after class; in the same way, a large wall in the student union adorned with photos of campus leaders but featuring few images of students of color can reduce underrepresented minority students' sense of belonging overall, and alienate them from positions of campus leadership. Student affairs educators who are serious about fostering supportive campus communities for all students must observe and attend to the influence of the physical environment and what it represents. Kinzie and Mulholland (2008), for example, describe the physical properties of the student union that contribute to or inhibit multicultural learning and inclusiveness, including the presentation of diverse images in campus photos and art, access to computer stations for students with physical challenges, among others, and suggest practical recommendations for making physical space more conducive to cross-cultural engagement and learning.

Viewing the college experience through the lens of the physical environment offers a perspective that student affairs educators can adopt to scan the environment and identify features that foster inclusion and support for learning and those that are counter to these goals.

Human Aggregate Environments

The second source of environmental influence identified by Strange and Banning (2001) addresses the human aggregate, or the impact of human characteristics on environments. This component refers to how the environment reflects the dominant characteristics of the people in it, and is akin to identifying the campus's "personality" or student culture. Human aggregate and, specifically, typology models define the patterned differences among students. Clark and Trow (1966) theorized four student subcultures based on the extent to which a student identifies with the institution and is involved with ideas: *academic, nonconformist, collegiate,* and *vocational.* For example, a collegiate subculture, defined by having extensive identification with the institution and little involvement with ideas, is a subculture the focuses on fraternity and sorority participation, parties, and football, with faculty and courses and grades in the background. A classic example of the collegiate subcultures is illustrated at Big Ten institutions such as Michigan State and Penn State, particularly during fall football weekend traditions and events that appeal to many students, but that make some students who are not interested feel disconnected from the dominant subculture and the campus as a whole.

The human aggregate largely determines a student's fit at a given institution. For example, the scholarly type, one of Astin's (1993b) seven empirically derived student types (Scholars, Student Activists, Artists, Hedonists, Leaders, Status Strivers, and Uncommited), displays a high degree of academic and intellectual self-esteem and high aspirations for academic success and advanced degree. The scholarly type fits with a campus environment with an intense intellectual milieu, emphasizes studying and academic commitment. The intense intellectual environment at selective, private liberal arts colleges such as Amherst or Williams College are most supportive of the scholarly type. Kuh, Hu, and Vesper (2000) further explored the relevance of typologies and identified ten types of students based on their engagement patterns, or the extent to which they dedicated effort to educationally purposeful activities. In addition to the role of type in influencing individual student fit, to the extent that one or more of these student types predominates at the campus, the human aggregate element of the environment exerts pressure to conform to the dominant type.

Another focus in human aggregate theory is person-environment interaction. Specifically, the degree of congruence between persons and their environment is important to the understanding of how someone will function within the environment and whether they will adapt to it, leave, it or try to change it. Holland's (1997) theory of vocational personalities and work environments identifies six personality types with parallel model environments and asserts that individuals actively seek out and select environments that are congruent with their personality types. The theory has been applied to study students' college choice, expectations about college, selection of academic major, socialization, and learning (Feldman, Ethington, & Smart, 2001; Pike, 2006; Smart, Feldman, & Ethington, 2000). Research employing Holland's model demonstrates that during the college choice process, students are making judgments about the alignment between their interests and the environment, and once they arrive on campus they are continuing to gauge the extent to which the campus environment encourages or is unsupportive of their types. College students seek educational environments that encourage them to develop further their dominant characteristic interests and abilities (Smart et al., 2000). This lens suggests that if an institution wishes to, for example, attract particular types of students, it may need to adapt programs, facilities, and community life to make the institution attractive to, and better align with, interests and needs of these student types.

A practical application of the person–environment interaction lens on college campuses is evidenced in assessments of the climate for under-represented students. Rankin's (2003) campus climate reports for gay, lesbian, bisexual, and transgender (GLBT) students documents that the campus community has not been an empowering place for GLBT people and that GLBT intolerance and harassment is prevalent. According to Rankin, assessments of campus climate illustrate that though institutional missions suggest that higher education values multicultural awareness and understanding and the creation of welcoming and inclusive climates, the college environment is a focused aggregate dominated by hetero-sexism, with dynamics that are incongruent with GLBT student interests and needs.

Human aggregate models and typologies help student affairs practitioners understand the evolving nature of college student characteristics and student types in a particular historical context. Even more, typologies provide a framework to reflect upon questions of alignment between institutional mission and culture and student interests, educational experiences, and outcomes. The assessment of institutional effectiveness needs to include an examination of student type and how students of various types progress toward their academic objectives during college. This frame can provide a tool for reflecting on institutional traditions, practices, and policies, and for gauging the extent to which they are aligned with student interests and efforts.

Organized Environments

The third component of campus environments is the organizational structure, defined as the patterns and processes that are created within the campus environment to get things done. Like all organizations, colleges and universities have been created to achieve particular goals in specific ways. Goals include educating students, creating and disseminating knowledge, serving the people of the state or region, and providing opportunities for civic and cultural enrichment for the community, among others. These goals influence how colleges and universities are organized, including the division of labor, distribution of power, and execution of policies and procedures. Decisions about how things are organized on campus affects the overall design of the environment, including how individuals function and feel in it.

Strange and Banning (2001) identify seven dimensions of organizational structure—complexity, centralization, formalization, stratification, production, efficiency, and morale—that contribute to degrees of flexibility or rigidity in the campus environment. Some of these dimensions are easy to understand and observe in campus environments; for example, the idea of organizational complexity in universities is demonstrated by the professional credentials and training required of various roles, such as the professional degrees required to work in academic departments or the counseling or career development office. Although aspects like production, which refers to the organization's products or services and productivity, may be difficult to see throughout the institution, they may be expressed in metrics such as enrollment yields, minority student enrollment, research grants received, advisee contacts, and job placement rates. These dimensions have implications for the college or university to meet its educational goals. Strange and Banning (2001) assert that to be responsive to students' learning needs, educational environments must have flexible structures that encourage innovation and engage students as meaningful participants.

The high-performing institutions identified by Kuh and colleagues (Kuh et al., 2010), demonstrate dynamic organizations with structures focused on student learning and success as a central purpose. At these institutions, student learning is the raison d'être for institutional policies, programs, practices, and the rationale for daily activities as well as broad institutional directions. Practices, policies, and programs foster (and even require) students to take advantage of resources designed to support student learning and success. Practices and policies that encourage students to take advantage of academic support services, writing centers, tutoring, leadership opportunities, and other educational programs are organizational structures that create and sustain a culture that promotes student success. Information about organizational productivity and the extent to which the environment supports student success, as monitored by measures such as the National Survey of Student Engagement (NSSE), or revealed in studies that identify curricular trouble spots (that is, courses with high fail or withdrawal rates), can point to areas of campus life that are problematic, or underperforming in general or for particular groups of students.

The organized environment frame emphasizes the benefits of considering how effectively the organizational form works to support student success, and in student affairs units, the extent to which it fosters flexibility, responsiveness, and collaboration to address student success needs. Manning, Kinzie, and Schuh (2006) theorized eleven organizational models for student affairs practice that take into account the campus culture and the current emphasis on student engagement and success. The organized environment frame provides a lens through which to thoughtfully consider the extent to which student affairs is positioned to help an institution fulfill expectations for all aspects of the learning environment to contribute to engaged and successful students.

Constructed Environments

The final component of campus environments relates to how the environment is perceived by individuals and how people make meaning in understanding the nature of the campus environment. Models of constructed environments assume that environments are perceptions or constructions of those who participate in them (Strange and Banning, 2001). In turn, the perceived characteristics influence behavior. For example, the collective perception among faculty and staff at Fayetteville State University (FSU) is a belief in "meeting students where they are"—which means developing students' talents, regardless of their academic preparation or background. This belief is not expressed explicitly in the mission or philosophy and value statements, yet the majority of faculty members understand that this is a part of the mission. Various maxims, such as "You have to reach them to teach them," or "You must teach the students you have, not the ones you wish you had," or "We don't want students to go through school, but for school to go through them," and "We will meet you where you are, but we will tell you where we want you to go" (Kuh et al., 2010, p. 78), illustrate perceptions of the campus environment that inform teaching and learning practices and the extent to which faculty are expected to challenge and support FSU students.

Constructed environments can be assessed through self-reports of participants activities and perceptions of institutional emphasis or by observers of the environment. This focus on both student and environmental factors related to college success became an important area of study for Pace (1964; 1979), who developed questionnaires for students to report on the college environment and in turn for the campus to understand the environment. Assessments of the campus environment identified three sources of environmental press: (1) administrative, which refers to perceptions of academic policies and conditions of facilities; (2) academic, or conditions of the curriculum, courses, and classroom practices; and (3) student sources, which refers to co-curricular programming, informal activities, and the attitudes of students. Pace's studies of college environments documented the influence of student and academic subcultures, programs, policies, facilities, among other factors, and how they vary among colleges and universities.

Another emphasis in constructed environments is on campus culture as a tool for describing and understanding college environments. Institutional culture is a multifaceted construct represented in part by deeply embedded, intertwined patterns of behavior, values, and beliefs shared more or less by members of the community (Kuh & Whitt, 1988). As an "invisible tapestry" (Kuh & Whitt, 1988), culture gives meaning to campus activities and events; provides a common language, purpose, and direction; and brings a measure of coherence to campus life (Kuh, Schuh, Whitt, & Associates, 1991; Kuh & Whitt, 1988; and Magolda, 2000; Manning, 2000). Culture is reflected in traditions, rituals, stories, ceremonies, myths, histories and interactions among members, policies, practices, and mission and philosophy.

The current focus on campuses to create a more student-centered culture suggests the importance of adopting a campus culture perspective of the college environment. Kuh and colleagues' identification of the features of high-performing institutions (Kuh et al., 2010) provides some illustration of the essential cultural properties in educationally effective or student-centered cultures. This work, combined with tried-and-true lessons from Chickering and Gamson (1987) regarding principles of good practice in undergraduate education, informed Kinzie and Kuh's (2007) identification of seven threads that are woven throughout the fabric of student-centered cultures:

1. Clear, coherent mission and philosophy
2. Unshakeable focus on student learning
3. High performance expectations for all students
4. Widespread use of effective educational practices
5. Human-scale settings
6. Collaborative, improvement-oriented ethic
7. Language and traditions that support student success

Institutions with strong student-centered cultures focus on students and their learning and present their students with rich and varied opportunities for learning inside and outside the classroom, challenge students to reach high levels of performance, and provide support to help meet students' academic and social needs. To create and sustain a student-centered culture, colleges and universities must understand the properties of campus cultures that foster student success and then work to ensure that they are in place and work for all students. To determine whether a campus is a student-centered culture, one must "make the familiar strange" (Whitt, 1993): that is, to look anew at the obvious, everyday patterns and activities and try to understand their meaning and influence on different groups—students, faculty from different departments, staff, and so on. To understand the culture and ascertain the extent to which it is student centered, it is necessary to go into natural settings and observe everyday activities. This approach is discussed more thoroughly in the next section of this chapter.

Theories of college and university environments provide a practical lens through which to view the undergraduate experience. More important, the models suggest how environmental components can positively influence students through physical features that are facilitative and welcoming, human aggregate characteristics that are affirming, organizational features that guide navigation, and aspects of the constructed environment that support positive perceptions and experiences. These frames are useful for student affairs professionals to understand and apply, particularly in situations where the environment is not supporting educational effectiveness.

Approaches to Assessing and Enhancing College Environments

Given the role that college environments play in the impact of college on students, it is essential for institutions to examine the environment and determine how it contributes to student success and the quality of learning experiences. Assessment results about the campus environment, including perceptions of students, faculty, and staff, considered in relation to environmental frameworks and combined with research about educational practices that support learning and success, can provide campus leaders with immediately useful information to inform efforts to improve educational quality. There are many approaches to assessing college environments including surveys, observation, focus groups, interviews, cultural audits, and ethnography.

Surveys are a popular approach for assessing the campus environment. One tool for assessing desirable aspects of the learning environment is the National Survey of Student Engagement, and the companion two-year instrument, the Community College Survey of Student Engagement (CCSSE). These assessment tools provide participating campuses valid, reliable information about students' engagement in educationally effective practices and their perceptions of the environment for learning. Student engagement results, combined with results from the Faculty Survey of Student Engagement (FSSE) about faculty practices and perceptions of student engagement, can provide institutions with a portrait of the student experience, the opportunity to disaggregate and explore by subpopulations, and to identify aspects of the learning environment misaligned with the institutional mission.

In addition to surveys of the total learning environment such as NSSE and CCSSE, more focused measures of campus climate (to assess climate for multiculturalism, or to study the experience of underrepresented student populations, and so on), and of particular environments (campus housing, the union, and so on), or for specific student subcultures (athletes, students in Greek life) are available. For example, the Higher Education Research Institute's Diverse Learning Environment (DLE) survey, which assesses the impact of the diverse environments that help shape student learning, captures student perceptions regarding the institutional climate, campus practices as experienced with faculty, staff, and peers, and student learning outcomes. Diverse student populations are at the crux of the survey, and the instrument is based on studies of diverse students and the complexity of issues that range from student mobility to intergroup relations (Hurtado, Arellano, Cuellar, & Guillermo-Wann, 2011; and Hurtado, Griffin, Arellano, & Cuellar, 2008). Another survey example is a suite of questionnaires available through Educational Benchmarking Inc. (EBI) to assess housing quality and the influence of different environmental conditions. By electing to use these more focused surveys, student affairs professionals can secure the information they need to evaluate performance, identify their contribution to professional standards and the institutional mission, and inform continuous improvement initiatives.

Although approaches using quantitative measures can provide helpful information to pinpoint strengths and shortcomings in the college environment, they do not fully capture all the elements of college environments, nor are they sufficient for collecting information about environmental aspects that can be readily observed, such as how students interact in the campus union, or how well a new learning commons is facilitating study groups. Student affairs professionals who can actively explore the environment with an eye toward inventorying what transpires in campus spaces, and to determine whether students are using spaces as intended, provide salient information about the campus environment. For example, concern about poor academic performance of students in a first-year student residence hall at an institution in the Midwest led to a study to explore residents' use of study space and study habits. Through observation and interviews with students, student affairs staff learned that the environment in the residence hall discouraged studying; as the hall nearest to the main academic buildings, it had high traffic and was known to all students as a place to socialize at all hours, and residents were advised to study someplace else. Following the environmental analysis, the campus designed a new social space to divert students from using the residence hall for this purpose, and invested in more flexible and quiet study space in the residence hall to support students' learning needs.

Analysis of campus environments demands the examination of all dimensions of the institution in order to begin to understand how students, faculty, and staff perceive the campus environment and how that influences the choices that people make on a daily basis. Observing everyday activities in natural campus settings and attempting to experience spaces from the vantage point of different student groups is a simple way to use an anthropological framework (Tierney, 1988) to better understand the influence of the environment on student learning and success.

The contextual conditions of a campus that influence learning and success can be better understood through an in-depth study of an institution's culture, policies, and practices. Institutional audits are labor-intensive processes for exploring the campus culture, but they can reveal detailed practice- and policy-relevant information that cannot be accessed by other means. One framework to help institutions work through an exploration of institutional effectiveness and take action to address the results of the examination is provided in the step-by-step guide, the Inventory for Student Engagement and Success (Kuh, Kinzie, Schuh, & Whitt, 2005). The process can be applied to areas within an institution, such as a school or college, or student affairs, and employs a set of diagnostic queries and interview protocols for students, faculty, and staff and administrators that focus on six properties and conditions common to high-performing colleges and universities. The practical approach advocated in this guide is a useful framework for conducting a self-study of institutional culture and for exploring elements of education effectiveness.

A culture audit is a comprehensive approach to discovering and documenting the conditions of the campus environment. The notion of assessing the campus environment through an audit process has been well documented (Kuh, 2009; Kuh & Whitt, 1988; Whitt, 1993; and Whitt & Kuh, 1991). Whitt (1993) defined a culture audit as providing insiders and outsiders with a means to systematically discover and identify the artifacts, values, and assumptions that comprise the culture. Culture audits allow student affairs educators to thoroughly examine the environment to assess the signals the institution is sending to its students. Audits can also be a way to more fully explore the context for cross division collaboration and the perceptions of faculty and student affairs staff relating to their own and each other's roles on campus.

Ethnography is a methodological tradition that can serve as a guide in pursuing the culture audit. Ethnographic work aims to uncover and explicate the ways in which people come to understand, account for, take action, and otherwise manage their day-to-day situations (Magolda, 1999). Key questions to consider include the following: "How have the people in this setting constructed reality? What are their reported perceptions, 'truths,' explanations, beliefs, and worldview?" (Patton, 2002, p. 96). The goal of ethnography is "to grasp the native's point of view, his relation to life, to realize his vision of his world" (Malinowski, 1922, p. 25). The focus of ethnography is on understanding the culture of the group, including how people experience and interpret the behaviors they have learned as members of a group. To understand a particular campus culture, it is necessary to explore ideas, beliefs, and knowledge that emerge as people interact and participate in shared activities.

In focusing on culture, attention is paid to the meanings that people give to events in a particular setting (Kuh & Whitt, 1988). Individuals within cultures develop lenses through which to view and interpret a situation at a particular time in a particular context. To understand a campus's environment, it is vital to uncover these lenses, understand how individuals make meaning from their particular lenses, and describe how people's many lenses connect and weave together. The discovery of these lenses involves engaging in participant fieldwork as well as gathering information through interviews, participant observation, and artifact analysis. Interviews can consist of both formally scheduled sessions with members of the community as well as informal, casual conversations (Patton, 2002). Participant observation focuses on everyday activities in which one observes people's behavior and inquires about the meaning behind the behavior by seeking participants' perspectives about why things happened (Fetterman, 1998). The third approach is artifact analysis, which involves examining documents relevant to the setting to discover patterns within the texts and to gain insights into espoused objectives. Throughout fieldwork, themes are developed to help explain one's interpretation of the culture. The goal of the audit is to help faculty, student affairs professionals, and students become more familiar with conditions of the campus environment from an insider's point of view. Information from a campus audit can provide critical insight about community members' experiences and interpretations that can then be used to inform efforts to encourage more students to take advantage of learning opportunities inherent in collegiate environments and to intentionally shape the environment to promote shared educational goals.

Considering the Impact of College Environments

Theories about college environments provide useful frameworks for understanding the distinctive elements of colleges and universities, and strategies to assess the environment provide a pathway to determine how campus settings contribute to student success. With theories and assessment strategies as backdrop, we now move to a discussion of the impact that the campus environment can have on student success and how environmental analysis with a focus on academic and student affairs collaboration can facilitate the development of a cohesive cross-divisional approach to undergraduate education.

The most comprehensive synthesis of college environment and impact research is found in the two volumes authored by Pascarella and Terenzini (1991, 2005). In 2005, the authors affirmed that although basic structural conditions of the undergraduate experience, such as institutional type, size, and locale, influence where students enroll, what really matters to student development and learning and the achievement of learning outcomes is the nature of the experiences students have, including college courses, instructional methods, interactions with peers and faculty, involvement in activities and meaningful educational experiences, and the extent to which students are supported in the social and academic systems at the institution. The nature and quality of the campus environment clearly influences student learning and success and makes it incumbent on student affairs educators to fully understand the total learning environment in which students interact with peers, the content, educators, and others, and the implementation of strategies that help guide the student toward the intended outcomes. Understanding the impact of the total environment demands that student affairs professionals attend to the whole environment, and in particular areas typically found outside the campus life division and the cross-institution collaboration that this perspective demands.

Research affirming the importance of the total quality of the campus environment to college impact suggests a broader frame for student affairs practice than is sometimes operationalized at most colleges and universities. It implies that student affairs educators adopt a wider lens and to think more holistically—from students' point of view—about the college experience. Seamless learning environments, advocated in the Student Learning Imperative (American College Personnel Association, 1996), require student affairs professionals and faculty to break out of their silos and develop integrated, complementary experiences for students. This philosophy suggests that the whole of the student experience is greater than the sum of its parts and that the distinction between in- and out-of-classroom learning blurs. It demands that student affairs educators work more with units and partners across campus to ensure that experiences are aligned and interconnected to support student success. To accomplish this goal, student affairs educators must understand the environment within which they work.

A useful framework for advancing this more comprehensive view of the college environment is described in *Learning Reconsidered* (NASPA, 2004), which portrays the entire campus as a learning community and defines learning as an activity that integrates both academics and student development. It also proclaims that student affairs educators explicate the learning derived from out-of-classroom experiences, commit to assessing the environment for learning, and be more accountable for the contributions these experiences make to advancing broad student learning outcomes. The Learning Partnership model (Baxter-Magolda and King, 2004) provides another helpful perspective, demonstrating the importance of adopting a holistic approach to integrating the multiple dimensions of campus life, including the need to help students make connections among ideas, experiences, contexts, people, and to make meaning of these experiences to develop an integrated sense of identity.

Despite the call for various units of higher education to collaborate to enrich the student experience, increased collaboration among campus units has been hampered by the distinct and sometimes disconnected cultures of student and academic affairs. Engstrom and Tinto (2000) note that student affairs professionals and faculty can struggle to comprehend one another's discourse and do not necessarily accurately understand each other's roles and responsibilities. The resulting cultural differences lead to misunderstandings, disrespect, and conflict. These sentiments are magnified when those at an institution focus on differences rather than on the commonalities that exist in their values and goals for educating students. Developing relationships, rather than focusing on the concept of the other, increases the likelihood of collaboration based on shared values and purpose (Rhoads & Tierney, 1992).

Bridging the gap between academic and student affairs divisions needs to be a high priority in order to develop campus environments that cultivate student success. It is important for the major players who shape the educational environment to work together to establish priorities to support learning. However, because the traditional college culture places faculty in the sole role of educator, this role is usually not assumed by student affairs professionals. In fact, narrow definitions of who is an "educator" can be one of the most significant barriers impeding a partnership between faculty and student affairs professionals, and it may be deeply embedded in the cultural norms of both divisions (Arcelus, 2008). Collaboration requires people on both sides to take the bold step and walk across the divisional border, and, through dialogue, to create relationships based on a moral responsibility to improve student learning (Magolda, 2005).

One established approach to encouraging cross-cultural discussion is through the interactive processes of intragroup (within-group) and intergroup (across-group) dialogue. Intragroup dialogue is consistent with Magolda's (2005) emphasis on the need for the subcultures of academic and student affairs first to understand themselves and to develop a deeper understanding of their own norms and values before embarking on an effort to learn about the other. Intergroup dialogue aims to develop trust and mutual understanding among different groups (Schoem, Hurtado, Sevig, Chesler, & Sumida, 2001). Schoem et al. (2001) define it as "a form of democratic practice, engagement, problem solving, and education involving face-to-face, focused, facilitated, and confidential discussions occurring over time between two or more groups of people defined by their different social identities" (p. 6). Once a foundation of mutual understanding is established through intergroup dialogue, discussion of collaborative initiatives has the potential to lead to successful, long lasting, and meaningful opportunities for student learning (Arcelus, 2011).

Pace, Blumreich, and Merkle (2006) provide an example of how intergroup dialogue was used at Grand Valley State University (GVSU) to foster greater understanding between the student and academic affairs culture, with the ultimate goal of increasing collaboration between academic and student affairs on efforts to reform liberal education. Their project, called "Claiming a Liberal Education," sought to develop opportunities for cross-divisional collaborations focused on student learning. GVSU administrators designed intergroup dialogues so that small groups of faculty and staff had the opportunity to discuss the meaning of liberal arts education and ways in which the two divisions might collaborate to support that education. Guided by facilitators, multiple groups of faculty, staff, and students met several times. The lead facilitators found that these meetings allowed people to learn about each other's roles, develop relationships that they planned to continue, and cultivate an appreciation for the importance of integrating the curricular and co-curricular components of students' education (Pace et al., 2006). Once this pivotal groundwork is accomplished, it is possible to implement collective initiatives. This example suggests that differences between student and academic affairs cultures can be bridged by striving to understand each other's culture through structured dialogue that allows for mutual understanding and the development of shared educational goals.

Conclusion

The distinct conditions of the collegiate environment influence the quality of students' experience, including how students feel and what they do, with consequences that may or may not be productive for learning and success. College environments exert their influence through a range of natural and synthetic physical features, collective characteristics of community members, the manner in which things are organized and done in the environment, and through the interpretations of people in the environment. Even more, the potency of the environment is a function of intentional design, what it intends to encourage and expects students to do, and what ends it services. Effective educational institutions actively consider the extent to which the physical, aggregate, organizational, and constructed environments encourage desirable behaviors and help students learn and succeed.

Student affairs professionals can enhance their environmental competence by developing a deeper appreciation for environmental theory and its influence on student success. The conceptual framework offered in this chapter provides an introduction to this approach for student affairs practice. Even more it suggests the promise of the framework as a way to broaden conceptualizations of learning in student affairs and to bridge the academic and student affairs cultures. Approaches including intragroup and intergroup dialogue and culture audits can be employed to understand the lenses and perspectives across campus divisions. Most important, environmental perspectives invite student affairs educators to imagine how the environment can be enhanced so more students do well, to help students from under-represented groups feel welcomed and affirmed, and to create more exciting learning environments that stimulate students to engage in high levels with the experiences that matter for learning and success.

Many aspects of the campus environment cited throughout this chapter make reference to current environments for higher education—including residential, urban, and commuter institutions. However, imminent issues—including more part-time, adult, and commuter students, coupled with greater mobility in students' enrollment, ease of transfer, and increased online platforms for learning, which increase heterogeneity in what constitutes an undergraduate education and creates a highly fragmented college experience—will make it increasingly more complex to apply college environment models. At institutions where students spend less time on campus, and more time in online courses or interacting via learning management systems, what does this suggest for academic success centers or for creating environments that help students feel supported in their learning? Some of the new features can be turned into advantages and ways to enrich the environment for student success. For example, the implementation of virtual student success centers and twenty-four-hour availability of online tutors to address the needs of online student populations prove beneficial for residential students as well.

Student affairs professionals are well positioned to advance a campus environment perspective as more institutions face the challenge of creating and maintaining environments that attract, satisfy, and engage students in the practices that matter for their learning and success. Although the responsibility for creating environments that support student learning rests with all campus educators, student affairs is uniquely equipped to access students' perspectives on the campus environment, to address features that inhibit student success, and to bridge campus divisions to achieve the holistic, student-centered cultures that promise to help more students learn and succeed.

References

American Association for Higher Education, American College Personnel Association, National Association of Student Personnel Administrators. (1998). *Powerful partnerships: A shared responsibility for learning (A joint report).* Washington, DC: Author.

American Council on Education. (2013). An open letter to college and university leaders: College completion must be our priority. Washington, DC: National Commission on Higher Education Attainment. American Council on Education. http://www.acenet.edu/news-room/Documents/An-Open-Letter-to-College-and-University-Leaders.pdf.

American College Personnel Association. (1996). *The student learning imperative: Implications for student affairs.* Washington DC: Author. http://www.acpa.nche.edu/sli/sli.htm

Arcelus, V. J. (2011). Transforming our approach to education: Cultivating partnerships and dialogue. In M. Baxter-Magolda & P. Magolda (Eds.), *Contested issues in higher education* (pp. 61–74). Sterling, VA: Stylus.

Arcelus, V. J. (2008). *In search of a break in the clouds: An ethnographic study of academic and student affairs cultures.* University Park: Pennsylvania State University.

Association of American Colleges and Universities (AAC&U). (2002). *Greater expectations: A new vision for learning as a nation goes to college.* http://www.greaterexpectations.org/.

Association of American Colleges and Universities (AAC&U). (2007). *College learning for the new global century: A report from the National Leadership Council for Liberal Education and America's Promise*. Washington, DC: Author.

Astin, A. W. (1985). *Achieving educational excellence*. San Francisco, CA: Jossey-Bass.

Astin, A. W. (1993a). *What matters in college? Four critical years revisited*. San Francisco, CA: Jossey-Bass.

Astin, A. W. (1993b). An empirical typology of college students. *Journal of College Student Development, 34,* 36–46.

Banning, J. H. & Bartels, S. (1997). A taxonomy: Campus physical artifacts as communicators of campus multiculturalism. *NASPA Journal, 35*(1), 29–37.

Baxter Magolda, M. B., & King P. M. (2004). *Learning partnerships: Theory and models of practice to educate for self-authorship*. Sterling, VA: Stylus.

Chickering, A. W., & Gamson, Z. F. (1987). Seven principles for good practice in undergraduate education. *AAHE Bulletin, 39,* 3–7.

Clark, B. R., & Trow, M. (1966). The organizational context. In T. M. Newcomb & E. K. Wilson (Eds.), *College peer groups: Problems and prospects for research* (pp. 17–70). Chicago: Aldine.

Engstrom, C. M., & Tinto, V. (2000). Developing partnerships with academic affairs to enhance student learning. In M. Barr (Ed.), *Handbook of student affairs administration* (pp. 425–452). San Francisco, CA: Jossey-Bass.

Feldman, K. A., Ethington, C. A., & Smart, J. C. (2001). A further investigation of major field and person-environment fit: Sociological versus psychological interpretations of Holland's theory. *Journal of Higher Education, 72,* 670–698.

Fetterman, D. M. (1998). *Ethnography: Step by step* (2nd ed.). Newbury Park, CA: Sage.

Hendrel, D. & Harrold, R. (2007). Changes in Clark-Trow subcultures from 1976 to 2006: Implications for addressing undergraduates' leisure interests. *College Student Affairs Journal, 27*(1), 8–23.

Holland, J. L. (1997). *Making vocational choices: A theory of vocational personalities and work environments* (3rd ed.). Odessa, FL: Psychological Assessment Resources.

Hurtado, S., Arellano, L., Cuellar, M., & Guillermo-Wann, C. (2011). *Diverse Learning Environments Survey Instrument: Introduction and Select Factors*. http://www.heri.ucla.edu/dleoverview.php

Hurtado, S., Griffin, K.A., Arellano, L. & Cuellar, M. (2008). Assessing the value of climate assessment: Progress and future directions. *Journal of Diversity in Higher Education, 1*(4), 204–221.

Kinzie, J., & Kuh, G.D. (2007). Creating a student-centered culture. In G. Kramer (Eds.), *Fostering student success in the campus community* (pp. 17-43). San Francisco, CA: Jossey-Bass.

Kinzie, J., & Mulholland, S. (2008). Transforming physical spaces into inclusive multicultural learning environments. In S. Harper (Ed.), *Creating inclusive campus environments for cross-cultural learning and student engagement* (pp. 103-120). Washington DC: NASPA

Kuh, G.D. (2009). Understanding campus environments. In G. McClellan & J. Stringer (eds.), *Handbook of student affairs administration* (3rd ed.). San Francisco, CA: Jossey-Bass.

Kuh, G. D. & Hall, J. E. (1993). Cultural perspectives. In G. D. Kuh (Ed.), *Cultural perspectives in student affairs work* (pp. 1–20). Lanham, Maryland: American College Personnel Association.

Kuh, G. D., Hu, S., & Vesper, N. (2000). "They shall be known by what they do": An activities-based typology of college students. *Journal of College Student Development, 41*, 228–244.

Kuh, G. D., Kinzie, J., Schuh, J. H., & Whitt, E. J. (2005). *Assessing conditions to enhance educational effectiveness: The inventory for student engagement and success.* San Francisco, CA: Jossey-Bass.

Kuh, G. D., Kinzie, J., Schuh, J. H., Whitt, E. J., & Associates. (2010). *Student success in college: Creating conditions that matter.* San Francisco, CA: Jossey-Bass.

Kuh, G. D., Schuh, J. H., Whitt, E. J., & Associates. (1991). *Involving colleges: Successful approaches to fostering student learning and personal development outside the classroom.* San Francisco, CA: Jossey-Bass.

Kuh, G. D., & Whitt, E. J. (1988). *The invisible tapestry: Culture in American colleges and universities* (ASHE-ERIC Higher Education Report No. 1). Washington, DC: Association for the Study of Higher Education.

Magolda, P. M. (1999). Using ethnographic fieldwork and case studies to guide student affairs practice. *Journal of College Student Development, 40*(1), 10–21.

Magolda, P. M. (2000). The campus tour ritual: Ritual and community in higher education. *Anthropology and Education Quarterly, 31*(1), 24–46.

Magolda, P. M. (2005). Proceed with caution: Uncommon wisdom about academic and student affairs partnerships. *About Campus, 9*(6), 16–21.

Malinowski, B. (1922). *Argonauts of the Western Pacific: An account of native enterprise and adventure in the Archipelagoes of Melanesian New Guinea.* London: Routledge.

Manning, K. M. (2000). *Rituals, ceremonies, and cultural meaning in higher education.* Westport, CT: Bergin & Garvey.

Manning, K. M., Kinzie, J. & Schuh, J. H. (2006). *One size does not fit all: Traditional and innovative models of student affairs practice.* New York: Routledge Press.

Moffatt, M. (1989). *Coming of age in New Jersey: College and American culture.* New Brunswick: Rutgers University Press.

Moos, R. (1979). *Evaluating educational environments: Procedures, methods, findings and policy implications.* San Francisco, CA: Jossey-Bass.

Moos, R. (1988). *University Residence Environment Scale manual* (2nd ed.). Palo Alto, CA: Mind Garden.

National Association of Student Personnel Administrators and American College Personnel Association (2004). *Learning reconsidered: A campus-wide focus on the student experience.* Washington DC: Author.

Pace, C. R. (1964). *The influence of academic and student subcultures in college and university environments.* Los Angeles: University of California.

Pace, C. R. (1979). *Measuring outcomes of college: Fifty years of findings and recommendations for the future.* San Francisco, CA: Jossey-Bass.

Pace, D., Blumreich, K.M., & Merkle, H. B. (2006). Increasing collaboration between student and academic affairs: Application of the intergroup dialogue model. *NASPA Journal, 43*(2), 301–315.

Pascarella, E. T., & Terenzini, P. T. (1991). *How college affects students: Findings and insights from twenty-years of research.* San Francisco, CA: Jossey-Bass.

Pascarella, E. T., & Terenzini, P. T. (2005). *How college affects students: A third decade of research.* San Francisco, CA: Jossey-Bass.

Patton, M. (2002). *Qualitative research and evaluation methods* (3rd ed.). Thousand Oaks, CA. Sage.

Pike, G. R. (2006). Vocational preferences and college expectations: An extension of Holland's principle of self-selection. *Research in Higher Education, 47*(5), 591–612.

Rankin, Susan R. (2003). *Campus climate for gay, lesbian, bisexual, and transgender people: A national perspective.* New York, NY: National Gay and Lesbian Task Force Policy Institute. www.ngltf.org.

Rhoads, Robert A., & Tierney, William G. (1992). *Cultural leadership in higher education.* University Park: The Pennsylvania State University, National Center on Postsecondary Teaching, Learning and Assessment.

Schoem, D., Hurtado, S., Sevig, T. Chesler, M. & Sumida, S. (2001). Intergroup dialogue: Democracy at work in theory and practice. In D. Schoem, S. Hurtado (Eds.), *Intergroup dialogue: Deliberative democracy in school, college, community and workplace* (pp. 1-22). Ann Arbor: University of Michigan Press.

Smart, J. C., Feldman, K. A., & Ethington, C. A. (2000). *Academic disciplines: Holland's theory and the study of college students and faculty.* Nashville, TN: Vanderbilt University Press.

Strange, C. C., & Banning, J. H. (2001). *Educating by design: Creating campus learning environments that work.* San Francisco, CA: Jossey-Bass.

Tierney, W. G. (1988). Organizational culture in higher education: Defining the essentials. *Journal of Higher Education, 59*(1), 2–21.

Whitt, E. J. (1993). Making the familiar strange: Discovering culture. In G. D. Kuh (Ed.), *Cultural perspectives in student affairs work* (pp. 81-94). Washington, DC: American College Personnel Association.

Whitt, E. J. & Kuh, G. D. (1991). The use of qualitative methods in a team approach to multiple institution studies. *Review of Higher Education, 14*, 317–337.

CHAPTER FOUR

FISCAL PRESSURES ON HIGHER EDUCATION AND STUDENT AFFAIRS

John H. Schuh

Although the fiscal environment in which student affairs has functioned over the past decade has been particularly daunting (Schuh, 2003, 2009, 2011), much of the twenty-first century has been challenging for higher education. As this chapter describes, many students are coming to our colleges and universities from economic and social backgrounds that place them at risk; the federal government's agenda for higher education has resulted in increased expenses for colleges and universities; and the cost of obtaining a higher education continues to escalate faster than the cost of living. Institutions of higher education face increased costs, as is the case for many enterprises similar to higher education, such as social service agencies and health services. As Archibald and Feldman conclude, "Higher education is not unique in facing both cost disease and the rising cost of a highly educated workforce. The same forces affect other important personal services, including dental, legal, and medical (to name a few), all of which have experienced cost pressures very similar to higher education" (2011, p. 37).

Fiscal policies, economic constraints, and social conditions have a profound effect on the programs, services, learning opportunities, and activities developed by and offered in the typical student affairs division. This chapter examines a variety of factors that influence the fiscal environment in which the student affairs division operates. First, the economic implications of selected demographic and social trends are presented. Second, several federal initiatives are identified in the context of their economic impact on institutions of higher education. Third, trends related to state support of higher education are provided. Finally, the cost to students of attending institutions of higher education and financial aid is discussed. Brief implications for student affairs are presented in each section.

Demographic and Social Trends

This section discusses selected demographic and social trends in the context of their financial implications for higher education. "Enrollment trends suggest that students are diverse in manifold sociodemographic categories, including sex, race, ethnicity, sexuality, and socioeconomic status" (Renn & Reason, 2013, pp. 24–25). In 1990 Kuh predicted that student affairs officers would have to deal with social issues that will affect the practice of student affairs in the future. Fifteen years later Reason and Davis reported, "To maximize student learning both in and out of the classroom, we must improve intergroup relations on campus and create an environment that nurtures all students equitably" (2005, p. 5). For reasons that are examined later in the chapter, many college students are at risk and may need additional support to be successful. This assistance will take the form of tutorial help, counseling, financial aid, and other assistance specific to individual campuses. Consider the following information about the students who are coming to college in the twenty-first century.

The Family

Family structure appears to have a relationship with whether or not the family members live in poverty. For example, according to federal data, families headed by a married couple are less likely to live in a state of poverty than families headed by a single person. "In 2011, 6.2 percent of married-couple families, 31.2 percent of families with a female householder, and 16.1 percent of families with a male householder lived in poverty" (DeNavas-Walt, Proctor, & Smith, 2012, p. 17). Trend data from 1980 to 2010 indicate modest growth in families headed by a single person (DeNavas-Walt et al., 2012, Table 59).

The percentage of married couple families with their own child under eighteen declined from 49.6 to 31.2 percent from 1970 to 2010 (Snyder &

Dillow, 2012, Table 23). During this same period of time the percentage of families headed by a male single head of household with at least one child under eighteen increased from 0.7 percent to 2.7 percent (Table 23). From 1970 to 2010 the percentage of families headed by a single woman with at least one child eighteen years of age or younger increased from 5.6 percent to 10.7 percent (Table 23).

The type of household in which a person lives has a relationship to income. For example, according to DeNavas-Walt et al., in 2011 median income for family households that consisted of a married couple was $74,130, while for a female householder with no husband present the median income was $33,637, and for a male householder with no wife present, the median income was $49,567 (2012, Table 1). Therefore, students seeking to attend college who come from family households where there is only one wage earner present may require significant financial assistance to pay for the cost of attendance. But, the composition of household is only one factor. Another important element is income distribution.

In terms of the percentage distribution of aggregate income, the lowest, second, third, and fourth quintiles saw their share of aggregate income decline from 1970 through 2009. The highest quintile and the top 5 percent of aggregate income saw their share of income increase from 1970 through 2009 (US Census Bureau, 2012, Table 694). "The share of aggregate income increased 1.6 percent for the highest quintile (from 50.3 percent to 51.1 percent [from 2010 to 2011]) and within the highest quintile, the share of aggregate income for the top 5 percent increased 4.9 percent (from 21.3 percent to 22.3 percent)" (DeNavas-Walt et al., 2012, p. 10). The concentration of wealth in the highest quintile will make it increasingly difficult for institutions of higher education to make higher education available to students from families other than those that have very robust economic circumstances. These statistics lead to a demographic trend that will affect students of the future: economic challenges.

Distribution of Wealth

According to data published in a recent federal report, an increasing number of children are living in poverty. *The Condition of Education 2013* (Aud, Wilkinson-Flicker, Kristapovich, Rathbun, Wang, & Zhang, 2013) reports that the percentage of children ages 5–17 living in poverty grew from 17 percent in 1990 to 21 percent in 2011. The growth in the percentage of students increased in all regions, although the percentage has increased the most in the South and Southwest, and has stayed relatively stable in the Plains states and New England (p. 27).

One measure of childhood poverty is eligibility of students to participate in free or reduced cost lunch programs in school. "The percentage of students eligible for free or reduced-price lunch (FRPL) under the National School Lunch Program provides a proxy measure for the concentration of low-income students within a school" (Aud et al., 2013, p. 80). In 1999–2000 45 percent of all public school students attended schools defined as "low poverty," meaning that "less than 25 percent of the students are eligible for the program" (p. 80) and 12 percent attended schools defined as high poverty, defined as "more than 75 percent of the students are eligible" (p. 80). By 2010–11 the percentage of students attending low poverty schools had declined to 24 percent while those attending high poverty schools had grown to 20 percent (Aud et al., 2013).

Students in the Future. The percentage of young people of color enrolled in elementary and secondary schools has grown dramatically over the past two decades and is an indicator of the composition of this century's college population. Unfortunately, young people from underrepresented minority groups do not enroll in institutions of higher education to the extent that they attend elementary and secondary schools, according to federal data. Whites comprised 78 percent of the enrollment in elementary and secondary schools in 1972, were 57 percent of the enrollment in 2004 (Snyder, Tan, & Hoffman, 2006, p. 342), and by 2010 they comprised 52 percent of enrollment in public elementary and secondary schools (Aud et al., 2013, p. 52). They comprised 82.8 percent of all college students in 1976, 68.3 percent in 2000, and 60.3 percent in 2010 (Snyder & Dillow, 2012, Table 237).

African Americans have increased their numbers from 15 percent of children attending elementary and secondary schools in 1972 to 16 percent of those enrolled in 2004 (US Department of Education, 2006b, p. 32) and remained at 16 percent in 2010 (Aud et al., 2013). But they constituted only 10 percent of all college students in 1976, 11.8 percent in 2000, and 14.8 percent in 2010 (Snyder & Dillow, 2012, Table 237).

Similarly, the representation of Latino/a youth has increased in elementary and secondary schools, but they are not enrolled proportionately in institutions of postsecondary education. The percentage of Latino/a children enrolled in elementary and secondary schools grew from 6 percent of all those enrolled in 1976 to 19 percent in 2006 (US Department of

Education, 2006b, p. 32) and increased to 27 percent in 2010 (Aud et al., 2013). These students, however, made up only 3.7 percent of all college students in 1976, 10.3 percent in 2000 and 14.1 percent in 2010 (Snyder & Dillow, 2012, Table 237). Students who are identified as Asians increased from 4 to 6 percent of public school enrollment from 2000 to 2011 (Aud et al., 2013).

Another dimension of the students of the future is worthy of note. Nine percent of students aged 5–17 in 2009 were enrolled as English Language Learners (ELL), and 10 percent of students in that age range in 2010 were ELL enrolled. Standardized reading test scores were dramatically different when one compares non-ELL students with ELL students. "In 2011, the achievement gap [as measured by reading test scores] between non-ELL and ELL students was 36 points at the 4th-grade level and 44 points at the 8th-grade level" (Aud et al., 2013, p. 56).

It is clear that colleges and universities of the future will enroll an increasingly larger percentage of students of color and students from families where English has not been spoken as the primary language. Additional financial investments may be required to provide staff time, perhaps staff members; and targeted programs for students from historically under-represented groups has been recommended many times in the student affairs literature (for example, Cuyjet, 1998; Fox, Lowe & McClellan, 2005; Howard-Hamilton, 2003; and Ortiz, 2004). Pope and Mueller (2011, p. 348) conclude "Multicultural competence is an integral component of student affairs work." Multicultural competence also is essential for all faculty and staff associated with institutions of higher education.

Federal Higher Education Initiatives

This section is dedicated to reviewing selected federal legislative and regulatory developments of recent years. Specific attention is given to the fiscal implications of these initiatives.

Access for Those With Disabilities

One category of ongoing federal regulatory interest in higher education is access for those with disabilities. With the passage of Section 504 of the Rehabilitation Act of 1973 (reauthorized in 1992) and the Americans with Disabilities Act (1990), colleges and universities incurred additional costs in the course of serving students who heretofore had not participated in campus life and who were entitled to reasonable accommodations in pursing their educational goals. The number of students receiving services under the Individuals with Disabilities Education Act (IDEA) legislation grew from 4.1 million in 1980–81 to 6.7 million in 2004–05. The number declined to 6.4 million in 2010–11 (Aud et al., 2013). The largest percentage of students had specific learning disabilities (37 percent), speech or language impairments (22 percent), or other health impairments (11 percent) (Aud et al., 2013, p. 58).

Among the implications of federal initiatives for student affairs officers are that as facilities are built or modified, accessibility for persons with disabilities will have to be assured; staff must be identified and programs developed to assist those with disabilities; accessible web sites, documents, brochures, and other printed material will have to be provided in formats to meet the needs of the visually impaired; interpreters will be needed for public events; assistive technology will need to be provided for learning-related activities such as classes or tutoring programs; and those with disabilities will expect student affairs officers to serve as their advocates.

Regulatory Compliance

Another category of federal initiatives deals with regulatory compliance. The burdens of some of these regulations are relatively light because all that is required is a certain degree of documentation. In other cases, a substantial amount of legislation has been passed that in turn requires institutions to engage in compliance activities that can be changed quite frequently, thereby incurring additional costs. For example, the Family Educational Rights and Privacy Act was enacted into law in 1974 and has been amended frequently since then. The regulations have become increasingly complex over the years (see US Department of Education, 2011) and the costs of compliance are borne by colleges and universities, not the federal government. The Clery Act, for example, applies to certain circumstances when institutions of higher education have a relationship with a military installation or has "an organized program of study and administrative personnel" in a foreign location (US Department of Education, 2011, p. 13). Basic elements of the act include reporting requirements (including annual reports) as well as emergency notification and evacuation procedures (US Department of Education, 2011, p. 8). The Violence Against Women Act, reauthorized in 2013, also applies to higher education and requires planning and services on the part of colleges and universities.

Consumer Protection

A third item on the federal agenda, which might be termed consumer protection legislation, has placed additional financial burdens on colleges and universities for the foreseeable future. Federal law has stipulated that institutions of higher education notify faculty, staff and students on a regular basis about the institution's substance-abuse policy, and laws have been enacted related to the use of alcohol and other drugs as well as the provision of programs available to provide assistance to those who seek help (Drug-Free Schools and Communities Act Amendments of 1989, Public Law 101-226). Starting with the 1992–93 academic year, institutions have been required to provide each current student and employee with information related to graduation rates, campus safety, and criminal activity. More recently federal regulatory initiatives have focused on issues of cost, completion rates, and career success of graduates. Failure to comply with Department of Education regulations can result in financial penalties for institutions.

The implications of consumer legislation include costs related to preparation and distribution of materials. For example, the law requires that every student receive information about campus crime each year. At a college where each student has a campus mailbox this requirement has minimal implications, but the costs associated with a commuter student body may be considerably greater. In addition to the costs of compliance, there can be considerable costs associated with noncompliance as a result of costs associated with investigations, litigation, or fines. Regardless of the form of compliance that an institution takes in complying with various federal requirements, the fact is that the requirements have become more complex over time and they require significant attention by institutional representations.

Issues Related to State Finance

Before reviewing specific factors and trends influencing the financing of higher education, it is useful to take a moment to describe some of the financial issues faced by the states. State governments have had to contend with a fundamental shift in their relationship with the federal government that has had dramatic implications for their budgets as manifested by unfunded mandates, (i.e., the federal government requires state governments to do certain things but do not provide the funding to do so). The pressures on state budgets are manifested by declining support for higher education as measured by the percentage of state appropriations received by public degree granting institutions. Consequently, many public institutions of higher education no longer are able to turn to their legislatures for substantial increases in funding. "In the past few years, a weak economy has put increasing pressure on state and institutional budgets. State appropriations for higher education have not been able to keep pace with increases in enrollment, and college prices continue to rise faster than average prices in the economy" (Baum & Ma, 2012, p. 1).

A number of the programs that have been transferred to the states have become competitors with higher education for state funding. Included in this group are hazardous waste control, transportation, and welfare. Added to this are the rising costs of operating prisons for an ever-growing population, health care and housing, PK–12 education, and a continuous pressure to reduce taxes.

The competition higher education faces for state support has become keen, indeed. When one examines sources of current fund revenue for public institutions of higher education, state appropriations in support of higher education declined from 1989–90 to 2011–12 (Baum & Ma, 2012). The percentage of revenue all public institutions receive from state appropriations declined from 23.85 percent to 20.59 percent from 2005–06 to 2009–10 (Snyder & Dillow, 2012, Table 366). For four-year public institutions the decline was from 22.51 percent to 19.64 percent, and for two-year institutions the decline was from 30.07 percent to 24.87 percent from 2005–06 to 2009–10 (Table 366). In constant dollars, the decline in state appropriations on a per student basis went from $6,811 in 2005–06 to $5,810 in 2009–10 (Table 366). Four-year institutions saw their per student state appropriations decline in constant dollars from $8,669 in 2005–06 to $7,551 in 2009–10, while two-year institutions have experienced a decline from $3,905 to $3,196 in constant dollars in the same time period (Table 366).

Private, not-for-profit institutions also have experienced economic pressures. Tuition income as percentage of total revenues increased from 24.58 percent in 1999–2000 to 33.41 percent in 2009–10 (Snyder & Dillow, 2012, Table 370). Tuition fees as a percentage of institutional income during this period ranged from 77.77 percent in 2008–09 to 24.58

percent in 1999–2000 (Table 370), in many cases reflecting declining investment income from the endowments of these institutions. In some years investment return has been negative. For example, investment return in 2008–09 was −92.96 percent (Table 370), reflecting negative returns in the stock market (Table 370). Investment income contributed 31.31 percent of institutional revenues in 1999–2000 (the highest for the years included in the table) but also had a negative return in 2008–09 of −92.96 percent (Table 370).

For-profit institutions have experienced more stability in revenue sources than state institutions or private, not-for-profit colleges and universities, primarily because of their dependence on tuition and fees for the majority of their funding. In 1999–2000 these institutions received 86.10 percent of their revenue from tuition and fees. By 2009–10, tuition and fees contributed 90.64 percent of these institutions' revenue (Snyder & Dillow, 2012, Table 372).

As institutions of higher education are adversely affected by state budget problems, student affairs units have been fortunate to maintain the status quo that marked public institutions' expenditures in the first decade of this century. For example, as a percentage of institutional expenditures in 2003–04, student affairs' expenditures at four-year public institutions represented 3.62 percent (Snyder & Dillow, 2012, Table 377). By 2009–10 the percentage was 3.80 percent (Table 377). In constant dollars the amount expended per student on student affairs was $1,271 in 2003–04 and $1,357 in 2009–10 (Table 377). Nevertheless, those student affairs units funded by general revenues (state support and tuition) will be in fierce competition with academic units for resources in the future. Those funded by user fees and fees for service (such as student housing or student unions) can expect to contribute more money to their institutions through overhead charges for human resources, accounting and purchasing services, security, and the like. Plus, those units funded by student fees will be subject to the vagaries of enrollment. If enrollment declines, fee revenue income will decline unless the fees are increased. Regardless of the funding source, student affairs units will be challenged to maintain an adequate funding base for the foreseeable future.

Private not-for-profit four-year institutions continue to spend a larger percentage of their institutional budget and more actual revenue on student affairs than public institutions. In 1999–2000 these institutions spent 7.02 percent on their total expenditures on student affairs ($2,880 per student in constant dollars) and by 2009–10 the percentage increased to 7.84 percent or $3,619 per student (Snyder & Dillow, 2012, Table 379).

Private for-profit institutions report expenditures for student services, academic support. and institutional support in the aggregate. In 1999–2000 four-year private for-profit institutions spent 54.58 percent of their expenditures on these categories (Snyder and Dillow, 2012, Table 381), in contrast to slightly more than 28 percent spent on the same categories of expenditures by private not-for-profit institutions in the same time period (Table 379). By 2009–10 the percentage spent on these categories by private for-profit institutions was 69.26 percent (Table 381), in contrast to slightly more than 30 percent spent by private not-for-profit institutions in the same time period (Table 379).

The Public-Private Dilemma

An especially vexing issue confronting the financing of higher education by state governments is the extent to which government ought to support private institutions. Although public institutions rely on state support to a much greater degree than private institutions, virtually every college or university in the country is affected to some degree by the amount of financing that the states can provide, whether through direct support to institutions or financial aid programs to students. There is little doubt that the competition between public and private institutions for state dollars—often revolving around whether states ought to provide direct support to students (through financial aid programs, thereby favoring private colleges) or direct support to institutions (thereby favoring public colleges)—has the potential to become more heated. In the next section we explore the cost of attendance in postsecondary institutions and the extent to which financial aid ameliorates access to higher education.

Cost of Attendance and Financial Aid Trends

In this section elements related to the cost of attendance to students and their parents are examined. Financial aid disbursements have continued to provide some relief for the ever-increasing cost of attendance, but the bottom line is that students and their families face increasing challenges to meet their financial obligations.

Revenues

Revenues have a dramatic and important effect on the financial status of colleges and universities. "Institutions generally rely on six main sources for revenues: students or parents, federal government, state government, private gifts, endowments, and auxiliary enterprises" (Toutkoushian, 2003, p. 27). Students and their families pay tuition, fees, and room and board expenses and buy books and supplies. State governments, as mentioned earlier, provide direct aid to public institutions and financial aid to students who attend private institutions. The federal government sponsors financial aid programs and supports research and creative activities. Individuals, foundations, and corporations furnish gifts and grants to colleges and universities; financial markets provide income for these institutions through revenue generated from investments of endowments and operating funds. In general, the mix of revenues has changed over time in that the cost to students, or students and their families, has increased more rapidly than income from other courses while state appropriations have declined. "At all types of public institutions, the average share of revenues coming from net tuition increased between 1999–2000 and 2009–10, while the share coming from state and local appropriations decreased" (Baum & Ma, 2012, p. 24).

Tuition. Tuition is the most important source of income for many not-for-profit degree-granting private institutions of higher education and has become increasingly important at public degree-granting institutions. Increases in tuition have been significant for a recent thirty-year reporting period. The average 2012–13 published tuition and fee prices for public four-year institutions was $8,655 in contrast to $2,423 in 1982–83. For private not-for-profit four-year institutions the average published price was $29,056, compared with $10,901 in 1982–83 (Baum & Ma, 2012, p. 15). All amounts are reported in 2012 dollars.

At public bachelor's and master's degree-granting institutions, net tuition and fee revenue was the largest revenue source in 2009–10, and tuition and fee revenue was a larger source of revenue than state appropriations at public doctoral universities (Baum & Ma, 2012, p. 24). "The share of total revenue for general operating expenses for higher education originating from net tuition revenue showed an increased from 31.6% in 2008 to 38.5% in 2011 and 42.5% in 2012. Tuition revenue collected by independent (private, not-for-profit) and for-profit institutions is not included in this total" (State Higher Education Executive Officers, 2013, p. 7). Net tuition and fee revenue is the largest source of revenue for all types of private institutions (Baum & Ma, 2012). Tuition and fee revenue is central to the funding of private, for-profit institutions. In 2008–09 tuition and fee revenue was 77.77 percent of total revenue of private not-for-profit institutions (Snyder & Dillow, 2012, Table 370).

Fund Raising

Private colleges depend more on private, foundation, and corporate contributions than do public institutions, but the latter have also begun to rely more on donations—a situation that puts them squarely in competition for these funds with the private not-for-profit sector of higher education. Revenues from investments reflect the fruits of gifts and donations. In some years the returns are relatively robust, but in other years, reflecting a difficult investment environment, returns may be disappointing, as was pointed out earlier, when investment return was −92.96 percent in 2008–09 at private not-for-profit institutions (Snyder & Dillow, 2012, Table 370). The implications of poor investment returns are obvious: less money may be available from one year to the next and, hence, other sources of funding to support an activity, a special project, or a scholarship would have to be identified through institutional reallocation of funds or tuition would have to be raised.

Student Costs

This section uses the term *costs* the way that students and their families typically use the word: the cost of attendance to them. Baum and Ma (2012) refer to the cost to students and their families as net price, defined as "what the student and/or family must cover after grant aid and savings from tax credits and deductions are subtracted" (p. 39). The cost of attending college continues to rise at a rate much higher than the commonly accepted measure of inflation, the Consumer Price Index. To illustrate the growth in student costs, Baum and Ma (2012, p. 14) provide the following conclusion:

> Over the 30 years from 1982–83 to 2012–13, average published tuition and fees at private nonprofit four-year institutions rose by 167%, from $10,901 (in 2012 dollars) to $29,056. The average published price at public two-year colleges rose by 182%, from $1,111 (in 2012 dollars) to $3,131, while the increase for in-state students at public four-year institutions was 257%, from $2,423 to $8,655.

The actual cost of attendance is less than the published cost. For example, the estimated net cost of tuition in 2012–13 at a public four-year university was $2,910 (Baum & Ma, 2012, p. 19) compared with the published figure of over $8,000 cited previously. The actual cost of attending a private not-for-profit four year institutions in 2012–13 was estimated to be

$13,380 (Baum & Ma). Actual cost reflects discounted tuition, meaning that institutions publish a tuition and fee schedule but will reduce the actual tuition and fees that are paid by individual student. The tuition discount rate can be defined as the difference between the published tuition and fee rate and the actual tuition and fees paid by the student body in the aggregate.

Cost of attendance varies widely along a number of dimensions: geographical location, state policy, type of control (public versus private), type of institution (such as regional baccalaureate-granting versus doctoral-granting with an international profile), and perceived prestige of the institution, among others. A student attending a private institution in one state very well could incur a lower cost of attendance than a student attending a public four-year institution in another. In-state students attending public four-year colleges in the South and Southwest, for example, face lower published tuition and fees and room and board costs than their colleagues who enroll at public universities in New England or the Middle States regions of the country (Baum & Ma, 2012, Figure 7). The range in 2012–13 for flagship state universities was from the University of Wyoming, $4,278, to Pennsylvania State University's University Park campus, which had a published tuition and fee charge of $17,266 (Baum & Ma, 2012).

Financial Aid Trends

Clearly, one of the responses to the growth in the cost of attendance has been the widespread development of financial aid programs. Sixty percent of all full-time undergraduate students who attended college in 1989–90 received some form of financial aid, but participation in financial aid programs increased to 74 percent in 1999–2000 (Wei, Li, & Berkner, 2004, p. 14). By 2009–10 the percentage of students who received some form of financial aid increased to 81.9 percent (Snyder & Dillow, 2012, Table 354). Students attending private not-for-profit institutions were more likely to participate in financial aid programs in 2009–10 (88.8 percent) than those attending public institutions (76.6 percent) (Snyder & Dillow, 2012, Table 354). This difference, in part, can be attributed to participation in institutional aid programs. More than three quarters of the students who attended private colleges and universities (78.2 percent) participated in institutional grant programs, compared with 26.3 percent of students who attended public institutions. These data reflect full-time enrollment (Snyder & Dillow, 2012, Table 354).

Loans

During the first decade of this century the most common form of financial aid for undergraduates has been loans. Fewer than half of all college students (40.1 percent) had loans in 2000–01, but by 2009–10, 51.1 percent had loans (Snyder & Dillow, 2012, Table 354). Students enrolled at private, not-for-profit institutions were more likely to have loans than students enrolled in public institutions, although the percentage of students with loans is increasing regardless of institutional type. In 2009–10, 38.6 percent of all students attending public institutions had loans, while 63 percent of all students enrolled in private, not-for-profit institutions had loans (Table 354).

At private for-profit institutions, loans are the most common form of financial aid. In 2000–01, 63.5 percent of all students attending private for-profit institutions had loans, and the percentage increased to 81.3 percent in 2010 (Snyder & Dillow, 2012, Table 354). Institutional grants grew from 6.2 percent of all students receiving this form of aid in 2000–01 to 15.1 percent in 2009–10 at private, for-profit institutions (Table 354).

In addition to the growth in the percentage of students who use loans to help finance their college education, the amount of money students borrow has increased over the past two decades. In the 1992–93 academic year, full-time undergraduates who borrowed at community colleges borrowed from all sources, on average, $2,530 (Snyder & Dillow, 2012, Table 359). At public four-year doctoral institutions, full-time undergraduate students borrowed, on average, $3,640. Full-time undergraduate students who attended private not-for-profit four-year doctoral institutions borrowed, on average, $4,880, and full-time undergraduate students who attended two-year and above private for-profit institutions who borrowed averaged $,5190 in federal and nonfederal loans (Table 359). By 2007–8, the amounts had increased substantially, as the following data reveal. Full-time undergraduates who borrowed at community colleges borrowed from federal and nonfederal sources, on average, $5,450. At public four-year doctoral institutions full-time undergraduate students borrowed, on average, $8,880. Full-time undergraduate students who attended private not-for-profit four-year doctoral institutions borrowed, on average, $13,300, and of all full-time undergraduate students who attended private for-profit two year and above institutions who borrowed averaged $10,670 in federal and nonfederal loans (Snyder & Dillow, 2012, Table 359). Dependent full-time full-year undergraduate students tended to borrow more on average as their family income increased. That is, such students from families who report higher incomes borrow more. For example, dependent students from families with a reported income of less than $20,000 borrowed on average a total of $7,050 in 2007–08, and the amount borrowed increased as income categories increased. Students from families with a reported income of over $100,000 borrowed on average $11,780 in 2007–08 (Snyder & Dillow, 2012, Table 355).

In terms of federal support of financial aid, recent data indicate that grants represent a larger percentage (51 percent) of student aid for undergraduates than federal and nonfederal loans (40 percent) (Baum & Payea, 2012, Figure 4A). In previous years, loans had been more common than grants (Figure 4A). It is important to note, however, that the amount of money borrowed has increased substantially in recent years. Baum and Payea (2012) note, "The total volume of education loans disbursed doubled from $55.7 billion (in 2011 dollars) to $113.4 billion between 2001–02 and 2011–12. This growth rate was slower than over the previous decade, when total borrowing increased by 150%, from $22.3 billion (in 2011 dollars) to $55.7 billion" (p. 17).

Students who do not begin to repay their loans within the parameters of the borrowing agreement are said to be in default and those who do not complete their degrees are at risk. "Students who leave school without completing a degree or certificate are significantly more likely than those who complete their programs to default on student loans" (Baum & Payea, 2012, p. 20). The default rate of borrowers varies by the type of institution they attended. In 2009 the three-year default rate ranged from 23 percent at for-profit institutions to 18 percent at public two-year colleges, to 8 percent at public four-year institutions to 7 percent at private not-for-profit four-year institutions (Baum & Payea). More on student loan default is included in later paragraphs in this chapter.

Work. In the twenty-first century, those from families with modest financial resources who are considering becoming college students are likely to be forced to work more hours to finance their educations, to take on greater debt burden, or both. In a study of the working poor, McSwain and Davis (2007, p. 6) concluded that youth from working poor backgrounds "often find themselves in a precarious position—reaching for the education that many of their parents have not attainted, yet lacking the financial and auxiliary support to help them achieve their goal."

Institutions seeking to attract students from families with modest financial resources will be confronted with the expenses related to offering additional financial aid, additional campus employment, and additional support services. Though it may have been possible for students in previous generations to finance most or at least a meaningful proportion of their college costs through work, such is not the case in contemporary higher education. Simply multiply the minimum wage by the number of hours worked per week by the number of weeks worked in a year and one can find that other than in rare circumstances, the net cost to students cannot be defrayed entirely by work. Work study, a federal program, declined by 24 percent as a source of financial aid from 2001–02 to 2011 to 2012, according to Baum and Payea (2012, Table 1). So in practical terms, work can help underwrite the cost of attendance, but it is not the solution to paying for college.

Nevertheless, work is very much a part of the lives of undergraduate students. Perna (2010) observes, "Most college students are now not only employed but also working a substantial number of hours, a fact not widely understood or discussed by faculty members and policy makers" (p. 3). She adds that about 80 percent of full-time college students work and recommends that "colleges and universities should consider ways to transform employment into an experience that can enhance students' intellectual development" (p. 7).

College Attendance and Income

One of the objectives of federal policy, almost regardless of which party holds the presidency, has been to provide greater access to postsecondary education for students from modest economic backgrounds. Current economic data suggest that achieving this objective will be difficult. For example, "Over the entire income distribution in the United States, average family incomes in 2011 were lower in inflation-adjusted dollars than they were a decade earlier. The largest declines were for the families in the lowest 20% of the population" (Baum & Ma, 2012, p. 28). Some financial aid programs were developed to increase college access for students, but in other cases institutional aid has been awarded to students from middle–high-income families in amounts that suggest using aid to recruit high-ability students regardless of their economic circumstance is as important to many institutions of higher education as is using institutional grants to help students from modest economic circumstances defray their cost of attendance. For example, according to the National Center for Education Statistics (National Center for Education Statistics, 2011, Table 2.1-B), in comparing the percentage of undergraduates receiving grant aid in 1995–96 with 2007–08, students from families with the lowest family income on average received $3,700 in 1995–96 and $6,500 in 2007–08 (Table 2.1B). Students from the highest 25 percent of family incomes received $3,600 in 1995–96 and $6,800 in 2007–08 (Table 2.1B). A larger parentage of students from the lowest-income group received grant aid over the years, 64.1 percent in 1995–96, and 74.7 percent in 2007–08 compared with 20.6 percent of students from the highest-income families in 1995–96 and 36.8 percent in 2007–08 (Table 2.1B). Nevertheless, these data illustrate that grant aid is used for purposes other than simply easing the cost of attendance for those from low-income families.

Federal Aid. The demographic trends noted in the first section of this chapter indicate that an increasing proportion of college students will be from low-income backgrounds. At one time Pell Grants covered the cost of tuition and fees, but that is no longer the case in many situations. Consider the following data. Pell Grants, the largest federal grant program, increased by 172 percent from 2001–02 through 2011–12 (Baum & Payea, 2012, p. 10). "The $5550 maximum Pell Grant in 2011–12 was about equal to the 1976–77 maximum grant of $1400 after adjusting for inflation" (Baum & Payea, 2012, p. 24). "The maximum Pell Grant covered 98% of average public four-year tuition and fees in 2002–03 but only 64% in 2012–13" (Baum & Ma, 2012, p. 25). The largest type of federal aid, however, included various forms of loans, totaling more than $105 billion in 2011–12, or more than double federal grant programs (Baum & Payea, 2012).

Institutional Aid. Institutional grants comprised about 18 percent ($32.8 billion) of undergraduate student aid in 2011–12. Private, not-for-profit institutions provide considerably more institutional grant aid on a per student basis than public institutions, but this is mitigated by a higher cost of attendance. The most selective institutions, public and private, provide more grant aid than those that are less selective. Institutional aid is used for a variety of purposes, some of which has to do with lowering the cost of attendance for needy students, but also for other reasons as pointed out earlier. Related to institutional merit aid, Woo and Choy (2011, p. 9, citing Gansemer & Schuh, 2006; Perna, 1998; St. John, 1992; Schuh, 2000) conclude, "Merit aid can serve institutions' purposes as well as help students. Researchers have found evidence that institutional expenditures on grants improve student retention and graduation rates and have a positive effect on student choice." Among these are to help students with inadequate financial resources to attend, but also to recruit students with strong academic credentials or other characteristics of importance (Baum & Payea, 2012).

Managing Debt

With an increase in the number of students who are borrowing, and the amount of money that students borrow increasing, a logical concern centers on the long-term effect of borrowing on the lives of the borrowers.

First we look at the amount of debt incurred by college graduates. In 1999–2000 54 percent of students completing a bachelor' degrees that year graduated with debt. "About 57% of students who earned bachelor's degrees in 2010-11 from the public four-year colleges at which they began their studies graduated with debt. Average debt per borrower was $23,800, up from $20,100 (in 2011 dollars) a decade earlier" (Baum & Payea, 2012, p. 23). Students completing their bachelor's degrees at private not-for-profit institutions were more likely to graduate with debt, and the amount of their debt was greater than their counterparts who graduated from public four-year institutions. Baum and Payea (2012, p. 23) provide the following data: "About 66% of students who earned bachelor's degrees in 2010–11 from the private nonprofit four-year colleges at which they began their studies graduated with debt. Average debt per borrower was $29,900, up from $23,400 (in 2011 dollars) a decade earlier."

As indicated in the previous paragraph, more students are borrowing to finance their education, and those who are borrowing are borrowing more money. Debt levels of bachelor's degree recipients have increased from 1999–2000 through 2010–11 for those students who have completed degrees at public four-year institutions and also at private nonprofit four-year colleges and universities (Baum & Payea, 2012). Baum and Payea add, "Students who earn their bachelor's degrees at for-profit institutions are more likely to borrow than those who attend public and private nonprofit colleges, and those who borrow tend to accumulate higher average levels of debt" (2012, p. 23).

Individuals who borrow to finance their educations but do not complete a degree differ from those who complete their degrees and borrow. First, they borrow more. "On a per credit, basis, noncompleters had borrowed more than completers as of 2009" (Wei & Horn, 2013, Figure 5). For example, at public four-year institutions, noncompleters borrowed, on average, $130 per credit compared with $90 per credit for completers (Figure 5). At four-year private, not-for-profit institutions, noncompleters borrowed $190 per credit compared with $120 per credit for completers (Figure 5). Second, they are less likely to be employed. "In 2009 [noncompleters] had lower rates of employment when they left post-secondary education than did completers at all four institution sectors" (public two- and four-year institutions, private not-for-profit and for-profit institutions) (Wei & Horn, 2013). Finally, the median ratio of debt-to-income (cumulative federal loan debt as a percentage of annual income) for noncompleters has continued to rise. "In 2009, the median ratio of cumulative federal student debt to annual income was 35 percent for all noncompleters, and ranged from 26 percent for those who started in public 2-year colleges to 51 percent for those who started in private nonprofit 4-year institutions. The median debt burden of noncompleters in for-profit institutions in 2009 (43 percent) was about double that in 2001 (20 percent)" (Wei & Horn, 2013, p. 11).

Predicting the financial future of higher education certainly is challenging, but several financial aid trends identified in this chapter may have a serious impact on higher education delivery systems of the future. The longitudinal data suggest the following:

- More students are participating in financial aid programs.
- More students are participating in institutional financial aid programs and are receiving institutional grants, particularly at private, not-for-profit institutions.
- More students are working, and they are working long hours to pay for their educations.
- More students are borrowing money to pay for their educations, and those who borrow are borrowing more money than in the past.

Fund Raising

One option that student affairs practitioners can employ to increase their resource base is to engage in fund raising. Fund raising can be conducted to create endowments for specific projects, such as securing support for the annual recognition dinner for student leaders, or for an ongoing project, such as scholarships for students who meet certain criteria—participation in community service, or being a single parent. Fund raising also can be targeted toward capital projects such as building new facilities, renovating buildings, purchasing equipment, and so on. A more detailed discussion of fund raising is included in chapter 29. Fund raising is noted in this chapter because it is an increasingly important source of funding in student affairs and needs to be noted as such.

Conclusion

This chapter has been developed during a period of relatively poor economic times. Unemployment rates have been stubbornly high, and state revenues have declined from the stronger economic years of the beginning of this century. Typically, in times of economic hardship, enrollments increase but state support for higher education declines. These phenomena—declining governmental support in face of rising enrollments—provide a set of challenges for institutions of higher education to resolve, although the typical approach has been to increase the cost of attendance at an accelerated rate, resulting in higher costs for students to manage. Although every institution's economic story is unique, one can take some comfort in higher education's resiliency and ability to manage financial challenges in the past. The economic experiences of the 1930s, the 1970s, and the latter part of the first decade of this century are examples of time periods when higher education leaders faced enormous financial problems and managed to address them in the face of increasing enrollments and demands by various stakeholders. On that point of relative optimism, one can hope that the past is prologue.

References

Americans with Disabilities Act of 1990. Public Law 101-336, 42 U.S.C. 12101–12132.
Archibald, R. B., & Feldman, D. H. (2011, January-February). Are plush dorms and fancy food plans important drivers of college cost? *Change, 43*(1), 31–37.
Aud, S., Wilkinson-Flicker, S., Kristapovich, P., Rathbun, A., Wang, X., & Zhang, J. (2013). *The Condition of Education 2013.* (NCES 2013–037). Washington, DC: U.S. Department of Education, National Center for Education Statistics.
Baum, S., & Ma, J. (2012). *Trends in college pricing.* New York: College Board.
Baum S., & Payea, (2012). *Trends in student aid.* New York: College Board.
Cuyjet, M. J. (Ed.). (1998). *Helping African American men succeed in college.* New Directions for Student Services, no. 80. San Francisco, CA: Jossey-Bass.
DeNavas-Walt, C., Proctor, B. D. & Smith, J. C. (2012). *Income, poverty, and health insurance coverage in the United States: 2011.* U.S. Census Bureau, Current Population Reports, P60–243. Washington, DC: US Government Printing Office.
Drug-Free Schools and Communities Act, Public Law 101-226.

Fox, M. J. T., Lowe, S. C., & McClellan, G. S. (Eds.). (2005). *Serving Native American students*. New Directions for Student Services, no. 109. San Francisco, CA: Jossey-Bass.

Howard-Hamilton, M. F. (Ed.). (2003). *Meeting the needs of African American women.* New Directions for Student Services, no. 104. San Francisco, CA: Jossey-Bass.

Kuh, G. D. (1990). The demographic juggernaut. In M. J. Barr, M. L. Upcraft, & Associates (Eds.), *New futures for student affairs: Building a vision for professional leadership and practice* (pp. 71–97). San Francisco, CA: Jossey-Bass.

McSwain C., & Davis, R. (2007). *College access for the working poor*. Washington, DC: Institute for Higher Education Policy.

National Center for Education Statistics (NCES). (2011). *Trends in student financing of undergraduate education: Selected years, 1995–96 to 2007–08*. (NCES 2011–218). Washington, DC: US Department of Education.

Ortiz, A. M. (Ed.). (2004). *Addressing the unique needs of Latino American students*. New Directions for Student Services, no. 105. San Francisco, CA: Jossey-Bass.

Perna, L. W. (2010, July August). *Understanding the working college student*. AAUP report. http://www.aaup.org/article/understanding-working-college-student# .UfFNv1OJRUM).

Pope, R. L. & Mueller, J. A. (2011). Multicultural competence. In J. H. Schuh, S. R. Jones, S. R. Harper & Associates, *Student services: A handbook for the profession* (5th ed., (pp. 337–352). San Francisco, CA: Jossey-Bass.

Reason, R. D., & Davis, T. J. (2005). Antecedents, precursors, and concurrent concepts in the development of social justice attitudes and actions. In R. D. Reason, E. M. Broido, T. J. Davis, & N. J. Evans (Eds.), *Developing social justice allies* (pp. 5–15). New Directions for Student Services, no. 110. San Francisco, CA: Jossey-Bass.

Renn, K. A., & Reason, R. D. (2013). *College students in the United States: Characteristics, experiences, and outcomes*. San Francisco, CA: Jossey-Bass.

Schuh, J. H. (Ed.). (2003). *Contemporary financial issues in student affairs*. New Directions for Student Services, no. 103. San Francisco, CA: Jossey-Bass.

Schuh, J. H. (2009). Fiscal pressures on higher education and student affairs. In G. S. McClellan, J. Stringer & Associates (Eds.), *The handbook of student affairs administration* (3rd ed., pp. 81–104). San Francisco, CA: Jossey-Bass.

Schuh, J. H. (2011). Financing student affairs. In J. H. Schuh, S. R. Jones, S. R. Harper & Associates, *Student services: A handbook for the profession* (5th ed., pp. 303–320). San Francisco, CA: Jossey-Bass.

Snyder, T. D., & Dillow, S. A. (2012). *Digest of Education Statistics 2011* (NCES 2012–001). Washington, DC: National Center for Education Statistics, Institute of Education Sciences, U.S. Department of Education.

Snyder, T. D. Tan, A. G., & Hoffman, C. M. (2006). *Digest of education statistics 2005* (NCES 2006–030). U.S. Department of Education, National Center for Education Statistics. Washington, DC: U.S. Government Printing Office.

State Higher Education Executive Officers. (2013). *State higher education finance FY 2012*. Boulder, CO: Author.

Toutkoushian, R. K. (2003). Weathering the storm: Generating revenues for higher education during a recession. In F. K. Alexander & R. C. Ehrenberg (Eds.), *Maximizing revenue in higher education*. New Directions for Institutional Research, no. 119. San Francisco, CA: Jossey-Bass.

US Census Bureau. (2012). *Statistical abstract of the United States.* Washington, DC: US Department of Commerce.

US Department of Education. (2006a). *A test of leadership: Charting the future of U.S. higher education.* Washington, DC: Author.

US Department of Education, National Center for Education Statistics. (2006b). *The condition of education 2006* (NCES 2006–071). Washington, DC: US Government Printing Office.

Wei, C. C., Li, X., & Berkner, L. (2004). *A decade of undergraduate student aid: 1989–90 to 1999–2000.* (NCES 2004–158). U.S. Department of Education, National Center for Education Statistics. Washington, DC: U.S. Government Printing Office.

Wei, C. C., & Horn, L. (2013). *Federal student loan debt burden of noncompleters.* NCES 2013–155. Washington, DC: US Department of Education.

Woo, J. H., & Choy, S. P. (2011). *Merit aid for undergraduates: Trends From 1995–96 to 2007–08.* (NCES 2012–160). Washington, DC: US Department of Education.

CHAPTER FIVE

ACCOUNTABILITY, ACCREDITATION, AND STANDARDS IN STUDENT AFFAIRS

Sherry L. Mallory and Linda M. Clement

Accountability is certainly not a new issue in higher education or student affairs. As noted by Wellman (2006), "Access, quality, and accountability have been framing the context for ... higher education in the United States since the 1950s" (p. 113). It is, however, an issue that has gained considerable attention in recent decades. From campuses to state houses, in news stories and in Congress, accountability is being discussed, and the general consensus is clear: greater transparency and accountability is needed in higher education.

Two key catalysts have served to up the ante in this discussion. The first, according to Levine (1996), was the higher education reform movement that began in the early 1980s with the publication of A Nation at Risk (National Commission on Excellence in Education, 1983). The second came in October 2005, when US Secretary of Education Margaret Spellings appointed a task force to lead a national conversation on issues of quality, access, affordability, and accountability in higher education. The resulting report, *A Test of Leadership: Charting the Future of U.S. Higher Education* (National Commission on the Future of Higher Education, 2006) painted a critical picture of higher education, and urged institutions to "become more transparent about cost, price, and student success outcomes" (p. 4).

Student affairs professionals must pay attention as this discussion continues to unfold. As Blimling (2013) asserts, although student affairs has "not been at the center of the criticism about higher education ... [we] have not escaped the demand for greater accountability" (p. 7). Student affairs must be able to show "how it contributes to the education of students, why its programs are important to students' education, why the investment in student affairs facilities and programs is worth the increased cost to students, and what system of performance measures is in place to ensure that students' money is spent efficiently" (Blimling, 2013, p. 13).

This chapter presents an overview of the growing accountability movement in higher education, with specific emphasis on the implications of this movement for student affairs. Three primary questions are considered: (1) To whom are we accountable? (2) For what are we accountable? and (3) More broadly, what constitutes accountability? To address these issues, we define accountability, provide a review of related literature, and discuss why accountability in higher education has become such a salient issue. We review who the stakeholders are and the areas for which student affairs is accountable. The chapter delves briefly into the accreditation movement and its role in accountability, and concludes with a summary of best practices and resources.

Accountability Defined

Accountability, in the context of higher education and student affairs, is difficult to define. It is not a monolithic concept; multiple definitions exist (Neave, 1980). Moreover, perspectives on higher education accountability have changed significantly over time (Leveille, 2013; McLendon, Hearn, & Deaton, 2006).

In the 1970s and 1980s, when higher education began to face increased public scrutiny, a primary focus of accountability was the responsible stewardship of resources. As Harpel (1976) noted, "Being accountable means being a good steward. We have been entrusted with physical and financial resources ... It is not unreasonable that we should be called upon periodically to account for our stewardship" (p. ii). During this period, accountability was primarily decentralized and institution-based, functioning without external oversight.

In the 1990s, as competition for public resources increased and criticism of higher education continued to grow, accountability focused more on institutional productivity and student performance. State governments took an active role in this process, defining performance indicators and requiring annual accountability reports. With an emphasis on such issues as student access, retention and graduation rates, and institutional efficiency (McLendon et al., 2006), accountability moved from being decentralized and institution-based, to being coordinated at the state level.

In recent years, accountability has shifted yet again, to what some have dubbed the "new accountability" (Burke & Minassians, 2002; Welsh & Metcalf, 2003). A key characteristic of this approach is its focus on institutions from the outside-in, rather than the inside-out. Public accountability for the public agenda, as Wellman (2006) refers to it, is less about the institution as a unit of performance, and more about the role it plays in meeting "general social, cultural, and economic needs" (p. 113).

Accountability, in this context, has become a public-oriented process, designed to "assure public constituents of the value, effectiveness, and quality of higher education" (Leveille, 2005, p. 3). It requires greater attention to "cross-sector measures of student academic preparation ... student flow across institutions, and measures of student learning outcomes" (Wellman, 2006, p. 115). According to Reville (2006), a key question of the movement is, "what specifically should students know and be able to do as a result of their education?" (p. 19).

It is no longer enough for institutions to measure the effectiveness of what they do, including the outcomes their students achieve. They must now be purposeful, aligning departmental goals with institutional goals, and institutional goals with state and federal goals. They must also share the information they have collected with a range of constituents, presenting it in ways that are both easy to understand and readily accessible. Put simply, accountability in higher education and student affairs has become about "publicly acceptable performance and results" (Ewell, 2004, p. 3).

Relevant Literature on Accountability

Upcraft and Schuh (1996) put it best when they posed the question, "Why all the fuss about accountability?" After all, "For about 350 years, our citizenry accepted as a matter of faith that ... higher education was doing its job, and doing it well" (p. 5).

A critical turning point for higher education came in the mid-1980s, with the publication of *A Nation at Risk* (National Commission on Excellence in Education, 1983), a scathing report on the state of education in the United States. Although the report focused primarily on K–12 education, the resulting cries for reform in public schools echoed "in calls for change on college campuses" (Burke & Minassians, 2002, p. 6) and became the impetus for an "increase in institutional reporting requirements imposed by the US Department of Education, by many state governments, and by virtually all regional accrediting agencies" (Blimling, 2013, p. 6).

Not long after, US Secretary of Energy James Watkins charged Sandia National Laboratories with examining the state of public education. The resulting *Sandia Report* (Sandia National Laboratories, 1993) shared a more positive view than *A Nation at Risk*, citing steady or slight improvement on a number of indicators of educational progress. Yet, it still called for "upgrading the quality of educational data" and making "major improvements … in the data used to analyze U.S. education" (Sandia National Laboratories, 1993, pp. 309–310).

In the early 1990s, the nation experienced a major recession. For the first time in decades, higher education faced a decline in state support. In 1993, the Wingspread Group on Higher Education released *An American Imperative: Higher Expectations for Higher Education* (Wingspread Group on Higher Education, 1993). The report charged higher education with failing to meet society's needs for a better educated, more skilled and more adaptable citizenry, and urged society to hold colleges and universities to higher standards. Calls for change began to intensify.

In recent years—prompted by rising costs, graduation rates that have not significantly increased over time, escalating student loan debt, and concerns that graduates do not have the skills necessary to succeed in the workplace—accountability in higher education has become an issue of national importance (Miller, 2003). Calls for change are clearly here to stay.

A number of events illustrate this. In April 2004, the Business-Higher Education Forum issued the report, *Public Accountability for Student Learning in Higher Education* (Business-Higher Education Forum, 2004). It called on colleges and universities to conduct rigorous learning outcomes assessments and publicly report their results. Less than a year later, in March 2005, the National Commission on Accountability in Higher Education issued the report, *Accountability for Better Results: A National Imperative for Higher Education* (National Commission on Accountability in Higher Education, 2005). It called for a new approach to accountability, grounded in public responsibility, and urged the creation of a system that emphasizes student learning.

The National Commission on the Future of Higher Education issued their final report in September 2006. In the report, the authors cited "inadequate … accountability for measuring institutional performance" and called on higher education to embrace and implement serious measures of accountability (National Commission on the Future of Higher

Education, 2006, p. 13). The Association of American Colleges and Universities and the Council for Higher Education Accreditation banded together a few years later to issue *New Leadership for Student Learning and Accountability: A Statement of Principles, Commitments to Action* (2008), which called on higher education to "constantly monitor the quality of student learning and development, and use the results to both improve achievement and demonstrate the value of our work to the public" (p. 1).

Why All the Fuss About Accountability?

So, why all the fuss about accountability? First, higher education represents a significant public investment. Each year, the United States spends roughly $220 billion on higher education at the state and federal level, primarily in the form of student financial aid (White House, 2013).

Second, the stakes are high. Shulock (2006) notes, "Problems of low college-going rates, low graduation rates, inadequate preparation among college graduates ... and persistent gaps in educational attainment across income and racial lines bode poorly for the future social and economic health of the nation" (pp. 1–2). The United States once ranked first in the world in both the proportion of its population that graduated from high school and the proportion that enrolled in postsecondary education; it now ranks twelfth and eighth, respectively (Organisation for Economic Co-operation and Development, 2013).

Third, despite the large amounts of data provided by colleges and universities to regional accrediting bodies, state governing boards, and the federal government in the name of accountability each year, significant change has yet to occur. Until higher education is able to get in front of the calls for accountability in ways that have meaning and motivate substantive change, it will likely continue to cause a fuss (Leveille, 2013; McCormick, 2007).

There are many involved in higher education and student affairs that are skeptical of the movement toward greater accountability. Reactions to a national push have ranged from "cynical hostility to blithe acquiescence" (Campbell, 2007, p. 99). Critics fear that institutions will be measured against a single template—a "one-size-fits-all" approach—that doesn't respect the diversity of our missions and goals, or the students we serve (Warren, 2004).

As noted by McCormick (2007), a well-designed accountability system can motivate substantive change. However, a system requiring institutions to use common assessments that measure common outcomes could "undermine useful diagnostic tools" and "seriously hamper efforts to improve college quality" (McCormick, 2007, p. 1–2) Notwithstanding critics, the drive for greater accountability in higher education remains a resounding imperative that will continue to be a focus for our institutions and for the student affairs profession.

Who Are the Stakeholders for Institutional Accountability?

There are three primary types of stakeholders in higher education: those who provide funding and support, those who ensure that institutions fulfill their various fiduciary and educational responsibilities, and those who are consumers of higher education. Each group has different expectations related to institutional accountability.

The federal government provides funding for student financial aid, as well as for research and development. State policymakers provide funding for operating and capital expenditures, as well as for need- and merit-based aid, for most public institutions and some private institutions. The business community, alumni, and the greater public provide support to institutions through tuition, gifts, and service. These stakeholders believe their investment should—among other desired outcomes—result in the development of "human capital" for the workforce, and view education as a key to remaining competitive in today's global society (Zumeta, 2001).

State higher education coordinating agencies and institutional governing boards, including Boards of Trustees, also have a stake. There is a fiduciary responsibility inherent in their roles, as well as a responsibility for making sure that institutions are achieving their missions. In exercising oversight, these stakeholders perform a service for the public and society as a whole. They play a clear role in ensuring that institutions are responsive to current realities (Zumeta, 2001).

Consumers of higher education are a diverse group, and include students, their families, and local communities served by higher education institutions, among others. With the costs of higher education rising, stakeholders in this group expect colleges and universities to produce well-educated individuals who can achieve their full potential to lead productive lives. Recently, authors and the popular media have begun to question whether the investment in higher education is worth the return—adding to the case for students and families as major stakeholders in the issue of institutional accountability (Bennett & Wilezol, 2013; Selingo, 2014).

We recognize that these are not rigid categories, and that there may be overlap among the groups in these categories. For instance, students and their families are also funders, while the business community is also a consumer.

For What Is Student Affairs Accountable?

Priorities and expectations have changed over time as student affairs has evolved. The *Student Personnel Point of View* (American Council on Education, [1937] 1949), a seminal document of the profession, urged the development of services; it also called for intentional assessment in order to improve services. The profession looked to measures of efficiency, like usage data and satisfaction, to assess success.

In the decades that followed, researchers began to develop theories about students' cognitive development (Gilligan, 1982; Perry, 1968), identity development (Chickering, 1969) and moral reasoning (Kohlberg, 1976). These theories were operationalized, as were the means for measuring them, and a body of literature around student development emerged. In 1972, Robert Brown published *Student Development in Tomorrow's Higher Education: A Return to the Academy*; in it, he advised student affairs professionals to fully embrace student development as their leading priority and integrate it into their daily practice.

Two decades later, in 1994, the *Student Learning Imperative* encouraged practitioners to be intentional about creating conditions that enhance student learning (American College Personnel Association, 1994). This was followed by the publication of *Learning Reconsidered: A Campus-Wide Focus on the Student Experience* (Keeling, 2004); *Learning Reconsidered 2: A Practical Guide to Implementing a Campus-Wide Focus on the Student Experience* (Keeling, 2006); and *Assessment Reconsidered: Institutional Effectiveness for Student Success* (Keeling, Wall, Underhile, & Dungy, 2008). All emphasized the role that student affairs plays as a partner in the broader campus curriculum, and the resulting positive impact on student learning.

It is clear that student affairs professionals need to accomplish these ends—to provide high-quality services delivered in an efficient manner, to facilitate students' development, and to contribute to student learning (Barham and Scott, 2006). However, there is much work yet to be done. As noted in *Envisioning the Future of Student Affairs*, the final report of the Task

Force on the Future of Student Affairs, "Examples of a culture of evidence in student affairs—such as outcomes-based planning and assessment or the systematic use of assessment data to support decision making—are few and far between. This must change" (American College Personnel Association and National Association of Student Personnel Administrators, 2010, p. 10).

The Role of the Accreditation Process

Accreditation, according to Eaton (2012a), is a "process of external quality review" created and used by higher education institutions in the United States "to scrutinize colleges, universities, and programs" (p. 1). Originally conceived by college presidents in the 19th century, it emerged "from concerns to protect public health and safety and … serve the public interest" (Eaton, 2012a, p. 1). The accreditation process—which, today, is carried out by nonprofit organizations designed for this specific purpose—has widespread buy-in among institutions of higher education because it involves peer reviewers, can be applied to all types of institutions, utilizes standards approved by the institutions themselves, and is primarily focused on improvement (Eaton, 2012a; Wolff, 2005). Over time, accreditation has become a high-stakes endeavor: "without accreditation from an agency recognized by the US Department of Education, no Title IV federal financial aid can flow into an institution" (Middaugh, 2012, p. 5).

Three approved types of institutional accreditation occur: regional, national, and specialized (or, discipline-based) accreditation. Regional accrediting agencies operate within geographical parameters—for example, Middle States or North-Central States—and are generally viewed as a stable and revered mechanism for accreditation. National accrediting agencies focus on specific types of institutions, such as faith-based institutions or those that offer programs primarily through distance education. Specialized accrediting agencies focus on specific disciplines, including architecture, business, engineering, nursing, and teacher education.

Accreditation processes typically involve a complex and intensive self-study, as well as a site visit by a team composed of faculty and key administrators. The costs for these processes are borne by the institution, in the form of annual dues and site visit expenses. Institutional responsibility for meeting accrediting standards has largely fallen to the academic sector of higher education institutions, although that has begun to change in recent years. According to Eaton (2011), "As faith and confidence" in higher education have diminished and "calls for greater accountability" have increased, the federal government has responded by "expanding regulation and oversight in many phases of U.S. life, including accreditation" (p. 9).

The 2008 reauthorization of the Higher Education Act and subsequent negotiated rule-making sessions resulted in "a larger government footprint in both accreditation and academic areas heretofore untouched by government action: transfer of credit, textbooks, student achievement, and distance learning" (Eaton, 2012b, p. 12). There has also been a push toward a greater focus on institutional performance, student achievement, and increased transparency.

In the past, accreditation tended to focus primarily on measurable inputs such as faculty characteristics, resources (for example, library books), and processes (for example, course approval). Today, the focus is primarily on measureable outcomes and results, often in the form of student learning outcomes. Defined by the Council for Higher Education Accreditation (2003) as "the knowledge, skills, and abilities that a student has attained at the end (or as a result) of his or her ... higher education experiences," these outcomes may include critical reasoning, written and oral communications, quantitative reasoning, information literacy, or technology fluency (p. 5).

As the emphasis on measuring student learning continues to grow, student affairs has a key role to play in the accreditation process. Accordingly, useful tools have been developed by the Council for the Advancement of Standards in Higher Education and others.

Council for the Advancement of Standards and Accountability

The Council for the Advancement of Standards in Higher Education (CAS) has responded to calls for increasing accountability in student affairs by developing a series of self-assessment guides (CAS, 2012a) and frameworks for assessing student learning and development (Strayhorn, 2006). With the CAS Professional Standards (CAS, 2012b), these self-assessment guides and frameworks represent a key force in responding to calls for accountability within student affairs. Examples of how CAS and other professional standards can be used as tools for promoting accountability are available in Dean (2013), Arminio (2009), and Whitt & Blimling (2000).

Accreditation by Student Affairs Professional Organizations

Utilization of the CAS Standards is voluntary. Currently, no national accreditation mechanisms exist within the student affairs profession. In an effort to be accountable, however, three health and wellness–related organizations—to which many student affairs professionals belong—have fashioned processes that are similar to those of regional, national, and specialized accrediting bodies. These include the International Association of Counseling Services, which accredits college and university counseling centers; the American Psychological Association, which accredits psychologist internship and training programs; and the American College Health Association, which provides a consultation service to help institutions navigate the accreditation process for student health centers.

Best Practices for Accountability in Student Affairs

Demands for greater accountability in higher education, according to Kinzie (2011a), "compel student affairs educators to demonstrate their contribution[s] to student learning and … assume greater responsibility for learning outcomes assessment" (p. 203). Recent publications have identified a number of institutions that are making solid progress in this area, by using assessment data to illuminate the role that programs and services provided by student affairs play in student learning and success. These include Colorado State University (Kinzie, 2011b), Isothermal Community College (Jones, 2009), Texas A&M University (Osters, 2009), and the University of Maine at Farmington (Schuh & Gansemer-Topf, 2010). Additional examples can be found in Baker, Jankowski, Provezis, and Kinzie (2012); Bresciani, Gardner, and Hickmott (2009); and Mallory and Clement (2009).

Additional Resources

As calls for accountability in higher education and student affairs have become more vocal, a number of key associations have weighed in, creating resources and undertaking initiatives to develop "common, voluntary standards of ... public disclosure" (Keller, 2012, p. 372). In this section, we describe several of these resources and initiatives.

National Institute for Learning Outcomes Assessment

In 2008, the National Institute for Learning Outcomes Assessment (NILOA) was established by coprincipal investigators George Kuh and Stan Ikenberry. Colocated at the University of Illinois and Indiana University, the primary mission of NILOA is to champion and support efforts by colleges and universities to obtain, use, and share evidence of student learning to strengthen student attainment and improve undergraduate education (National Institute for Learning Outcomes Assessment, 2013).

New Leadership Alliance for Student Learning and Accountability

In 2009, the Association of American Colleges and Universities (AAC&U) and the Council for Higher Education Accreditation (CHEA) joined together to create the New Leadership Alliance for Student Learning and Accountability. The advocacy-focused organization leads and supports voluntary efforts to move the higher education community toward gathering, reporting on, and using evidence to improve student learning (New Leadership Alliance for Student Learning and Accountability, 2012).

University and College Accountability Network

In 2007, the National Association of Independent Colleges and Universities (NAICU) launched the University and College Accountability Network (U-CAN). The website, designed to give prospective students and their families concise, consumer friendly information on private colleges and universities, includes information on student demographics, graduation rates, most common fields of study, faculty information, class sizes, tuition and fee trends, average loan debt, and campus safety (University and College Accountability Network, 2013).

Voluntary Framework of Accountability

In 2009, the American Association of Community Colleges (AACC) partnered with the Association of Community College Trustees (ACCT) and the College Board to develop the Voluntary Framework of Accountability (VFA). The objectives of the VFA project—which is structured as a three-phase initiative—are to identify a common set of readiness, progress, and outcomes measures that allow community colleges "to benchmark their data against peers and...give stakeholders critical information on institutional performance" (Keller, 2012, p. 381).

Voluntary System of Accountability/College Portrait

In 2007, the Association of Public and Land-Grant Universities (APLU) and the American Association of State Colleges and Universities (AASCU) unveiled the Voluntary System of Accountability (VSA). Through a common web report—*College Portrait*—the system seeks to demonstrate accountability and stewardship to the public by providing information on student and faculty characteristics, popular majors, average class sizes, estimated costs, gains in student learning, and campus safety (Voluntary System of Accountability, 2013).

Conclusion

It has become clear—in recent years—that accountability in higher education and student affairs is here to stay. As asserted by Mundhenk (2006), "Higher education is being asked by many groups, both within and outside higher education, to be publicly accountable and demonstrate its worth to stakeholders" (p. 44).

For student affairs professionals, this means not only providing high-quality services delivered in a cost-efficient manner, facilitating students' development, and contributing to student learning (Barham & Scott, 2006), but also finding ways to measure the effectiveness of these activities and share the results with a variety of stakeholders—including students, parents, state and federal government, higher education coordinating agencies, and governing boards—in ways that are both easy to understand and readily accessible.

Lee Shulman (2007) has likened the growing volume of calls for accountability in higher education to a powerful current. As noted by Shulman, we have three options for responding: we can "paddle upstream, resisting all the way"; we can "go with the flow, adopting a stance of minimal compliance"; or we can "take the approach that a skilled whitewater rafter or canoeist would—negotiating the rapids by paddling faster than the current" (p. 25).

It is time, Shulman asserts, for higher education to take control. Accordingly, we must "summon the creative energy and ambition to take advantage of the momentum (and resources) unleashed by [this movement] ... and exploit them to initiate the long-overdue progress in assessment needed to improve the quality of learning in higher education" (p. 25).

We must also continue to take initiative to ask the critical questions, to inform and educate, and to ensure that accountability is moving higher education toward a place of meaningful change. It is critical that we continue to advocate for approaches to accountability that are not "one size fits all" and that take into consideration the diversity of our institutions, our communities, and the students that we serve. It is time for us to embrace accountability, on our own terms; to make it our own, and to tell—as noted by Shulman (2007)—the "full range of stories about [the] learning and teaching" that is occurring on our campuses (p. 25).

References

American College Personnel Association. (1994). *The student learning imperative: Implications for student affairs.* Alexandria, VA: Author.

American College Personnel Association and National Association of Student Personnel Administrators. (2010). *Envisioning the future of student affairs.* Report of the Task Force on the Future of Student Affairs. Washington, DC: Authors.

American Council on Education. (1949). *The student personnel point of view.* Washington, DC: Author. (Originally published 1937)

Arminio, J. (2009). Applying professional standards. In G. S. McClellan & J. Stringer (Eds.), *The handbook of student affairs administration* (3rd ed.) (pp. 187-205). San Francisco, CA: Jossey-Bass.

Association of American Colleges and Universities and Council for Higher Education Accreditation. (2008). *New Leadership for student learning and accountability: A Statement of principles, commitments to action.* Washington, DC: Author.

Baker, G. R., Jankowski, N. A., Provezis, S., & Kinzie, J. (2012). *Using assessment results: Promising practices of institutions that do it well.* Urbana: University of Illinois and Indiana University, National Institute for Learning Outcomes Assessment.

Barham, J. D., & Scott, J. H. (2006). Increasing accountability in student affairs through a new comprehensive assessment model. *College Student Affairs Journal, 25*(2), 209–219.

Bennett, W. J., & Wilezol, D. (2013). *Is college worth it?: A former United States Secretary of education and a liberal arts graduate expose the broken promise of higher education.* Nashville, TN: Thomas Nelson.

Blimling, G. S. (2013). Challenges of assessment in student affairs. In G. S. Blimling (Ed.), *Selected contemporary assessment issues.* New Directions for Student Services, no. 142. San Francisco, CA: Jossey-Bass.

Bresciani, M. J., Gardner, M. M., & Hickmott, J. (Eds.). (2009). *Case studies for implementing assessment in student affairs.* New Directions for Student Services, no. 127. San Francisco, CA: Jossey-Bass.

Brown, R. D. (1972). *Student development in tomorrow's higher education: A return to the academy.* Student Personnel Series, no. 16. Washington, DC: American Personnel and Guidance Association.

Burke, J. C., & Minassians, H. P. (2002). The new accountability: From regulations to results. In J. C. Burke & H. P. Minassians (Eds.), *Reporting higher education results: Missing links in the performance chain.* New Directions for Institutional Research, no. 116. San Francisco, CA: Jossey-Bass.

Business-Higher Education Forum. (2004). *Public accountability for student learning in higher education: Issues and options.* Washington, DC: American Council on Education.

Campbell, K. J. (2007). Assessment advice for beginners. *PS: Political science and Politics, 40*(1), 99.

Chickering, A. (1969). *Education and identity.* San Francisco, CA: Jossey-Bass.

Council for Higher Education Accreditation. (2003). *Statement of mutual responsibilities for student learning outcomes: Accreditation, institutions, and programs.* Washington, DC: Author.

Council for the Advancement of Standards in Higher Education (CAS). (2012a). *Self-assessment guides* (Version 5.0) [CD]. Washington, DC: Author.

Council for the Advancement of Standards in Higher Education (CAS). (2012b). *CAS professional standards for higher education* (8th ed.). Washington, DC: Author.

Dean, L. A. (2013). Using the CAS standards in assessment projects. In G. S. Blimling (Ed.), *Selected contemporary assessment issues.* New Directions for Student Services, no. 142. San Francisco, CA: Jossey-Bass.

Eaton, J. S. (2011). U.S. accreditation: Meeting the challenges of accountability and student achievement. *Evaluation in Higher Education, 5*(1), 1–20.

Eaton, J. S. (2012a). *An overview of U.S. accreditation.* Washington, DC: Council for Higher Education Accreditation.

Eaton, J. S. (2012b). The future of accreditation. *Journal of the Society for College and University Planning, 40*(3), 8–15.

Ewell, P. T. (2004). *The changing nature of accountability in higher education.* Paper prepared for the Western Association of Schools and Colleges (WASC) Senior Commission, Alameda, CA. November 2004.

Gilligan, C. (1982). *In a Different Voice.* Cambridge, MA: Harvard University Press.

Harpel, R. L. (1976). Planning, budgeting, and evaluation in student affairs programs: A manual for administrators. *NASPA Journal, 14*(1), i–xx.

Jones, K. K. (2009). Isothermal community college. In M. J. Bresciani, M. M. Gardner, & J. Hickmott (Eds.), *Case studies for implementing assessment in student affairs.* New Directions for Student Services, no. 127. San Francisco, CA: Jossey-Bass.

Keeling, R. P. (Ed) (2004), *Learning reconsidered: A campus-wide focus on the student experience.* Washington, DC: American College Personnel Association and National Association of Student Personnel Administrators.

Keeling, R. P. (Ed.). (2006). *Learning reconsidered 2: A Practical guide to implementing a campus-wide focus on the student experience.* Washington, DC: American College Personnel Association, & Others.

Keeling, R. P., Wall, A. F., Underhile, R., & Dungy, G. J. (2008). *Assessment reconsidered: Institutional effectiveness for student success.* Washington, DC: International Center for Student Success and Institutional Accountability.

Keller, C. M. (2012). Collective responses to a new era of accountability in higher education. In R. D. Howard, G. W. McLaughlin, & W. E. Knight (Eds.), *The handbook of institutional research* (pp.371-385). San Francisco, CA: Jossey-Bass.

Kinzie, J. (2011a). Student affairs in the age of accountability and assessment. In P. M. Magolda & M. B. Baxter Magolda (Eds.), *Contested issues in student affairs: Diverse perspectives and respectful dialogue* (pp.202-214). San Francisco, CA: Jossey-Bass.

Kinzie, J. (2011b). *Colorado State University: A comprehensive continuous improvement system* (NILOA Examples of Good Assessment Practice). Urbana: University of Illinois and Indiana University, National Institute for Learning Outcomes Assessment.

Kohlberg, L. (1976). Moral stages and moralization: The cognitive-developmental approach. In T. Lickona (Ed.), *Moral development and behavior: Theory, research, and social issues* (pp.31-53). New York, NY: Holt, Rinehart & Winston.

Leveille, D. E. (2005). *An emerging view on accountability in American higher education* (Research and occasional paper series: CSHE.8.05). Berkeley: University of California.

Leveille, D. E. (2013). *Accountability in postsecondary education revisited* (Research and occasional paper series: CSHE.9.13). Berkeley: University of California.

Levine, A. (1996). Education reform: Designing the end game. *Change: The Magazine of Higher Learning, 28*(1), 4.

Mallory, S.L., & Clement, L.M. (2009). *Accountability.* In G.S. McClellan and J. Stringer (Eds.), *The handbook of student affairs administration* (3rd ed., pp. 105-119).). San Francisco: Jossey-Bass.

McCormick, A. C. (2007, April). First, do no harm. *Carnegie perspectives.* http://www.carnegiefoundation.org/.

McLendon, M. K., Hearn, J. C., & Deaton, R. (2006). Called to account: Analyzing the origins and spread of state performance-accountability policies for higher education. *Educational Evaluation and Policy Analysis, 28*(1), 1–24.

Middaugh, M. F. (2012). Introduction to themed PHE Issue on accreditation in higher education. *Journal of the Society for College and University Planning, 40*(3), 5–7.

Miller, C. O. (2003, May 13). Is there a need for a new approach to higher education accountability? Testimony Provided to the US Committee on Education and the Workforce.

Mundhenk, R. T. (2006). Embracing Accountability. *American Academic, 2*(1), 39–53.

National Commission on Accountability in Higher Education. (2005). *Accountability for better results: A national imperative for higher education.* Denver, CO: State Higher Education Executive Officers.

National Commission on Excellence in Education. (1983). *A nation at risk: The imperative for educational reform.* Washington, DC: US Government Printing Office.

National Commission on the Future of Higher Education. (2006). *A test of leadership: Charting the future of U.S. higher education.* Washington, DC: U. S. Department of Education.

Neave, G. (1980). Accountability and control. *European Journal of Education, 15*(1), 49–60.

National Institute for Learning Outcomes Assessment. (2013, October). *About Us.* http://www.learningoutcomesassessment.org/AboutUs.html.

New Leadership Alliance for Student Learning and Accountability. (2012). *Committing to quality: Guidelines for assessment and accountability in higher education.* Washington, DC: Author.

Organisation for Economic Co-operation and Development. (2013). *Education at a glance 2013: OECD Indicators.* Paris, France: Author.

Osters, S. (2009). Texas A&M University. In M. J. Bresciani, M. M. Gardner, & J. Hickmott (Eds.), *Case studies for implementing assessment in student affairs.* New Directions for Student Services, no. 127. San Francisco, CA: Jossey-Bass.

Perry, W. G. Jr. (1968). *Forms of Intellectual and ethical development in the college years: A scheme.* New York, NY: Holt, Rinehart, & Winston.

Reville, S. P. (2006). Coming soon to a college near you: Accountability. *Connection: New England's Journal of Higher Education, 20*(5), 19.

Sandia National Laboratories. (1993). Summary of issues. *Journal of Educational Research, 86*(5), 309–310.

Schuh, J. H., & Gansemer-Topf, A. M. (2010). *The role of student affairs in student learning assessment* (Occasional paper no. 7). Urbana: University of Illinois and Indiana University, National Institute for Learning Outcomes Assessment.

Selingo, J. J. (2014). *College unbound: The future of higher education and what it means for students.* New York, NY: Houghton Mifflin Harcourt.

Shulman, L. S. (2007). Counting and recounting: Assessment and the quest for quality improvement. *Change: The Magazine of Higher Learning, 39*(1), 20–25.

Shulock, N. B. (2006). Editor's notes. In N. B. Shulock (Ed.), *Practitioners on making accountability work for the public.* New Directions for Higher Education, no. 135. San Francisco, CA: Jossey-Bass.

Strayhorn, T. L. (2006). *Frameworks for assessing learning and development outcomes.* Washington, DC: Council for the Advancement of Standards in Higher Education.

University and College Accountability Network. (2013, October). *About U-Can.* http://www.ucan-network.org/about-u-can.

Upcraft, M. L., & Schuh, J. H. (1996). *Assessment in student affairs: A guide for practitioners.* San Francisco, CA: Jossey-Bass.

Voluntary System of Accountability. (2013, October). *About VSA.* http://www.voluntarysystem.org/.

Warren, D. (2004, April 8). Appropriate accountability. Testimony before the National Commission on Accountability in Higher Education. http://archive.sheeo.org/account/comm/testim/NAICU Testimony.pdf.f

Wellman, J. V. (2006). Accountability for the public trust. In N. B. Shulock (ed.), *Practitioners on making accountability work for the public.* New Directions for Higher Education, no. 135. San Francisco, CA: Jossey-Bass.

Welsh, J. F., & Metcalf, J. (2003). Administrational support for institutional effectiveness activities: Responses to the new accountability. *Journal of Higher Education Policy and Management, 25*(2), 183–193.

White House. (2013, October). Fact sheet on the president's plan to make college more affordable: A better bargain for the middle class. http://www.whitehouse.gov/the-press-office/2013/08/22/fact-sheet-president-s-plan-make-college-more-affordable-better-bargain-.

Whitt, E. J., & Blimling, G. S. (2000). Applying professional standards and principles of good practice in student affairs. In M. J. Barr & M. K. Desler (Eds.), *The handbook of student affairs administration* (2nd ed., pp. 612-618). . San Francisco, CA: Jossey-Bass.

Wingspread Group on Higher Education. (1993). *An American imperative: Higher expectations for higher education*. Racine, WI: Johnson Foundation.

Wolff, R. A. (2005). Accountability and accreditation: Can reforms match increasing demands? In J. C. Burke (Ed.), *Achieving accountability in higher education: balancing public, academic and market demands* (pp.78-103). San Francisco, CA: Jossey-Bass.

Zumeta, W. (2001). Accountability challenges for higher education. *The NEA 2000 almanac of higher education*. Washington, DC: National Education Association.

CHAPTER SIX

STUDENT AFFAIRS AND SERVICES IN GLOBAL PERSPECTIVE

Brett Perozzi and Enrique Ramos

Higher education and student affairs and services are inextricably linked to globalization and internationalization. Douglass, King, and Feller (2009) went so far as to entitle their work on these concepts *Globalization's Muse*, given that higher education is such a suitable platform for internationalization efforts and exploration. As the purview of global tertiary education, research output, community impact, and, above all, talent development are key elements of a globalized society. Student affairs work ties directly to supporting these aims and helping students succeed at the highest level (Nuss, 1996).

This chapter addresses the concepts of globalization and internationalization as they relate to higher education generally and to student affairs and services specifically. The stage is set by describing and discussing the concepts within individual cultural contexts and by using examples from around the world. Student and staff learning are explored in relation to various concepts such as cultural competence and skill/knowledge development. For those working in student affairs roles globally, many of whom come from a variety of both educational and experiential backgrounds, organizations and professional associations exist in some parts of the world to provide professional development and educational programs and services, in addition to locally produced programs. Against this vast global backdrop, working with students is the common denominator among various student affairs and services structural models and diverse paradigms that help students succeed in the higher education environment.

The terms *higher education* and *tertiary education* are variously used throughout the world; in this chapter the term *higher education* is used. Although work with students is typically referred to as "student affairs" or "student services," in this chapter the term *student affairs* is used. This is not to dilute or homogenize the vernacular, as in many regions of the world there are various conceptualizations and different labels for the work being done with students. For example, in Latin America, this emerging area may be called *student life* or even *student wellness,* both of which have broad conceptualizations, more like what might be called student affairs in other parts of the world.

Globalization and Internationalization

Globalization may be defined as a host of social and economic forces that combine to bring about phenomena that affect people and organizations across the globe. Knight (2008, p. 208) defines *globalization* as "the flow of technology, economy, knowledge, people, values, and ideas ... across borders." Globalization has led to the concept of internationalization in higher education, which Osfield and Terrell (2009, p. 121) define as the "process of fostering intentional, multidimensional, and interdisciplinary leadership-driven activities that expand global learning, for example, knowledge, skills, and attitudes."

With globalization feeding the growth of internationalization in the higher education sector, during the past fifteen years colleges and universities have been expanding their horizons, with many operating campuses in other countries (Knight & Morshiti, 2011). Major shifts in approach within regions and new collaborative agreements among countries now has far-reaching impact.

For example, despite the economic challenges of several Western European countries, such as Ireland and Spain, the European Union remains a key economic and policy leader in global higher education, as demonstrated by the forward thinking and collaborative Bologna process and Erasmus Program. By harmonizing curricula across the European Higher Education Area (EHEA), the Bologna process has made transferability a logical and simple option for students across dozens of countries. The Bologna process is an initiative to align higher education across the newly created EHEA, allowing for ease in the transfer of credit, consistent outcomes among majors, and congruence in time to degree completion. The Erasmus Program's primary aim, in concert with Bologna, is to further encourage student mobility, allowing for the free flow of students among countries in the EHEA (Teichler, 2012). In other regions such as Latin America, institutions have sought accreditation from US or other country's accreditation bodies to help be attractive destinations for students. Even as massive open online courses (MOOCs) continue to gain in popularity, many countries such as China and Brazil are investing in building their educational infrastructure to accommodate their populations' growing appetites for higher education.

Influencing the curriculum and permeating the basic college and university experience, an increased attention to global issues has affected higher education as an industry. Recruitment of international students has become big business, accounting for significant changes in national policies around immigration and access to education. A global economy and shrinking traditional resource bases for higher education have heightened the need for student affairs and services to embrace an expanding role (Ping, 1999) and widening international lens. Given advances in communication technologies, reaching and interacting with those from other countries has become effortless, and even placeless. The challenges and paradigm changes associated with increased communication, exploding mobile technologies, changing student demographics, MOOCs, and a host of other globally relevant issues present a need for higher education and student affairs to become or remain relevant within their social contexts.

Therefore, it is important for student affairs to have a critical view of internationalization. As stated by Marmolejo (2011), "While most practitioners see internationalization as something good for individuals and institutions, specific initiatives can have wide-ranging effects on the parties involved, some positive and some negative" (p. 2).

Globalization, Internationalization, and Student Affairs

Since the previous edition of this book (2009), there have been more than 100,000 students added to the rolls of international study in just the United States alone, where international enrollments are increasing at a greater average rate than overall US higher education enrollment (Institute of International Education, 2013). There are also massive increases in student mobility spawned by the European Erasmus program (Teichler, 2012) and ground-breaking initiatives to send students abroad by countries such as Chile, Brazil, and Saudi Arabia (Horden, 2012). Although the global number of mobile students has topped 4 million, it still represents fewer than 2 percent of the global student population (Teekens, 2013). Increasing attention is being paid to world higher education institution ranking schemes, which show that the top 700 world universities are attracting massive numbers of international students (Q.S., 2012). As a result, the traditional view of the student affairs role in shaping students' experiences needs to be reconceptualized to include the role student affairs plays in the education of students from other countries and cultures.

The need has never been greater for student affairs administrators to understand the impact of globalization and internationalization on higher education, including the ramifications for student affairs. Evolving global issues create a sense of urgency for student affairs scholars and practitioners. Are programs and services for students organized to support students in a global context? Do staff members have the skills and knowledge to appropriately lead internationalization initiatives on individual campuses? And, are the key factors and skills identified so that the path to global learning can be followed?

Regional and National Contexts

"What is true is that while internationalization of higher education is here to stay, there is considerable variation in the way it unfolds over time on the regional, institutional, and individual level. Because it is an evolving phenomenon, its meaning can be difficult to pin down" (Marmolejo, 2011, p. 2). Major changes in tuition fees policies in countries such as The Netherlands (UNICAS, 2013) and the United Kingdom (Blick, 2010), capacity and infrastructure realities in China and India (Goswami, 2012), and federal government policy decisions in countries such as Australia (Tani, 2012; and Trounson, 2013) have wreaked havoc on governments, the higher education sector, and students. These issues combined with the aggressive recruitment of international students globally, are generating a new and increasingly similar global context for student affairs personnel, yet at the same time these concepts play out differently within regional cultural contexts.

A series of personal interviews conducted by the authors supports the notion that there is considerable variability among world regions and individual countries regarding the philosophical approach and delivery of student affairs and services (Ramos & Perozzi, 2014). The interview data represent the countries of Azerbaijan, Canada, Germany, Japan, Lebanon, Lithuania, Mexico, Qatar, Spain, and the United States. From providing essential services to students through accommodation (housing) and catering (food service), to measuring the extent to which students gain knowledge and develop skills, the practice and philosophical underpinnings of student affairs differs dramatically based on regional and country cultures and values (Ramos & Perozzi, 2014).

There also are important regional and national differences regarding the extent to which student affairs is established as a profession or as a formal structure within higher education institutions. In many world regions student affairs is perceived to be an emerging or evolving concept. Few countries outside of the United States and Canada have student affairs educational preparation programs or offer master's or doctoral degrees in student affairs and higher education. In most countries, those working in student affairs typically have a background in an academic discipline, or another field outside of higher education (Seifert, Perozzi, Bodine Al-Sharif, Li, & Wildman, 2014).

Many countries and regions do not have a body of literature on student affairs nor is research regularly conducted on students of that country or region. However, more is known now about how to account for "culture, intersectionality, context, self-identification, and many other factors" (Carpenter & Haber-Curran, 2013, p. 5) when using research conducted on students in other countries. Research on students exists in the United States and some other countries, but is it transferable to the varied needs and aspirations of students globally? Counseling is a student service offered quite widely around the world, yet do counselors work within and understand the context of student affairs? Should they?

These existing and emerging issues are embraced differently and impact the local practice of student affairs disparately. For example, although student affairs in countries such as the United States and Germany emphasize the importance of student autonomy, Latin American countries place more emphasis on student wellness and the role that family plays in student development. Despite these differences, student affairs professionals interviewed by Ramos and Perozzi (2014) agree, to a great extent, on an important set of student centered values such as: diversity, leadership development, self-exploration, experiential learning, problem solving, and character building that student affairs professionals embrace and promote.

Although not possible to provide commentary here on a country by country or region by region basis, general tenets and highlights of student affairs delivery and philosophy of five countries/regions are presented to provide some basis for discussion and comparison. Those presented here are Europe, Latin America, the Middle East, South Africa, and the United States and Canada. For in-depth information on these countries and regions, readers are referred to *Student Affairs and Services in Higher Education: Global Foundations, Issues and Best Practices* (Ludeman, Osfield, Iglesias, Oste, & Wang, 2009).

Student Affairs in Europe. Several European countries, specifically, France, Germany, and Italy, provide students with essential services through administrative structures that are organized outside of the higher education institutions themselves. Each of these countries has local or regional student services organizations that provide services to university students. In some cases, one regional service provider may provide services to multiple higher education institutions. This model is not necessarily an outsourced model as conceptualized in the United States. Rather, it is an approach that combines a loosely cooperative arrangement between the higher education institution, the student services provider, and federal and/or state governments. The extent to which the student services agencies are or are not aligned with institutions and governments varies by country, yet the combination of government and student funding is present across all schemes. Services such as accommodation, catering, and counseling (broadly construed) are subsidized for students using government fiscal standards, which allow for very low costs to students for these services.

Student Affairs in North America. The United States and Canada have fairly well-established student affairs traditions and philosophical underpinnings. Although present in various forms earlier, the history of modern student affairs in the United States dates back to the early 1900s (Rhatigan, 2009), and Canadian student affairs continues to evolve (Canadian Association of College and University Student Services, 2012). These countries offer advanced degrees in university administration and student affairs. Although delivery and philosophy of programs and services varies dramatically across the spectrum of higher education institutions, basic concepts are generally accepted. American student affairs ideology grew out of a tradition of supporting students in their success by providing high-quality services within each institution. Over time that concept expanded to helping students develop as a whole person and to gain critical skills and knowledge necessary for future success (Keeling, 2006), and today that concept is further extended to focus the delivery of programs and services on helping students learn critical skills that will allow them to be successful in a global community. For a more complete discussion of the history of student affairs in higher education in the United States, see chapter 1 in this volume.

Student Affairs in Latin America. Student affairs functions across Latin America differ in name, construct, structure, resources, and services provided depending on the country. The closer the country is to the United States the more similar to the American model the student affairs structure and services provided by the country are. Because of its proximity to the United States, Mexico emphasizes, through student affairs areas, that student development is a central element of mission and purpose. Furthermore, several practitioners in Mexico have a closer relationship with student affairs associations in the United States; these relationships have led to the establishment of an International Summer Symposium sponsored by four important Mexican higher education institutions. The symposium has provided student affairs staff in Mexico with important developmental opportunities. In addition, the Tecnologico de Monterrey offers an online masters program in higher education with emphasis on student affairs.

In most Central and South American countries student affairs is a much more loosely constructed concept, which varies in terms of structure, functions, and services provided to students, depending on each country. No formal academic programs are offered for student affairs personnel and no professional associations related to student affairs exist in South America. Student affairs and services in South America are typically referred to as *student wellness, student life,* or *student relations.* In general, student affairs in South America could be conceptualized more as a student services area, with provided services including counseling, sports and cultural activities, alcohol and drug prevention programs, dining, and housing. Some institutions also provide student retention, orientation, and financial aid programs.

Student Affairs in South Africa. Student affairs in South Africa is expanding at a rapid rate, and the first professional journal for the continent of Africa was published in November, 2013. Professional associations serving student affairs personnel have been in existence for many years, indicating a significant level of evolution for student affairs as a profession. There are currently 12 professional associations, of which seven are active (Gugulethu Xaba, personal communication, September 18, 2013). These associations are helping to create a common ideology, share experiences, and provide some level of coordination among those working in a student affairs capacity. Practitioners come from various backgrounds with few formal educational programs in higher education and student affairs (Luescher-Mamashela, Moja, & Schreiber, 2013). There is a wide range of programs and services offered to students that might include any of the following: financial aid, student governance, health services, chaplaincy, clubs and organizations, counseling and careers services, HIV/AIDS services, student leadership, international student services, sports and recreation.

A Common Agenda

No common frame of reference or agreed-upon philosophy of student affairs currently exists globally. In some countries there is debate as to whether student affairs is a field or a profession, rather than a practice of working with students within specific cultural contexts. There are efforts underway to gather input from student affairs personnel on a common ideology, and bring together thought leaders from around the world to work through shared elements of student affairs work that can potentially unite the field across borders. The philosophy must capture the essence of student affairs work in a way that embraces cultural nuances and multiple values systems. The shared understanding must be succinct enough to describe the core and heart of student affairs work, but contain a breadth that expresses the spirit of the work that allows individual regions or countries to see how they are encompassed within the statement and aligned with the philosophy. It is possible to build capacity for student affairs within countries while strengthening global ties and understanding. In this process both the means and the end represent a valuable learning opportunity for all involved. Becoming part of the process can be achieved by reaching out to global colleagues, participating in an exchange or internship, or coauthoring an article, all of which can help increase understanding and comprehension about the context-specific role of student affairs.

Professional associations and institutions with established student affairs traditions play an important role in demonstrating the profession. However, these organizations must seek to understand cultural context, rather than providing answers or solutions. Student affairs around the world can develop international initiatives through partnerships and collaboration "measuring success in terms of mutual benefit and global action" (Sutton & Deardorff, 2012, p. 16). Professional associations can help organize the work of leaders at local and international levels, and provide a host of programs, services, and volunteer opportunities to enrich their members' roles and careers. For example, the National Association of Student Personnel Administrators (NASPA), has held an International Symposium for the past two decades that gathers student affairs leaders from across the globe to engage in meaningful dialog about international student affairs. NASPA has also established an international advisory board (IAB) to more closely involve international members and to help define and understand NASPA's role in this emerging global setting. The American College Personnel Association (ACPA) offers a range of international programs and involvement opportunities for its members, and many other content-specific associations such as the Association of College and University Housing Officers-International provide programming around international topics. Furthermore, the International Association of Student Affairs and Services (IASAS) has recently been chartered in Brussels. This organization intends to provide its members with opportunities to develop worldwide partnerships and share best practices.

Professional Associations

Devoid of a common agenda or agreement about how, and even if, there should be overarching understandings and decisions made about common ideology—for example, a shared philosophy or common student and staff competencies—developing deep connections among student affairs practitioners in different countries is challenging. There is strong and natural allegiance to how student affairs is carried out in specific countries, based on local cultural ideals, customs, and mores. There is also significant sensitivity to Western conceptualizations of student affairs being regarded as prevailing, or good, or better than other or regional conceptualizations of student affairs. There is no one group, council, or association that sets policy or standards for student affairs globally, nor is there necessarily agreement that such a body should exist.

Many student affairs professional associations globally, such as NASPA in the United States, provide options for the international involvement of practitioners. Associations can provide a context for the work of practitioners and also developmental opportunities to keep professionals current, help with exposure to best practices, and generate critical content for journals and other publications. These associations can provide a network of practitioners and help connect people around common issues and ideas.

These factors combine to create a critical and exciting time for student affairs globally, and the official chartering of IASAS is a symbolic and significant step forward. This organization is the first truly global association for student affairs practitioners. The chartering outside of North America was intentional, to signify the commitment to colleagues in countries and regions with emerging paradigms of student affairs, as opposed to countries that have a traditional or a Western orientation to student affairs. IASAS can provide a platform for discussion and communication about critical issues related to global philosophy, organization, and delivery of student affairs.

NASPA and IASAS partnered to host the Global Summit on Student Affairs and Services in 2012 in Washington, D.C., and 2014 in Rome, Italy. These summits brought together more than fifty senior student affairs representatives from more than twenty-five countries. There was general agreement at the first summit that several factors inhibit the full development of student affairs in different parts of the world including a "lack of sufficient funding, the lack of recognition as a profession, few opportunities for staff training and continuing education, a possible lack of professional associations, and a general misunderstanding of the field by the academic community" (Callahan & Stanfield, 2012, p. 2).

Delegates to the 2012 Global Summit agreed that many issues, including the massification of higher education, are critical in shaping student affairs globally. Fiscal issues were prevalent with many countries reporting increased government influence, competition for scarce resources, and concern over the availability of financial aid. Other factors presented were student diversity, access and persistence of students, and decreasing incoming student preparedness. The need to understand student affairs context, remain current in one's position, and learn new skills and knowledge to best serve students and educational institutions were evident during the Global Summit and also in current research (Seifert et al., 2014).

Staff and Student Development

Evolving global issues present both challenges and opportunities for student affairs scholars and practitioners. On the one hand, these issues represent an opportunity to understand and support students with different perspectives, backgrounds and needs—on the other hand, they represent a challenge to develop programs and services in order to support student development in both global and local contexts. Therefore, development of staff members becomes increasingly important in order to have the skills and knowledge to appropriately support institutional internationalization and to adequately enhance student development.

Staff Development

In the international context, student affairs practitioners should be trained to attend to the needs of all students and to function in a multicultural and international environment. Globalization is a wide-ranging concept, and countries and individual institutions are affected in different ways. "The integration of the environment external to higher education has a substantial influence on the success of students and the ability of higher education to meet the needs of an ever-changing student population" (Torres & Walbert, 2010, p. 5).

Despite the fact that academic programs are in place for student affairs practitioners in some countries, little attention has been placed on the requirements for student affairs staff to deal with a more globalized society. As Ping (1999) asserts:

> The preparation for this expanded role requires study, reflection, and, most critically, direct experience with other cultures. The base for this preparation is an interest in the world and its diverse peoples, in geography, in global history, and in the contemporary political and economic realities of various regions in the world. (pp. 20–21)

Furthermore, Dalton (1999) reminds us that faculty members have a long history of engagement in international exchanges and professional activities, whereas student affairs practitioners have more recently begun to develop these types of relationships in order to develop a wider and international perspective. In this regard, Pope and Reynolds (1997) argue that student affairs literature shows an increased interest in the development of multicultural skills and core competencies required for stronger professional practice.

Student affairs practitioners around the world must continue to learn and develop critical skills. Although the role and approach with students may differ, meeting student expectations is important. Yakaboski and Perozzi (2014) and Latham and Dalton (1999) provide several overlapping suggestions for staff development around international issues. These include:

- Conduct research on and/or write about relevant student affairs international issues.
- Participate in curricular or non-curricular-based study abroad or travel programs offered by the institution, civic organizations, or professional associations.
- Develop cultural competency through professional travel.
- Regularly interact with those doing international work on your campus, and stay abreast of relevant issues.
- Learn another language.
- Stay current on international issues, especially as they relate to the local situation.

To continue learning and developing international skills, staff can also consider the following.

- Develop new programs that include a global perspective.
- Engage international students in program development.
- Engage with international students by inviting them to take on leadership positions.
- Start or support international clubs and student organizations.
- Encourage international students to present about their home countries' higher education systems, cultures, and so on.
- Host exchanges, trips, and outings.

Student Development

Different theories have provided student affairs professionals with frameworks for understanding the way students develop during their college experience (Evans, Forney, Guido, Patton, & Renn, 2009). Far from what could be considered an established paradigm that students only attend college in order to obtain knowledge related to their academic discipline, it could be argued from a student affairs perspective that college attendance is crucial for students' personal and professional growth. It is advised that theories established using subjects from the United States be used only as general reference for understanding development of students globally. Research should be replicated in other countries to be tested and/or adapted as contextually appropriate.

Graduate competencies are the set of knowledge, skills, and abilities that students gain during their time at university. Defining agreed-upon competencies is essential for student affairs so that staff can support students and faculty in the pursuit of fulfilling the competencies. These graduate skills have various labels across the world, including soft skills (Cinque, 2012), core competencies, and graduate learning outcomes. The name of the concepts may not be as important as the identification and common pursuit of the ideals. The methods used to achieve the outcomes vary, and the role that student affairs plays varies even more substantially. However, the ability to leverage the collective strength of student affairs across borders allows staff to be recognized as key partners on the path to students' success.

In recent years, higher education institutions around the world have shown an interest in demonstrating the impact of their activities on students by compiling specific and concrete evidence. By collecting direct evidence of student achievement (Maki, 2010), programs and services provided by student affairs can be directly linked to student learning and development.

Hard Skills and Soft Skills

During college, students acquire hard skills—technical or operative competencies required to take a specific assignment to its appropriate end. Students should also develop a set of soft skills that are required in social interactions or are related to communication processes or processes of interpersonal influence (Lozano, 2013).

Within the context of higher education, hard skills are developed or acquired primarily inside the classroom, whereas soft skills can be acquired or developed in different settings throughout students' college experience, which include cognitive elements found in nonacademic activities. From the job market standpoint, soft skills are more critical than ever before in this era of information and communications technology (Vishal, 2009).

Student affairs personnel in many countries actively engage with employers to learn about the competencies required and sought in their companies and organizations. Employers find it desirable for current and future employees to possess high levels of proficiency in soft skills so that they can effectively communicate and interact with others (Cinque, 2012). To what extent can this synergy assist with competency development? Although colleges and universities must provide graduates who have competencies desired by employers, they also have a responsibility to develop socially conscious citizens of the world. Some competencies needed by employers immediately upon graduation may differ from those needed throughout a lifetime. This leads to significant debate about what constitutes an educated person.

From the development of oral communication skills to abilities for team work, many competencies are developed through out-of-class programs and services in student affairs, such as student organizations, varsity and intramural sports, and cultural and recreational activities. According to Vishal (2009), seven soft skills are usually associated with higher education: communicative, thinking and problem solving, team work, lifelong learning and information management, entrepreneur, ethics and morals, and leadership. An appropriate assessment methodology is required to measure the extent to which student affairs affect students' soft skill development.

Developing Global Competence

Global competency is a specific and critical skill for college students to develop in order to compete and excel in a rapidly shrinking world. Professional associations and other organizations promote methodologies for teaching and assessing global competency achievement of students, and these skills and abilities are variously defined and promoted to students. Cultural competence and intercultural competence are other terms or skills closely associated with global competency. The American Association of Colleges and Universities has created the Global Learning Value Rubric (2014) that is called Intercultural Knowledge and Competence. In reviewing the definitions of global competency, Hunter, White, and Godbey (2006) assert that there is little commonality among current definitions.

One example of developing global competence from Moss, Manise, and Soppelsa (2012) focuses on preparing globally competent teachers by focusing on the following learning outcomes: understanding of one's own cultural identity; valuing diverse cultures and learning from them; understanding the world as one interdependent system; understanding prevailing world conditions, process of change, and emerging trends; and developing skills for constructive participation in a changing world. Another example is Florida International University's global learning outcomes. Components include global perspective: the ability to view the world from multiple perspectives; global awareness: knowledge of the interconnectedness of issues, trends, and systems; global engagement:

willingness to address local, global, international, and intercultural issues (Redden, 2013).

What role does student affairs play in helping students achieve global or cultural competency? Day (2013) advocates that elements of a liberal arts education can assist with engaging in critical conversations that lead to global competency. He presents five core areas to help student affairs professionals engage students in these conversations: personal resource management; physical and behavioral health; interpersonal relationships and conflict resolution; ethics, values clarification, and spiritual centering; and global civic engagement.

It is important to remember that the student affairs approach to working with students varies based on cultural values and philosophical perspectives. Different regions or countries will employ an approach to providing programs and services to students, and it may not necessarily include helping students understand global competence. That said, higher education helping students learn about and experience international perspectives can lead to significant learning on the part of students. And, providing basic services to students allows them to focus their attentions on learning and be fully engaged in their academic environment.

Conclusion

The impact of globalization on higher education is real and ubiquitous. Internationalization is no longer defined by the simple mobility of students, but by a much deeper, core change in paradigm around content and course delivery and programs and services for students. Student affairs must recognize the new realities for students and institutions and adapt accordingly. The impact of globalization will be variously felt in different world regions, and the thrust of internationalization will unfold in myriad ways at individual institutions. Remaining up to date and knowledgeable about how these forces are affecting local communities is important for student affairs practitioners.

Regional and cultural contexts remain a central driver in the conceptualization and delivery of student affairs programs and services. It is important to understand that Western interpretations of work with students are not always appropriate in different contexts. Indeed, even in some Western countries, student services are not delivered in a traditionally Western model. This variation in ideology is energizing, and the global student affairs community endeavors to come together to explore common ground. Students are the central concern for student affairs globally, which provides a common denominator upon which to build. Expanding from the core understanding of student affairs necessarily varies given local values and cultural expression. Developing a learning process or frameworks for student support must remain locally unique while united across borders by individual threads of a common tapestry.

Student affairs on individual campuses must reexamine current relationships and partnerships to be sure that they are appropriately addressing the expanding needs of current students and serving the globalized marketplace. Students have access to massive amounts of information and experiencing different cultures is far easier than it once was. This expanded view and opportunity that many students bring to college necessitates an intentional focus on continuous improvement and assessment of student affairs work. Working across an institution and across divisions in collaborative ways is essential, and integrating with local communities is paramount. The localized context serves as the backdrop for growth and development of students around the world. Role modeling this connectivity among groups for students will help them understand the multiple lenses on world issues and how to embrace and celebrate differences. Student affairs can reach out to employers, governments, and community agencies to share in the responsibility of educating a global citizenry by working together and providing an integrated environment that mirrors the greater society.

Students, faculty, and staff working together to achieve the competencies necessary to flourish in our shrinking, globalized society is critical to the success of these emerging leaders. Understanding the role that student affairs plays both locally and globally to leverage the talent development of students also is essential for society. The core learning domains and critical skills required to be globally competent are clearly within the purview of student affairs, to support what students learn in the classroom, provide space for them to exercise their knowledge and skills, and help them learn and refine a set of essential global competencies. The support and learning opportunities provided by student affairs sets students on a course for successful, meaningful careers and a life of engaged citizenry and continuous learning.

The global stage is set for the student affairs play to commence. Actors are communicating across boundaries and organizing bodies are choreographing large scale scenes. Understanding which partners to engage globally is an important element in the continued development of international student affairs. Additional research and broad conversation must be undertaken to fully understand the current global context, and to anticipate future needs of students and student affairs globally.

References

Association of American Colleges and Universities. (2013). *Global learning VALUE rubric*. Paper presented at the Association of International Education Administrators Conference. New Orleans, LA, February 18.

Blick, A. (2010, December). *The controversy over university student finance: The EU perspective*. The Federal Trust for Education and Research. http://www.fedtrust.co .uk/filepool/FedT_Student_Finance_in_the_EU.pdf.

Callahan, K. & Stanfield, D. (2012). Global summit on student affairs and services: Executive summary and proceedings. Washington, DC: NASPA.

Canadian Association of College and University Student Services. (2012, April 29). *Reflections on the CACUSS Identity Project: What we've learned since Leaders in Learning*. Toronto, Ontario.

Carpenter, S., & Haber-Curran, P. (2013). The role of research and scholarship in the professionalisation of student affairs. *Journal of Student Affairs in Africa, 1*, 1–10.

Cinque, M. (2012). *Soft skills in action: Halls of residence as centres for life and learning*. Brussels, European University College Association.

Dalton, J. C. (1999). *The significance of international issues and responsibilities in the contemporary work of student affairs*. New Directions for Student Services, no. 86, 3–11. San Francisco, CA: Jossey-Bass.

Day, P. K. (2013) Reconnecting higher education to the world: Student affairs must take leading role in defining a new model. *Leadership Exchange* (Spring). Washington, DC: NASPA.

Douglass, J. A., King, C. J., & Feller, I. (Eds.). (2009). *Globalization's muse: Universities and higher education systems in a changing world*. Berkeley: University of California Press.

Evans, N., Forney, D., Guido, F., & Patton, L. (2009). Student development in college: theory, research, and practice. San Francisco, CA: Jossey-Bass.

Goswami, R. (2012, July 13). Economic growth and higher education in India and China. *East Asia Forum*. http://www.eastasiaforum.org/2012/07/13/economic-growth-and-higher-education-in-india-and-china/.

Horden, B. B. (2012, May 31). International educators see South America as a red-hot market. Universityworldnews.com, no. 224. http://www.universityworldnews.com/article.php?story=20120531081659355.

Hunter, B., White, G. P., & Godbey, G. (2006). What does it mean to be globally competent? *Journal of Studies in International Education, 10*(3), 267–285.

Institute of International Education. (2013). *Open Doors Data*. http://www.iie.org/research-and-publications/open-doors/data.

Keeling, R. (2006). *Learning reconsidered 2: Implementing a campus-wide focus on the student experience*. Washington, DC: ACPA/NASPA.

Knight, J. (2008). Internationalization: Concepts, complexities and challenges. In James J. F. Forest & Philip G. Altbach (Eds.), *International handbook of higher education* (pp. 207-227). Dordrecht, The Netherlands: Springer.

Knight J. & Morshiti, S. (2011). The complexities and challenges of regional education hubs: focus on Malaysia. *Higher Education, 62*(5), pp. 593-606.

Latham, S., & Dalton, J. (1999). *International skills and experiences for a global future.* New Directions for Student Services, no. 86. San Francisco, CA: Jossey-Bass.

Lozano, A. y Herrera. (2013). *Diseño de programas educativos basados en competencias.* Monterrey: Editorial Digital Tecnológico de Monterrey.

Ludeman, R., Osfield, K., Iglesias, E. I., Oste, D., & Wang, H. (2009). *Student affairs and services in higher education: Global foundations, issues and best practices.* Paris: UNESCO.

Luescher-Mamashela, T., Moja, T. & Schreiber, B. (2013). Towards a professionalisation of student affairs in Africa. *Journal of Student Affairs in Africa, 1,* vii–xiii.

Maki, P. (2010). *Assessing for learning: Building a sustainable commitment across the institution.* Sterling, VA: Stylus.

Marmolejo, F. (2011, August 30). The future of higher-education internationalization. *Chronicle of Higher Education.* http://chronicle.com/blogs/worldwise/defining-internationalization/28615.

Moss, D. M, Manise, J., & Soppelsa, B. (2012). *Preparing globally competent teachers.* Background paper for CAEP commissioners. Washington, DC: NAFSA.

Nuss, E. 1996. The development of student affairs. In S. Komives & E. Woodard (Eds.), *Student services: A handbook for the profession* (3rd ed., pp. 22-42). San Francisco, CA: Jossey-Bass.

Osfield, K. J., & Terrell, P. S. (2009). Internationalization in higher education and student affairs. In G. S. McClellan & J. Stringer, (Eds.). *The handbook of student affairs administration in higher education* (pp. 120-144). San Francisco, CA: Jossey-Bass.

Ping, C. J. (1999). *An expanded international role for student affairs.* New Directions for Student Services, no. 86 San Francisco, CA: Jossey-Bass.

Pope, R., & Reynolds, A. (1997). Student affairs core competencies: Integrating multicultural awareness, knowledge, and skills. *Journal of College Student Development, 38,* 266–277.

Q.S. (2012, September). *Top universities.* [http://www.topuniversities.com/university-rankings-articles/world-university-rankings/increase-number-international-students].

Ramos, E. & Perozzi, B. (2014). *Student affairs and services staff interviews.* Unpublished report.

Redden, E. (2013, February 20). The 'I' in FIU. *Inside Higher Ed.* https://www.insidehighered.com/news/2013/02/20/florida-international-university-attempts-infuse-global-learning-across-curriculum.

Rhatigan, J. (2009). From the people up: A brief history of student affairs administration. In G. S. McClellan & J. Stringer (Eds.), *The handbook of student affairs administration* (3rd ed., pp. 3-18). San Francisco, CA: Jossey-Bass.

Seifert, T., Perozzi, B., Bodine Al-Sharif, M.A., Li, W., & Wildman, K. (2014). *Student affairs and services in global perspective: A preliminary exploration of practitioners' background, roles and professional development.* Toronto: International Association of Student Affairs and Services.

Sutton, S., & Deardorff, D. K. (2012, February/March). Internationalizing internationalization: The global context. *IAU Horizons*, pp. 16–17.

Teekens, H. (2013, June 15). Internationalisation at home—Crossing other borders. *University World News* (no. 276). http://www.universityworldnews.com/article.php?story=20130613084529186.

Tani, M. Does immigration policy affect the education-occupation mismatch? *Evidence From Australia*. (IZA DP no. 6937). Accessed on July 22, 2015 at http://ftp.iza.org/dp6937.pdf.

Teichler, U. (2012, October). International Student Mobility in Europe in the Context of the Bologna Process. *Journal of International Education and Leadership*, 2(1). http://www.jielusa.org/wp-content/uploads/2012/01/International-Student-Mobility-inEurope-in-the-Context-of-the-Bologna-Process1.pdf.

Torres, V. & Walbert, J. (2010). *Envisioning the Future of Student Affairs*. Final Report of the Task Force on the Future of Student Affairs. Appointed jointly by ACPA and NASPA. Accessed on July 22, 2015 at https://www.naspa.org/images/uploads/main/Task_Force_Student_Affairs_2010_Report.pdf.

Trounson, A. (2013, October 30). Canberra to ease student visa rules. *Australian*. http://www.theaustralian.com.au/national-affairs/education/canberra-to-ease-student-visa-rules/story-fn59nlz9-1226749278450.

Yakaboski, T. & Perozzi, B. (2014). Globalization and college unions. In D. DeSawal, D., & T. Yakaboski (Eds.), *The State of the College Union: Contemporary Issues and Trends* (pp. 79-90). New Directions for Student Services, no. 145. . San Francisco, CA: Jossey-Bass.

Vishal, J. (2009, February). Importance of soft skills development in education. *Schools of Educators*. http://schoolofeducators.com/2009/02/importance-of-soft-skills-development-in-education.

PART TWO

FRAMEWORKS FOR PROFESSIONAL PRACTICE

Just as our professional practice takes place in a variety of contexts, so too is it conducted within multiple frameworks. These frameworks provide professionals, regardless of their specific roles within the profession, a series of guideposts that can be used to point the way to educated practice. Terrell Strayhorn in chapter 7 discusses how various theories and models relate to the practice of student affairs administration. He indicates that both foundational theories and newer perspectives can assist practitioners in understanding students' developmental processes, learning styles, and identities. Peter Magolda and Tony Ribera in chapter 8 stress the educational role of student affairs educators. They describe the impact of both internal and external forces on the co-curriculum and offer ideas to assist us in providing meaningful learning opportunities beyond the formal curriculum. In chapter 9, Lori Varlotta encourages us to stretch our understanding of student success in college. Though the prevailing contemporary defines success for both students and institutions as gradua-tion, she suggests that there are some situations in which a student and an institution might have achieved success despite the fact that the student did not earn a degree. Ethical practice is a key framework for professionals in any field, and student affairs is no exception. In chapter 10, Jon Dalton, Pam Crosby, Aurelio Valente, and David Eberhardt review the ethical guidelines of several student affairs professional associations, and present a conceptual framework for examining ethical issues and making moral decisions. Additional standards that provide models of professionalism are presented by Stephanie Gordon in chapter 11. She delineates the value of utilizing the standards and guidelines promulgated by the Council for the Advancement of Standards in Higher Education to assist institutional efforts to achieve continuous quality improvement. In chapter 12, the final chapter in the frameworks part of the volume, Nancy Evans and Jessica Ranero-Ramirez discuss professional associations in student affairs, including their functions, history, and structure.

CHAPTER SEVEN

AN OVERVIEW OF RELEVANT THEORIES AND MODELS OF PRACTICE

Terrell L. Strayhorn

Sofia Petrillo, the eldest fictional character in the hit TV series *Golden Girls*, was known for beginning all of her personal anecdotes, long-winded stories, and Italian parables with two simple words: "Picture it." Borrowing from her classic approach, several vignettes are offered that will prove instructive over the course of this chapter:

> Picture it: A dean of students at a small, liberal arts college has been asked to coordinate a campus strategic planning process that will organize all units and programs around a few carefully selected learning outcomes that seem central to the university's mission such as appreciation of diversity, purposeful life, cognitive complexity, and active participation in democracy, to name a few. Before convening the steering committee, she asks herself: How do college students learn and grow in these domains? What do college student educators assume about student learning and how it is nurtured?
>
> Picture it: Black students at a large, predominantly White university adamantly protest a recent decision to convert the long-standing Black Cultural Center into a diversity resource office for all historically underrepresented students on campus including ethnic minorities,

sexual minorities, and those who hail from low-income families, among other groups. In a meeting of several vice presidents regarding the protest, Dr. Adam Hampton (vice president of academic affairs) remarked: "Keep in mind folks, we're here to educate students in ways that carry out our mission ... not to host social parties. It seems to me that whatever Black students derived from the cultural center can be gained from the diversity office." To what extent, if any, do you agree with Dr. Hampton's conclusion? What do we know about individuals' need for affiliation and belonging in college contexts? And, what academic outcomes are realized in social spaces where students' interact purposefully with those who share core aspects of their identity?

Picture it: Kanye James, a member of the transgender community, was recently hired by DuBois University, a historically Black college located in the southwestern region of the country, to establish and lead the university's first-ever gay, lesbian, bisexual, and transgender (GLBT) resource center. The GLBT resource center, for which Kaleidoscope is the proposed name, will offer academic and social support services for the campus' growing GLBT population comprised of students, faculty, and staff. One of Kanye's initial priorities is to secure funds for hiring additional staff, especially an assistant director and program coordinator who understand the peculiarities that characterize the lived experiences of diverse GLBT populations; he has long- believed that traditional models of GLBT identity development have limited applicability to the stories of ethnic or international GLBT students and staff with whom he has worked. To what extent, if any, do you agree with Kanye's assertion? What do you know about the process through which individuals assume GLBT identities? How are the stories—or lived realities—of some gay people of color different from the dominant norm that typically informs traditional models and theories? How might Kanye, and other educators like him, reconcile his tensions with traditional models and use such information in this scenario about hiring staff?

At the core of each vignette listed above are questions about the purpose and role of theory, including the rich theoretical bases that shape student affairs professionals' current understanding of the whole [college] student (American Council on Education, 1983). Just as questions about theory abound, so too do the various models and theories that educators can bring to bear in their work with students. Some of these, theories of intellectual development, are foundational and have stood the test of time, while others, such as intersectionality, represent newer perspectives for understanding college students' identities, learning processes, and structural inequalities in social spheres like education.

Given the swelling menu of theories available to those who work with college students, both novice and experienced professionals may experience difficulty in identifying an informative theoretical frame, recalling its major assumptions and key concepts, and applying the theory to practice so as to promote optimal students' learning and development. A number of factors have been identified as sources of professionals' difficulty with theory: lack of knowledge of various frames, insufficient time for reading and contemplating theory's relevance to practice, and inadequate preparation for using theory effectively in educational practice, to name a few (Strayhorn, 2006). In fact, a number of individuals with whom I spoke while writing this chapter admitted that they had little command over the theoretical constructs embedded in most developmental theories and could say little about concepts borrowed from psychology, sociology, anthropology, and other disciplines that might relate to their day-to-day work in student affairs. Even those with backgrounds and/or degrees in student affairs struggled to recall the theorists, core elements, and major assumptions of models they studied in graduate school. The present chapter was written with these challenges and gaps in mind.

The purpose of this chapter is to provide an overview of relevant theories and models of practice that can be used in college educators' work with students, especially among those working in student affairs. Specifically, the chapter was organized around two questions and several major sections: (1) What is theory? (2) Why do we use theory? (3) Overview of theories and models (4) Applying theory to practice, and (5) Recommendations for practice and research. A final section presents a few questions and activities for guided practice.

What Is Theory?

Theory is a term with many meanings. One definition of theory is "a set of interrelated constructs, definitions, and propositions that presents a systematic view of phenomena by specifying relations among variables, with the purpose of explaining and predicting phenomena" (Kerlinger, 1986, p. 9). Another definition is "a set of propositions regarding the interrelationship of two or more conceptual variables relevant to some realm of phenomena" (Rodgers, 1980, p. 81). And, as yet another example, I vividly recall a moment in graduate school when I was called upon by my doctoral advisor (Don Creamer) to answer the question: "What is theory?" Caught off-guard but determined to satisfy the request of my advisor-mentor, I stuttered: "A theory is a plausible explanation of observable, oftentimes social, phenomena." His smile signaled approval and he replied affirmatively: "Well, that's exactly right … a classic textbook definition, if you will."

Just as it is necessary to attend to basic definitions of theory, it is equally as important to recognize the array of terms used in reference to theory. For example, scholars tend to employ various terms such as conceptual frames (Merriam, 1998); propositions (Argyris & Schön, 1974); abstract categories (LeCompte & Preissle, 1993); conceptual maps (Ausubel, 1963); models (Parker, 1977); stances (Crotty, 1998); frameworks (Anfara & Mertz, 2006; Strayhorn, 2013a); postulations (Astin, 1984); and hypothesized relationships (Lewin, 1936). Indeed, there are subtle (and not-so-subtle) distinctions between these terms and the authors intended meaning; *conceptual frames* and *frameworks* often refer to plausible explanations that can be helpful to seeing something old in a new way or making the mundane somewhat miraculous by intentionally adopting a different perspective. Other terms, such as postulation map, underscore the explanatory power of theories for forming hypotheses or predicting possible outcomes.

While definitions and terms vary, theories are useful in that they generally simplify or explain phenomena that might otherwise remain incomprehensibly abstract, unnecessarily complex, or too vague to be operationalized in our day-to-day work with college students. Several book-length volumes have been devoted to this topic (Evans, Forney, & Guido-DiBrito, 1998; Strayhorn, 2012, 2013a). However, theory's power is constrained by what Parker (1977) and others call one of the paradoxes of theory—any attempt at simplifying the complex gives up a degree of accuracy. Theories, by design, account for the common denominators or what's generalizable about a particular phenomenon and may certainly miss subtle nuances in the story. Moreover, theories are social constructions and, therefore, "typically reinforce the *status quo* or societal power relationships such as racism, heterosexism, and classism" (Jones & Abes, 2011). That's not to say that theory cannot challenge the status quo or transform societal relations—in fact, that's the principal aim of many critical theories, such as critical race theory, which will be reviewed later in the chapter. In short, theory is a tool that can be used for important purposes.

Why Use Theory?

There are several reasons why practitioners and scholars use theory, six of which are outlined in this section. Theory is used to:

- Describe
- Explain
- Predict
- Produce outcome
- Assess programs and practices
- Generate new knowledge through research (McEwen, 2003)

Generally speaking, theories can be put to one or more uses at any point in time, although some theories might satisfy the goals of a particular purpose better than others. For example, Astin's (1984) theory of student involvement was posited to help college student educators design more effective learning environments in order to maximize student potential through involvement. According to Astin, student involvement refers to the amount of physical and psychological energy that the student devotes to the college experience. His conception of involvement is largely behavioral and lends itself to application across a broad array of issues and opportunities in student affairs practice. For instance, Astin argued that the quality of any educational program or service is proportional to its ability to engender student involvement.

There are other theories that are best used for a specific aim. For instance, intersectionality is a theoretical perspective—not a theory per se—that can be used to contest existing ways of looking at structures of inequality, thereby resisting the urge to look at them in isolation but rather to pay close attention to the ways in which they intersect, converge, and inform one another (Strayhorn, 2013b). Intersectionality is typically used to describe, sometimes explain, and generate new knowledge through research but generally not put to use for prediction or program assessment, as it currently lacks assumptions about causal relations, temporal ordering of events, and empirical testing of underlying tenets.

A primary example of how intersectionality has been used to generate new knowledge through research on Black collegians is Strayhorn's (2013b) edited volume *Living at the Intersections: Social Identities and Black Collegians.* Therein, Fries-Britt, Johnson, and Burt (2013) use intersectionality to shed light on the experiences of Black physics students and the role that social class plays in their success. Despite the researchers' initial hunch that race would be most prominent for all students, what they learned by viewing students' experiences intersectionally is that race is an important factor but social class combined with race creates a relatively unique set of circumstances under which Black low-income students in physics must thrive. Think back to Kanye's questions about the experiences of marginalized GLBT populations in the opening vignettes.

Another chapter uses qualitative portraits to break new ground in our understanding of Black first-generation women in college and the ways in which race, gender, and social class intersect with other dimensions of identity to create both unique and shared experiences among such students. Indeed, generating new knowledge through research is an important use of theory in student affairs. Using theory appropriately in practice and research is another concern for educators. With these definitions and uses in mind, let's proceed with an overview of relevant theories and models of practice in the field of higher education and student affairs.

A Review of Theories and Models

Given the important roles that theory plays in professional practice and research in higher education and student affairs, it seems useful to review a few of the theoretical frames that have been productively employed in our work with students. A close, exhaustive review of these is beyond the scope of the present chapter but that has been done in a number of other volumes (including Evans et al., 1998; Strayhorn, 2013a), which should be consulted by those who desire more details. A brief summary of a few extant theories is offered here using a classification system that may be useful to readers who need a framework for organizing the large body of theories available for use in student affairs.

Generally, theories can be organized into seven major categories: psychosocial, cognitive, moral/ethical, faith/spiritual, college impact, student success, and emerging theoretical perspectives. Other conceptualizations exist (Creamer & Associates, 1990; Evans et al., 1998; Jones & Abes, 2011) that may be helpful to readers too. Before describing each major category, let's discuss a few features that characterize most theories.

Key Features of Theory

Fundamentally, all educators are concerned about student learning and development. Development occurs in different ways at various times across the lifespan for all populations. As a subset of human development frames, student development theories have been posited to facilitate understanding of students' maturation. For instance, psychosocial theory attempts to explain developmental processes such as identity and personality formation. Another line of plausible explanations is often referred to as cognitive-structural theories. The works of Jean Piaget, William Perry, Lawrence Kohlberg, and Carol Gilligan are "highly respected benchmarks for investigating cognitive development over the lifespan" (Strayhorn, 2006, p. 12). Despite differences in the outcome or social process they attempt to describe, virtually all theories of this kind are based on the premise that phases or parts arise from each other, each part has its time of ascendancy, and movement from one phase to the next implies growth or development. This is what Erikson (1968) called the *epigenetic principle.*

Psychosocial Development

One major category of theories is comprised of models that relate to psychosocial development. Psychosocial development refers to the process of an individual's psychological growth in, and interaction with, a social environment. Generally, psychosocial development theories are grounded in the work of Erik Erikson. Whereas cognitive theories (which will be discussed in the next section) focus on the meaning that one makes of experiences and the complexity of thoughts, psychosocial theories focus on the content of individuals' concerns in different time periods of life. For example, some psychosocial theories examine aspects of identity, interpersonal relations, career and work life, as well as values. Erikson (1968) described development throughout the life span using eight distinct stages, each marked by a basic conflict that ultimately plays a major role in the development of personality. His model posits development as growth from infancy (birth to 18 months), characterized by a basic conflict between trust and mistrust, to preschool (3 to 5 years), characterized by conflict between initiative and guilt, onward to young adulthood (19 to 40 years), marked by conflict between intimacy and isolation, arriving at maturity (65 to death), marked by conflict between ego integrity and despair.

As another example, Chickering (1969) described seven vectors of development that lead to establishing one's identity: developing competence, managing emotions, moving through autonomy toward interdependence, developing mature interpersonal relationships, establishing identity, developing purpose, and developing integrity. His model focuses principally on identity development during the college years (Chickering & Reisser, 1993). Chickering's model is not rigidly sequential, like most others, and he noted that students tend to move through these vectors at different rates; vectors can interact with one another over time

FIGURE 7.1 CHICKERING'S SEVEN VECTORS

Stage	Process
1	Developing intellectual, physical, and interpersonal competence
2	Managing emotions
3	Moving through autonomy to interdependence
4	Developing mature interpersonal relationships
5	Establishing identity
6	Developing purpose
7	Developing integrity

and students often revisit issues associated with vectors they had previously seemed to resolve, which is often referred to as developmental regression. For a graphical representation, see Figure 7.1.

Cognitive Development

Cognitive development or cognitive-structural theories are grounded in the work of Jean Piaget (1952) and focus on the complexity of thought or cognitive structures that leads to the content of those psychosocial issues mentioned in the prior section such as identity, values, and relationships. Cognitive structures refer to the mental capacities that act as a filter through which individuals make meaning of experiences and encounters in the social world; typically these structures develop from profoundly simple to increasingly complex. Cognitive-structural theories tend to be organized hierarchically and sequentially, whereby each stage arises from the previous one and represents a more complex way of sense making, meaning making, or thinking about the world, also referred to as cognitive complexity (see the opening vignettes, for example).

A corpus of studies has posited that students make meaning of life experiences and issues of identity in varied and complex ways. One example of a cognitive-structural theory that explains the stages through which individuals make sense of social experiences that serves as a foundation for those used in student affairs is William Perry's (1981) intellectual development theory. Perry described nine developmental positions that can be grouped into four major categories: (1) dualism, (2) multiplicity, (3) relativism, and (4) commitment. Generally, his theory is characterized by a logical progression from simple meanings to more complex modes of reasoning. Dualist thinkers devote much time to learning the right-and-wrong answers, whereas relativists come to accept multiple realities and competing possibilities so they learn to evaluate solutions.

There are other cognitive-structural models. For instance, Loevinger (1976, 1998) also explained cognitive growth but as ego development. By ego, she refers to that aspect of personality that assigns meaning to experiences. The term ego development refers to hierarchical interrelated patterns of cognitive, interpersonal, and ethical development that create a cohesive epistemology or worldview (Weathersby, 1981). Therefore, each worldview (or stage) represents a qualitatively different way of responding to or making meaning of life experiences. Loevinger's description of the milestone sequences of ego development consists of: "impulsive, self-protective, conformist, conscientious-conformist, conscientious, individualistic, autonomous, and integrated. Each transition from a previous stage to the next represents an individual's restructuring of personality" (Strayhorn, 2006, p. 38). Final stages are marked by the ability to respect other's autonomy and a heightened respect for individuality, for instance (Loevinger & Wessler, 1970). Remember, cognitive development is less concerned with the content of one's beliefs and thoughts but rather focuses on the meaning making processes through which one works to arrive at such beliefs, thoughts, and values. It's entirely possible for two individuals to share common beliefs or values (that is, the content of what they believe) about, say, capital punishment but for one to be more advanced than the other in their ability to arrive at such beliefs through a more complex process of sorting information, weighing available options, balancing options with internally-derived commitments, and so on.

Moral/Ethical Development

Many theories of moral and ethical development are also considered cognitive-structural frames, although they are often treated as a separate category (Jones & Abes, 2011). For instance, Kohlberg (1969) explored the cognitive dimensions of moral reasoning. Building upon the work of Piaget (1977), Kohlberg posited three levels of moral reasoning: preconventional, conventional, and postconventional. He argued that each level of this model represented a qualitatively different orientation toward the self and society. Essentially, the theory describes a shift from an inward, individual perspective towards a more external, universal stance.

Faith and Spiritual Development

Another domain of human development that has been explained through theories used in student affairs is faith and spiritual development. For instance, Fowler (1981) posited spirituality as a universal process of meaning making aimed toward understanding self and the lived experience. His six-stage model explains faith development as growth from intuitive-projective (stage 1) through synthetic-conventional (stage 3) to universalizing faith (stage 6), which very few people reach. Parks (2000), like Fowler before her, referred to faith development as a progressive process of seeking patterns, order, and coherence between seemingly disparate elements of human life. Both Fowler and Parks differentiated faith development from spirituality, which is the personal search for spirit or the animating force at the core of life. Struggling to find meaning and perhaps divine providence in early life experiences (for example, how one was raised), strained relationships, prior educational experiences, and where one is located at midlife can be framed as part of faith development.

In sum, student development theories (that is, psychosocial, cognitive-structural) have been gainfully employed in studies of majority students, women, as well as African American students' problem solving skills in chemistry (Atwater & Alick, 1990); American Indian students' academic persistence (Brown & Robinson Kurpius, 1997); lesbian, gay, bisexual, and transgender (LGBT) student leaders (Renn, 2006); and even first-year students' adjustment to college (Martin, Swartz-Kulstad, & Madson, 1999). For example, Renn (along with her colleague, Bilodeau) conducted several studies of LGBT student leaders and found evidence "that leaders of LGBT student organizations grew in both sexual orientation identity and leadership identity" (2006, p. 1) which are the focus of several psychosocial identity development models.

Yet, there are other questions that educational researchers engage. Not only are higher education researchers principally concerned with student development, quite often they want to study students' personal histories or demographic backgrounds and how their capital reservoirs affect short-term and long-term outcomes. Here college impact models tend to be useful, supplying necessary language, constructs for talking about how college affects students, and explanations about how this all occurs.

Impact of College on Students

A large number of higher education studies are designed to estimate the net effect of college on students (Pascarella & Terenzini, 1991, 2005). In estimating the effects of college programs, services, and experiences on students, a number of conceptual and theoretical frameworks are employed (Astin, 1993; Chickering & Reisser, 1993; Weidman, 1989). These models underscore that "the impact of college on nearly any student outcome is the result of multiple influences" (Cruce, Wolniak, Seifert, & Pascarella, 2006, p. 367). These influences include precollege background traits, precollege experiences, organizational character of one's institution, academic experiences in college, and nonacademic or social experiences to name a few.

Traditional college impact theory suggests that college affects students' behaviors, decisions, and educational outcomes, generally speaking. Impact theories tend to concentrate on the origins of change rather than detailed accounts of the processes through which change occurs. Although they are often referred to as theoretical frameworks or theoretical models, constructions of college's impact on students are less of an attempt to explain the how and why of students' development than a conceptual guide to understanding students and their experiences (Pascarella & Terenzini, 2005).

Astin (1991) developed one of the first college impact models which is now commonly referred to as the input-environment-outcome (I-E-O) model. According to this model, student outcomes are functions of two factors including inputs such as demographic traits and environment or students' experiences in college. Several studies have adopted this conceptual frame to examine the effects of background and/or environment influences on student change and growth in college as well as their propensity to behave in certain ways (Strayhorn, 2008a). For instance, students who enter college academically ready (input)—likely scoring high on the college entrance exam and earning high grades in school—and attend colleges that provide adequate academic support such as writing centers, intrusive advising, and tutoring (environment) tend to fare well in college (outcome).

Other college impact theories represent modified versions of the model described above. That is, several authors have used expanded frameworks to specify inputs or to identify specific outcomes such as student learning or cognitive development. For instance, Terenzini, Springer, Yaeger, Pascarella, and Nora (1996) posited a version of the college impact model that consists of three phases, moving from students' college expectations through one's transition between high school or work and college to the impact of college on student outcomes such as learning, achievement, or degree attainment. The model is longitudinal in nature and it is built upon the same premise as Astin's (1991) original conceptualization.

The model can be further distilled into six constructs: precollege traits, curricular patterns, in-class experiences, out-of-class experiences, institutional context, and learning outcomes. College experiences, too, can be further understood as both in- and out-of-class experiences. The take home message is simple—the influence of college (represented by variable X) on any dependent outcome (represented by variable Y) (for example, learning, attainment, satisfaction, retention) is multifaceted and complex. College impact theory was developed in an attempt to make the complex simple, realizing that any attempt to render sophistications as simple gives up a degree of accuracy in exchange for simplicity. This goal is related to the current chapter's purpose.

Student Success Models

A final category of theories encompasses a broad array of models that attempt to explain how college students change, grow, or learn in ways that facilitate their success in school. For instance, Tinto (1993) posited a theory of college student departure that frames departure decisions as a function of individuals' initial and subsequent goals and commitments, academic and social integration into the life of college, and individuals' backgrounds characteristics and traits. Figure 7.2 is a graphical representation of retention theory.

Another theoretical model that relates to student success is sense of belonging, defined as membership, feelings of acceptance, being cared

FIGURE 7.2 TINTO'S (1993) COLLEGE STUDENT RETENTION THEORY

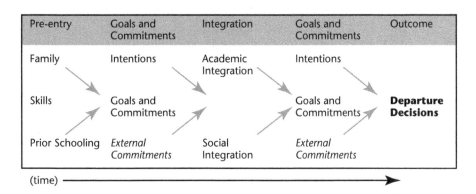

Pre-entry	Goals and Commitments	Integration	Goals and Commitments	Outcome
Family	Intentions	Academic Integration	Intentions	
Skills	Goals and Commitments		Goals and Commitments	**Departure Decisions**
Prior Schooling	*External Commitments*	Social Integration	*External Commitments*	

(time) ⟶

about or part of a group. It's an assessment of one's perceived sense of support in educational contexts such as college campuses and the extent to which one feels connected to others. Osterman (2000) referenced belonging as "a feeling that members matter to one another and to the group, and a shared faith that members' needs will be met through their commitment to be together" (p. 324). One common survey item used to measure sense of belonging is: My friends would miss me if I left college (Strayhorn, 2012).

Sense of belonging has been framed as a key ingredient for college student success (Strayhorn, 2012). According to the model, there are seven core elements of sense of belonging:

1. Sense of belonging is a basic human need.
2. Sense of belonging is a fundamental motive, sufficient to drive human behavior.
3. Sense of belonging takes on heightened importance in certain contexts, at certain times, and among certain populations.
4. Sense of belonging is related to and seemingly a consequence of mattering.
5. Social identities intersect and affect college students' sense of belonging (which, in some ways, is related to intersectionality).
6. Sense of belonging engenders other positive outcomes.
7. Sense of belonging must be satisfied on a continual basis and likely changes as circumstances, conditions, and contexts change.

Belonging may be a useful heuristic for thinking through Dr. Hampton's response to Black students' protests about the multicultural center (see opening vignettes).

Emerging Theoretical Perspectives

Several emerging theoretical perspectives have proven useful to new interpretations of college student development and the college experience, although they were not originally created for college students. Three are discussed below including critical race theory, intersectionality, and cultural/social capital.

Critical Race Theory. Critical race theory (CRT) has its roots in legal scholarship, specifically Black feminist writers who sought to reveal and challenge the practices of subordination. CRT is based upon the premise that race and racism are permanent, central fixtures in America. It was established to critique historical and structural conditions of oppression and seeks transformation of material conditions.

CRT is composed of five central tenets: (a) centrality and intersectionality of race and racism, (b) challenge of dominant ideologies (for example, colorblindness, meritocracy, neutrality of law), (c) commitment to social justice and elimination of oppression (Matsuda, 1991), (d) legitimacy of experiential knowledge of people of color, and (e) use of an interdisciplinary perspective grounded in both historical and contemporary contexts (Villalpando & Delgado Bernal, 2002).

CRT has been employed in previous research, including education. Bell (1995) used CRT to explain why gross socioeconomic disparities exist in America. His analysis suggests that many Whites will accept huge inequities among Whites as long as White superiority over Blacks (and other minorities) is maintained. DeCuir and Dixson (2004) used CRT to interrogate the racialized experiences of Black students in an elite academy and unveiled the permanence of racism even among the affluent. And, quite candidly, the author of this chapter used CRT, almost unknowingly, to help advise leaders of a campus through a hate crime that involved White students throwing bananas and racial epithets at Black students on campus with very few eyewitnesses. Despite initial disbelief that racism of that kind exists nowadays and no first-hand witnesses to affirm the testimony (or what CRT might call "counterstories") of victims, CRT provided a frame for starting in a different place—a point that admits upfront race and racism are real and permanent fixtures in American society and college campuses as microcosms of the larger world.

Intersectionality. Drawn from critical race feminism and legal scholarship (Crenshaw, 1991), intersectionality provides a framework for acknowledging that individuals hold multiple social identities simultaneously and that the confluence of those identities shapes the way in which they navigate interlocking systems of oppression such as sexism and racism, as well as how they experience the world socially, economically, and politically (Collins, 2000). Intersectionality has been articulated as a framework for analyzing the way in which multiple social locations and identities mutually inform and constitute one another (Collins).

A core concept of intersectionality is that the process of identification with more than one social group in any specific context produces altogether new forms of subjective experience that are unique and non-additive. For example, if women experience X, referring to some social phenomena shared by those whose biological assignment at birth was female, and Black people experience Y, referring to a social experience common to those whose ancestral origins lie in the African Diaspora, intersectionality helps us understand that Black women's experiences are not necessarily equal to X + Y but rather a more complicated function of X and Y that leads to a unique, non-additive subjective experience. Intersectionality may be useful to Kanye in the opening vignette as a way of extending or revising existing LGBT theories to apply to the experiences of LGBT people of color on campus.

Social and Cultural Capital. Increasingly, researchers in higher education employ or augment existing theories with notions borrowed from social, cultural, and human capital theories. Generally speaking, human capital theory posits that individuals make investments in education or training to gain additional knowledge, skills, and abilities that are often associated with increased income, higher occupational status, or other monetary benefits. Broadly conceived, human capital, on the one hand, refers to the "information, knowledge, skills, and abilities of an individual that can be exchanged in the labor market for returns such as salary, financial rewards, and jobs" (Strayhorn, 2008b, p. 31). It is generally assumed the more education an individual attains, the more human capital one accumulates and thereby the more benefits one can accrue.

Social capital, on the other hand, refers to the information-sharing networks or instrumental, supportive relationships that an individual may have that provide access to information and opportunity (Ceja, 2006). In addition, social capital refers to the social norms, values, and behaviors that affect an individual (Coleman, 1988). Such relationships may lead to advantageous behaviors, opportunities, or outcomes within a social stratum or system such as clubs or groups where membership is open to the affluent only. As Coleman described: "[social capital] makes possible the achievement of certain ends that in its absence would not be possible ... and it exists in the relations among people" (p. 98–101).

Cultural capital is the system of beliefs, tastes, and preferences derived from one's parents or guardians, which typically define an individual's class standing (Bourdieu, 1977; McDonough, 1997). Understanding cultural capital is important in educational research as a number of scholars have shown that upper-class students inherit, acquire, and develop substantially different forms of cultural capital than working-class youth (Bensimon, 2007; Lareau, 2003). This is problematic because schools generally reward, acknowledge, and privilege the cultural capital of the dominant classes and systematically devalue that of nondominant groups (Villalpando & Solórzano, 2005). Quite often, students activate their social capital (for example, relationships and networks) to acquire the cultural capital necessary to succeed in college (Pascarella & Terenzini, 1991, 2005).

In sum, these theories allow us to see and understand how human, social, and cultural factors operate independently in certain domains such as education, coalesce and simultaneously influence each other, and influence important outcomes such as annual earning, job satisfaction, or occupational status, to name a few (for example, see Strayhorn, 2008b).

Applying Theory to Practice

To illustrate how theory might be applied to professional practice, turn back to the vignettes that opened this chapter. Recall the dean of students at the small liberal arts college who pondered how students learned and the assumptions that educators hold about college student development. Here the dean of students might apply Perry's (1981) model of intellectual development to the matter at hand to understand cognitive complexity as development from simple right-and-wrong perspectives to more advanced ways of thinking that admit multiple possibilities and require evaluating various solutions. Theory also might reveal how learning can be facilitated through cognitive dissonance created by problems or challenges for which one's current cognitive script is found insufficient or inadequate for the problem at hand; students grow intellectually as they struggle to develop what is needed for the present situation. The dean of students might offer committee members a summary of Perry's model, a diagram of cognitive-structural theories like those found in this chapter, or invite a learning specialist who can offer ideas about catalyzing development of higher-order ways of thinking.

Turn now to the scenario involving Dr. Hampton's reaction to Black students' protests about the conversion of the Black cultural center. Regardless of whether one agrees with Dr. Hampton, one might use sense of belonging theory to describe the process of affiliation, connectedness, and community and how it applies to students' sense of place on campus, as well as the role that belonging plays in college students' educational success. Reading through prior research on sense of belonging, college student educators can identify the academic, social, and psychosocial outcomes of college that are achieved when one's need to belong is satisfied. For instance, students who feel as if they belong in a college also tend to engage in purposeful activities, feel confident in their abilities and skills, derive satisfaction from such learning environments, earn higher grades, stay in school, and go on to complete their degrees. All of this relates to questions before Dr. Hampton's committee. Sense of belonging theory also may be helpful for assessing the veracity of his statement about Black students deriving the same benefits from a diversity resource office that they gain from a Black cultural center—belonging theory suggests that feelings of belonging take on heightened importance in certain contexts and must be satisfied on a continual basis, all of which may suggest that Dr. Hampton's assumption is false. What we expect from a Black cultural center may not be reasonably expected of a diversity resource office and vice versa.

Conclusion

The information presented in this chapter is useful to several audiences. It is written for both student affairs practitioners and graduate students enrolled in higher education, student affairs administration, college student personnel, and related degree programs. Students should benefit from the number and type of theories addressed in this chapter. It is helpful to find brief summaries of so many widely used theories in a single publication. This can potentially reduce the amount of time that students and administrative professionals spend in the library hunting for the lens that permits them to see what might otherwise go unnoticed or completely concealed in a particular crisis or scenario.

Faculty who teach graduate-level courses on student affairs administration might also find material in this chapter useful for instruction. For example, graduate students (especially at the master's level) often yearn for opportunities to apply classroom learning to real-life situations. Faculty may find that this chapter serves as a useful complement to classroom teaching or lectures about administrative challenges, professional dilemmas, or how practitioners can nurture the development of college students generally and vulnerable populations in college specifically. Some faculty members may wish to consider using this text in conjunction with Jones and Abes's (2011) chapter on the nature and uses of theory; although related, these two chapters differ in their organization, scope, and the specific theories that are explained in depth. Taken together, they strike a balance between traditional theories and newer perspectives that inform our work with the diverse array of students enrolled in higher education today.

There is at least one other group who might benefit from this chapter: educational researchers. Those who study college students using both qualitative and quantitative methods and analytic techniques stand to gain from the open, frank discussion of theory that characterizes this chapter (Strayhorn, 2013a). For instance, picture it: A higher education researcher is interested in knowing how a group of students come to understand themselves as Muslim Americans and whether or not their ethnic identity is centrally important to them during college. They might consider information presented in this chapter, or elsewhere (Jones & Abes, 2011; Strayhorn, 2013a), to design a study using ethnic identity theory (Phinney, 1996) or the model of multiple dimensions of identity (Jones and McEwen, 2000) to interrogate students' academic and social experiences in college. Without a theoretical frame, the study might seem aimless, too broad, or unconnected to be useful, whereas theory acts as glue to link seemingly disparate parts together into a cohesive whole. As many of my former students come to realize, theory is the glue that links all of the individual parts together to explain what you're looking at. It helps you better understand a problem or design a study. In fact, it is theory that increases the rigor of empirical research studies, thereby increasing the worth of a study's findings. Theory is a powerful tool. Next time you're confronted with a problem in your work with students use theory to "picture it."

References

American Council on Education. (1983). The student personnel point of view. In G. L. Saddlemire & A. L. Rentz (Eds.), *Student affairs—A profession's heritage: Significant Articles, authors, issues, and documents* (pp. 122–140). Carbondale: Southern Illnois University Press.

Anfara, V. A., & Mertz, N. T. (2006). *Theoretical frameworks in qualitative research.* Thousand Oaks: Sage.

Argyris, C., & Schön, D. A. (1974). *Theory in practice: Increasing professional effectiveness.* San Francisco, CA: Jossey-Bass.

Astin, A. W. (1984). Student involvement: A developmental theory for higher education. *Journal of College Student Personnel, 25,* 297–308.

Astin, A. W. (1991). *Assessment for excellence: The philosophy and practice of assessment and evaluation in higher education.* New York, NY: MacMillan.

Astin, A. W. (1993). *What matters in college: Four critical years revisited.* San Francisco, CA: Jossey-Bass.

Atwater, M. M., & Alick, B. (1990). Cognitive development and problem solving of Afro-American students in chemistry. *Journal of Research in Science Teaching, 27,* 157–172.

Ausubel, D. P. (1963). *The psychology of meaningful verbal learning.* New York, NY: Grune & Stratton.

Bell, D. (1995). Racial realism—After we've gone: Prudent speculations on America in a post-racial epoch. In R. Delgado (Ed.), *Critical race theory: The cutting edge* (pp. 2–8). Philadelphia: Temple University Press.

Bensimon, E. M. (2007). Presidential address: The underestimated significance of practitioner knowledge in the scholarship on student success. *Review of Higher Education, 30*(4), 441–469.

Bourdieu, P. (1977). *Outline of a theory of practice.* Cambridge: Cambridge University Press.

Brown, L. L., & Robinson Kurpius, S. E. (1997). Psychosocial factors influencing academic persistence of American Indian college students. *Journal of College Student Development, 38,* 3–12.

Ceja, M. (2006). Understanding the role of parents and siblings as information sources in the college choice process of Chicana students. *Journal of College Student Development, 47*(1), 87–104.

Chickering, A. W. (1969). *Education and identity.* San Francisco, CA: Jossey-Bass.

Chickering, A. W., & Reisser, L. (1993). *Education and identity* (2nd ed.). San Francisco, CA: Jossey-Bass.

Coleman, J. S. (1988). Social capital in the creation of human capital. *American Journal of Sociology, 94* Supplement, 95–120.

Collins, P. (2000). *Black feminist thought: Knowledge, consciousness, and the politics of empowerment* (2nd ed.). New York, NY: Routledge.

Creamer, D. G., & Associates. (1990). *College student development: Theory and practice for the 1990s.* Washington, DC: American College Personnel Association.

Crenshaw, K. (1991). Mapping the margins: Intersectionality, identity politics, and violence against women of color. *Stanford Law Review, 43*(6), 1241–1299.

Crotty, M. (1998). *The foundation of social research: Meaning and perspective in the research process.* Thousand Oaks, CA: Sage.

Cruce, T.M, Wolniak, G.C., Seifert, T.A., & Pascarella, E.T. (2006). Impacts of good practices on cognitive development, learning orientations, and graduate degree plans during the first year of college. *Journal of College Student Development, 47*(4), pp. 365-383.

DeCuir, J. T., & Dixson, A. D. (2004). "So when it comes out, they aren't that surprised that it is there": Using critical race theory as a tool of analysis of race and racism in education. *Educational Researcher, 33*(5), 26–31.

Erikson, E. H. (1968). *Identity: Youth and crisis.* New York, NY: Norton.

Evans, N. J., Forney, D. S., & Guido-DiBrito, F. (1998). *Student development in college: Theory, research, and practice.* San Francisco, CA: Jossey-Bass.

Fowler, J. (1981). *Stages of faith: The psychology of human development and the quest for meaning.* San Francisco, CA: Harper & Row.

Fries-Britt, S., Johnson, J., & Burt, B. (2013). Black students in physics: The intersection of academic ability, race, gender, and class. In T. L. Strayhorn (Ed.), *Living at the intersections: Social identities and Black collegians* (pp. 21–39). Charlotte, NC: Information Age.

Jones, S. R., & Abes, E. S. (2011). The nature and uses of theory. In J. Schuh, S. R. Jones, & S. R. Harper (Eds.), *Student services: A handbook for the profession* (5th ed., pp. 149–167). San Francisco, CA: Jossey-Bass.

Jones, S. R., & McEwen, M. K. (2000). A conceptual model of multiple dimensions of identity. *Journal of College Student Development, 41*(4), 405–414.

Kerlinger, F. N. (1986). *Foundations of behavioral research* (3rd ed.). New York, NY: Holt, Rinehart, & Winston.

Kohlberg, L. (1969). Stage and sequence: The cognitive developmental approach to socialization. In D. A. Goslin (Ed.), *Handbook of socialization theory and research* (pp. 347–480). Chicago: Rand McNally.

Lareau, A. (2003). *Unequal childhoods: Class, race, and family life.* Berkeley: University of California Press.

LeCompte, M. D., & Preissle, J. (1993). *Ethnography and qualitative design in educational research* (2nd ed.). San Diego: Academic Press.

Lewin, K. (1936). *Principles of topological psychology.* New York, NY: McGraw-Hill.

Loevinger, J. (1976). *Ego development: Conceptions and theories.* San Francisco, CA: Jossey-Bass.

Loevinger, J. (1998). History of the Sentence Completion Test (SCT) for ego development. In J. Loevinger (Ed.), *Technical foundations for measuring ego development: The Washington University Sentence Completion Test.* Mahwah, NJ: Lawrence Erlbaum Associates.

Loevinger, J., & Wessler, R. (1970). *Measuring ego development: Construction and use of a sentence completion test* (Vol. *1*). San Francisco, CA: Jossey-Bass.

Martin, W. E., Swartz-Kulstad, J. L., & Madson, M. (1999). Psychosocial factors that predict the college adjustment of first-year undergraduate students: Implications for college counselors. *Journal of College Counseling, 2,* 121–133.

Matsuda, M. (1991). Voices of America: Accent, antidiscrimination law, and a jurisprudence for the last reconstruction. *Yale Law Review, 100,* 1329–1407.

McDonough, P. M. (1997). Choosing colleges: How social class and schools structure opportunity. Albany: State University of New York Press.

McEwen, M. K. (2003). The nature and uses of theory. In S. R. Komives, D. B. Woodar Jr., & Associates (Eds.), *Student services: A handbook of the profession* (4th ed., pp. 153–178). San Francisco, CA: Jossey-Bass.

Merriam, S. B. (1998). *Qualitative research and case study applications in education.* San Francisco, CA: Jossey-Bass.

Osterman, K. F. (2000). Students' need for belonging in the school community. *Review of Educational Research, 70*(3), 323–367.

Parker, C. A. (1977). On modeling reality. *Journal of College Student Personnel, 18*(5), 419–425.

Parks, S. D. (2000). *Big questions, worthy dreams: Mentoring young adults in their search for meaning, purpose, and faith.* San Francisco, CA: Jossey-Bass.

Pascarella, E. T., & Terenzini, P. T. (1991). *How college affects students.* San Francisco, CA: Jossey-Bass.

Pascarella, E. T., & Terenzini, P. T. (2005). *How college affects students: A third decade of research* (Vol. 2). San Francisco, CA: Jossey-Bass.

Perry, W. G. (1981). Cognitive growth and ethical growth: The making of meaning. In A. W. Chickering (Ed.), *The modern American college* (pp. 76–116). San Francisco, CA: Jossey-Bass.

Phinney, J. S. (1996). Understanding ethnic diversity: The role of ethnic identity. *American Behavioral Scientist, 40*(2), 143–152.

Piaget, J. (1952). *The origins of intelligence in children.* New York, NY: International Universities Press.

Piaget, J. (1977). *The moral judgement of the child* (M. Gabain, Trans.). Hardmondsworth, UK: Penguin.

Renn, K. A. (2006). Identity and leadership development in lesbian, gay, bisexual, and transgender student organizations. *Concepts and connections: A publication for leadership educators, 14*(1), 1–3.

Rodgers, R. F. (1980). Theories underlying student development. In D. G. Creamer (Ed.), *Student development in higher education: Theories, practices, and future directions* (pp. 10–95). Alexandria, VA: American College Personnel Assocation.

Strayhorn, T. L. (2006). *Frameworks for assessing learning and development outcomes.* Washington, DC: Council for the Advancement of Standards in Higher Education (CAS).

Strayhorn, T. L. (2008a). How college students' engagement affects personal and social learning outcomes. *Journal of College and Character, 10*(2), 1–16.

Strayhorn, T. L. (2008b). Influences on labor market outcomes of African American college graduates: A national study. *Journal of Higher Education, 79*(1), 29–57.

Strayhorn, T. L. (2012). *College students' sense of belonging: A key to educational success.* New York, NY: Routledge.

Strayhorn, T. L. (2013a). *Theoretical frameworks in college student research.* Lanham, MD: University Press of America, Rowman & Littlefield.

Strayhorn, T. L. (Ed.). (2013b). *Living at the intersections: Social identities and Black collegians.* Charlotte, NC: Information Age.

Terenzini, P. T., Springer, L., Yaeger, P. M., Pascarella, E. T., & Nora, A. (1996). First generation college students: Characteristics, experiences, and cognitive development. *Research in Higher Education, 37*(1), 1–22.

Tinto, V. (1993). *Leaving college: Rethinking the causes and cures of student attrition* (2nd ed.). Chicago, IL: University of Chicago Press.

Villalpando, O., & Delgado Bernal, D. (2002). A critical race theory analysis of barriers that impede the success of faculty of color. In W. A. Smith, P. G. Altbach, & K. Lomotey (Eds.), *The racial crisis in American higher education: Continuing challeges for the twenty-first century* (rev. ed., pp. 243–270). Albany: State University of New York Press.

Villalpando, O., & Solórzano, D. G. (2005). The role of culture in college preparation programs: A review of the research literature. In W. G. Tierney, Z. B. Corwin & J. E. Colyar (Eds.), *Preparing for college: Nine elements of effective outreach* (pp. 13–28). Albany: State University of New York Press.

Weathersby, R. P. (1981). Ego development. In A. W. Chickering & Associates (Eds.), *The modern American college: Responding to the new realities of diverse students and a changing society* (pp. 51–75). San Francisco, CA: Jossey-Bass.

Weidman, J. (1989). Undergraduate socialization: A conceptual approach. In J. C. Smart (Ed.), *Higher education: Handbook of theory and research* (Vol. 5). New York, NY: Agathon.

CHAPTER EIGHT

TEACHING AND LEARNING BEYOND THE CLASSROOM

Responding to the Internal and External Challenges Facing Student Affairs

Peter Magolda and Tony Ribera

At a recent national conference, residence lifers declared they were now "equal partners" with faculty in higher education. They characterized residence life in the old days as being concerned merely with "programming activities," while under the new "curricular model," res lifers, like faculty members, act as teachers. Teachers of what? And by what means? It is much in the interest of faculty members everywhere to begin posing these questions.

—*National Association of Scholars, 2008*

The elitist and condescending undertones embedded in the two questions posed by the National Association of Scholars in *Rebuilding Campus Community: The Wrong Imperative* remind readers that some faculty neither understand nor agree with student affairs' emphasis on teaching and learning outside the classroom. To educate skeptics and, more important, students, student affairs professionals, regardless of department and institution type, must answer the question, "What do I need to know and do in order to successfully design and implement a progressive co-curriculum that focuses on learning and supports collegians' quests for meaningful learning opportunities beyond the classroom?" We argue in this chapter that student affairs professionals must view themselves as educators, take a learning-centered approach to their work, and recognize that the scholarship of teaching and learning is a professional obligation.

The student affairs profession emerged as a result of evolving faculty roles and responsibilities in higher education (Garland & Grace, 1993; Nuss, 2003). Faculty—who had once overseen students' entire college education, including tutoring and monitoring discipline—were becoming more specialized and focused on classroom teaching and research (Creamer, Winston, & Miller, 2001; Fenske, 1980; Hartley, 2001; Rudolph, 1977; Schroeder & Mable, 1994). This shift sparked the need for a new kind of campus professional charged with promoting the development of students and coordinating their out of class activities (Garland & Grace, 1993; Schroeder & Mable, 1994). Student affairs professionals have gradually and intentionally redefined their emphases from providers of customer service to development specialists (that is, tending to the affective, personal, social, intellectual, cognitive, and vocational dimensions of students' development) and ultimately to educators concerned about learning (Ender, Newton, & Caple, 1996; Magolda & Quaye, 2010).

In defining functions and goals of student affairs professionals, the American Council on Education (ACE) in *The Student Personnel Point of View* (1937, 1949) initially envisioned these individuals as educators charged with helping students discover their strengths and interests. Later, scholars (for example, Brown, 1972) not only called student affairs professionals to educate students but also to assess student learning and understand the strengths and weaknesses of their programs and services (American College Personnel Association, 1975). Today, contributing to student learning is the primary responsibility of the field (Creamer et al., 2001; Roper, 2003). Regardless of the functional area or institutional type, universities call upon all professionals in the field of student affairs to function as student affairs educators (SAEs) by developing educational programs based on specific learning outcomes (American College Personnel Association, 1994; Keeling, 2004) and offering intentional co-curricular programming focused on enhancing student knowledge and skills (Saunders & Cooper, 2001).

Despite these responsibilities, SAEs often encounter and will continue to encounter challenges in fulfilling their educational responsibilities. This chapter focuses on these challenges by discussing three issues: (1) the influences of the ever-changing university on the student affairs profession and the co-curriculum; (2) external influences—namely, the dwindling fiscal resources, rising operating costs, and universities' responses to these budgetary woes—that complicate SAEs efforts to teach; and (3) innovative initiatives aimed at ensuring collegians' quests for meaningful learning opportunities beyond the classroom.

Colleges and Universities in Transition

Hanson (1980), asserted, "The question is not *whether* we [SAEs] should teach, for we have a rich heritage of doing so—one we will probably continue for some time. Rather, our emphasis must be on *how* we should teach. What makes for good, effective teaching? What ideas, attitudes, and skills help others learn?" (p. 267). Hanson correctly predicted more than thirty years ago that teaching would be an integral aspect of SAEs' identities and work responsibilities. Yet, continually evolving and responsive universities have necessitated that SAEs regularly revisit Hanson's two questions—because good teaching practice and support practices aimed at enhancing learning are fluid. Two brief examples support this claim.

Over the past two decades, shifts in student demography (for example, social class, race, gender, ethnicity, age, and sexual orientation), which favor diverse learners from various cultures with varied learning preferences, have had far-reaching educational implications for SAEs as they continually assess what makes for good effective teaching and modify the co-curriculum to address these needs. Today, SAEs realize it is neither feasible nor wise to offer, "one size fits all academic advising" for first-generation, nontraditional-age, and part-time students. They have effectively redesigned co-curricula to address changing demographics.

New technologies, too, have dramatically altered SAEs' co-curricular offerings and delivery methods (Connolly, 2011; Martinez-Aleman, 2011). The Internet, social media, and smartphone/tablet technologies provide collegians greater access to information, essentially upending conventional college curricula, pedagogies, and student-teacher roles. Now, virtual orientations allow international students to become acquainted with their new American universities from their homeland, long before they arrive on campus; likewise, American students can learn about their study abroad destinations long before they travel, which enhances learning. Distance education and virtual faculty office hours allow students working full time to enroll in online seminars and regularly interact with faculty without having to physically visit campus. Facebook and Twitter have replaced conventional resident assistant–residents modes of acquaintanceship and communication, such as flyers, newsletters, and face-to-face hall meetings (Eberhardt, 2007). These social media have empowered students to become worldwide teachers and learners.

Fortunately, SAEs have recognized the importance of influences such as demography and technologies (Morrison, 2005) and attend to issues such as these when answering Hanson's two teaching questions: "What makes for good, effective teaching?" and "What ideas, attitudes, and skills help others learn?" Unfortunately, SAEs have paid far less attention to other subtle, powerful macro-issues, such as economics and politics that also influence the academy. Higher education's dwindling fiscal resources, rising operating costs, and political responses to these challenges impact SAEs and the co-curriculum. Declining fiscal support for higher education as well as universities' subsequent declining support for student affairs dramatically influence what SAEs teach, how they teach, and what collegians learn outside the classroom.

Economic Calamities and Co-curricular Challenges

Schrecker (2010) summarized the aftermath of the 2008 worldwide economic collapse on higher education:

> When the economic tsunami washed over them in 2008, almost every institution of higher learning, from the Ivy League to the community colleges, feared that it was in trouble. States cut back their funding, while endowments plummeted. Though each school handled the loss of income in its own way, their early responses indicate that the current crisis will only intensify many of the deleterious trends … Most strove, it is true, to avoid laying off tenured and tenure-track faculty members and instead resorted to hiring freezes, tuition increases, pay cuts, and reductions in everything from pension contributions to trash collection. (p. 225)

Economic influence on the academy persists. In 2012, California public higher education received 12 percent of its budget (a record low) from the State, down from 54 percent in 1987 (Rapold, 2013). In September 2013, President Barack Obama, during a speech, reminded Americans that this higher education crisis persists and change is inevitable:

> Families and taxpayers can't just keep paying more and more and more into an undisciplined system where costs just keep on going up and up and up. We'll never have enough loan money, we'll never have enough grant money, to keep up with costs that are going up 5, 6, 7 percent a year. We have got to get more out of what we pay for. (Jaschik, 2013, p. 4)

External support for higher education will not likely increase anytime soon and efforts to rein in spending will persist. Becoming more businesslike (Tuchman, 2009) is a common university response to the challenges (for example, rising operating costs, dwindling external revenue streams) that President Obama raised during his speech. Examples of the adaptation of businesslike practices include unconditional customer service, branding, cutting costs, downsizing staff, increasing productivity, encouraging competition, outsourcing, and evaluation (to ensure quality and accountability) (Tuchman, 2009).

As noted earlier in this chapter, Schrecker (2010) highlighted American universities' typical response to these challenges, which mirrored most of Tuchman's businesslike criteria. Decisions to protect faculty from budget cuts symbolically conveys that learning will not be compromised; students' relationship with faculty will not be jeopardized (ensuring high customer satisfaction); and a university's commitment to teaching, research, and intellectual pursuits will not be diminished. To the not-so-discerning observer, these businesslike responses appear prudent, logical, rational, and normal.

Yet, to the discerning, numerous concerns are obvious. Nonfaculty must cope with their diminishing status and influence evidenced by budget cuts, downsized staffs, increasing job responsibilities, and the devaluing of campus life beyond the classroom. This faculty versus all other campus community members dichotomy illuminates seminal institutional values: (1) the most important learning takes place in classrooms, (2) faculty are the most valued human resource on campus, and (3) "life of the mind" trumps developing the "whole student." Such dynamics harm morale of nonfaculty educators.

From the vantage point of student affairs, businesslike decisions such as these signal higher education's desire to return to its wayward past: insular, fragmented, antiquated, and unequal organizational structures as well as a bifurcated division of labor between student affairs and academic affairs (that is, faculty teach—focusing on cognitive and intellectual matters and student affairs administrators provide support services). Indeed, resurrecting such practices is not in the best interest of students and a serious threat to student learning.

Why should SAEs care about seemingly tangential issues such as the adaptation of businesslike practices to solve problems? Giroux (2005) succinctly synthesized concerns:

Colleges and universities do not simply produce knowledge for students; they also play an influential role in shaping their identities, values, and sense of what it means to become citizens of the world. If colleges and

universities are to define themselves as centers of teaching and learning
vital to the democratic life of the nation and globe, they must
acknowledge the real danger of becoming mere adjuncts to big business,
or corporate entities in themselves. (p. 5)

Giroux posited that the adaptation of businesslike or corporate ideals
is not merely a set of technical, bureaucratic, or administrative practices
resulting from objective analysis of the situation, but instead a moral and
a political ideology that shapes identities and statuses within the campus
community. For example, exempting faculty from personnel and budget
cuts or disproportionally cutting student affair budgets reveals a university's
responses to the question, "What is good?" A response to this question is
political and reveals institutional core values.

Issues such as economics, politics, morality, and ideology seem far
removed from the topic of teaching and learning in the co-curriculum;
but they are not. SAEs need to understand the influences of larger social
systems on their everyday work. Framed metaphorically, SAEs need to see
the proverbial forest (for example, the political and moral implications
of declining fiscal support from the federal government on higher
education and subsequently student affairs) *and* the proverbial trees (for
example, co-curricular refinements to respond to demographic shifts and
technology innovations). Economic, moral, and political matters have and
will have a profound influence on student learning.

Acknowledging and Avoiding Typical Coping Strategies

Admittedly, grappling with budget shortfalls and the larger campus
community's lack of understanding of the centrality of learning to
SAEs' daily work are familiar challenges—hardly unique or noteworthy.
Yet, responses to these challenges, during austere economic times, are
significant, predictable, and detrimental. When uncertainty reigns and
trouble is imminent, a natural inclination is for SAEs to either hunker
down to outlast the crisis or attempt to get back to basics (for example,
simply providing essential services). With fewer student affairs staff and
declining status within the university, it is easy to comprehend these coping
strategies. Yet, such actions (1) deemphasize student learning and instead
advocate a return to the good old days that emphasized student services;
(2) yield short-term and simple solutions to perennial and complex
problems; (3) foster adversarial rather than collaborative interactions with

the "other" (for example, faculty and students); and (4) spawn simplistic assessment metrics that create the illusion of measuring and evaluating worth. Instead, readers are invited to consider some counterintuitive solutions. A brief example and analysis will illuminate these dangers and possibilities.

For Office of Ethics and Conduct staff, an understandable, although dangerous, response to staff downsizing and budget cuts is to temporarily (that is, until the crisis subsides) shift its focus from educating students about their errant behaviors to simply sanctioning (that is, punishing) them for their inappropriate actions. Sanction-oriented administrative hearings are more efficient when measured by time spent per case rather than those that focus on learning and development. Yet, this short-term and simple solution has long-term negative consequences. If students do not fully understand how their actions harm the larger community and themselves, repeat offenders are likely. A disciplinary hearing centering on punitive sanctioning tends to be more adversarial than a hearing that places education at the epicenter of the meeting and where collaboration is the course of negotiating and mutually agreeing upon an appropriate sanction is the norm.

To protect the office from future budget cuts, office staffs devise satisfaction surveys measuring student perceptions of the fairness of proceedings to demonstrate their worth, while ignoring more important data such as assessing what students learned from the disciplinary process. This example illustrates that crises (for example, budget shortfall, shifting priorities) and responses (for example, efficiency) make it even more important for SAEs to recommit themselves to their roles as educators.

What do SAEs need to know and what actions must they initiate to enact these "solutions"? The authors posit: educating, not administering; collaborating, not competing; being progressive, not reactionary; engaging with, not retreating from the scholarship of teaching and learning; and assessing what is important, not convenient; moving forward, not backward. These last three issues are discussed in the remainder of this chapter.

Contributing to and Consuming the Scholarship of Teaching and Learning

Although SAEs serve in different functional areas at different kinds of institutions with diverse missions, sustaining an emphasis on teaching and learning, despite local and global challenges, is essential. Scholarship is a commonality that unites SAEs as professionals (Carpenter, 2001). Student affairs professionals committed to student learning must possess knowledge about different types of scholarship (Young, 2001)—such as a scholarship of practice (Carpenter, 2001), integration (Fried, 2002), and application (Schroeder & Pike, 2001)—to optimize student learning.

Despite heightened rhetoric in the student affairs literature about the importance of teaching and learning, scholar-practitioners who contribute to and consume the scholarship of teaching and learning (any effort to gather, analyze, interpret, and disseminate evidence of teaching and learning for individual improvement, institutional improvement, and the advancement of the larger profession in student affairs) remain the exception, not the rule. In grim economic and politically turbulent times, with fewer staff, heightened responsibilities, and less time for professional development, SAEs may become more reactive or concentrate on comfort areas or operate from the seat of their pants rather than generating, disseminating, and consuming knowledge—a process that aligns with professional responsibilities and is vital to the advancement of the profession.

Despite these challenges, it is prudent for SAEs to produce and circulate insights gained from their co-curricular teaching and learning experiences. Regardless of how they envision their role as educators— scientist-practitioners (Winston et al. 2001), pedagogical researchers (Kuh, 1996), or scholar-practitioners (Komives, 1998)—gathering, analyzing, interpreting, and disseminating evidence of teaching and learning are professional obligations (ACPA, 2006; NASPA, n.d.).

Huber and Hutchings (2005) proposed four defining features of the scholarship of teaching and learning: (1) questioning, (2) gathering and exploring evidence, (3) trying out and refining new insights, and (4) going public. These features align with calls from the student affairs scholars/researchers/authors. SAEs have been called to ask tough questions about teaching and learning (for example, Schuh & Gansemer-Topf, 2010), engage in systematic inquiry of teaching and learning (for example, Pascarella & Whitt, 1999), and use evidence of teaching and learning to improve their efforts (for example, Brigman & Hanson, 2000). If SAEs expect students, who participate in the co-curriculum, to question, gather and explore evidence; try out and refine new insights; and go public with their view (as Huber and Hutching propose)—SAEs must, too, embrace and model these values.

Publicly disseminating evidence of teaching and learning for the advancement of the profession is a key feature of the scholarship of teaching and learning. Although the scholarship of teaching and learning is similar to other practices (that is, action research), it is the dissemination of this work that makes it distinct (Gurung & Schwartz, 2009). Huber and Hutchings (2005) write, "The scholarship of teaching and learning is about more than individual improvement and development—it is about producing knowledge that is available for others to use and build on" (p. 27). In the American College Personnel Association's (2006) *Statement of Ethical Principles & Standards*, contributing to the profession through scholarly research is described as a responsibility of SAEs in the field. Specifically, SAEs have been charged with sharing effective teaching methods and evidence of teaching and learning to the larger profession (Moore & Blake, 2007).

Technological innovations have revolutionized ways for SAEs to share good teaching and learning practices. Prior to the Internet, the "chosen few" (for example, journal and book publishers) were the knowledge gatekeepers who determined what counted as scholarship, what scholarship would be disseminated, and how consumers would access knowledge. These gatekeepers' goodness criteria (for example, scholar-generated, national, empirical, and formal research studies) trumped local, informal essays showcasing best practices. These criteria complicated SAEs' efforts to disseminate their teaching and learning insights as well as limited the kinds of scholarly works they could access. Yet, Internet innovations such as blogs, wikis, listservs, and social networks greatly diminished the power of gatekeepers and subsequently empowered SAEs, making more egalitarian the generation, dissemination, and consumption of knowledge. These social media augment, not replace, more conventional means to generate and disseminate knowledge such as peer-reviewed journals or books. Contemporary technologies simplify and diversify ways SAEs can share information regardless of the scale and focus of the study (for example, a best practices essay summarizing an informal campus-based intervention), which foster collaboration and make it less likely that insular SAEs will reinvent the wheel.

As colleges and universities move from a teaching-centered to a more learning-centered paradigm, faculty members have assumed a greater level of ownership for student learning and recognized the need for evidence of student learning (Barr & Tagg, 1995; Cross, 1986). Institutions and departments have supported this inquiry about teaching and learning and encouraged collaboration among faculty (Chism, Sanders, & Zitlow, 1987). The scholarship of teaching and learning has grown in academe as a result of this larger learning-centered paradigm shift, with faculty seeking to improve the effectiveness of their teaching and further facilitate student learning (Gittens, 2007; Hutchings, Huber, & Ciccone, 2011).

Like their faculty colleagues, many SAEs have gradually embraced a learning-centered approach to their work (Cross, 1981) and been encouraged to engage in the scholarship of teaching and learning (Ribera, Fernandez, & Gray, 2012). Although professional development opportunities and departmental/institutional incentive structures would further ensure both faculty and SAEs seamlessly integrate the scholarship of teaching and learning into their daily routines, SAEs must prioritize this scholarship and learning-centeredness under the assumption that these opportunities and rewards may not be present with their departments and institutions.

Professionals engage in the scholarship of teaching and learning for three distinct reasons as defined by Shulman (2000): (1) pragmatism, (2) policy, and (3) professionalism. One gains new insights into the student population and effective teaching strategies. Not only do they use evidence to improve their individual efforts, but they also help shape larger institutional policy. Additionally, by disseminating this evidence one advances the profession by sharing new perspectives on teaching and learning.

Assessment in Student Affairs

SAEs are considered pedagogical specialists who, guided by student needs and clearly articulated learning objectives, apply different pedagogies to promote student learning (Creamer et al., 2001). However, in order to answer the questions originally posed by Hanson (1980), SAEs require more than an understanding of the defining features of the scholarship of teaching and learning; they require a familiarity with assessment methods and skills in conducting meaningful assessment. The American College Personnel Association and the National Association of Student Personnel Administrators (2010) write:

> All student affairs practitioners, regardless of functional area, must approach their work with the assumption that all aspects of it must be supported by evidence gathered through accepted modes of assessment and consistent with the research about college student success. (p. 10)

Assessing student learning is a professional obligation of SAEs (ACPA, 2006; NASPA, n.d.), as well as a competency with which individuals should enter the profession (ACPA, 2007). Unfortunately, although common position responsibilities for new SAEs entering the profession have teaching and learning implications, assessment is an area they are less competent in and is rated lower in importance among all their responsibilities (Burkard, Cole, Ott, & Stoflet, 2005). SAEs seldom emphasize assessment is their daily practices and they struggle to show evidence of effective teaching and student learning (Pascarella & Whitt, 1999). Blimling and Whitt (1999) echo this sentiment, writing:

> One of the greatest weaknesses in student affairs organizations has been their inability to demonstrate how their efforts influence student learning. Although research on college impact provides ample indications that there are such influences, too few student affairs professionals take the time to examine how—or whether—their programs and practices contribute to student outcomes. (p. 182)

During economic downturns, SAEs often take on additional responsibilities and become overextended as a result. It is common when forced to decide which practices to emphasize in daily work for one to focus on areas they are more comfortable with or perceive they have more skills in. Yet, if SAEs diminish their emphasis on assessment (even if they can justify it), their capacity to assess student learning decreases as its vulnerabilities related to its standing in the university increase.

Considering the research literature regarding assessment in student affairs, SAEs may lack confidence in their assessment abilities. This could lead to them emphasizing assessment less in their daily practice or to remove it from their list of responsibilities. However, SAEs contribute to the larger academic mission of higher education, and abandoning assessment should not be perceived as a viable option, much like an SAE would never contemplate not advising individual students or student groups, not supervising staff members, not scheduling conduct hearings, and so on. If SAEs abandon assessment, they will not know if they are making a difference and will not be able to improve their efforts to further promote student learning.

Through meaningful assessment, SAEs can gain greater clarity of the extent to which they promote student learning (Upcraft & Schuh, 1996) and use findings to better identify areas in need of attention (American College Personnel Association and National Association of Student Personnel Administrators, 1997). These efforts should align with larger departmental initiatives as student affairs divisions have been called to "develop and implement a comprehensive plan for assessment of student learning and the role of student affairs in that learning" (Pascarella & Whitt, 1999, p. 109). In addition to seeing themselves as part of a department and institution, SAEs should not fail to recognize that they are also part of a larger profession.

Meeting the Challenges

Despite the shifting educational landscape, an unstable economy, and businesslike solutions, it is both necessary and possible to sustain learning at the center of student affairs practice by promoting learning, contributing to and consuming the scholarship of teaching, and assessing whether students meet learning outcomes. Here is an extended example of how one university met this challenge.

California State University, Northridge (CSUN), in the context of "increasing enrollments, a rising and urgent demand for baccalaureate and graduate education, and an eroding financial base for public universities" (Koester, Hellenbrand, & Piper, 2005, p. 11), undertook a campuswide initiative to transform itself into a learning-centered institution. Among the principles they adopted were "a learning-centered university establishes learning outcomes for each of its programs"; "a learning-centered university uses assessment to feed results back to faculty, staff and administrators so that they can replot what they are doing"; and "a learning-centered university measures its success by how well its students meet learning objectives". (p. 11)

CSUN student affairs educators focused on learning, engaged in the scholarship of teaching and learning, assessed learning and forged meaningful partnerships with faculty. For example, the Department of Residential Life "partnered with academic departments to create living learning communities that blur the lines between learning inside the classroom and learning outside the classroom, and that bring to life the learning-centered university principle that students learn best when they work together to solve problems in applied settings" (Koester et al., 2005, p. 16). This long-term transformative initiative resulted in

- Creating a unified vision that binds this initiative with other important activities like the university's planning efforts and upcoming reaccreditation
- Increasing cross-divisional collaboration that is critical to the success of the effort

- Using evidence to assess programs and as a basis for moving forward
- Transforming the campus culture
- Facing the challenges of campus leadership, to ensure the university continues to focus on the goal of becoming more learning-centered while remaining attentive to other internal and external demands (Koester et al., 2008, p. 13)

This brief exemplar draws on both CSUN faculty and SAEs' professional obligations to educate and gather, analyze, interpret, and disseminate evidence of teaching and learning and assessment and bridge gaps between academic and student affairs by: establishing learning outcomes to guide practice, organizing practice around those learning outcomes (using knowledge of the teaching and learning process), assessing progress on the outcomes, and using the assessment to further inform practice. These reflect reorienting practice to focus on learning, and making that practice central to the institution. This makes partnering with other educators (that is, faculty) easier given the common language of learning. Even with a shifting educational landscape, and an unstable economy, CSUN sustained learning at the center of student affairs practice.

Conclusion

In 1994 *The Student Learning Imperative* indicated, "If learning is the primary measure of institutional productivity by which the quality of undergraduate education is determined, what and how much students learn also must be the criteria by which the value of student affairs is judged" (p. 3). The authors of *The Student Learning Imperative*, challenge what the National Association of Scholars (2008) suggest in *The Wrong Imperative* by positing that learning is central to the work of everyone in the academy—including student affairs educators. To meet the challenges of contemporary higher education and answer the question, "What do I need to know and do in order to successfully design and implement a progressive co-curriculum that focuses on learning and support collegians' quests for meaningful learning opportunities beyond the classroom?" student affairs educators must:

- View themselves as educators, first and foremost
- Continually pose and answer the questions: "What makes for good, effective teaching?" and "How do my actions enhance student learning?"

- Be attentive to both micro-and macro-internal and especially external challenges that influence the ever-changing university and could threaten student learning outside the classroom
- Recognize that teaching and learning is not simply a technical or administrative exercise, but a moral and political one, as well
- Become generators, disseminators, and consumers of the scholarship of teaching and learning even when opportunities and rewards may not be present
- Recognize that assessing student learning is a professional obligation
- Increase cross-campus collaboration with faculty and students

Simply stated, student affairs work in higher education is all about learning.

References

American College Personnel Association. (1975). A student development model for student affairs in tomorrow's higher education. *Journal of College Student Personnel, 16*(4), 334–341.

American College Personnel Association. (1994). *The student learning imperative: Implications for student affairs.* Washington, DC: Author.

American College Personnel Association. (2006). Statement of ethical principles standards. http://www.myacpa.org/au/documents/Ethical_Principles_Standards .pdf.

American College Personnel Association. (2007). *Professional competencies: A report of the steering committee on professional competencies.* Washington, DC: Author.

American College Personnel Association and National Association of Student Personnel Administrators. (1997). *Principles of good practice for student affairs.* Washington, DC: Authors.

American College Personnel Association and National Association of Student Personnel Administrators. (2010). *Envisioning the future of student affairs: Final report of the task force on the future of students affairs appointed jointly by ACPA and NASPA.* Washington, DC: Authors.

American Council on Education. (1937). *The student personnel point of view.* American Council on Education Students (Series 1, Vol. 1, No. 3). Washington, DC: Author.

American Council on Education. (1949). *The student personnel point of view* (rev. ed.). American Council on Education Students (Series 6, No. 13.) Washington, DC: Author.

Barr, R. B., & Tagg, J. (1995). From teaching to learning: A new paradigm for undergraduate education. *Change, 27*(6), 13–25.

Blimling, G. S., & Whitt, E. J. (1999). Using principles to improve practice. In G. S. Blimling, & E. J. Whitt (Eds.), *Good practice in student affairs: Principles to foster student learning* (pp. 179–204). San Francisco, CA: Jossey-Bass.

Brigman, S. L., & Hanson, G. R. (2000). Making things happen in higher education: Dissemination of student affairs research results. In J. W. Pickering & G. R. Hanson (Eds.). *Collaboration between student affairs and institutional researchers to improve institutional effectiveness.* New Directions for Institutional Research (No. 108, pp. 49–61). San Francisco, CA: Jossey-Bass.

Brown, R. D. (1972). *Student development in tomorrow's higher education—A return to the academy.* Washington, DC: American Personnel and Guidance Association.

Burkard, A., Cole, DC, Ott, M., & Stoflet, T. (2005). Entry-level competencies of new student affairs professionals: A Delphi study. *NASPA Journal, 42*(3), 283–309.

Carpenter, S. (2001). Student affairs scholarship (re?)considered: Toward a scholarship of practice. *Journal of College Student Development, 42*(4), 301–318.

Chism, N., Sanders, D., & Zitlow, C. (1987). Observations on a faculty development program based on practice-centered inquiry. *Peabody Journal of Education, 64*(3), 1–23.

Connolly, M. R. (2011). Social networking and student learning: Friends without benefits. In P. Magolda & M. B. Baxter Magolda (Eds.), *Contested issues in student affairs: Diverse perspectives and respectful dialogue* (pp.122–134). Sterling, VA: Stylus.

Creamer, D. G., Winston Jr., R. B., & Miller, T. K. (2001). The professional student affairs administrator: Roles and functions. In R. B. Winston, Jr.,, D. G., Creamer, & T. K. Miller (Eds.), *The professional student affairs administrator: Educator, leader, and manager* (pp.3–38). New York, NY: Brunner-Routledge.

Cross, K. P. (1981). Planning for the future of the student personnel profession. *Journal of College Student Personnel, 22*(2), 99–104.

Cross, K. P. (1986). A proposal to improve teaching or what "taking teaching seriously" should mean. *AAHE Bulletin, 39*(1), 9–14.

Eberhardt, D. M. (2007). Facing up to Facebook. *About Campus, 12,* 18–26.

Ender, S. C., Newton, F. B., & Caple, R. B. (1996). Contributions to learning: Present realities. In S. C. Ender, F. B. Newton, & R. B. Caple (Eds.), *Contributing to learning: The role of student affairs.* New Directions for Student Services (No. 75, pp. 5–17). San Francisco, CA: Jossey-Bass.

Fenske, R. H. (1980). Historical foundations. In U. Delworth & G. R. Hanson (Eds.), *Student services: A handbook for the profession* (pp. 3–24). San Francisco, CA: Jossey-Bass.

Fried, J. (2002). The scholarship of student affairs: Integration and application. *NASPA Journal, 39*(2), 120–131.

Garland, P. H., & Grace, T. W. (1993). *New perspectives for student affairs professionals: evolving realities, responsibilities and roles* (ASHE-ERIC Higher Education Report no. 7). Washington, DC: George Washington University, School of Education and Human Development.

Giroux, H. (2005). Academic entrepreneurs: The corporate takeover of higher education. *Tikkun, 20*(2), 18–28.

Gittens, W. (2007). Shifting discourse in college teaching. *International Journal for the Scholarship of Teaching and Learning, 1*(1), 1–5.

Gurung, R. A. R., & Schwartz, B. M. (2009). *Optimizing teaching and learning: Practicing pedagogical research.* West Sussex, UK: Wiley-Blackwell.

Hanson, G. R. Instruction. (1980). In U. Delworth & G. R. Hanson (Eds.), *Student services: A handbook for the profession* (pp. 267–295). San Francisco, CA: Jossey-Bass.

Hartley, M. (2001). Student learning as a framework for student affairs—Rhetoric or reality? *NASPA Journal, 38*(2), 224–237.

Huber, M. T., & Hutchings, P. (2005). *The advancement of learning: Building the teaching commons.* A Carnegie Foundation Report on the Scholarship of Teaching and Learning in Higher Education. San Francisco: Jossey-Bass.

Hutchings, P., Huber, M. T., & Ciccone, A. (2011). *The scholarship of teaching and learning reconsidered: Institutional integration and impact.* San Francisco, CA: Jossey-Bass.

Jaschik, S. (2013, July 25). *Shake up for higher ed.* http://www.insidehighered.com/news/2013/07/25/obama-vows-shake-higher-education-and-find-new-ways-limit-costs.

Keeling, R. P. (Ed.). (2004). *Learning reconsidered: A campus-wide focus on the student experience.* Washington, DC: National Association of Student Personnel Administrators and American College Personnel Association.

Koester, J., Hellenbrand, H., & Piper, T. D. (2005). Exploring the actions behind the words "learning-centered institution." *About Campus, 10*(4), 10–16.

Koester, J., Hellenbrand, H., & Piper, T. D. (2008). The challenge of collaboration: organizational structure and professional identity. *About Campus, 13*(5), 12–19.

Komives, S. R. (1998). Linking student affairs preparation with practice. In N. J. Evans & C. E. Phelps Tobin (Eds.), *The state of the art of preparation and practice in student affairs: Another look* (pp. 177–200). Lanham, MD: University Press of America.

Kuh, G. D. (1996). Guiding principles for creating seamless learning environments for undergraduates. *Journal of College Student Development, 37*(2), 135–148.

Magolda, P. M., & Quaye, S. J. (2010). Teaching in the co-curriculum. In J. H. Schuh, S. R. Jones & S. R. Harper (Eds.), *Student services: A Handbook for the profession* (5th ed., pp. 385–398). San Francisco, CA: Jossey-Bass.

Martinez-Aleman, A. M. (2011). Social media and learning: A profile. In P. Magolda & M. B. Baxter Magolda (Eds.), *Contested issues in student affairs: Diverse perspectives and respectful dialogue* (pp.135–140). Sterling, VA: Stylus.

Moore, E. L., & Blake, J. H. (2007). Articulation, communication, dissemination: SHARING your experiences with others. In E. L. Moore (Ed.), *Student affairs staff as teachers.* New Directions for Student Services, no. 117. San Francisco, CA: Jossey-Bass.

Morrison, J. (2005). U.S. higher education in transition. *On the Horizon, 11*(1), 6–10.

National Association of Scholars. (2008, October). Rebuilding campus community: The wrong imperative. http://www.nas.org/polArticles.cfm?Doc_Id=251.

National Association of Student Personnel Administrators. (n.d.). *Standards of professional practice.* http://www.naspa.org/about/standards.cfm.

Nuss, E. M. (2003). The development of student affairs. In S. R. Komives & D. B. Woodard, Jr., (Eds.), *Student services: A handbook for the profession* (4th ed., pp. 65–88). San Francisco, CA: Jossey-Bass.

Pascarella, E. T., & Whitt, E. J. (1999). Using systematic inquiry to improve performance. In G. S. Blimling & E. J. Whitt (Eds.), *Good Practice in student affairs: Principles to foster student learning* (pp. 91–112). San Francisco, CA: Jossey-Bass.

Rapold, N. (2013, Sept. 3). Looking at modern campus life minus keg parties. *New York Times*, pp. C–6.

Ribera, T., Fernandez, S., & Gray, M. (2012). Assessment matters: Considering the scholarship of teaching and learning in student affairs. *About Campus, 16*(6), 25–28.

Roper, L. D. (2003). Teaching. In S. R. Komives & D. B. Woodard Jr., (Eds.), *Student services: A handbook for the profession* (4th ed., pp. 466–483). San Francisco, CA: Jossey-Bass.

Rudolph, F. (1977). *Curriculum: A history of the American undergraduate course of study since 1636.* San Francisco, CA: Jossey-Bass.

Saunders, S. A., & Cooper, D. L. (2001). Programmatic interventions: Translating theory to practice. In R. B. Winston, Jr., D. G., Creamer, & T. K. Miller (Eds.), *The professional student affairs administrator: Educator, leader, and manager* (pp. 309–340). New York, NY: Brunner-Routledge.

Schrecker, E. (2010). *The lost soul of higher education: Corporatization, the assault on academic freedom, and the end of the American university.* New York, NY: New Press.

Schroeder, C. C., & Mable, P. (1994). Residence halls and the college experience: Past and present (Eds.). In C. Schroeder & P. Mable (Eds.). *Realizing the educational potential of residence halls* (pp. 3–21). San Francisco: Jossey-Bass.

Schroeder, C. C., & Pike, G. R. (2001). The scholarship of application in student affairs. *Journal of College Student Development, 42*(4), 342–355.

Shulman, L. S. (2000). From Minsk to Pinsk: Why a scholarship of teaching and learning? *Journal of Scholarship of Teaching and Learning, 1*(1), 48–53.

Tuchman, G. (2009). *Wannabe U: Inside the corporate university.* Chicago, IL: University of Chicago Press.

Upcraft, M. L., & Schuh, J. H. (1996). *Assessment in student affairs: A guide for practitioners.* San Francisco, CA: Jossey-Bass.

Winston, R. B. Jr., Creamer, D. G., Miller, T. K. (Eds.). (2001). *The professional student affairs administrator: Educator, leader, and manager.* New York, NY: Brunner-Routledge.

Young, R. B. (2001). A perspective on the values of student affairs and scholarship. *Journal of College Student Development, 42*(4), 319–337.

CHAPTER NINE

MEASURING STUDENT SUCCESS

Models and Metrics

Lori Varlotta

The prevailing public narrative regarding the state of student affairs for US higher education in general, and public higher education in particular, is largely framed by five seemingly straightforward terms: *retention, graduation, student success, institutional effectiveness,* and *institutional efficiency*. In everyday parlance these terms, and the normative dialogue they shape, circulate without much scrutiny. It is plausible, for example, that educators could imagine hearing many of their constituents—prospective and current students, their parents, elected officials, and community leaders—engaging in conversations that go something like this: "Retention refers to students who stay at an institution to pursue their studies; graduation refers to those who have been retained long enough to complete degree requirements; and student success refers to those students who graduate with a degree in hand." It is conceivable that these same stakeholders might continue this line of thought by assuming that "effective institutions are those that graduate large numbers of students and efficient ones are those that facilitate timely progress to degree." Although this chapter does not address theories of retention, or models of practice relating to retention, there are numerous resources related to the aforementioned topics (see the retention resource list located at the end of this chapter).

On the surface, it seems natural, and inconsequential, for the public to deduce that a simple definition exists for each term and that the situation each describes is a monolithic one. From this vantage point, student success and institutional effectiveness and efficiency may be thought to look more or less the same from college to college. It also might seem innocuous for the public to assume that a causal relationship connects these concepts such that one leads to another: retention → graduation → student success → institutional effectiveness. Most educators, however, would agree that such perceptions are disturbingly simplistic ones that have the potential to shape a public dialogue that becomes normative (a good institution should have at least an 80 percent graduation rate; a successful student should be able to graduate in four years) and a state allocation process that glosses over the complex realities and variations at hand. To reduce the chances of perpetuating an uninformed public dialogue that may influence the way stakeholders, including legislators, reconfigure emerging funding models, this chapter urges readers to define these terms more explicitly and conceptualize the relationships that connect them. It is hoped that readers of this chapter will discover a counternarrative that brings into focus the intricacies and nuances that the prevailing narrative obscures. Toward that end, this three-part chapter gives readers the rhetorical, formulaic, and conceptual tools they need to sharpen their thinking, refine their rhetoric, and deliver to their own stakeholders a more accurate and detailed presentation of the enrollment situation unfolding in most of today's colleges and universities.

The chapter opens by presenting the prevailing graduation/degree completion narrative that circulates in many public and policy circles, including those at the highest levels of government. This commentary largely reflects a public consciousness that perpetuates one-dimensional definitions of terms such as *retention, graduation, student success,* and *institutional effectiveness* and infers causal relationships between them. Cognizant of the complexities that are glossed over through the unexamined use of these terms, several contemporary scholars have analyzed these terms in-depth. Many of these writers have refined a professional terminology that more accurately captures the enrollment patterns of today's students and informs the modern enrollment reports that are disseminated broadly throughout many university communities.

The chapter then uses the conceptual refinements introduced earlier to problematize the widely utilized Integrated Postsecondary Education Data System (IPEDS) federal graduation rate model. This graduation model was developed as part of the 1990 US Student Right-to-Know Act

(SRTK) to track and measure the progress of a very narrow cohort of students: first time, full-time students who begin their studies in the fall term. Concerned that a focus on such a narrow cohort limits and distorts the ways higher education's constituents think about, talk about, and advocate for education, five newer models that contextualize graduation rates in more sophisticated ways are shared. The Actual-to-Expected Graduation Rate Model, the Actual-to-Peer Graduation Model, the Disaggregated Graduation Rate approach, the Voluntary System of Accountability's (VSA) Undergraduate Success and Progress Rate (S&P), and the Student Achievement Measure (SAM) can potentially affect not only public rhetoric and academic modeling but also public policy.

Next, the chapter poses stretch questions that may make many internal and external stakeholders squirm. What if the two most important linkages explored in this chapter—the one between student success and graduation and the one between graduation and institutional effectiveness—are decoupled? To what extent can and should educators work to craft a definition of student success that does not have the earned degree as the ultimate goal? To what extent should educators consider an institution successful even if its graduation rate is very low? The chapter concludes by suggesting that there are some situations where a student and an institution might have achieved success despite the fact that the student did not earn a degree.

The Prevailing Student Success Narrative

This section presents the contemporary definitions of key educational terms and how they come together as "given" to shape the prevailing narrative in many general public and policy circles. In most of these circles, both the terms themselves—*retention, graduation, student success, and institutional effectiveness and efficiency*—and the relationships between them go unexamined. Although remaining somewhat unexamined at the general public level, several scholars have scrutinized these terms in detail.

The writings of Hagedorn (2012), Astin (1971), and Tinto (1987), for example, decouple artificial dichotomies such as retention/dropout that limit both rhetoric and accurate descriptions of reality. In doing so, they also expose the problems of conflating student success with graduation. Works like theirs help to explain why the cohort measured via the federal graduation rate erases the progress, success, and, sometimes, the graduation of what is likely to be the majority of today's college students.

Additionally, this body of literature prompts educators to hone in on the "standpoint" from which a term or measure is constructed and used.

Decoupling Artificial Dichotomies

To illuminate the dynamics of the binary rhetoric used in public discourse, Hagedorn (2012) probes the terms *retention* and *dropout*. Though typically used as antonyms to depict opposite situations—*retention* to describe staying in school until the degree is completed and *dropping out* to describe leaving school prematurely—in today's reality, they are not necessarily contradictory. Alexander Astin (1971) indicates, "A perfect classification of dropouts versus non-dropouts could only be arrived at when all of the students had either died without finishing college or had finished college" (p. 83). Like Astin, Hagedorn explains that dropout can only be temporarily defined since dropouts may become non-dropouts and vice-versa, depending on the specific snapshot of time when the data are reported.

From these perspectives, the retention/dropout dichotomy is a false one: students are often not simply one or the other. The college pathways traveled by today's students are often too complex and divergent to be demarcated by such a binary. Which students in the scenarios below, for example, are dropouts? Which students are retained?

Student A, who enrolls in a university, remains for one year, and stops out to return six years later

Student B, who enrolls in a university, remains for one year, and transfers to another university to complete the degree

Student C, who enrolls in college but does not complete any credits The next year the student re-enrolls part time and remains continuously enrolled to degree completion.

Students who enroll in college directly after high school, maintain full-time status, and earn degrees four years later are no longer in the majority. Instead, the students in the examples above represent the preponderance of students nationwide. Therefore, rather than rely on artificial binaries that erase the enrollment complexities of today's students, contemporary educators should construct terms that can tell their story, metrics that can chart their progress (even if their path is circuitous), and enrollment models that can capture their success.

Questioning Causal Relationships

A common assumption for many is that retention leads to graduation and graduation leads to (or is the most significant form of) student success. Often, the two latter phenomena—student success and graduation—become conflated. Although a few conversations at the university level have questioned whether graduation is a necessary or sufficient marker of student success, conversations at the public level have promulgated the notion that completing the bachelor's or associate's degree or attaining some type of certificate is the gold standard in student success.

A strong contemporary indicator of the link in the public consciousness between graduation and student success is President Barack Obama's (2009) American Graduation Initiative (AGI). A key part of Obama's AGI plan was to "fund innovative strategies to promote college completion. [These strategies were meant to include efforts to] increase college graduation rates and close achievement gaps" (White House: Office of the Press Secretary, 2009, p. 17). Obama's emphasis on college completion, that is, graduating from a university or earning a certificate from a community college, intensifies the public impulse to attach student success to graduation."

Expanding Cohorts That Count

One of the many problems of equating student success to graduation is related to the way that the US government requires universities and colleges to report their institution's graduation rate. The graduation rate that is tracked and reported via the widely used Integrated Postsecondary Education Data System (IPEDS) Graduation Rate Survey (GRS) is based on the data from a very narrow cohort of university enrollees: first time, full-time degree-seeking students who enrolled as part of a fall cohort and graduated within 150 percent of the normal time for completion (defined as six years for four-year institutions and three years for two-year institutions).

Having a mandated federal graduation rate that tracks this particular cohort only works well for a small cross section of US institutions—residential colleges that attract mostly traditional college-age students who enroll full-time and stay put. "But for many colleges and universities, that population is practically nonexistent, and for many others, that population is shrinking" (Jaschik, 2013, p. 4). Unfortunately, this means that despite its continued and broad use, the federal graduation rate is more of an artifact of a previous era than an accurate, contemporary measure or illuminator of present day reality.

Because the GRS model excludes from its data compilation and reporting functions students who are more typical these days, such as students A-C discussed earlier, it also excludes them from being considered as part of the higher education success story. The GRS survey and its graduation rate also fail to capture differences in institutional missions, not to mention differences in student goals and educational intentions. Since there appear to be few, if any, models that capture a student's own educational intentions and allow a student's personal goals to shape the evaluation of where he or she has ended his or her journey, the next subsection unearths the issues that grow out of this void.

Identifying Perspectives and Standpoints

In the minds of many educational stakeholders, leaving college before a degree is earned is a mark of failure for the student. Similarly, these same stakeholders probably perceive an institution's lack of ability to retain a student as a failure on the part of that institution. In the public policy dialogue, then, students starting college but not graduating is indeed a failure—two times over.

Such a view, however, may not be the one held by students who *stop out* temporarily or even those who leave college altogether. In terms of a stop out, consider Miesha who departs Institution X after her first semester when she is diagnosed with a serious health issue. She is unable to return. The following fall, Institution X counts her, in its formal enrollment report, as a dropout. After moving back to her parents' house and receiving a two-year series of medical treatments, Miesha attempts, once again, to pursue her degree. She enrolls as a part-time student at nearby Institution Y and earns a bachelor's degree six and one-half years later. Labeled a dropout by Institution X, will Institution Y label her a completer? Maybe, or maybe not: many institutions do not report the graduation rates for those students who protract their studies beyond the 150 percent of normal time measured by the GRS (Hagedorn, 2012, pp. 87–88). Hence, it may be the case that neither institution's reporting structures identified Miesha's educational journey or attainment of a degree as a success. Miesha, however, may beg to differ.

To accurately portray Miesha's journey, educators could look more carefully at how they employ terms and report out data. Institution Y's graduation rate, for example, could measure degree completion at time intervals that extend beyond the four- and six-year periods. Educators might also avoid using the words *persistence* and *retention* interchangeably.

Pointing to the definitions used by the National Center for Education Statistics (NCES), Hagedorn highlights a crucial difference between them. Along with NCES, Hagedorn argues retention is an *institutional* measure to describe one who stays at a particular college or university. Persistence is a *student* measure that describes a student's ongoing academic pursuits, continual or interrupted (and perhaps within or beyond the original institution) (2012, pp. 2–3). In this example, Institution X did not retain Miesha; still, Miesha persisted elsewhere and eventually earned the degree.

According to retention scholar Vincent Tinto (1987), students who leave college on a permanent basis similarly may not see themselves as failures (which the term *dropout* most often implies) or see their time at the university as squandered. Instead, they may view their time in postsecondary education as an important part of a healthy and productive process of self-discovery that has helped them mature socially and intellectually. Consider Sanjay, a licensed electrician, who has accompanied his wife to a US Air Force base across the country where she is scheduled to serve for two years. Shortly after the move, Sanjay enrolls in an open-access university to take classes in accounting, marketing, and finance because he has long-term plans to start a small electrical repair business. When Sanjay departs that institution two years later, as planned, he has successfully completed fifteen courses in the areas he intended to study. Is Sanjay a dropout? Is his story one of failure?

To get a handle on issues such as these, John Bean (1990) suggests that retention needs to somehow take into account student goals—that dropping out or failing to continue should be "defined in comparison to student outcome versus original intent" (p. 5). The vitally important part of the examples mentioned here is that they point to the necessity of stepping back and thinking about educational terms and assessments from a particular person's or agent's standpoint. Since the standpoint from which an enrollment journey is charted and measured has a direct impact on how the endpoint is described and evaluated, educators must ask: From whose vantage point is the story being told?

Neither Miesha nor Sanjay would be tracked via the GRS, let alone be considered a GRS success since neither of them falls into the cohort the GRS studies. It also appears that the GRS and the data it compiles and disseminates have no capacity to account for students' intentions; these inadequacies are problematic. But as it turns out, the GRS data may be able to tell a more contextualized graduation story if it is dissected in some of the ways promoted by newer models. The next section of the chapter presents several of those models and their potential impact on public policy.

Emerging Models and Metrics

To mitigate the shortcomings of focusing on the narrow cohort adopted by the GRS and the single graduation rate measure it advances, several national organizations and foundations are tweaking the graduation rate model to drill down to more complex, nuanced sets of data. Five such models are discussed next.

The first three models use the same GRS cohort but each one articulates the data in a specific way to highlight a more contextualized part of the graduation story (American Association of State Colleges and Universities [AASCU], 2006, p. 4). The first model weighs certain characteristics such as the academic readiness and socioeconomic status of an institution's first time, full-time students to calculate and compare the expected graduation rate at that particular institution with its actual graduation rate. The second model displays how the GRS graduation rates of like institutions compare to the rates of their peer institutions. The third model hones in on disaggregated data to identify and report the graduation rates of certain subgroups of first time freshmen such as under-represented minorities or Pell Grant–eligible students.

The fourth model, dubbed the Voluntary System of Accountability's (VSA) Undergraduate Success and Progress Rate (S&P), expands the cohort measured by the GRS to include transfer students and those students who enroll at terms other than the fall term. The College Portrait also supplements the graduation rate measure itself with a new student success metric called the Student Success and Progress (S&P) rate. The fifth model, Student Achievement Measure, pushes the VSA's S&P metric further as it tracks the two cohorts included in the S&P rate plus two cohorts of students seeking associate degrees and certificates. SAM also reports on multiple success measures for each cohort and uses more varied time frames than the federal system. The section concludes with an overview of the Tennessee model, which uses student and institutional characteristics and metrics developed in the other five models to evaluate institutional effectiveness and allocate funds.

Model 1: Actual-to-Expected Graduation Rate Model

The Actual-to-Expected Graduation Model, created by the Higher Education Research Institute at University of California, Los Angeles (UCLA) using Cooperative Institutional Research Program (CIRP) Freshman Survey data, identifies key inputs (for example, high school GPA and parental education) that are correlated with graduation rates and assigns a weight to those characteristics to determine the expected graduation rates for a particular institution. An institution can then compare its expected rate of graduation to its actual rate of graduation. The impact of such a comparison is seen in the hypothetical situation that follows.

A daily paper has just published the graduation rates of its two hometown institutions of higher learning. One is a private liberal arts college and the other is a large metropolitan university. Interestingly, both institutions have a 55 percent graduation rate. It may appear that both institutions are doing an equally effective (or ineffective) job of graduating students. However, when the characteristics of each institution's first time, full-time freshmen are considered, a different picture emerges. Based on the predictors of college completion and weighted inputs, "the liberal arts college would be expected to graduate 68% of its first time, full-time freshmen while the public university would be expected to graduate only 40%. According to this [model], the public university is performing better, [at least in terms of graduation rates], than the [liberal arts college]" (AASCU, 2006, p. 4). The public university's actual graduation rate far exceeds its expected one; the liberal arts college's actual rate, however, is much lower than its expected rate.

A form of the actual-to-expected graduation rate model can also be used to compare universities that are part of a single public system. An example of a comparison between two University of Tennessee campuses is presented later in this section.

Model 2: Actual-to-Peer Graduation Rate Model

The Actual-to-Peer Graduation Rate Model, developed by the Education Trust, a national nonprofit organization that promotes academic achievement (AASCU, 2006, p. 4), compares the IPEDS GRS graduation rates of one university to its peer institutions. Peer institutions share similar student demographics and have the same Carnegie classification (the country's most popular framework for describing institutional diversity).

To help the public make such comparisons, the Education Trust created a resource called College Results Online (College Results Online, 2013). This web-based tool compares graduation rates of any four-year college in the country to similar institutions based on 11 factors ranging from college admission exam scores to Pell Grant recipients. Designers of the model argue that its data are not only beneficial in identifying high-performing colleges and universities after taking into account factors such as mission, demographics, and financial resources but also useful for institutions with lower graduation rates to identify and address issues to improve their rates (AASCU, 2006, p. 4).

As an example of how this model might be useful, consider this scenario. The parent of a California high school junior with a 3.4 GPA and a 1200 SAT score is trying to determine to which public universities her daughter should apply. She knows her daughter is unlikely to be admitted to a top University of California campus like UC Berkeley or UCLA, but she is confident that her daughter will be admitted to a number of California State University (CSU) campuses. To get an inkling of how California State University, Northridge, for example, compares to San Jose State or San Francisco State, this mother and daughter may find the college results website (Education Trust, 2013) very helpful since it compares these campuses.

Model 3: Disaggregated Graduation Rate Approach

The Disaggregated Graduation Rate Approach also uses the GRS first time, full-time freshman cohort but it peels back the layers to consider cohort subgroups such as under-represented minorities, and Pell Grant–eligible students. This model can then compare the overall graduation rate of first-time, full-time students with the disaggregated graduation rates for subcohorts.

Research shows, for example, that low-income students often graduate at lower rates than high-income students. Therefore, a university could create a disaggregated graduation model that compares the graduation rates of students who have (1) full Pell Grant eligibility (typically those from the lowest socioeconomic backgrounds); (2) partial Pell Grant eligibility; (3) partial subsidized loan eligibility; and (4) no Pell Grant or subsidized loan eligibility (typically those from the highest socioeconomic backgrounds). The model would then allow educators to compare the graduation rates of these four subsets against themselves and against the GRS cohort at a single institution (AASCU, 2006, pp. 4–5).

The disaggregated rates could also be used in a cross-institution comparison to show how the graduation rates of low-income students at Institution A compare to the graduation rates of similar types of students at Institution B. Hence, the model allows two institutions to better understand how they stack up against each other when serving a similar group of students. It is conceivable, for example, to imagine that a Historically Black Master's Large may do as good a job, or better, of graduating African

American male students as the more selective Research I campus within the same system.

Model 4: The Voluntary System of Accountability's Undergraduate Success and Progress Rate

The Voluntary System of Accountability (VSA) is a national initiative by American Association of State Colleges and Universities (AASCU) and Association of Public and Land-Grant Universities (APLU) to design a voluntary accountability model for four-year public universities. The model has at its crux an electronic template called the College Portrait (College Portrait of Undergraduate Education, 2011) that member institutions use to populate data about their institution. 280 member institutions have posted their version of the College Portrait on their university's webpage so that prospective students, their parents, policy makers, and other stakeholders can access the information it contains.

A promising metric included in the College Portrait is the Success and Progress (S&P) rate. The S&P rate expands the GRS graduation rate metric by measuring the progress of two critical cohorts: first time, full-time students (like the GRS measures) and full-time transfer students. Other differences between the S&P rate and the federal graduation rate include:

The S&P rate counts both a two- and four-year degree as a completion.

The S&P rate continues to track students who graduate with a two-year degree and re-enroll at a four-year university, allowing the four-year degree to replace the two-year degree so that no completer is double counted.

The S&P rate is calculated for an academic year versus the fall term so that it can count students who enroll throughout the year.

The S&P rate includes students from the cohort who are still enrolled in a two-year or four-year institution six years later (even if they have not yet graduated).

Figures 9.1 and 9.2 illustrate the S&P rate.

Since the S&P tracks more than one cohort it has more students and more types of students in its purview than does the GRS. This means that larger numbers of students, including those who traveled circumlocutory paths, may count as a success. Expanding the groups of students who get tracked, whose paths get charted, and whose degrees count are crucial moves toward reshaping a narrative that heretofore erased them.

FIGURE 9.1 FIRST-TIME FULL-TIME STUDENTS STARTING FALL 2006

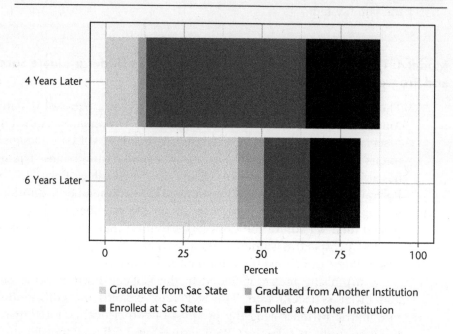

FIGURE 9.2 FULL-TIME TRANSFER STUDENTS STARTING FALL 2006

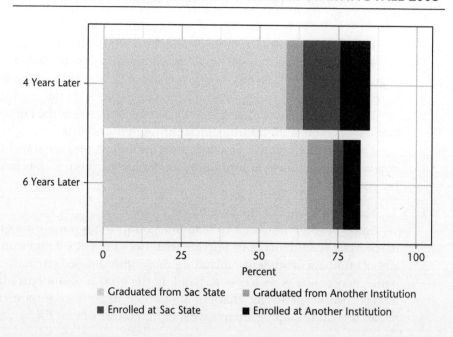

Model 5: The Student Achievement Measure

The VSA's College Portrait and its S&P metric vastly improve the limited methodology undergirding the federal graduation rate, but since the College Portrait was designed by organizations that focus on four-year public institutions, it was not intended to report out on the success rates of students attending other types of institutions. To address this part of the void, six national organizations representing four-year public, private, and independent colleges and community colleges collaborated in 2013 to design the Student Achievement Measure (Student Achievement Measure, 2013), a model that appears to be the most expansive one to date. Financially supported by the Gates and Carnegie Foundations, the Student Achievement Measure prompts myriad segments of higher education to work together on improving student success methodologies and reporting functions. The cohorts, outcomes, and time frames covered by SAM are well summarized by Scott Jaschik (2013).

For bachelor's degrees, SAM examines:

Full-time students attending college for the first time
Full-time students [transferring] to the reporting institution

For each group, SAM records who

Graduated from the reporting institution
Is still enrolled at the reporting institution
Transferred to/graduated from one or more subsequent institutions
Transferred to/is still enrolled at a subsequent institution
Has unknown current enrollment or graduation status

Data are reported for periods of four, five, and six years after enrollment.

For associate and certificate programs, SAM examines:

Full-time [native and transfer students] attending the reporting institution for the first time
Part-time [native and transfer students] attending the reporting institution for the first time

For each group, SAM records who:

Graduated from the reporting institution
Is still enrolled at the reporting institution
Transferred to one or more subsequent institutions
Has unknown transfer, current enrollment, or graduation status

The associate and certificate data are provided for periods of six years after enrollment (Jaschik, 2013).

SAM went live in October 2013, and a number of universities uploaded their data at that time. Although SAM is a somewhat newer model, its future potential is positive and far reaching.

The Tennessee Model

The models described above help educators and other stakeholders compile, analyze, and disseminate graduation data in ways that tell a more complete and contextualized success and progress story than the one told by the federal graduation rate. The models can do more than tweak rhetoric; however, they can also inform how policy makers and other decision makers allocate resources.

Tennessee was one of the first states to develop graduation models that are linked to resource allocation. In 2010, Tennessee Governor Phil Bredesen signed into law the Complete College Tennessee Act to bolster public financial support of higher education. The CCTA reflects a comprehensive educational reform agenda, but it has at the heart a clear and unapologetic college completion agenda (Tennessee Higher Education Commission, 2013).

Before CCTA, Tennessee, like the majority of states, made allocations to its public universities based on the commonly employed enrollment/full-time equivalent (FTE) model. When using such a model, a university's state allocation is largely determined by the number of students it enrolls. This type of enrollment model incentivizes enrollment growth or access—getting as many students as possible through the proverbial door. Since it focuses almost exclusively on the number of students admitted, it prompts little examination of and gives little reward for the number or percentage of students a university graduates, the output. To redirect a focus on output, the state of Tennessee has begun to incentivize, via a formal budget allocation formula, graduation rates over enrollment growth. Impressively, the state did not proceed with a performance pay plan that simply rewarded the ultimate outcome (graduation) with little regard to input. Instead, Tennessee set out to reward graduation rates, while taking into account the incoming students' attributes, characteristics, and backgrounds. Tennessee now funds its public institutions "through a form of performance pay that incentivizes progression and graduation with adjustments for adult and low-income student progression as well as weights that reflect the Carnegie Classification and unique mission of each institution"

(Wright, Fox, Murray, Carruthers, & Thrall, 2012, p. 22). This type of model is called an "input-adjusted outcome model."

The model recognizes that there is no simple or singular way to increase graduation rates across diverse institutions and that there is no one size fits all approach to identifying, comparing, and rewarding good graduation rates. Based on these very accurate realizations, myriad metrics—and weighted ones at that—have been born out of the CCTA's graduation model. For example, the weights given to the metrics of doctoral degrees and research activity are much higher at University of Tennessee, Knoxville, the system's selective Research University, than at University of Tennessee, Martin, a Master's Medium University.

The Tennessee Model is not a perfect one, but its features elicit several points that prompt educators to reexamine how they think about, talk about, and fund public higher education. First, the model uses contextualized or adjusted outcomes based on student characteristics and attributes in the calculation of institutional success and progress. Conversely, it reminds educators that raw measures of student outcomes that do not control for such inputs produce misleading signals of student success and institutional effectiveness. A second point is that the model factors institutional diversity into the calculation of graduation and success. In other words, what counts as a good, effective, and efficient institution may vary from one type of institution to another. Third, because the model recognizes the diversity of each institutional mission, it may be likely to ward off any push for access-oriented universities to raise graduation rates by adjusting upward their admission criteria and thereby reducing the very student population they were meant to serve. The next section of the chapter helps readers further contemplate points such as these.

Redefining Student Success

As part of a 2013 congressional hearing, Tracy Fitzsimmons, president of Shenandoah University, urged members of the House Education and Workforce Committee *not* to focus simply on graduation rates: "There are a number of members on this committee that did not graduate from college and clearly they have been highly successful" (Laitinen, 2012, p. 3). Fitzsimmons's testimony—a bit jarring in places—makes an impassioned case that many dropouts are indeed successful. Even if readers do not align completely with Fitzsimmons, they, like this chapter, may be searching for a model that views the graduation rate as a viable but incomplete metric for student success. To conceptualize a more far reaching definition of student success, this chapter suggests that educators capture, analyze, and report out on one or more of the student inputs and outcomes described below.

Student Intention

A student's own intentions should matter (at least somewhat) in the calculation of success. It is conceivable to consider Sanjay a successful student. After all, he set a clear, measurable, ambitious goal, and he achieved it in the time and manner he had hoped. If the student's intention is not to earn a degree per se but to learn X, Y, and Z from a certain cluster of classes, educators need to use a model that can measure goals achieved against original or revised intentions.

Self-Reported Accounts of Success and Satisfaction

A student's self-evaluation or report of what she has accomplished could feasibly be part of a success metric. In the assessment world, for example, there is some credibility in measuring and analyzing indirect learning outcomes, what a student says she has learned and the extent to which she is satisfied with what was offered and learned.

Direct Learning Objectives or Demonstrated Outcomes

The demonstrated outcomes (as compared to self-reported ones) are important components of a more comprehensive model for student success. Some postsecondary institutions (Northern Arizona, Southern New Hampshire University's new College for America, an associate degree-granting institution, and Capella University) have launched credential programs that include a competency-based transcript. As one example, students enrolled in a Northern Arizona online bachelor's program will receive two official transcripts: the conventional one and a competency report. The latter one is meant to be shared with potential employers even though it includes no courses or grades. Instead, it includes a list of lessons and concepts mastered and assigns a level of achievement attained (Fain, 2013).

This type of competency-based reporting gives educators and higher education stakeholders a glimpse of how formal credentialing might be changing. It also reinforces observations like those from *New York*

Times columnist John Friedman (2013), who says that we now live in a world where there will be "less interest in how you acquired the competency ... and more demand to prove that you mastered the competency" (2013, p. 6). If competency becomes a primary metric for success then it will be imperative to evaluate students beyond or in addition to degree completion. Friedman calls for institutions to embrace a model that goes beyond traditional metrics to capture "stuff learned" versus "time served" (p. 6).

Self-Directed Learning

The emergence of Massive Open Online Courses (MOOCs) is rapidly redefining the way people think about education and success. A 2013 study by the Duke Center for Instructional Technology and the Office of the Provost revealed that learner intent is a critical metric for measuring MOOC success rates. In a pre- and postsurvey assessment of Duke University's first MOOC, researchers determined that student intent, course satisfaction, and course outcome were better barometers of student success than course completion. Although MOOCs differ from traditional courses and degree programs, they may be the catalyst educators need to connect intentionality and learning outcomes to student success.

Student Financial/Career Status

Students, their parents, and other educational stakeholders may be quick to identify financial security and job security as two other markers of student success. A success model that can accurately capture or reinforce the findings of the US Census Bureau might be helpful. For example, the 2012 US Census Report estimates the lifetime earnings of a high school graduate to be about $1.371 million compared with $2.422 million for a bachelor's degree graduate. This gives a college graduate a lifetime earnings advantage of more than $1 million (Farnen, n.d., p. 3). Additionally, a model that compared job earnings and employment statistics to student loan indebtedness would also be valuable. A 2012 study conducted by policy and communications consulting firm Hamilton Place Strategies found that the median income for all college graduates was $46,412 while average student loan debt was $28,720 (Fairchild, 2013, p. 2).

Although it is crucial for educators to get a better handle on student success, it is equally important to nuance and contextualize institutional success. In a 2012 *Texas Tribune* article, the University of Texas at El Paso (UTEP) was criticized for its low four- and six-year graduation rates. The president of UTEP, Diana Natalicio, rebutted by asserting that "the graduation rate is much more about the demographics of [an institution's] student population than it is about the [institution's] efficiency or performance" (Hamilton, 2012, p. 11). Aligned with Natalicio's sentiment, this chapter continues to look for models that take one or more of the factors below into account when calculating institutional success.

Actual-to-Expected Rates. If institutional success is to be measured accurately, it must consider the demography of any given institution's student population. Student demography is a vital component for reflecting institutional mission and for measuring institutional performance.

Extended Time Frames. Although most graduation models measure degree completion at the four- and six-year mark, they do not readily broadcast completions that occurred beyond those time frames. For institutions with a large number of low-income students, adult learners, and full-time workers, a longer time frame would provide a more accurate measure of completers.

Student Transfer. As institutional swirl becomes a more common phenomenon, educators must be able to track and follow the circuitous pathways that many students travel. This is especially important for students who toggle between community colleges and universities in an effort to get the classes they need to complete their degree.

Peer Comparisons. For all of the reasons alluded to in this section of the chapter, it is edifying to judge one institution against others in a similar peer group. Comparing the graduation rates of a research intensive university against an open-access university makes little sense.

Postgraduation Outcomes. Institutional success may also in part be determined by how well graduates or even departers do after they leave the institution. A model that captures the type of statistics related to job placement, annual salary, and civic/community engagement activities, statistics that have been notoriously difficult to collect, would be a practical and productive tool.

Conclusion

This chapter challenges readers in three ways. First, it asks readers to probe the prevailing narrative to dismantle dichotomies, question causal relationships, expand cohorts who count, and identify standpoint. Second, it asks readers to explore how models and metrics could be redesigned to reconfigure funding formulae for public institutions. Finally, it asks readers to contemplate the controversial—ponder the extent to which student and institutional success need to be connected to graduation. These ideas are broached in the spirit of helping students, educators, stakeholders, policymakers, and other decision makers consider how insufficient terminology and overly simplistic thinking can influence all of our beliefs about student and institutional success. Finally, this chapter encourages readers from the academy to go one step further and move this way of thinking into action. Hopefully readers will use the refined concepts, models, and metrics presented here to reframe the way their institution thinks about and formulates its own policies and goals around student success.

References

American Association of State Colleges and Universities (AASCU). (2006). Graduation rates and student success: Squaring means and ends. *Perspectives*, 1–14.

Association of Public and Land-Grant Universities (APLU). (2008). *Voluntary system of accountability (VSA) methodology for calculating the success and progress rate*. https://cp-files.s3.amazonaws.com/7/SP_Methodology.pdf.

Astin, A. W. (1971). *Predicting academic performance in college: selectivity data for 2300 American colleges.* New York, NY: Free Press.

Bean, J. P. (1990). The strategic management of college enrollments. In J. P. Bean (Ed.), *Why students leave: Insights from research.* San Francisco, CA: Jossey-Bass.

Belanger, Y., and Thornton, J. (2013, February). *Bioelectricity: A quantitative approach. Duke University's first MOOC.* http://dukespace.lib.duke.edu/dspace/bitstream/handle/10161/6216/Duke_Bioelectricity_MOOC_Fall2012.pdf.

Carnegie Classification of Institutions of Higher Education. (2010). http://classifications.carnegiefoundation.org. College Portrait of Undergraduate Education. (2011). *Voluntary system of accountability.* http://www.Collegeportraits.org.

Education Trust. (2013). *College results online.* http://www. collegeresultsonline.org.

Education Trust. (2013). *College rankings online.* http://www.collegeresults.org/collegeprofile.aspx?institutionid=110608.

Fain, P. (2013, August). Competency-based transcripts. *Inside Higher Ed.* http://insidehighered.com/news/2013/08/09/northern-arizona-universitys-new-competency-based-degrees-and-transcripts.

Fairchild, C. (2013, July). Student loan debt will exceed median annual income for college grads by 2023: Analysis. *Huffington Post.* http://www.huffingtonpost.com/2013/07/10/student-loan-debt-median-income_n_3573683.html.

Farnen, K. (n.d.). How much more money does a college graduate make than just a high school graduate? *Global Post.* http://everydaylife.globalpost.com/much-money-college-graduate-make-just-high-school-graduate-8703.html.

Friedman, T. L. Mar. (2013). The professors' big stage. *New York Times.* http://nytimes.com/2013/03/06/opinion/friedman-the-professors-big-stage.html?_r=0.

Hagedorn, L. S. (2012). How to define retention: A new look at an old problem. In A. Siedman (Ed.), *College student retention: Formula for student success* (pp. 81-100). Lanham, MD: Rowman & Littlefield.

Hamilton, R. (2012, March). UTEP seeks success beyond graduation rate. *Texas Tribune.* http://www.texastribune.org/2012/03/02ut-el-paso-looks-success-beyond-graduation-rates/.

Jaschik, S. (2013, June). New measure of success. *Inside Higher Ed.* http://www.insidehighered.com/news/2013/06/24/college-associations-introduce-new-ways-measure-student-completion.

Laitinen, A. (2012, September). Great news? Reports of College completion crisis grossly overstated. *Higher Ed Watch.* http://higheredwatch.newamerica.net/blogposts/2012/great_news_reports_of_college_completion_crisis_grossly_overstated-71985.

National Center for Education Statistics (NCES). (2003). *The integrated postsecondary education data system (IPEDS).* http://www.nces.edu.gov/ipeds/.

Student achievement measure. (2013). http://www.studentachievmentmeasure.org.

Student Right-to-Know and Campus Security Act, Public Law 101–542 (1990).

Tennessee Higher Education Commission. (2013). http://tn.gov/thec/complete_college_tn/ccta_summary.html.

Tinto, V. 1987. *Leaving college: Rethinking the causes and cures of student attrition.* Chicago, IL: University of Chicago Press.

White House: Office of the Press Secretary. (2009, July). President Obama's American graduation initiative in Warren, Michigan. http://www.whitehouse.gov/the_press_office/Excerpts-of-the-Presidents-remarks-in-Warren-Michigan-and-fact-sheet-on-the-American-Graduation-Initiative/.

Wright, D. L., Fox, W. F., Murray, M. N., Carruthers, C. K., and Thrall, G. (2012, September). College participation, persistence, graduation, and labor market outcomes: An Input-adjusted framework for assessing the effectiveness of Tennessee's higher education Institutions, report of HCM Strategists' *Context for Success Project.* Washington, D.C.: HCM Strategists. http://www.hcmstrategists.com/contextforsuccess/papers.html.

Resources

TABLE 9.1 RESOURCES FOR THEORIES, PRACTICES, AND PROGRAMS RELATED TO STUDENT RETENTION

Resource	Description	Publisher/URL
American College Personnel Association (ACPA)	ACPA hosts conferences and publishes scholarly materials (*Journal of College Student Development*) related to a variety of student affairs topics. At any given time, a conference or publication may be related to student retention.	http://www2.myacpa .org/publications
Association of American Colleges and Universities (AAC&U)	AAC&U hosts meetings, institutes, and posts and publishes materials related to a variety of topics in higher education, including student success. At any given time, a publication may feature articles related to student retention.	http://www.aacu.org/
Association of College and University Housing Officers-International (ACUHO-I)	ACUHO-I hosts regional and international conferences and offers publications (*Journal of College and University Student Housing*) related to a variety of student housing topics including retention. ACUHO-I also utilizes a web-based blog for critical topics including a blog dedicated to retention topics.	http://www.acuho-i .org
Center for the Study of College Student Retention	The Center for the Study of College Student Retention, founded by Dr. Alan Seidman, is an online resource that provides a list of the major retention theories and an extensive list of references related to student retention.	http://www.cscsr.org/ about.htm

(continued)

TABLE 9.1 (*continued*)

Resource	Description	Publisher/URL
The Education Trust	The Education Trust hosts conferences and offers publications in an effort to promote student success as well as close the achievement gap among underrepresented minority students. The Education Trust's publications often feature articles and research related to student retention and success.	http://www.edtrust.org
Journal of College Student Retention: Research, Theory & Practice	The *Journal of College Student Retention: Research, Theory & Practice*, edited by Dr. Alan Seidman, provides current research and articles related to student retention.	Published by Baywood Publishing Company. https://www.baywood .com/journals/ previewjournals.asp? id=1521-0251
National Academic Advising Association (NACADA)	The NACADA website includes the Association's Clearinghouse of Academic Advising Resources, which contains links to articles and resources related to academic advising—a topic that is routinely connected to issues of retention. Related periodicals include the *NACADA Journal* and *Academic Advising Today: Voices of the Global Community*.	http://www.nacada.ksu .edu/
National Association of Student Personnel Administrators (NASPA)	NASPA hosts regional and national conferences and offers publications related to student affairs. At any given time, NASPA may release publications that feature articles and research related to student retention.	http://www.naspa.org/ publications
Association for Orientation, Transition and Retention in Higher Education (NODA)	NODA holds conferences and offers publications (*Journal of College Orientation and Transition*) related to orientation, college transitions, and student retention.	http://www.nodaweb .org/? page=Publications

TABLE 9.1 (*continued*)

Resource	Description	Publisher/URL
National Resource Center for the First-Year Experience and Students in Transition	The organization hosts conferences and offers publications related to first-year experience and other transition periods associated with the undergraduate experience. Successful transitions are routinely connected to issues of retention. Related periodicals include the *Journal of the First-Year Experience & Students in Transition* and *E-Source for College Transitions*.	http://www.sc.edu/fye/
Student Services: A Handbook for the Profession (various editions)	This handbook—updated regularly—provides information on a wide range of student affairs topics, including retention issues.	Recent editions published by Jossey-Bass, San Francisco

CHAPTER TEN

MAINTAINING AND MODELING EVERYDAY ETHICS IN STUDENT AFFAIRS

Jon C. Dalton, Pamela C. Crosby, Aurelio Valente, and David Eberhardt

Janice Jenkins hung up the phone and reflected on the words of the vice president: "I need your help on this, Janice," he said. "The faculty is very concerned about student cheating, especially by athletes, and I think we need to be very firm in handling this situation. Your recommendation of disciplinary probation may be too lenient, and I would like for you to consider suspension in this case. Please get back to me on this matter by tomorrow."

Janice Jenkins, dean of students at Eastland College, had called her supervisor to tell him that she had completed her formal review of an academic conduct code violation by Rod Simmons, a freshman member of the football team who had been found guilty of plagiarizing an English paper from an Internet source. Based on her review, she was recommending that the student be placed on probation because of his first offense, his lack of familiarity with rules for using source material for writing assignments, and his apparent genuine remorse. She did not anticipate the vice president's disagreement with her proposed sanction.

She stared at the student's open folder before her and thought about the vice president's words, "I need your help ... ," and "consider suspension in this disciplinary case." Janice was troubled by conflicting thoughts: Have I been unreasonable in my review of this student's conduct? Am I being consistent with what I have done in the past? How would my actions affect the well-being of the student? Do I owe the vice president my loyalty when he asks for my help? Should his judgment about this situation trump my own? What will happen to me if I disagree with him? What is my duty as dean of students? For the first time since becoming dean, Janice was vacillating, unsure of what she ought to do and afraid of making a wrong decision.

Sooner or later, every student affairs professional comes to grips with a compelling ethical situation that can become a defining moment in his or her professional and personal life. Such questions are unavoidable given that the work of student affairs is steeped in ethical considerations and conflicts. Examples of common ethical questions in student affairs include:

- How do I balance punishment and forgiveness when disciplining a student?
- How do I determine responsibility in a sexual assault complaint in which the alleged victim was intoxicated?
- When does providing equal opportunity for disadvantaged students require special considerations and efforts?
- Should college athletes be compensated for the use of their images?
- Should colleges restrict activities on major religious holidays out of respect for religious traditions and student religious practices?
- Should birth control resources be provided by the student health service?
- Should students' online communications be treated as purely personal and private?
- Is it appropriate to date a student?
- Should I side with students in a complaint against the college?
- On what grounds should I give someone "special consideration"?
- When should I intervene in the life of a troubled student?
- Can I be loyal to my supervisor and still disagree with her or him?
- Should I tell the whole truth about student binge drinking to the local television reporter?
- When should I encourage students to compromise their convictions for the sake of the common good?
- Should students enrolled in massive open online courses (MOOCs) have the same rights and privileges as campus-based students?
- Was I right to suspend the fraternity?
- Should I fire an unproductive long-time employee who has several young children?
- What should I do when my conscience conflicts with institutional rules and policies?

This chapter provides an introduction to the role of ethics in student affairs work in higher education. We identify and discuss examples of everyday ethical issues to assist practitioners in recognizing and understanding the moral terrain of professional work. We also present and discuss a conceptual framework for examining ethical issues and making moral decisions. We offer and discuss practical examples for applying the conceptual model in professional roles. In order to illustrate the variety of approaches to ethics that are utilized and emphasized in the profession, we review professional ethics statements of several student affairs national organizations. Finally, we offer observations and recommendations to assist student affairs professionals when confronting difficult ethical issues and decisions.

What Is Ethics?

Ethics is the study of how individuals ought to act in moral conflict situations where issues of right and good are at stake. Ethics centers on an examination of two moral questions. *What ought I to do? What is my responsibility?* These questions are at the heart of ethics because they require that a judgment of right or wrong, good or bad, be made and that the criteria used to make the judgment be clearly evident and justified. Ethical issues arise from those situations that generate questions about the rights and welfare of individuals or of one's moral character (Callahan, 1988).

Failure to act ethically can call into question one of the most important qualities an individual can possess as a professional: personal integrity. Consequently, ethics lies at the heart of professional competence and is an indispensable trait of effective student affairs practice. Richard Niebuhr (1999) used the analogy of driving a car to describe the complexities of ethical decision making. When driving a car, he argued, one has to obey the rules of the road, keep control of the vehicle, respond to unexpected situations that may arise, avoid harming others, and still successfully manage to reach one's destination. In much the same way, moral decisions, like driving a car, have to be made in the context of dynamic circumstances in which many things are happening and one must try to keep things under control, avoid harming others, and reach a desirable outcome. While it is possible to study ethical dilemmas as isolated and static cases, real-life ethical decision making always takes place in dynamic situations in which moral decisions, like driving down the highway, must be managed in the context of some very fluid and often compelling circumstances.

We use the phrase "everyday ethics" to refer to the types of ethical problems that are common to college student affairs work as well as to the application of some practical principles and strategies that can help staff to resolve ethical issues in their work.

Ethics as the Art of Making Wise and Responsible Decisions

Managing ethical problems is more of an art than a science. Fletcher (1966) noted that there are no formulas, prescriptions, or instructions that guarantee correct moral decisions. While guidelines and principles can help to illuminate the process of ethical decision making, they do not guarantee moral outcomes. Making wise and responsible ethical decisions depends in part upon experience, practice, and reflection in much the same way that becoming a good driver requires both considerable training and practice. Moreover, ethical decision making must be responsive to unique situations that vary from case to case so that moral maxims must be translated to ever-changing contexts. The goal of ethical decision making is, therefore, to determine how to be responsible in the midst of unique and changing circumstances involving issues of right and wrong.

The dynamic and contextual nature of everyday ethics requires regular practice, discussion, and reflection in real-life circumstances of professional practice. Aristotle (Bostock, 2000) argued that skill in moral judgment is developed through the regular exercise of making practical ethical decisions in daily life. One becomes competent in ethical decision making through practice over time in many different situations. Effective training in ethics enables one to think quickly and automatically without having to rely upon an authority to point out specific steps.

Why Be Concerned About Ethics?

There are several practical reasons for paying attention to ethics in the work of student affairs:

- Ethical conflicts represent some of the most complex and difficult situations confronted in professional life. Issues such as sexual assault; academic cheating; racial and ethnic injustice; and alcohol abuse threaten institutional integrity and professional credibility.
- Effectiveness as a professional is judged in part by one's ability to make ethical decisions in a competent, fair, and consistent manner.

- Student affairs professionals are expected to act in accordance with established professional ethics that define the moral norms of good practice.
- Personal integrity, the bedrock virtue of an individual's credibility and authenticity, depends upon the ability to maintain and model ethical reasoning and behavior.
- Finally, good ethical practice helps to ensure that all who are involved in moral conflict situations receive fair and equal consideration.

Paying attention to ethics, therefore, is an intrinsic aspect of being a capable leader, an effective professional, and a good human being.

Five Domains of Ethical Responsibility

When managing any serious ethical issue, student affairs professionals usually find themselves engaged with five different types or domains of ethical responsibility. These five domains represent critical relationships with individuals, groups, and institutions to which they have a special duty and obligation as student affairs professionals. These five domains of ethical responsibility include (1) student welfare, (2) the institution, (3) the profession, (4) the community, and (5) personal conscience. All of these domains of duty and responsibility represent critical relationships in which a special ethical claim is made upon student affairs staff. These five domains of ethical responsibility are illustrated in Figure 10.1.

Each of these domains of professional work represents an area of professional responsibility and obligation. Each of them lays some claim to the ethical obligations of student affairs professionals and may at times compete and conflict in their claims. These five ethical domains are briefly described following.

The Student

The holistic welfare of students is the moral center of student affairs work. Students, as individuals and in groups, are where one begins in efforts to determine how to manage and model ethics in professional practice. Although there are a number of competing priorities in professional responsibilities, the first and most important moral obligation is the welfare and development of students. It is important to stress this moral

FIGURE 10.1 DOMAINS OF ETHICAL RESPONSIBILITY

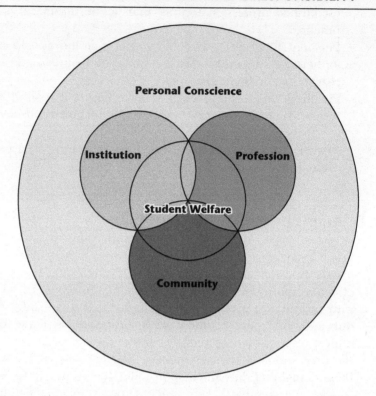

priority because students generally have so little power in higher education and are so transient.

> *Scenario.* Janice, the dean of students, has an ethical responsibility to do all she can to promote the holistic welfare of Rod Simmons, the new student athlete who has violated the school's academic honor code. She must consider his needs and welfare as a student, a new student, an athlete, and a human being. She must also consider the impact of his conduct and her disciplinary sanction on the holistic welfare of other students in the university.

The Institution

The institution that employs student affairs professionals has a strong claim on their ethical responsibilities through the employer-employee relationship, but even more strongly, it can be argued, through the institution's stated mission and values. By accepting employment with a college or university, a student affairs professional affirms and agrees to promote actively the institution's mission and values.

Scenario. The dean of students must consider her responsibilities to her supervisor and the institution she both works for and represents. She must determine what her proper duty is to both of them and how she can fulfill those expectations in a manner consistent with the holistic welfare of the student involved.

The Profession

By joining professional associations and subscribing to their standards of ethical practice, student affairs professionals agree to be guided by the standards of conduct determined by practitioners in the field. Subscribing to a profession's ethics is one of the ways in which professionals assure the public that their occupation will be performed in accordance with certain standards (Boylan, 2000).

When they join professional associations, student affairs staff are required to consider the association's ethical principles and rules when confronting ethical problems and issues in their work. Some professional organizations have disciplinary procedures to address violations of their standards and some do not. Procedures for documenting good standing and managing disciplinary procedures are especially important in situations where licensure or certification is required for professional practice.

Some student affairs staff work in professional positions but do not join professional associations. They, too, have a responsibility to observe the ethical standards of the professional group associated with their area of work, but this responsibility is less formal and documented.

Scenario. The dean of students has an obligation to apply the standards of ethical practice endorsed by her primary professional organization that apply to situations like the one she is confronting. As a consenting member and representative of the profession association, she has made a commitment to implement their ethical standards in professional practice.

The Community

Student affairs professionals work in the context of a surrounding community that includes a broad network of laws, rules, relationships, and mores. For student affairs professionals, this community consists of parents, local police and health officials, community service agencies, state agencies, news media, homeowners, bar owners, alumni, school officials, and a host of other individuals, organizations, and groups that are connected to the institution in a variety of different ways. This community exerts legal, moral, and political influence on student affairs professionals and can affect the manner in which ethical issues are discussed and decided. Some aspects of the community adhere to particular values and moral beliefs and expect student affairs professionals to observe them in their activities.

> *Scenario.* The dean of students must be aware of and considerate of the moral, social, and legal standards of the surrounding community of which she is both a member and an official, particularly as these standards may relate to the situation she is confronting. Community values and standards usually have less direct influence on professional practice, but they provide an important context for moral decision making that should be considered.

Individual Conscience

In addition to the previously discussed four domains of ethical responsibility, it is important to include the fifth domain, individual conscience, in our discussion of managing and modeling ethics in professional practice. Conscience is the domain of one's most deeply held personal beliefs and convictions that are formed by life experiences and commitments. Conscience is highly individual and deeply rooted in both emotion and reason. It bridges the realms of rationality and emotion but is not entirely grounded in either. Conscience is the individual's internal court of last resort that reflects his or her deepest convictions about what is fundamentally right and wrong. Conscience is important in ethics because it provides an integrative function in ethical decision making that helps to define personal responsibility. It helps to interpret, integrate, and balance the various realms of responsibility we have previously discussed.

In deciding how to proceed with a professional ethical problem, student affairs professionals should be guided by these five domains of ethical responsibility. The first four domains of responsibility—that is, student holistic welfare, institution, profession, and community—are viewed through the lens of conscience, which provides a necessary personal context and helps one weigh priorities and claims using ethical principles guided by conscience.

Personal conscience also provides what one might call a "comfort fit" in exploring ethical responsibilities. Do I feel right about this course of action? Can I be proud of this decision? Would I feel good about explaining this decision to people I respect? Thus, conscience helps to integrate the process of moral decision making by providing a lens through which to interpret moral responsibilities and decisions.

Personal conscience can and should trump other moral considerations in certain situations. If student affairs professionals believe that a decision or action would compel them to violate a sacred personal belief or value, then they must decide whether to follow their conscience. Student affairs professionals must cultivate and use their best personal judgments when deciding how to apply stated standards of ethical practice in particular situations so as to bring about maximum benefit to all involved. However, there is no free ride in commitment to conscience. When deciding to follow one's conscience, the student affairs professional must also weigh and accept the practical consequences of acting on the basis of individual conscience.

> *Scenario.* The dean of students tries to separate her purely personal beliefs and values as much as possible from the circumstances of the problem she is seeking to resolve. In the end, however, she knows she must be true to her deepest personal convictions about what is right and good to do in this situation. These convictions may at times run counter to what is endorsed by the institution, her profession, and her community and require courage to act on conscience and to accept the consequences of that moral stance.

Ethics in the Student Affairs Profession

To guide student affairs professionals in ethical decision making and conduct, a number of professional organizations have developed ethical standards and codes of ethics. These standards and codes are intended to do three primary things: (1) promote the interests and welfare of those who are served by professionals, (2) protect the professional, and (3) advance the profession. Ethical standards help to insure the greatest good for those who are served and to protect against self-interest and personal gain that can undermine professional credibility as well as the credibility of the profession.

The professional field of student affairs work is currently comprised of more than forty different professional associations (Council for the

Advancement of Standards in Higher Education, 2012). Many of these professional associations have adopted formal ethical codes of professional practice that prescribe ethical standards for their members. While there is considerable overlap in the ethical standards of these student affairs associations, there are also considerable differences. Discussion continues as to whether or not student affairs can rightfully be understood as a profession (Blimling, 2001; Carpenter, 2001), but for the purposes of this chapter it is treated as one. Certainly there is much common agreement about the ethical responsibilities of student affairs professionals, as this chapter demonstrates.

In an effort to identify ethical principles that are shared in common by the various student affairs professional associations, the Council for the Advancement of Standards in Higher Education (CAS) conducted a study of professional ethical codes. Their review identified seven ethical principles that are shared across the various student affairs professional groups in higher education (CAS Statement, 2006). These shared ethical principles include:

1. *Autonomy:* Respecting freedom of choice
2. *Nonmalfeasance:* Doing no harm
3. *Beneficence:* Promoting the welfare of others, especially students
4. *Justice:* Being fair and respectful to others
5. *Fidelity:* Being faithful to our word and duty
6. *Veracity:* Being truthful and accurate
7. *Affiliation:* Fostering community and the public good

There are several interesting aspects about these commonly shared ethical principles. First, they encompass the five ethical principles identified by Kitchener (1985) that are widely utilized in the profession today. Second, they have the advantage of recognition by CAS as well as endorsement by all of the member professional associations that have professional ethical codes. These seven shared ethical principles do not supplant the individual ethical codes of student affairs professional groups, but they do offer a foundation of core ethical standards for the student affairs profession as a whole. The seven CAS principles are used in this chapter as normative ethical standards that can be useful in addressing ethical issues.

Because CAS standards must be general enough to represent the shared core values of thirty-five associations, CAS's summary of ethical principles cannot depict all of the specificity of interests and values that are unique to particular associations. As principles become more general and inclusive of diverse organizations, they necessarily become increasingly abstract, providing more silhouette and shadow and less context and detail. Following is a brief overview of the ethics statements of four student affairs organizations that are members of CAS. The overview illustrates some of the differences in approach to professional ethics and the special emphasis placed upon the importance of the holistic welfare of students in student affairs work. The ethical statements and/or core values of these four organizations illustrate the diverse ways that values or domains are structured and the many ways that students are emphasized.

ACPA's Statement of Ethical Principles and Standards

The American College Personnel Association (ACPA) is made up of members from both public and private colleges and universities in the United States and abroad, and includes administrators and faculty who work, teach, and/or research in the areas of student affairs as well as graduate students who pursue degrees in student affairs and higher education administration.

The purpose of ACPA's *Statement of Ethical Principles and Standards* is to provide a context for thinking about ethical issues relating to student affairs practice and to assist members to acquire sensitivity to problems relating to potential ethical dilemmas. The *Statement* also clarifies expected standards of behavior and helps members to monitor their own conduct. Finally, it helps to increase an awareness of standards of behavior in others through a spirit of collegiality (American College Personnel Association [ACPA], 2006). The *Statement* is based on Kitchener's (1985) ethical principles, as noted earlier.

In contrast to the organization of CAS principles, whose standards are presented according to value statements, ACPA's *Statement* consists of four standards, each representing what has been identified in this chapter as a *domain of ethical responsibility*:

1. Professional responsibility and competence
2. Student learning and development
3. Responsibility to the institution
4. Responsibility to society (ACPA, 2006)

Subsumed under each standard are specific statements describing ethical actions that embody the standard. For example, under "Student

Learning and Development" are indicator statements of moral actions including:

> 2.3 Abstain from all forms of harassment, including, but not limited to, verbal and written communication, physical actions and electronic transmissions,
>
> 2.4 Abstain from sexual intimacy with clients or with students for whom they have supervisory, evaluative, or instructional responsibility,
>
> 2.5 Inform students of the conditions under which they may receive assistance. (ACPA, 2006, p. 3)

The fact that an entire section is devoted to issues focusing on the treatment of, and interaction with, students, reflects ACPA's emphasis on the importance of student growth and development, a domain central to its mission. ACPA underscores its commitment to accountability to students by stating, "Student development is an essential purpose of higher education. Support of this process is a major responsibility of the student affairs profession" (ACPA, 2006, p. 3).

NASPA's Guiding Principles

NASPA—Student Affairs Administrators in Higher Education (NASPA) is a professional organization of student affairs administrators, faculty, and graduate students. NASPA describes itself as an association committed to serving ""a full range of professionals," who help to "cultivate student learning and success in concert with the mission of our colleges and universities" (NASPA, n.d., p. 1).

Reference to ethical standards is markedly general and described in the phrase "Committed to high moral principles exhibiting authentic, honest, just, and ethical behavior" and subsumed under *integrity*, which is one of the four guiding principles; the other three are *innovation, inclusion*, and *inquiry* (NASPA, n.d., col. 2). There is no specific interpretation of how those principles are to be operationalized. Therefore, it is clear that NASPA relies on individual institutions to apply these principles to and incorporate these principles into their own specific contexts and daily practice.

ACUI's Core Values and Code of Ethics

The Association of College Unions International (ACUI) is a professional organization that encourages college union and student activities professionals to build strong campus communities through educational resources and programs. Its members include students as well as professionals in college student union administration who may be, for example, student union directors, program directors, or food service administrators, among others.

The purpose of ACUI's core values of *unconditional human worth, joy, caring community, innovation, communication,* and *integrity* (ACUI, n.d., para 3), as well as their *Code of Ethics,* is to articulate the organization's expectations of members' "professional behavior" (ACUI, n.d., p. 3). Under each core value are indicator statements.

One subsection under the core value *integrity* is devoted specifically to students and is entitled, "Students as Individuals." It includes the following:

- Members view each student as a unique individual with dignity and worth, and with the ability to be self-directed.
- Members are concerned for the welfare of all students and work to provide an environment that encourages personal growth, effectiveness, creativity, and responsible citizenship.
- Members respect the rights of students and promote responsible behavior.
- Members respect the privacy of students and hold in confidence personal information obtained in the course of the staff/student relationship. (ACUI, n.d.)

ACUI emphasizes that its professional members serve students in many different roles, including as "teachers" and "role models" (ACUI, n.d.).

NODA's *Statements of Ethical Standards*

The National Orientation Directors Association (NODA) is an association of professionals in the field of orientation, transition, and new student programs in the academic community. NODA's professional standards are intended to be used as a "benchmark for ethical practices" (NODA, n.d., p. 2). The purpose of NODA's *Statements of Ethical Standards* is to lend support to its members in choosing actions that will further college students' "positive educational outcomes" (NODA, n.d., p. 1).

NODA's *Statements of Ethical Standards* are organized by domains of ethical responsibility. Six domains focus on the accountability of orientation professionals to the following groups with whom they interact: students as staff members and students in transition; parents, guardians, and families of students in transition; professional colleagues; the institution; higher education and student development as a profession; and corporate sponsors or partners with whom the orientation program has established contractual relationships. Of the six domains, two are devoted especially to ethical decisions focusing on students: student staff members and students in transition. For example, the standard that pertains to interactions with students in transition, stipulates that professionals should

- Ensure that students receive accurate and adequate information necessary for decision making
- Ensure that students have access to relevant materials, and that materials are available in multiple formats, including text, Web resources, and other adaptive technologies when possible
- Recognize the diversity of experiences of students in transition, and work to meet the various needs of new students, transfer students, adult learners, and other special populations (NODA, n.d., p. 7)

As the examples here illustrate, there are differences in approach and emphasis among the various student affairs professional organizations in how they articulate ethical standards and priorities. Despite these differences, they share a strong commitment to the welfare and development of college students, and this commitment forms the foundation of the profession's ethics.

The Holistic Welfare of Students as the Moral Focus of Student Affairs Work

Most professions claim a guiding moral purpose and have an ethical focus that helps to define their deepest values (Anderson, 1980). The medical profession, for example, affirms the moral principle of preserving life as central to professional practice. The legal profession emphasizes the core principle of justice, while journalists claim truth as their guiding moral purpose. These defining ethical principles serve to guide practitioners of these professions and to anchor their practice to a strong moral foundation.

The enduring central moral purpose of student affairs work has been and continues to be the holistic welfare of college students. This central and defining ethical purpose provides the basic moral foundation that guides our profession and is the beginning point for the examination of professional ethics. From the inception of the profession in American higher education, student affairs practitioners have stressed the importance of learning in the context of students' holistic needs and development.

This holistic educational focus runs deep in the profession's history and legacy and has played an important role in shaping contemporary student affairs professional practice. Bryan, Winston, and Miller (1991) note that "above all, student affairs practitioners are engaged in the business of helping students improve their lives" (p. 10).

A professional ethics grounded in an ethic of care for students' holistic welfare emphasizes that the well-being and development of every student are a central purpose of professional practice. Starting with this core purpose provides an important moral foundation for constructing the ethics for the profession. Although the student affairs profession has grown rapidly in scope and complexity over the past century, its moral focus, its ethical center, continues to be on students and the values associated with their welfare, learning, and development.

A Multi-lens Perspective on Managing and Modeling Everyday Ethics

Ethics is often viewed from a top-down perspective, in which particular normative ethical principles are identified and then applied to specific moral situations in professional work. This approach has been used often in the past and is examined in several publications on ethics in the student affairs profession (Canon & Brown, 1985; Fried, 2003; Kitchener, 1985; and Lampkin & Gipson, 1999). Kitchener's (1985) five ethical principles mentioned earlier have been especially influential among student affairs practitioners and are widely cited in student affairs literature and utilized in professional ethics statements (for example, American College Personnel Association).

Normative ethical constructions like Kitchener's have the advantage of viewing ethics from a conceptual framework of relatively fixed ethical principles that provide continuity and clarity across many different kinds of ethical issues. Using the principles-based approach is appealing to some because it provides unchanging standards or guidelines for making ethical decisions. Those who use normative ethics treat similar cases similarly and pay less attention to the particular circumstances of the individuals involved (Laney, 1990). To use the analogy of driving, ethical principles are like the rules of the road that guide our choices and behaviors while driving down the highway.

The disadvantage of normative ethics can be, however, that approaching moral conflicts from the vantage point of relatively fixed moral principles can sometimes be abstract and disconnected from the everyday ethics of professional work. Normative ethical approaches also give less recognition to some powerful human motivations that can in some ethical situations overwhelm reason. Moreover, people can interpret abstract principles so differently that professionals may make considerably different decisions in similar situations and thus not treat those affected equally. Rules of the road are less useful when one is contemplating how fast to drive in the growing dusk on a little used, unmarked, and unfamiliar side road.

At the other end of the continuum in approaches to ethics is the perspective of contextualism or situation-oriented ethical decision making. In this approach, sometimes called the "case-based" orientation (Lampkin & Gipson, 1999, p. 75) more emphasis is placed on the unique circumstances and conditions of specific moral situations that confront the professional. Considerable attention is also given to the personality and psychology of the individual facing an ethical dilemma (Laney, 1990). This perspective offers much greater flexibility and relevance in particular cases than the moral principles approach, but it has a serious downside in that there is much less continuity, uniformity, and predictability from one ethical decision to the next.

The practical work of solving everyday ethical problems in student affairs work requires both a situation-specific understanding of moral problems and decision makers and the ability to apply relevant normative ethical principles. Consequently, solving everyday ethical problems is facilitated by the use of both normative and contextual ethical approaches. The authors refer to this method of incorporating both approaches in managing ethical issues as a "multi-lens perspective" because it starts with a perspective on the individual circumstances of moral situations and also incorporates the perspective of relevant moral principles in the process of decision making in ethical situations.

Moreover, we argue for a bottom-up approach, in which one begins ethical deliberation by first examining the practical moral situations and responsibilities that student affairs professionals confront in their everyday work. As much as possible ethical deliberation should be kept as closely connected to the real ethical issues, roles, and responsibilities that student affairs professionals encounter in their everyday responsibilities.

It is also important to connect professional ethics to the broader moral and social context in which professional practice takes place. As Thompson (2007) notes, ethics tends to focus on individuals, but ethical issues are very often connected to the broader social and political environments of institutions and communities.

The Moral Landscape of Student Affairs Work

Ethical practice in student affairs work requires an understanding of the moral landscape of ethical problems that one is likely to confront in his or her professional responsibilities. In this section of the chapter, some of the most characteristic everyday ethical issues that student affairs staff encounter in their work are examined. In order to ensure that this approach to ethics is grounded in the real-life experiences of student affairs staff, we reviewed the literature on ethics in student affairs and conducted an online survey of student affairs professionals using several professional and regional Internet listservs. The survey asked student affairs colleagues to identify examples of ethical issues they had encountered in their work and the domains of ethical responsibility involved. In all, more than 150 unique ethical conflict situations were identified using this process.

Approximately half of respondents indicated they were in middle management positions, and about one third indicated they were new professionals in entry-level positions. The remaining respondents identified themselves as serving in senior leadership positions. Most respondents reported that they worked for four-year public institutions; however, community colleges, professional, and proprietary institutions were also represented among the respondents.

An important observation that can be drawn from this review of ethical issues is that many of the ethical dilemmas one encounters in the moral landscape of student affairs work are not unique to this field. The ethical conflicts that arise in the work of student affairs encompass many of the same ethical problems—such as dilemmas involving dishonesty, deception, integrity, loyalty, conflict of interest, and favoritism—that are common in other professions. What makes these issues distinctive in student affairs work are the special contexts and circumstances in which they occur and the unique moral status accorded the holistic welfare of college students.

Common Ethical Issues in Student Affairs Work

The following ethical issues are culled from the literature and from the issues most frequently mentioned in the online survey conducted by the authors. The list is by no means exhaustive.

Institutional Alcohol Policies and Practices. One of the most common student affairs ethical dilemmas arises out of the conflict of trying to serve students' welfare on one hand while also promoting institutional rules and values on the other. This conflict can be seen especially in the area of institutional alcohol policies and enforcement. Colleges and universities generally have strict policies restricting alcohol consumption by students. Often these policies are ignored or downplayed by institutions at alumni and student events on home football game weekends or on other special college occasions. Student affairs staff thus find themselves teaching and enforcing a set of college rules and policies that students quickly learn are unevenly applied. Colleges and universities have rules and policies that prohibit underage alcohol consumption but, in practice, often look the other way when underage students party. Inconsistent application and enforcement of institutional policies on alcohol presents a common type of ethical dilemma for student affairs staff.

Bias and Prejudice on Campus. Over the past half-century colleges and universities have become increasingly diverse and plural. Major efforts have been made by institutions to accommodate and integrate an increasing diversity of college students. Nevertheless, many college students continue to be stigmatized and victimized on campuses because of racial, ethnic, religious, and class bias and prejudice. When this happens, students are oppressed and unjustly denied a level playing field for success in college. Prejudice and bias disenfranchise students from many important opportunities for learning and development that college offers and can cause hurtful insult and injury. Bias and prejudice can also disrupt the social fabric of a campus and create considerable conflict. Sometimes bias and prejudice are expressed in overt forms of intolerance, but often they are conveyed through unintentional institutionalized practices and social rituals that create a culture of insensitivity and bias. Practicing justice and equality in the treatment and care of college students is one of the most important moral obligations of student affairs staff and other college staff. In an age of increasing globalism and diversity, this moral imperative will continue to be crucial for higher education and student affairs staff to follow.

Sexual Misconduct. An often cited statistic notes that 20–25 percent of traditional-age female students will be victims of some type of sexual misconduct during their time in college (White House Task Force, 2015; Wilson, 2014), indicating the seriousness of this issue and the likelihood that student affairs professionals will deal with this issue in their roles.

Sexual misconduct has received much attention nationally in recent years through government action, including strongly-worded guidance (Ali, 2011) and subsequent investigations of dozens of campuses by the US Department of Education's Office of Civil Rights (Kelderman, 2014), a White House task force that labeled sexual violence on college campuses a national epidemic (White House Task Force, 2015), and legislative measures like the Campus Sexual Violence Elimination Act (Campus SaVE), which demanded greater reporting of incidents (Clery Center, 2013). Advocacy groups and defendants' rights organizations have added their own critiques of institutions for doing both too little or too much regarding these issues (Kelderman, 2014; Wilson, 2014). These external actions, and the significant media coverage that has accompanied them, have created immense pressures on college officials regarding their response to incidents of sexual misconduct.

Many institutions have responded with new or revised policies and conduct procedures about sexual violence that intensified the challenging ethical dilemmas. Included among these challenges are significant tensions between priorities for survivors' privacy and accommodation of their needs, while meeting respondents' rights and demands for fair and impartial hearings. In addition, officials must try to increase awareness of sexual violence incidents on campus while attending to the public perceptions of institutions, and balance their allocation of resources toward preventive educational efforts along with providing meaningful support for response to incidents. Student affairs practitioners are uniquely poised to handle these pressures on campuses and the dilemmas they create. Increased national attention and the resulting emerging resources have provided student affairs professionals both the support and opportunity to lead institutions in addressing sexual misconduct issues and navigating the challenges involved, but they must be prepared to do so, relying on the mission and values of promoting student welfare.

Personal Relationships with Students. A pervasive ethical dilemma that challenges professionals in student affairs involves personal relationships with students. Student affairs staff are often young themselves and not far removed in age from college students. Moreover, student affairs staff probably spend more time with students than anyone else on campus (Kuh, 1991). These circumstances often lead to close personal relationships between staff and students and can sometimes cross, or appear to cross, the boundary of propriety and ethical responsibility. Ethical dilemmas easily arise when student affairs staff enter into romantic relationships with students or socialize with students in ways that seem to compromise professional standards or responsibilities. Because of their close rapport with students, student affairs staff often are seen as powerful role models and mentors, and this special relationship makes ethical conduct especially important.

Confidentiality and Privacy. Other common ethical dilemmas for student affairs staff involve confidentiality and privacy of student information. Institutional policies regarding confidentiality of student information are grounded in federal and state laws as well as professional codes of ethics that are intended to foster student privacy and welfare. However, when student affairs staff become aware of physical, mental, or emotional health problems, such as clinical depression, learning disabilities, or diabetes, of specific students, they often feel a sense of responsibility to help these students. Yet privacy policies restrict the information that can be divulged to any other individuals including parents and guardians. Alerting other university officials who come in contact with these students could help avert serious problems, but to do so could compromise students' confidentiality and privacy. Defining the limits of student confidentiality and privacy in electronic communications has posed many new ethical considerations for student affairs staff.

Exception, Privilege, and Favoritism. Another common type of ethical dilemma presents itself when student affairs staff are asked to make exceptions to policies for students in special situations. For example, a popular or well-connected student, such as the relative of an institutional trustee, becomes involved in a disciplinary situation. The judicial affairs department receives a phone call from the president's office asking to be kept informed of the case. In such a situation student affairs officials then face dilemmas about how to proceed, how to appropriately discipline the student, and to whom to report their findings and actions once decisions are made.

A similar type of ethical dilemma is created when a staff member is asked to consider an exception to an admission denial decision. For example, an influential parent threatens to sue a college or university for denying enrollment to his son or daughter. The college dean responds by applying subtle pressure on the student affairs leader chairing the admissions appeals committee to admit the student through the appeal procedures. Since many prospective students with much stronger academic credentials have already been denied through the appeal process, the staff member faces a serious ethical decision.

Punishment. Student affairs staff are often responsible for student conduct and judicial procedures on campus and also carry responsibility for administrative operations which must be enforced through procedures and regulations. Consequently, student affairs staff frequently find themselves in situations in which they must administer sanctions and penalties for violations of one type or another. Determining the most appropriate discipline for students can be especially problematic for student affairs staff, since they are strongly oriented to the holistic welfare of students and may be uncertain about the uses of punishment.

Fairness and Justice. Many of the ethical conflicts student affairs staff face are related to situations that challenge their sense of fairness in the workplace. For example, professionals often must consider challenging policies, supervisors, or practices they may believe are not ethical in nature. When staff members feel that a departmental policy is unfair or unevenly applied, should they challenge it when doing so may compromise their professional standing? Such policies may include unfair hiring and promotion decisions, inequities in applying and distributing compensation and vacation time, and inappropriate use of departmental funds. Ethical issues involving concerns about fairness and justice are among the most common and difficult ethical issues that confront student affairs staff. They call into question an administrator's commitment to equal treatment and consideration of all parties involved in a conflict situation.

Uses and Misuses of Computer Technology and Social Media. A new arena of ethical issues has arisen in the past twenty years associated with the expansion of computer technology and its uses and misuses. The pervasive use of cell phones, social media, online videos, photographs, and blogs by college students has generated many ethical problems such as cyberbullying, sexual harassment, racial and ethnic intolerance, academic cheating, and privacy concerns among others. While many of these ethical issues are not new to higher education they are often framed and communicated in highly public and volatile ways by the new technology. In order to respond effectively to these issues student affairs staff must understand not only the ethical issues involved but also the new technology that mediates and frames the content of these ethical problems.

Finally, although practitioners generally share a common moral focus on student welfare, individuals within the same department may differ on how they view ethical issues and come to different conclusions about what is required ethically. Moreover, as student affairs staff progress through positions of increasing responsibility, they may interpret ethical issues differently depending on their experience, responsibilities, and judgment.

Deciding and Acting in Ethical Conflict Situations

The goal of ethics is to enable an individual to act on the basis of moral reflection and commitment. Using ethical principles and reason to determine ethical responsibility in moral conflict situations must finally be affirmed in behavior in order to be judged ethical. The requirement of acting on ethical decisions is also a reminder that courage is always a necessary virtue of ethical decision making and behavior. Ethical decision making, like driving a car, requires action in order to be responsible. Failure to act in an ethical situation as well as in driving has real consequences.

A multi-lens approach to ethics consists of (1) identifying and understanding the nature of the ethical conflict with which one is presented, (2) examining the appropriate domain(s) of ethical responsibility that are entailed, (3) applying appropriate ethical principles to the moral conflict, and (4) deciding and acting on the basis of one's ethical conclusions. Table 10.1 summarizes these four components of ethical action.

TABLE 10.1 COMPONENTS OF ETHICAL DELIBERATION AND ACTION

Everyday Ethical Issues*	Domains of Responsibility	Ethical Principles	Decisions/Actions
Rules/Policies	Students	Autonomy	Specific actions
Confidentiality	Institution	Nonmalfeasance	taken in ethical
Relationships	Profession	Beneficence	conflict situations
Punishment	Community	Justice	based on
Fairness	Conscience	Fidelity	multi-lens
Truthfulness		Veracity	approach
		Affiliation	

*Most common types of ethical issues

Using a Moral Compass in Everyday Ethics

This chapter has examined the knowledge, processes, and skills that constitute the components of a student affairs professional's moral compass. A compass points the way to some known objective or goal and is used when one is uncertain about current position or direction. A moral compass points the way to what is right or good when one is uncertain about the right thing to do in any situation. A moral compass utilizes established ethical benchmarks and decision-making criteria to point the way to one's moral responsibility in specific situations.

While using a moral compass helps student affairs professions to navigate through ethical dilemmas, some individuals succeed and some fail when faced with tough moral choices. There are at least four common reasons or explanations that account for success or failure when confronting ethical conflicts.

First, some student affairs staff have a moral compass that helps them to recognize very early that a situation involves serious ethical considerations. Some individuals, however, lack the moral sensitivity to recognize that an issue is ethical in nature, and this oversight can inhibit them from taking appropriate action quickly and effectively. Thus, the ability to perceive quickly that a problem has a serious ethical consideration is important for helping student affairs staff to anticipate ethical problems. The sensitivity of one's moral compass is developed by studying ethics, observing ethical role models, and managing real-life ethical conflicts.

Second, some student affairs staff develop a feeling or sensitivity for the specific domain(s) or type of ethical responsibility that is implicated in the ethical situation confronting them. Others may recognize that a situation involves ethical issues but not be able to determine which specific domains of ethical responsibility make the greatest claims on their attention and commitment.

Third, some student affairs staff are aided in acting in morally responsible ways by taking advantage of the conceptual tools of ethical analysis and reflection or, in essence, learning how to use their moral compass. Others can fail to reason clearly about the appropriate application of ethical principles in ethical situations so that principles fail to be effective guides and illuminators to understanding and decision making.

Fourth, some student affairs staff act with conviction and courage in situations that test one's moral fiber. Others lack the will or courage to act on what they determine to be the right thing to do. Self-interest, fear, and uncertainty can erode one's best intentions to do the right thing. Thus, managing and modeling ethics in student affairs require skills in perceiving, feeling, thinking, and acting in ethical situations.

Conclusion

Acting ethically keeps the professional's work on track. A moral compass points the way to what matters most in professional work. It helps one to make tough decisions and gives continuity to leadership and example. Striving to do the right thing helps keep order in the wide array of choices that one must face in professional work and makes it possible to sleep at night after agonizing over conflicts and dilemmas. Being an ethical professional makes it possible to take unpopular stands when taking the easy way is so inviting. Being ethical gives one an enduring place to stand in the midst of constant change. Ethical competency is indispensable for student affairs professionals who are both blessed and burdened with being among the most influential role models and mentors for today's students in higher education.

References

Ali, R. (2011, April 4). Letter to colleague from assistant secretary for civil rights. Washington, DC: Department of Education, Office of Civil Rights. http://www2.ed .gov/about/offices/list/ocr/letters/colleague‐201104.pdf.

American College Personnel Association. (2006). *Statement of ethical principles and standards.* http://www.myacpa.org/au/documents/Ethical&uscore;Principles& uscore;Standards.pdf.

Anderson, R. M. (1980). Applied ethics: A Strategy for fostering professional responsibility. [Special Issue]. *Carnegie Quarterly, XXVII* (2&3).

Association of College Unions International. (n.d.). *Mission of the association.* http:// www.acui.org/content.aspx?menu&uscore;id=90&id=186& amp;ekmensel=c580fa7b&uscore;90&uscore;0&uscore;186&uscore;1.

Bostock, D. (2000). *Aristotle's ethics.* Oxford: Oxford University Press.

Blimling, G. S. (2001). Uniting scholarship and communities of practice in student affairs. *Journal of College Student Development, 42,* 381–396.

Boylan, M. (2000). *Basic ethics.* Upper Saddle River, NJ: Prentice Hall.

Bryan, W., Winston, R., & Miller, T. (1991). *Using professional standards in student affairs.* New Directions in Student Services, no. 53. San Francisco, CA: Jossey-Bass.

Callahan, J. C. (1988). *Ethical issues in professional life.* New York, NY: Oxford University Press.

Canon, H. J., & Brown, R. D. (1985). *Applied ethics in student services*. San Francisco, CA: Jossey-Bass.

Carpenter, D. S. (2001). Student affairs scholarship (re?)considered: Toward a Scholarship of practice. *Journal of College Student Development, 42*, 301–318.

Clery Center for Security on Campus. (2013). The Campus Sexual Violence Elimination (SaVE) Act. http://clerycenter.org/campus‐sexual‐violence‐elimination‐save‐act.

Council for the Advancement of Standards in Higher Education. (2006). *CAS Statement of Shared Ethical Principles*. Washington, DC: Author.

Council for the Advancement of Standards in Higher Education. (2012). *CAS professional standards for higher education* (8th ed.). Washington, DC: Author.

Fletcher, J. (1966). *Situation ethics: The new morality*. Philadelphia, PA: Westminster Press.

Fried, J. (2003). Ethical standards and principles. In S. R. Komives, D. B. Woodard, & Associates (Eds.), *Student services: A handbook for the profession* (pp.107–127). San Francisco, CA: Jossey-Bass.

Kelderman, E. (2014, Fall). College lawyers confront a thicket of rules on sexual assault. *In context: Campus sexual assault*. Special Report from the *Chronicle of Higher Education*. http://chronicle.com/items/biz/pdf/sex&uscore;assault&uscore;brief&uscore;fall2014.pdf.

Kitchener, K. (1985). Ethical principles and ethical decisions in student affairs. In H. Canon & R. Brown (Eds.), *Applied ethics in student services*. New Directions for Student Services, no. 30. San Francisco, CA: Jossey-Bass.

Kuh, G. D. (1991). Characteristics of involving colleges. In G. D. Kuh & J. H. Schuh (Eds.), *The role and contributions of student affairs in involving colleges* (pp. 34–48). Washington, DC: National Association of Student Personnel Administration.

Lampkin, P., & Gipson, E. (1999). *Mountains and passes: Traversing the landscape of ethics and student affairs administration*. Washington, DC: National Association of Student Personnel Administrators.

Laney, J. T. (1990).Through thick and thin: Two ways of talking about the academy and moral responsibility. In W. W. May (Ed.), *Ethics and higher education* (pp.49–66). New York, NY: Macmillan.

National Orientation Directors Association. (n.d.). *NODA statements of professional ethics*. http://www.nodaweb.org/?page=ethical&uscore;standards.

NASPA—Student Affairs Administrators in Higher Education. (n.d.). *About NASPA*. http://www.naspa.org/about/default.cfm.

Niebuhr, H. R. (1999). *The responsible self: An essay in Christian moral philosophy*. Louisville, KY: Westminster: John Knox Press.

Thompson, D. (2007). *What Is Practical Ethics?* http://www.ethic.harvard.edu/welcome&uscore;practical.php.

White House Task Force to Protect Students From Sexual Assault. (2015). *Not alone: The first report of the white house task force to protect students from sexual assault*. http://www.whitehouse.gov/sites/default/files/docs/report&uscore;0.pdf.

Wilson, R. (2014, Fall). Presumed guilty. *In context: Campus sexual assault*. Special Report from the *Chronicle of Higher Education*. http://chronicle.com/items/biz/pdf/sex&uscore;assault&uscore;brief&uscore;fall2014.pdf.

CHAPTER ELEVEN

APPLYING PROFESSIONAL STANDARDS

Stephanie A. Gordon

A profession is defined by the principles, guidelines, and practices of the individuals who work in that career. A standard is "something considered by an authority or by general consent as a basis of comparison; an approved model" (Dictionary.com, 2013). Professional standards serve as a framework for professional practice, help socialize new members to the field, provide a structure for self-regulation of the occupation, and offer the public a means through which they can understand and evaluate the programs and services offered by persons in the field.

This chapter provides an overview of professional standards in student affairs. The chapter begins by situating student affairs professional standards within the broader context of standards in K–12 and higher education. Next, the historical origins of professional standards in student affairs are briefly discussed before turning to an extended discussion of professional standards for contemporary practice in student affairs. Finally, the chapter offers three case illustrations for ways that a student affairs administrator can assess their institutional effectiveness, provide a departmental focus on standards, and apply professional standards to their own personal professional development. With the increased scrutiny on higher education, it is even more important that the established standards and guidelines provide a framework for practice and benchmarks that can be assessed and evaluated throughout the year.

Standards in K–12 Education

Standards in education at the K–12 sector have focused on the establishment of learning standards for students, the creation of assessments to measure students' achievements, and imposing sanctions if those standards or learning goals are not met. "Standards-based reform is a strategy that includes specifying [not only] what is to be learned, [but also] devising tests to measure learning, and establishing consequences of performance" (Betts & Costrell, 2001, p. 1). Many states have tied public funding to the results of a standards evaluation and the negative consequences often have an impact on the schools with the most to lose. There is great controversy over standards-based reform, as increased standards for high school graduate have served to detain some students from earning diplomas (Betts & Costrell, 2000).

The Common Core State Standards (CCSS) were developed through a collaborative effort of the states, community leaders, and parents. Implemented in 2010, CCSS are intended to focus on helping students succeed in college and beyond. There is much controversy about the CCSS and individual states are beginning to opt out of the program and use their own standards.

As K–12 continues to evolve the standards on which they base their curriculum, it is important that higher education also work to understand the CCSS and how the continuum of learning can develop with standards of professional practice. Higher education must take heed of how the standards reform process has occurred in the K–12 environments, as the challenge of student learning and success has arrived at the doorsteps of US colleges and universities.

Standards in Higher Education

In comparison to standards in other professions, standards related to higher education are fairly new because "there were relatively few colleges and universities, only a small portion of the population attended and the curriculum was not of concern to many" (Alstete, 2004, p. 7, and Arminio, 2009). Interest in standards and accreditation began in the early twentieth century due to the great inconsistency and confusion regarding the preparation necessary for college admission. Because creating a national admissions process consistent with criteria was beyond the scope of state governments and because the federal government had no authority at the same time to intervene, regional intra-institution associations began to set minimal standards for accreditation of an institution (Alstete, 2004; and Arminio, 2009). Accreditation came to be defined as a systemized process for recognizing institutions that have met a prescribed level of performance by an established formalized authoritative body to engender public trust (Mable, 1991).

Alstete (2004) offered the following timeline and eras regarding standards and institutional accreditation:

- 1880s–1900s: Admissions standards formalized, postsecondary institutions defined
- 1900s–1970s: Specialized discipline standards established and promulgated
- 1970s–present: Focus on self-study, coordinated evaluations and periodic review

According to Murray (2012), with approximately seventy nongovernmental and voluntary agencies, American higher education's accreditation process serves some or all of the following purposes including consumer protection, the fair and accurate public disclosure of higher education institutions and programs, and the continuous improvement of those institutions and programs (p. 53). There are six regional accreditation organizations which publish a set of standards intended to promote quality and improvement in higher education in all 50 states and territories (See Table 11.1).

Although each operates independently, the organizations collaborate and are members of the Council on Higher Education Accreditation (CHEA), which advocates for the voluntary system of accreditation with the government and provides information to the public on accreditation outcomes (Saunders, 2011; and Stoops & Parsons, 2003). Many educators are critics of the accreditation process because an assumption is made that the evaluations are focusing on the wrong processes and procedures to assure quality. Most critics note that the focus should be on student success and competent graduates and not on the managerial aspect of university operations. Student learning and competent graduates may mean different things to different people, and so the discrepancies remain.

Over the years, student affairs at various colleges and universities have played a larger role in higher education accreditation. The need for standards in student affairs was evident in the 1970s. Rather than

TABLE 11.1 REGIONAL ACCREDITATION ORGANIZATIONS' JURISDICTION

Name	Regional Authority	URL
Middle States Commission on Higher Education	Washington, DC, New York, Pennsylvania, Delaware, Maryland, New Jersey, Puerto Rico, US Virgin Islands	http://www.msche.org
New England Association of Schools and Colleges	Connecticut, Maine, Massachusetts, New Hampshire, Rhode Island, Vermont, Canada	http://www.neasc.org
North Central Association of Colleges and Schools	Arizona, Arkansas, Colorado, Illinois, Indiana, Iowa, Kansas, Michigan, Minnesota, Missouri, Nebraska, New Mexico, North Dakota, Ohio, Oklahoma, South Dakota, West Virginia, Wisconsin, Wyoming	http://www .ncahigherlearningcommission .org
Northwest Commission of Colleges and Universities	Alaska, Washington, Oregon, Idaho, Montana, Nevada, Utah	http://www.nwccu.org
Southern Association of Colleges and Schools	Alabama, Florida, Georgia, Kentucky, Louisiana, Mississippi, North Carolina, South Carolina, Tennessee, Texas, Virginia	http://www.sacscoc.org
Western Association of Schools and Colleges	California, Hawaii, Guam, Pacific Basin	http://www.wascsenior.org/wasc

Source: Adapted from Saunders (2011, p. 23).

having "outsiders" define the roles and responsibilities for student affairs, thirty-two professional associations hoping to establish and promulgate professional standards and guidelines which encouraged state-of-the-art thinking about educational programs and services joined together to establish the Council for the Advancement of Standards in Higher Education (CAS) in 1979 (CAS, 2012).

Standards provide a framework for education, models for professionalism, connection to the ethical actions and interactions of individuals, as well as a conglomeration of what is valued within the profession. As referenced in chapter 1, *The Student Personnel Point of View* (SPPV), written by Esther Lloyd-Jones, H. E. Kawkes, and L. B. Hopkins in 1937, established that student personnel work in American higher education was "major concern, involving the cooperative effort of all members of the teaching and administrative staff and the student body" (American Council on Education, 1937, p. 5). Throughout a subsequent revision in 1949 and a follow-up perspective in 1987, the basic tenet remains: the profession of student affairs is integral to the higher education experience. Although the SPPV was not meant to be used as a standards-setting document, it provided an outline for the importance of student affairs in supporting the academic mission, advocating for student learning, and providing an environment that supports individuality and community engagement. For many years, it was debated whether or not student affairs was a field or actually a profession (Penney, 1972), but it is clear that the work of student affairs educators has a positive impact on student learning and therefore, standards for the profession are a necessary reality for individuals in the field.

Standards in the Contemporary Context of Student Affairs

The significant changes in higher education over the past ten years have brought about new ways of working with students through full-time student affairs assessment professionals, case managers, campus intervention teams, and online student services. Due to concerns about acts of violence, generational changes with posttraditional students and returning student veterans, the technological changes, and more legal and compliance issues than ever before, what is considered a "standard" in student affairs must be reexamined based on the new body of knowledge. Student affairs professionals have a number of ways to use standards, including program development, continuous improvement, self-study for accreditation or review, staff development, student development program planning, program evaluation, acceptance of and education about student affairs services and programs, political maneuverability, budgetary assistance, ethical practice, and standardized language in functional areas (Arminio & Gochenauer, 2004; Bryan & Mullendore, 1991; Jacobs, Hayes-Harris, Lopez, & Ward, 1995; Mann, Gordon, & Strade, 1991; and Winston & Moore, 1991).

In "Professional Standards: Whither Thou Goest?" Miller (1984) noted that it would be important that the creation of professional standards become an integral part of any forward movement in the student affairs profession. Although the student affairs profession does not have one authoritative body that governs the profession, standards in student affairs are continually evolving.

In 1990, the NASPA—Student Affairs Administrators in Higher Education (NASPA) Board of Directors endorsed the *Standards of Professional Practice* for student affairs. The association outlined eighteen different standards. Through the standards, the association's leadership sought to "promote student personnel work as a profession which requires personal integrity, belief in the dignity and worth of individuals, respect for individual differences and diversity, a commitment to service, and dedication to the development of individuals and the college community through education" (National Association of Student Personnel Administrators, 1990, p. 1). It was decided that these standards were general enough so that any student affairs professional could implement them throughout their career.

In 1996, ACPA—College Student Personnel Educators International (ACPA) and NASPA collaborated to draft the *Principles of Good Practice for Student Affairs*; though not explicitly expressed as standards, the associations intended for this document to guide student affairs practice. "The principles are grounded in the research on college students, experiences with effective educational institutions, and the historical commitment of student affairs to students and their learning" (American College Personnel Association and National Association of Student Personnel Administrators, 1996, pp. 5–6). These following principles outline that an individual who demonstrates good practice:

1. Engages students in active learning
2. Helps students develop coherent values and ethical standards
3. Sets and communicates high expectations for student learning
4. Uses systematic inquiry to improve student and institutional performance
5. Uses resources effectively to achieve institutional missions and goals
6. Forges educational partnerships that advance student learning
7. Builds supportive and inclusive communities.

Both the NASPA *Standards of Professional Practice* and the ACPA/NASPA *Principles of Good Practice for Student Affairs* highlight the importance of continual assessment either through personal inventories or through the CAS standards assessment process, which is outlined later in this chapter. Blimling and Whitt (1999) also discuss the good practices in student affairs in their book noting that it is the action of student affairs educators that helps to improve student learning and success.

Standards of Student Affairs Competencies

In 2009–10, the NASPA Board of Directors and the ACPA Governing Board called together the Joint Task Force on Professional Competencies and Standards to develop a set of professional competencies that would help guide the continuing education of student affairs administrators, and ultimately, have an impact on how the student affairs profession does business. Each association had similar competencies outlined, but there had not been a comprehensive review and integration of these competencies until the task force.

In reviewing the seminal documents of student affairs practitioners, an analysis by Weiner, Bresciani, Hickmott, and Felix (2009) provided a summary of the documents and research of student affairs competencies and standards. The research team looked at a set of nineteen documents, including the *CAS Standards and Guidelines.*

Competencies relate to student affairs professional standards by connecting an individual's ability to develop the skills necessary to be a successful student affairs administrator. The relationship between individual competence and practice in student affairs continues to further define the standards that guide student affairs work. The Joint Task Force on Professional Competencies report to the ACPA and NASPA boards was titled *ACPA/NASPA Professional Competencies for Student Affairs Practitioners* (2010). This document provided a list of ten competencies for which every student affairs practitioner should hold a basic competency. Komives and Carpenter outline the competencies, including the basic, intermediate, and advanced levels of competence, in chapter 20 of this volume. As the field continues to evolve, both ACPA and NASPA boards have committed to revising and improving the competencies so that the varied knowledge, skills, and experience can match the work that needs to be accomplished on campus.

Ethical Standards Within Student Affairs

One cannot discuss professional standards without considering the ethical implications of those standards. It is to the benefit of the student affairs profession, the institutions served, student learning, and the community as a whole that individuals follow ethical principles of practice. While the role of student affairs administrators is often influenced by both the nature of the institutions for which they work and by individual specialties within student affairs, nearly all student affairs professional organizations have endorsed the Council for the Advancement of Standards *Statement of Shared Ethical Principles.* These shared principles allow educators to begin with a basis of ethics and integrity in practice. As outlined in chapter 10, having an ethical lens through which to view their work on campus provides individuals a way to keep their activities central to student learning and development.

Council for the Advancement of Standards in Higher Education

The discussion about how the profession should speak with one voice and begin to create standards in student development started with the Council of Student Personnel Associations in Higher Education (COSPA), which specifically focused on ten student affairs associations and student development topics. COSPA dissolved in 1976 because of political disagreements within the council (CAS, 2012). Shortly thereafter, in 1979, the Council for the Advancement of Standards in Higher Education was established "in direct response to the emerging profession's need to establish standards to guide both practice and preparation" (CAS, 2012, p. 1). The consortium of eleven charter-member professional associations joined together with a goal of "developing and promulgating professional standards to guide both student affairs practices and academic preparation of those who administer student support programs and services" (CAS, 2012, p. 2).

The first CAS standards were published in 1986, and new and revised standards have been published seven times since that date, with the last update published in 2012. At the core of the CAS philosophy is that self-regulation is the responsibility of the institution, division, or unit to commit to continual improvement. Although there is no outside authority or governmental agency that requires a CAS review, self-assessments of functional areas using CAS standards can provide a framework to prepare for an accreditation review. For more than thirty-five years, CAS standards have reflected the evolution of student affairs and provided guidelines for continual improvement and assessment of programs and services.

CAS Standards and Guidelines. Paterson and Carpenter (1989) stated that CAS standards represented a "major step forwards in the efforts toward becoming a profession" (p. 125). By establishing standards, "student affairs clearly announced its determination to control its own destiny" (Bryan & Mullendore, 1991, p. 29). The Council for the Advancement of Standards' Board of Directors, which is made up of individual representatives of each professional organization member, revises and edits the standards every five to seven years in order for them to remain "evolving documents" (p. 29). The scheduled revisions for each standard allow for updates to both the CAS General Standards and the functional area standards on a regular basis. The credibility of these standards is based on the interassocation consensus on the purpose of establishing professional standards for student development services and for graduate school preparation of professionals entering the field of student affairs (Council for the Advancement of Standards, 1980).

In addition, new standards are added and updated as the profession evolves. For example, CAS General Standards published in 2011 included the recognition of family education history (for example, first generation to attend college) in its standard on discrimination and the addition of distance learning as a pervasive aspect of higher education. In addition, "major revisions [were] made to the structure of the General Standards reduc[ing] the 14 sections to 12 by combining and renaming sections where common or related elements existed" (CAS, 2012, p. 28).

CAS Domains of Learning Outcomes. In 2003, CAS articulated sixteen domains of learning outcomes that encouraged CAS members to focus on learning, as well as standards. After the publication and widespread adoption of *Learning Reconsidered* (Keeling, 2004), the learning outcomes were revised to be more congruent with learning outcomes described in what was articulated as "higher education's new playbook" (Fried, 2007, p. 2). CAS now organizes learning in six broad categories: knowledge acquisition, construction, integration, and application; cognitive complexity; interpersonal development; interpersonal competence; humanitarianism and civic engagement; and practical competence. These domains were embedded in each functional area standard. Programs and services must identify relevant and desirable learning from these domains, assess relevant and desirable learning, and articulate how their programs and services contribute to domains not specifically assessed. An important aspect of the CAS standards is that they provide guidance in the assessment and review of programs and services which in turn can assist student affairs administrators in developing programs which result in intentional learning outcomes (Komives & Arminio, 2011). For example, if a user wanted to conduct a study of measuring the growth of students' cognitive complexity, CAS offers illustrations of ways that students demonstrate achievement in this area. These include (1) applies previously understood information to new situations or settings, (2) uses complex information from a variety of sources to form a decision, and (3) formulates new approaches to problems (Arminio, 2009).

Applying CAS Standards. At the core of the CAS philosophy is that self-regulation presumes the responsibility of the institution, division, or unit to commit to continual improvement. CAS Self-Assessment Guides (SAGs) offer standards as criteria measures in an assessment rating form for conducting a self-study and implementing the standards that are endorsed by the CAS Board of Directors. SAGs were first published in 1988, are evaluated and updated when a particular standards is revised, and allow for easier utilization of the CAS standards (Bryan & Mullendore, 1991). The self-assessment guides "provide the perfect means to judge compliances" with standards (Gold, 1995, p. 68). Each CAS functional area has a SAG which outlines the process and ratings for individuals to conduct a self-study. The time frame for a typical self-study in a complex student affairs division is six to nine months. The self-study is broken down into twelve parts, and each part can be used to review a single aspect of a program or plan for professional development activities. CAS suggests that organizations conducting a CAS review implement the following steps (CAS, 2012):

1. *Establish and Create a Self-Assessment Team.* The review team should include representatives from the institutional community such as professional staff, faculty, and any individuals on whom the service or unit has an impact. Some institutions choose to have students serve on the team as well. Establishing the self-assessment team is also an opportunity to educate those who may be critical of the service provided. Choosing the chair of the self-assessment team is as equally important to the process as determining team members. Ideally, the director of the service or program should not be the chair, and if at all possible, it would be best if that person does not serve on the committee. Constituting the self-study team from across an institution would allow the selection of a chair based on experience in the self-assessment process rather than leadership within a particular department or division.

2. *Embark on Self-Study.* Beginning the self-study is a two-tiered approach, both through individual review and group analysis, which

helps to determine whether or not the unit meets the CAS standard. Any available documentation or related data should be collected and given to the team to review. This data should be gathered systematically each year, rather than just within the year that the CAS review takes place. Each member of the assessment team would then individually rate each criterion measure noting the evidence that supports the rating.

3. *Identify and Summarize Evaluative Evidence.* Once individual team members have completed their ratings, a collective review of the results is necessary. The individual ratings are compiled so that the team can view the evaluation data in aggregate. The self-assessment team can then determine if the unit under review is meeting the requirements of the standard and may highlight the strengths and/or weaknesses within the programs and services provided.

4. *Identify Discrepancies Between Practice and CAS Standards.* After the team rating is compiled, the committee can determine individual differences in perspectives in order to come to a common understanding in the ratings. A clear and transparent review process would include meetings with the staff from the functional area to help clarify misunderstandings and provide additional information that might refine the ratings and recommendations. The role of the committee is to help determine areas of weakness so that improvements can be implemented.

5. *Determine Appropriate Corrective Action.* An important aspect of the self-study is the resulting recommendations on what must be done to meet CAS standards in the functional area reviewed. The goal is to generate the information necessary to develop a plan for improvement and to bring the unit into compliance. The SAGs provide worksheets which guide the team through this process and provide action steps to be implemented.

6. *Recommend Steps for Program Enhancement.* A CAS standards self-assessment process would not be complete without the additional aspect of program enhancement. The SAG process is not meant to just provide a list of what is insufficient or lacking, but to identify areas that could use additional attention which would further strengthen the program and/or service provided. Self-study can offer the opportunity to both evaluate and celebrate the positive contributions to the institution and its students. Identifying the program enhancements in order of priority would assist the staff in setting aspirational goals.

7. *Prepare an Action Plan.* An assessment cycle without an action plan represents an incomplete process (Barham & Scott, 2006). Along with creating the right team to complete the self-study, a detailed action plan with realistic goals, timelines, and designation of responsible staff is essential.

The self-assessment team and the staff who will implement the changes and enhancements should meet in order to fully understand the recommendations and nuances of the study. The action plan should be a living document which is evaluated and revised throughout the unit's annual activities.

Continued Research on the Use of CAS Standards. Although the CAS Standards and Guidelines have been published and evolving for the past thirty-five years, the research in the awareness, use, and implementation of the CAS standards continues to develop. In 1989, Marron found that the distribution of the standards was not sufficient. Hence, only minimal utilization was found and the long-term effects were not predictable. Later, Mann et al. (1991) found that 51 percent of senior student affairs officers used the standards, 33 percent did not use them, and 16 percent were unaware of the CAS standards. In the comments section of their survey, fifteen examples of specific use of CAS standards were noted. Using a larger random sample of individuals who are members of CAS consortium associations, including new professionals as well as directors, deans and vice presidents, Arminio and Gochenauer (2004) found that 61 percent of respondents in general and 85 percent of vice presidents and associate vice presidents have heard of CAS. Twenty-seven percent of respondents, regardless of job title, indicated that they had read the standards, 33 percent used the standards as a program guide, and 18 percent used the standards for assessment (Arminio, 2009).

The research questions discussed by Creamer in 2003 remain:

- What student learning and development outcomes are associated with the use of CAS standards and guidelines by practitioners within a specific functional area?
- What behaviors of staff are associated with the implementation of CAS standards and guidelines in their functional area?
- Do practitioners perceive that the use of CAS standards and guidelines effectively improves their performance?
- Do student users of selected programs and services who are guided by the use of CAS standards and guidelines perceive a benefit of their learning and development?
- Are educational programs and services that are guided by CAS standards and guidelines more effective than similar programs and services that are not guided by CAS standards and guidelines?

Laura Dean, former president of the CAS Board of Directors noted that "there is still a need for further research to better understand the conditions and outcomes related to its use" (Dean, 2013, p. 27). More individuals are aware of the CAS standards at this point in the evolution of student affairs practice, but there are still many questions about their implementation, use, and overall effectiveness.

Other Organizations Promulgating Standards Related to Student Affairs Practice

Although the number of associations who have joined CAS has increased from the original eleven in the consortium to the forty-one varied organizations that now collaborate on the standards, there are still student affairs professional associations that are not members. Many higher education associations have created standards that are specific to their practice and they do not necessarily align with the overarching functional standards outlined in the CAS publication. The member organizations continue to support and advocate for the general functional area guidelines, but the specific areas of expertise or unique requirements of their content may require additional standards. For example, The National Intramural Recreation Sports Association (NIRSA) is a member of CAS and promotes CAS standards for generic use in recreational sports but has established specific standards in areas such as facilities management and student conduct of club members (Arminio, 2009). In addition, the Association of College and University Housing Officers—International (ACUHO-I) has incorporated the CAS standards for housing and residential life services and additional information from the American Council on Education (ACE) Statement entitled "Achieving Reasonable Campus Security" in order to develop its own standards that are available for free on its website. CAS supports using both the functional area guidelines and those specific standards that support continual improvement of programs and services.

Case Illustrations

Following are a few case illustrations that provide context to the discussion of professional standards within student affairs. After the cases, there is a brief analysis of how standards and competencies apply in each example.

Case 1   Creating a Divisionwide Assessment Program

George is a senior student affairs officer (SSAO) who needs to create a divisionwide assessment program in order to demonstrate student learning and success in preparation for the university's regional accreditation process. As a new SSAO, George has joined a campus where there are varied abilities of the student affairs staff and limited formal survey data available. A set of learning outcomes and goals have been established for the entire university, but the student affairs division and functional areas range from having no individual learning outcomes at all to a comprehensive strategy in one department. The university has many duplicative programs, across many divisions, which are each attempting to meet the needs of a distinct group of students. In addition to implementing the divisionwide assessment process, George must also work across the institution to connect the new student affairs assessment processes with the academic affairs units, which already have a comprehensive assessment plan. What are the challenges that George will face in developing the divisionwide assessment process? What literature and resources might George consult to assist him in his efforts?

Case 2 Establishing a Professional Development Plan

Tonya recently graduated from her master's degree program and is a new professional in residence life. While she was in graduate school, Tonya was a graduate assistant in student activities where she worked advising student groups, managing the concert venue, and coordinating the student ambassador group for the admissions office. She has never worked in residence life and her new role includes staff development and training, where her responsibilities include developing a resident advisor training program, managing the resident student association, and coordinating student conduct hearings for the residence halls. Tonya was selected for the position in residence life at her new campus because, in her interview, she was able to articulate the similarities between the roles including coordination of budgets, management of training programs, and conflict resolution skills that she had in dealing with individual conduct concerns. Now that she is in the residence life position, she is not sure what resources she will use to actually implement what she articulated in her interview. She is at a small college where the director of residence life does not have the resources to send Tonya to multiple conferences that would help her develop the knowledge and skills necessary to fulfill her position responsibilities. What are the resources she might consult to provide a framework for her new role and responsibilities?

Case 3 Managing Evolving Specialties in Student Affairs

Jennifer is the director of commuter and off-campus programs for a large urban institution in the Midwest. For the last four years, she and her two assistant directors have created and implemented a new orientation and student activities process for commuter students who attend the institution. They are very proud of their programs and even built in the learning outcomes and assessment process while developing the services provided. The professional staff has always had a focus internally on the institution and engaging students in what activities are available for a typical eighteen- to twenty-five-year-old commuter student. They have four years of data available regarding students who participated in programs and those who did not. For the participants of the program, Jennifer and her staff have seen a dramatic increase in the satisfaction and learning through the quantitative and qualitative data collected. However, the numbers of nontraditional students and returning student veterans have increased substantially. They have noticed a decrease in use of these services by these new students. Jennifer does not have experience with student veterans and all of her previous institutional experiences have been with traditional-age college students. At this time, there is no funding for a student veterans office or an office for nontraditional students, so Jennifer and her staff must learn how to provide support for these increasing student populations through their current programs and services. What literature and resources are available to help Jennifer and her staff understand what they need to do to both improve their current offerings and expand to serve these new populations?

These are three illustrations regarding how standards can be incorporated in the development, evaluation, and implementation of programs and services in higher education. There are several seminal documents in student affairs that would help each individual inform their next steps. From the *Standards of Professional Practice in Student Affairs* to the CAS standards and individual professional competencies, these documents can guide all three individuals, who are at varying experience levels, to the right course of action for their specific situations.

In the first case study, George's task has implications across the university. With the varied abilities of the student affairs staff, he must create both a learning environment and an action-oriented assessment culture. He must determine leaders within his organization who can help develop the skills or knowledge to create rubrics, connect learning outcomes to assessment strategy, and implement change on campus. Once he establishes the team that will help lead the charge, they could consult with *Learning Reconsidered* and the CAS Standards and Guidelines to assist in creating a consistent plan for goal setting, action plans, and outcomes reporting. As a new vice president, it is important for George to establish that his division understands the value of aligning the learning outcomes for his division to the overall mission and vision of the institution. As an additional item of note, the institution does not have consistent data and evidence to support what they are currently doing, so it is important for George to communicate the types of data that must be regularly collected to inform their practice.

In Tonya's situation, she must seek out the information regarding the varied functional standards of her new content area. Tonya is experiencing the change from her graduate assistantship to the multiple perspectives that one position can hold at an institution. Many student affairs administrators hold multiple roles within one division, especially at small colleges and universities. Although she worked in student activities, the standards and literature of housing and residential life program development have different requirements for learning and support. Her specific role is in training and development within residential life, but she also has responsibilities for the student conduct hearings that have an entirely different set of standards. In addition, it is important that she recognize that the residential student conduct process is a part of the overarching student conduct philosophy at the institution. She must collaborate across departments in order to better determine the student development process that can demonstrate learning and improve compliance with university conduct standards. Tonya should also review her individual competencies and complete a self-assessment to determine where she falls in the basic, intermediate, and advanced areas of the *ACPA/NASPA Professional Competencies for Student Affairs Practitioners.* This self-assessment will help Tonya articulate her professional development needs to her supervisor. With the combination of the self-assessment of her individual competencies and the knowledge of the standards she must meet in each functional area, Tonya can develop an individual action plan to improve her knowledge and understanding of her new role on campus.

Jennifer is experiencing what many student affairs practitioners have in the last ten years—the shrinking of available resources alongside the increase in student demand for specialized services on campus. On the surface, Jennifer and her staff have done everything right by developing activities with the foundation of learning outcomes, assessment plans, and data gathering. Although the programs and services seem to work for the traditional-age college student, the increase in posttraditional students and student veterans arriving on her campus provide a challenge to her well-established processes. Jennifer should consult the new *CAS Standards and Guidelines for Veterans' Programs and Services* and understand how she can implement some of those practices into her commuter and off-campus offerings. Because her institution is not able to provide a specific office for these student populations, it is important that Jennifer review the current roles and responsibilities of the staff and determine if they need additional professional development to assist them in their evolving responsibilities. In addition, Jennifer and her staff can evaluate the program data to decide what programs may need to end in order to divert efforts to this new population of students.

Conclusion

Higher education is under more scrutiny than ever before. Accountability, affordability, value, access, and student success are the buzzwords for today's administration and the US Department of Education. As traditional higher education tries to remain relevant and well funded in the world of shrinking resources and virtual learning, professional standards and quality assurance are more important than ever. It is not the time to rest on the traditional model of higher education and simply declare that a college degree is "worth it." Higher education professionals must demonstrate, through data and analysis, comprehensive student learning outcomes and how they are reached, how services provided are being improved, and the success of their college graduates in the workplace.

The Council for the Advancement of Standards in Higher Education and many professional associations have provided the structure for student affairs practitioners to establish an environment of continual quality improvement. However, it works only if practitioners know the standards exist, develop their individual competencies, and implement research and evaluation of programs and services provided on campus. Student affairs is changing and evolving as higher education propels forward in a world where students are less place-based and the demographics of those coming to college are no longer the traditional eighteen- to twenty-five-year-olds. The standards on which we currently operate provide a solid framework for what is happening today, but it is important to look ahead in order to be prepared for future changes and gather the evidence that will be required to keep student affairs a relevant and integral part of the higher education experience.

References

Alstete, J. W. (2004). *Accreditation matters: Achieving academic recognition and renewal* (ASHE-ERIC Higher Education Report, Vol. 30, no. 4). San Francisco, CA: Jossey-Bass.

American College Personnel Association and National Association of Student Personnel Administrators. (1996). *Principles of good practice for student affairs, 1998.*

http://www.naspa.org/images/uploads/main/Principles_of_Good_Practice_in_Student_Affairs.pdf.

American Council on Education. (1937). *The student personnel point of view.* Washington, DC: Author,

Arminio, J. (2009). Applying professional standards. In G. S. McClellan & J. Stringer (Eds.), *The handbook of student affairs administration* (3rd ed.). San Francisco, CA: Jossey-Bass.

Arminio, J., & Gochenauer, P. (2004). After sixteen years of publishing standards, do CAS standards make a difference? *College Student Affairs Journal, 24,* 51–65.

Barham, J. D., & Scott, J. (2006). Increasing accountability in student affairs through a new comprehensive assessment model. *College Student Affairs Journal, 25*(2), 209–219.

Betts, J. R., & Costrell, R. M. (2001). *Incentives and equity under standards-based reform.* Brookings Papers on Educational Policy. Washington, DC: Brookings Institution. http://mus.jhu.edu/journals/brookings_papers_on_educational_

Blimling, G. S., & Whitt, E. J. (Eds.). (1999). *Good practices in student affairs: Principles to foster student learning.* San Francisco, CA: Jossey-Bass.

Bryan, W. A., & Mullendore, R. H. (1991). Operationalizing CAS standards for program evaluation and planning. In W. A. Bryan, R. B. Winston Jr., & T. K. Miller (Eds.), *Using professional standards in student affairs.* New Directions for Student Services, no. 53. San Francisco, CA: Jossey-Bass.

Council for the Advancement of Standards in Higher Education. (2012). *CAS professional standards for higher education* (8th ed.). Washington, DC: Author.

Council for the Advancement of Standards. (1980). *By-laws.* Washington, DC: Author.

Creamer, D. G. (2003). Research needed on the use of CAS standards and guidelines. *College Student Affairs Journal, 22,* 109–124.

Dean, L. A. (2013). Using the CAS standards in assessment projects. In J. Schuh (Ed.), *Selected contemporary assessment issues.* New Directions for Student Services, no. 142. San Francisco, CA: Jossey-Bass.

Dictionary.com. Aug. (2013). Standard. http://dictionary.reference.com/browse/standard?s=t.

Fried, J. (2007). Higher education's new playbook: Learning reconsidered. *About Campus, 12*(1), 2–7.

Gold, J. A. (1995). Criteria for setting allocation priorities. In D.B. Woodard, Jr. (Ed.), *Budgeting as a tool for setting policy in student affairs.* New Directions for Student Services, no. 70. San Francisco: Jossey-Bass.

Jacobs, B. C., Hayes-Harris, M., & Ward, J. A. (1995). Maintaining an ethical balance in orientation programs. *College Student Affairs Journal, 15,* 44-53.

Keeling, R. P. (Ed.). (2004). *Learning reconsidered: A campus-wise focus on the student experience.* Washington, DC: National Association of Student Personnel Administrators and the American College Personnel Association.

Komives, S. R., & Arminio, J. (2011). Promoting integrity through standards of practice. In R. B. Young (Ed.), *Advancing the integrity of professional practice* (Special Issue). New Directions for Student Services, no. 135. San Francisco, CA: Jossey-Bass.

Mable, P. (1991). Professional standards: An introduction and historical perspective. In W. A. Bryan & R. B. Winston (Eds.), *Using professional standards in student affairs.* New Directions for Student Services, no. 53. San Francisco, CA: Jossey-Bass.

Mann, B. A., Gordon, S. E., & Strade, C. E. (1991). The impact of the CAS Standards on the practice of student affairs. *College Student Affairs Journal, 10,* 3–9.

Miller, T.K. (1984). Professional standards: Whither thou goest? *Journal of College Student Development, 25,* 412-416.

Murray, F. B. (2012). Six misconceptions about accreditation in higher education: Lessons from teacher education. *Change: The Magazine of Higher Learning, 44*(4), 52–58.

Paterson, B. G., & Carpenter D. S. (1989). The emerging student affairs profession: What still needs to be done. *NASPA Journal, 27,* 123–127.

Penney, J. F. (1972). *Perspective and challenge in college personnel work.* Springfield, IL: Charles C Thomas.

Saunders, L. (2011). *Information Literacy as a student learning outcome the perspective of institutional accreditation.* Santa Barbara, CA: Libraries Unlimited.

Stoops, J. A., & Parsons, M. D. (2003). Accreditation in the United States. In J. W. Guthrie (Ed.), *Encyclopedia of education* (2nd ed., Vol. 1, pp. 28–35). New York: Macmillan Reference USA.

Weiner, L., Bresciani, M., Hickmott, J., & Felix, E. (2009). *ACPA, NASPA and CAS professional standard document analysis.* NASPA/ACPA/CAS Joint Task Force on Professional Standards. Washington, DC: National Association of Student Personnel Administrators.

Winston, R. B., & Moore, W. (1991). Standards and outcomes assessment: strategies and tools. In W. A. Bryan, R. B. Winston Jr. & T. K. Miller (Eds.), *Using professional standards in student affairs.* New Directions for Student Services, no. 53. San Francisco, CA: Jossey-Bass.

CHAPTER TWELVE

THE ROLE OF PROFESSIONAL ASSOCIATIONS

Nancy J. Evans and Jessica J. Ranero-Ramirez

New student affairs graduate students and professionals are almost immediately bombarded with acronyms of professional student affairs associations, both generalist in nature and specific to the functional areas in which they are employed. It can be overwhelming to determine what all these organizations do, how they are related to the work of student affairs, and which groups, if any, are worth joining. This chapter provides information about professional associations in student affairs, including their functions, history, and structure. Various types of associations, the benefits of membership, and opportunities for involvement are also discussed.

The Functions of Professional Associations

The website of the American Society of Association Executives (ASAE) and the Center for Association Leadership (American Society of Association Executives and the Center for Association Leadership, 2011) explains that professional associations consist of individuals who voluntarily join the group because they share common interests and goals. The ASAE website lists a variety of purposes to which associations commit themselves, including (1) education and professional development of their members,

(2) provision of information about the field or area they represent, (3) the establishment of ethical and professional standards, (4) a vehicle for discussion of issues and concerns in the profession, (5) volunteer and service opportunities for members in their areas of interest, and (6) the development of a community of people who share common interests for support and networking.

These purposes are reflected in the work of student affairs associations, which serve individual student affairs professionals, institutions of higher education, and the profession as a whole. An increasingly critical role of student affairs associations is lobbying government officials regarding issues and legislation important to the profession and its members. Student affairs professional associations also provide information to the general public through websites, media interviews, and publications (Moore & Neuberger, 1998).

The History of Student Affairs Professional Associations

Professional associations started to appear in the early 1900s to provide support, professional development, and a voice for individuals in the emerging field of student affairs (Nuss, 2003). The deans of women and deans of men, who were the most visible student affairs professionals at this time, had little preparation for assuming their new roles and few colleagues who understood their role on campus (NASPA—Student Affairs Administrators in Higher Education, 2008). The need to discuss the issues facing them in their new positions provided the impetus for the development of two early associations.

National Association of Women in Education

The deans of women were the first to see the value of organizing. In 1903, eighteen women deans came together informally at a meeting at Northwestern University (Bashaw, 2001a). The group formally organized in 1916 as the National Association of Deans of Women (NADW). In the early years of NADW, the organization's focus was on the role and responsibilities of deans of women, and later, on issues facing women in education and the women students they served (Hanson, 1995). In 1938, NADW began publishing a journal to disseminate research on these topics.

In response to "demotion and dismissal" (Bashaw, 2001b, p. 263) of college deans of women during the conservative atmosphere following World

War II, many questioned the need for a gender specific association; in 1952 NADW considered combining with other student affairs organizations but decided to remain separate to ensure that ongoing equity issues in higher education and the unique needs of women educators and students were addressed (Bashaw, 2001b; Hanson, 1995). However, to better reflect the roles being played by women in education at this time, the organization's name was expanded in 1956 to the National Association of Women Deans and Counselors (NAWDC) (Hanson, 1995). NAWDC also partnered with the National Association of Student Personnel Administrators (NASPA) and the American College Personnel Association (ACPA) to address issues facing the student affairs profession as a whole.

In 1973, the association's name was changed to the National Association of Women Deans, Administrators, and Counselors (NAWDAC) and the association for the first time offered membership to men (Hanson, 1995). Intentional initiatives to create a more inclusive organization resulted in the development of committees for graduate students and young professionals, women of color, disability issues, and lesbian and bisexual issues. In 1991, the association's name was changed to the National Association of Women in Education (NAWE) to better reflect its focus on issues facing women working in all educational settings (Hanson, 1995; Moore & Neuberger, 1998). Despite serving as a valued professional home for many women in student affairs and other areas of education, decreases in membership and conference attendance resulted in the decision of the leadership and membership of NAWE to dissolve the association in 2000 (Nuss, 2003).

NASPA—Student Affairs Administrators in Higher Education

The deans of men first met at the University of Wisconsin in 1919 with six men present (NASPA, 2008). From that meeting until 1929, this gathering was called the Conference of Deans and Advisors of Men. In its early years, meetings of the association were held on college campuses and provided an opportunity to informally share ideas and discuss issues facing male students.

In 1929, the name of the organization was changed to the more formal National Association of Deans and Advisors of Men (NADAM) and conferences from 1929 on were held at off-campus sites (NASPA, 2008). In 1932, institutional membership was established, with each member school having one official representative who voted on association business. However, institutions could send additional delegates to the conference.

As the title dean of men disappeared on campuses, an increasing need was felt for an organizational name that reflected the broader roles of NADAM's membership (NASPA, 2008). In 1951, the name National Association of Student Personnel Administrators (NASPA) was adopted and new members were actively recruited to join. However, the main target audience of NASPA remained senior student affairs officers and their senior staffs (Moore & Neuberger, 1998). In the 1960s, NASPA developed a system of regional meetings paralleling the national accreditation regions, with each region having a vice president who served on the executive committee of the national organization. Because of its size, Region IV was split into IV-East and IV-West; thus, there are seven NASPA regions (NASPA, 2008).

Although women had attended association meetings earlier, it was not until 1958 that the first woman served as an institutional representative and 1966 when a woman first served on the executive committee (NASPA, 2008). In 1976, NASPA elected its first woman president, Alice Manicur (NASPA, 2008). Between 1990 and 2013, sixteen of the twenty-three presidents were women (NASPA, 2013e). Student affairs professionals of color and those working in community college settings also became more prevalent in the overall NASPA membership and in leadership positions in the late twentieth century (NASPA, 2008).

In 1967, a national office was established to coordinate the association's activities and NASPA appointed its first executive director in 1975. In 1985, the national office was permanently moved to Washington, D.C. (NASPA, 2008). In recent years, NASPA has expanded the role of its national office with regard to member services, moved into a new building in Washington, D.C., and added an updated tag line, "Student Affairs Administrators in Higher Education."

NASPA now has just over 13,000 members (NASPA, 2013a). The association's stated mission is "to be the principal source for leadership, scholarship, professional development, and advocacy for student affairs" (NASPA, 2013a). NASPA has led the way with online publications and Web-based knowledge communities. It is also recognized for its timely response to current issues in the field (Coomes, Wilson, & Gerda, 2003). NASPA's Undergraduate Fellows Program (NUFP), the purpose of which is to increase the number of persons of colors, persons with disabilities, and/or persons who identify as lesbian, gay, bisexual, and transgender in student affairs and higher education, has been the impetus for many highly qualified and competent undergraduate students to pursue graduate education in student affairs (NASPA, 2013d). Other notable NASPA programs include the Alice Manicur Symposium for women aspiring to become chief student affairs officers, Institute for New Chief Student Affairs Officers, James E. Scott Academy addressing executive excellence for senior student affairs officers, and Multicultural Affairs Institute (NASPA, 2013b).

ACPA—College Student Educators International

The other generalist student affairs association, ACPA, began as the National Association of Appointment Secretaries (NAAS) in 1924 (ACPA—College Student Educators International [ACPA], 2013d; Bloland, 1972). Appointment secretaries served as placement officers, assisting graduating students to find positions. The purpose for which NAAS was founded was to promote and develop the work of appointment offices across the United States, emphasizing cooperation, research, and service. In 1929, NAAS became the National Association of Placement and Personnel Officers (NAPPO) to better reflect the expanding work responsibilities of its members (Bloland, 1972).

Two years later, in 1931, the name American College Personnel Association (ACPA) was adopted to encourage a broader membership and mission—one that included student affairs professionals with a wide variety of responsibilities. Sections, later called "commissions," were established to deal with different aspects of student affairs work and an emphasis was placed on professional development of student affairs personnel. State branches of ACPA were also formed (ACPA, 2013d; Evans & Powell, 2002).

A desire to bring together the major guidance organizations led to the formation of the American Personnel and Guidance Association (APGA, later the American Association of Counseling and Development [AACD]) in 1952; ACPA led this initiative and became the first division of this new association (Bloland, 1972). As the student affairs profession became increasingly complex, taking on educational and administrative responsibilities as well as work with individual students, ACPA's need to focus on these changing roles became apparent (Evans & Powell, 2002; Steffes, 2001). In 1991, ACPA leaders and members voted to disaffiliate from AACD. The separation became effective in 1992 when ACPA moved into its own office space at the National Center for Higher Education in Washington, D.C. and hired an Executive Director (Evans & Powell, 2002). In 2007, ACPA reorganized its governance structure to more efficiently accomplish its goals and has added the tagline, "College Student Educators International" to the ACPA acronym to better reflect the educational and international initiatives that have become increasingly important parts of its mission. Office staffing and technology were also expanded to ensure effective and efficient service to the organization's members (ACPA, 2013d).

ACPA's current membership is around 7,500 (ACPA, 2013a). According to its mission statement, "ACPA supports and fosters college student learning through the generation and dissemination of knowledge, which informs policies, practices and programs for student affairs professionals and the higher education community" (ACPA, 2013b). ACPA's roots are in the counseling tradition of student affairs, and it has been a welcoming home for professionals in many functional areas of student affairs (Evans & Powell, 2002). Throughout its history, ACPA has been recognized for its commitment to inclusion and advocacy for underrepresented groups. Its leadership reflects this value, with Executive Council positions overwhelmingly held by women and people of color in recent years (Steffes, 2001). ACPA also has a long history of scholarship (Evans & Powell, 2002). In addition to publishing the premier research journal in the student affairs field, the *Journal of College Student Development,* many of the foundational documents of the field were generated as ACPA projects or by scholars affiliated with ACPA. The Senior Scholars and Emerging Scholars programs also help to keep scholarship at the forefront in ACPA (Coomes et al., 2003). ACPA's strong standing committees and commissions provide many educational and leadership opportunities for the association's members (ACPA, 2013c, 2013h) and extensive use of social media has been particularly attractive to ACPA's younger members. Recent ACPA initiatives include Next Generation Conference; Donna M. Bourassa Mid-Level Management Institute; Institute on Social Justice, and Institute on Sustainability (ACPA, 2013g).

Efforts to Consolidate

Throughout their histories, student affairs associations have collaborated on programming, held joint conferences, and cooperated to address major issues facing the student affairs profession (Bloland, 1972; Moore & Neuberger, 1998), including the recent development of the ACPA/NASPA Professional Competencies for Student Affairs Practitioners (ACPA, 2013f). While a number of attempts have been made to consolidate or merge associations to increase visibility, respect, and effectiveness in addressing the issues facing the student affairs field (Bloland, 2002; Coomes et al., 2003; Moore & Neuberger, 1998), none has been successful, including a recent attempt to combine ACPA and NASPA into one organization (Lipka, 2011).

Although ACPA and NASPA share many commonalities in their missions, values, functions, and goals; differences in organizational structure, priorities, and culture are also apparent (Coomes et al., 2003). Given the 2011 vote of the associations not to consolidate, it is unlikely that a merger will happen in the near future. However, ACPA, NASPA, and other associations have committed to collaboration on projects to more efficiently serve the student affairs field and address student needs.

Confederations

Somewhat more successful than attempts at consolidation have been confederations of organizations to achieve specific goals, starting in the 1960s with the development of the Council of Student Personnel Associations in Higher Education (COSPA), a confederation of student affairs associations designed to facilitate communication among the different associations. This group developed several position pieces related to the role of student affairs, issues facing the profession, and professional preparation (Caple, 1998; Crowley, 1964). More recently, the Council for the Advancement of Standards in Higher Education (CAS), founded in 1979, has representatives from nearly forty professional student affairs associations (Council for the Advancement of Standards in Higher Education, 2013b). CAS has developed and continuously revises standards for professional practice in a wide variety of areas of student affairs practice as well as professional preparation. In addition, the Washington Higher Education Secretariat (HES), a group of approximately fifty chief executive officers of national higher education associations that meets monthly under the auspices of the American Council on Education (Washington Higher Education Secretariat, 2013), and the Council of Higher Education Management Associations (CHEMA), a group of equivalent size convened twice a year by the National Association of College and University Business Officers (NACUBO), focus on collaborative initiatives and governmental lobbying related to issues relevant to member associations (Council of Higher Education Management Associations, n.d).

Specialty Associations

In addition to the generalist higher education associations, NASPA and ACPA, numerous professional associations have been initiated that focus on specific subdivisions of student affairs. The Council for the

Advancement of Standards in Higher Education (CAS) includes more than forty different associations with a variety of specializations within the field of higher education, which are listed in Exhibit 12.1 (Council for the Advancement of Standards in Higher Education, 2013a). In addition, StudentAffairs.com, an online resource, provides a list of more than seventy professional associations (StudentAffairs.com, 2013).

EXHIBIT 12.1 A SAMPLE LISTING OF PROFESSIONAL ASSOCIATIONS

American Association for Employment in Education (AAEE)
American College Counseling Association (ACCA)
American College of Health Association (ACHA)
American College Personnel Association (ACPA)
American Counseling Association (ACA)
Association for Student Judicial Affairs (ASJA)
Association of College Unions International (ACUI)
Association of College and University Housing Officers-International (ACUHO-I)
Association of Collegiate Conference & Events Director-Int'l (ACCED-I)
Association of Fraternity Advisors (AFA)
Association of Higher Education and Disability (AHEAD)
Canadian Association of College and University Student Success (CACUSS)
Collegiate Information and Visitor Services Association (CIVSA)
Consortium of Higher Education LGBT Resource Professionals (Consortium)
Cooperative Education and Internship Association (CEIA)
Council for Opportunity in Education (COE)
International Association of Campus Law Enforcement Administration (IACLEA)
National Academic Advising Association (NACADA)
National Association for Campus Activities (NACA)
National Association for Developmental Education (NADE)
National Association of College Auxiliary Services (NACAS)
National Association of Colleges and Employers (NACE)
National Association of College and University Food Services (NACUFS)
National Association of College Stores (NACS)
National Association of International Educators (NAFSA)
National Association of Student Affairs Professionals (NASAP)
National Association of Student Financial Aid Administrators (NASFAA)
National Association of Student Personnel Administrators (NASPA)
National Clearinghouse for Leadership Programs (NCLP)
National Council on Student Development
National Institute for the Study of Transfer Students (NISTS)
National Intramural and Recreational Sports Association (NIRSA)
National Orientation Directors Association (NODA)
National Society for Experiential Education (NSEE)
National Women's Studies Association (NWSA)
The Network: Addressing Collegiate Alcohol and Other Drug Issues (The Network)
Southern Association for College Student Affairs (SACSA)

Source: Council for the Advancement of Standards in Higher Education (2013a).

Organizations such as the Association of College and University Housing Officers-International (ACHUO-I), the National Orientation Directors Association (NODA), the National Association for Campus Activities (NACA), the Association of Fraternity Advisors (AFA), the Association for Student Judicial Affairs (ASJA), and the National Academic Advising Association (NACADA) were established to focus on specific areas of student affairs. The structure and mission of each organization vary because of their specializations, but they share similar goals of disseminating information and providing opportunities for networking and professional development. In addition, state and regional associations, sometimes affiliated with national associations and sometimes independent, serve the needs of professionals in specific geographical regions.

More recently, associations focused on the needs of underrepresented and constituent groups have been established. The National Association of Student Affairs Professionals (NASAP) was founded in 1954 by the merger of two gender-specific associations established earlier to serve student affairs professionals in Historically Black Colleges and Universities: the National Association of Deans of Women and Advisors of Girls in Colored Schools and the National Association of Personnel Deans of Men at Negro Educational Institutions (Dungy & Gordon, 2011). Today, NASAP focuses on promoting research, professional development, and effective student affairs programs. It also hosts an annual student leadership institute (National Association of Student Affairs Professionals [NASAP], n.d.).

The Association on Higher Education and Disability (AHEAD) was founded in 1977 to ensure universal accessibility to higher education for persons with disabilities (Association on Higher Education and Disability [AHEAD], 2012). AHEAD accomplishes its mission through trainings, workshops, publications, and consultation. Similarly, the Consortium of Higher Education LGBT Resource Professionals was founded in 1997 to ensure that lesbian, gay, bisexual, and transgender members of the college community have equity and equal access to higher education (Consortium of Higher Education LGBT Resource Professionals, 2012).

The Asian Pacific Americans in Higher Education (APAHE) was established to ensure that national attention was given to the issues affecting a particular constituent group. APAHE was founded in 1987 to address discriminatory admissions policies that were directed against Asian Pacific Americans at several research universities across the country. Currently, APAHE's goal is to address issues that affect Asian Pacific American students, faculty, staff, and administrators (Asian Pacific Americans in Higher Education, 2013). The American Association of Hispanics in Higher Education (AAHHE) is an outgrowth of the American Association of Higher Education's Hispanic Caucus. The mission of AAHHE is to advocate for increased access for Hispanics in higher education and to increase the number of Hispanics attending and completing graduate programs in higher education (American Association of Hispanics in Higher Education, 2013). The National Association of Diversity Officers in Higher Education (NADOHE) is an association that also focuses on diversity. NADOHE began with an informal meeting in 2003 of a few senior diversity officers in higher education and business sectors. Out of the meeting grew an interest in continued dialogue, which led to the official establishment of NADOHE in 2006 and its first conference in 2007 (National Association of Diversity Officers in Higher Education, 2012). The purpose of NADOHE is to create a network of senior diversity officers and multicultural experts in order to create more inclusive colleges and universities.

Other associations developed to focus on colleges and universities that primarily serve under-represented populations. The American Indian Higher Education Consortium (AIHEC) serves tribal colleges and universities by focusing on public policy, advocacy, research, and program initiatives that strengthen higher education for American Indians (American Indian Higher Education Consortium, 2013). AIHEC currently represents thirty-seven tribal colleges and universities in the United States and Canada. The National Coalition for the Advancement of Natives in Higher Education (NCANHE) is a new organization that aims to bring together practitioners and scholars to support the success of Native students (NCANHE, 2013a, 2013b). NCANHE hosted its first national conference in the fall of 2013 and had a series of workshops that focused on the three pillars of the coalition: practice, policy, and research (George McClellan, personal correspondence.). The Hispanic Association of Colleges and Universities (HACU) is a resource for college administrators who work at Hispanic Serving Institutions (Hispanic Association of Colleges & Universities, 2011). HACU was established in 1986 and currently represents more than four hundred college and universities. In addition, HACU advocates for Hispanic-serving institutions through public policy, student scholarships, and student internship programs (Hispanic Association of Colleges & Universities, 2011). The counterpart to both AIHEC and HACU is the National Association for Equal Opportunity in Higher Education (NAFEO) (National Association for Equal Opportunity in Higher Education, 2010). NAFEO was established in 1969 and serves as an umbrella organization for Historically Black Colleges and Universities (HBCUs) and Predominantly Black Institutions (PBIs). As such, NAFEO advocates for the preservation and enhancement of its member organizations and serves as a source of information for student affairs professionals working at HBCUs and PBIs.

Other associations, including the Consortium of Liberal Arts Colleges (CLAC), National Council on Student Development (NCSD), and Association of Private Sector Colleges and Universities (APSCU, 2013), also focus on specific types of institutions. CLAC was established in 1986 and currently has many of the top liberal arts colleges in the United States as its members (Consortium of Liberal Arts Colleges, 2013). CLAC holds an annual conference, collects and shares benchmark data, and has an active listserv that members can use to exchange ideas and information on a national level. NCSD is an affiliate council of the American Association of Community Colleges (AACC) (National Council on Student Development, 2013). As an affiliate of AACC, NCSD focuses on serving as a resource for student affairs professionals working at community colleges. NCSD hosts an annual conference and a leadership institute that is designed to prepare student affairs administrators who are interested in senior leadership positions. APSCU serves student services administrators working at for-profit colleges and universities. APSCU has approximately 1,700 members and provides its members with information about relevant national and state policies as well as hosting an annual convention.

Organizations also exist to support student affairs professionals who work at religiously affiliated colleges and universities. The Jesuit Association of Student Personnel Administrators (JASPA) was founded in 1954 to promote the mission of Jesuit higher education (Jesuit Association of Student Personnel Administrators, 2013). In 1999, the Association for Student Affairs at Catholic Colleges and Universities (ASACCU) was founded by student affairs professionals working at Catholic institutions (Association for Student Affairs at Catholic Colleges and Universities, 2010). The Council for Christian Colleges and Universities (CCCU) was established in 1976 to "advance the cause of Christ-centered higher education" (Council for Christian Colleges and Universities, 2013). All of these associations provide their members with opportunities to share resources through conferences, workshops, websites, and various other activities.

Although there has been an increase in the number of organizations that focus on the needs of underrepresented populations, there are still gaps. For example, there is no association that is dedicated to the work of multicultural affairs offices on college campuses. Though NADOHE was established in 2006, its primary focus is on issues facing senior diversity officers, which are often different from the work of multicultural affairs offices. Conferences such as the National Conference on Race and Ethnicity in American Higher Education (NCORE) and the Creating Change Conference sponsored by the National Gay and Lesbian Task Force provide additional resources regarding diversity in higher education.

The increase of specialized student affairs professional associations presents a number of benefits. As the profession continues to grow, there is an increased need to understand the complexities of the various areas within student affairs, which these specialized associations address. The creation of new organizations has also contributed to an increased awareness of the vast needs of diverse students.

Despite these gains, there are some concerns that increased specialization in student affairs is threatening the strength of the profession. Sandeen (1998) stated that specialization contributes to professional isolation by creating challenges to communication among professionals in the field. In addition, upward mobility within the profession may become more difficult because student affairs professionals are no longer seen as having a generalist skill set, but instead are now seen as experts within a specific area. Furthermore, collaboration within and outside of student affairs may become more difficult because of competing needs (Sandeen, 1998).

In the current higher education environment, student affairs professionals must challenge themselves to be both generalists and specialists. As Sandeen (1998) stated, it is the duty of student affairs professionals to work toward the holistic development of students, which requires a general knowledge of the overall university system and the field of student affairs as well as the specific needs of student populations. To gain the necessary knowledge and skills, both generalist and specialty organizations are needed.

The Structure of Professional Associations

In addition to sharing similar functions, most student affairs associations are volunteer-based organizations. They have elected governing boards that consist of volunteers who take on leadership roles within the associations. The governing boards are charged with responsibilities that include the oversight of policies and procedures, budget management, and the development of strategic plans. Most associations also have special interest committees or task forces that focus on special interests and specific constituent groups, as well as state or regional divisions that hold their own conferences to provide additional opportunities for professional development.

There are a few associations, including ACPA and NASPA, that have central offices with paid full-time staff who are responsible for seeing that the activities of the association are carried out and who represent the association in various settings. They manage membership and conference planning, as well as the finances of the organization. Associations are primarily funded through membership dues, although grants from corporate sponsors and revenue from conferences and workshops bring in additional funding. Larger professional organizations, including NASPA, ACPA, NACA, and ACUHO-I, have affiliated foundations that seek philanthropic support for association activities such as scholarships, research, innovative programs, study tours, and leadership development (ACPA Foundation, 2013; NACA, 2012; NASPA, 2013c; ACUHO-I, 2013).

Benefits of Membership in Professional Associations

Becoming involved in student affairs professional associations can be time consuming and expensive. When one considers that student affairs professionals often work more than forty hours a week at their jobs and are not highly paid, why would a person want to invest extra time and money in professional association membership and activity? For most people, fortunately, the benefits outweigh the costs. Professional organizations offer opportunities for professional development, networking, job seeking, and member discounts (ACPA, 2013e).

Membership in professional associations indicates to employers that one has a commitment to the profession beyond the institutional level. Attendance at national, regional, and/or state conferences as well as enrollment in specialized workshops or Web-based seminars involves a commitment of time and additional cost, which sometimes is covered by one's institution and sometimes not. However, it provides an opportunity for active learning and engagement.

Professional associations offer extensive opportunities for professional development. Annual conferences provide educational sessions, major speakers, and opportunities to talk with and learn from other professionals. Attending conferences is a good way to stay up to date on current issues and learn about cutting-edge practice and theory. Professional associations also offer regional, national, and Web-based seminars on specific topics of importance in student affairs. These intensive seminars allow participants to learn from experts in specific areas and to interact with other professionals interested in the same topic.

Professional associations also offer networking opportunities. Interaction among professionals at conferences and workshops fosters the exchange of ideas and the development of connections that can be helpful in career advancement. Listservs also provide opportunities for communication with other members who share similar interests or job responsibilities. Publications sponsored by professional associations offer professional development opportunities by keeping members informed about current research and scholarship in the field and also provide publication outlets for those who are engaged in scholarly endeavors. ACPA, NASPA, and many specialty associations offer on-site placement services at national and regional conferences and/or Web-based career information and job postings. Many associations offer member discounts on publications, workshops, professional insurance, and merchandise. Conference registration is significantly discounted for members.

Involvement and Leadership Opportunities

There are many levels of involvement in professional associations, ranging from passive membership to extensive involvement in leadership positions. Most student affairs associations are very welcoming of volunteer assistance, and professionals can be as involved as they choose to be. Individuals need to carefully assess their time and interests to ensure that they will be able to competently carry out any assignments they undertake, as professional reputations, both positive and negative, are often built on reliability and effectiveness in professional association activities.

Participation in a committee or commission is a way to get more actively involved in a professional association. Opportunities include serving on conference-planning committees, reading program proposals, developing new initiatives, editing newsletters, maintaining websites, and a myriad of other possibilities. Presenting at a conference is an additional kind of active involvement professionals take on. This type of activity requires preparation of a proposal for a program session on a topic that the presenter believes will be of benefit to other professionals. Submitted proposals undergo review by the conference committee and the best are chosen for presentation. Although it can be intimidating to present to one's peers, it is also a good way to test out one's ideas. Professional writing is another way to be involved in the profession. Submitting a newsletter article is a low-risk way to get started in this arena. Professional journals are always looking for strong research-based articles, and many associations also publish books of interest to their membership. Editorial boards of association-sponsored journals and books are usually very willing to assist new authors with the writing process. Serving on editorial boards is another way to contribute to the field.

Running for elected office is the most visible and time-consuming type of involvement, but serving as an officer of a professional association is also very rewarding. Testing the waters by serving as an elected officer of a commission, standing committee, knowledge community, or state or regional executive council is a way to determine whether being involved in governance is manageable given one's institutional responsibilities. All associations eagerly welcome individuals who wish to be involved in governance; in fact, it is often difficult to find people willing to take on this type of role.

Serious thought should be given to the type and degree of involvement a professional undertakes. Professional involvement can be seductive because of the visibility, recognition, and personal fulfillment it provides. It is easy to overcommit to activities in several associations and find that one does not have the time to devote to all of them and complete one's job responsibilities on campus as well. If one has the financial resources, being a member of a number of associations is certainly beneficial for keeping up to date on current issues in various areas of student affairs. It is generally advisable to be involved in one of the generalist associations, usually ACPA or NASPA, to stay current with the profession as a whole, and one specialty association that serves the area of student affairs in which one is working or interested in working. Involvement in an association focused on a specific identity group is also an important option for many professionals. It is generally not possible or advisable to be deeply involved in more than one association at the same time. In any case, discussing professional involvement responsibilities with one's institutional supervisor is important to ensure that appropriate support is available and there are no misunderstandings about how the individual is spending his or her time.

Conclusion

For any professional, professional involvement is both a responsibility and opportunity. The level and timing of such activity is a personal decision. Every professional has an obligation to stay current in the field and to continue to develop the skills necessary to be effective in her or his position. Regardless of level of involvement, professional associations provide many and varied opportunities for professional development.

At different points in a person's career, different types of involvement may be of interest and viable. Generally, new professionals begin their careers by joining professional associations and attending conferences. They may use the placement services associations provide to secure employment. Later, presenting and volunteering provide ways to engage with other professionals and contribute to the profession. As the individual progresses professionally, writing for publication and running for office may have appeal.

At any career stage, networking with other engaged professionals and being exposed to innovative ideas are important benefits of professional association involvement. Less obvious benefits also result. In her study of women involved in leadership in ACPA, Steffes (2001) found that the association provided critical personal and professional support for these leaders. Indeed, many of them used the word *family* to describe the association.

References

ACPA—College Student Educators International. (2013a). *2011–2012 annual report.* http://www2.myacpa.org/images/about-acpa/docs/acpa_2011_12_annualreport .pdf.

ACPA—College Student Educators International. (2013b). *About ACPA.* http://www2 .myacpa.org/about-acpa.

ACPA—College Student Educators International. (2013c). *Commissions.* http://www2 .myacpa.org/commissions.

ACPA—College Student Educators International. (2013d). *History of ACPA.* http:// www2.myacpa.org/about-acpa/history.

ACPA—College Student Educators International. (2013e). *Resources.* http://www2 .myacpa.org/professional-development/resources.

ACPA—College Student Educators International. (2013f). *Membership.* http://www2 .myacpa.org/membership.

ACPA—College Student Educators International. (2013g). *Signature professional development opportunities.* http://www2.myacpa.org/professional-development/ professional-development-opportunities.

ACPA—College Student Educators International. (2013h). *Standing committees.* http://www2.myacpa.org/standing-committees.

ACPA Foundation. (2013). *About the Educational Leadership Foundation.* http://www .acpafoundation.org/about-educational-leadership-foundation.

ACUHO-I—American College and University Housing Officers-International. (2013). *Foundation.* http://www.acuho-i.org/foundation.

American Association of Hispanics in Higher Education. (2013). *About us.* http://www .aahhe.org.

American Indian Higher Education Consortium. (2013). *About AIEHEC.* http://www .aihec.org/about/index.cfm.

American Society of Association Executives and the Center for Association Leadership. (2011). *Associations FAQ.* http://www.asaecenter.org/Advocacy/ contentASAEOnly.cfm?ItemNumber=16341.

Asian Pacific Americans in Higher Education. (2013). *About.* http://www .apahenational.org?page_id=2.

Association for Student Affairs at Catholic Colleges and Universities. (2010). *About us.* http://www.asaccu.org/index.php?option=com_content&view=section& layout=blog&id=8&Itemid=212.

Association of Private Sector Colleges and Universities. (2013). *About APSCU.* http:// www.career.org/about/.

Association on Higher Education and Disability. (2012). *About AHEAD.* http://www .ahead.org/about.

Bashaw, C. T. (2001a). "Reassessment and redefinition": The NAWDC and higher education for women. In J. Nidiffer & C. T. Bashaw (Eds.), *Women administrators in higher education: Historical and contemporary perspectives* (pp.157-182). Albany: State University of New York Press.

Bashaw, C. T. (2001b). "To serve the needs of women": The AAUW, NAWDC, and persistence of academic women's support networks. In J. Nidiffer & C. T. Bashaw (Eds.), *Women administrators in higher education: Historical and contemporary perspectives* (pp. 249-270). Albany: State University of New York Press.

Bloland, P. A. (1972). Ecumenicalism in college student personnel. *Journal of College Student Personnel, 13,* 102–111.

Caple, R. B. (1998). *To mark the beginning: A social history of college student affairs.* Lanham, MD: American College Personnel Association.

Consortium of Higher Education LGBT Resource Professionals. (2012). *About us.* http://www.lgbtcampus.org/about-us.

Consortium of Liberal Arts Colleges. (2013). *About CLAC.* http://www.liberalarts.org/ about.

Coomes, M. D., Wilson, M. E., & Gerda, J. J. (2003). *Of visions, values, and voices: Consolidating ACPA and NASPA.* Paper presented at the NASPA Annual Conference. St. Louis, MO, March 2003.

Council for Christian Colleges and Universities. (2013). *About CCCU.* https://www .cccu.org/about.

Council for the Advancement of Standards in Higher Education. (2013a). *Member associations.* http://www.cas.edu/.

Council for the Advancement of Standards in Higher Education. (2013b). *Professional services.* http://www.cas.edu/.

Council of Higher Education Management Associations. (n.d.). Home page. http:// www.chemanet.org/.

Crowley, W. H. (1964). Reflections of a troublesome but hopeful Rip Van Winkle. *Journal of College Student Personnel, 6,* 66–73.

Dungy, G., & Gordon, S. A. (2011). The development of student affairs. In J. H. Schuh, S. R. Jones, S. R. Harper, & Associates (Eds.), *Student services: A handbook for the profession* (5th ed., pp. 61-79). San Francisco, CA: Jossey-Bass.

Evans, N. J., & Powell, T. (2002). *ACPA? NASPA? What's the difference?* Paper presented at the American College Personnel Association Convention, Long Beach, California, March 2002.

Hanson, G. S. (1995). The organizational evolution of NAWE. *Initiatives, 56*(4), 29–36.

Hispanic Association of Colleges & Universities. (2011). *HACU 101.* http://www.hacu .net/hacu_101.asp.

Jesuit Association of Student Personal Administrators. (2013). *About JASPA.* http:// www.jesuitstudentaffairs.org.

Lipka, S. (2011, April 27). Two student-affairs groups vote not to merge. *Chronicle of Higher Education.* http://chronicle.com/article/2-Student-Affairs-Groups-Vote/ 127282/

Moore, L. V., & Neuberger, C. G. (1998). How professional associations are addressing issues in student affairs. In N. J. Evans & C. E. Phelps Tobin (Eds.), *The state of the art of preparation and practice in student affairs: Another look* (pp. 61-80). Lanham, MD: American College Personnel Association.

NACA—National Association for Campus Activities. (2012). *The NACA foundation.* http://www.naca.org/Scholarships/Pages/default.aspx.

National Association for Equal Opportunity in Higher Education. (2010). *About NAFEO.* http://www.nafeo.org/community/web (2010/about.html.

National Association of Diversity Officers in Higher Education. (2012). *History.* http://www.nadohe.org/history.

National Association of Student Affairs Professionals. (n.d.). *Upcoming events.*

NASPA—Student Affairs Administrators in Higher Education. (2008). *History.* http:// www.naspa.org/about/history.cfm.

NASPA—Student Affairs Administrators in Higher Education. (2013a). *About us.* http://www.naspa.org/about/default.cfm.

NASPA—Student Affairs Administrators in Higher Education. (2013b). *Events and programs.* http://www.naspa.org/programs/default.cfm.

NASPA—Student Affairs Administrators in Higher Education. (2013c). *NASPA foundation.* http://www.naspa.org/fdn/default.cfm.

NASPA—Student Affairs Administrators in Higher Education. (2013d). *NASPA undergraduate fellows program.* http://www.naspa.org/programs/nufp/default.cfm.

NASPA—Student Affairs Administrators in Higher Education. (2013e). *Past presidents.* http://www.naspa.org/about/pastpres.cfm.

National Council on Student Development. (2013). *Mission.* http://www.ncsdonline .org/home/index.html.

NCANHE—National Coalition for the Advancement of Natives in Higher Education. (2013a). *Welcome.* http://ncanhe.wordpress.com/welcome/.

NCANHE. (2013b). National Coalition for the Advancement of Natives in Higher Education 2nd annual meeting. http://eventful.com/rapidcity/events/national-coalition-advancement-natives-higher-edu-/E0-001-061991283-2.

Nuss, E. M. (2003). The development of student affairs. In S. R. Komives & D. B. Woodard Jr. (Eds.), *Student services: A handbook for the profession* (4th ed, pp. 65-88.). San Francisco, CA: Jossey-Bass.

Sandeen, A. (1998, May–June). Creeping specialization in student affairs. *About Campus*, 2–3.

Steffes, J. S. (2001). *The experiences of women in leadership in the American College Personnel Association.* Unpublished doctoral dissertation, University of Maryland, College Park.

StudentAffairs.com. (2013). *Professional associations.* http://studentaffairs.com/web/professionalassociations.html.

Washington Higher Education Secretariat. (2013). *About WHES.* http://whes.org/aboutwhes.html.

PART THREE

STUDENTS: THE PURPOSE OF PROFESSIONAL PRACTICE

There are many pathways to positions in student affairs and a myriad of professional specialties. What all practitioners have in common is a commitment to enriching the college experience for our students. Part 3 focuses on students, and includes chapters addressing student diversity, developing international and multicultural campus communities, helping students prepare for lives of purpose, fostering collaboration to help students be healthy and fit, and serving students online and at a distance. In chapter 13, Anna Ortiz and Stephanie Waterman explore how the makeup of the student bodies on our campuses is changing. They broadly define student diversity and challenge student affairs professionals to stay attuned to demographic changes in their student populations in order to continue to serve all of their students well. The theme of student diversity continues with chapter 14, in which Jason Laker and Tracy Davis explore the ways that student affairs professionals can effectively promote equitable multicultural and international communities with significant and wide-ranging educational benefits. They argue that student affairs professionals must accept the mandate to become multiculturally skilled and commit themselves to the long-term process of developing more inclusive campuses. In chapter 15, Michele Murray and Robert Nash explore the centrality of meaning making to the college student experience. They offer pedagogical strategies and tools student affairs educators can use to guide students in their search for meaning and purpose. Chapter 16, authored by Joy Gaston Gayles, Tiffany J. Davis, and Mary Howard Hamilton, focuses on the interconnected roles of intercollegiate athletics, recreation, and student affairs. They postulate that student affairs professionals should collaborate with other campus educators to develop opportunities for students to develop habits of physical fitness that will prepare them to take active and healthy roles in society. In the final chapter in this section, Anita Crawley and Andy Howe reflect on the tremendous growth of online learning and the challenge of serving students online and at a distance. Chapter 17 addresses the role of student affairs in supporting online learners and offers strategies innovative institutions have used to improve the retention, success, and completion of online students.

CHAPTER THIRTEEN

THE CHANGING STUDENT POPULATION

Anna M. Ortiz and Stephanie J. Waterman

The changing demographic landscape of the United States has important implications for higher education and student affairs. The often-cited projection that by 2050 the United States will no longer have a non-Hispanic White majority population continues to hold in census cohort-component models. In fact, although White Americans will continue to be the largest racial group, their proportion of the population will drop to 46.3 percent, representing a decrease of 35 percent from 2015 and 2050. African American, Native American, and Native Hawaiian/Pacific Islanders will see slight increases in their proportions of the population. Asian Americans will see an increase of 65 percent between 2015 and 2050, and Hispanics will experience a 59 percent increase. By 2050 Hispanics will be the largest non-White ethnic group, with 30 percent of the population, well over double the size of the next non-White racial group, African Americans, at 13 percent in 2050 (Guarneri & Ortman, 2009). Every state showed increases in the diversity of their populations between the 2000 and 2010 censuses. In 2010, Texas joined California, Hawaii, and New Mexico as minority majority states. Seven states (Idaho, Iowa, Maine, New Hampshire, Minnesota, Nebraska, and Nevada) saw their minority populations increase more than 50 percent (Humes, Jones, & Ramirez, 2011). With the exception of Nevada, these states remain overwhelmingly White, but the increases in the diversity of their states surely signals an important change for all states, not only those with traditionally high minority populations.

This chapter explores the multiple ways in which the national collegiate student population is changing and postulates how student affairs professionals need to lead campuses in meeting the needs of a multitude of students. The importance of this leadership cannot be overstated because maintaining or increasing racial and ethnic diversity in the face of shrinking resources and limited access is a challenge. Students are diverse in more ways than ever before, calling student affairs professionals, especially those trained in our graduate preparation programs, to consider the multitude of ways in which our students will change.

Defining Diversity

Traditionally, when we speak of diversity in higher education, the discussion is limited to the participation of racial and ethnic groups, as well as gender equity. However, a number of student characteristics can be considered as adding to the diversity of higher education. In this chapter we broaden the definition of student diversity to include socioeconomic status, ability status, sexual orientation, veteran status, immigration-generational status, generational status in college, transfer students, gender, religious status, and nontraditional-age students. Although we do not attempt to thoroughly discuss participation rates and current issues regarding each of these important student characteristics, we do attempt to update the most important information about these students.

Scholarly Works on Student Diversity

The profession is fortunate that scholarship exploring the diversity of students in higher education has exploded in recent years. Since the 2009 publication of the previous volume of this handbook, a wealth of material has been published. These texts more thoroughly describe specific groups and recommend how student affairs professionals can better serve them. Reason and Renn (2012) examine trends in student outcomes considering institutional type, gender, sexual orientation, race, and family income. Winkle-Wagner and Locks (2013) use an intersectional approach, connecting race, class and gender to cover a range of college experiences.

Cuyjet, Howard-Hamilton, and Cooper, (2011) offer detailed information on multiple cultural groups and explore associated issues such as multicultural awareness and oppression. Bonner, Marbley, and Howard-Hamilton, (2011) focus on how diverse student groups experience the millennial phenomena. Ortiz and Santos (2009) report on the ethnic identity and college experiences of four pan-ethnic groups. Shotton, Lowe, and Waterman (2013) offer a book about Native American college students. Ching and Agbayani (2012) bring authors together to discuss the experiences to specific Asian American and Pacific Islander groups. Laker and Davis (2011) join Harper and Harris (2010) in extending the discussion of gender to masculinities in higher education. Hamrick, Rumann, and associates (2012) present one of the first extensively researched volumes on veterans in higher education. Though this list is long, it is but a selective list of all the work that has been done on specific student populations since 2009. The in-depth examination in each of these volumes provides ample opportunity for student affairs professionals to expand their knowledge base and gives them information they need to develop expertise to serve diverse student groups through direct service delivery and program development.

Yesterday, Today, and Tomorrow

The changing college student population has always influenced the collegiate environment. This section begins with a short overview of the changing student body of the past, discusses today's student characteristics, and offers projections for the future.

Yesterday

Although change comes slowly to higher education, shifts in the student body have always been a factor in changing educational institutions. After the Civil War, African American demand for education resulted in the establishment of Black colleges throughout the South, although some northern institutions opened their doors to a limited number of Black college students (Anderson, 1988). Civil Rights Era activists demanded equal educational opportunities that increased college access for African Americans beyond the Historically Black College and Universities (HBCUs) increasing their enrollments.

The women's rights movement that coincided with the civil rights movement also demanded access to higher education, resulting in increases in women attending college (Eisenmann, 2006). After World War II the GI Bill resulted in a rapid increase in nontraditional students and expansion of college and universities to support returning soldiers (Thelin, 2004).

Underrepresented students also made their presence known in Hispanic-Serving Institutions (HSIs) and in Tribal Colleges and Universities (TCUs). HSIs are a prime example of the changing students' influence on higher education. HSIs are "accredited degree-granting colleges and universities with Hispanic students accounting for 25 percent or more of the undergraduate enrollment" (Gasman, 2008, p. 23). HSIs were not created specifically for the Hispanic population; the increased Hispanic student enrollment changed the institution. TCUs, however, were established for and by, Native American communities starting with Navajo Community College (now Diné College) in 1965. Tribal Colleges have developed into institutions that serve their communities in multiple ways, demonstrating the significant role that institutions of higher education can play in the ongoing community development (Benham & Stein, 2003). HBCUs, HSIs, and TCUs are often discussed under the umbrella term of minority-serving institutions.

In addition to the development of minority-serving institutions, multicultural student support offices, women's centers, and LGBTQ centers have been created in response to the increase in enrollment of these students and student demand.

Today

There are more than 20 million students enrolled in institutions of higher education (Chronicle of Higher Education, 2013). Of these, 55 percent are White Americans, 13.3 percent are African Americans, 12.8 percent are Hispanic, 5.4 percent are Asian, .3 percent are Pacific Islander, .8 percent are Native American and 1.9 percent are bi- or multiracial. Women continue to outpace men in higher education participation, with 57 percent of the national student population. And for Black, Hispanic, and Native American women, their participation can be up to 20 percent higher than men of their race or ethnic group (Chronicle of Higher Education, 2013). Slightly more students attend four-year public institutions (37 percent) than two-year colleges (36 percent), with much fewer attending four-year private institutions (18 percent), and four-year for-profit institutions (fewer than 1 percent). Just over 20 percent of students attend a minority-serving institution, with most of those attending a

HSI (18 percent). The remaining attend HBCUs (1.5 percent), women's colleges (.4 percent), and tribally controlled colleges (.09 percent). Native American enrollment in predominantly white institutions and four-year institutions has increased (DeVoe, Darling-Churchill, & Snyder, 2008). In 2012, 66 percent of all high school graduates enrolled in higher education (Fry & Taylor, 2013). Eighty-five percent of students attend college full-time (Fry & Taylor, 2013).

In 2011, the year for which there is latest data, more than 1.6 million students earned bachelor's degrees (Chronicle of Higher Education, 2013). Of these graduates, 64.3 percent are White, 9.4 percent African American, 8.4 percent Hispanic, 6.4 percent Asian Americans, .5 percent Native American, and .2 percent Native Hawaiian and Pacific Islander. Notably, Whites and Asian Americans are the only ethnic or racial groups to have a larger share of bachelor's degrees awarded than their own share of the student population, indicating that for other racial and ethnic groups, graduation rates lag behind those of these two groups. Perna and Jones (2013) cite National Center for Education Statistics data that indicate "only 5 percent of Black and 8 percent of Hispanic high school graduates in 2009 took a rigorous academic curriculum" (p. 18). With an emphasis on testing in the K–12 environment, resources often target test performance rather than "activities that more directly promote college enrollment" (p. 19). Research on access and college knowledge note a widening gap between nontraditional and communities of color and White middle-class communities (Perna & Jones, 2013; Perna, Rowan-Kenyon, Bell, Thomas, & Li, 2008).

In 2012, 30.9 percent of all persons in the United States over the age of twenty-five had bachelor's degrees or higher. Ethnic and racial differences in the proportion are significant: Asian Americans in this age group have the highest postsecondary attainment at 50.7 percent, Whites at 34.5 percent, African Americans at 21.4 percent, and Native American and Hispanic at 16.7 percent and 14.5 percent, respectively (NCES, October 2012). With clear advantages associated with educational attainment—lower crime rates, fewer health problems, a more secure income, and reported life satisfaction (Baum, Ma, & Payea, 2010)—it is imperative that all student affairs professionals prepare themselves to support all students in their efforts to complete a college degree.

Tomorrow

Enrollment projections show that the number of students enrolling in post-secondary education will continue to grow, though not as rapidly as in the past. For example, enrollment growth from 1996 to 2010 increased by 46 percent, but predicted growth between 2010 and 2021 is only 15 percent (Husser & Baily, 2013). Traditional-age college students will continue to outnumber older age cohorts, but their growth will be slower (10 percent growth between 2010 and 2021). Nontraditional students, such as students over the age of twenty-five, parents, single parents, and veterans will continue to increase, similar to the increase they enjoyed between 2000 and 2010 (NCES Fast Facts, 2012). More specifically, students ages twenty-four to thirty-four will grow by 20 percent, and those over thirty-five will grow by 25 percent. Though both men and women will see growth patterns through 2021, women will continue to outpace men by 8 percent (Husser & Baily, 2013).

Hispanics, projected to be the country's largest non-White ethnic group by 2050, will also have the youngest population of any single racial or ethnic group, making their presence in K–12 education and higher education even more significant. Their projected growth from 2010 to 2021 is 42 percent (Guarneri & Ortland, 2009). Though not as dramatic as the growth of the Hispanic population, other ethnic and racial groups will also experience growth: Whites at 4 percent, African Americans at 25 percent, Asian Americans at 20 percent, and Native Americans at 1 percent. Multiethnic or biracial populations, which have only recently been segmented in the census, will double their numbers between 2015 and 2050 (Guarneri & Ortman, 2009).

Students attending high school and college simultaneously will be an increasing presence on our campuses. More than half of all postsecondary institutions reported that high school students took courses for credit either on their own or through dual enrollment programs (Marken, Gray, & Lewis 2013). Most of these courses were taught on the college campus and more than half of the students paid a discounted tuition rate. Although most campuses rely on the high schools to provide academic support for these students, 4 percent of institutions with dual enrollment programs offer them specifically to high school students in academic difficulty, complete with a full complement of support services.

Trends in Student Characteristics

The diversity of today's college students is also evident in trends that are seen in who and how students are attending college. These trends reflect the broad range of experiences and backgrounds that students bring with them to the college environment and also reflect the burgeoning body of research on college students in general. This section highlights significant trends that suggest departures from our traditional knowledge base concerning students.

Community College Students

With enrollment of students in two-year colleges nearly matching that of four-year public universities, it is not surprising that 28 percent of bachelor degree earners began their higher education careers in community colleges (Mullin, 2012). Hispanics are more likely to attend community colleges than any other ethnic or racial group, with 44 percent enrolling directly in a community college after high school (Fry & Taylor, 2013). Students who begin their higher education careers at community colleges are more successful in transfer when they are deeply engaged in their academic plans. Bradburn and Hurst (2001) found that transfer was most likely when students met the following criteria: were enrolled in twelve or more credits, began taking courses toward their bachelor degrees in their first year, and were pursuing academic majors. Success of community college transfer is not only the responsibility of student affairs professionals in those institutions. Student affairs professionals at receiving universities need to be equally concerned because transfer students are more successful when they are focused on transfer success (Mullin, 2012). Forty-seven percent of all college graduates have taken at least one course in a community college (Mullin, 2012), making the community college experience a needed area of interest for student affairs professionals.

Today's students seem to be more mobile than previous cohorts. The rising cost of higher education and the poor job climate likely play a role in student mobility rates. Hossler, Shapiro, and Dundar (2012a, 2012b) recently completed a groundbreaking study of student mobility in higher education. Tracking students over a five-year time period, they were able to gain important insights into college students who began college in 2006. They found that one third of all American college students transferred at least once during their college careers, and that 25 percent of those students "did so more than once" (p. 9). Although most students transferred in their second semester, 25 percent of students who transferred did so in their third year. Students did not transfer exclusively from community colleges; movement was lateral, as well as reverse, or back transfer. *Reverse transfer* refers to movement from a four-year institution to a two-year institution (Kajstura & Keim, 1992). Hossler et al, (2012b) report that 14 percent students reverse transferred and that 5 percent of those students were taking courses at community colleges in the summer to return to their four-year institutions. Summer sessioners can reduce cost by taking course requirements at the community college for cheaper tuition or to improve a grade point average without incurring the added costs of the four-year institution. Students who transferred also did so across state lines, with 22 percent of two-year college transfers moving out of state, and with 26 percent of four-year college transfers also doing so. Although they have yet to release a comprehensive community college transfer rate for the 2006 cohort, they have found that 20 percent of all students who started at a two-year college made their first transfer to a four-year college. Student affairs professionals play critical roles in student mobility in two ways. First, they are key players in student retention through their work directly with students and through the environments they create. Second, students who transfer to other institutions during their college careers need transition services, including tailored academic advising, as they seek to integrate into their new home institutions while optimizing coursework they have already completed for degree attainment.

Students and Immigration

Twenty-three percent of the undergraduate student population are either children of immigrants or immigrants themselves (Staklis & Horn, 2012). The majority of these students are of Hispanic or Asian origin, with more than 90 percent of all Asian American undergraduates falling into this category. These data are significant for student affairs professionals as first and second generation Americans have important distinctions when compared to college students whose families have a longer history in the country. Immigrants or children of immigrants are more likely to have English as their second language and are more likely to come from families where parents do not have experience in American colleges and universities (Portes & Rumbaut, 2006).

Although it is difficult to accurately count the number of undocumented students in higher education, their presence and student affairs professionals' interest in better serving them is a major development since the last edition of this handbook. Although their population is relatively small—up to 13,000 (Educators for Fair Consideration, 2012) in one estimate, to more than 60,000 in another (Immigration Policy Center, 2012)—their needs are high. Undocumented students, or DREAMers (in reference to the federal and various state Development, Relief and Education for Alien Minors legislation [DREAM Act]), face a continually changing legal and political landscape, encounter significant financial burdens in gaining a college education, and may experience isolation on our campuses.

Students and Ability Status

Eleven percent of the college population reports having one or more disabilities as defined by the American with Disabilities Act (NCES, 2012). Institutions report that learning disabilities are most frequently reported (33 percent), followed by ADD/ADHD (18 percent), mental illness/psychological or psychiatric conditions (15 percent), and health impairments/conditions (11 percent) (Raue & Lewis, 2011). Most of these would be considered *hidden disabilities* making it likely that their numbers are underreported and also making it likely that students need to be served in different ways. Wolf and Brown (2014) recommend that student affairs professionals be especially vigilant in helping students with hidden disabilities with self-regulation, potential substance abuse, development of appropriate social skills, and gaining work experience, all in addition to services that help them manage their particular disability. Although veterans make up only 6 percent of all students with disabilities (NCES, 2012), Mikelson (2014) reminds us that these numbers, too, may be underreported because of the complicated nature of diagnosis through the Veterans Administration and the stigma attached to help-seeking among veterans. Undoubtedly, as stigma against help-seeking and disability in general declines, student affairs professionals can expect to serve more students who meet the various diagnosis standards.

Military Students

Military students (active duty, reservists, and veterans) make up approximately 4.0 percent of college enrollments, and 95 percent were considered independent students. The average veteran or active service member tends to be a white male, over the age of twenty-four and married (Radford & Weko, 2011). DeSawal (2013) outlines several elements of military life that may sometimes be at odds with the norms and culture of higher education institutions. Military norms such as discipline, hierarchy, and structure—can conflict with autonomy, independent decision making, exploration, and experimentation—expectations institutions may have of their traditional-age students. In Barry, Whiteman, & Wadsworth's (2014) analysis of more than a decade of research on veteran students, they found that despite the confidence and self-reliance they may have experienced in active service, veteran students with post-traumatic stress disorder were inclined to experience binge drinking, suicide ideation, and alienation on campus. They also found that veterans perceived less emotional support from their peers and often had to bear insensitive questions about their active duty. Nearly all institutions who enroll military service members, veterans, or their dependents have an office or staff member dedicated to offering or facilitating specialized services, with the most popular being benefit and financial aid counseling and referral services (Queen & Lewis, 2014). These programs certainly assist in helping veteran students navigate the college environment. However, initiatives such as the VetNet Ally Programs also help mitigate the negative stereotypes and subtle discrimination many veterans feel on campus. Through these programs faculty and staff are educated about the common issues veterans face in higher education and extend the campus network of support (Thomas, 2010).

Students and Gender

In the past, when student affairs professionals discussed college students in terms of gender, it was usually in the context of women's programs or gender equity. Contemporary work with college students and gender still includes women's programs and increasingly a variety of issues related to Title IX, but also includes a growing attention to men and masculinity and to transgendered students.

Harper and Harris's (2010) extensive volume on men and masculinity covers diverse issues such as men's identity development, race or ethnicity, sexual orientation, bad behavior, health and wellness, and sports. Laker and Davis (2011) followed with a similar volume. These editors and authors challenge student affairs professionals to consider the complexity of identity and behavior of men to better work with them to effectively promote positive development and to learn better strategies to recruit and retain men, especially African American men and Latinos. Additional work may be needed to encourage a higher proportion of men to attend college. Although men from all ethnic groups attend college at higher rates than 1967, women's rates have outpaced and surpassed those of men (US Department of Education, 2013).

Student affairs professionals have an increased interest in understanding and providing appropriate programming and support for transgendered students. The work of Beemyn and Rankin (2011), based on one of the largest studies of transgender people, helps us to understand the identity milestones for diverse transgender groups: feeling different from a young age, seeing to present as the gender assigned to them, repressing their identity in the face of hostility or isolation, initially misidentifying their identity, learning about and meeting other transgender people, changing their outward appearance, establishing new relationships, and developing a sense of wholeness. Attention to the unique needs and experiences of transgender students is needed, as many campuses combine programming and services for transgender students with Lesbian, Gay and Bisexual students (Dugan, Kusel, & Simounet, 2012).

Low-Income Students

Low-income students often come to college with characteristics that have been shown to be a challenge to attaining a higher education, but simultaneously they often have an incredible drive to do well to improve their life chances and raise the status of their families. Most are first-generation college students with limited models and support for navigating higher education institutions (McDonough, 1997). They are also more likely to come from PK–12 educational environments that did not prepare them well for college-level coursework. In a recent study (Mullin, 2012), it was reported that 36 percent of those who came from families with incomes of less than $25,000 graduated from high school with less than a 3.0 grade point average.

Today's increasingly diverse students will need skilled student affairs professionals. Scholars have found "widespread beneficial effects" of diversity (Astin, 1993, p. 15), both academically and socially (Gurin, Dey, Hurtado, & Gurin, 2002). However, challenges remain, some of which are discussed in the next section.

Challenges to Diversity

Challenges to diversity are a recurring theme in higher education. From misappropriation of funds for Native American students by the colonial colleges (Carney, 1999); to laws prohibiting the education of African Americans; to questionable college application forms for Jewish, Asian, and "nondominant" groups of the past (Lucas, 1996); to the current era's push-back in the courts (for example, *Regents of the University of California v. Bakke,* 438 US. 265 (1978); *Grutter v. Bollinger, et al.,* 539 U.S. 982 (2003); and *Fisher v. University of Texas at Austin* 560 U.S. (2013)), gains in diverse student participation are under continual scrutiny.

Recent court cases have challenged race as a consideration in college applications without acknowledgment that race and social economic status are closely linked. Students of color tend to come from poorer communities and schools with fewer resources, advanced courses, experienced teachers, and less college preparation (McDonough, 1997). The economic downturn of 2008 increased the gap between the rich and poor in the United States (Sherman & Stone, 2010), affecting women and communities of color more severely (Jank & Owens, n.d.). Despite these gaps, programs such as TRIO are under continuous threat of cuts (Field, 2013).

A challenge to diversity that is different from the past is the majoritarian push-back against immigration and ethnic studies. Political gridlock on immigration reform and passage of the DREAM Act delay enrollment for many Latino and immigrant groups (Downes, 2015)). Although the debate continues, Latino/a students, in particular, are being discouraged from entering higher education, and undocumented students are being deported. Ethnic studies at the K–12 level were banned in Arizona schools and upheld by a US Circuit Court Judge in March 2013 (Collom, 2013). Students entering higher education from these schools will not have the multicultural history and social understanding necessary to thrive and work well with others. This is a future challenge for higher education, and only time will tell if ethnic studies will be challenged at the college level in Arizona and elsewhere.

Diversity is also being challenged in ways that show themselves in micro-agressions perpetuated by students, faculty, and staff toward students from under-represented groups, including well-publicized incidents of bullying or the harassment of LGBT students. The recent mandates to universities to respond appropriately to reports of gender-related violence via Title IX also highlight the difficulty institutions encounter in managing the complexities of diverse campus environments.

Diversity as a Global Issue in Higher Education

Much of the discussion in this chapter has centered on diversity issues in US higher education; however, higher education institutions around the globe are also grappling with diversifying their systems and institutions. The European Education Community continues to refine efforts to increase student mobility across its 28 member countries. Though students continue to study in other countries at relatively low rates, the trend definitely shows upward movement (Brandenburg et al., 2013). Many European countries are beginning to grapple with access and equity issues, much like the United States. The economic crisis of 2008 caused countries to reconsider their nearly full funding of higher education. Although countries such as Denmark, Germany, Austria, and Sweden continue to offer free or very low tuition, others, such as Great Britain, the Netherlands, and Ireland, have begun to charge tuition at levels approaching and exceeding those in the United States (Brandenberg et al., 2013). It is early to determine how this will affect the diversity of student populations at those nations' most prestigious institutions, but the question needs to be considered.

Student activism in Arab countries, associated with the Arab Spring in 2011, brings attention to the need to reform higher education in the Middle East and North Africa (MENA) region. Nearly two thirds of the Arab population is under twenty-five. High-skilled jobs for them are scarce, and many find that universities cannot accommodate their numbers or needs (Grove, 2011). There is also concentrated interest to modernize systems of higher education across the region by developing new classifications systems guided by the Carnegie Corporation (Bhandhari & El-Amine, 2012). These efforts may increase access, promote expansion of higher education, and facilitate effective transition from university to the workforce.

International students make up 3.7 percent of the US student population, which represents a reversal of a ten-year trend of declining international student enrollments and restores the pattern of international undergraduates outnumbering their graduate student counterparts (Institute of International Education, 2012). China continues to send more students to the United States than any other nation (25 percent of all international students), increasing its numbers by 23 percent in just one year, from 2010 to 2011. India and South Korea follow, with Saudi Arabia coming in fourth, increasing their numbers by 50.4 percent from 2010 to 2011.

In 2010–11 nearly 300,000 US college students studied abroad, less than half the number of international students who come to study in the United States (Institute of International Education, 2012). The top destinations for these students are the United Kingdom, Italy, Spain, and France. Study abroad continues to be a predominantly White experience (77.8 percent), though there is a very slight upward trend for racial and ethnic groups since 2005. Most students either study abroad for a semester or the summer term, though since 2004 there are slight increases in short-term programs.

Recommendations

Like the technology they utilize, college student populations change. Higher education was slow to embrace social media and had to catch up with college students' social media knowledge, expertise, and savvy. Student affairs professionals should never be in that position with respect to their knowledge about students. The following recommendations are intended to help the profession keep up with the changing student:

1. *Be aware of who is on your campus.* Get to know students by looking beyond appearances. Data from the institution's research office may provide a demographic picture, and talking with students provides valuable information beyond statistics. Look for "hidden" information about students that can help you serve them better, such as ability status, immigration experiences, socioeconomic status, and family higher education experience.

2. *No matter the functional area in which a professional is housed, make academic achievement the center of your work.* Become concerned about remediation, wise major and career choices, and engage with students regarding their academic successes and challenges.

3. *Attend multicultural and ethnic studies programming.* Engage with those departments and encourage your staff to participate as well. Encourage students to academically engage in multicultural studies courses.

4. *Conduct a campus climate assessment* to discover where students experience pockets of prejudice, discrimination, and/or a general lack of belonging. Find the key supports for students and support those areas.

5. *Learn about the DREAM Act and immigration and your state's and institution's policies and opportunities.* Be discreet with any confidential information students may share.

6. *Stay abreast of demographic changes and know the latest research about student experiences and outcomes.* Take the initiative to provide information to faculty members and other academic affairs personnel.

Conclusion

In order to support college students, student affairs professionals must understand their students. This chapter and others in this volume seek to inform our profession in order to support *all of* our students well. This chapter explored how the changing student body and external forces have changed higher education and will likely continue to do so.

This chapter indicated how student demographics have changed, and postulated how they will in the future. Higher education and student affairs personnel need to keep up with their student populations, learning about who they and their concerns are. Ways to do this include professional development through workshops, conferences, and coursework. It is also likely that for many student affairs professionals, the current students with whom they work will not be like those of the future in a multitude of ways. All campuses will experiences shifts in demographics, but students will also generate their own changes in how they identify, how they prefer to experience college, and what they seek to gain from their college educations. Staying abreast of these changes requires deep engagement—listening to students, inviting communities to share knowledge, and going to communities to learn about their issues and realities: essential skills in the past, present, and future.

References

Astin, A. (1993). What matters in college? *Liberal Education, 4*, 4–15.

Anderson, J. D. (1988). *The education of Blacks in the South, 1860–1935*. Chapel Hill: University of North Carolina Press.

Bhandari, R., & El-Amine, A. (2012). Higher education classification in the Middle East and North Africa: A pilot study. Carnegie Corporation. http://www.iie.org/ Research-and-Publications/Publications-and-Reports/IIE-Bookstore/MENA-Institutional-Classification-Study.

Barry, A. E., Whiteman, S. D., & MacDermid Wadsworth, S. (2014). The current evidence base for student service members/veterans in higher education: A systematic review. Forthcoming. *Journal of College Student Development, 51*(1), 30–42.

Baum, S., Ma, J., & Payea, K. (2010). *Education pays, 2010: The benefits of higher education for individuals and society*. Trends in Higher Education Series. New York, NY: College Board Advocacy and Policy Center.

Beemyn, G. & Rankin, S. (2011). *The lives of transgender people*. New York, NY: Columbia University Press.

Benham, M.K.P. & Stein, W. J. (Eds.). (2003). *The renaissance of Native American higher education: Capturing the dream*. Mahwah, NJ: Lawrence Erlbaum.

Bonner, F., Marbley, A., & Howard-Hamilton, M. (2011). *Diverse millennial students in college: Implications for faculty and student affairs*. Sterling, VA: Stylus.

Bradburn, E. M., Hurst, D. G., & Peng, S. S. (2001). *Community college transfer rates to 4-year institutions using alternative definitions of transfer*. US Department of Education, Office of Educational Research and Improvement, National Center for Education Statistics.

Brandenburg, U., McCoshan, A., Bischof, L., Kreft, A., Storost, U., Leichsenring, H., Neuss, F., ... & Noe, S. (2013). *Delivering education across borders in the European*

Union. European Commission. http://ec.europa.eu/education/library/study/borders_en.pdf.

Carney, C. M. (1999). *Native American higher education in the United States*. New Brunswick, NJ: Transaction.

Ching, D., & Agbayani, A. (2012). *Asian Americans and Pacific Islanders in higher education*. Washington DC: NASPA Student Affairs Administrators in Higher Education.

Chronicle of Higher Education. (2013). *The almanac of higher education 2013–14*. http://chronicle.com/section/Almanac-of-Higher-Education/723/.

Collom, L. (2013, March 11). Judge upholds most of Arizona law banning ethnic studies. *Arizona Republic*. http://www.azcentral.com/news/politics/articles/20130311arizona-ethnic-studies-ban-ruling.html.

Cuyjet, M., Howard-Hamilton, M., & Cooper, D. (2011). *Multiculturalism on campus: Theory, models, and practices for understanding diversity and creating inclusion*. Sterling, VA: Stylus.

DeSawal, D. Contemporary student veterans and service members. In F. Hamrick, F. Rumann, & Associates. (2013). *Called to serve: A handbook for student veterans and higher education*(pp. 71-86). San Francisco, CA: Jossey-Bass.

DeVoe, J. F., Darling-Churchill, K. E., & Snyder, T. D., (2008). *Status and trends in the education of American Indians and Alaska Natives 2008*. Washington, D.C.: US Department of Education, National Center for Education Statistics, Institution of Education Sciences.

Downes, L. (2015, January 9). Behold the Republican immigration strategy: Mass deportation. *New York Times*. http://takingnote.blogs.nytimes.com/2015/01/09/behold-the-republican-immigration-strategy-mass-deportation/.

Dugan, J., Kusel, M., & Simounet, D. (2012). Transgender college students: An exploratory study of perceptions, engagement, and educational outcomes. *Journal of College Student Development, 53*(5), 719–736.

Educators for Fair Consideration. (2012). Fact sheet: An overview of college-bound undocumented students. http://e4fc.org/images/Fact_Sheet.pdf.

Eisenmann, L. (2006). Higher education for women in postwar America, *1945–1965*. Baltimore, MD: Johns Hopkins University Press.

Field, K. (2013, September 30). An advocate for access reflects on decades of political battles. *Chronicle of Higher Education*. http://chronicle.com/article/An-Advocate-for-Access/141957.

Fry, R., Taylor, P. (2013). High school drop-out rate at record low Hispanic high school graduates pass whites in rate of college enrollment. *Pew Research Center*. http://www.pewhispanic.org/files/2013/05/PHC_college_enrollment_2013-05.pdf.

Gasman, M. (2008). Minority-serving institutions: A historical backdrop. In M. Gasman, B. Baez, & C. S.V. Turner (Eds.), *Understanding minority serving institutions* (pp. 18–27). Albany: State University of New York Press.

Grove, J. (2011, September 22). Potential of the "Arab."Spring *Inside Higher Ed*. http://www.insidehighered.com/news/2011/09/22/conference_on_europe_and_the_arab_spring.

Guarneri, C., & Ortman, J. (2009). *United States population projections: 2000 to 2050*. http://www.census.gov/population/projections/files/analytical-document09.pdf.

Gurin, P., Dey, E.L., Hurtado, S., & Gurin, G. (2002). Diversity and higher education: Theory and impact on educational outcomes. *Harvard Educational Review, 72*(3), 330–366.

Hamrick, F.A., & Rumann, C.B. (Eds.). (2012). *Called to serve: A handbook of student veterans and higher education.* San Francisco: Jossey-Bass.

Harper, S., & Harris, F. (2010). *College men and masculinities.* San Francisco, CA: Jossey-Bass.

Hossler, D., Shapiro, D., & Dundar, A. (2012a). *Signature report No. 2: Transfer and mobility: A National view of pre-degree student movement in postsecondary institutions.* Herndon, VA: National Student Clearinghouse Research Center.

Hossler, D., Shapiro, D., & Dundar, A. (2012b). *Signature report No. 3: Reverse transfer: A National view of student mobility from four-year to two-year institutions.* Herndon, VA: National Student Clearinghouse Research Center.

Humes, K., Jones, N., & Ramirez, R. (2011). *Overview of race and Hispanic origin: 2010.* US Department of Commerce Economics and Statistics Administration US Census Bureau. http://www.census.gov/prod/cen2010/briefs/c2010br-02.pdf.

Hussar, W., & Bailey, T. (2013). *Projections of education statistics to 2021.* National Center for Education Statistics. http://nces.ed.gov/pubs2013/2013008.pdf.

Immigration Policy Center, College Board Advocacy. (2012). *Undocumented student statistics.* http://www.statisticbrain.com/undocumented-student-statistics/.

Institute of International Education. (2012). International student enrollment trends, 1949/50–2011/12." *Open Doors Report on International Educational Exchange.* http://www.iie.org/Who-We-Are/News-and-Events/Press-Center/Press-Releases/2012/2012-11-13-Open-Doors-International-Students.

Jank, S., & Owens, L. (n.d). *Inequality in the United States: Understanding inequality with data.* The Stanford Center on Poverty and Inequality. fromhttp://www.stanford.edu/group/scspi/slides/Inequality_SlideDeck.pdf.

Laker, J., & Davis, T. (2011). *Masculinities in higher education theoretical and practical considerations.* New York, NY: Taylor & Francis.

Lucas, C. J. (1996). *American higher education: A history.* New York, NY: St. Martin's Press.

Kajstura, A. & Keim, M. C. (1992). Reverse transfer students in Illinois community colleges. *Community College Review, 20,* 39–44.

Marken, S., Gray, L., & Lewis, L. (2013). *Dual enrollment programs and courses for high school students at postsecondary institutions: 2010–11.* (NCES 2013–002). U Washington, DC: S Department of Education, National Center for Education Statistics.

McDonough, P. M., (1997.) *Choosing colleges: How social class and schools structure opportunity.* Albany: State University of New York Press.

Mikelson, J. (2014) .Wounded warriors. In M. Vance, N. Lipsitz, & K. Parks (Eds.). *Beyond the Americans with Disabilities Act.* Washington DC: NASPA-Student Affairs Administrators in Higher Education.

Mullin, C. M. (2012, October). *Transfer: An indispensable part of the community college mission* (Policy Brief 2012–03PBL). Washington, DC: American Association of Community Colleges.

NCES Fast Facts. (2012). *Digest of education statistics. Table 200. Total fall enrollment in degree-granting institutions, by attendance status, sex, and age: Selected years, 1970 through 2020.* http://nces.ed.gov/programs/digest/d11/tables/dt11_200.asp.

National Center for Education Statistics. (2012, October). *Percentage distribution of undergraduate students enrolled in postsecondary institutions, by disability status and selected student characteristics.* https://nces.ed.gov/fastfacts/display.asp?id=60.

National Center for Education Statistics. (2012, October). *Percentage of first-year undergraduate students who took remedial education courses, by selected student and institution characteristics: 2003–04 and 2007–08.* http://nces.ed.gov/programs/digest/d10/tables/dt10_241.asp.

National Center for Education Statistics. (2012, July). *Enrollment, staff, and degrees/certificates conferred in all postsecondary institutions participating in title iv programs, by level and control of institution, sex of student, type of staff, and type of degree: Fall 2010, fall 2011, and 2010–11.* http://nces.ed.gov/programs/digest/d12/tables/dt12_219.asp.

National Center for Education Statistics (2012, October). *Percentage of persons age 25 and over with high school completion or higher and a bachelor's or higher degree, by race/ethnicity and sex: Selected years, 1910 through 2012.* https://nces.ed.gov/programs/digest/d12/tables/dt12_008.asp.

National Center for Education Statistics. (2012, December). *Fall enrollment and degrees conferred in degree-granting tribally controlled institutions, by state and institution: Selected years, fall 2000 through fall 2011, and 2009–10 and 2010–11.* http://nces.ed.gov/programs/digest/d12/tables/dt12_280.asp.

Ortiz, A. M., & Santos, S. J. (2009). *Ethnicity in college.* Arlington, VA: Stylus.

Perna, L. W., & Jones, A. P. (2013). *The state of college access and completion: Improving college success for students from underrepresented groups.* New York, NY: Routledge.

Perna, L. W., Rowan-Kenyon, H., Bell, A., Thomas, S. L., & Li, C. (2008). A typology of federal and state programs designed to promote college enrollment. *Journal of Higher Education. 79*(3), 243–267.

Portes, A., & Rumbaut, R. (2006). *Immigrant America.* Berkeley: University of California Press.

Queen, B., & Lewis, L. (2014). *Services and support programs for military service members and veterans at postsecondary institutions, 2012–13.* (NCES 2014–017). US Department of Education, National Center for Education Statistics, Washington, DC: US Government Printing Office.

Radford, A. W., & Weko, T. (2011). *Military service members and veterans* (NCES 2011–163). US Department of Education, National Center for Education Statistics. Washington, DC: US Government Printing Office.

Raue, K., & Lewis, L. (2011). *Students with disabilities at degree-granting postsecondary institutions* (NCES 2011–018). US Department of Education, National Center for Education Statistics. Washington, DC: US Government Printing Office.

Reason, R., & Renn, K. (2012). *College students in the United States: Characteristics, experiences, and outcomes.* San Francisco, CA: Jossey-Bass.

Sherman, A., & Stone, C. (2010, June 25). *Income gaps between very rich and everyone else more than tripled in last three decades, new data show.* Center on Budget and Policy Priorities. http://www.cbpp.org/files/6-25-10inc.pdf[cbpp.org.

Shotton, H. J., Lowe, S. C., & Waterman, S. J. (2013). *Beyond the asterisk: Understanding Native students in higher education.* Sterling, VA: Stylus.

Staklis, S., & Horn, L. (2012). New Americans in postsecondary education a profile of immigrant and second-generation American undergraduates. *Stats in Brief. US Department of Education.* http://nces.ed.gov/pubs2012/2012213.pdf.

Thelin, J. R. (2004). *A history of American higher education*. Baltimore, MD: Johns Hopkins University Press.

Thomas, M. W. (2010). A safe zone for veterans: Developing the VET NET Ally program to increase faculty and staff awareness and sensitivity to the needs of military veterans in higher education. California State University, Long Beach, 2010, 133; 3425191.

Thomas, S. L., & Perna, L. W. (2004). The opportunity agenda: A reexamination of postsecondary reward and opportunity. In J. C. Smart (Ed.), *Higher education: Handbook of theory and research* (Vol. 19, pp. 43–84). Dordrecht, The Netherlands: Kluwer Academic.

US Department of Education. (2013). Digest of Education Statistics, Table 302.60. Washington, DC. Available at: http://nces.ed.gov/programs/digest/d13/tables/dt13_302.60.asp

Winkle-Wagner, R., & Locks, A. M. (2013). *Diversity and inclusion on campus: supporting racially and ethnically underrepresented students* (Core concepts in higher education). New York: Routledge.

Wolf, L., & Brown, J. (2014). Fostering success for students with hidden disabilities. In M.L. Vance, N.E. Lipsitz, and K. Parks (Eds.), *Beyond the Americans with Disabilities Act*. Washington DC: NASPA-Student Affairs Administrators in Higher Education.

Court Cases and Legislation

20 U.S.C. Sections 1681–1688
Abigail Noel Fisher v. University of Texas at Austin et al. U.S. 570 (2013)
Barbara Grutter, Petitioner v. Lee Bollinger, et al., 539 U.S. 982 (2003)
H.R. 1751 (111th): American Development, Relief, and Education for Alien Minors Act
Introduced: March 26, 2009 (111th Congress, 2009–2010)
Status: Died (Referred to Committee)
Title IX, Education Amendment of 1972
University of California Regents v. Bakke, 438 U.S. 265 (1978)

CHAPTER FOURTEEN

UNFINISHED BUSINESS, DIRTY LAUNDRY, AND HOPE FOR MULTICULTURAL CAMPUS COMMUNITIES

Jason A. Laker and Tracy L. Davis

D iversity, access, equity, and inclusion continue to be among the most pervasive, complex, and contentious issues facing higher education communities today. Even the terminology used when discussing these subjects is contested. It is not uncommon for conflicts to arise over particular words or phrases, including questions about who is being intimated or excluded by them. To be sure, the language we use is important because it allows people to vividly describe lived experiences and to frame questions, problems, or goals. Nonetheless, there are many who dismiss such disagreements as political correctness gone too far; that in turn provokes those who see substantive implications vested in language. Most readers have experienced situations when debates about semantics sidelined efforts to make progress on resolving problems or achieving important goals associated with social justice. There is a philosophical foundation in taking time to excavate assumptions and to deal with word choices as sites on inquiry. For people whose social identities subject them to marginalization, oppression, or violence, the deliberative process (or lack of one) in a college community can itself exacerbate the barriers interfering with dignity, learning, and success. Giving space and attention to that experience can be restorative, even if the initial period is rife with mistrust, frustration, and resentment. The commitment to being with each other through the hard stuff builds trust and respect. We discuss practical applications in more detail, but this assertion is rooted in the oft-repeated mantra of social justice, perhaps informed by the Prayer of Saint Francis, seek first to understand, then to be understood. Take a few moments to reflect upon your own college experiences: particularly instances when someone offered you time to express your feelings and thoughts even if they were not completely formed, and to do so without judgment. Perhaps you have no such memories, and this remains a painful legacy of your education. Or, you might immediately remember such an instance with fondness, recognizing it as a critical and positive experience. In any case, this commitment to staying with difficult dialogues is essential and has potential fostering transformation of relationships and the cultivation of actionable wisdom.

Student affairs work includes many disparate responsibilities, but the shared interest in students' holistic development frequently situates student affairs professionals in the middle of identity conflicts. The challenges are formidable, even intimidating at times. After all, people and institutions are complex and relationships can be messy. This is only defeatist if one thinks of the goals of diversity and multiculturalism as achieving a state of happiness where everyone is comfortable. It is worth reflecting on the extent to which contentment has been the implicit ambition of diversity work by many well-intentioned colleagues. An often-unintended result of such reactions is to disarm or distract expressions of anger or hurt, but this tends only to delay or possibly ignite an even more consuming dispute. Institutional leaders and stakeholders such as trustees and alumni are instrumental in determining the climate for honesty, debate, and disagreement, for better or worse. Many ethical dilemmas arise between the desire to make room for honest conflict and sharing one's truth on the one hand, and the hope to keep one's job or standing on the other.

However, when the complexity and untidy nature of achieving social cohesion among an incredibly diverse group of people is seen as a natural business condition rather than a problem to be solved, new and hopeful possibilities emerge for the prospect of a truly multicultural campus community. This includes the recognition that it is in the very definition of diversity that there will be disagreements: disengagement, paradox, and debates present within an educational community.

Student affairs practitioners are possibly—though not assuredly—in a position to make meaningful impacts on creating and sustaining a welcoming and diverse environment. First, they can influence the level of inclusiveness on their campuses for students already present. Second, they can create opportunities for students to develop a deeper understanding and commitment to such issues in order to actively work for social justice.

Third, they can influence policies and institutional structures that promote systematic organizational change that push campus diversity and equity efforts to more meaningful levels. Fostering equitable international and multicultural campus communities will require strategies that account for and address complexities related to individual developmental processes, epistemological frameworks that undergird professional practice, and often deeply embedded institutional policies and structures. This chapter, therefore, explores the ways that student affairs professionals can effectively promote equitable multicultural and international communities by challenging and supporting at the individual level, routinely interrogating static professional belief systems, and transforming cosmetic institutional diversity initiatives.

Moreover, we suggest some conceptual and theoretical lenses to deepen analysis of social identity issues. Such an analysis is necessary for developing complex and more effective efforts to achieve inclusive campus communities. We also suggest structural efforts that reflect the concepts discussed here. One of these, which is actually best mentioned at the beginning of the chapter, is the practice of expressing one's positionality. Takacs (2003) describes positionality through a question: "How does who you are shape what you know about the world?" The authors have been good friends and colleagues for more than twenty years, and we have spent many hours grappling with this question and sharing it with our students. We are both Caucasian, *cisgendered* (a term used to indicate a lived experience of gender identity consistent with the sex assigned to them at birth [Crethar & Vargas, 2007]), males who identify as heterosexual. One of us identifies his ethnicity as Jewish, and the other as Italian. We are both approaching middle age and have long answers to the question of our faith identities. We are both middle class, presently without disabilities, married to female partners, and are parents. We have reflected upon and discussed how these various identities may shape how we experience our work and the societies in which we live, at times stimulating a great deal of self-consciousness about our privileges and creating hesitation about making any assertions about identities. When we wrote an earlier version of this chapter that appeared in the previous edition, we concluded that people with marginalized or oppressed identities are often coerced into doing so-called diversity work, and that such work is made more difficult when people with privileged identities do not share the risk and labor of doing it. We also recognized that spending a lot of time talking about our self-consciousness is indulgent, yet we also believe it is important for each person to have somewhere to explore such experiences. For this reason, we have offered such space to each other while also trying to be transparent with our friends, colleagues, and students across identities, both for accountability and to model the process. It is in this spirit that we have shared this passage. It also begins to explain where we are coming from—our positionality—and why we wrote this chapter.

Identity: A Critical Individual-Institutional Nexus

"An identity is established in relation to a series of differences that have become socially recognized. These differences are essential to its being...Identity requires difference in order to be, and converts difference into otherness in order to secure its own self-certainty" (Connolly, 2002, p. 64). Connolly speaks to the ways in which identities are co-constructed and to the power relations that situate identities in dynamic and hierarchical positions. Social identities are commonly discussed in student affairs circles in terms of privilege and oppression, and in particular the idea that the holders of a majority identity enjoy privilege, whereas those whose identity is in the minority are targeted for oppression. The implication is that each person is either privileged or oppressed.

Although it is critical to incorporate complexities of the co-construction of identities in the context of institutional oppression, emerging scholarship challenges the binary equation posed by such descriptions (for example, hooks, 2004; and Kaufman, 1999). That is, the either/or conceptualization of privilege and oppression essentializes identities in a manner that does not adequately address their multidimensional nature or the reality that students vary widely in terms of how deeply they identify with particular identities. Discussing identity as unilaterally privileged or oppressed not only fails to capture the complexity of lived identities, but it may also situate those with oppressed identities against those with privileged identities in some mythic binary debate that tends to close, rather than promote, discussion. In order to understand how to genuinely create multicultural communities we need to move beyond the frameworks that currently dominate student affairs discourse. According to Caryn McTighe Musil, Association of American Colleges and Universities vice president for Diversity, Equity, and Global Initiatives, speaking at the 2006 Diversity and Learning Conference, diversity education has outgrown its frameworks while practitioners hesitate to leave the structural, political, and intellectual shells they have so painfully crafted (Peltier Campbell,

2007, p. 1). Moreover, Barcelo (2007) argues that "to be effective leaders we must be willing to reevaluate the structures of knowledge, the patterns of relationships, and the organizing principles of institutional life" (p. 3).

Few would argue that we have achieved the kind of educational equity required by our missions and outlined by law in our democracy. Carnevale and Fry (2002), for example, demonstrate that college students from historically under-represented populations often have differential access to resources before college that hinders educational attainment during college. In order to move beyond cosmetic changes that cover discrimination with a cloak of diversity, educators need to constantly question the assumptions that support our equity efforts, the meaning-making frameworks that deflect our focus toward simplistic solutions, and the assessment strategies that measure trivia. One of the purposes of this chapter, then, is to interrogate existing conceptual professional frameworks in order to explore roles and offer strategies that student affairs professionals might use in extending the journey toward inclusive and equitable international and multicultural campus communities. Accordingly, we assume that language like *community, international,* and *multicultural* connote meanings that cannot be understood in static or final ways, but rather are contextual and dynamic—and often quite personal and politically charged. Readers are encouraged to reflect upon and grapple with the ambiguous and at times contested discussion in this chapter, noting instances in which deeply held views are challenged and remaining open to the possibility of refining these views (or ultimately reinforcing them with additional depth of understanding). This is analog to the discussions readers will be encouraged to foster at their respective institutions—moving from esoteric and frustrating to understandable and still frustrating. Our experience is that finding solidarity in the experience of frustration about identity and institutional oppression offers liberating opportunities for agreement and/or connection among diverse groups of people, important ingredients of inclusive communities.

Despite the ambiguity associated with learning about identities, we cannot remain moral relativists with regard to the social commitments incumbent upon institutions of higher education. Colleges and universities must forcefully enact commitments to promoting understanding, and to nurturing cross-cultural and interidentity engagement for the purpose of underwriting a society in which all members have agency within, and access to an education. Doing so will take action to make both epistemological and fundamental structural changes.

Pedagogical Issues at the Individual Level

So, what is a well-meaning and well-educated student affairs practitioner to do when trying to understand the meanings and implications of equity work? Indeed, the contexts of college campuses are growing more complex. As discussed in chapter 13, the demography of higher education is dynamic, increasing in complexity, and thus poses profound challenges for practitioners. Accepting and effectively engaging the challenges, however, is a professional mandate. Fortunately, there is clear evidence that the struggle pays significant returns in terms of promoting learning and development.

There is general agreement in the literature that engagement across identities fosters cognitive development (Milem, Chang & Antonio, 2005; Pascarella, Edison, Nora, Hagedorn, & Terenzini, 1996; Smith & Associates, 1997; and Terenzini, Pascarella, & Blimling, 1996) and psychosocial growth (Antonio, 1998; Chang, 1996; Hurtado, 1997; and Smith & Associates, 1997), and that students learn more effectively in such environments. According to Gurin (2007), for example, "Complex thinking occurs when people encounter a novel situation for which, by definition, they have no script, or when the environment demands more than their current scripts provide. Racial diversity in a college or university student body provides the very features that research has determined are central to producing the conscious mode of thought educators demand from their students" (p. 2). From this perspective, fostering international and multicultural communities is quite simply an educational mandate for preparing citizens in a pluralistic democracy. We know, however, that although the rationale for creating diverse communities is clear, the work of advancing multicultural communities is anything but simple. Educational community participants' understanding of, and willingness to interact with, those who are different from themselves is not assured. Because engaging in the learning process is requisite, "a sustained and coordinated effort regarding diversity is necessary to increase the positive effects on student development and learning" (Chang, 2005, p. 15). Educational benefits do not accrue simply by bringing together diverse groups. Research (Chang, Denson, Saenz, & Misa, 2006; Jayakumar, 2008; Milem, Chang, & Antonio, 2005) demonstrates that campuses must provide engaging coursework covering historical, cultural and social bases for diversity and community, and there must be concurrent opportunities, encouragement, and expectations outside of the classroom for students to interact across identity differences.

Moreover, guiding and mediating the conflicts that naturally occur from such interactions are skills that require more than multicultural awareness and knowledge. Although awareness and knowledge about cultures and cultural differences is necessary, it is not sufficient to effectively negotiate the rocky terrain of establishing genuinely celebratory multicultural communities (Pope, Reynolds, & Mueller, 2004). An example of this complexity is evident in Jones and McEwen's (2000) original Multiple Dimensions of Identity (MDI) Model. In their model, sexual orientation, race, culture, class, religion, and gender are dimensions central to one's identity. The salience of a particular dimension to one's core identity depends on changing contexts that include current experiences, family background, sociocultural conditions, and career decisions and life planning. This model offers a template for gauging both individual interventions with, and institutional programs for, students, whether generally, or with respect to particular subpopulations. Moreover, Dolby (2000) challenges, "Instead of probing what identities are and how they structure experience (or what identities a person has), the critical questions revolve around how difference is produced in a particular situation, how it is explained, circulated, and reproduced, and how 'difference' as a construct interfaces with various structures of power" (p. 901).

As a practical tool for promoting multicultural understanding and development, student affairs professionals can use the MDI as a mental framework to avoid making assumptions about the individuals with whom they are working. This tool encourages professionals to consider how intersections of sexual orientation, race, culture, religion, class, and gender might affect a student. Moreover, the MDI offers a model for promoting discussion beyond an oversimplified dualistic conception of oppression to consider questions like how are we positioned differently and how this difference is being negotiated within the context of power. White, heterosexual, men, for example, are presumed to hold privilege. Although men with these identities generally hold racial, sexual, and gender privilege (depending on cultural context), focusing on the identity intersections such as class and gender or religion and race helps to more accurately capture not only how oppression works, but also how it needs to be navigated in order to be effective (Reed, 2008). Fine, Weis, Addelston, and Hall (1997), for example, in their qualitative research on men and boys in White working-class neighborhoods found that "white working-class men … scramble to reassert their assumed place of privilege on a race-gender hierarchy in an economy that has ironically devalued all workers" (p. 77). Further complicating the discussion is the need to understand that class too often goes unnamed in our multicultural discussions, and it is much more complicated than just level of income. It includes language usage, dress styles, educational level, occupations seen acceptable, how leisure and social time is spent, and so on (Longwell-Grice, 2002; Reed, 2008). The complexity of identity dimensions, their diverse intersections, and the intricate contexts in which they are performed illustrates the absurdity of "essentializing" identity and the necessity of using newer critical approaches. Reinforcing this idea, Kaufman (1999) persuasively argues, "Our whole language of oppression is in need of overhaul for it is based on simple binary oppositions, reductionist equations between identity and social location, and unifocal notions of self" (p. 70).

Promoting multicultural and international communities at the individual level will also require patience and empathy with those who have not seriously engaged issues of human diversities and institutional oppression. Learning about these issues is not simply an intellectual process, but also a profoundly emotional and psychological one. Although it is understandable to be frustrated and angry at the lack of knowledge about differences and the systems that privilege some and oppress others, we should not be surprised when we encounter resistance. In fact, it is incumbent upon those of us in the educational enterprise to meet students and peers where they are and aim learning interventions at appropriate developmental levels and to do so with sensitive, thoughtful responses. Reason, Broido, Davis, and Evans (2005), for example, provide the theoretical foundation and practical strategies to effectively foster the development of social justice allies, specifically addressing pedagogical issues related to negotiating sexual orientation, gender, disability and race. Davis and Harrison (2013), furthermore, outline critical pedagogical strategies for effectively meeting community members' resistance in a manner that increases potential for enlisting them in the battle for social justice and equity.

Student affairs professionals need a broader and more complex understanding of the larger political and sociohistorical context in which learning and development occur. Communication and interpersonal skills, though necessary, need to be matched with a fundamental understanding of inclusion and power. Who on a campus should have the power to decide that there is indeed an issue? Who gets to decide the issue is resolved? Does resolution require that all stakeholders are satisfied with the outcome? What about those who are regarded not as stakeholders, but instead as bystanders? Should their views inform answers to these questions?

By the time students arrive at college, they have been subject to at least eighteen years of supremacist ideologies along every category of identity. Whether they hold majority or marginalized identities in any one of these categories, the messages are present within their minds. Educators should understand and ideally become forgiving of the fact that both their own and students' worldviews will not simply become free of *-isms* during the time they are enrolled or employed. This is not a call for complicity, but rather for approaches that incorporate understanding, respect, patience, and a willingness to stay in the conversation. We need to expect that the work of fostering inclusion will be rife with confusion, fear, guilt, shame, anger, resentment, frustration, and mistrust. Occasionally, and ideally, the work can achieve both hope and justice. However, those who do the work must first respect the complexity and continually evolving understanding of identities in order to put issues in perspective and to avoid indulging in either self-congratulatory or indignant stances.

The Conversation Must Become More Uncomfortable for All

It is well past time for holders of majority identities to work harder, and to contribute more significantly to achieving inclusive campus communities. What, then, has been preventing this from happening? In relation to the earlier statement about socialization, some might argue that those who hold majority identities (in the United States, typically Caucasians, men, heterosexuals, upper- and middle-class people, able-bodied people, and Christians) simply do not wish to cede the privilege and power afforded them and thus will act to affirm their position. This argument may be extended by discussing the supremacist notions inculcated into the majority population both subtly (for example, media images, product labels depicting mostly majority identities) and overtly (for example, racist, sexist statements in the public sphere) with respect to their particular identities. In short, they believe overtly or have adopted subconsciously that it is both just and appropriate for them to be secure in their position. Although understanding how privilege is mostly invisible and normalized is necessary, this explanation does not fully illuminate the harmful effects of these processes, nor offer any hopeful alternative or solution.

One possible area for attention, albeit politically loaded, is to explore how systems of privilege and oppression might harm those in the privileged role. Consider, for instance, how hooks (1984) discusses this with respect to gender: "Men are not exploited or oppressed by sexism, but there are ways in which they suffer as a result of it. This suffering should not be ignored. While it in no way diminishes the seriousness of male abuse and oppression of women, or negates male responsibility for exploitative actions, the pain men experience can serve as a catalyst calling attention to the need for change" (p. 73). She goes on to discuss the harmful effects of rigid gender role scripts on women, but also on men. There are analogs across identities. How, for instance, does the faith of a Christian get diminished when Jews, Muslims, and other religious minorities are made invisible in its shadow or in its practice? How does White Privilege interfere with a Caucasian's knowing oneself as a racial being and thus undermine both identity formation and the ability to form authentic relationships with a wider range of people?

Student affairs practitioners are in an important position to help with this dilemma by raising difficult questions. Undoubtedly, it is difficult to consider offering a majority person a compassionate ear when one is either profoundly affected by oppression, or deeply wounded from it. Ironically, the authors argue, taking this time can create a mutually liberating transformation. People of majority identities generally, and student affairs staff with these identities in particular, should seriously consider the potential gains associated with being the first person to offer this to students. The old model, in which we diminish students by demanding that they get in touch with their privilege, or call them homophobic, sexist, and/or racist (whether we do so to their face or to our colleagues outside of their view), has yet to yield the change we claim to want. If we want to foster self-awareness, growth, and change, then we will need a different approach. Although it may be justifiable and even valid to become enveloped in historical injuries, beliefs, personal issues, shame, guilt, and even fear, we must support each other in this difficult work, and hold each other compassionately accountable in order to model the change we wish to experience.

Student affairs professionals with agent or majority identities must also learn to effectively tolerate discomfort. Rather than performing a "you got me all wrong—I'm an ally!" stance, majority members need to tolerate the understandable anger from people who have been marginalized because of targeted identities. Although sometimes imprecisely directed, anger because of past experiences of marginalization and the agent/majority members' willingness to listen nondefensively can provide a painful but positive catalyst toward authentic relationships. Moreover, majority members' focus on "being a good one" can lead to complicity with superficial expectations and accolades for doing the work that we all should be doing for the sake of promoting both individual development and institutional community. To do otherwise risks a presumption of charity and thus reinscribes supremacy and privilege.

Language Matters

Another dimension of the constraints undermining inclusive multicultural campus communities is simply that our language tends to be too imprecise to articulate a problem accurately or convincingly. Words such as *racism*, *sexism*, and *homophobia* are used by student affairs practitioners and others to describe dynamics and behaviors ranging from subtle cultural misalignments in structures or policies to overt acts of hate violence. To be sure, any place along that continuum can result in deep hurt, marginalization, or exclusion of people of oppressed identities. In terms of remedying or preventing the situations, however, it is necessary to more clearly name what is happening. Given the espoused values of the student affairs profession, we should be accountable to be more sophisticated in our analysis. For instance, words like *normative*, and *centric*, whether used alone or as suffixes can be somewhat clearer. For example, an environment may be Anglocentric, referring to a space in which Caucasian imagery and its constituent ethnicities' practices and customs are socially normalized and dominant. A heteronormative environment thus could be described as containing images, customs, and expectations that assume heterosexual identity among its members, which in turn privileges those who enact that identity and oppresses those who do not. In this example, even heterosexual people who do not conform to the heteronormative image of gender performance can experience marginalization, social pressure to perform their gender identity according to dominant norms, or even violence and oppression. When we describe a place as homophobic, our framing may be reductionist because there are a wide range of dynamics and nuances that could be subsumed into that broad category. We might be missing an opportunity to recognize and respond to a dynamic that is centric but not actively hostile. Clarifying language is important for identifying the issues, their influences, lived experiences, impacts, and possible remedies.

There are at least two risks to avoid when seeking precision. The first one is the risk of getting so caught up in semantics or wordsmithing that it overtakes the initial reason for the process, which is to give voice to experiences and to move toward improvements, social inclusion, and cross-cultural engagement. The second risk is to slip into a dysfunctional competitiveness of debating which oppressive dynamic is worse than another, and who has the more horrid or less bad experience. In this regard, a preliminary and periodic conversation about process and perhaps ground rules can be helpful toward keeping first principles in the forefront of the effort.

Looking Inward: Student Affairs and Identity Politics

As mentioned earlier, serious challenges have been leveled that educators have become too complacent in accepting stagnant and self-serving mental frameworks that fail to effect change with regard to diversity. We need to apply this critique to the field of student affairs and question whether we have been languishing in outdated and insular, or at least limiting paradigms that often undermine practitioners' abilities to facilitate inclusive communities. Stier (2006), for example, challenges us to consider how much we remain emotionally distant and intellectually abstract in our engagement with others on issues of diversity when he says, "Undoubtedly, there is a thin line between being a critical observer, interculturally competent participator and a self-righteous educator. In short, ambitions must not end with merely analyzing the actions and perspectives of others but must be followed by continuous scrutiny of his or her own [actions and perspectives]" (p. 5). From this perspective knowledge about various cultures and awareness of human differences is book knowledge that is by nature static. As Dewey (1938) forcefully articulated over three quarters of a century ago, book knowledge "is taught as a finished product with little regard either to the ways in which it was originally built up or to changes that will surely occur in the future" (p. 19). Our explicit challenge in education, in general, and in diversity education, in particular, is to routinely interrogate our static mental frameworks and personal perspectives in order to "evoke curiosity and passion for new cultural experiences and knowledge that dissolves our own cultural imaginaries" (Stier, 2006, p. 8).

These are decidedly process, not content, issues. As such, process competence requires intrapersonal skills of "viewing oneself in the position of the other (empathy); acting as both insider and outsider roles (consciousness to positionality); coping with problems that arise originating from intercultural encounters; and keeping flexible and open with a receptive mind, noting cultural peculiarities without either valuing them automatically or uncritically" (Stier, 2006, p. 7). If we do not take on this critical, process-oriented frame of mind, student affairs professionals may unintentionally and continuously reproduce the very systems of oppression we aim to deconstruct.

Promoting Structural Transformation

Wilkinson and Rund (2000) stated that organizational "structures should be reviewed periodically to determine their effectiveness… (since) the majority of campuses continue to follow the more traditional organizational constructs" (p. 592). Static organizational structures, like stagnant knowledge and mental frameworks, need to be routinely reviewed. Davis and Harrison (2013) describe how conventional organizational practices steeped in hierarchy and technical rationality can be challenged by mindful strategies that incorporate equitable and inclusive processes. Murray's (2006) Global Fund for Women is offered as a model that uses organizational approaches congruent with culturally inclusive policies and practices. The Global Fund for Women, for example, focuses on issues raised by women in developing countries rather than those identified by the so-called experts. Another strategy is to enfranchise those traditionally disenfranchised by giving them structural leadership positions within the organization. Central to the process of promoting multicultural campus communities is reconsidering our organizational charts, recruitment processes, curricula, and ways of keeping those in leadership positions accountable.

Chief Diversity Officer

A variety of institutions, such as the University of Minnesota, Providence College, the University of Virginia, Anne Arundel Community College, and the University of California-Berkeley have modeled mindful attention to the changing landscape of higher education by revisiting organizational needs and structures and appointing senior level diversity officers. As Nancy "Rusty" Barcelo (2007), the first vice president for Access, Equity, and Multicultural Affairs at the University of Minnesota, points out, by creating these positions "institutions not only illustrate their renewed commitment to diversity but, more importantly, assert that diversity will be 'at the table', informing policy in formal ways at key meetings with senior officials" (p. 2).

Although the practice of establishing a chief diversity officer holds promise, Barcelo (2007) contends that its success depends upon the following important aspects of infrastructure: "research and data management; development and grant writing; communications, public relations and a website; a senior staff member who focuses on administrative and personnel issues, community development outreach, faculty and staff development, student outreach, and retention; a central budget that is base funded; a staff of diverse multiculturalists; and, diversity units that report to the CDO and provide direct services to their constituencies and resources to the campus and community" (p. 3). If colleges and universities are genuinely committed to promoting international and multicultural campuses, our organizational charts and staffing structures need to reflect those values.

Curricula and Co-curricula

A recent review of the past decade of research related to diversity experiences provides consistent evidence that interactions with and about people from varying cultures and ethnic identities have positive net effects on a wide variety of cognitive and psychosocial outcomes (Pascarella & Terenzini, 2005). This analysis found, for example, that critical thinking, complexity of thought, self-concept, locus of control, civic engagement, and openness to intellectual challenge are all positively influenced by exposure to diversity experiences. Although causal relations are not yet completely clear, Pascarella and Terenzini report that "the evidence is mounting that structural diversity (the racial-ethnic representation among students and faculty on campus) is a necessary if not sufficient condition for educational impact" (p. 638).

Quite simply, our in-class and out-of-class curricula must reflect the emerging needs of a global economy and multicultural world. Although monocultural Western structures of knowledge are still relevant, they need to be interrogated and matched by exposure to philosophies, epistemological assumptions, and cultural ways of knowing outside of the traditional canons. For example, traditional student development interventions in the residence halls focused on large come-one-come-all programming could be replaced by funding smaller, more collaborative dialogues aimed at exploring controversial issues in the news related to cultural dynamics.

In addition, current educational offerings could be evaluated based on the following questions related to Ukpokodu's (2007) suggestions for campuswide diversity curriculum infusion: How do our interventions help prepare students to live and work in today's multicultural democracy and interdependent world? What issues of diversity, social justice, and civic engagement are infused in our out-of-class offerings and how? How inclusive are our selected materials? How do student and staff worldviews, learning styles, and teaching strategies match, and how are students' learning styles accommodated? And, how diversified are staff strategies for facilitating learning?

Although offering programs that reflect attention to these questions is a first step, we must also bring diverse students together to interact across racial and other social identities. It is easier and less risky for students to gravitate to others with similar identities. According to Chang (2005), "When students retreat from the rich and complex social and learning opportunities offered by a diverse campus and settle into institutional spaces that are more homogenous, they are likely to miss out on the important benefits derived from diversity" (p. 3). It our experience that there is no substitute for sustained and meaningful (and often mediated) dialogue among people with different social identities both in terms of promoting learning about these issues and sustaining multicultural campus communities.

Effective Recruitment and Retention Processes

Given the clearly demonstrated educational benefits of learning environments that both contain diverse representation and foster active engagement across difference, it follows that our recruitment and retention strategies for establishing a diverse human aggregate is critical. Traditional methods for recruiting and retaining a diverse staff and student population, like proactive advertising in diverse media, direct contact with diverse colleagues, and effective multicultural training of all staff, still need to be utilized, but we must go further. Planning for diversity tends to take on a chicken-and-egg framework—do we recruit diverse populations to achieve some critical mass that sustains diversity, or do we work on establishing programs that might then attract people not currently present on the campus? The authors argue that though both of these are important, institutions rarely invest significantly in fostering an inclusive sensitivity in the majority populations already on the campus. This is arguably a linchpin issue. Building resource centers and appointing support staff offer refuge, but from what? It is the daily reinscription of who matters and who doesn't that creates the climate. In truly multicultural places, even those in the majority population depart from the subconscious (or conscious) notion that they constitute normalcy and tread into a worldview in which there is a genuine interest and effort to know each identity present as a means of learning about life and a lens to more deeply understand any subject of interest. That can be particularly difficult in academe, because the social and emotional dimensions are not easily or adequately explained by the intellectual and analytical ones.

So, to create a multicultural and inclusive campus environment, recruiting a diverse staff is just one of many important steps. It should be noted, though, that a critically self-aware and multiculturally skilled student affairs organization will be a place in which staff can express their worldviews, work styles, and be safe to model authentic sharing without paying a personal cost of marginalization within the workplace. As Pope et al. (2004) argue, addressing interpersonal and structural dynamics within the environment will help create a welcoming and nurturing environment that facilitates both multicultural retention and recruitment. From this perspective, all of the strategies we implement that effectively promote a multicultural campus are part of our retention and recruitment efforts. Effectively designed and targeted advertising or aggressive recruitment strategies aimed at developing a diverse candidate pool cannot mask an environment that does not truly welcome diverse voices, life experiences, and backgrounds for students and for the staff who work with them.

Assessment Strategies Toward Accountability

As mentioned earlier, one of the criticisms that has been leveled at traditional efforts to promote inclusive and diverse campus environments is that those efforts have resulted too frequently in only cosmetic changes. For example, so-called climate studies are often used to investigate the extent to which particular campus populations experience acts of oppression and discrimination, and they invariably point to bad news. One of us has argued that if there are calls for a climate study, we already know there is a climate problem. This is not intended to be sarcastic, but rather to point out that climate studies have significant limitations in practice.

Experiences of a campus are situational, contextual, and dependent on the identities and circumstances of those being asked about it. Even if a climate study were to determine, for instance, that 85 percent of respondents agree or strongly agree that a campus is inclusive, we are left to wonder about the other 15 percent, and, for that matter, how experiences of inclusion fluctuate and for what reasons. Static metaphorical snapshots are wholly inadequate for understanding dynamic conditions and experiences. In addition, it is common for climate studies to be conducted in the wake of bias incidents, their methodologies thus rooted in deficit paradigms at a very vulnerable moment for all concerned. By conducting such a study in the wake of an incident, administrators are likely to encounter politically charged reactions and to activate defensiveness among already mistrustful (for understandable reasons) people. Beyond that, it is not particularly thoughtful, because critical incident investigations are no substitute for honest climate appraisals.

An investigation focusing on places where particular populations feel most affirmed might yield more valuable information. To be clear, this is not a call for sugar coating or avoiding difficult truths, but rather a genuine interest in learning where an organization's best places reside, how and why. First, it allows for a nondefensive, positive and asset-based approach to the questions. Second, it points to specific and potentially reproducible and/or scalable locations of institutional strength. Third, it assumes the reality that there are places that don't feel affirming and removes that question from debate. This is especially valuable because a debate about whether an experience actually happened (or is currently happening) only serves to further silence and demoralize those who have been hurt.

We need, then, to implement effective assessment strategies that distinguish meaningful progress from superficial change. Student affairs professionals looking for checklist or purely quantitative strategies for assessing the effectiveness of our progress in creating multicultural campuses need to acknowledge that the nature of the phenomena being evaluated does not lend itself to simple designs. Pope (1995) suggests using a systematic Multicultural Organizational Development (MCOD) strategy for improving and assessing institutional effectiveness in eliminating social oppression and supporting socially just campus communities. Rather than viewing assessment as a static snapshot, the MCOD processes help transform organizations through questioning and evaluating underlying beliefs, routine practices, and core values. For example, the Student Affairs MCOD Template is an assessment tool that can be used by student affairs departments or divisions (Reynolds, Pope, & Wells, 2002, as cited in Pope, Reynolds, & Meuller, 2004). The assessment template identifies ten key areas for multicultural intervention: mission statement, leadership, policy review, recruitment and retention, multicultural competency in training, scholarly activities, programs and services, physical environment, assessment, and inclusiveness in the definition of multicultural. Specifically, for example, the target area of multicultural competency expectations and training focuses attention on opportunities for staff to attend diversity-oriented workshops and conferences, the supervision competencies of professional staff, professional development interventions aimed at diversity training, clarity of expectations regarding multicultural responsibilities of all staff, and annual evaluation of both individual and department diversity goals.

A team at Loyola Marymount University has implemented another assessment strategy. This group used an equity scorecard to support their strategic plan which aimed in part to actively promote diversity in the student body, faculty, and staff (Robinson-Armstrong, King, Killoran, Ward, Fissinger, & Harrison, 2007). The scorecard was developed by Estela Bensimon's (2004) team at the University of Southern California to address the problem of measuring equity. She claims that although valued in principle, equity is not routinely measured in relation to educational outcomes for specific groups of students. Bensimon describes the scorecard as an assessment tool that can "foster institutional change in higher education by helping to close the achievement gap for historically underrepresented students" (p. 45). The scorecard essentially promotes a consultative process that values both the broad needs of an institution and the goals of specific units and programs. Attention is given to access, retention, educational excellence, and institutional viability. Although quantitative data is used to assess these four dimensions, qualitative perspectives are not ignored. Educational excellence and institutional viability, for example, can be defined in a manner that accounts for contextual distinctions and other meaningful peculiarities. Data are then reviewed by local teams to develop and implement programmatic responses when necessary. Individual units, therefore, maintain control of equity initiatives and are held accountable for progress by either their supervisor or the president.

Conclusion

The philosophical and pragmatic challenges in this chapter do not promise quick or easy solutions. Professionals looking for shortcuts around the messy, uncomfortable, and emotionally charged discussions that need to occur in order to effectively interrogate our current models for implementing multicultural campus communities will have to look elsewhere for solutions, and are sure to be disappointed. If, however, we are willing to accept the educational mandate to become multiculturally skilled (as opposed to the static limitations of "competence"), we need to develop our "ability to reflect over, problematise, understand, learn from, cope emotionally with and operate efficiently in intercultural interaction situations" (Stier, 2006, p. 9).

Multiculturally diverse campus communities have significant and wide-ranging educational benefits for students. The stakes, therefore, are high and the pitfalls are legion. We must begin by critically reflecting on the assumptions with which we enter the discussion and taking inventory of our own understanding and capacity to meaningfully engage the issues discussed in this chapter. The structural suggestions offered grow out of an interrogation of these issues, but context matters. The strategies need to be adapted to the cultural context of specific institutions. Moreover, those in leadership positions need to understand and model the processes inherent in the journey toward truly multicultural campus communities.

Student affairs professionals, by virtue of their direct relationships with students and the eclectic nature of their responsibilities, are well positioned to address these important issues. However, the profession's capacity to do so is currently mitigated by serious limitations that require our attention. In particular, we contend that the current discourses in student affairs are stagnated because the binary notions of privilege and oppression have not advanced to an analysis of the nuances of lived identities, intersections between identities, ways in which individuals participate in co-constructing identities, and in turn how these influence a campus culture. In short, there are no simple or final answers to questions about diversity, access, and inclusion, yet much of the discourse is framed as if there are. It is critical, therefore, that student affairs practitioners not only become versed in the professional literature, but also in interdisciplinary scholarship (for example, gender studies, critical White studies, queer studies). Moreover, practitioners must have the courage to resist demands for cosmetic and short-term fixes and engage in more complex approaches to building inclusive campuses. In order to identify, implement and institutionalize processes, policies, structures, programs, and services that are experienced as inclusive, practitioners need to understand critical theoretical lenses related to diversity, access, and inclusion, as well as the processes associated with translating concepts into meaningful applied efforts.

References

Antonio, A. L. (1998). *Student interaction across race and outcomes in college.* Paper presented at the American Educational Research Association Conference, San Diego, CA.

Barcelo, N. (2007). Transforming our institutions for the twenty-first century: The role of the chief diversity officer. *Diversity Digest, 10*(2). http://www.diversityweb .org/digest/vol10no2/barcelo.cfm.

Bensimon, E. M. (2004, January/February). The diversity scorecard: A learning approach to institutional change. *Change,* 44–52.

Carnevale, A. P., and Fry, R. A. (2002). The demographic window of opportunity: College access and diversity in the new century. In D. E. Heller (Ed.), *Condition of access: higher education for lower income students* (pp. 137-151). Westport, CT: Praeger.

Chang, M. (2005, Winter). Reconsidering the diversity rationale. *Liberal Education,* 1–6. http://www.aacu.org/publications-research/periodicals/reconsidering-diversity-rationale.

Chang, M. (1996). *Racial diversity in higher education: Does a racially mixed student population affect educational outcomes?* Unpublished doctoral dissertation, University of California, Los Angeles.

Chang, M. J., Denson, N., Saenz, V., & Misa, K. (2006). The educational benefits of sustaining cross-racial interaction among undergraduates. *Journal of Higher Education, 77,* 430–455.

Connolly, W. E. (2002). *Identity/Difference: Democratic negotiations of political paradox.* Minneapolis: University of Minnesota Press.

Crethar, H. C., & Vargas, L. A. (2007). Multicultural intricacies in professional counseling. In J. Gregoire & C. Jungers (Eds.), *The counselor's companion: What every beginning counselor needs to know.* Mahwah, NJ: Lawrence Erlbaum.

Davis, T., & Harrison, L. M. (2013). *Advancing social justice: Tools, pedagogies, and strategies to transform your campus.* San Francisco, CA: Jossey-Bass.

Dewey, J. (1938). *Experience and education.* New York, NY: Collier Books.

Dolby, N. (2000). Changing selves: Multicultural education and the challenge of new identities. *Teachers College Record, 102*(5), 898–912.

Fine, M., Weis, L., Addelston, A., & Hall, J. M. (1997). In secure times: Constructing White working-class masculinities in the late 20th century. *Gender & Society, 11*(1), 52–68.

Gurin, P. (2007). New research on the benefits of diversity in college and beyond: An empirical analysis. *Diversity Digest, 10*(2). http://www.diversityweb.org/digest/ vol10no2/gurin.cfm.

Hooks, B. (2004). Men: Comrades in struggle. In M. S. Kimmel & M. A. Messner (Eds.), *Men's lives* (6th ed., pp. 68–83). Needham Heights, MA: Allyn & Bacon.

Hurtado, S. (1997). *Linking diversity with educational purpose: College outcomes associated with diversity in the faculty and student body.* Cambridge, MA: Harvard University, Harvard Civil Rights Project.

Jayakumar, U. M. (2008). Can higher education meet the needs of an increasingly diverse and global society? Campus diversity and cross-cultural workforce competencies. *Harvard Educational Review, 78*(4), 615–651.

Jones, S. R., & McEwen, M. K. (2000). A conceptual model of multiple dimensions of identity. *Journal of College Student Development, 41*(4), 405–414.

Kaufman, M. (1999). Men, feminism, and men's contradictory experiences of power. In J. A. Kuypers (Ed.), *Men and power* (pp. 59–85). Halifax, Nova Scotia: Fernwood Books.

Longwell-Grice, R. M. (2002). *Working-class and working college: A case study of the first generation, working class, first year, White male college students.* Unpublished doctoral dissertation, University of Louisville.

Milem, J. F., Chang, M. J., & Antonio, A. L. (2005). *Making diversity work on campus: A research-based perspective.* Washington, DC: Association of American Colleges and Universities.

Murray, A. (2006). *Paradigm found: Leading and managing for positive change.* Novato, CA: New World Library.

Pascarella, E. T., Edison, M., Nora, A., Hagedorn, L. S., & Terenzini, P. T. (1996). Influences on students' openness to diversity and challenge in the first year of college. *Journal of Higher Education, 67*(2), 174–195.

Pascarella, E. T., & Terenzini, P. T. (2005). *How college affects students: A third decade of research.* San Francisco, CA: Jossey-Bass.

Peltier Campbell, K. (2007). Diversity and learning: A defining moment. *Diversity Digest, 10*(2). http://www.diversityweb.org/digest/vol10no2/campbell.cfm.

Pope, R. L. (1995). Multicultural organizational development: Implications and applications in student affairs. In J. Fried (Ed.), *Shifting paradigms in student affairs: Culture, contexts, teaching and learning* (pp. 233–249). Washington, DC: American College Personnel Association.

Pope, R. L., Reynolds, A. L., & Mueller, J. A. (2004). *Multicultural competence in student affairs.* San Francisco, CA: Jossey-Bass.

Reason, R. D., Broido, E. M., Davis, T. L., & Evans, N. J. (2005). *Developing social justice allies.* San Francisco, CA: Jossey-Bass.

Reed, B. (2008). *Patterns of gender role conflict in white working-class males.* Unpublished manuscript, University of Virginia, Charlottesville.

Robinson-Armstrong, A., King, D., Killoran, D., Ward, H., Fissinger, M. X., & Harrison, L. (2007). Creating institutional transformation using the equity scorecard. *Diversity Digest, 10*(2). http://www.diversityweb.org/digest/vol10no2/robinson-armstrong.cfm.

Smith, D. G., & Associates. (1997). *Diversity works: The emerging picture of how students benefit.* Washington, DC: Association of American Colleges and Universities.

Stier, J. 2006 Internationalisation, intercultural communication, and intercultural competence. *Journal of Intercultural Communication, 11*, 1–11.

Takacs, D. (2003, Summer). How does your positionality bias your epistemology? *Thought and Action.* http://ww.nhea.org/assets/img/PubThoughtAndAction/TAA_03_04.pdf.

Terenzini, P. T., Pascarella, E. T., & Blimling, G. S. (1996). Students' out-of-class experiences and their influence on learning and cognitive development: A literature review. *Journal of College Student Development, 37,* 149–162.

Ukpokodu, O. N. (2007). A sustainable campus-wide program for diversity curriculum infusion. *Diversity Digest, 10*(2). 1–2. http://www.diversityweb.org/digest/vol10no2/robinson-armstrong.cfm.

Wilkinson, C. K., & Rund, J. A. (2002). Supporting people, programs, and structures for diversity. In M. J. Barr & M. K. Desler (Eds.), *The Handbook of Student Affairs Administration* (2nd ed., pp 580–96). San Francisco, CA: Jossey-Bass

CHAPTER FIFTEEN

HELPING STUDENTS PREPARE FOR LIVES OF PURPOSE

Michele C. Murray and Robert J. Nash

Today's college students began coming of age during a severe economic downturn when unemployment rates were a regular feature of the nightly news. They started their college search process amid growing national concern over the rising costs of college attendance and related student debt. Given the clouds of uncertainty that shaded their financial futures, it is no wonder that first-year students entering college in 2012 listed getting a better job and making more money among the top reasons for college attendance (Pryor, Eagen, Blake, Hurtado, Berdan, & Case, 2012). In that same year, the personal goal "being well off financially" reached an all-time high, with more than 80 percent of students identifying it as "essential" or "very important" (Pryor et al., 2012). These understandably practical responses to ever-shifting economic realities belie another truth about today's college students: they are in active pursuit of purpose and meaning in their lives (Astin, Astin, & Lindholm, 2011).

This chapter presents the centrality of meaning-making to the student experience and makes the case for readying student affairs educators to respond appropriately. We explore meaning-making as part of the spiritual journeys common to a majority of college students and as the foundation on which they can develop a sense of purpose. We offer pedagogical strategies and tools student affairs educators can use to guide students' search for meaning and purpose, and we conclude with a discussion of the role of mentors and the ethics of mentoring for meaning. Above all else, we intend the information in this chapter to be straightforward and ultimately useful in guiding professional practice.

Lives of Meaning, Lives of Purpose

With their near-hyper focus on future earning potential as both motivation and goal for college attendance, the class entering in 2012 may be caught short by Viktor Frankl's (1979) famous admonition: "The truth is that as the struggle for survival has subsided, the question has emerged—survival for what? Ever more people today have the *means* to live, but no *meaning* to live for" (p. 77). Frankl's (1963) horrendous living nightmare of subsisting in Nazi concentration camps gave him a window onto the human spirit that may not be readily accessible to the majority of new college students. Frankl's experiences and observations led him to understand that survival—and even joy—belonged not to the fittest, as Charles Darwin's (1869) research allowed, but rather to those who sought gratitude and human connection. In another oft-quoted take on means and meaning, Nietzsche offered, "He [sic] who has a *why* to live can bear almost any *how*" (in Frankl, 1963, emphasis added). The philosophies of both Nietzsche and Frankl emphasized developing a meaning for life over material wealth or comfort. In direct contrast to these philosophies, the primary concerns for new college students revolve around the means their baccalaureate degrees will help them attain rather than the meaning that undergirds their values and choices.

For some students, inattention to their whys for living can lead to prolonged bouts with meaninglessness, or the sense that nothing they do really matters to anyone or anything (Nash & Murray, 2010). Although fleeting encounters with meaninglessness are a common human experience (Yalom, 1980, 2002, 2008), persistent feelings of meaninglessness easily lead to depression and anxiety. National College Health Assessment results from a representative sample of more than 76,000 undergraduate students across all institution types indicated that today's students dabble in persistent meaninglessness (American College Health Association, 2012). A majority of students in the study reported signs of hovering over depression and anxiety, and many reported more serious—and perhaps chronic—mental health difficulties during the twelve months preceding the survey.

- 86 percent felt overwhelmed.
- 82 percent felt exhausted, other than from physical activity.
- 62 percent felt very sad.
- 58 percent felt very lonely.
- 52 percent felt more than average or tremendous stress.
- 51 percent felt overwhelming anxiety.
- 47 percent felt hopeless.
- 38 percent felt overwhelming anger.
- 32 percent felt so depressed that it was difficult to function.

Despite the signs of depression and anxiety in a majority of students, only 20 percent reported that they had been diagnosed or were under the care of a medical or mental health professional. The likelihood that today's students are struggling with understanding their "why to live" is enough reason for student affairs educators to develop a few pedagogical skills to assist students with their meaning-making.

Recent research addressing the spirituality of college students confirms college students' deep desires to develop meaning and purpose. Astin et al. (2011) found that undergraduates in their junior year demonstrate a considerable rise in the attention they give toward questions of meaning, authenticity, and spiritual mystery. According to the data, students in the middle of their college careers are twice as likely to report an increase in their search for meaning and purpose as they are to report a decrease in the same activity. The researchers concluded that questions of meaning and purpose become more prominent for students as they progress through their college years. Although students may maintain a focus on their financial futures, or their means to live, they are also growing in their ability and desire to engage and their interest in the "big" philosophical questions and the greater purpose of their lives.

Meaning and Purpose: Two Sides of the Same Coin

Though often used interchangeably, we understand *meaning* and *purpose* as fundamentally different, yet related, terms. Marinoff (1999) and Nash and Murray (2010) distinguish between meaning and purpose in the following ways: *purpose* is related to one's goals and objectives, while *meaning* has to do with the interpretations, values, and beliefs one uses to understand the events, people, and circumstances that populate one's life. Similarly, Parks (2000) recognizes meaning as involving the "search for a sense of connection, pattern, order, and significance" (p. 14). The meanings one creates lend worth and justification to the purposes one pursues (Nash & Murray, 2010), or in Kant-like terms: "Purpose without meaning is empty, yet meaning without purpose goes nowhere" (Nash & Murray, 2010, p. xx). Meaning and purpose go hand in hand. Ultimately, meaning is what sustains us when obstacles block the path to fulfilling our purpose.

Additionally, we support Haidt's (2006) distinction between purpose and meaning. For Haidt, there is an upper-case Purpose *outside* of our individual, day-to-day lives that might be based in the natural, supernatural, or metaphysical. But there is also a lower-case purpose *inside* our individual lives that gives us meaning. Purpose helps us to look at our lives from the outside; meaning helps us to look at our lives from the inside. For Haidt, happiness is more likely to occur when both Purpose and meaning align.

Another way to understand the differences between meaning and purpose as well as how they relate to one another is through life's "big questions." As reported in Nash and Murray (2010) and Astin et al. (2011), the big questions are existential, bordering on the practical. Big questions explore the unknown and that generative space between the real and the ideal. These questions emerge in a powerful way during the collegiate years, and they continue to hover throughout adult life. Some common big life questions include:

- Who am I, and who am I becoming?
- What, if anything, am I passionate about?
- Why do innocent people suffer?
- What is my responsibility to those around me, and does that responsibility differ between strangers and close relations?
- Why do some people experience lives of privilege and others lives of privation? Which describes my life?
- What is my relationship to the transcendent?
- What is sacred to me?
- What do religion and faith have to do with one another, and what do either have to do with me?
- Where do my talents lie?
- How should I define success?
- Why am I here now? What is my purpose in life?
- How will I know what type of career is best for me?
- Why do I hurt so much when a relationship ends?
- Can I be a good person without religion?
- What is my responsibility to clean up the messes of the world? And is it even any use to try because, after all, I am only one person?

Questions about which career to pursue are related to purpose, whereas the deep-seated reasons behind pursuing a particular career path are related to meaning. How students begin to answer the constellation of these and similarly provocative questions helps shape the ways in which they understand their life's goals, or purpose, as do the relative weights they assign to each question. The point is not for students to develop cookie-cutter understandings of the big questions. Rather, we recommend that students have multiple opportunities to contemplate the questions and incorporate their understanding of their values, beliefs, and interpretations into their evolving life's purpose.

The Universality of Meaning and Purpose

Recent research on college student spirituality (Astin et al., 2011) confirms a phenomenon we have long believed to be true: The big questions of life that fuel a search for meaning transcend age, gender, racial, religious, and socioeconomic class divisions. Specifically, Astin et al. (2011) note that despite the vast differences in their backgrounds, the 112,000 students in their study from 236 four-year public and religiously affiliated institutions reported remarkably similar spiritual concerns, hopes, and desires for connection to self, others, and the transcendent. In other words, the big questions of life are part and parcel of the human condition, and we are sure that students, regardless of demographic background or academic major, struggle to ask and answer them. As such, student affairs educators must be prepared to engage and assist students in their quest for meaning and purpose.

The next section outlines a series of tools and strategies that we have found useful for inviting students to engage and learn from the questions that will guide meaning and purpose in their lives.

Pedagogies for Making Meaning and Defining Purpose

The big questions at the heart of meaning-making are the big questions of life. Although they may first emerge in late adolescence and early adulthood, the big questions circle around again and again until they meet adequate answers or until the question asker meets her or his end (Baggini, 2005; de la Chaumiere, 2004; Nash & Murray, 2010; Yalom, 2008). Unfortunately "Once and done," "Been there, done that," and other mottos of conquest do not apply to the meaning-making process of asking and understanding big life questions. There is, however, good news to be found in a never-ending cycle of questions that prompt deep psychospiritual reflection. With each cycle, the possibility exists to develop familiarity with the questions themselves as well as with the process of encountering and sifting through them.

For college students, the big questions often arise from tough personal issues they encounter for the first time in their undergraduate years, including catastrophic family illness, dissolving relationships, identity development, failure, uncertainty about the future, encountering difference, and the like. Hard-hitting concerns—racial or religious conflict, natural disaster, and war, for example—that challenge communities and nations also generate big questions of meaning. As anxiety-provoking as these global and personal matters can be, they also are foundational fodder for understanding one's identity and making meaning of the world and one's place in it (Kegan, 1994; Magolda, 2008). The unique spaces student affairs educators occupy position them well to help students address the meaning challenges students confront regularly.

As college students begin to wrestle with the existential questions that will lend meaning to, and shape the purpose of, their lives, they need user friendly approaches to reflection. The practical methods outlined below are but a few of the pedagogical tools and strategies that assist students in making meaning. No one tool is right for every student or for every existential crisis. Therefore, we advocate for educators to develop and maintain several methods for opening conversation, inviting reflection, and encouraging meaning-making. (See Nash and Murray, 2010, for a more in-depth treatment of the meaning-making strategies outlined.)

Tell Powerful Stories

Each of us conceals a nagging need to tell some kind of truth about our lives. When, and if we are ready, then the best way to convey a truth, and to create a meaning, is to tell a story. A story is always profoundly personal and unique to some degree, never replicated in exactly the same form by anyone else. But if others can hear our truths within the context of their own personal stories of meaning-making, then they might be better able to find a corollary in their own stories. One of the best ways to make meaning and find purpose is to tell personal stories. A story helps us to make connections of the disparate events, and people, that appear in our lives. A story creates order out of chaos. A story teaches, elevates, and inspires. According to Peter Brooks (1985), "Our very definition as human beings is inextricably bound up with the stories we tell about our own lives and the world in which we live. We cannot, in our dreams, our daydreams, our ambitious fantasies, avoid the imaginative imposition of form on life" (p. 19).

One of our favorite pedagogies for helping students create lives of purpose is to teach them to write their stories and to draw both personal and general meaning from them. We call this type of re-search /me-search—Scholarly Personal Narrative (SPN) writing (Nash, 2004; Nash & Bradley, 2011; Nash & Viray, 2013). Scholarly Personal Narrative writing:

- Tells a good story and/or many good stories.
- Features a clear point of view, an organizing theme, and/or a coherent argument.
- Starts with the "I" and proceeds outward to the "you" and the "they." The author's distinct and honest voice is key. The author's ideas are only as strong as the voice that delivers them. By the same token, absent the ideas, the personal voice can sometimes be seen as self-indulgent or overly confessional.
- Uses personal stories to deliver the message.
- Strives for an ideal mix of particularity and generalizability, concreteness and abstractness, practice and theory.
- Presents the author's voice as personal, clear, fallible, and honest; it is also humble and open-ended.
- Generously cites other authors' works and ideas.
- Shows some passion. SPN is not a detached, "objective" examination of a topic. Rather it is a thoughtful, first-person attempt to make a point or teach a lesson by drawing on the author's own life experiences to provide context.
- Helps others see the world a little differently, from the storyteller's personal point of view.
- Is editorially and technically meticulous.
- Takes personal risks.
- Begins with the self-confidence that the author has a personal story worth telling and a point worth making.

Ask Philosophical Questions

As university educators, we witness firsthand the need for students of all ages, both traditional and nontraditional, to have something coherent to believe in, some centering values and goals toward which to strive. Students need strong background beliefs and ideals to shore them up during times of geopolitical, economic, or environmental uncertainty. On a more personal level, students need to make sense of the turmoil that results when their lives get turned upside-down; when their work grows tedious and unsatisfying; or when they become disillusioned by a sense of unfulfillment or broken relationship. Few opportunities exist on most college campuses for students to develop these strong background beliefs and ideals.

Meaning-making during the young adult developmental cycle (Nash & Murray, 2010) is a concern almost totally absent from most classrooms and nonclassroom venues on campus. We try never to miss an opportunity to draw out the philosopher who resides within each student. A philosopher is a lover of wisdom, someone who asks questions based on a sense of wonder, someone who thinks deeply, and someone who needs some enriching meaning to hold onto. And we believe, as did Socrates, that, as educators, we function as philosophical "midwives" who help our students to give birth to themselves.

Here are some further examples of philosophically oriented, pedagogical questions that we find to be especially helpful when examining and analyzing particular texts, situations, or experiences:

- What does this mean for *you* right now as you struggle with constructing your own sense of meaning and purpose?
- What is your personal take given your unique belief system?
- What sense do you make for your own life and for that of others?
- What are the personal and social contexts you bring to your understanding?
- What are some of the implications for your evolving philosophy of life, work, relationships, and professional identity?

In response to these types of questions, and many others that come up in our teaching and conversations with students, we work hard to help them understand, and navigate, their meaning-making journeys. All students are capable of answering for themselves the deepest questions they might be asking about the inner meaning of their lives as well as the outer purpose of their existence. What they need from educators is an open mind, compassion, vulnerability, trust, and continual encouragement.

Create Intentional Silence

The concept of silence seems incompatible with the postindustrial, digital age in which our students (and we) live. Smartphones and tablet computers are near-constant companions with which students keep up with current events and their friends, listen to music, play games, tape lectures, conduct research, create videos, and take notes. Add the busy-ness of daily living to the electronic noise, and it is no wonder that students (and we) are distracted and feel fragmented. For distracted minds, the static and interruptions of modern life are poisonous to the meaning-making process. Fortunately silence is a healthy, free antidote.

Regular silence clears psychological and emotional space to think anew and gain perspective. The gift of silence is the opportunity to counteract the rush and whir that lead to the compartmentalization of thoughts and actions and the separation of self from others and, sometimes, from self (Nash & Murray, 2010). As Pico Iyer (1993) observed, "In silence, we often say, we can hear ourselves think; but what is truer to say is that in silence we can hear ourselves *not* think, and so sink below ourselves into a place far deeper than mere thought allows" (p. 74).

As much as silence can be a source of connection and renewal, it also can be a source of tension and agitation. To be alone with one's thoughts, free from the distractions that fill nearly all waking moments, is rare for most students, and may be unwelcome for some. To the uninitiated student—even for the introverted—silence can be a fearful, loathsome thing. Silence, like all habits of heart and mind, takes practice before comfort with it develops and its utility comes to fruition. When intentionally using silence as a meaning-making tool, student affairs educators can help students acquire familiarity, experience real benefit, and begin seeking silence on their own (Nash & Murray, 2010).

Silence as Pause. Student affairs educators can wield the tool of silence in two powerful ways. The first is as a temporary retreat from the noise of daily life. Brief pauses of silence offer the opportunity to become fully present to self and others by actively setting aside the distractions that fracture thought and attention. Silence provides the space to call to mind individual or collective purpose and invites greater intentionality for engaging the specific moment. Educators can call for moments of silence at any time—beginning, middle, or end—of a gathering or as a regular feature of a class or meeting. When done with enough regularity, silence becomes a welcome respite that students come to expect and create for themselves.

Silence as Process. A second powerful use of silence is as a deliberate break in conversation or activity in order to give ample consideration to a thought, idea, or feeling (Nash & Murray, 2010). The silence-as-process strategy is especially useful during contentious debate, confrontation of an ethical dilemma, or other highly emotionally charged interaction. These moments are rife with meaning but require purposeful attention if students are to access the meaning available to them. The student affairs educator who listens acutely for the questions hidden in the static and calls appropriately for silence can seize the opportunity to turn frustrating, even potentially explosive, situations into opportunities for growth and greater understanding. Silence provides students the opportunity to momentarily disengage from their "locked-in" positions and invites perspective taking. In these moments silence creates breathing room and asks students to thoughtfully consider how they would like to proceed.

Invite Honest Reflection

As a pedagogical tool for making meaning and defining purpose, reflection is an obvious choice. Creating space for students to reflect on their experiences and learning invites them to dig beneath the carefully constructed *persona* they want the world to see and begin to reveal the *person* that hides just beneath the surface. Honest reflection makes it possible for students to see their thoughts, actions, and feelings for what they truly are, to confront contradictions between word and deed, and to discover the sources of both joy and discontent. Reflection also helps students internalize what they learn and experience, develop a deeper sense of who they are, and, in turn, be able to author their own lives (Kegan, 1994; Magolda, 1998, 2008). Although all reflection can be helpful in the meaning-making process, not all reflective activities are equivalent. The quality of reflection ranges from the cursory and superficial to the deeply insightful and profound. On the shallower end of the spectrum are quick, evaluative processes that provide opportunities for students to connect what they are learning with their reactions and feelings. Student affairs educators might close a meeting or program with students by asking students to offer a word, phrase, or sentence that captures and summarizes their thoughts. Alternately, educators might ask students a series of questions.

1. What went well? Or, what did you learn?
2. What could have gone differently? Or, what questions remain?
3. How will you incorporate what we have discussed? Or, how will you approach this topic/scenario/opportunity differently?

These short evaluations help reveal questions and concerns percolating within students as well as the ideas that hold personal resonance for them.

For deeper reflection, writing is an excellent tool. Journals and reflection papers are excellent for wrestling with ideas, events, and relationships. The process of writing brings forth the oft-hidden internal world, highlighting places of alignment or incongruence. Reflective writing allows students to come face to face with thoughts, perspectives, and feelings that are otherwise inaccessible or too jumbled to decipher. The self-knowledge students develop as a result aids their ability to discern their paths and make meaning of their experiences. As informative a process as reflective writing can be, it does not come easily to some. Encouraging journal keeping, including reflection questions in learning portfolios, and assigning reflection papers as a judicial sanction all provide opportunities for students to become comfortable with the process of deep reflection.

When done regularly, intentional reflection of either variety—short evaluations or longer writings—can reveal patterns in thought and behavior. The information students record acts like data points, creating a verbal scatterplot that points toward trends. As constructive trends develop, students receive confirmation that they are living in alignment with their values and meanings. Likewise, identifying destructive trends empowers students to make different choices and decisions. Honest and regular self-reflection invites students to know themselves more deeply and, in knowing themselves, experience greater agency in their lives (Kegan, 1994; Magolda, 1998, 2008).

Have Moral Conversation

Meaning-making, purpose-guiding conversations require an infinite supply of patience, vulnerability, respect, support, encouragement, and reciprocity. We call our approach to talking about hot topics *moral conversation*, and we have written about this at great length (Nash, Bradley, & Chickering, 2008; Nash, Johnson, & Murray, 2011). In a nutshell, moral conversation is predicated on the assumption that more people tend to speak their mind in a group when they feel safe and supported (Bain, 2004; Isaacs, 1999; Yankelovich, 1999). They respond less defensively when they are affirmed rather than when they are attacked. They listen more carefully to alternative points of view. Conversations are livelier.

In our continual moral conversations with students, we stipulate the following:

• Our dialogue needs to be unbounded in the sense that everything is up for grabs. There is no a priori prohibition against talking about particular issues or taking particular philosophical, educational, political, or religious positions that might at first appear politically incorrect or heretical.

• While it is true that all ideas need to be dissected, challenged, and critiqued, they also have a right to be *respected*, at least initially. Moreover, the people who hold these ideas have a right, at all times, to be listened to, drawn out, and treated with the utmost kindness and generosity.

• We need always to find the truth in what we oppose, and the error in what we espouse, *before* we proclaim the truth in what we espouse and the error in what we oppose.

• We need always to make the other person look good by resisting the ever-present temptation to make ourselves look good at the expense of others. We are not about winning arguments, making points, or showing off our brilliance.

• We need always to avoid the temptation of becoming a zealot on behalf of our favorite political, religious, philosophical, educational, and so on, causes. Unfortunately, the more passionate we become in advancing our ideologies and causes, the more likely we are to "preach, screech, and leech," especially when we talk about our favorite "causes." Moral conversationalists are pragmatists. They ask this question: What communication style is most likely to create allies to our causes rather than enemies behind our backs? Communication research shows time and time again that guilting, accusing, bullying, and assuming the high moral ground creates enemies, not friends. The challenge is to find ways to communicate our enthusiasm and commitment to a cause in such a way that turns others on rather than off. We believe that moral conversation achieves this objective.

One of the great pedagogical rewards for us and for our students in engaging in moral conversation together is the discovery of commonality between and among each and everyone of us, no matter what our surface differences might be. We are reminded again and again of the ancient Roman playwright, Terence, whose wisdom is profound: "I am human, I consider nothing human alien to me" (Barsby, 2001, p. 231). There is a great deal of overlapping narrative in our lives. When, in moral conversation, we commit ourselves to discovering, expanding, and deepening this overlap, then this is a significant signal that we are starting to click, maybe even to bond with one other, to become less strangers and more friends. Moral conversation, when it is working well, provides an opportunity for all of us to come together to create meanings, both individually and collectively, personally and professionally, philosophically and politically. We are able to retain our individual uniquenesses while learning to become communitarians in search of meaning and purpose.

Mentoring for Meaning

At its core, meaning-making is a deeply personal journey. Collective or shared experiences may fuel a student's meaning-making process, but the work of sorting and sifting, reflecting and contemplating, is highly individual. Yet the process of making meaning and reaching new understandings is not necessarily a solitary one. As the pedagogies outlined here suggest, influential others can shape and guide a student's meaning-making process. This section is devoted to intentional mentoring for meaning-making and addresses both the role of "meaning mentors" (Nash & Murray, 2010) and the associated ethical considerations.

The Role of Meaning Mentors

In her seminal work addressing young adults' search for meaning, purpose, and faith, Parks (2000) championed need for mentors at this critical juncture in their lives. Parks observed that the meaning-making process is hampered by the rapid pace of change and ensuing uncertainty in our "cusp time" (p. 9.), and she warned that too many young adults struggle with complex and difficult questions of meaning without the benefit of mentors and mentoring communities. Given the status of higher education as a cultural institution dedicated to reflection and inquiry, educators have a distinct opportunity and a particular responsibility to shepherd students through their formative and defining moments (Parks, 2000). Parks urged educators to recommit to sharing their wisdom through intentional and strategic mentoring relationships with young adults. We agree wholeheartedly.

A student's meaning process benefits from an external, but connected, other—a mentor who can offer feedback in a way that respects the student's sovereignty and who can assert herself or himself appropriately into the student's process. A meaning mentor listens for unspoken questions, welcomes the exploration of ideas, and discourages premature commitment to one way of thinking or believing over another. A meaning mentor invites the unadulterated self to "just be." Farrington (2003) described this type of mentor as a "soul friend." Soul friends, she wrote:

> Know our faults and difficulties—what "games" we tend to play in our own hearts and minds. But they understand and care for us in a profound way, so much so that we are willing to trust them with our soul's concerns and desires. They are also people who see with the eyes and ears of the heart, with compassion, concern, and clarity. They are the ones who, when we think our only choices are to go forward or backward on the wheel, can help us discover ... a whole new direction. (pp. 119–120)

In many ways, the work of student affairs educators aligns with these descriptions of meaning mentors and soul friends. However, as Parks (2000) indicated, mentoring must be intentional to be effective.

The Ethics of Mentoring for Meaning

Before any type of meaning-making conversation occurs, it is crucial for all participants to agree on a code of ethics, made up of a set of mutual rights and obligations that governs the process. A safe conversational space is a critical prerequisite for encouraging students to open up about their past and present experiences as well as their personal failures and successes. Students need to do more than show up and show off, as most tend to do in their usual classroom settings. If we set the right tone, and create the most secure environment, our students will feel free, perhaps for the first time in a college classroom or campus office space, to be candid and forthright in their self-disclosures. They will learn very quickly not to waste time on impression management (Nash, 2002; Nash & Murray, 2010).

When meaning-making conversation is real, we enter unchartered ethical territory in our educational spaces. Thus, we need to proceed with caution. As the authors of chapter 10 point out, student welfare is a primary moral obligation. Following, we have created a conversational code of ethics that can be shared directly with students in order to help them interact respectfully with one another, and with us, when talking about meaning and purpose:

- Treat each person fairly, impartially, and equitably.
- Whenever in doubt, always remember the principle of "primum non nocere"—first, do no harm.
- Treat each person in the group always as an end, and never as a means.

- Abstain from ad hominem and ad feminam attacks, and ganging up on individuals with unpopular views.
- Respect, do not violate, students' rights to privacy.
- Keep confidences.
- Do not foist personal beliefs on others.
- Seek informed consent in everything you do.
- Understand that not everyone is ready to be a vulnerable meaning-maker; avoid imposing vulnerability on others.
- Know when students might need professional therapy and counseling.

Also, we need to trust the process in conversations about meaning. In addition to introducing a code of ethics for conducting conversations about meaning, educators must exercise prudent leadership throughout the conversation by gently and persistently keeping people on track. At the same time, we must also be ready to get out of the way whenever possible. We need to avoid pushing students beyond their comfort levels. We need to be careful not to make overt judgments of approval or disapproval of what students have to say. We must beware of practicing beyond our competence, and covering up our *preaching* by calling it *teaching*.

Conclusion

What we have written about in this chapter by way of educating about meaning-making on college campuses holds the promise of giving a plugged-in generation of students permission to stop and pause in the middle of tweeting, texting, electronic gaming, YouTubing, and Facebooking. We want to enable students to talk about the deeper questions and universal life issues openly and honestly, and face to face, with significant others on campus. As a stepping stone for meaning-making, we urge higher education to provide resources, facilitate discussions, and introduce a variety of traditional and innovative pedagogies to encourage critical thinking and deep, existential reflection on what gives individual and collective lives meaning. We would like to go even further and propose an all-university, senior capstone experience (which might even offer academic credit) before students graduate. This capstone would help them to put together a tentative life plan based on their ongoing meaning-making explorations.

Today's college students are asking existential questions of meaning. As Viktor Frankl suggested, many students might have the "means to live," but what they are in search of is a "meaning to live for." Their questions are timeless and yet reflect the age in which they live. As we have suggested throughout this chapter, these questions are a fascinating admixture of the abstract and the practical, the universal and the particular. They represent well the tensions that exist for so many college students who seek to find the delicate balance that exists in the difficult space between idealism and realism; between macro- and micro-meaning. It is time for us to help students to find that delicate balance.

We can almost guarantee that, sooner rather than later, some aspect of way-finding, meaning-making, and discernment of purpose will be an obligatory part of the collegiate experience for all students. More and more students are actively seeking, and welcoming, opportunities to make meaning. One thing is sure: their processes of making meaning and developing purpose will be far less bewildering if they have reliable and responsible mentors to accompany them. The question remains, however, whether student affairs educators will be prepared to help guide and mentor students as they struggle to ask, and answer, some of life's big questions. We stand firm that because of their interdisciplinary professional training and profound understanding of student development, student affairs educators are more than ready to become meaning-making guides and mentors.

References

American College Health Association. (2012, Spring). Undergraduate students: Reference group executive summary. http://www.acha-ncha.org/docs/ACHA-NCHA-II_UNDERGRAD_ReferenceGroup_ExecutiveSummary_Spring2012.pdf. July 2015.

Astin, A. W., Astin, H. S., and Lindholm, J. A. (2011). *Cultivating the spirit: How college can enhance students' inner lives*. San Francisco, CA: Jossey-Bass.

Bain, K. (2004). *What the best college teachers do*. Cambridge, MA: Harvard University Press.

Baggini, J. B. (2005). *What's it all about? Philosophy and the meaning of life*. New York, NY: Oxford University Press.

Barsby, J. (Ed.). (2001). *Terence. The woman of Andros. The self-tormentor. The eunuch.* Cambridge, MA: Harvard University Press.

Brooks, P. (1985). *Reading for the plot*. New York, NY: Random House.

Darwin, C. (1869). *On the origin of species* (5th ed.) Oxford: Oxford University Press.

de la Chaumiere, R. (2004). *What's it all about? A guide to life's basic questions and answers*. Sonoma, CA: Wisdom House.

Farrington, D. K. (2003). *Hearing with the heart: A gentle guide to discerning God's will for your life*. San Francisco, CA: Jossey-Bass.

Frankl, V. (1963). *Man's search for meaning: An introduction to logotherapy.* New York, NY: Simon & Schuster.

Frankl, V. (1979). *The unheard cry for meaning: Psychotherapy and humanism.* New York, NY: Touchstone.

Haidt, J. (2006). *The happiness hypothesis: Finding modern truth in ancient wisdom.* New York, NY: Basic Books.

Isaacs , (1999). W. *Dialogue and the art of thinking together.* New York, NY: Doubleday.

Iyer, P. (1993). *Falling off the map: Some lonely places of the world.* New York, NY: Vintage.

Kegan, R. (1994). *In over our heads: The mental demands of modern life.* Cambridge, MA: Harvard University Press.

Magolda, M.B.B. (1998). Developing self-authorship in young adult life. *Journal of College Student Development, 39*(2), 143–156.

Magolda, M.B.B. (2008). Three elements of self-authorship. *Journal of College Student Development, 49*(4), 269–284.

Marinoff, L. (1999). *Plato not Prozac: Applying eternal wisdom to everyday problems.* New York, NY: HarperCollins.

Nash, R. J. (2002). *Spirituality, ethics, religion, and teaching: A professor's journey.* New York, NY: Peter Lang.

Nash, R. J. (2004). *Liberating scholarly writing: The power of personal narrative.* New York, NY: Teachers College Press.

Nash, R. J., & Bradley, D. L. (2011). *Me-search and re-search: A guide for writing scholarly personal narrative manuscripts.* Charlotte, NC: Information Age.

Nash, R. J., Bradley, D. L., & Chickering, A. W. (2008). *How to talk about hot topics on campus: From polarization to moral conversation.* San Francisco, CA: Jossey-Bass.

Nash, R. J., Johnson, R. G. III,, & Murray, M.C. (2011). *Teaching college students communication strategies for effective social justice advocacy.* New York, NY: Peter Lang.

Nash, R. J., & Murray, M.C. (2010). *Helping college students find purpose: The campus guide to meaning-making.* San Francisco, CA: Jossey-Bass.

Nash, R. J., & Viray, S. (2013). *Our stories matter: Liberating the voices of marginalized students through scholarly personal narrative writing.* New York, NY: Peter Lang.

Parks, S. D. (2000). *Big questions, worthy dreams: Mentoring young adults in their search for meaning, purpose, and faith.* San Francisco, CA: Jossey-Bass.

Pryor, J. H., Eagen, K., Blake, L. P., Hurtado, S., Berdan, J., & Case, M. H. (2012). *The American freshman: National norms for Fall 2012.* Los Angeles: University of California-Los Angeles, Higher Education Research Institute.

Yalom, I. D. (1980). *Existential psychotherapy.* New York, NY: Basic Books.

Yalom, I. D. (2002). *The gift of therapy: An open letter to a new generation of therapists and their patients.* New York, NY: Perennial.

Yalom, I. D. (2008). *Staring at the sun: Overcoming the terror of death.* San Francisco, CA: Jossey-Bass.

Yankelovich, D. (1999). *The magic of dialogue: Transforming conflict into cooperation.* New York, NY: Touchstone.

CHAPTER SIXTEEN

INTERCOLLEGIATE ATHLETICS AND RECREATION ON COLLEGE CAMPUSES

Joy Gaston Gayles, Tiffany J. Davis, and
Mary Howard-Hamilton

The purpose of higher education is to provide students with a well-rounded learning experience that prepares them to take active roles in society as responsible citizens. Part of this involves leading a healthy lifestyle. According to the Centers for Disease Control and Prevention, individuals who are physically active and lead healthy lives live longer and enjoy a better quality of life. Further, maintaining a healthy lifestyle reduces physical and psychological stress that can trigger disease (Wartell, 2012).

This chapter focuses on the important role that intercollegiate athletics and recreation plays in the lives of students on college campuses. We begin with a discussion of the benefits of intercollegiate athletics and recreation on a college campus, followed by an overview of the organization of these units and their programs and services. The chapter concludes with a discussion about opportunities for partnerships among student affairs, intercollegiate athletics, and recreation.

Benefits of Intercollegiate Athletics and Recreation

There are numerous benefits for all constituents associated with intercollegiate athletics in higher education. Although the intercollegiate athletic model is not perfect, the United States is the only country in the world that has a system in which student-athletes have the opportunity to compete at the college level before advancing to elite levels of competition. Connecting sport to higher education in this way benefits individuals and society in important ways. Individuals have the opportunity to be rewarded for their athletic prowess and at the same time gain skills to become educated citizens. Ideally, when individuals retire from playing sports they will have college degrees and can take on active roles in society as responsible, educated citizens. In addition to individual and societal benefits, intercollegiate athletics brings the community and the college campus together in a unique way. Consider football game day Saturdays; the college campus and surrounding community come together for a common goal—a concept that is often unheard of any other day of the week when there are issues that cause the campus and community to be divided.

Student-athletes who participate in intercollegiate athletics benefit from learning good sportsmanship, how to win and lose, teamwork, and communication skills (Shor, Dunkle, & Jaworski, 2012). Further, given the diversity of student athletes who participate in college sports, there is evidence to suggest that colleges and universities might learn from intercollegiate athletics how to facilitate openness to diversity and effective interaction across people who are different from one another (Wolf-Wendel, Toma, & Morphew, 2001).

Some scholars are concerned about the extent to which student-athletes benefit from the college experience relative to their non-athlete peers (Gayles & Hu, 2009; Gayles, Rockenbach, & Davis, 2012; Umbach, Palmer, Kuh, & Hannah, 2006). Although there are issues with admitting student athletes with low grades and test scores (Bowen & Levin, 2005; Shulman & Bowen, 2001), there is also evidence to suggest that student athletes are as engaged and experience gains in cognitive and affective development when compared to their non-athlete peers (Gayles & Hu, 2009; Gayles et al., 2012; Umbach et al., 2006).

Intramural and recreation programs for college students also have many benefits. Regular exercise and physical activity contribute to life balance and wellness, which are precursors to an overall sense of well-being and high-level functioning (Shor et al., 2012). Developing an overall sense of well-being encompasses more than being free of disease and sickness. In addition, it includes training and caring for the mind, body, and spirit. There is growing concern about the behavioral norms in our country such as sitting in the same place for hours at a time with little to no bodily movement, that reinforce a sedentary lifestyle, (Fakhouri, Hughes, Burt, et al., 2014; Strand, Egebergy, & Mozumdar, 2010). Many people in society have jobs and careers that require them to sit in front a computer or stand in one place for an extended amount of time. Within the college culture, students spend large amounts of time sitting in classes, while studying, and when playing video games (Strand et al., 2010).

College, however, is a transitional time for adolescents to explore and establish positive behaviors and attitudes that can have a lasting impact on establishing healthy lifestyles for years to come (Shor et al., 2012). Thus, infusing health and fitness activities into the campus culture has the potential to shape the lives of students in positive ways. In addition, establishing good health and fitness habits early in life has the potential to prevent health issues from developing later in life (National Center for Chronic Disease Prevention and Health Promotion, 2011).

Participating in athletic competition between peers can foster character values such as teamwork, sportsmanship, communication, organizational skills, and leadership. Such values are lifelong, transferable skills that individuals need to be successful in the workforce and in life. The same skills that are developed playing sports can be used in other areas of life, both personally and professionally. Further, participating in intramural sports allows students to effectively channel excess energy that could otherwise be distracting when trying to focus on academics. Regular exercise has the potential to release endorphins that promote increased energy and overall well-being (Centers for Disease Control, 2008).

Overview of Intercollegiate Athletics and Recreation

Intercollegiate athletics is a major part of the campus culture at many colleges and universities around the country. The first athletic competition was a rowing match between Harvard and Yale universities in 1852 (Rudolph, 1962). Students organized their practices, scheduled competitions, and developed training programs for themselves (Ridpath & Abney, 2012). Intercollegiate athletics quickly grew from a student-driven activity to the big-business enterprise that now exists on many large college campuses. In essence, intercollegiate athletics has morphed into a highly competitive, commercialized enterprise, particularly at Division I institutions.

Four-year colleges and universities with athletic programs are typically associated with either the National Collegiate Athletic Association (NCAA) or the National Association of Intercollegiate Athletics (NAIA). Athletic programs at the community college level fall under the National Junior College Athletic Association (NJCAA). The NCAA is the largest governing body of intercollegiate athletics, with more than a thousand member institutions across its three divisions. Each division is further divided into athletic conferences to which member institutions also belong. Athletic conferences under the NCAA have historically been divided by region (although that is changing for reasons related to funding and perceived prestige) and largely determine in-season competition schedules because teams within conferences must compete against each other during the regular competition season. Conferences also sponsor championships, and the outcome determines which teams move forward to the NCAA championships by sport. Both the conference and national-level organizations award scholarships to outstanding student-athletes who both perform well academically and excel within their sports.

The NAIA was established in 1937 and is the governing body for intercollegiate athletic programs at small colleges. Both four-year and two-year institutions that award bachelor's degrees can become members of the NAIA. The NAIA is a much smaller association compared to the NCAA, with only about three hundred member institutions. The NAIA has two divisions, with twenty-three conferences across the two divisions. In the 1980s and 1990s, the NAIA lost 125 member institutions to the NCAA and was expected to dissolve (Pennington, 2007). Around that time NAIA president Jim Carr stated he was confident about the future of the NAIA and indicated there were no plans to dissolve the association (Pennington, 2007). More recently, Carr acknowledged the continuing challenges faced by the association and the importance of rebranding and taking advantage of opportunities in the midst of changes across intercollegiate athletics (Hawes, 2013).

Student athletes at NCAA institutions can participate in intercollegiate athletics at one of three levels: Division I, II, or III. The major differences between athletic divisions are the type and number of sport programs offered, size of facilities, and level of attendance and whether or not athletic scholarships are awarded. Division I athletic programs offer the most athletic opportunities for men and women and also have the largest stadiums and arenas for revenue-producing sports: football and men's basketball. Division I institutions are largely made up of large research institutions around the country. Division I and II institutions offer athletic scholarships, whereas Division III athletic programs do not offer scholarships to student-athletes. Many Division II and III institutions are small liberal arts colleges.

There are many challenges associated with intercollegiate athletics on college campuses today, particularly at NCAA Division I institutions. Unfortunately, discussing all of the challenges that plague intercollegiate athletics is beyond the scope of this chapter. Many of the challenges involve governance and control of big-time college sports on university campuses. Institutional control involves the extent to which colleges and universities comply with the rules and regulations enforced by the governing association (Ridpath & Abney, 2012). Over the years, concerns about academic integrity and other gross acts of misconduct have increased in severity. Instances of academic dishonesty on the part of student-athletes (or on the part of others on behalf of student-athletes), gambling scandals, poor handling of student-athlete conduct issues, improper benefits to student-athletes, and perceived indifference on the part of colleges and universities to issues related to the welfare and appropriate compensation of student-athletes have eroded the public's confidence in intercollegiate athletics as well as higher education institutions as a whole. Some universities are considering adding or even deleting football programs because they requires a major financial commitment. Football programs have the potential to generate revenue for institutions and increase alumni support and giving; yet, football programs require greater resources for support staff, equipment and practice facilities, and travel and meals. These issues are primarily problematic for Division I institutions because they have the highest levels of commercialism and visibility through television contracts and advertising; however, these issues are also important considerations for smaller athletic programs who aspire to move up or compete at a higher level. It can be argued that NCAA Division III and NAIA athletic programs represent the purest form of amateurism in college sports because of lack of scholarship awards, low visibility, and little to no commercialism.

Campus Recreation

Engaging in athletic competition is a tradition that is deeply embedded within the college culture. During the colonial period, students resorted to playing games and engaging in competitions between classes to offset stress from the rigors of academia (Rudolph, 1962). Class competitions became a part of the norm on college campuses and eventually led to the establishment of social clubs and intercollegiate athletics. Students took pride in organizing and participating in athletic competition against peers at their own institution and against peers at other colleges. During the colonial period, faculty did not approve of any activity that took students time and attention away from academic pursuits. Over time, however, college presidents saw the value of athletic competition, particularly in alumni involvement and giving. Thus, as opposed to allowing students to organize and participate in sports on their own, university administrators deemed it more effective to provide oversight to support and supervise athletic competition for liability purposes as well as to capitalize on revenue generated through sport competition.

Intramurals on college campuses today consists of competitive games such as flag football, basketball, softball, kickball, and ultimate Frisbee. Students form teams to compete against one another throughout the academic year. In most cases, intramural games are played using teams of students from the same school and students who participate in intramural sports do not receive scholarships for participation and spectators do not pay a fee to watch intramural games on campus. Students organize and coach intramural teams, and the university provides support for intramural programs through the campus recreation departments. The department institutes rules and instructions for play, provides referees and game officials, allows access to venues for play, and schedules competitions and events.

Some of the challenges associated with running an intramural program on campus include how to deal with the intensity of competition between students, unsportsmanlike conduct, and unethical behaviors such as cheating. Although these issues are challenging, they also represent an opportunity for student growth and development. Managing emotions is an important psychosocial task for students to grapple with during the college years (Chickering & Reisser, 1993). Learning how to win and lose while maintaining good sportsmanship and character are valuable life skills.

Club sports are another avenue for athletic participation during college. Such programs are often coordinated through campus recreation departments, yet they are governed by a national association. For example, the National Intramural-Recreational Sports Association (NIRSA) hosts club divisions of both men and women's basketball, soccer, and tennis that culminate in national championships and the National Federation of Collegiate Club Sports Leagues, LLC (CollClubSports), a group of governing bodies that oversee basketball, football, track and field, softball, and baseball. Club sport teams offer students the opportunity to play at a competitive level against other college teams, yet require a more reasonable time commitment than that of NCAA intercollegiate athletics.

Health and Wellness

Although distinct from recreation, health and wellness programs are (or at least ought to be) closely aligned with them. Fitness has been a part of the campus culture since the 1860s, when the first course on physical fitness and hygiene was offered (Strand et al., 2010; Swinford, 2002). By the 1960s nearly every four-year college campus offered and required physical fitness courses for degree completion (Hensley, 2000; Strand et al., 2010). Wellness issues, particularly concerning young adults, have shifted over the years. The American College Health Association (2007) conducted a National College Health Assessment across 117 institutions with more than 94,000 student participants. The findings from this assessment identified five major health related issues on college campuses: (1) alcohol, tobacco, and drug use; (2) sexual health; (3) weight, nutrition, and exercise; (4) mental health; and (5) personal safety and violence. Wellness and fitness programs focus on these critical issues and others by offering a wide range of events and program initiatives for students, faculty and staff. At minimum most institutions provide exercise facilities, which are a basic necessity for any health and wellness program. Through the exercise facility, aerobic group fitness classes and weight training equipment may be provided for faculty, students, and staff. Some facilities may also include walking paths and programs for running, swimming, and biking. Other types of health and wellness programming include health education, open gym, fitness programs and sports, swimming, and racquet sports. Campus administrators should aim to make sure exercise facilities are conveniently located to maximize student access on the college campus.

The organizational structure of health and wellness programs varies by institution. On some campuses these programs are affiliated with the health and physical education and recreation department on campus. On other campuses the programs might be aligned with the health center, student affairs unit, or medical school. Many of the facilities that house health and wellness programs are auxiliary services that are self-supporting through receipts collected for programs and services offered (see chapter 25 for full discussion on auxiliaries). Some of the most popular types of programming offered through health and wellness programs include blood pressure screenings, body composition and assessment, agility and flexibility testing, personal training, weight control classes, nutrition and dietitian services, and strength assessments (Dinger, Watts, Waigandt, & Whittet, 1992; Sivik, Butts, Moore, & Hyde, 1992).

There are some challenges associated with operating a health and wellness program on a college campus, but many of the challenges can be viewed as opportunities to facilitate student development and opportunities for partnerships among departments on campus. A common question that arises is whether or not students, faculty, and staff should use the same facilities and participate in the same programming. It would be quite costly for institutions to build separate facilities. Further, many institutions are challenged with space issues that would prevent the likelihood of two facilities.

Although some programming may be offered separately for employees, opportunities for students, staff, and faculty to exercise together should be encouraged. Exercising together can serve as a great opportunity for staff and faculty to interact with students outside of the classroom, which has been linked to fostering student development, success, and retention (Astin, 1993; Tinto, 1993). For example, students having an opportunity to work out with the vice president for student affairs could be a positive source of motivation for students and send a strong message about the importance of health and fitness at all ages. Indeed, some campuses have developed wellness initiatives wherein staff and students create teams and compete against each other in weight loss challenges, pedometer steps races, indoor triathlons, or physical activity and fitness education participation. Further, working out together provides a great opportunity for administrators, faculty, and staff to mentor and establish connections to students outside of the classroom. However, ground rules should be established and clearly communicated about appropriate dress and behaviors to avoid and lessen the likelihood of awkward experiences among students, staff, and faculty.

Another common issue with health and wellness programs is the extent to which separate facilities should exist for intercollegiate athletes or whether all students should use the same facilities. Student-athletes are a unique population, particularly at Division I institutions. Given the role that exercise and weight training plays in becoming conditioned to compete at a high level, it makes sense for student-athletes to have separate facilities, exercise programs, and equipment.

Intercollegiate Athletics, Recreation, and Student Affairs

In a time of scarce resources and reduced funding for higher education, the need for partnerships and collaboration between units on campus is necessary and critical for sustainability. Chapter 21 discusses partnerships between student affairs and academic affairs, and some of the same principles apply to partnerships in the arenas of recreation and athletics. It makes good sense for most departments that serve students to collaborate and partner whenever possible. The goals and contextual values of student affairs as a profession call for partnership and collaboration among the various functional areas on campus. Student affairs divisions consists of an array of functional areas, including housing, orientation, student activities, campus recreation, Greek Life, and multicultural affairs. On larger campuses, these units are separate functional areas, whereas on smaller campuses one office or administrator may be responsible for several of these functions.

Given the vast array of student services, senior-level college administrators are concerned about cutting cost and avoiding duplication of programs and services. The danger of having so many functional areas on campus is the temptation to work in silos, in which each office provides programs and services without considering or knowing what other functional areas are doing on the campus. Duplication of services is costly and a waste of limited resources. Collaboration and partnership among functional areas is beneficial to both the institution and the students. Collaboration is beneficial for students because it provides opportunities for bringing different groups of students together that might not otherwise interact. This represents a great way to build community on campus. Partnerships between student affairs units is beneficial for institutions because costs can be cut if programs and services are cosponsored. Fortunately, there is a natural connection among student affairs, recreation, health and wellness, and intercollegiate athletics that make partnerships and collaborating fairly easy to do.

Partnerships Between Intercollegiate Athletics and Student Affairs

Intercollegiate athletics, particularly on large campuses, is often criticized for isolating the student-athlete population. Questions have been raised about the extent to which student-athletes benefit from the college experience in ways similar to their peers, as well as the extent to which the goals and values of intercollegiate athletics align with the goals and values of higher education (Bowen & Levin, 2005; Clotfelter, 2011; and Shulman & Bowen, 2002).

Student-athletes are students first, and attending to their academic success should be a top priority for all campus administrators, faculty, and staff. In recent years there has been a shift in reporting lines for directors of academic support services for student-athletes. Instead of reporting to the athletic director, the trend has shifted to having them report to the vice provost for academic affairs (Gaston-Gayles, 2003). This alignment is critical to ensure that the academic needs of student-athletes are met and that it is not the sole responsibility of the athletic department to provide academic support and attend to student-athletes' academic issues. Further, there may be less pressure on the director for academic support when reporting to the vice provost as opposed to solely reporting to the athletic director, particularly when an unfavorable event occurs.

Co-curricular programming for students on campuses is designed to facilitate student development and learning. Recreation and intercollegiate athletics can play an important role in the process, and there are many opportunities for collaboration and partnership between and among these areas and student affairs units. For example, student groups and organizations, such as fraternities and sororities, frequently participate in intramural programs to promote teamwork, bonding, and unity. Further, it provides an excellent form of exercise and a healthy outlet for dealing with stress and managing emotions such as anger and frustration. Student groups and organizations are full of student leaders on campus; student leaders across organizations should be encouraged to collaborate and cosponsor programs that involve student service offices on campus as well as the community. What follows are additional areas of partnerships that are promising and demonstrate collaboration is possible in a myriad of ways irrespective of institutional size, type, division affiliation, or reporting structures.

Residence Life and Housing. Community building is a key goal of residential living, and collaborations between intercollegiate athletics and college recreation can assist in its development and maintenance. Residence hall teams often form for campus intramurals, and these teams often bring together students across different majors, backgrounds, and social groups. In addition, a friendly residence hall competition for group attendance to an athletic event can not only increase community building and hall pride but also serve to bolster attendance at less visible and traditionally less attended sporting events. Mutually beneficial partnerships are more likely to be sustained.

Alternatively, with respect to student learning and development for student athletes, integration into the general student body through residential living represents powerful opportunities for programming, combating student-athlete isolation, and facilitating greater and more positive interactions with staff and non-athlete peers to counter negative perceptions. While NCAA regulations provide guidance for residence life administrators with respect to housing patterns, student affairs professionals have a responsibility to ensure inclusive environments for student-athletes who are housed on campus. Thus, it is necessary to forge positive relationships with athletic coaches and athletic support offices to encourage effective communication as well as provide professional development training for professionals and paraprofessionals who seek to understand the complex and unique lives of student-athletes.

Identity Centers. Student affairs professionals cannot forget that *athlete* is just one of many possible intersections of identity for the student-athlete and must explore how these multiple identities may affect their experiences. Davis and Cooper (2014) urged student affairs professionals to embrace the intersectionality in Black male student-athletes, specifically, by acknowledging the ways in which their racial, gender, sociocultural, and academic identities intersect with their athletic identity to affect their collegiate development and success. Culture centers focusing on issues related to gender, race/ethnicity, and sexual orientation and offices of multicultural and intercultural affairs are necessary to allow an affirming space for all students, especially student-athletes.

Student Volunteerism. NCAA's Life Skills Program offers a natural space for partnerships between offices of volunteerism and/or service learning to occur, as one of the core commitments is that of community service. Life Skills views and promotes campus and community services opportunities as valuable aspects of the student-athlete experience. Seeking shared service and reflection experiences between athletics and volunteerism offices can only enrich the experience. Athletics can benefit from having access to the functional area expertise and community connections of the volunteerism professionals, while the offices of volunteerism can benefit from engaging with a special population. Such collaborative efforts also give functional areas more opportunities to extend their reach on the campus. In addition, student-athlete involvement in the campus community can often spark greater involvement from other students because of their high-profile leadership status.

Volunteerism offices might also capitalize on student interest in sport and recreation by providing opportunities for students to engage with community members through coaching or supporting recreational leagues and/or after-school programs that have a focus on developing teamwork, leadership, and discipline among children through sport participation. Moreover, First Lady Michelle Obama's "Let's Move" (2010) campaign to combat the epidemic of childhood obesity has been in the national spotlight. This campaign has mobilized schools and community agencies to develop comprehensive and collaborative initiatives to promote and encourage healthy lifestyles. College students who are active in college sports and recreation could serve as excellent role models, volunteers, and mentors for children.

Student Conduct Offices. As student affairs professionals, we play a unique role in shaping the experience, engagement, and learning of today's college students. For some, this learning takes place, not through positive curricular and co-curricular involvement, but as students are held accountable to upholding community values, expectations, and responsibilities through the student conduct process. There has been growing concern over the high incidence of interpersonal violence, alcohol and drug abuse, hazing, and bullying taking place on today's college campus. Unfortunately, Division I institutions with prominent athletic and Greek life systems seem to be disproportionately plagued by these issues. Therefore, partnerships with student conduct offices can be useful beginning with prevention and outreach efforts to clarify and articulate community standards and expectations to ensure a fair and ethical process of resolving campus discipline issues, especially since those involving student-athletes can attract media attention.

The manner and process in which conflicts are resolved when they arise may differ based on institution, sport (whether intercollegiate, club, or intramural), divisional affiliation, and severity of the situation. In some situations, coaches work closely with the student affairs division, and quite often athletic directors are called in when intercollegiate student athletes feel as the though the decision is not fair. In other situations, divisions and governing bodies respect the institution's adherence to the rules, regulations, and policies of the institution when handling the situation. In the context of intramural and club sports, it is increasingly important for there to be clear and consistent messaging to and training for students, who frequently coordinate and officiate in these programs, about policies and procedures as well as appropriate behavior both on campus and when traveling for competitions.

Health and Wellness Programs. Health and wellness programming is essential for all students, and campus wellness programs' effectiveness often hinges on successful partnerships with other areas because of its primary function of outreach and advocacy. For example, student groups might partner with the wellness office to cosponsor a health fair for the campus and surrounding community. Cultural and identity centers might be particularly interested in raising awareness around health issues and disparities that exist within the various populations. Some of these include diabetes and high blood pressure within the African American community, heart disease and cancer for women, and growing body image issues among men and athletes. Residence halls provide a captive audience for both passive and active programming targeted on a variety of issues, including healthy eating, sleep habits, and mental health. To accomplish these goals, utilizing peer education has become commonplace at many institutions. Peer education not only serves a vital role in educating the campus community but also provides leadership opportunities for the students who get involved at this level.

Conclusion

In conclusion, intercollegiate athletics, recreation, and wellness are all a part of the campus culture and play a valuable role in facilitating the development of healthy and active lifestyles as well as fostering student development and learning. Understanding the roles, functions, and organizational structures of these departments can lead to increased collaboration and opportunities for partnerships with other student affairs units on campus.

References

American College Health Association. (2007). *American College Health Association—National College Health Assessment (ACHA-NCHA)*. http://www.acha-ncha.org/data_highlights.html.

Astin, A. W. (1993). *What matters in college: Four critical years*. San Francisco, CA: Jossey-Bass.

Bowen, W. G., & Levin, S. A. (2005). *Reclaiming the game: College sports and educational values*. Princeton, NJ: Princeton University.

Chickering, A. W., & Reisser, L. (1993). *Education and identity* (2nd ed.). San Francisco, CA: Jossey-Bass.

Centers for Disease Control. (2008). *Physical activity and health: A report from the surgeon general*. Washington, DC: Author.

Clotfelter, C. T. (2011). *Big time sports in American universities*. New York, NY: Cambridge University.

Davis, T. J., & Cooper, J. N. (2014). *Embracing intersectionality in Black male student athletes: A call for support.* Knowledge Communities Publication. Washington, DC: NASPA-Student Affairs Administrators in Higher Education.

Dinger, M. K., Watts, P. R., Waigandt, A., & Whittet, C. (1992). A nationwide survey of college wellness and university student wellness programs. *National Intramural Recreation Sports Association Journal, 16*(4), 44–48.

Fakhouri, T.H.I., Hughes, J. P., Burt, V. L., et al. (2014). *Physical activity in U.S. youth aged 12–15 years, 2012* (NCHS data brief, no. 141). Hyattsville, MD: National Center for Health Statistics.

Gaston-Gayles, J. L. (2003). Advising student athletes: An examination of academic support programs with high graduation rates. *NACADA Journal, 23*(1 & 2), 50–57.

Gayles, J. G., & Hu, S. (2009). The influence of student engagement and sport participation on college outcomes among division I student athletes. *Journal of Higher Education, 80*(3), 315–333.

Gayles, J. G., Rockenbach, A. B., & Davis, H. A. (2012). Civic responsibility and the student athlete: Validating a new conceptual model. *Journal of Higher Education, 83*(4), 535–557.

Hawes, K. (2013, April 21). NAIA ready for opportunity: State of the association panel focuses on opportunities amid change. *NAIA e-news.* http://www.naia.org/ViewArticle.dbml?ATCLID=207356860.

Hensley, L. D. (2000). Current status of basic instruction programs in physical education at American colleges and universities. *Journal of Physical Education, Recreation and Dance, 71*(9), 30–36.

National Center for Chronic Disease Prevention and Health Promotion. (2011, February 16). *Physical activity and health: The benefits of physical activity.* http://www.cdc.gov/physicalactivity/everyone/health/index.html.

Pennington, B. (2007, February 13). N.A.I.A.'s future looms large for division III. *New York Times.* http://www.nytimes.com/2007/02/13/sports/othersports/13naia.html.

Ridpath, B. D., & Abney, R. (2012). Governance of intercollegiate athletics and recreation. In G. S. McClellan, C. King, & D. L. Rockey (Eds.), *The handbook of college athletics and recreation administration* (pp. 127-152). San Francisco, CA: Jossey-Bass.

Rudolph, F. (1962). *The American college and university: A history.* New York, NY: Knopf.

Shor, D. A., Dunkle, J. H., & Jaworski, C. A. (2012). Health and wellness issues. In G. S. McClellan, C. King, & D. L. Rockey (Eds.), *The handbook of college athletics and recreation administration* (pp. 336-354). San Francisco, CA: Jossey-Bass.

Shulman, J. L., & Bowen, W. G. (2002). *The game of life: College sports and educational values.* Princeton, NJ: Princeton University.

Sivik, S. J., Butts, E. A., Moore, K., & Hyde, S. (1992). College and university wellness programs: An assessment of current trends. *National Association of Student Personnel Administrators Journal, 29*, 136–142.

Strand, B. N., Egeberg, J., & Mozumdar, A. (2010). The prevalence and characteristics of wellness programs and centers at two-year and four-year colleges and universities. *Recreation Sports Journal, 34*, 45–57.

Swinford, P. L. (2002). Advancing the health of students: A rationale for college health programs. *Journal of American College Health, 50*, 309–312.

Tinto, V. (1993). *Leaving college: Rethinking causes and cures of student attrition* (2nd ed.). Chicago, IL: University of Chicago Press.

Umbach, P. D., Palmer, M. M., Kuh, G. D., & Hannah, S. J. (2006). Intercollegiate athletes and effective educational practices: Winning combination or losing effort? *Research in Higher Education, 47*(6), 709–733.

Wartell, M. A. (2012). A CEO's perspective of athletics and recreation. In G. S. McClellan, C. King, & D. L. Rockey (Eds.), *The handbook of college athletics and recreation administration* (pp. 303-320). San Francisco, CA: Jossey-Bass.

Wolf-Wendel, L., Toma, J. D., and Morphew, C. C. (2001). "There's no 'I' in team": Lessons from athletics on community building. *Review of Higher Education, 24*(4), 369–396.

CHAPTER SEVENTEEN

SUPPORTING ONLINE STUDENTS

Anita Crawley and Andy Howe

Higher education is experiencing a transformation to which online learning is making a significant contribution. In just a little more than a decade, online learning has spurred exciting changes in teaching and learning at colleges and universities. As more and more students take advantage of online learning, providing face-to-face services for all students is becoming an increasingly challenging model of delivery. Because of this transformation, it is critical to learn new ways of delivering services to support online student success.

Professionals in student affairs are helping to shape the transformation by using innovative applications of technology to support online students. Some examples that enhance the student experience include using social media to build communities of online learners, gamification to engage learners, and reward-driven actions such as badges (Anderson & Rainie, 2012). Although student affairs professionals use technology to support on-campus students, more effort needs to be made to support students who are unwilling or unable to come to campus.

This chapter addresses growth of online learning, services needed to support online learner success, the role of student affairs in supporting online learners, benefits of cross-departmental collaboration, and the potential of a seamless online learning environment. The chapter concludes with sections about accountability and innovative strategies institutions have used to improve student retention, success, and completion.

Growth of Online Learning

According to the eleventh annual report on the state of online learning in US higher education, 7.1 million college students are taking at least one online course. This reflects a 6.1 percent growth rate over the previous year, representing 400,000 additional students participating in an online learning course (Allen & Seaman, 2013). For more than a decade, growth in online enrollments has been fueled by institutions seeking to expand access to education and students demanding more convenient ways of earning certificates and degrees. Although those reasons for increasing enrollments will persist, institutions may face additional pressure from secondary school students who come to college having already had an online experience and who want more (Project Tomorrow, 2013). With more students taking advantage of online learning options, institutions will need to deal with the concomitant demand for innovative ways of supporting students' academic and personal success.

Who Is Learning Online?

To be sure, learning online is now a well-accepted way of pursuing degrees and certificates. However, the greatest number of online enrollments will not come from freshmen enrolling directly from high school and living on campus. The 2013 University of California at Los Angeles Freshman Survey found that low percentages of students expect to take a course exclusively online (3.9 percent from private universities, 5.8 percent from private four-year colleges, 6.7 percent from public universities, 8.0 percent from public four-year colleges, and 13.9 percent from Historically Black Colleges and Universities). Interesting, 25 percent of the students who frequently used online instructional materials as high school seniors expect to take online courses (Hurtado, Eagan, & Stolzenberg, 2014).

During spring 2012, a nationwide study was conducted with 1,500 individuals who were at least eighteen years old and recently enrolled, currently enrolled, or planning to enroll in a fully online undergraduate or graduate degree, certificate, or licensure program (Aslanian & Clinefelter, 2012). This survey provides a snapshot of who is learning or planning to learn online. Twice as many women as men enroll in an online course, 40 percent are twenty-nine years old or younger, and 40 percent do not work full time. Surprisingly, 25 percent of undergraduate online students have already earned bachelor's degrees or higher, and their primary reason for enrolling in an online course, certificate, or program is to qualify for a work promotion or salary increase. Close to 75 percent intend to earn a degree. The full-time/part-time breakdown shows 60 percent of online undergraduates and 40 percent of online graduate students attend school full time. More than 80 percent of those undergraduates have previously earned college credit (Aslanian & Clinefelter, 2012).

How close online students live to campus has much to do with whether they are likely to come to campus for support services. Eighty percent of the students in the Aslanian and Clinefelter study live within 100 miles of campus or a learning center, and a little more than half of those students live within 50 miles (Aslanian & Clinefelter, 2012). Online students from the same study report the most positive things about online learning are the ability to study anywhere/anytime and to be able to study at home. The three top negative features of online learning are lack of direct contact and interaction with instructors and students, inconsistent or poor contact and communication with instructors, and students' lack of motivation, attention, or focus. These results highlight the importance of engaging online students to help them feel connected to the institution.

Students completing this survey identified the following as the most important student services:

- Online library and research (74 percent)
- 24/7 technical support (67 percent)
- Academic advising (58 percent)
- Career placement (50 percent)
- Career coaching and planning (49 percent)
- Student support and coaching (49 percent)
- Writing assistance and tutoring (43 percent)
- Math assistance and tutoring (41 percent)

Institutions might use this snapshot of online learners and the services they consider the most important for their success as they prioritize the design and development of online student services.

Scope of Online Student Services

To succeed in the online environment, online students need the same services as students taking courses in traditional formats, as well as a few specialized services. In many cases, the content is the same; only the method of delivering those services is different. Student-centric services delivered online do not need to follow the organizational structure of any particular institution, but it would be good for institutions to plan services with the students' needs in mind in order to facilitate a seamless online experience (Shea, 2007).

This chapter divides online student services into four categories: enrollment services, technical services, academic services, and personal services. Enrollment services include academic advising and education planning, admission and records, application, assessment and placement testing, bookstore, college catalog, course registration, financial aid, orientation to online learning, schedule of courses, transcript request, evaluation, and payment. Students may need some or all of these services prior to enrolling in an online course. Students may also need to know basic computer skills, how to download plug-ins, hardware and software requirements, how to access help desk support, how to use the learning management system (LMS), and where to find technical support prior to the beginning of an online course as well as during the term. Students need academic and personal support services throughout their enrollment. Academic services not previously mentioned include tutoring and other supplemental instructional support (such as study skills, time management, and organizational skills), library and research services, prior learning assessment, test proctoring, tutoring, writing and math support. Personal support services include career and placement, disability support services, financial planning, health and wellness, personal counseling, and services specific to the needs of population segments (such as veterans, students of color, and first-generation, basic-skills, and low-income students). Online students may want to become involved in online student activities.

These categories and time frames serve as organizational frameworks to help the reader understand the scope of services online students may need. A one-size-fits-all approach will not meet the needs of online students. One strength of delivering services online is that students can participate in the services at a time when they are best able to benefit from the information. Just-in-time delivery can be very effective, especially for those who are learning around the clock and from anywhere in the world. The following sections provide details and examples of good practices in each category.

Enrollment Services

Included in the enrollment services category are information, resources, and services students need to get started and to continue matriculation at a college or university. Many of these services are closely tied to the student information system and have been among the first services to be put online (Shea, 2005). Students (114,138) from 104 institutions report the convenience and quality of online registration, billing and payment, financial aid, and flexible pacing for completing a program are of prime importance and may influence the decision to enroll in a program (Noel-Levitz, 2013). Once enrolled, it is essential to prepare students to succeed in the online environment (Ali & Leeds, 2009). However, only 22 percent of institutions responding to the Managing Online Education Survey administered by the Western Interstate Commission for Higher Education (WICHE) require online students to take an orientation prior to their first online course (WICHE, 2013b).

First-time online learners need a comprehensive orientation program exemplified by Richland Community College's orientation to online learning (Jones, 2013). In 2009, Richland Community College (RCC) began mandating an online orientation for all students taking an online or hybrid course for the first time. To develop the orientation, RCC gathered feedback from online learning staff, faculty, and students. RCC gathered data from help desk tickets, examined online student retention rates, and reviewed the literature to determine what content would best prepare students for success in the online courses. The orientation, which is self-paced and delivered using the learning management system, is available to students within an hour after they register for an online course. Each of the ten modules ends with an interactive learning activity that students must complete before they can advance to the next module. Students must score 80 percent or higher on the cumulative examination before they gain access to their online course.

Online orientation student evaluations at RCC indicated students were confident or very confident they

- Know how to properly configure their computer for an online course (90 percent)
- Understand what it takes to be a successful online learner (87 percent), and
- Have the ability to navigate and use the LMS (93 percent)

Prior to implementation of the mandatory online orientation, retention rates were 71 percent; after the first year they increased to 79.5

percent, and were 80–84 percent for the three subsequent years. Faculty members report that students seem to be more prepared to learn, and the help desk reports a decrease in the number of tickets during the first two weeks of the semester (Jones, 2013). The Richland experience demonstrates the importance of institutions making effective orientation programs available, and perhaps mandatory, to students before their first online course.

Technical Services

Online student success depends on excellent technical resources and support. Students need to learn how to use the learning management system and have basic computer skills such as using a word processing program and managing their files. They need to own or have access to an adequate computer or other electronic device from which to learn, and possess the software required for their online courses (Muilenburg & Berge, 2005). Students may encounter technical difficulties throughout their online enrollment. With students studying at all hours, having around-the-clock technical support and resources to troubleshoot problems may be the ideal, but it is found only at 30 percent of institutions (WICHE, 2013b). Although institutions may have difficulty justifying the cost of twenty-four-hour live technical support, they typically provide answers to frequently asked questions and create multimedia tutorials to assist students during off hours.

Student affairs professionals sometimes leave responsibilities for technical support to the IT (information technology) and distance learning offices. Leslie Dare and Kyle Johnson (2012) call for the development of student affairs technology officer positions to provide student affairs leadership in the areas of strategic planning, project management, technology evaluation, data management, and technology education for student affairs professionals. North Carolina State University provides an example of developing a collaborative framework that includes student affairs representation in leadership roles. The Academic Technology Subcommittee at North Carolina State University is composed of members from IT, distance learning, library, various colleges within the university, faculty development, student affairs, faculty senate, and students (Dare & Johnson, 2012).

Academic Services

Academic support services are essential to an online student's success. Remotely located online students need to be able to fully participate in these services using Web-based services. Only 59 percent of colleges and universities provide online tutoring, whereas 79 percent provide online advising (WICHE, 2013b). Academic advising is the service online students most want institutions to make available at a distance (Noel-Levitz, 2009). The National eAdvisor, an online service from Arizona State University, provides information to help students understand academic program requirements and monitor their progress through specific programs (Phillips, 2013). The eAdvisor also provides alerts to students, faculty, and staff when student progress is off track. Degree progress reports, academic status updates, holds, and task lists provide personalized information to support online and on-campus students. In the first five years of eAdvisor's full implementation, freshman-to-sophomore retention rates improved by 8 percent and graduation rates by 10 percent. This online, personalized support has allowed advisors to work with online students more holistically. Because much of the administrative work is automated and analytics provide information about academic progress, advisors can focus on psychosocial influences that hinder progress while increasing student engagement (Phillips, 2013).

Personal Services

Institutions strive to connect with their online students to support their personal needs. Student affairs professionals are well aware that effective services in this category can and do facilitate academic success. The institutional challenge is to develop a means of delivering "high-touch" services using "high-tech" delivery methods while abiding by confidentiality and other ethical requirements of the profession. The National Board of Certified Counselors (NBCC), Center for Credentialing and Education has partnered with ReadyMinds to train career and mental health counselors to provide fully online services (Malone, Miller, & Walz, 2009). The NBCC code of ethics recognizes telephone, e-mail, chat, video conferencing, and social networks as possible methods for providing professional services. NBCC has established twenty standards for professionals providing services at a distance that offer guidance for appropriate delivery (NBCC, 2012). The National Association of Colleges and Employers (NACE) Career Services Survey of Colleges and Universities found that 98 percent of the reporting career centers have a website and sponsor online job postings, and 64 percent offer online counseling. This represents about 586 institutions that make online career counseling available to their students (NACE, 2013). Institutions that combine live online career counseling with robust Web-based career and job placement tools are providing good online career services.

Century College in Minnesota created the GPS Life Planning guide as a comprehensive program intended to help students plan their future (Century College, 2008). GPS Life Plan is now supported by the Minnesota State Colleges and Universities and used at several institutions throughout the state. This Web-based tool has three components: the Life Plan modules (career, education, finance, leadership, and personal), an electronic portfolio (eFolio), and links to relevant campus-based activities and events. Each module is introduced with a multimedia overview. The modules consist of information, checklists, and links to online and on-campus workshops and seminars. This comprehensive tool serves as a vehicle for blending online and on-campus student support services.

The needs of online students are similar to the needs of other students. The few unique needs relate to preparing students to learn online. Students need to understand how to use the technology that is required to succeed in the online environment, how to navigate the course and meet the instructor's expectations, and that online learning demands more self-discipline, initiative, and responsibility than traditionally taught courses. Some online students will need few additional support services; others will need many.

Online Student Services: The Stepchild

Institutions new to online learning typically focus on making technology decisions, developing online courses, and training instructors to teach online. Providing online support services is sometimes an afterthought. The results of the Instructional Technology Council (ITC) Annual Survey (2013) confirm that distance education program administrators understand the importance of providing services for online students that are equivalent to those available for on-campus students. For two years in a row, those administrators indicate that providing adequate services for online students was their number one challenge (Mullins, 2013). Although the challenge of providing equivalent services for online students is well documented, the solution is not. Even though individual institutions and sometimes consortia are addressing components of the problem, comprehensive solutions are difficult to find. Perhaps the California Community Colleges Online Education Initiative will provide a model for online student services that are fully integrated inside an educational management platform. The vision is to provide an ecosystem in which students who are learning online can easily access the support tools and services directly from the platform they are using to take their online course (Raths, 2014).

Role of Student Affairs

For years, student affairs professionals have used student information systems, educational planning tools, online college application and registration systems. That they are actively using technology is demonstrated by the results of the National Association of Student Personnel Administrators (NASPA) Survey of Technology Usage in Student Affairs (NASPA, 2013). Professionally, respondents use social media platforms (Facebook, 71 percent; Twitter, 63 percent; and YouTube, 49 percent), Microsoft Office (99 percent), presentation software such as PowerPoint or Prezi (86 percent), and cloud drives to store documents and information (58 percent). Virtually all respondents believe that Facebook (95 percent) and Twitter (93 percent) are important for engaging students (NASPA, 2013).

There is a strong demand for student affairs professionals to increase their support of online students. Some insight is provided by a joint study by University Professional, Continuing, and Online Education (UPCEA), NASPA, and InsideTrack (Fong, 2014). Participants, including student affairs and continuing education leaders from UPCEA and NASPA, were surveyed in the fall of 2013. For UPCEA respondents, 20 percent indicated a significant increase and 46 percent indicated some increase in the use of student services by online adult students, while only 1 percent of NASPA respondents indicated a significant increase and 23 percent indicated some increase. To address this increased demand for online services, about 50 percent of UPCEA and 14 percent of NASPA membership have added staff. More than 60 percent of UPCEA respondents use technology and have added new processes (for NASPA, only 39 percent use technology and 24 percent have added new processes) to become more efficient in managing the growth of services for online learners. These results suggest differences between how institutions serving adult students and traditional students support online learners. Institutions primarily serving adult students seem to be more responsive to supporting the needs of online students than institutions serving students who enroll directly from high school (Fong, 2014).

As online enrollments grow, institutions may want to create dynamic, remotely delivered services while maintaining the important interpersonal aspects of student services. For example, effective online advising is clearly more complex than merely sending students a link to a degree audit tool. Because advisors understand that students have a range of academic advising needs, they may want to consider three types of students. First, there are those students who are satisfied with an interactive multimedia academic advising tutorial that explains how to read their degree audit. These students are motivated, tech savvy, and certain of their education decisions and may prefer serving themselves. Second are a group of students who are selecting or changing their majors or have other complex questions. These students may benefit from online tools but want additional services that include interacting with an advisor, a blend of self-service and professional support. The third group of students may want and need intensive professional support. They may not benefit from Web-based information, and if they are not able to come to campus, will need to be served exclusively by live online meetings. For these students, student affairs professionals can use the phone, Skype, or videoconferencing tools such as Blackboard Collaborate to provide comprehensive online services. Videoconferencing tools most closely approximate in-person meetings and can be used to provide individual appointments, walk-in office hours, group meetings, seminars, and workshops. Institutions have been concerned about whether students would use videoconferencing as a means of receiving support services. In a study of undergraduate student use of information technology, 40 percent responded that they would like to communicate using two-way audio/video interaction (Educause, 2013).

Student affairs professionals may want to consider alternative approaches in order to provide effective remotely delivered support services. Communication is significantly different when students and professionals are not in the room together or participating in the service at the same time. Neither can take advantage of nonverbal cues, body language, and voice intonation. However, professionals may use a variety of strategies for expressing a caring attitude and developing a meaningful relationship both in person and online.

The more personal the online education environment is for students, the more likely they will be engaged throughout their enrollment and will stay connected to the institution as alumni. Professionals can convey a caring tone and attitude by the way they present text through e-mail, on a website, or in an online course (Betts, 2009). They may provide a welcoming online presence by creating video greetings and multimedia tutorials. Professionals may also want to use the videoconferencing tool that would allow staff to use a more personal approach to their interactions with remotely located students.

Institutions might consider which solutions are most appropriate for their setting by answering some of these questions. How will student affairs professionals identify students who need or want a more interpersonal approach to online support services? What approaches can these professionals take to make online student services more personal so they more closely resemble the human interaction of in person services? How can these services be made readily available to online students who are learning around the clock?

Effective Collaboration

To implement these innovative approaches for supporting online learners, institutions might foster collaboration among student affairs, academic affairs, information technology, and other departments. Effective collaboration is achieved when all players work together for a common purpose and achieve established goals in a timely manner. Effective collaboration can reinforce mission, increase communication and build trust, and foster a healthy organization. For individuals, effective collaboration can increase morale and productivity, develop skills and competencies, and expand one's professional network.

However, institutions may encounter barriers that hinder effective collaboration. These barriers include limited resources and time, unclear purpose and individual roles, no visible champion, lack of senior leadership, scope that is either too narrow or broad, and distrust (Kezar & Elrod, 2012). When student and academic affairs professionals begin to collaborate, they may sense a lack of understanding or respect between the two divisions, no clear understanding of student learning, and competition between which division "owns" student learning (Schroeder, 1999). If these problems are not resolved, they can substantially decrease effectiveness and stall innovation.

Institutions might emphasize that effective collaboration fosters a seamless learning environment for online learners. Staff and faculty can all play roles in creating effective collaboration. Meeting staff in other departments and understanding their responsibilities can foster effective collaboration, informed leadership about policies that support collaboration, identify barriers, and educate the communities about the benefits of effective collaboration. Successful collaboration can result in the development of seamless learning environments that best serve the needs of online learners.

Online Seamless Learning Environment

Institutions sometimes duplicate their organizational structures in the online environment, creating silos and disjointed experiences for online students. Institutions might want to foster a learning environment where student affairs professionals are an integral part of the design, development, and implementation process. For example, student affairs staff might work with course instructors to create online tutorials that can be integrated with the academic curriculum to be used as supplemental instruction. Instructors and student affairs professionals can create learning environments where students develop academically and personally through interaction with each other, with the instructor, with student affairs professionals, and with other support personnel. This community-centered environment can promote the achievement of learning outcomes and personal growth.

Institutions recognize the diverse needs of students taking online courses. In an online seamless learning environment, institutions can adapt services to provide personalized support directly to each student. Traditional student support services generally offer a package of services requiring students go to individual offices to receive the services available from that office. In an online seamless learning environment, support services can be personalized to each student's needs, as supplemental material related to a topic is embedded into the course, and human support engages students in deeper learning.

Institutions may want to unbundle services and support roles from the package of student services. Unbundling means removing certain content or services from each other so that they can be used in different situations and can target the individual needs more readily. For example, academic advisor responsibilities could be unbundled by separating the administrative responsibilities from the advising responsibilities, allowing advisors more time with students, while using technology to automate the task of monitoring student progress.

Institutions might have difficulty creating such an environment and unpackaging services. Initially student affairs professionals might identify concrete information about individual services that is easily explained online. This type of information is likely already included on student affairs office websites. Student service planners might ask whether technology can support the process of students completing transactions online. More and more, the answer is yes. Online applications to college, financial aid applications, registration, and bill payment are commonplace. The often-overlooked final factor is the element of human contact that has traditionally accompanied support services. Successful institutions find ways to integrate "high-touch" interpersonal elements with electronically delivered student services.

Delivery Methods

Institutions have three options available for delivering online student services: self-service support, blended support services, and services integrated into the online classroom. Each option provides opportunities for institutions to develop personalized online services.

Self-Service Support

Although students have access to learning anytime and from any location, many of the services to support those students are not available around the clock (WICHE, 2013b). Most students expect to receive the support they need when they need it from the computers or mobile devices from which they are learning. Online students learn during times that fit their busy schedules and from different time zones throughout the world. These times are frequently beyond the normal office hours of US colleges and universities.

From the beginning of Web-based learning, regional accrediting commissions and organizations such as NASPA and the American College Personnel Association (ACPA) have sent consistent messages that online students need to receive support services similar to those received by all other student populations (Crawley, 2012). Support services for online learners that are available only on campus cannot be considered equivalent. To effectively support the growing population of online students, student affairs might conceive of new ways to support students beyond traditional time frames, one of the guiding principles identified in the report, *Envisioning the Future of Student Affairs* (NASPA, 2010).

Because some online students are unable or unwilling to come to campus, institutions might develop new ways of delivering services. Access to the college website is always available to students. One method of providing around-the-clock student services is to develop dynamic multimedia tutorials. When institutions make student support tutorials available from the public websites, the student portal, or the learning management system, students are able to obtain just-in-time information exactly when they need it.

Fully online schools have been doing this for years. Capella University's iGuide offers a comprehensive series of videos organized as follows: support services, technical support, financial aid resources, advising, career center, disability services, military support, academic tutoring, tutorials, free seminars, and frequently asked questions. All sections have well-designed and engaging tutorials. In many cases, students use the tutorials for self-assessment to determine whether they have learned the material. Some tutorials are always visible from each page of a section. For example, on all pages of the technical section, a video tour of iGuide (the virtual campus) and Capella Mobile are always visible. Most pages of the iGuide provide students with a method of contacting a person for live support (Chow & Chmura, 2010).

Blended Student Support Services

Not all students are best served by fully online self-services. Some students may want to begin with the services described here but will then want to interact with a professional. In order to scale online student services, institutions may want to encourage students to be as self-sufficient as possible by encouraging them to first use self-service tutorials and then provide options for interacting with professionals online, or, if possible, have students come to campus.

Institutions might want to adopt a blended approach to delivering student services. Such an approach

- Maximizes the effectiveness and efficiency for students and the professional staff
- Provides intensive services only to those students who need them
- Makes some services available to students around the clock
- Empowers students to become more self-determined and independent
- Utilizes professional staff for the students with the most complicated needs

Support Services Integrated into the Online Course

Another promising practice is for institutions to incorporate support information and supplemental material into the online course room. Online students enjoy seamless and relevant learning environments in which embedded and unbundled content appears at the moment the student needs it. Online courses might include academic or career advising modules related to specific course content. The learning management system welcome page can include links to academic support, tutoring, and library modules.

Institutions that embed support service professionals into online courses successfully engage students and improve student learning, development, and success. Some institutions have embedded academic advisors, success coaches, tutors, and/or librarians into online courses. For example, Walden University has implemented a peer-tutoring program in quantitative research courses. Advanced graduate students who have demonstrated outstanding competencies in statistics and analysis are assigned to work with learners one on one in the course room, while other tutors are assigned to facilitate small-group tutoring sessions and conduct webinars that provide supplemental instruction. Walden found that courses with both embedded peer mentors and small-group instruction generally had a higher grade distribution, learner satisfaction, and retention rates compared to courses that did not (Online Writing Center, 2014). Institutions that provide just-in-time support expand the concept of a seamless and relevant learning environment for online students.

Success and Retention

Remotely delivered support services are essential for online student success and retention. Sixty-five percent of the institutions responding to the 2012 Educause Core Data Service Report indicate that they provide special support services for distance education (Educause, 2012). However, retention rates for online students are lower than the rates for students taking courses in the classroom. The Instructional Technology Council survey reports that the gap between online and face-to-face course completion rates has narrowed over the previous year, with 45 percent of the responding institutions reporting they have achieved equivalency. A mere

4 percent report retention rates are higher in online courses, and 50 percent report online retention rates are lower (Mullins, 2013). Even with these improvements over the previous year, with half the respondents reporting lower online course retention, professionals charged with the support of online students have more work to do.

Some institutions try to improve retention rates only when students begin to fail. Institutions might consider using early alert systems that help identify at-risk students before they fall too far behind. Some institutions use analytical tools to identify patterns of student behavior within the online course room. When a student meets predetermined criteria, automated status notifications are sent to faculty, support staff, and students. These notifications typically include suggested methods for remediating the situation. For example, a system can send to a student a personalized message indicating that academic performance is below par and provide contact information for online tutoring. Alternatively, the offer for academic support might come directly from a tutor. Institutions use learning management systems, like Desire2Learn and Blackboard, that provide data and analytics to make it easy for faculty and support staff to identify at-risk students. Using early alert systems, institutions provide a means to identify a specific student need and provide interventions targeted to meet those needs.

Institutions may improve student success and retention rates in online courses by using learning analytics, described as "the analysis of electronic learning data which allows teachers, course designers and administrators of virtual learning environments to search for unobserved patterns and underlying information in learning processes" (Agudo-Peregrina, Elrod, Conde-González, & Hernández-García, 2014). Learning analytics holds much promise for helping students make informed decisions about course selection and academic success. For example, Austin Peay State University has developed a system that can predict with 90 percent accuracy whether a student will get a C or better in certain courses. Students are encouraged to take courses in which they have the greatest chance of success (Denley, 2013). The initial system used filters based on a student's unmet degree requirements and past academic performance. The improved system added criteria that consider a student's life circumstances such as juggling family and work responsibilities. Desire2Learn, a learning management system, has purchased this product and includes it as part of their portfolio of predictive analytics and student success (Denley, 2013).

Institutions participating in the Predictive Analytics Reporting (PAR) Framework have done promising work. PAR is a nonprofit multi-institutional data mining collaborative of two- and four-year, public, private, for- and not-for-profit institutions of higher education (WICHE Cooperative for Educational Technologies, 2014). The goals of PAR are to identify points of student loss and effective practices that improve online student retention. Sixteen member institutions have provided 1,700,000 student records and 8,100,000 course level records to be analyzed using the PAR Framework. The PAR proof of concept pilot program supported the method for identifying common variables likely to influence student retention and progress toward completion, as well as institutional points of potential loss and opportunities for proactively improving student success. Key findings from the pilot program are

- More concurrent online courses can lead to lower chance of passing.
- Any developmental education course reduces the likelihood of a student passing the course.
- First-time college students are less likely to pass an online course.
- Prior withdrawals predict subsequent withdrawals.
- Past success predicts future success.

In addition to identifying loss points and high-risk factors, the PAR Framework has created a Student Success Matrix. Interventions are organized based on the possible cause of the problem (learner characteristics, learner behaviors, academic integration, social/psychological integration, other learner support, course/program characteristics, and instructor behavior/characteristics). The specific intervention is based on the type of problem and where the student is in the academic cycle. The sixteen participating institutions are collecting data about how helpful specific interventions may be in improving rates of success and retention (Wagner & Davis, 2013).

Accountability

The eight regional accrediting commissions working with the Western Cooperative for Educational Telecommunications (WCET) provided best practice standards for supporting online students (WICHE, 2001). During the ensuing years, each regional accrediting commission has further explicated and supported the initial principles that online students deserve equivalent services and that those services should be delivered electronically (WICHE, 2013a). Along with the regional accrediting commissions, various other organizations like the Council for the Advancement of Standards in Higher Education (CAS) set quality standards for online support services. Although these organizations initially developed separate standards and benchmarks for distance learning programs (including student support), they now apply the same standards to all services no matter what delivery method is used.

The Council for the Advancement of Standards in Higher Education (CAS), eighth edition, eliminated the support of distance education students as a separate functional area and now includes the support of students learning at a distance in all functional areas. CAS has recognized the pervasiveness of distance learning and the need for all functional areas to provide access to information about programs and services, staff members who can address questions and concerns and provide counseling, advising, and other forms of assistance. The CAS standards are voluntary, but they apply to all institutions that offer distance education (CAS, 2012).

College and university departments also measure the quality of student support services. Student affairs professionals use several means to measure quality, including usage, satisfaction, student development, and learning that results when students participate in traditionally delivered services; however, it is unclear how many student affairs offices are measuring these elements for services delivered at a distance. Academic affairs professionals at some institutions have attempted to isolate satisfaction and learning in the online environment by administering student evaluations from within online courses; however, those measures rarely include an assessment of online student services.

Online learning administrators are using a variety of instruments to measure quality of online learning courses and programs. Quality Matters (QM), a rubric used to evaluate online course design, includes four learner support standards: technical support, academic support (library, testing, tutoring, writing and math centers, and supplemental instruction), support services (advising, registration, financial aid, student life, counseling), and tutorials and/or help files. QM recommends that all learner support services be made available to students from inside the online course.

The Sloan-C Quality Scorecard for the Administration of Online Programs (the Scorecard) also measures the quality of online programs. Based on quality indicators from the Institute for Higher Education Policy study, *Quality on the Line: Benchmarks for Success in Internet-Based Distance Education* (2000), the Scorecard was later validated through a six-round Delphi study, in which forty-three administrators of online education agreed on seventy quality indicators (Shelton, 2010). Moore and Shelton (2013) labeled eighteen of the seventy quality indicators as relating specifically to the support of online students and organized them into four categories:

1. Encouraging a sense of community for students
2. Introducing students to online learning
3. Supporting students' use of technology
4. Providing ongoing support for learning, research, resources, and guidance

Moore and Shelton (2013) identify good practices that institutions use to meet benchmarks in each category. For encouraging community, Rio Salado Community College uses data mining and predictive modeling to proactively reach out to students. The University of Maryland University College introduces students to online learning by providing a free introductory online course that helps students evaluate whether online learning is right for them. State University of New York, Delhi provides students an always available technical portal, using mostly free Google tools to provide comprehensive online technical support (Moore & Shelton, 2013). Ongoing support for learning, research, resources, and guidance is a catchall category that includes services traditionally delivered by student affairs professionals and others. The Lone Star College System provides a comprehensive student support system for online students (Britto & Rush, 2013). The comprehensiveness and organizational structure of the Lone Star College System website are good and provide a model that other institutions might use to develop more dynamic online student services.

Conclusion

Online learning can contribute substantially to increasing the educational achievements of college students, but only if online students are supported throughout their time in college. Online learning is now an integral part of many institutions' academic offerings. Although an increasing number of students are registering for online courses, the success and retention rates are not as strong as rates in traditionally delivered instruction. To correct this deficiency, institutions might consider developing dynamic online student services that provide support before a student's first online course and throughout the time they spend at the college or university.

Student and academic affairs might collaborate to develop effective support of online students and to make those support services available through a seamless learning environment. Students benefit when services are developed and delivered using the expertise of professionals who work together to assure that students successfully complete their online courses and programs.

Student affairs professionals have been slow to assume responsibility for creating dynamic services for remotely located online students. As this population increases, student affairs professionals will assume a leadership role in developing services that support the success of online students.

References

Agudo-Peregrina, Á. F., Elrod, S., Conde-González, M., & Hernández-García, Á. (2014). Can we predict success from log data in VLEs? *Computers in Human Behavior, 31,* 542–550.

Ali, R., & Leeds, E. (2009). The impact of face-to-face orientation on online retention: A pilot study. *Online Journal of Distance Learning Administration, 12*(4). http://www.westga.edu/~distance/ojdla/winter124/ali124.html.

Allen, I. E., & Seaman, J. (2013). *Grade change: Tracking online education in the United States.* Babson Park, MA: Babson College.

Anderson, J., & Rainie, L. (2012). *The future of gamification.* Pew Research Center's Internet & American Life Project. http://www.pewinternet.org/2012/05/18/the-future-of-gamification/.

Aslanian, C. B., & Clinefelter, D. L. (2012). *Online college students 2012: Comprehensive data on demands and preferences.* Louisville, KY: Learning House.

Betts, K. (2009). Lost in translation: Importance of effective communication in online education. *Online Journal of Distance Learning Administration, 12*(2).http://www.westga.edu/~distance/ojdla/summer122/betts122.html.

Britto, M., & Rush, S. (2013). Developing and implementing comprehensive student support services for online students. *Journal of Asynchronous Learning Networks, 17*(1), 29–43.

Century College. (2008). GPS *LifePlan.* http://www.gpslifeplan.org/century/.

Council for the Advancement of Standards in Higher Education. (2012). *General standards.* http://www.cas.edu/generalstandards.

Chow, T., & Chmura, A. (2010). Implementing a virtual community of interest at Capella University. In *Proceedings of the 2010 ACM Conference on Information Technology Education* (pp. 59–64). New York, NY: Association for Computing Machinery. doi.acm.org/10.1145/1867651.1867668.

Crawley, A. (2012). *Supporting online students: A Practical guide to planning, implementing, and evaluating services.* San Francisco: Jossey-Bass.

Dare, L. & Johnson, K. (2012). Emerging roles and responsibilities of the student affairs technology officer position. In A. Tull & L. Kuk (Eds.), *New realities in the management of student affairs: Emerging specialist roles and structures for changing times.* Sterling, VA: Stylus.

Denley, T. (2013). Degree compass: A course recommendation system. *Educause Review Online*. http://www.educause.edu/ero/article/degree-compass-course-recommendation-system.

Educause. (2012). *Core Data Service, 2012*. Washington, D.C.: Educause Center for Analysis and Research.

Educause. (2013). *ECAR study of undergraduate students and information technology, 2013*. Washington, D.C.: Educause Center for Analysis and Research.

Fong, J. (2014). *It takes more than a village for online learning*. Washington, D.C.: University Professional and Continuing Education Association.

Hurtado, S., Eagan, K., & Stolzenberg, E. B. (2014). *The freshman survey, 2014*. Los Angeles: University of California Los Angeles, Higher Education Research Institute.

Institute for Higher Education Policy. (2000). *Quality on the Line: Benchmarks for Success in Internet-Based Distance Education*. Washington, D.C.: Author.

Instructional Technology Council. (2013). Annual Survey 2013 *Washington*, D.C.: Author.

Jones, K. R. (2013). Developing and implementing a mandatory online student orientation. *Journal of Asynchronous Learning Networks, 17*(1), pp. 43-45.

Kezar, A., & Elrod, S. (2012, January–February). Facilitating interdisciplinary learning: Lessons from Project Kaleidoscope. *Change: The Magazine of Higher Learning*. http://www.changemag.org/Archives/Back%20Issues/2012/January-February%202012/Facilitating-learning-full.html.

Malone, J. F., Miller, R. M., & Walz, G. R. (2009). A review of distance counseling: Expanding the counselor's reach and impact. *Journal of Technology in Human Services, 27*(3), 252–255.

Moore, J. C., & Shelton, K. (2013). Social and student engagement and support: The Sloan-C quality scorecard for the administration of online programs. *Journal of Asynchronous Learning Networks, 17*(1), 53–72.

Muilenburg, L. Y., & Berge, Z. L. (2005). Student barriers to online learning: A factor analytic study. *Distance Education, 26*(1), 29–48.

Mullins, C. (2013, April). *Trends in eLearning: Tracking the impact of eLearning at community colleges, 2013*. Instructional Technology Council. http://www.itcnetwork.org/attachments/article/87/AnnualSurveyApril2013.pdf.

National Association of Colleges and Employers. (2013). *2012–13 Career services benchmark survey for college and universities*. Bethlehem, PA: Author.

National Association of Student Personnel Administrators. (2010). *Envisioning the future of student affairs*. Washington, DC: Author.

National Association of Student Personnel Administrators. (2013). *A survey of technology usage in student affairs*. Washington, D.C.: Author.

National Board of Certified Counselors. (2012). *Policy regarding the provision of distance professional services*. Greensboro, NC: Author.

Noel-Levitz. (2009). *Academic advising highly important to students, National Research Report 2009*. Coralville, IA: Author. http://www.eric.ed.gov/ERICWebPortal/detail?accno=ED541564.

Noel-Levitz. (2013). *Adult and online learner satisfaction-priorities reports*. Coralville, IA.: Author.

Online Writing Center. (2014). Walden University. *Writing Tutor*. http://academic guides.waldenu.edu/content.php?pid=531652.

Phillips, E. D. (2013). Improving advising using technology and data analytics. *Change: The Magazine of Higher Learning*.

Project Tomorrow. (2013). *2013 Trends in online learning: virtual, blended and flipped classrooms*. Washington, DC: Author.

Raths, D. (2014, February 26). California community colleges joining forces for online success. *Campus Technology*. http://campustechnology.com/articles/2014/02/26/california-community-colleges-joining-forces-for-online-success.aspx?=ct21.

Schroeder, C. C. (1999). *Partnerships: An imperative for enhancing student learning and institutional effectiveness*. New Directions for Student Services, no. 87. San Francisco: Jossey-Bass.

Shea, P. (2007). Student services rethought for all students. In S. Johnstone (Ed.), *Advancing campus efficiencies: A companion for campus leaders in the digital era*. Bolton, MA: Anker.

Shea, P. A. (2005). *Serving students online: Enhancing their learning experience*. New Directions for Student Services, no.112. San Francisco: Jossey-Bass.

Shelton, K. (2010). A quality scorecard for the administration of online education programs: A Delphi study. *Journal of Asynchronous Learning Networks, 14*(4), 36–62.

Wagner, E., & Davis, B. (2013). The Predictive Analytics Reporting (PAR) Framework. *Educause Review Onlin,*. http://www.educause.edu/ero/article/predictive-analytics-reporting-par-framework-wcet.

Western Interstate Commission for Higher Education. (2001). *Best practices for electronically offered degree and certificate programs*. Boulder, CO: WCET/WICHE Cooperative for Educational Technologies.

Western Interstate Commission for Higher Education. (2013a). *Guidelines for the review and evaluation of distance education links to guidelines and policy statements from the regional accrediting commissions*. Boulder, CO: WCET/WICHE Cooperative for Educational Technologies. http://www.wcet.wiche.edu/advance/resources.

Western Interstate Commission for Higher Education. (2013b). *Managing online education 2013: Practices in ensuring quality*. Boulder, CO: WCET/WICHE Cooperative for Educational Technologies, 2013.

WICHE Cooperative for Educational Technologies. (2014). *Predictive Analytics Reporting (PAR) Framework*. Western Interstate Commission for Higher Education/Western Cooperative for educational Communications. http://wcet.wiche.edu/par.

PART FOUR

HUMAN RESOURCES IN PROFESSIONAL PRACTICE

The organization, recruitment, selection, supervision, and development of human capital, including our own capital, is an essential
endeavor for the successful practice of student affairs administration.
This part of the handbook addresses these important human resources
issues. Linda Kuk begins the section in chapter 18 by presenting a variety
of organizational models for student affairs. She discusses organizational
issues to consider in order to positively respond to ever-changing student
demographics and institutional imperatives. The quality of student affairs
departments is highly dependent on effective professional staff in place
who can create and deliver the programs and services needed and desired
by students. In chapter 19, Zebulun Davenport offers practical suggestions
for the recruitment, selection, supervision, and retention of capable
professional staff. The human resources theme continues in chapter 20, in
which Susan Komives and Stan Carpenter discuss the connection of professional competencies to the need for lifelong professional learning. They
propose a model for individual and group professional development, offer
suggestions about how to implement a comprehensive strategy for professional development, and highlight distinctive professional development
activities.

CHAPTER EIGHTEEN

ORGANIZATIONAL AND ADMINISTRATIVE MODELS WITHIN STUDENT AFFAIRS

Linda Kuk

Student affairs as an organizational unit within higher education can play an integral role in both student and institutional success. A student affairs presence can be found on nearly every campus within higher education throughout the United States and, with increasing frequency, throughout the world. As student affairs has developed, its mission and purpose have evolved to focusing on serving the needs of students, to fostering the academic success and personal development of students, and to creating campus environments that support the educational mission of collegiate institutions (Dungy, 2003; Hirt, 2006, 2009; & Kuk, 2009).

The organizational complexity within student affairs organizations has its origins in the tremendous growth in the number, diversity, and needs of students accessing higher education after World War II. From the late 1950s through the mid-1970s, higher educational institutions created separate student services structures to more specifically address the needs of students (Knock, 1985).

Over time, the growth and complexity have been sustained by the demands of consumer-oriented students and their families for greater access, greater educational and service amenities, and more individualized programs and services. In order to compete, higher educational institutions have added services, programs, and facilities to attract and retain students, and to maintain and enhance their educational reputations. (Dungy, 2003; Hirt, 2006, 2009; Manning, Kinzie, & Schuh, 2006; Rhatigan, 2009; and Sandeen, 2001).

Over the past decade student affairs organizations have experienced considerable turbulence, new challenges, and significant loss of both fiscal and human resources. Many of the emerging challenges have been fueled by rapidly changing technological developments and their applications (Dungy 2003; and Kruger, 2009). The pressure for change in student affairs organizations has also been intensified amid resource losses resulting from the economic downturn of the most recent recession. These resource losses have occurred in the midst of increasing enrollments and shifting demands for increased and more complex services and programs aimed at meeting the needs of an increasingly diverse student body. In most cases, student affairs operations have been seriously challenged in their efforts to maintain their funding and service base, and this pressure is likely to continue (Schuh, 2009).

Student affairs organizations now face intensified student consumer-oriented expectations of service delivery in a world of 24/7 communication, social media, and new approaches to learning-centered pedagogies (Dungy, 2003; Hartley, 2001; Kuk, Banning, & Amey 2010; and Manning et al., 2006). During this time, student affairs organizations and their institutions have also experienced the fears and trauma associated with increasing disruption, violence, and terrorism that have significantly eroded perceptions of once safe, friendly, and learning-focused campus environments (Jackson & Terrell, 2007). In the midst of these challenges student affairs organizations now face a relatively new consciousness of the importance of their organizational structure, design, and functionality, and how they contribute to institutional success.

As we look to the future, there is a growing need to focus on how student affairs might more effectively reorganize programs and services to serve the changing needs of students and other constituent groups, in addition to more effectively addressing institutional and divisional strategic goals (Kezar & Lester, 2009; and Tull & Kuk, 2012). This chapter focuses on what we know about current student affairs organizational models, as well as related research and theory in the area of student affairs organizational design. It also offers several pertinent considerations for crafting effective student affairs organizational models for the future.

Organizational Design Issues in Student Affairs

Most student affairs operations within American higher education institutions have historically been structured both hierarchically and functionally (Barr, 1993). As the needs for services and programs have grown, units were created and added to the existing organizational structures (Ambler, 1993; Dungy, 2003; and Rhatigan, 2009). Most of the student affairs organizational models utilized today are the result of institutional history, institutional type, state law, and institutional financial policies, as well as the individual preferences of institutional leadership (Barr, 1993; Dungy, 2003; and Sandeen, 2001).

Over time, the structural issues of which units should constitute student affairs, how these units should be organized, to whom they should report, and how they should be managed have continued to evolve. There is no one organizational model that fits all, yet there appear to be some common elements that exist across institutional type that greatly affect student affairs organizational structures and their effectiveness (Dungy, 2003; Hirt, 2006, 2009; Kuk, 2012; Kuk & Banning, 2009, 2012; and Manning et al., 2006).

What Units Constitute Student Affairs

There are some distinct differences in what service and support units are a part of student affairs at various institutions (Dungy, 2003; Hirt, 2006, 2009; and Kuk & Banning, 2009, 2012). The ongoing issue of what constitutes student affairs as an organizational unit within higher education is not directly related to any obvious organizational factors other than organizational history, mission, and the desires of institutional leadership (Ambler, 2000; Barr, 1993; and Sandeen, 1989). Kuk and Banning (2009, 2012) found that differences in which institutional units reported to student affairs, and which did not, were found across all types of institutions. There was no evident or consistent pattern of what units constituted student affairs by size or type of institution, although there were some similarities by type of institution.

Research Universities. The student affairs divisions in research universities appear to be the most visibly different from the others. They tend to have larger numbers of units in their divisions, more personnel, more levels within the organizational structure, the presence of a middle management level (assistant and associate vice presidents) that manage many functional units within the organization and report to the senior student affairs officers (SSAOs), as well as smaller numbers of people who report directly to the SSAO. However, the type of units within student affairs organizations varies considerably; the majority are units traditionally associated with student affairs functions. The divisions in research institutions are also distinctly different from those in the other types of institutions by the frequent inclusion of technology services for student affairs and auxiliary services in their units. Many also report to a provost or the executive vice president, while nearly all of the SSAOs from the other types indicted in the Kuk and Banning studies (2009, 2012) reported directly to the president.

Four-Year Master's-Level Institutions. The student affairs divisions in four-year master's-level institutions are close to those in the research universities in numbers of service units in their divisions, but are much flatter in organizational structure, with almost no indication of a middle management layer, and nearly all of those reporting directly to the SSAO being unit directors. Kuk and Banning found no consistent pattern regarding which service units were in student affairs. Institutions in this category are the most consistent in organizational structure and have the most traditional student affairs units within their divisions, including residential-based programs and services, fraternities and sororities, college unions, counseling, dean of students, student conduct, and student leadership. As a result, they are the most similar with regard to the type of service units within their student affairs organizations.

Community Colleges. The student affairs organizations in community colleges are distinct from the other types in that nearly all of them supervise academic advising services, enrollment management, TRIO programs, and international student services. For the most part, the other three institutional types do not. Very few of the community college SSAOs supervise college unions, commuter and off-campus living programs, housing and residence life, services for under-represented populations, sorority and fraternity advising, or health centers. Most of the SSAOs at the other types of institutions supervise these units as part of their divisions.

Liberal Arts Colleges. Student affairs structures in liberal arts colleges are about the same as in the community colleges in number of service units and staff within the student affairs divisions. However, the units that report within student affairs are very different; they consist mostly of traditional student affairs units, including residential-based programs and services such as fraternities and sororities, college unions, residence halls and housing, counseling, dean of students, student conduct, and student leadership. Their organizational structures resemble those of institutions in the community college and four-year master's categories, being flatter in structure with a larger number of staff, most of whom are unit directors, reporting directly to the SSAO. Kuk and Banning found an occasional assistant dean or associate vice president title in liberal arts colleges, but most role incumbents were unit heads and not the type of middle managers found in research university structures.

How Student Affairs Is Organized

Kuk and Banning (2009, 2012) studied how senior student affairs officers conceptualized their current student affairs structures. In examining the organizational models utilized by student affairs divisions across a variety of institutional types, the models used were essentially functional in nature, with distinct functional units reporting through a varied number of hierarchical levels. Although the specific individual functional units within student affairs divisions varied greatly, the organizational structures looked very similar, with some differences by type of collegiate institution. All of the structures were hierarchical and pyramid-shaped in design. No other variations in organizational structure were reported within student affairs.

Some of the larger organizations, mostly research institutions, appeared to have a form of a "hybrid-matrix" structure integrated across their primary functional structures, but these structures were not a prominent part of the organization's design, and the existence of this aspect of the structural model was not consciously noted by any respondent. It is likely that these structures were added to enable increasingly complex and specialized organizations to communicate across the existing organizational units and to create greater efficiency in commonly used resources and services.

The smaller organizations, notably the community colleges, liberal arts colleges and four-year master's-level universities, appeared to address the communication and efficiency issues by having staff assume some generalist and crossover responsibilities among functional areas and by having a flatter, less complex structure. The smaller student affairs organizations appeared to have more generalists engaged in a variety of responsibilities, while the larger and more complex organizations had a greater level of specialization of professional roles and responsibilities. As a result, the larger organizations appeared more complex, with more hierarchical layers and staff performing more specialized functions, resulting in more overall units in the organization. The organizations differed in which units reported to which higher level within the structure and how many hierarchical levels were represented in the organizational structure. Hence, the research institutions had the most distinctive structures.

In addition to the wide variation in which functional units were included in student affairs, the biggest differences in structural design across all types of institutions appeared in the areas of span of control and hierarchical levels. The number of direct reports to SSAOs appeared to be diverse, spanning from four to seventeen people, and the number of levels within the organizations also varied. Most of the organizations, including nearly all of the liberal arts colleges, community colleges, and four-year master's-level universities, appeared to have three hierarchical levels within the student affairs division, but many research institutions had four or five levels of hierarchy.

However, the availability of resources (either as a matter of perception or reality) may be a factor that has influenced the design of student affairs organizations among all types of institutions, especially in relation to levels of hierarchy and spans of control. Kuk and Banning (2009) found that the SSAOs' perceptions about the amount and quality of existing human resources within their organizations in relationship to their perceived level of need may have influenced both their organizational spans of control and the number of levels within the organizational hierarchies. When the SSAO respondents expressed concern about the shortage of or need for more staff within their organizations, the student affairs organizations appeared to be flatter, and the SSAOs and their directors appeared to have more units reporting directly to them. In most of these cases, the SSAOs also expressed concerns about having too many direct reports, or no resources to hire a desired associate or assistant senior level staff person. Also, in most of these cases, the directors of the organization reported directly to the SSAO without a level of management in between. This relationship between structure and perception of resources was present in all types of institutions regardless of institutional size or type and may also have been exacerbated by recent resource losses.

Where Student Affairs Reports

Where student affairs organizations report within the greater institution may also have some relationship to institutional type (Hirt, 2006, 2009;

and Kuk & Banning, 2009, 2012). As institutional growth and complexity has increased, the relationship of student affairs to institutional decision making has tended to change, and in some cases become increasingly submerged within academic organizational units. This seemed to occur most frequently in research universities and some private liberal arts institutions. In these cases, student affairs reported to either the provost or other key academic administrator. Shuffling of units within, and in and out of student affairs to other areas within an institution was found to be a common occurrence and was reported to be the most common organizational change process affecting student affairs organizations.

Organizational Change and Redesign

In Kuk and Banning's (2009) study, and reinforced by their study in 2012, only a small number of the respondents indicated that they had redesigned their current student affairs organizational structure at some time during their tenure as the SSAO. Those who did report changes indicated that these changes occurred when the SSAOs first assumed their roles at their institution. It was also reported that the organizational changes made were very modest, such as shifting reporting lines among various units or moving units in or out of student affairs.

The majority of SSAOs indicated that they were happy with their organizational structures and/or did not intend to make any major organizational changes in the near future. Only two SSAOs reported conducting major organizational audits and implementing major organizational changes when they first took over as the SSAO at their institution. Some SSAOs reported that, although they desired to make changes in their organizational structure, they believed that the political consequences were too great or they needed to wait for some of their staff to retire before they could make desired changes.

When asked about reasons they had or would use for deciding to redesign their student affairs divisions, the responding SSAOs identified five reasons they used for making organizational changes. They included (1) to address financial concerns; (2) to meet strategic priorities; (3) to enhance efficiencies and effectiveness; (4) to promote teamwork and collaboration; and (5) to reduce hierarchical approaches to decision making. None of the SSAOs indicated they would redesign the organization to work differently or to collaborate differently. No one indicated that they were thinking about an organizational model that was different than the hierarchical, functional structures they were presently utilizing.

Shifting Dynamics in Student Affairs Organizations

For many, the concept of organizational models or structures has traditionally been captured in a rigid and static organizational chart. However, student affairs organizations are becoming increasingly more dynamic and process oriented. Although the mission and functions of student affairs organizations have remained substantially the same in recent decades, how they are managed and organized is beginning to shift (Dungy, 2003; Kezar & Lester, 2009; and Tull & Kuk, 2012). Student affairs leaders are beginning to implement new organizational designs in response to the demands of new challenges and decreasing resources. Changes that have been made to organizational structures have generally appeared as adaptive shifts occurring out of necessity, often urgently and in isolation, and have not been widely shared within the profession (Kuk & Banning, 2009; and Tull & Kuk, 2012).

Adrianna Kezar and Jaime Lester (2009) argue that higher education needs to be reorganized to ensure that collaboration and cross-organizational communication processes are built into organizations. Most student affairs organizations have retained their functional characteristics of structure, the use of committees, task forces, work groups, and cross-functional teams, as well as hybrid structures (Kezar & Lester, 2009; and Tull & Kuk, 2012). However, many are enhancing communication and collaboration across unit and department boundaries, especially in relation to faculty and academic affairs administrators. Unfortunately, most of these structural additions and changes are short-lived and relational in nature, and as a result not imbedded into the fabric of the organization.

Theory and Research Related to Organizational Design in Higher Education

Most of the early writing on organizational design in higher education and student affairs assumed that having functional structures was the only way to organize student affairs. Many previous writers focused on variations of this basic organizational paradigm. Recent higher education and student affairs literature contains more diverse general philosophical models and guiding principles related to organizational design issues and strategies. Some of these are discussed following.

Robert Birnbaum (1988) applied the concepts of systems and used five typological models of organizational functioning to describe the various ways college and university organizations function: (1) the collegiate institution, (2) the bureaucratic institution, (3) the political institution, (4) the anarchical institution, and (5) the cybernetic institution. George Kuh (1989) identified four conventional models for examining different organizations. These models are (1) the rational model, (2) the bureaucratic model, (3) the collegiate model, and (4) the political model. These models closely resemble the four organizational frames of theory and research outlined by Bolman and Deal (2003): (1) the structural frame, (2) the human resource frame, (3) the political frame, and (4) the symbolic frame.

Unfortunately, there has not been a great deal of research and attention given to understanding organizational design and structural models within student affairs organizations. Although early references to student personnel services were descriptive of the types of services and programs that should be provided, these efforts did not clearly discuss what organizational structure or reporting lines were used to organize and provide these programs and services.

David Ambler (1993) conducted a survey of more than one hundred student affairs divisions and found a wide variety of unique and different organizational structures. Ambler (2000) later repeated the distribution of the survey to the same sample of student affairs programs and found that many had experienced institutional changes that had affected their divisions' structures. Some of these changes included the adoption of the provost model, establishment of an executive officer for enrollment management, increased use of technology, and the privatization of some services. He found that despite these changes, four basic models of management structures for student affairs remained in the institutions he surveyed. These are (1) the revenue source model, (2) the affinity of services model, (3) the staff associates model, and (4) the direct supervision model. Ambler strongly supported the use of the corporate model for student affairs management.

Kathleen Allen and Cynthia Cherrey (2000) applied the ideas of systems and learning organizations to student affairs organizations, leadership, structures, and student affairs practice. They discussed the idea of fragmentation and its application to traditional hierarchical organizations. They offered the idea of connectivity and networking as a more systems-focused view of how student affairs organizations could become more effective. They discussed a vision based on new ways of relating, influencing change, learning, and leading. Allen and Cherrey also argued that student affairs practitioners' thinking needed to change in several ways in order to integrate these new dimensions of organizing and implementing student affairs practice.

Carney Strange and James Banning (2001) created a comprehensive model for student friendly and learning-supportive environments. They focused on the dimensions of organizational environments, the organization's structural anatomy, dynamics, and the relationship to these environmental dimensions that created effective learning environments within college campuses.

In their work on rethinking student affairs practice, Patrick Love and Sandra Estanek (2004) used organizational development theory and new science ideas to challenge student affairs practitioners to think differently about their work, student affairs structures and processes, and to adopt new models for change. They provided four conceptual lenses: (1) valuing dualism, (2) transcending paradigms, (3) recognizing connectedness, and (4) embracing paradox.

Recent Student Affairs Organizational Models

There are distinctive differences in how student affairs work is carried out at institutions of different types and what differing skills and understandings are needed to be effective practitioners. Joan Hirt (2006, 2009) has focused on understanding the professional life of student affairs practitioners at different types of higher educational institutions. See chapter 2 for her description of the ways in which institutional mission influences the practice of student affairs administration.

Kathleen Manning, Jillian Kinzie, and John Schuh (2006) discussed the organization of student affairs work based on a study of twenty high-performing colleges and universities. This work highlighted the history of student affairs organizations as well as contemporary issues that have had an impact on organizational structures within student affairs. They suggested that there are three approaches to student affairs work that influence the organization of student affairs: student services, student development, and student learning. Manning et al. build a strong case for asserting that the structure of student affairs should be closely shaped and aligned with the mission of the institution.

From their analyses of the interviews and their review of student affairs literature, they identified eleven student affairs organizational models. Six traditional models were developed through an analysis of the student affairs literature, and five new innovative models grew out of the Documenting Effective Educational Practices (DEEP) Project they conducted. Tables 18.1 and 18.2 summarize the two sets of models.

Manning et al. (2006) concluded that there are several ways to practice student affairs work and that there is no single best organizational model for student affairs practice. "Rather careful consideration of the campus culture, hard work, thoughtful reflection, and a clear understanding of how student affairs can facilitate student success are essential ingredients in developing student affairs organizations that truly are effective" (Manning et al., 2006, p. 34). This work provides a sound philosophical framework for linking student affairs organizational design to the educational focus and strategic mission and goals of student affairs organizations, but it does not provide guidance or models on how to restructure organizations to ensure the creation of this vital link.

In a recent study (Kuk & Banning, 2009), SSAOs were asked to ascertain which of the philosophical practice organizational models identified by Manning et al. (2006) they were utilizing within their student affairs organizations. The most frequently used model was reported to be the co-curricular learning model. Many respondents also indicated that their organizational structure was reflected in the seamless learning model.

When asked which model they would choose if they could redesign their division to reflect a new model, nearly half of the respondents indicated that they would not pick a different model. Other SSAOs responded that they would change to one of three models: the seamless learning model, the academic-student affairs collaboration model, or the co-curricular learning model. The other models were not indicated.

These findings seem somewhat curious. Student affairs organizations, especially at the larger public institutions, appear to have retained the complex hierarchical, functional structures that have evolved over the past several decades, and there is little indication that there is a desire to change these structures very much, if at all. Yet, the philosophies and perceptions of organizational models being used by student affairs divisions to define their practice seem to have shifted away from the extracurricular and administrative organizational models that were traditionally used within student affairs operations (Manning et al., 2006) to philosophical models that are learning and academic centered.

Ashley Tull and Linda Kuk (2012) presented a variety of strategies for addressing change in student affairs organizations. They offered a variety

The Handbook of Student Affairs Administration

TABLE 18.1 TRADITIONAL MODELS OF STUDENT AFFAIRS PRACTICE

Models	Description	Assumptions
Extracurricular model	Student affairs is organized to provide student life and student development.	Student affairs is entirely separate from academic affairs.
Functional silos model	Student affairs operates from a management and leadership approach rather than student development.	Units perform their functions and services as discrete entities, and integration and communication is achieved through loose coordination.
Student service model	Organizations operate from management and leadership services, often clustered together with the focus on providing quality programs and services, with close coordination of like units.	There is minimal if any integration of programs with academic units.
Competitive/Adversarial model	Student affairs units operate independently of academic units.	Student affairs and academic affairs units are concerned with what students learn and how they grow, but there is little acknowledgment of the contribution of the other.
Co-curricular model	Student affairs and academic affairs have complementary yet different missions; both acknowledge the contributions of the other to student learning.	Both student affairs and academic affairs units are concerned with student learning.
Seamless learning model	Student learning experiences are conceived as integrated and continuously happening across all aspects of the student experience and campus life.	Every member of the institution and the student affairs organization can contribute to learning. The mission of the institution and all its units are dedicated to the total student learning experience.

Source: Adapted from Manning et al. (2006).

TABLE 18.2 INNOVATIVE MODELS OF STUDENT AFFAIRS PRACTICE

Models	Description	Assumptions
Student-centered, ethic of care model	Organizations center on care and relationships, with a fundamental response to addressing what students need to be successful. The goal is to facilitate student success through the integration of service, policies, and programs.	All practices are centered on the ethic of care. This model focuses on students who have the most need of support.
Student-driven model	Organizations value students as integral members of the campus community, and student involvement and leadership serve are core organizing principles. Rephrase to clarify valuing students as integral members of the community. Students have a strong voice in governing the organization. Students drive campus activities and make key decisions about campus life.	Student learning is enhanced by greater student involvement and engagement, and identification with the institution contributes to student persistence and success.
Student agency model	Students assume as much responsibility as possible in the development of their learning experiences by managing campus life and helping to design curriculum. Students serve as workers, providing a wide range of student services and programs.	Students have the primary role and responsibility for their learning and their education. Students are completely responsible for student life, and they perform as full and equal partners with faculty and staff in these efforts.
Academic/student affairs collaboration model	Student affairs and academic affairs emphasize mutual territory and combine efforts to engender student engagement and success. The work between academic and student affairs is supported with tightly coupled student affairs structures and philosophies that support student learning and success.	Student affairs and academic affairs units place student learning at the center of their goals and activities and create institutional coherence about student success. The model assumes seamless collaboration between student affairs and academic affairs units on a routine basis.

(continued)

TABLE 18.2 (*continued*)

Models	Description	Assumptions
Academic-centered model	Student affairs functions are organized around the academic core and promote the academic experience over co-curricular activities. Student affairs serves as a support to the academic focus of the institution and is almost invisible in the academic focus.	Student affairs and academic units place student learning at the center of their goals and activities. Both share responsibility for student success.

Source: Adapted from Manning et al. (2006).

of specialist roles and hybrid organizational models as possible options for addressing the emerging challenges that student affairs organizations are facing and will continue to face in the near future. A variety of specialist roles and job descriptions represent examples of new roles that are emerging in the changing environmental context of student affairs, and also provide a way of addressing the needs for cross-organizational collaboration and more efficient use of resources. They highlight the use of a particular type of hybrid organizational structure, the matrix structure, as a means of integrating these new roles and responsibilities into existing student affairs organizations. The matrix structure can use the critical features of traditional functional structures and overlay this model with a matrix that also focuses on cross-unit collaboration and communication as well as more efficient use of organizational resources.

Currently it is unclear whether student affairs organizations will be able to adapt their current functional structures to effectively implement the new philosophical models they have adopted or can recreate new organizational structures in order to be effective in addressing the changing demands placed on student affairs organizations. Most of the recent research and theory about organizational viability and survival conducted within the business sector would suggest that such shifts are not generally possible or easy to accomplish (Ashkenas, Ulrich, Jick, & Kerr, 2002; Galbraith, 2002; Hesselbein, Goldsmith, & Beckhard, 1997). Additional research needs to occur about student affairs organizations to better understand their changing dynamics and to determine how leaders might craft their organizations to better accomplish their changing missions and goals.

Alternative Approaches to Organizational Design and Structure

In today's student affairs world, organizational structures and models do not have to be silo grounded and functionally fixed. In fact, the current approach may not be the most effective way to organize student affairs organizations in the future. More recent research and theory on organizational design (Ashkenas et al., 2002; Galbraith, 2002; and Hesselbein et al., 1997) suggest modern organizations need to be flexible, responsive, collaborative, and adaptive.

There is no single correct way to structure student affairs organizations (Ambler, 2000; Barr, 1993; Sandeen & Barr, 2006). But this does not mean that there is not a need to engage in structural change and organizational redesign. In fact, student affairs organizations should be structured to address the strategic mission of the institutions and the divisions they serve (Hirt, 2009; Kuk, 2012; Kuk & Banning 2009; Tull & Kuk, 2012). At the same time, the structure should fit with the needs of the institution and the surrounding external environment in which it exists (Galbraith, 2002; Kuk, 2012; Kuk, Banning, & Amey, 2010).

Fluidity and adaptability are key characteristics in future organizational designs (Galbraith, 2002; Hesselbein et al., 1997, 1997; and Senge 1990, 2006). Organizational structure is concerned with how individuals, groups, and systems organize their time, energy, and resources to accomplish goals. Adaptive organizations continually align resources and strategies to address institutional and divisional strategic goals and attempt to become more efficient and effective in the allocation and deployment of resources, especially human resources. Fluidity, in this regard, refers to being able to adapt easily, such as by changing priorities, strategies, and resources in the midst of shifting organizational direction. The notion that structure assumes a fixed or stationary position for indefinite periods of time is no longer realistic.

Different types of institutions may have different environmental, political, and economic issues that affect the design and structure of student affairs. The goal of any design process should be to craft an organizational structure that best fits the environmental needs of the institution. Efforts to design effective student affairs organizations should take into consideration the needs and challenges presented by the diversity among the students and other constituent groups it serves. For example, residential campuses might create a very different structure than commuter-oriented student affairs organizations. Institutions with large numbers of traditionally underserved or disadvantaged populations might create different structures than organizations that serve more traditional or economically advantaged students. Urban institutions might have different structural needs than rural institutions. As student needs change and the demographic dimensions of students shift, the organizational structure of student affairs will need to adjust. The days of simply adding more specialty functional units that serve very distinct populations is not likely to remain the preferred response to changing demands. Given the restraints on new resources and increasing accountability, the student affairs organizations of the future are more likely going to be asked to restructure existing resources to serve changing needs and new student demands instead of receiving new allocations.

Kezar and Lester (2009) have built a very strong case for organizational restructuring based on the need for stronger and more institutionally crafted channels for lateral collaboration across both department and institutional boundaries. This shift in focus from hierarchical decision making and communications to a structure that includes both hierarchical and horizontal decision making and communication processes will likely require new ways of structuring roles and responsibilities within student affairs organizations.

A Systematic Approach to Organization Structural Design

Student affairs leaders and their staffs may want to step back and assess their current organizational structures in terms of organizational effectiveness. Are the current functional silos that permeate the organizational structures of most student affairs units really the most effective way to realize the institutions' and divisions' strategic missions and goals? Do emerging assessment plans adequately provide for assessing organizational design and structural effectiveness? What is on the horizon that will demand new ways of providing student-focused programs and services, and how will student affairs adapt to these demands and expectations? How can student affairs leaders think differently about how to organize, deliver, and coordinate their services and programs?

Not many senior student affairs officers have the opportunity to start from scratch as they craft the organizational structure for their divisions. Most inherit an organizational model, and they are clearly limited by the available resources, both human and fiscal. Neither of these factors needs to become deterrents to making necessary and effective changes. In fact, limitations on resources may present a sound and compelling reason for a student affairs organization to undergo an organization redesign process. Applying an effective change strategy that is well thought out and crafted, and includes securing staff and organizational buy-in, are critical to the success and sustainability of any redesign process. The following are points for consideration as plans for organizational structure assessment and redesign are contemplated.

Strategic Plan

Student affairs leaders might want to create or update their strategic plans to ensure that they are in line with the institution's mission and strategic goals. This plan provides the basis and guiding map for examining and redesigning an organizational structure. An organization's structures should grow out of its strategic priorities.

Organizational Strengths

It is critical to conduct and maintain a thorough and comprehensive assessment of resources (human, financial, facilities, and so on). It is essential that the leadership within student affairs determine the strengths of the organization and the individuals within the organization. Uncovering and building on the strengths of an organization is a productive way of securing buy-in and of helping to dispel negative fears and threats to change. Too often leaders focus on the negative or problems and miss opportunities to build on strengths through which they can create new learning opportunities for individual staff and the entire organization.

Priorities and Resources

Successful redesign first requires a realistic determination of what needs to be done to accomplish the strategic plan. Second, it requires a careful alignment of resources to address the strategic priorities. This process should not be defined or held hostage by what an organization does not have in terms of new resources. A common mind-set that change can happen only by adding more resources often inhibits the ability to make constructive and creative change. It is easy to become paralyzed by the notion that there are not enough resources.

Organizational redesign and structural changes can very successfully be accomplished with very little or no additional resources. What is required is getting people in the organization to think differently about what they do and how they do it. This process requires a willingness to reconfigure organizational resources and approach establishing institutional and divisional priorities openly and honestly. More fundamentally, it requires leaders to think very differently about how work is done, who does it, and how it is rewarded. This type of redesign might require an investment in professional development, retooling, and cross-training of staff. But these costs can usually be recaptured through realignment and rethinking work, structure, and organizational priorities.

Leadership

The student affairs leadership should be responsible for crafting the agenda of what needs to be redesigned within the organization and will likely want to involve the various divisional units in the process. It is easy for such a process to get sidetracked or derailed without a clear and consistent focus. The leadership may want to secure the assistance of an outside consultant to help frame the difficult and important issues that need to be faced when matching and reallocating resources and in setting priorities and helping to steer the change process. A neutral, guiding perspective can help the process retain its integrity and its focus.

Consideration of Structural Options

Once the desired roles within the organization are defined and aligned to work responsibilities, a variety of organizational philosophical and structural models might be considered and appropriately adopted to align the roles to work effectively together. It is critical to think outside of the box. It is at this point that organizational structure takes shape and should reflect the changing nature and requirements of the student affairs organizational goals and expectations. Structures and/or structural elements other than just siloed, functional structures should be strongly considered and integrated into the design as appropriate.

Such approaches might include organizational models that incorporate both the hierarchical and horizontal organizational (process) dimensions in the structure (Kezar & Lester, 2010; Kuk, 2012; and Tull & Kuk, 2012). The process component of this model can take many forms, but it focuses essentially on the complete lateral flow of work, collaboration, and communication across the organization. Such an organizational design might appear as a team-oriented structure in which the team is given complete end-to-end responsibility for a work product. It can also take the form of a hybrid-matrix structure in which cross-organizational specialist positions are laid upon a predominantly hierarchical functional structure. The role of the cross-organizational specialist is to ensure that communication and collaboration across department and organizational unit boundaries become incorporated into the day-to-day structural functioning of the organization. These types of positions, as indicated earlier in the chapter, have already begun to appear in some student affairs units (Tull & Kuk, 2012).

A third type of organizational redesign takes into account the need for ongoing change as an essential part of the day-to-day life of the organization and its members. This type of redesign involves both restructuring and professional development of the student affairs staff. The focus of this redesign involves crafting a flatter, more fluid organization in which responsibilities, rewards, and recognition are structurally flattened, and cross-training of responsibilities and incorporation of change is built into the organization as part of everyday life. In this type of design the organization attends to more of a horizontal organizational focus. Decision making is moved to the point of interaction through the use of teams, and collaboration and change become part of performance and reward structures, with less focus on hierarchical approval processes. The role of the leader becomes more of a visionary, coach, and enabler than a day-to-day decision maker.

Assessment

As student affairs leaders consider the elements of redesigning they might also consider how they want to assess the organization's ongoing effectiveness. How will effective performance and progress toward achieving the mission and goals be measured and rewarded? How will the change process be managed, and who will be assigned accountability for various elements within the change process and the implementation of the final plan? Assessment is a very critical component of the design process in that it enables the organization to both gauge its effectiveness and to know when and how it needs to adapt structurally in the future.

Conclusion

Organizational structure and design is dynamic. Structures should facilitate organizational environments that maximize opportunities for creativity and achievement of goals and strategies. They should be able to adapt to change, effectively meet constituent needs and demands, and ensure that resources are efficiently allocated in the interests of students and the institution's mission.

References

Allen, K. E., & Cherrey, C. (2000). *Systemic leadership: Enriching the meaning of our work.* Lanham, MD: American College Personnel Association and the National Association for Campus Activities.

Ambler, D. (2000). Organizational and administrative models. In M. J. Barr & M. K. Desler (Eds.), *The handbook of student affairs administration* (2nd ed., pp. 119–134). San Francisco, CA: Jossey-Bass.

Ambler, D. A. (1993). Developing internal management structures. In M. J. Barr (Ed.), *The handbook of student affairs administration* (pp. 107–120). San Francisco, CA: Jossey-Bass.

Ashkenas, R., Ulrich, D., Jick, T., & Kerr, S. (2002). *The boundaryless organization: Breaking the chains of organizational structure.* San Francisco, CA: Jossey-Bass.

Barr, M. J. (1993). Organizational and administrative models. In M. J. Barr (Ed.), *The handbook of student affairs administration* (pp. 95–106). San Francisco, CA: Jossey-Bass.

Birnbaum, R. (1988). *How colleges work.* San Francisco, CA: Jossey-Bass.

Bolman, L. G., & Deal, T. E. (2003). *Reframing organizations: Artistry, choice and leadership* (3rd ed.). San Francisco, CA: Jossey-Bass.

Dungy, G. (2003). Organizations and functions of student affairs. In S. R. Komives & D. B. Woodard Jr. (Eds.), *Student services: A handbook for the profession* (4th ed., pp. 339–357). San Francisco, CA: Jossey-Bass.

Galbraith, J. R. (2002). *Designing organizations: An executive guide to strategy, structure and process.* San Francisco, CA: Jossey-Bass

Hartley, M. (2001). Student learning as a framework for student affairs: Rhetoric or reality? *NASPA Journal, 38,* 224–236.

Hesselbein, F., Goldsmith, M., & Beckhard, R. (1997). *The organization of the future.* San Francisco, CA: Jossey-Bass.

Hirt, J. B. (2006). *Where you work matters.* Lanham, MD: University Press of America.

Hirt, J.B. (2009). The importance of institutional mission. In G. S. McClellan & J. Stringer (Eds.). *The handbook of student affairs administration* (3rd ed.,pp. 19–40). San Francisco, CA: Jossey-Bass.

Jackson, J. F. L., & Terrell, M. C. (2007). *Creating and maintaining safe college campuses.* Sterling, VA: Stylus.

Kezar, A., & Lester, J. (2009). *Organizing higher education for collaboration: A guide for campus leaders.* San Francisco, CA: Jossey-Bass.

Knock, G. H. (1985). Development of student services in higher education. In M. J. Barr & L.A. Keating (Eds.), *Developing effective student services programs: Systemic approaches for practitioners* (pp.15–42). San Francisco, CA: Jossey-Bass.

Kruger, K. (2009). Technology: Innovations and implications. In G. S. McClellan & J. Stringer (Eds.), *The handbook of student affairs administration* (3rd ed., pp. 586–601). San Francisco, CA: Jossey-Bass.

Kuh, G. D. (1989). Organizational concepts and influences. In U. Delworth & G. R. Hanson (Eds.), *Student services: A handbook for the profession* (2nd ed., pp. 209–242). San Francisco, CA: Jossey-Bass.

Kuk, L. (2009). The dynamics of organizational models within student affairs. In G. S. McClellan & J. Stringer (Eds.), *The handbook of student affairs administration* (3rd ed., pp. 313–332). San Francisco, CA: Jossey-Bass.

Kuk, L. (2012). The changing nature of student affairs. In A. Tull & L. Kuk (Eds.), *New realities in the management of student affairs: Emerging specialist roles and structures for changing times* (pp. 3–12). Sterling, VA: Stylus.

Kuk L., & Banning J. H. (2009). Designing student affairs organizational structures: Perceptions of senior student affairs officers. *NASPA Journal, 46* (1) 94–117.

Kuk, L., & Banning J. H. (2012). *The ecology of student affairs leadership*. Colorado Springs, CO: Colorado State University.

Kuk, L., Banning J. H., & Amey, M. (2010). *Positioning student affairs for sustainable change: Achieving organizational effectiveness through multiple perspectives*. Sterling, VA: Stylus.

Love, P. G., & Estanek, S. M. (2004). *Rethinking student affairs practice*. San Francisco, CA: Jossey-Bass.

Manning, K., Kinzie, J., & Schuh, J. (2006). *One size does not fit all: Traditional and innovative models of student affairs practice*. New York, NY: Routledge, Taylor & Francis Group.

Rhatigan, J. J. (2009). From the people up: A brief history of student affairs administration. In G. S. McClellan & J. Stringer (Eds.), *The handbook of student affairs administration* (3rd ed., pp. 3–18). San Francisco, CA: Jossey-Bass.

Sandeen, A. (1989). Issues influencing organizations. In U. Delworth & G.R. Hanson (Eds.). *Student services: A handbook for the profession* (2nd ed.,pp. 45–460). San Francisco, CA: Jossey-Bass.

Sandeen, A. (2001). Organizing student affairs divisions. In R. B. Winston Jr., D. G. Creamer, & T. K. Miller (Eds.), *The professional student affairs administrator* (pp. 181–210).

Sandeen, A., & Barr, M. J. (2006). *Critical issues for student affairs: Challenges and opportunities*. San Francisco, CA: Jossey-Bass.

Schuh, J. (2009). Fiscal pressure on higher education and student affairs. In G. S. McClellan & J. Stringer (Eds.), *The handbook of student affairs administration* (3rd ed., pp. 81–104). San Francisco, CA: Jossey-Bass.

Senge, P. (1990). *The fifth discipline: The art and practice of the learning organization*. New York, NY: Doubleday/Currency.

Senge, P. (2006). The leader's new work: Building learning organizations. In J. V. Gallos (Ed.), *Organization development* (pp.765–792). San Francisco, CA: Jossey-Bass.

Strange, C. C., & Banning, J. H. (2001). *Educating by design: Creating campus learning environments that work*. San Francisco, CA: Jossey-Bass.

Tull, A., & Kuk, L. (Eds.). (2012). *New realities in the management of student affairs: Emerging specialist roles and structures for changing times*. Sterling, VA: Stylus.

RECRUITING, SELECTING, SUPERVISING, AND RETAINING STAFF

Zebulun R. Davenport

Although the functions of recruiting, selecting, supervising, and retaining staff are often considered as discrete, they should be viewed as related phases in a contiguous process with interconnected stages. These activities are fairly common and ubiquitous across the industry of higher education. There are, however, components of the phases that are unique to each campus, hiring manager, and employee, including institutional type and mission, employee's work preference regarding student population and campus culture, and espoused values versus values in practice. Ultimately, the entire process is something that every hiring manager, supervisor, leader, and employer must complete. Regardless of who is hiring, being hired, or the level of the position, each individual can benefit from a deeper understanding of the processes discussed in this chapter.

Each of the phases can be arduous and time consuming. If the necessary attention and care are not taken with each phase, it can result in wasted time, energy, and effort, not to mention unsatisfactory results and perhaps even legal proceedings. However, when executed properly, this process can be among the most professionally rewarding activities with which one will ever be involved. In order to successfully recruit, select, supervise, and retain quality staff, the hiring manager must understand the complexity of each phase and what it takes to navigate them. This chapter seeks to support such understanding through sharing thoughts for consideration when recruiting, selecting, supervising, and retaining quality professional staff.

Recruiting

The practice of successful hiring begins with a thorough recruitment process. Recruiting quality professional staff is more complex and sophisticated than simply creating a job description and posting it on a website or placing it in a publication. There are a number of components in the recruitment process to consider that will increase the chances of success. These components include, but are certainly not limited to, the following: understanding the institution and its needs; clearly stating the necessary knowledge, skills, and qualities the ideal candidate must possess to successfully perform the specified duties; and developing an effective recruitment plan. When the aforementioned are adequately addressed, the chances for a successful recruitment process increase.

Understanding the Institution and Its Needs

It may seem obvious, but institutions of higher education are similar to other institutions in some ways and different in other ways. Hiring managers often overlook or fail to consider this component when seeking an ideal candidate.

There are also many types of institutions, and matching the desired work environment with the employee is crucial. The differences between postsecondary institutions are considerable, and these differences can affect both the nature and the manner of work done by student affairs professionals (see chapter 2). Among the most obvious differences are degrees granted, size, funding sources, and mission. As discussed extensively in chapter 2, the Carnegie Foundation classifies colleges and universities into various categories, including public; private; for profit; nonprofit; two-year; four-year; associate degree granting; baccalaureate degree granting; master's/professional degree granting; research focused; and specialized institutions. These institutions can be located in rural, suburban, or urban settings; are classified as small, medium, or large; and can be selective, moderately selective, or open access. All of these elements help to create the culture of the institution and affect what is important to and valued by the institution's constituents. As a result, when recruiting to fill a position, the hiring manager must first understand the type of institution for which he or she is seeking employees, and, second, be able to articulate this culture clearly to the potential candidates. Congruency between the employee and the institution will increase the probability of a positive work environment and a more satisfied and productive employee.

Although most educational institutions have similar goals related to student success, the definition of success may vary from institution to institution. Many institutions align with definitions of success that focus solely on retention and graduation rates. However, there are institutions that have missions that are focused on moving students toward certificate completion or even transferability (Davenport, Rhine, & Martinez-Saenz, 2012). Consequently, to increase the probability of a good match for the applicant and the institution, the recruitment process should start with a clear description and explanation of the institution's mission and values.

When recruiting staff, managers must be able to articulate the missions of their institutions and the types of students they serve. Working for a large, Research I, urban metropolitan institution, and serving a wide variety of traditional and nontraditional first-generation students is very different than working at a midsize comprehensive, metropolitan institution, or even at a comprehensive institution mainly serving high-achieving traditional-age students located in a small college town. These three examples alone provide for very different and unique opportunities and challenges. Knowing what to expect from each type of educational environment allows the hiring manager as well as the potential employee to be better prepared to face the challenges and opportunities that each environment offers.

Another component in successful recruitment focuses on clarity of vision, mission, and the purpose of the division, department, or unit. Akin to this clarity is alignment to the institution's mission. The mission of a given unit in student affairs (for example, student life) can vary by the type and mission of the larger institution. Some institutions may not support the co-curricular/out-of-classroom learning that focuses on cognitive nonacademic learning constructs, while others may more strongly value the integration of the curricular and co-curricular. Having an awareness of the focus and the values of the institution will pay major dividends on the back end of the hiring process. When misalignment occurs, there are many adverse effects. Most important, the student affairs division may be out of sync, resulting in frustration among those who work there.

Position Description

A clear and complete position description is important in helping assure successful recruitment. Important elements of a position description include title, position classification, reporting relationships, and functions or duties of the position. In addition to identifying all of the functions or duties of the position, the level of responsibility for each function or duty should also be noted. For example, a position description for a coordinator of leadership development programming might include mention of supervising student paraprofessional staff for the office and assisting in the development of new leadership programs offered through the office.

It is obviously the case that position descriptions are created when new positions are proposed. Position descriptions should be reviewed any time a search will be held to fill the job. It is important, however, that position descriptions are kept current even when no change in personnel is taking place. Positions tend to change over time. These changes can come about as a result of intentional action, but they may also come about inadvertently or without particular thought. A regular review of position descriptions helps assure alignment of effort to mission, equal distribution of workload across all members of a staff, and fair compensation for duties being performed.

Knowledge, Skills, and Qualities

With regard to knowledge and skills, it can be helpful to keep in mind that student affairs is a discipline similar to any other discipline in higher education in that, for one to experience success in this discipline, there are specific and fundamental concepts that one must know. Having basic theoretical knowledge of and practical experience with the issues faced by professionals in student affairs is paramount. There is no substitute for knowing and understanding student development theory, key concepts of administration, basic counseling skills, leadership competencies, as well as other aspects of this profession. There are many graduate preparation programs in student affairs or higher education that are specifically designed to teach professionals about the discipline and prepare them for this discipline, and recruiting individuals who have completed such a program can help assure applicants' familiarity with fundamental concepts. Indeed, as Winston and Creamer (1997) note, there are many hiring managers who consider recruiting only individuals with educational credentials from student affairs or higher education programs. That said, there can be high-performing, highly successful professionals in this discipline who have not come through the traditional preparation programs or professional pathways. So, thoroughly reviewing each candidate for what knowledge, skills, and competencies each possesses is critical. This may also involve educating the search committee to look for transferrable skills and competencies for those candidates who come from outside of student affairs.

Recruitment Plan

A successful recruitment plan allows the hiring manager to attract the candidate with the desired skills, the appropriate level of professional experience, and the ideal personality for the position. It should also be designed to help meet the goals of the department and institution to have a diverse group of employees. A recruitment plan should include a timeline for the search process, budget for the search process, and list of methods to be used in posting the position. Methods for posting vary based on the type of position available. The specific methods included should assure that the position is presented to appropriate pools of potential candidates and may include print or digital media. Common examples include print ads in local papers or professional periodicals; Web or social media postings on institutional, professional, or commercial sites; announcements on listservs; mailings to graduate preparation programs or professional peers in student affairs or higher education; listings at professional conferences or student affairs recruitment events; and use of informal networks. Effective recruitment can occur through informal yet professional networks. Former colleagues and students can often generate referrals who become qualified candidates for potential positions.

Selection

The selection of the right candidate is one of the most important things any hiring manager can do. The hiring manager should make the case to the institution that they should fail the search and not fill the position versus hiring a person who is not the right fit. Filling a position with the wrong person can cause major problems for that division or unit. These problems can range from poor service and program delivery, confusion in the department, negative effects on staff morale, personnel problems, legal issues, and even negative impressions of the division among colleagues around the campus. So, due diligence must be taken when selecting candidates.

Winston and Creamer (1997) identified potential challenges or pitfalls when selecting staff that include campuswide policies or regulatory agencies dictating staffing practices other than at the division level, the absence of clarity regarding the expectations of the position, limited number of quality candidates in the marketplace, insufficient finances to support the growing market, and limited ability to deviate from the protocol for hiring new staff. Hiring protocols serve several important purposes, but there may be extenuating circumstances in which deviating from the norm may be important to complete the hiring process.

The selection processes for most positions have certain fundamental components that are common among most colleges and universities. Included in these components are selecting a search committee, exhibiting ethical treatment of all candidates during the search process, reviewing and interviewing candidates, and identifying and hiring the desired candidate. The next few paragraphs further explain the importance of the aforementioned components as well as provide sample questions and situational examples for potential use.

Selecting a Search Committee

The hiring manager should make sure a search committee for a position is representative of the constituents with whom the selected candidate will work. The size and makeup of a search committee may vary based upon the position and the politics associated with the position. The ideal number of committee members will vary. Five to seven members, including the chair, can work very well for many searches. The higher the position is in the institution or the more politically charged the position is, the larger the search committee may become. Committee membership may include students, members of the community, representatives of other units or divisions with whom this person will work, colleagues in academic affairs, peers from the division, and the chair.

It is a good idea to partner with the institution's human resources department, office of affirmative action, human rights compliance office, or whatever similar resources are available to seek training for those directly involved in the search. Usually, these offices have a recommended format to follow and instructions on how to conduct legal and ethical searches, as well as modules for training that may include antidiscrimination, appropriate conduct during searches, proper documentation of search committee meetings, and other topics.

It is usually a good practice for the hiring manager to meet with the search committee prior to beginning the search. During this meeting, the hiring manager should charge the committee with developing a qualified pool of applicants, winnowing that pool down to a group of finalists, and assisting in gathering feedback from various constituents about the finalists (and *not* to make the actual hiring decision). In the course of this work, the search committee may also be asked to play a role in describing the desired qualification of a successful candidate (typically based on a draft developed by the hiring manager), and help to develop the timeline for the various steps in the search process (meeting a deadline or goal set by the hiring manager for concluding the process).

It is neither common nor politically prudent to forgo use of a search committee. However, depending upon extenuating circumstances, the hiring manager may elect to do so. These circumstances may include, but are not limited to, the following situations: an interim has been in the position and has performed the requirements in a satisfactory manner; the desired candidate is known and a search of any kind would be unnecessary or even unethical; and the hiring manager may desire to manage the search process because of environmental or political sensitivities associated with the position. A decision to forego a search committee should always be vetted with the human resources office, office of equal opportunity, and supervisor of the hiring manager.

In addition to utilizing a search committee, institutions may also choose to make use of a search firm to assist in the process of filling a position. Sometimes institutions or hiring managers use search firms to assist them in identifying qualified candidates. Typically, search firms are used for positions with high visibility, such as senior-level and/or executive-level positions. Other times search firms may be used when the institution wants to avoid a biased or narrowly focused search. Finally, a search firm might be used if there are political ramifications associated with the hire. Otherwise, an institutionally run search process is most commonly used.

Searches may be classified as internal only or closed searches. This usually means that the selection pool is restricted to candidates associated with the institution. Another type of search is an external-only search. External-only searches seek candidates only from outside the institution. Finally, there are open searches in which all qualified candidates are invited to apply.

Exhibiting Ethical Treatment of Candidates

It is crucial to maintain the ethical treatment of candidates during a search process. This treatment starts from the moment candidates submit their applications and ends when the hiring manager appropriately notifies each candidate of the hiring decision. Maintaining the respect, dignity, and privacy of each candidate is a sign of a high-quality institution and hiring manager. Too often, searches are completed and the unsuccessful candidates never hear back from the hiring manager or even get a courtesy note from the institution. Another component of ethical treatment is maintaining an open line of communication with the candidates. Once a candidate is given a timeline for the search process, the ethical thing to do is to maintain that timeline. If a timeline has to be altered, a representative from human resources or the search committee chair should contact the candidates and inform them of the change.

Providing training for the search committee is another key component of the ethical treatment of candidates. The hiring manager should ensure that all of those who are directly involved with the search process understands the appropriate manner with which to conduct themselves. This conduct should be expected from the beginning of the search process until its conclusion. Ensuring the fair and equitable treatment of all candidates is inclusive of legal as well as ethical matters.

Maintaining confidentiality of the candidate pool is essential. It is not the search committee's role to share or discuss any information involving a search with anyone not on the search. Often, candidates are conducting selective searches, and until the pool is made public, this confidentiality should be maintained. Following this step increases the chances of a successful search.

Reviewing and Interviewing Candidates

Reviewing candidates for qualifications and fit is very important. The process of determining whether a candidate is qualified for a position is a part of the process of determining whether they fit within the organization. Candidate review may include any and all of the following: evaluation of application materials; pre-campus interviews; reference checks; one or more in-person interviews (either off-site or on campus); and post-interview or off-line reference checks. Often, the level of the position dictates which or whether all of the aforementioned steps are executed. If resources and time are not issues, it is suggested to use as many steps as possible when reviewing candidates.

Application Materials. Evaluation of application materials should make use of a systematic process that includes a rubric or rating scale to compare the desired qualifications of a position to the submitted materials. This assists the search committee with narrowing the candidate pool to the most qualified individuals.

Pre-campus Interview. The next step in the review process is usually a pre-campus interview. Telephone or videoconference conversations are common forms of pre-campus interviews, a cost-efficient step that can provide valuable supplementary information to a search committee and assist in further narrowing the candidate pool prior to investing resources in bringing applicants to campus. Pre-campus interviews can also be helpful in taking an additional look at candidates who are on the bubble following the review of application materials; vetting congruence between candidates' written statements in the application materials and in their comments during the conversation; getting a sense of candidates' interpersonal skills; and providing candidates with an opportunity to gain additional information from the committee regarding the position, campus, and community.

Reference Checks. Reference checks are the next step in the review process. Reference checks should provide additional information and should be designed to obtain information that is not obvious or easily accessible during the initial screening and phone interview. Although some hiring managers conduct reference checks prior to investing in campus interviews, other hiring managers elect to conduct reference checks afterward. Regardless as to when this step is initiated, it is essential work. No selection process should conclude without a thorough reference check. It should be made known to candidates at what point references will be contacted. The best way to conduct a reference checks is to use it in a way that allows the hiring manager to obtain information that will assist in ascertaining the candidates' fit. Asking questions that provide information about the potential candidate's intangible skills and abilities is advisable. Suggested questions include:

- Would you tell me how this candidate responds to critical feedback?
- How does this candidate relate to colleagues within the division and across the campus?
- Can you provide an example of how this candidate took a risk and what was the result of that risk?

- How does the candidate respond when making mistakes?
- What do students think about this candidate?
- Would you rehire this candidate if you had the opportunity?

It also may be desirable to conduct off-list reference checks using social media (for example, Twitter, LinkedIn, or Facebook) or the Internet (using Google or another search engine). There is much that can be gained by viewing potential candidates' social media feeds. If an individual's espoused values and values in practice are not congruent, it may be exhibited in their expression of opinion regarding various topics via social media outlets. Although this should not be the determining factor in making a hiring decision, it can certainly be a part of the data-gathering process. Additionally and of equal importance are off-list reference calls. Higher education, and particularly the field of student affairs, is a tight-knit field. There are an abundance of opportunities to connect with former coworkers, supervisors, students, and other contacts. Obtaining information about potential candidates through mutual and trusted colleagues is a common practice. The most ethical way to conduct this method of data gathering is to inform the potential candidate what this step will ensue and seek their permission before proceeding. It is also most ethical to ask questions that do not put either the candidate or the source in a compromising position. Personnel matters should be reserved for the candidate to disclose. Finally, a good general guideline is to use information only that is of such a nature that it can be confirmed and repeated.

Campus Interviews. Many authors have explored steps on conducting an interview well (Davis & Herrera, 2013; Howard & Johnson, 2010; McConnell, 2003). Interviews frequently include dinner with the hiring manager and chair of the search committee, a group session with divisional peers, a group session with campus peers, meeting or lunch with students, a session with the department or unit for which the person in the position will work, an open session for the campus (perhaps with a presentation), a follow-up with the hiring manager, and feedback forms.

During the interview process, it is extremely important to listen for answers to questions that are truthful and thoughtful. If the answers are appropriate and the candidate is authentic, chances are greater that the best candidate for the given position will emerge.

Further exacerbating the complexity of hiring the right candidate for the position and institution is the issue of identifying and isolating important intangible qualities that differentiate mediocre candidates from great candidates. Effectively identifying intangible qualities include the ability to discern nonverbal cues, picking up on communication patterns that suggest scripted responses, listening for what is not said versus what is said, and evaluating fit.

Being consciously aware of what a person is communicating through body language and other nonverbal cues can provide solid information to complement what the candidate is communicating verbally. Many studies (Ishikawa, Hashimoto, Kinoshita, Fujimori, Shimizu, & Yano, 2006; and Woods, 2012) have been conducted on messages sent through nonverbal communication. Subramani (2010) found that there are clear distinctions between the words we use and the meanings we give off in nonverbal signs. This study concluded that around 65 percent of the social meanings of the messages are exchanged with others nonverbally. In another study conducted by Mehrabian (1971), it was determined that approximately 93 percent of all messages are communicated by nonverbal expressions (voice infection and body language). Regardless of which study is most accurate, it is clear that much of what is communicated is done nonverbally.

Listening for scripted and rehearsed responses, candidates' follow-up questions, as well as for what is not said are other important intangibles of which to be aware. Human beings are creatures of comfort. We are habitual by nature and we operate in patterns. We usually have the same preparation patterns and daily routines. Just as this is the case, when interviewing for positions, most prepared candidates will have scripted and rehearsed answers to anticipated questions. Most anticipate the usual prompts like "Tell me about yourself, what are your strengths and weakness, what would people say about you, how would you describe your leadership style," and so on. There are techniques like *hooking, bridging, redirecting,* and other common communication practices designed to assist respondents with answering anticipated questions. These techniques are designed to assist the respondent with directing answers in a manner that allows him or her to control the interview. Therefore, it is always good when selecting a candidate to ask a series of nontraditional questions to determine the candidates' ability to think creatively. Here are a few examples of behavioral-based inquiries:

- Describe a time when you had to lead a team to achieve an outcome. What role did you play and how did you resolve conflict among the team members?
- Describe a time when members of your team disagreed with a decision you made. What did you do to resolve the disagreement?

- How have you motivated members of teams with which you have led to accomplish a goal you set for the team?
- If you have to choose between completing a project on time and providing a higher quality of work, which would you choose and why?"
- What are the signs that an employer is a good one with whom to work?
- Describe the biggest risk you have ever taken and why.
- What is the last book you have read on (fill in the blank—leadership, change management, assessment, policy, and so on)? Would you recommend it and why or why not?
- What three words would best describe you?
- If you were hired here, what would be your legacy at you current institution?

Avoidance or diverting the topic is another form of communication. People often say a lot by not uttering a word or not directly answering a question. When asked a question, they may avoid answering or respond with statements that do not directly address the question at all. Regardless, during an interview or selection process, if incongruent verbal and nonverbal cues are detected, the interviewer should at least inquire about what the interviewee is experiencing. The hiring manager owes it to him- or herself, his or her staff, his or her department, and to the candidate to be open and honest. Moderately probing by asking appropriate follow-up questions and then progressing to more direct questions allows an interviewer to uncover the real or underlying message. For example, if the topic of discussion involved a working relationship with a coworker or a supervisor, prompts like "Tell me more about your relationship/s with your former supervisor or coworkers." "If your coworkers were asked about this topic, how do you think they would describe things?" "It appears that you are experiencing a level of discomfort with this topic, is this accurate?" If the answer is "no," then move on. If the answer is "yes," then the interviewer might ask the following question: "Are you comfortable sharing more about how you are feeling?" If the candidate refuses to respond or is even more uncomfortable, move on to the next set of questions but note that interaction.

It is also important to allow the candidate to ask questions. This process can be a very telling aspect of the interview process. If the candidate does not have questions or the questions are not well thought out, it may be an indication that this candidate is not well prepared and an indication of his or her work habits. Finally, it is crucial to include feedback forms in the interview process. It is important to provide all of those who have participated in the interview an opportunity to provide feedback via some type of formalized process. There is much that can be gained from the perceptions and insight of those who have participated in on campus interview. When considering feedback from participants, use thematic responses rather than focusing on the outlying responses.

Choosing the Desired Candidate and On-Boarding

Selecting the right person for a position can be very complex. It does not always mean choosing the person who answered all of questions correctly or who on paper is the most qualified candidate. The right candidate is a person who works well with others, brings strengths to the team that do not already exist, complements the team, appropriately challenges processes and others, responds well to direction, asks appropriate questions, is accountable, knowledgeable, dependable, professionally mature, and possesses the necessary level of intelligence for the sought-after position. It is difficult in an interview to determine whether a person possesses all of these tangible and intangible skills. This is why it is essential to listen for verbal cues, watch for nonverbal cues, ask appropriately probing questions, conduct thorough reference checks, and most important, with the consent of the candidate, conduct Internet searches and off-list reference checks. It is also helpful to have a formal process for discerning the strengths and weaknesses of the candidate as well as a process for the hiring manager to determine whether the candidate's tangible and intangible skills and competencies complement the team with which he or she will work. If all of these variables align and the desired candidate is hired, the next step is the "on-boarding" or orientation process. This process should begin prior to the arrival of the new hire. Efforts to on-board must be intentional, appropriate, and should begin almost immediately after the offer is made and accepted and should continue well beyond the start date of the new hire. This process should involve including the new hire on departmental and divisional e-mail correspondences, providing the candidate with appropriate resources and contacts to assist in making a smooth transition into the workplace, a schedule for the first week, follow-up meetings with human resources if necessary as well as with other appropriate offices that will help with this transition. Tull, Hurt, and Saunders (2009) offer a number of effective strategies, research, and curricular suggestions to create a structured and appropriate orientation program for new hires.

Supervision

After recruiting and selecting the right person for the position, it is critical that effective supervision ensue. The hiring manager must recognize and understand that upper-level professionals have different needs, expectations, and requirements that mid-level and entry-level professionals. There is a fair amount of literature that exists that can teach, help, and guide supervisors on how to work effectively with employees. There are several examples included later in this section. However, there is not much, if any, information written on how to supervise senior- or executive-level employees. The fact is, college presidents are not publishing information regarding the effective supervision of executive-level higher education administrators such as provosts, vice presidents and vice chancellors, and other cabinet-level positions.

A distinction must be made when providing supervision for individuals at various levels. There is a certain level of autonomy that should be given to senior-level professionals versus entry- and mid-level professionals responsible for direct service and program delivery. With novice supervisees, a high degree of support and a low amount of challenge or confrontation is advisable (Howard, Nance, & Myers, 1986). However, regardless of the level of the professional who is being supervised, there are some fundamental components to supervision that every supervisor should know. There is an abundance of literature about tangible skills and techniques needed to be an effective supervisor (Arminio & Creamer, 2001; Manathunga, 2005, 2007; Sutcliffe, 1999). Instead of reiterating what can be found in most books or articles on effective supervision, this section highlights tips acquired from the author's personal experiences over the past twenty-five-plus years of supervising staff, making mistakes, and learning from mentors on how to be an effective coworker, supervisor, and leader. It draws largely from experiences, skills, and techniques that have been effective in maximizing the strengths of employees and helping them to grow in areas in which they need improvement. To provide a broader perspective of suggested approaches to take when supervising staff, some of the responses included here were solicited directly from coworkers regarding the effectiveness and ineffectiveness of the author's supervision and leadership styles. It is important to maintain that though the role of a supervisor is to lead and guide his or her supervisees, it is even more important to be able to allow the individual strengths of each employee to emerge. However, there are some hires that are made with the intention of developing and preparing the person for future opportunities. Equally important to the aforementioned is the converse. It is not wise to hire a person who needs development or is not ready for the identified position if the supervisor does not have the time to invest in the employee. If the person is considered a project and you don't have the time, don't make the hire.

Effective supervision must begin with building a solid relationship. Building this relationship starts with establishing a high level of trust and mutual respect between the supervisor and the supervisee. The premise for this is drawn from John Maxwell's sentiment that people don't care how much a person knows until they understand how much that person cares (Maxwell, 1998). If the supervisor shows the supervisee that she or he is genuinely concerned about the supervisee's well-being and is willing to invest in him or her, the supervisee is generally more willing to commit and work harder for the good of the cause. To build trust and respect with an employee or supervisee, the supervisor must be willing to be cautiously vulnerable, appropriately transparent, and trusting. Each employee is different; therefore, unique relationships will be developed and should be fostered accordingly. Operating from the perspective of being fair, honest, and consistent with everyone pays great dividends. It is important to remember that fair does not always mean equal, and, just like students, staff come to us with different needs and at various developmental stages. As a result, each relationship should be treated as an individual relationship. However, holding people accountable, expecting quality work, and effectively communicating expectations should be consistent for everyone and it should happen no matter at what point the employee is in his or her professional development. It is also important to listen and provide clear and direct feedback at all times. When being direct, it is crucial to couple it with diplomacy. In the context of communicating, diplomacy involves skillfully articulating a message in a manner that can be heard and received by the recipient. Diplomacy is a vital component in the communication process. As a supervisor, it is important to recognize the vulnerabilities of each staff member and balance listening to him or her with open and honest feedback. This maximizes the potential for learning. Finally, when communicating, always remember to maintain an even balance of intellect and emotion. Too much of either one can distort the message. When passion is used to communicate a point, the message can get lost in the emotion. So, never forget: "I before E"— intellect before emotion in communication increases the probability that your message is received.

The following lessons have been learned over my twenty-five-plus years from being supervised and supervising others. These are shared as suggestions to effectively lead and supervise others, regardless of your level in the organization.

• Provide a thorough on-boarding process for new employees. Proper training and orientation to the culture of an institution, division, and department play a vital role in how the employee moves forward in the position. This process can be an ongoing and progressive process. However, it must be intentional and have specific outcomes.

• Provide an environment that has a balance of challenge and support.

• Lead by example, especially when asking people to practice certain values.

• Do not ask people to do anything you are not willing to do yourself.

• It is alright to lead with your head and your heart. This makes you human. In return, people will be open and honest in their communication.

• Be visible. Visit with departments during tough times and good times. People need to see their leader.

• Make sure your staff can relate to you and vice versa. Do not be untouchable, and do not lose sight of the work being done at *all* levels.

• Have a clear vision and purpose and frequently communicate it to others at every level.

• When possible, create a shared vision so that others can see themselves in it. People are more likely to support what they help to create.

• When setting annual goals, both personal and or professional for each employee, be clear about expectations and provide guidance and support to assist in reaching them.

• Provide regular and timely feedback, both praise and areas for improvement.

• Recognize employees who perform at high levels and praise that behavior.

• Be diplomatically direct in offering suggestions for improvement.

• If an employee is willing to learn and to allow you to hold a mirror up for them, the opportunity for self-reflection and growth is great; however, it is crucial to know whether the employee is ready to hear the feedback. Again, it is important to provide a balance of challenge and support along the way.

• Do not push too hard in the area of personal growth if the employee is not ready or chooses not to go here. It may have a negative impact.

• Be reasonable with expectations about the skills needed to achieve results.

- Make sure the person being asked to perform can realistically achieve the goal.
- Challenge staff to operate outside of their comfort zones to allow for learning to occur, and support them as they take risks. Tailor each approach to the needs of the employee. Some people do not welcome direct challenges.
- Consider the strengths of your employee and position the person for success in the organization. This increases their confidence, often resulting in them wanting to achieve more.
- Invest in your employees. If money is a problem, provide suggested articles, books, journals, online resources, webinars, podcasts, social media chat sessions, and even time for the employee to do some of this during work hours, as well as discussions following to create opportunities for development.
- There are formal and informal ways for accountability of learning. These include one-on-one discussions, presentations, reports, role-modeling good leadership skills, and sharing relevant student affairs literature that can be important in developing new staff and mentoring seasoned professionals.
- Regularly seek input and feedback about your supervision style. Always ask the question, "What can I do to be a better supervisor?"

Retention

Generally speaking, in contrast to working in other occupational settings, higher education has been associated with lower levels of stress and higher levels of job satisfaction, resulting in greater levels of retention. French, Caplan, and Van Harrison (1982) purport that higher levels of job satisfaction are found in postsecondary education as a result of higher levels of autonomy, clarity of work, and a collegiate culture emphasizing consensual decision making and shared values. Even though many professionals in higher education struggle with work/life balance, the flexibility in the job still allows for greater levels of job satisfaction. However, as a result of increased workloads, higher expectations, higher levels of accountability, lower pay levels, and longer workweeks, more attention must be given to retaining staff. There are several factors that affect retention. Some can be controlled, and others are beyond a manager's control. Every employee has reasons for wanting to leave or stay with an organization. These reasons can be personal or professional; some are positive and some are not. Employees may be motivated by things like bonuses, promotions, flexible working conditions, campus climate, community support, financial stability in the workplace, or additional paid time off. Some increases in retention can be attributed to employees who are fulfilled just by what they do and where they are. They do not have aspirations of moving anywhere. Additionally, some job-related retention may be attributed to "outside" conditions that require individuals to stay in an area or a region. Whatever the reason, employees must find satisfaction in their work or they will become unhappy and unproductive. Regardless of the environmental factors that exist, managers who invest in employees have higher rates of retention. This is supported by Heathfield (2011), who suggests that the quality of supervision is directly related to employee retention. She postulates that people leave managers more frequently than they leave jobs. Conversely, people also follow good supervisors. Consequently, managers must find ways to understand what drives each individual employee within the context of his or her role in the organization and either work to nurture that or help an employee transition on to their next professional role.

Retention rates for new professionals in student affairs, however, are not good. Renn and Hodges (2007) reported an estimated 50 percent to 60 percent of new professionals leave the field of higher education before their fifth year. Cilente, Henning, Skinner Jackson, Kennedy, and Sloan (2006) conducted a mixed-methods self-reported study to determine the developmental needs of new professionals (five years or fewer). It was found that the following six developmental needs were identified and ranked highest by respondents: (1) receiving adequate support, (2) understanding job expectations, (3) fostering student learning, (4) moving up in the field of student affairs, (5) enhancing supervision skills, and (6) developing multicultural competencies. It was suggested that a more comprehensive orientation, better supervision, and more intentional staff development opportunities result in higher levels of staff retention.

Keeping employees engaged and motivated is the key to a successful, highly productive workforce. There are many outside factors that affect employee retention, and many resources (Buck & Watson, 2002; Butler & Felts, 2006; and St. Onge, Ellett, & Nestor, 2008) the reader may consult on this topic. However, retaining quality employees can be enhanced by putting into practice the information presented in this chapter. The first step is effective recruitment. Knowing what you are looking for in a qualified candidate and then hiring the best-qualified person to fulfill the requirements of the position is most important. The best-qualified person must have the fundamental professional experiences necessary, understand the institutional type, and fit the team with which he or she will be most closely working. Next is selecting the right candidate for the place. In this context, the place refers to the position, department, division, and the institution. The right candidate is a person who works well with others, brings missing attributes to the team, complements the team, appropriately challenges processes and others, responds well to direction, asks appropriate questions, is accountable, knowledgeable, dependable, professionally mature, and possesses the appropriate level of intelligence for the desired position. The third step is effective supervision. Remember Maxwell's axiom that people do not care how much their supervisor knows until they know, understand, and believe how much their supervisor cares. Building a solid relationship with the employee through establishing a high level of trust and mutual respect helps in the retention process. Finally, investing in the employee's development is a major component of retention. This sends a clear message that the supervisor is concerned about the employee's professional growth and development. Often resources to fund travel and other types of professional development are limited, so these kinds of actions pay major dividends in the employee's emotional bank account.

Professional Development

Meaningful and effective professional development plans must include a number of key components. First, aligning the programmatic ideas with student affairs competencies such as the ACPA/NASPA Professional Competency Areas for Student Affairs Practitioners (2010) validates the experience. This set of competencies, developed by a joint task force, is "intended to define the broad professional knowledge, skills, and, in some cases, attitudes expected of student affairs professionals regardless of their area of specialization or positional role within the field" (p. 3). A curriculum aligned with the Professional Competency Areas included in this document provides a framework for defining professionalism in your unit or division. These competency areas are extensively discussed in chapter 20. Professional development must be grounded in learning and should incorporate a needs assessment that addresses the desires of the professionals in your unit or division. This data-gathering process should be all-inclusive, from the administrative staff to the senior leaders. In an effort to understand and meet the developmental needs of staff, a comprehensive data-gathering process, including surveys, focus groups, and one-on-one discussions, is advised. The results of the assessment should be shared to ensure accuracy and obtain support for the identified topics. Then, these topics can be turned into a curriculum designed for all levels of the staff in the unit or division. To better serve staff needs, dividing these topics into levels such as entry-level, mid-level, senior-level, and support staff ensures that programs are appropriate for the participants.

Conclusion

In summary, the major purpose of higher education is to assist students to achieve success. Our jobs as student affairs professionals are to assist students with achieving their desired goals while simultaneously helping them realize their maximum potential. In many cases, this means assisting them with successful matriculation into and through our institutions. Student affairs professionals contribute to their learning by providing quality co-curricular programs and services that teach students cognitive nonacademic or human relations skills and competencies. The ability to have the greatest impact on student learning starts with competent professionals. As a result, the strength of any student affairs division begins and ends with employing capable professional staff responsible for creating and delivering these programs and services. The quality of the staff is directly related to the hiring manager's ability to recruit, select, supervise, and retain talented professionals. The resources, examples, and recommendations provided in this chapter are designed to assist managers to successfully achieve these important responsibilities.

References

American College Personnel Association and National Association of Student Personnel Administrators. (2010). *ACPA/NASPA Professional competencies areas for student affairs practitioners*. Washington, DC: Authors.

Arminio, J., & Creamer, D. (2001). What supervisors say about quality supervision. *College Student Affairs Journal, 21*(1), 35–44.

Buck, J. M., & Watson, J. L. (2002). Retaining staff employees: The relationship between human resources management strategies and organizational commitment. *Innovative Higher Education, 26*(3), 175–193.

Butler, M., & Felts, J. (2006). Tool kit for the staff mentor: Strategies for improving retention. *Journal of Continuing Education in Nursing, 37*(5), 210–213.

Cilente, K., Henning, G., Skinner Jackson, J., Kennedy, D., & Sloan, T. (2006). *Report on the new professional needs study*. Washington, DC: American College Personnel Association. http://www.myacpa.org/research/newprofessionals.php.

Davenport, Z., Rhine, L. & Martinez-Saenz, M. (2012). The student success conundrum. In B. Bontrager (Ed.), *Strategic enrollment management: Transforming higher education* (pp. 25-50). Washington, DC: American Association of Collegiate Registrars and Admissions Officers.

Davis, C. E., & Herrera, A. (2013). Preparing for the job interview: The interviewers' responsibility. *Strategic Finance, 95*(3), 47–51.

French, J.R.P., Caplan, R. D., & Van Harrison, R. (1982). *The mechanisms of job stress and strain*. Buckingham, UK: Open University Press.

Heathfield, S. M. (2011). *The bottom line for employee retention*. http://humanresources .about.com/.

Howard, A., & Johnson, J. (2010). If you were a tree, what kind would you be? The surprising truth about interviewing. *Catalyst, 39*(2), 13–21.

Howard, G. S., Nance, D. W., & Myers, P. (1986). *Adaptive counseling and therapy: An integrative, eclectic model*. The Counseling Psychologist, *14*, 363–442.

Ishikawa, H., Hashimoto, H., Kinoshita, M., Fujimori, S., Shimizu, T., & Yano, E. (2006). Evaluating medical students' non-verbal communication during the objective structured clinical examination. *Medical Education, 40*(12), 1180–1187.

McConnell, J. (2003). Preparing for and conducting interviews. *Hunting Heads,* 101–137.

Manathunga, C. (2005). The development of research supervision: "Turning the light on a private space." *International Journal for Academic Development, 10*(1), 17–30.

Manathunga, C. (2007). Supervision as mentoring: The role of power and boundary crossing. *Studies in Continuing Education, 29*(2), 207–221.

Maxwell, J., C. (1998 and 2007). *The twenty-one irrefutable laws of leadership*. Nashville, TN: Thomas Nelson.

Mehrabian, A. (1971). Silent messages, Wadsworth, California: Belmont.

Renn, K., & Hodges, J. (2007). The first year on the job: experiences of new professionals in student affairs. *NASPA Journal, 44*(2), 367–39.

St. Onge, S., Ellett, T., & Nestor, E. M. (2008). Factors affecting recruitment and retention of entry-level housing and residential life staff: Perceptions of chief housing officers. *Journal of College and University Student Housing, 35*(2), 10–23.

Subramani, R. R. (2010, February). Insight through body language and non-verbal communication references in Tirukkural. *Language in India, 10*(2), p. 261.

Sutcliffe, N. (1999). Preparing supervisors: A model of research awards supervision training. In G. Wisker & N. Sutcliffe (Eds.), *Good practice in supervision* (pp. 139–147). Birmingham: SEDA.

Tull, A., Hirt, J. B., & Saunders, S. A. (2009). *Becoming socialized in student affairs administration: A guide for new professionals and their supervisors*. Sterling, VA: Stylus.

Winston, A. W. Jr., & Creamer, D. G. (1997). *Improving staffing practices in student affairs*. San Francisco, CA: Jossey-Bass.

CHAPTER TWENTY

PROFESSIONAL DEVELOPMENT AS LIFELONG LEARNING

Susan R. Komives and Stan Carpenter

Illinois Wesleyan University once sent an invitation to alumni weekend with the bold announcement, "Your Degree is Now Obsolete!" The same could be said for all of our undergraduate and graduate degrees. The half-life of information is shortening; it requires our continued learning to stay updated, competent, and visionary. Indeed, "workers and practitioners in virtually all industries and disciplines must remain students for life to stay current in their skills and knowledge" (Cantor, 2006, p. 28).

Although grounded in bodies of knowledge from our formal study in higher education, student affairs, or student development, today's times require that professionals acquire new information to approach contemporary challenges. More than twenty years ago, wise scholar, Peter Vaill (1991) wrote that in these rapidly changing times we must become comfortable being beginners again and again as we face new situations. He forecast, "It is not an exaggeration to suggest that everyone's state of beginnerhood is only going to deepen and intensify so that ten years from now each of us will be even more profoundly and thoroughly settled in the state of being a perpetual beginner" (p. 81). Professionals may not need competency skills for this kind of lifelong learning, but they do need comfort with incompetency skills—acknowledging what we do not know or know how to do with the confidence that we know how to learn (Vaill, 1996). Paradoxically, we build our capacity when we admit we do not know something and we have the efficacy to know we can learn it.

In the sections that follow, we assert the need for lifelong professional learning and identify the complexity of skills and competencies needed in the field. We advance a notion of professional development, propose a model for thinking about individual and group professional development, offer some suggestions about how to implement a comprehensive professional development plan, and share some exemplary professional development activities.

Lifelong Professional Learning

The complexity of problems student affairs professionals face daily, the rapid influx of new information, the need for knowledge management (Cantor, 2006), the nature of evolving technologies, and the importance of examining diverse frameworks and perspectives clearly signal that no individual ever has all the information or personal skills to address the complexity of today's challenges in professional practice. For these and many other reasons, professional student affairs administrators and student development educators are obligated to a personal commitment to socialization and regeneration (Carpenter, 2003), especially initial preparation and lifelong learning (Carpenter, 1991). The juxtaposition of knowledge and skills necessary for the practice of any profession, together with the intricacy of student affairs practice, leads to a discussion of the knowledge and learning requirements for lifelong professional education.

Professional Competencies

Student affairs professionals have been guided by numerous models of professional competencies that reflect the evolution of the field (ACPA Steering Committee on Professional Competencies, 2007; Council for the Advancement of Standards in Higher Education [CAS], 2012c; Janosik, Carpenter, & Creamer, 2006; Pope, Reynolds, & Mueller, 2004). Studies frequently compare and contrast the competency expectations of new professionals held by senior student affairs offices and graduate faculty (that is, Swen et al., 2011). Herdlein, Riefler, and Mrowka's (2013) recent meta-analysis of nearly twenty years of scholarship on competencies in student affairs from an analysis of twenty-two articles found "a developing consensus in student affairs toward a more administrative focus to complement human facilitation skills" (p. 250). Their analysis revisited a similar methodology used by Lovell and Kosten in 2000. Lovell and Kosten identified competencies of student development (70 percent), unit responsibility (13 percent), academic background (13 percent), organizational development (9 percent), federal policies (9 percent), and student needs (4 percent). The Herdlein et al. (2013) study found multicultural/diversity (86 percent), student development (68 percent), research/assessment (55 percent), legal issues (55 percent), budget and finance (50 percent), and ethics (50 percent). High levels of agreement (50–86 percent) in the Herdelein et al. study reflect a growing consensus of competencies needed in the field with critical recognition of multicultural and diversity competence (not even noted in the top six categories in 2000) leading the list in the 2013 study.

The most recent comprehensive list of competencies was published in 2010 in a joint project from the two premier general associations in student affairs: ACPA: College Student Educators International and NASPA: Student Affairs Administrators in Higher Education. Both chapter authors served on this project team. The ten competency areas are (1) advising and helping, (2) assessment, evaluation, and research, (3) equity, diversity, and inclusion, (4) ethical professional practice, (5) history, philosophy, and values, (6) human and organizational resources, (7) law, policy, and governance, (8) leadership, (9) personal foundations, and (10) student learning and development. Each of the ten competency areas is presented in three levels of competence (that is, basic, intermediate, advanced). These levels are not based on years in the field but experience levels that may vary by positions held and skill levels sought by employers and professionals themselves. All student affairs professionals should be competent at least at a basic level in each of the ten areas. This list is an exceptionally useful tool for an individual who seeks to develop a professional development program to be effective within a current role or to stretch to play a new role. It could also be useful in designing meaningful job descriptions that identify the level of competency needed for any particular position. ACPA has published a set of rubrics for assessing each of the competency and key skill areas. An abridged competency list is presented in Table 20.1; the complete list can be found on the ACPA and NASPA websites. The competency areas are presented alphabetically. Technology, sustainability, and globalism are threads that run through each competency and should be a focus of professional development programs.

TABLE 20.1 ACPA AND NASPA PROFESSIONAL COMPETENCY AREAS

Advising and Helping: Addresses the knowledge, skills, and attitudes related to providing counseling and advising support, direction, feedback, critique, referral, and guidance to individuals and groups.

Basic	Intermediate	Advanced
Examples: Exhibit active listening skills; facilitate reflection to make meaning from experience; facilitate problem solving; know and use referral sources ... and exhibit referral skills in seeking expert assistance.	*Examples*: Perceive and analyze unspoken dynamics in a group setting; manage conflict; demonstrate culturally appropriate advising, helping, coaching, and counseling strategies; appropriately mentor students and staff.	*Examples*: Provide effective counseling services to individuals and groups; exercise institutional crisis intervention skills, and coordinate crisis intervention and response processes.

Assessment, Evaluation, and Research (AER): Focuses on the ability to use, design, conduct, and critique qualitative and quantitative AER analyses; to manage organizations using AER processes and the results obtained from them; and to shape the political and ethical climate surrounding AER processes and uses on campus.

Basic	Intermediate	Advanced
Examples: Differentiate among assessment, program review, evaluation, planning, and research and the methodologies appropriate to each; facilitate appropriate data collection assessment and evaluation efforts using up-to-date technology and methods.	*Examples*: Construct basic surveys and other instruments with consultation; use culturally appropriate terminology and methods to conduct and report AER findings.	*Examples*: Effectively use assessment and evaluation results in determining accomplishment of missions/goals, reallocation of resources, and advocacy for more resources.

Equity, Diversity, and Inclusion: Includes the knowledge, skills, and attitudes needed to create learning environments that are enriched with diverse views and people. It is also designed to create an institutional ethos that accepts and celebrates differences among people, helping to free them of any misconceptions and prejudices

Basic	Intermediate	Advanced
Examples: Integrate cultural knowledge with specific and relevant diverse issues on campus; demonstrate fair treatment and change aspects of the environment that do not promote fair treatment.	*Examples*: Supervise, challenge, and engage in hiring and promotion practices that are fair, inclusive, proactive, and nondiscriminatory.	*Examples*: Ensure individuals throughout the institution are treated respectfully, justly, fairly, and impartially.

TABLE 20.1 (*continued*)

Ethical Professional Practice: Pertains to the knowledge, skills, and attitudes needed to understand and apply ethical standards to one's work. While ethics is an integral component of all the competency areas, this competency area focuses specifically on the integration of ethics into all aspects of self and professional practice.

Basic	Intermediate	Advanced
Examples: Identify ethical issues in the course of one's job; assist students in ethical decision making.	*Examples*: Address and resolve lapses in ethical behavior among colleagues and students; articulate and implement a personal protocol for ethical decision making.	*Examples*: Ensure those working in the unit or division adhere to identified ethical standards.

History, Philosophy, and Values: Involves knowledge, skills, and attitudes that connect the history, philosophy, and values of the profession to one's current professional practice.

Basic	Intermediate	Advanced
Examples: Describe the foundational philosophies, disciplines, and values on which the profession is built; articulate the principles of professional practice.	*Examples*: Explain how today's practice is informed by historical context; explore new philosophical contexts and approaches.	*Examples*: Contribute to the research and scholarship of the profession; demonstrate visionary and forward thinking.

Human and Organizational Resources: Includes knowledge, skills, and attitudes used in the selection, supervision, motivation, and formal evaluation of staff; conflict resolution; management of the politics of organizational discourse; and the effective application of strategies and techniques associated with financial resources, facilities management, fund raising, technology use, crisis management, risk management and sustainable resources.,

Basic	Intermediate	Advanced
Examples: Demonstrate familiarity in basic tenets of supervision; describe campus protocols for responding to significant incidents and campus crises.	*Examples*: Assist and/or direct individuals to develop professional development plans.	*Examples*: Effectively intervene with employees in regard to morale, behavioral expectations, and conflict and performance issues; teach resource stewardship to others.

(*continued*)

TABLE 20.1 (*continued*)

Law, Policy, and Governance: Includes the knowledge, skills, and attitudes relating to policy development processes used in various contexts, the application of legal constructs, and the understanding of governance structures and their impact on one's professional practice.

Basic	Intermediate	Advanced
Examples: Describe how policy is developed in one's department and institution, as well as the local, state/province, and federal levels of government; explain the concepts of risk management and liability reduction strategies.	*Examples*: Explain the legal theories connected with torts and negligence and how they affect professional practice; implement best practices with respect to access, affordability, accountability, and quality.	*Examples*: Develop institutional policies and practices consistent with contract law; participate effectively in the governance system of one's institution.

Leadership: Addresses the knowledge, skills, and attitudes required of a leader, whether a positional leader or a member of the staff, in both an individual capacity and within a process of individuals working together effectively to envision, plan, effect change in organizations.

Basic	Intermediate	Advanced
Examples: Identify one's strengths and weaknesses as a leader and seek opportunities to develop one's leadership skills; describe and apply the basic principles of community building.	*Examples*: Identify potential obstacles or points of resistance when designing a change process; share data used to inform key decisions.	*Examples*: Display authenticity and congruence between one's true self and one's positional roles; inform other units about issues that may affect their work.

Personal Foundations: Involves the knowledge, skills, and attitudes to maintain emotional, physical, social, environmental, relational, spiritual, and intellectual wellness; be self-directed and self-reflective; maintain excellence and integrity in work.

Basic	Intermediate	Advanced
Examples: Articulate meaningful goals for one's work; identify positive and negative impacts on psychological wellness and, as appropriate, seek assistance from available resources.	*Examples*: Recognize needs and opportunities for continued growth.	*Examples*: Attend not only to immediate areas of growth, but also those areas relating to one's anticipated career trajectory.

TABLE 20.1 (*continued*)

Student Learning and Development: Addresses the concepts and principles of student development and learning theory.

Basic	Intermediate	Advanced
Examples: Identify the limitations in applying existing theories and models to varying student demographic groups; identify and construct learning outcomes.	*Examples*: Design programs and services to promote student learning and development that are based on current research on student learning and development theories.	*Examples*: Explain theory to diverse audiences ... and use it effectively to enhance understanding of the work of student affairs.

Source: Adapted from American College Personnel Association and National Association of Student Personnel Administrators. (2010). *ACPA/NASPA professional competency areas for student affairs practitioners*. Washington, DC: Authors.

Studies of competencies in the field often compare those competencies advanced by graduate preparation programs as well as those competencies preferred in practice. The Council for the Advancement of Standards in Higher Education published the first standards for master's preparation in student affairs and higher education in 1986. Many graduate preparation programs use these standards for their program design and are in voluntary compliance with this approach to professional preparation. Table 20.2 outlines the key areas presented by CAS (2012c): foundational studies, professional studies, and supervised practice. Bodies of knowledge for each area are identified in this table. Graduate preparation is recognized as preparing new professionals well for their entry-level jobs (Cuyjet, Longwell-Grie, & Molina, 2009), with practical competencies

TABLE 20.2 THE CAS CURRICULUM

Areas of Study	Specific Curriculum
Foundational studies	Historical higher education and student affairs foundations
	Philosophical higher education and student affairs foundations
Professional studies	Student development theory
	Student characteristics and effects of college on students
	Individual and group interventions
	Organization and administration of student affairs
	Assessment, evaluation, and research
Supervised practice	Practica and internships covering two different experiences

Source: Adapted from CAS (2012c). p. 353.

such as budgeting needing more attention. The combination of good graduate preparation and good learning experiences in assistantships or work sites can enrich the entry-professional's competence.

These lists also represent a remarkable convergence of needed skills and competencies in professional student affairs practice. These competencies are complemented by the general and personal qualities advanced by CAS in their document, "Characteristics of Individual Excellence for Professional Practice in Higher Education" (CAS, 2012a), which are clustered as general knowledge and skills, interactive competencies, and self-mastery. This compilation is available on the CAS website and serves as a useful self-assessment to guide a personalized professional development plan.

Student affairs has the distinct challenge of being made up of professionals from diverse backgrounds (for example, health care, accounting, recreation) working together in a student affairs division. In addition, student affairs work occurs across the entire campus (for example, advising centers, internship offices, admissions) and may not be in the formal student affairs division. Blimling (2001) applied the idea of communities of practice to student affairs, noting that we do not have one culture and literature to pay homage and attention to, but several. Respecting each of these communities and studying the interesting ways in which they intersect and interact are necessary for contemporary student affairs practice.

Learning Reconsidered (Keeling, 2004) recognized that many professionals contribute to student learning who may not have formal preparation in student affairs (for example, accountants, doctors, coaches, social workers). The authors wrote, "While the educational preparation of student affairs professionals must focus on in-depth knowledge of these topics, it is equally important that other members of the academic community understand ... " (p. 25):

- The context of higher education
- Theories of student development and learning
- Factors that contribute to student success and retention
- Characteristics and needs of diverse student populations

Learning Reconsidered advocated that "since many academic administrators and advisors do not receive formal education in these areas, institutions of higher education must provide professional development to assist them in gaining this knowledge base" (p. 25).

With the quantity and complexity of information needed and the personal qualities required, it is no wonder that we feel like continual beginners! The question really is not whether one should engage in professional development, but how can one stay truly ready? The answer lies, as most things in education do, in a commitment to lifelong learning.

Defining Professional Development

Carpenter and Stimpson (2007) explored scholarly practice, professionalism, and professional development, concluding that intentional practice (research, peer review, and experience driven) demands career-long learning. Further, such learning should be reflective of the best thinking in the field. Student affairs work has a proud history of scholarship interacting with practice. Hence, there is an imperative for professionals to participate in lifelong learning and reflection, organized according to the standards of the profession (Webster-Wright, 2009). As just one example that this idea is gaining broad currency, the first volume of the *Journal of Student Affairs in Africa* is devoted to professionalization and professional development, including a piece on the importance of data-driven practice and up-to-date training and information using the values of rigorous scholarship in peer reviewed journals and other outlets (Carpenter & Haber-Curran, 2013).

In addition, professionals need to identify their basic philosophical orientations to their work roles. Komives (1998) explored the notion of a continuum, including "practitioner-practitioner; practitioner-scholar; scholar-practitioner; and scholar-scholar" (p. 179), suggesting that either extreme is suboptimal. The *practitioner-practitioner* has no theoretical grounding and operates without regard to applications of theory and research to his work. Likewise, the *scholar-scholar* is solely interested in theory and the generation of research without connection to practice or to policy or to student development questions that need understanding. The *practitioner-scholar* leads with her skill in application but is informed and understands the theoretical and research bases of practice. The *scholar-practitioner* is motivated by advancing theory and research from the context of practice and actively studies and assesses practical outcomes and experiences. Understanding the range of these orientations to professional work is useful for the group to design appropriately targeted professional development programs.

One way to look at professional development is to compare it to identity formation. Miller and Carpenter (1980) took this tack, reasoning

TABLE 20.3 THE NATURE OF PROFESSIONAL DEVELOPMENT

1. Professional development is continuous and cumulative in nature, moves from simpler to more complex behavior, and can be described via levels or stages held in common.
2. Optimal professional development is a direct result of the interaction between the total person striving for professional growth and the environment.
3. Optimal professional preparation combines mastery of a body of knowledge and a cluster of skills and competencies within the context of personal development.
4. Professional credibility and excellence of practice are directly dependent upon the quality of professional preparation.
5. Professional preparation is a lifelong learning process.

Source: Adapted from Miller and Carpenter (1980), p. 84.

that professional development ought to conform to human development principles, and derived five propositions (Table 20.3) that clearly support (indeed, demand) a commitment to learning from the beginning of one's career to the end.

Carpenter (2003) later modified the model derived from these propositions to consist of the formative, application, and additive stages. The *formative stage* is characterized by a more external locus of control, as the beginning professional looks to more seasoned ones to guide her training and orientation into the field. The dominant activity in this stage is learning. The *application stage* features a transition from external to internal locus of control, as the professional trusts himself and his judgment more and more. This stage is concerned most clearly and concisely with doing. Similarly, the *additive stage* professional is in a position of contributing to student affairs practice in any number of ways: humane and informed supervision, role modeling, policy making, professional association leadership, scholarly productivity, and other exemplary activities. These stages represent macro-versions of what Carpenter (2003) called the "cycle of professional development" (p. 582). Another interesting way to look at this cycle is in a micro way. The learning, doing, and contributing motif is a good way to think about every aspect of practice, almost as if this simple sequence operates as a kind of fractal, describing and guiding everything from the smallest structures of our daily interactions with colleagues and students to the largest aspects of organizational and scholarly productivity. We are what we learn, do, and contribute to clients, colleagues, the profession, and society!

This more fundamental and complex way of looking at professional development is consonant with the scholarship in the field of continuing and professional education. Departing from what Cervero (2000) suggested was a sort of pause in the progress of continuing professional education in the 1990s, Dirkx, Gilley, and Gilley (2004) argued for a much more subjective and contextual view, decrying a narrow focus on "simple" skill and competency development, presumably especially when "transmitted in a didactic fashion and offered by a pluralistic group of providers (workplaces, for-profits, and universities) that do not work together in any coordinated fashion" (Cervero, 2000, p. 4). To Dirkx and others, professional development is mediated by experience and vice versa. Further, borrowing the concept of developmental readiness from recent literature on leadership development, a particular professional development activity or content area may not be appropriate for individuals at the same positional or experience level (Dugan, 2013; Hannah & Avolio, 2010). Knowledge and skills, as well as the need for further development, evolve for each professional, meaning that formal professional development becomes an integral part of professional practice and identity.

In the next section of the chapter, we explore a model that reflects these characteristics. If professional development programs are to flourish, a "continuum of professional practice" (Knox, 2000, p. 16) must be adopted that views professional education as a lifelong process. Knox views the continuum as being an organized, coordinated effort that focuses on "goals, learning activities, providers, resources, context, and negotiation" (p. 17) concerning the aspects of professional development. Professional development activities should be application focused (which helps with the differential preparation issue), without losing sight of theory. Finally, professional development activities should receive support from all parties, including administrators, learners, and policymakers (Knox, 2000). Organizational learning often changes the culture of the organization and makes it possible to address complex issues and accomplish transformative change (Vahey, 2011).

A Model of Professional Development

Given the considerations discussed, modern professional development in a student affairs work context should have certain characteristics, whether designed for individual learning or group and unit development, captured here in a mnemonic fashion. Professional development activities should be

> *Purposeful, intentional, and goal related.* Professional development should result from a felt need, a desire to get better at particular aspects of practice. Professionals and groups should continually strive to improve and understand that this usually requires more learning.

Research, theory, and data based. Appropriate professional development, like any other professional activity, should have a rational basis in theory and ideally has been demonstrated to have value through disciplined inquiry. Using techniques or approaches that are not theory and research based is risky, at best, and may be wasteful or even harmful.

Experience based. Less experienced professionals should take opportunities to learn from more experienced ones. This dictum applies to both content and mode and is not age related, as noted in the three levels of the ACPA/NASPA competencies; for example, very young professionals may have technological expertise to bring to a division or team. Professionals should take advantage of established professional development modes, perhaps with occasional individual changes for context.

Peer reviewed. An underutilized resource in student affairs is peer review. In the context of professional development, it is particularly important to get some "organized help" in the form of individual opinions and analysis, committee efforts, departmental or divisional programs, professional association curricula or models, or many other sources. It is unnecessary and inefficient to ignore the judgment of other professionals when considering one's own professional development, and it seems especially unwise when mechanisms for doing so are readily available.

Assessed. Taking all the preceding factors into account, one must still check out the feasibility, likely cost and benefit(s), likelihood of achieving the purpose, level of challenge, and availability of needed resources, including time and energy. Simply stated, is the proposed activity going to result in the desired learning? It should go without saying that this assessment should be done in advance.

Reflected upon and reflected in practice. Every professional development activity, as any other educational endeavor, requires reflection to complete the learning loop. Schön's (1991) conception was that one's practice should include a significant amount of reflection, that continual reexamination, learning, and even intuition are necessary elements in any profession. Time and methods should be built in for thinking about and carefully applying lessons learned.

Evaluated. Did the activity result in what was expected? If not, was the result better or worse, and how can the former be maximized and the latter minimized in the future? If the needs or goals were not met, the professional should fold that knowledge into the ongoing plan for professional development. Similarly, if the goals were met, what is the next step?

It is necessary to **PREPARE** throughout one's entire career. In keeping with the notion that professional preparation is akin to identity development and is constructivist in nature, even formal preparation is subject to the same considerations as traditional professional development. For example, a formative-stage professional, engaging in a formal academic program, would also be involved in heavily supervised practice activities in the form of an assistantship or practicum (Carpenter, 2003). The overall program and every aspect of the experiences could be analyzed using the **PREPARE** framework. Formative-stage individuals not in formal preparation programs are equally dependent upon supervision and mentorship for a period of time. Obviously, the considerations of the model need to be evaluated and analyzed by someone with a fair amount of experience in the field—people new to the profession could not be expected to do so with any accuracy or comprehensiveness.

In the application stage (Carpenter, 2003), the professional would take more and more ownership for his or her own professional growth and development path, still asking for and getting help and guidance from mentors and supervisors, in addition to responding to professional associations and literature. The application-stage person also grows in the ability to understand that professional development often interacts with practice in unpredictable ways. Reflection, with the help of a colleague or alone, can lead to great insight. In the additive stage (Carpenter, 2003), one is usually responsible not only for personal professional development decisions but also for creating environments that facilitate the development of others, whether the student affairs division, the institution, or profession-wide. A great way to add or contribute to the profession is to participate in designing and delivering high-quality professional development experiences on one's campus and beyond.

The professional development activities subject to the considerations detailed in the simple model presented here would ideally be part of a larger context. One's personal plan should be as detailed and long term as possible, given one's experience and knowledge, which obviously grow with time. Similarly, the employing institution should offer a carefully thought-out and extensive professional development plan that encompasses all levels of professional development for a wide variety of student affairs generalists and specialists, with the hallmark being individual responsibility and intentionality.

Professional development activities can be short term, long term, or incidental. Table 20.4 illustrates how sample professional development activities can be framed as intentional, developmental experiences.

The real key is not single activities but organized programs, encompassing individual and group plans and activities, on-campus and off-campus activities, formal and informal programs, as well as opportunities to participate in association leadership at the state, regional, and national levels. Student affairs divisions, especially, have a responsibility and obligation to provide opportunities and encouragement to individual practitioners and to work unit learning. Professional development has many benefits to the individual, clearly, but it benefits the organization and the clientele (students) even more by fostering an ever-more-accomplished workforce. Winston and Creamer (1997) captured this triple benefit idea best in their book on staffing practices in student affairs, proposing "synergistic supervision" that is "a radically different perspective on supervision ... a helping process, which is designed to support staff as they seek to promote the goals of the organizations and to advance their professional development" (p. 194).

The PREPARE model offers a way to frame the plans and conversations necessary for synergistic supervision to occur. With this mind-set, it is easy to see how professional development benefits both the person and the organization, which means that students are better served. Taking this notion one step further and combining it with the ideas of Dirkx et al. (2004) that professional development and practice contexts are interactive, we arrive at the fundamental position that professional practice *is* professional development, and vice versa. Professionals need to be intentional, theory based, cognizant of history, responsive to peer review, reflective, and evaluative in *all* that they do, whether working with students or sharpening their own knowledge and skills.

There is no limit to creative opportunities for specific professional development activities. In addition to activities individuals or offices might design for themselves, Cantor (2006) identified four distinct categories of common sources for professional continuing education (PCE), often in competition in the marketplace for the training dollar. These four categories are professional associations, commercial vendors, proprietary schools and colleges, and not-for-profit organizations. Using a revised version of Cantor's taxonomy, Table 20.5 presents examples of the range of professional development opportunities in the student affairs or higher education fields.

TABLE 20.4 SAMPLE PROFESSIONAL DEVELOPMENT ACTIVITIES AND THE PREPARE MODEL

Dimension of Quality	Research Teams/Writing Groups	Internships/Job Sharing/Job Swapping	Book Clubs	Institute Attendance
Purposeful	Advance knowledge in the field; build personal research/writing skills; product oriented	Support career goals or skill-building goals	Identify books that relate to campus needs or individual needs and interests	Supports job needs or professional development plan
Research/ Theory based	Grounded in review of scholarship	Learn scholarship that applies to new functional areas of interest	Provide new scholarly understanding to apply to practice	Makes theoretical frames transparent
Experience based	Follow guidelines of successful projects in the past	Seek guidance from supervisors, mentors, and colleagues about how to gain maximum benefit	Discuss with peers to make application	Offers immersion experience for 2–3 days of institute; plan transference; vetted by professional association
Peer reviewed	Involve peer debriefers; submitted for formal peer review	Might use application process for selection; guidelines for program created by committee of colleagues	Assures quality experience; books have undergone some peer-review process in order to be published	Quality implied through sponsoring organizations
Assessed	Work pace important to writing time commitments; identify skill deficits (for example, analysis methods)	Check fit, willingness, meaningful involvement; make it time limited	Use criteria for book selection	Justify fit with personal goals and organizational needs
Reflected	Process experience with team	Provide developmental supervision on site	Expect application of material to work context	Require debriefing, report, or presentation upon return to campus
Evaluated	Team evaluated; productivity identified	Use 360-degree feedback strategies (that is, supervisor, peer, subordinate); process with regular supervisor	Evaluate learning after each reading cycle	Require institute impact to be addressed in annual review

TABLE 20.5 EXAMPLES OF CONTINUING PROFESSIONAL DEVELOPMENT BY PRIMARY SOURCES OF DELIVERY

Category of Sources	Sample Activities
Professional associations [see chapter 11]	Attend and present at international, national, regional, and local conferences (CEU credits often are possible)
	Become involved in diverse associations (including specialties outside student affairs)
	Attend and present at special institutes and workshops (for example, ACUHO-I's National Housing Training Institute (NHTI); NASPA's Richard Stevens Institute for Senior Student Affairs Officers; ACPA's Donna M. Bourassa Mid-Level Management Institute; NCLP, ACPA, and NASPA's Leadership Educators Institute)
	Experience e-learning courses; MOOCs; webinars; teleconferences
	Participate in international study tours
	Read and write for publications (for example, journals, magazines)
	Develop mentors/sponsors/peer supports/networks through associations
	For lists of higher education associations, see the CAS website
Commercial vendors	Explore the portfolios of such e-vendors as Magna, PaperClip, studentaffairs.com
	Hire consultants and consulting firms
	Work with a personal coach
	Enroll in Web-based short courses and seminars
Not-for-profit organizations	Identify programs and involvement in: • Chamber of Commerce • Public libraries • American Red Cross • Faith-based organizations • Heritage-based organizations • Service learning • Specialized institutes like the Social Justice Training Institute
Colleges and universities	Participate in campus-based opportunities such as: • Select graduate or undergraduate courses • Certificate programs or degree programs [see chapter 19] • Office of human resources/personnel programs • Center for Teaching Excellence programs • Office of technology programs • Seminars and institutes • Internships, postgraduate fellowships, and sabbaticals • Job exchanges or cross-training • Teaching courses • Book groups, reading groups, or case study groups • Research teams • Alternative spring break programs • Mentors and peer supports • Proprietary college programs in management, technology, or human services
International experiences	Become more globally minded through such experiences as: • Sponsoring study abroad experiences • Association study trips • Semester-at-Sea • Fulbright appointments • Peace Corps

Good Practices in Professional Development

Many institutions have developed outstanding professional development programs that provide examples to emulate. The ones mentioned here are the result of a quick poll the authors conducted of a very limited group of professionals from several listservs, with no pretense of comprehensiveness. No slight of any institution not mentioned is intended. Programs are typically offered through a staff committee and facilitated by at least one staff member. It is exciting to see a trend of student affairs divisions assigning full-time professionals and other resources to professional development efforts. One example is the University of California-Berkeley establishing a learning and development department with four full-time staff members focusing on organizational consulting, employee engagement, and talent management within the division; see the UC Berkeley student affairs website for details.

The University of South Carolina requires each professional to have a plan on file with the division that responds to one or more core competency areas and to be evaluated on it annually. Salary increases and travel funds, among other things, are contingent upon success with the plans, which can include attendance at the speaker series hosted by the division, conference and association attendance and leadership activity, formal coursework, service to the community, cross-training, and a variety of other activities.

Many campuses sponsor some kind of regular conversation groups or brown-bag lunch symposia like the monthly "Inclusion Conversations" at Cornell of Iowa, where the student affairs staff gathers to discuss their observations and reactions to a particular identity group.

Other good examples of cross-division collaboration include models in which staff interact with others across their divisions (for example, assistant director programs at University of Maryland, Lehigh University, University of North Carolina-Wilmington). Wheaton College (Massachusetts) starts the year with "Blenders," groups of student affairs division staff who are mixed together (about six groups of ten) for several meetings per year involving content and discussions.

Resident life departments have a large number of professional staff and often offer extensive professional development opportunities. The Association of College and University Housing Officers-International (ACUHO-I) has a long-standing annual institute for professionals with three to five years of full-time housing experience, built on a set of fifty competencies identified and refined over the years by housing professionals.

Each of these programs exists within a larger context, of course, but would be excellent parts of an overall plan (Swett, 2011). Multilevel offerings are essential to address differing needs of staff. Roberts (2007) concluded

> Results of this research indicate that staff [members] use interactive methods such as consulting with colleagues and mentoring more so than taking sabbaticals and online courses. New professionals were most likely to rely on their preparation program course, while mid-managers find value in professional conference sessions, and senior student affairs officers read professional journals and books. (p. 371)

Conclusion

In a review of ethics statements by the Council for the Advancement of Standards in Higher Education of its member associations, it was clear that, as one dimension of professional autonomy, it is an ethical practice to "engage in continuing education and professional development" (CAS, 2012b, p. 1). By implication, not to do so would be unethical. Both ACPA and NASPA advance professional development in their ethics statements.

Developing professionally must be viewed as a daily activity of learning and applying new perspectives as a way of being. One should have a clear and active plan, and so should one's unit, department, division, and institution. Professional development is so intertwined with appropriate, intentional student affairs practice that the two can be thought of as mutually constructed—it makes little sense to talk about one without the other. Ultimately, however, Kruger (2000) is absolutely right that professional development is the responsibility of each individual practitioner. It is ethical and desirable for individual offices and student affairs divisions to support, expect, and promote continuing education in diverse forms, but even if the employer does not provide reasonable supports to make that happen, individual professionals must ensure their own capacity building and renewal.

References

American College Personnel Association. (2007). *Professional competencies: A report of the steering committee on professional competencies.* http://www.myacpa.org/au/governance/.

American College Personnel Association & National Association of Student Personnel Administrators. (2010). *ACPA/NASPA professional competency areas for student affairs practitioners*. Washington, DC: Authors.

Blimling, G. S. (2001). Uniting scholarship and communities of practice in student affairs. *Journal of College Student Development, 42*, 381–396.

Cantor, J. A. (2006). *Lifelong learning and the academy: The changing nature of continuing education* (ASHE Higher Education Report, no. 32). San Francisco, CA: Jossey-Bass.

Carpenter, D. S. (2003). Professionalism. In S. R. Komives & D. Woodard Jr. (Eds.), *Student services: A handbook for the profession* (4th ed., pp. 107–127). San Francisco, CA: Jossey-Bass.

Carpenter, D. S. (1991). Student affairs profession: A developmental perspective. In T. K. Miller & R. B. Winston Jr. (Eds.), *Administration and leadership in student affairs* (2nd ed., pp. 253-269). Muncie, IN: Accelerated Development.

Carpenter, S., & Haber-Curran, P. (2013). The role of research and scholarship in the professionalization of student affairs. *Journal of Student Affairs in Africa, 1*(1 & 2), 1–9.

Carpenter, S., & Stimpson, M. (2007). Professionalism, scholarly practice, and professional development in student affairs. *NASPA Journal, 44*(2), 265–284.

Cervero, R. M. (2000). Trends and issues in continuing professional education. In. V. W. Mott & B. J. Daley (Eds.), *Charting a course for continuing professional education: Reframing professional practices*. New Directions for Adult and Continuing Education, no. 86. San Francisco, CA: Jossey-Bass.

Council for the Advancement of Standards in Higher Education. (2012a). *CAS characteristics of individual excellence*. Washington, DC: Author. http://www.cas.edu/.

Council for the Advancement of Standards in Higher Education. (2012b). *CAS statement of shared ethics*. Washington, DC: Author. http://www.cas.edu/.

Council for the Advancement of Standards in Higher Education. (2012c). Master's level student affairs administration preparation programs. In *CAS professional standards for higher education* (8th ed.). Washington, DC: Author. http://standards.cas.edu/getpdf.cfm?PDF=E86DA70D-0C19-89ED-0FBA230F8F2F3F41

Cuyjet, M. J., Longwell-Grice, R., & Molina, E. (2009). Perceptions of new student affairs professionals and their supervisors regarding the application of competencies learned in preparation programs. *Journal of College Student Development, 50*, 104–119.

Dugan, J. P. (2013). Developmental readiness: Framing the extant literature. *Concepts and Connections, 19*(3), 18–20.

Dirkx, J. M., Gilley, J. W., & Gilley, A. M. (2004). Change theory in CPE and HRD: Toward a holistic view of learning and change in work. *Advances in Developing Human Resources, 6*, 35–51.

Hannah, S. T., & Avolio, B. J. (2010). Ready or not: How do we accelerate the developmental readiness of leaders? *Journal of Organizational Behavior, 31*, 1181–1187.

Herdlein, R., Riefler, L., & Mrowka, K. (2013). An integrative literature review of student affairs competencies: A meta-analysis. *Journal of Student Affairs Research and Practice, 50*(3), 250–269. doi:10.1515/jsarp-2013–0019.

Janosik, S., Carpenter, S., & Creamer, D. (2006). Beyond professional preparation programs: The role of professional associations in ensuring a high quality work force. *College Student Affairs Journal, 25*(2), 228–237.

Keeling, R. P. (Ed.) (2004). *Learning reconsidered: A campus-wide focus on the student experience.* Washington, DC: National Association of Student Personnel Administrators and the American College Personnel Association.

Knox, A. B. (2000). The continuum of professional education and practice. In. V. W. Mott & B. J. Daley (Eds.), *Charting a course for continuing professional education: Reframing professional practice.* New Directions for Adult and Continuing Education, no. 86. San Francisco, CA: Jossey-Bass.

Komives, S. R. (1998). Linking student affairs preparation with practice. In N. J. Evans & C. E. Phelps Tobin (Eds.), *The state of the art of preparation and practice in student affairs* (pp. 177-200). Washington, DC: American College Personnel Association.

Kruger, K. (2000). New alternatives for professional development. In M. J. Barr & M. K. Desler (Eds.), *The handbook of student affairs administration* (2nd ed., pp. 535–553)). San Francisco, CA: Jossey-Bass.

Lovell, C. D., & Kosten, L. A. (2000). Skills, knowledge and personal traits necessary for success as a student affairs administrator: A meta-analysis of thirty years of research. *NASPA Journal, 37*(4), 1–18.

Miller, T. K., & Carpenter, D. S. (1980). Professional preparation for today and tomorrow. In D. Creamer (ed.), *Student development in higher education.* ACPA monograph series. Washington, DC: American College Personnel Association.

Pope, R. L., Reynolds, A. L., & Mueller, J. A. (2004). *Multicultural competence in student affairs.* San Francisco, CA: Jossey-Bass.

Roberts, D. M. (2007). Preferred methods of professional development in student affairs. *NASPA Journal, 44*(1), 561–577.

Schön, D. A. (1991). The *reflective practitioner: How professionals think in action* (2nd ed.). London, UK: Ashgate.

Swen, A., Hoffman, J., Anan, P., Brown, K., Vong, L., Bresciani, M.J., Monzon, R., & Hickmott, J. (2011). Comparison of senior student affairs officer and student affairs preparatory program faculty expectations of entry-level professionals' competencies. *Journal of Student Affairs Research and Practice, 48*(4). 463–479. doi:10.2202/1949–6605.6270.

Swett, D. (2011). Building a comprehensive professional development program. *Student Affairs Leader, 39*(7), 4–6.

Vaill, P. B. (1991). *Permanent white water: The realities, myths, paradoxes, and dilemmas of managing organizations.* San Francisco, CA: Jossey-Bass

Vaill, P. B. (1996). *Learning as a way of being: Strategies for survival in a world of permanent white water.* San Francisco, CA: Jossey-Bass.

Vahey, K. E. (2011). *Transformational learning for organizational change: Exploring employee experiences with a student affairs workplace professional development program.* Published doctoral dissertation, University of Northern Colorado.

Webster-Wright, A. (2009, June). Reframing professional development through understanding authentic professional learning. *Review of Educational Research, 79*(2), 702–739.

Winston, R. B. Jr., & Creamer, D. G. (1997). *Improving Staffing Practices in Student Affairs.* San Francisco, CA: Jossey-Bass.

PART FIVE

INTERPERSONAL DYNAMICS IN PROFESSIONAL PRACTICE

Interpersonal dynamics play a pivotal role in the successful practice of student affairs administration. This part of the handbook addresses aspects of these dynamics. In chapter 21, Adrianna Kezar and Sean Gehrke discuss how student learning is supported and enhanced by strong collaboration between student affairs administrators and academic colleagues. They offer action steps designed to help educators develop rich partnerships on their campuses. Shannon Ellis follows this discussion in chapter 22 by discussing the political dimensions of decision making. She articulates the necessity for student affairs leaders to develop a political mind-set, connects political activity to effective institutional governance, and offers practical considerations for successful political practice in higher education. Penelope Wills addresses partnerships and relationships from an institutional perspective in chapter 23. She explains the essence of all successful alliances, whether they are inside an institution or forged between an institution and external partners. Finally, this part of the handbook concludes with a discussion of the role of conflict in organizational enrichment. In chapter 24, Dale Nienow and Jeremy Stringer discuss various approaches to conflict, and review processes that might utilize the opportunities presented by conflict to develop and maintain healthy individuals and organizations.

CHAPTER TWENTY-ONE

SUPPORTING AND ENHANCING STUDENT LEARNING THROUGH PARTNERSHIPS WITH ACADEMIC COLLEAGUES

Adrianna Kezar and Sean Gehrke

More than seventy-five years after the *Student Personnel Point of View*, the student affairs profession remains focused on educating the whole student (Guthrie, 2012). The student experience is not one that consists of two parts—one inside and one outside the classroom—but rather a total experience in which these aspects of college life blend and overlap, much in the same way that students' cognitive and psychosocial learning is intertwined (American College Personnel Association [ACPA], 1994). This acknowledgment necessitates an approach to higher education that encourages and fosters partnerships between academic and student affairs. Partnering with academic colleagues might have been considered a controversial and difficult activity in the past, but it has now become relatively commonplace on college campuses across the country (Kezar, 2001). In 1999, Kuh noted that, historically, collaboration had been more espoused than enacted. However, the landscape has changed, and national surveys have documented that partnerships between academic and student affairs are happening at thousands of institutions and across institutional types and sectors (Kezar, Hirsch, & Burack, 2001; Kolins, 1999).

This sea of change in higher education has occurred, in large measure, as a result of the national conversation begun by ACPA and the National Association of Student Personnel Administrators (NASPA). This dialogue gained prominence in 1994 with the publication of *The Student Learning*

Imperative (ACPA) (Bourassa & Kruger, 2001) and was furthered with subsequent publications, *Powerful Partnerships: A Shared Responsibility for Learning* (American Association for Higher Education [AAHE], ACPA, & NASPA, 1998) and *Learning Reconsidered: A Campus-Wide Focus on the Student Experience* (Keeling, 2004). Taken together, these reports heralded a powerful call to higher education to break down barriers on campus to form seamless learning environments across organizational boundaries (ACPA, 1994), insist that academic and student affairs colleagues share responsibility for student learning through cooperation toward common educational goals (AAHE, ACPA, & NASPA, 1998), and acknowledge that all areas of student engagement are venues for students' learning and development (Keeling, 2004). It is exciting to observe that the field has moved from describing the importance of partnerships and discussions of obstacles (which dominated the discourse of the 1980s and 1990s) to examining the best strategies for developing partnerships and understanding some of the best models for collaboration.

This chapter synthesizes the literature and research about partnerships spawned by *The Student Learning Imperative*. The chapter is aimed at helping practitioners by shedding light on barriers, benefits, strategies, and promising practices for partnerships. We first situate our discussion of partnerships by reviewing relevant terminology and presenting a framework for conceptualizing the variety of partnerships. We then present four reflections that set a foundation to understand the current context around collaboration. The reflections are followed by action steps on ways to create and sustain collaborative partnerships.

Defining and Framing Partnerships

It is important to consider definitions. People use the words *collaboration, partnerships, cooperation,* and *coordination* interchangeably. It is important to keep in mind, however, that there are distinctions. Coordination or cooperative arrangements typically involve sharing information or working on tasks together, but usually do not fundamentally alter the work itself (Hagadoorn, 1993; Lockwood, 1996). Partnership or collaboration involves joint goals, a reliance on each other to accomplish those goals, joint planning, and often power sharing. In order to be considered collaboration, there must be an interactive process (relationship over time) and the groups must develop shared rules, norms, and structures that often become their first work together. When practitioners talk about partnerships, they are usually referring to either coordination or collaboration. This process usually begins with coordination and then, if it makes sense, there is an effort to move toward collaboration. These terms are used generically in the chapter, as practitioners typically do; this distinction is made within the research literature.

With this terminology in hand, we now explore a framework for understanding collaborative efforts between student and academic affairs. Streit, Dalton, and Crosby (2009) characterize seven types of interaction between faculty and student affairs practitioners on a continuum from structured to unstructured contacts. The interactions and their descriptions are shown in Table 21.1. This framework is a useful heuristic for understanding the wide range of contact with academic affairs that can occur through work in student affairs. Although much of the research on student affairs–academic affairs partnerships focuses on structured collaboration (for example, learning compacts), it is important to recognize that this wide range of interaction among student and academic affairs colleagues allows for relationship building that can contribute to forming the formal compacts described in the research in this chapter (Guthrie, 2012; Streit et al., 2009).

Regardless of the type of interactions student affairs educators have with faculty colleagues, several factors set the stage for fruitful collaborations. The four reflections following help to frame the current context for enhancing student learning through academic partnerships.

Reflection 1: Remember History

In the past, interactions between academic and student affairs were limited to coordination (Guthrie, 2012). In order to meet the needs of a growing student body for much of the past century, student affairs coordinated with academic affairs to ensure a holistic experience for students. However, the nature of the work remained separate; most interactions that may have occurred between academic and student affairs were toward the unstructured end of the continuum (Streit et al., 2009). Student affairs practitioners were used to collaborating across their functional areas, and early discussions about collaboration with academic affairs were dominated by student affairs practitioners who felt that they were second-class citizens to academic affairs practitioners (Bloland, 1997; Hyman, 1995; Smith, 1982).

If you are on a campus that is still struggling with its past, it might be important to have people on campus read *Envisioning the Future for Student*

TABLE 21.1 SEVEN TYPES OF STUDENT AFFAIRS-FACULTY INTERACTION

	Interaction	Definition	Examples
Structured	Learning compact	Initiatives are focused on student learning and development and require collaboration between faculty and student affairs practitioners to achieve their goals	Living learning communities; service learning programs; first-year experience programs; career development classes
	Research	Student affairs and faculty engaging in common research projects and sharing resources and access to students	Research on career development and technology; drug and alcohol abuse; test anxiety and stress; civic engagement and voting patterns
	Consultation	Focused and often temporary interaction to utilize expertise toward a specific objective	Learning outcomes assessment and evaluation; strategic and long-range planning; faculty presentations at staff training and retreats; student affairs staff serving in adjunct faculty positions
	Advising	Faculty and academic practitioners serving in advisory roles for student groups and organizations whose programs are often coordinated by student affairs practitioners	Sports clubs; Greek letter organizations; service organizations; departmental clubs; major campus events
	Committees/ Task forces	Work groups that utilize expertise of both student affairs and academic affairs practitioners and faculty, allowing for interaction on specific issues of importance to the institution	Academic calendar committee; admissions committee; graduate enrollment committee; crisis management committee; judicial board; orientation committee
	Shared use of facilities/ resources	Facilities and resources, often managed by student affairs, allowing for interaction with faculty who utilize them for academic and administrative purposes	Residence halls; student unions; recreation centers; health centers; movie theaters; conference centers; dining facilities
Unstructured	Informal contacts	Unstructured interactions that naturally occur on college campuses as a result of attending activities and working in a common location	Sports and recreation; sporting events; awards and recognition programs; campus dining; student activities; campus entertainment; volunteer service activities

Source: Adapted from Streit, M. R., Dalton, J. C., & Crosby, P. C. "A Campus Audit of Student Affairs–Faculty Collaborations: From Contacts to Compacts." *Journal of College and Character*, 2009, 10(5), 1–14.

Affairs (Task Force, 2010), *Learning Reconsidered* (Keeling, 2004), or *Powerful Partnerships* (AAHE, ACPA, & NASPA, 1998) in order to understand the important roles that both student and academic affairs play and also to help address biases that people may hold about student affairs work. One promising strategy might be to form a campus reading group. Research on reading groups (Eckel, Kezar, & Lieberman, 1999) has demonstrated that if cross-campus teams read articles and information in common and then have discussions on this material, they are more likely to develop a shared understanding of each other, to share cognitive frameworks, and to move toward change and better working relationships. Doing so improves the chances of moving toward more structured interaction in order to improve learning goals (Streit et al., 2009).

Reflection 2: Logic Overcomes Barriers

Schroeder (1999c) and Knefelkamp (1991) describe how college and university campuses have evolved into structures in which collaboration is difficult. For example, the hierarchical, bureaucratic organizational structure, specialization of knowledge, fragmentation of campus work, and deterioration of work into separate silos make educators less able to participate in partnerships. As Schroeder (1999b) notes, "These vertical structures, while often effective at promoting interaction within functional units, create obstacles to interaction, coordination and collaboration between units" (p. 137). Historically, one significant obstacle to collaboration and partnerships appears to have been specialization. This occurs when people focus increasingly on a very specific issue related to student learning or organizational functioning. As a result of specialization, professionals may become more and more distanced from each other, sharing fewer and fewer values and goals. These different values systems create distinctive cultures on campus, and the result is that student and academic affairs administrators have difficulty communicating and relating to or understanding each other's work. Faculty members on most four-year campuses have tremendous pressures to publish and have less time for students or for collaborating with staff on campus. Thus, they are not even able to participate in collaborative activities. In addition, academic and student affairs are often in competition for funding, which also prevents them from collaborating on goals.

One way to overcome these barriers is to create a compelling logic for collaboration and to help student affairs educators to see their connection to the academic mission. A host of texts and reports beginning in the 1990s helped underscore the importance of collaboration and why it was critical for student affairs to form partnerships (AAHE, 1998; Engstrom & Tinto, 2000; Fried, 2000; Hyman, 1995; Keeling, 2004; Kezar, 2001; Kezar & Lester, 2009; Martin & Murphy, 2000; Potter, 1999; Schroeder, 1999a, 1999b). Partnerships have the capacity to create a seamless learning environment—settings in which in-class and out-of-classroom experiences are mutually supporting and in which institutional resources are marshaled and channeled to achieve complementary learning outcomes (Nesheim et al., 2007). Partnering can improve student outcomes, enhance service, better capitalize on resources, create better decisions, improve graduation rates, enhance retention, revive undergraduate education, improve institutional communication, create a culture of trust and better campus relationships, increase student satisfaction, and improve organizational functioning and service, for example, more effective advising (Engstrom & Tinto, 2000; Schroeder, 1999a, 1999b; Schuh & Whitt, 1999).

Although the logic has been developing for years, we now have much greater research support and evidence that partnerships live up to their suggested benefits. For example, recent research by Kuh, Kinzie, Schuh, and Whitt (2005; 2011) found that shared responsibility for educational quality and student success is related to stronger levels of student engagement. Although earlier research suggested that collaborations and partnerships would increase student learning, we now have research that has found a relationship between the use of partnerships and higher levels of student engagement, which is a proxy for student learning. Also, a variety of studies have been conducted on specific types of programs and partnerships that academic and student affairs work on together. For example, research on learning communities—a collaboration between academic and student affairs administration—demonstrates they produce improved learning outcomes and improve retention (Smith & McCann, 2001; Westfall, 1999). First-year interest groups help to improve retention (Schroeder, Minor, & Tarkow, 1999). Programs designed jointly between academic and student affairs to retain special populations such as African American or low-income students have shown greater success than programs designed by one unit (Jackson, Levine, & Patton, 2000; Williams & Wilson, 1993).

Much attention has been given to the way collaborations improve student outcomes, but there is also research about its organizational benefits. One of the most important studies, conducted by Bensimon and

Neumann (1993), found that working collaboratively in cross-functional teams creates cognitive complexity, innovation, and learning between units and improves organizational functioning. Cognitive complexity relates to the ability of decision makers to come up with better decisions because they have more perspectives to bring to bear on an issue. In their research, campuses that drew on the expertise across units that typically do not work together were able to make better decisions that increased the organizational functioning of the campus. These teams also use the expertise from diverse areas to inform each other, creating organizational learning and improving functioning on other tasks and activities. This learning (a result of bringing together perspectives that are not usually coalesced) also led to innovation within in the partnership itself as well as innovation on a campus more generally.

Another outcome or benefit of collaboration is that it creates better service within a college (Schroeder, 1999a). Although organizations set up individual units to handle and manage a discrete set of activities, processes cut across organizational units. Because information is shared among offices and communication is open, each office has a better chance of serving the students and helping them understand what other office they need to interact with to resolve a problem. This also helps to address student concerns more quickly, creating greater efficiency as well as effectiveness. It is important to create a strong customer service environment, especially in light of calls for greater accountability on campus. See chapter 5 for a discussion of pressures for greater accountability in higher education.

Knowledge of the recent research in support of collaboration can be helpful on any specific campus. In fact, one of the most cited reasons for successful collaboration is leaders who are knowledgeable and can articulate the benefits of partnerships (Schroeder, 1999b; Westfall, 1999). Recognizing that many campuses have overcome these formidable challenges and engage in multiple partnerships between academic and student affairs should provide inspiration to those campuses early in their journey to collaboration. Also, research results demonstrate that one successful collaboration leads to others (Kezar, 2001). You may have skeptical colleagues on your campus who resist collaboration between student affairs and academic affairs or who have been involved in unsuccessful attempts at collaboration between the two. However, sharing the compelling logic of collaboration and the recent research evidence with colleagues can help even those who have had a negative experience to envision a different outcome and to try again.

Reflection 3: Fortuitous Timing

Culture is never static. As student affairs leaders have been focusing on how their work can relate more directly to student learning and the importance of partnering, faculty and academic affairs leaders have been engaged in a variety of changes that makes them much more amenable to partnerships. For example, many faculty are involved in a variety of teaching and research activities that are more collaborative, such as interdisciplinarity, team teaching, service learning, action or participatory research (in which faculty partner with other groups such as community members to conduct research) (Kezar, Chambers, & Burkhardt, 2005). Also, academic administrators are trying to determine ways to create greater collaboration among faculty members through research institutes, interdisciplinary departments, and multidisciplinary teaching configurations. Academic leaders have also been reading about the importance of cross-functional teams and reconfiguring operations to have deans and department chairs work together on a more ongoing basis. Many of the recent publications and books for academic administrators have challenged the siloed organization of college campuses and advocated for more collaborative forms of work (Ferren & Stanton, 2004; Kezar & Lester, 2009). Incentive and reward systems are changing on some campuses to encourage more collaboration and cooperative endeavors (Diamond, Bronwyn, & Adam, 2004).

Beyond these changes in academic culture, broader changes in higher education necessitate continued focus and emphasis on academic and student affairs partnerships. The effects of the recession of 2008 were felt by higher education institutions for years after the recession officially ended (Oliff, Palacios, Johnson, & Leachman, 2013; Zumeta, 2010). Colleges and universities continue to cut budgets in response to the greatest financial downturn in recent years. In conjunction with tightening budgets, "government and philanthropic organizations exhort the enterprise to confer more degrees to insure a vibrant democracy, keep the country's economy competitive, and prepare the current and next generation of college students for an ever-expanding global workplace" (Kuh et al., 2011, p. 13), all for less cost than in previous years. Despite these pressures, Kuh et al. found that campuses that held steady in their commitment to collaboration across the campus were able to sustain effective educational practices and were better able to weather these difficult times.

State and federal governments and major foundations have made significant commitments in recent years to increase graduation and retention rates; these draw attention to the need for stronger academic and student affairs partnerships. Examples include President Barack Obama's 2020 College Completion Goal plan, which intends to double the number of American college students, and efforts such as the Lumina Foundation's Goal 2025 to increase the percentage of Americans with high-quality degrees and credentials to 60 percent by 2025. To meet these ambitious goals, higher education needs to respond and change in new ways, as there is limited, if any, new funding coming to incentivize such growth. Collaboration among units is a central way to further these goals, as we know collaboration tends to increase student success. Divisions will need to work together to develop solutions, including greater use of technology, to deliver education and support students.

Reflection 4: Collaboration Is Deepening

In the past, most partnering occurred around orientation or advising and was limited in scope (Kezar, 2001). For example, campuses recognized the need to coordinate services for first-year students. Staff from both academic and student affairs broke traditional work boundaries and partnered to offer orientation programming and worked together to develop the overall program. More recently, student affairs has played a partnership role in important curricular programs, including first-year experience seminars, learning communities, living and learning environments, service learning, senior capstone, citizenship education, intergroup dialogues, and leadership. All of these curricular innovations have been demonstrated to improve student learning and are gaining in popularity on campuses across the country. This movement from semi-structured to structured interactions is indication that partnerships are deepening and leading to stronger partnerships (Streit et al., 2009). This section of the chapter details three of these curricular programs: first-year seminars, service learning, and learning communities. More detail on these curricular innovations can be found in a variety of texts (see Jacoby, 1996; Kezar, 1999; Schuh & Whitt, 1999).

On many campuses, first-year experience seminars emerged exclusively in either student or academic affairs. If they emerged in student affairs, they were often in the form of noncredit courses that were offered optionally and that focused on issues of time management, social involvement, and study skills. First-year seminars that emerged in academic affairs focused on a particular content area, such as understanding human experience, and brought in content from psychology, sociology, and anthropology. They also included information relevant to first-year students, such as evaluating the status of their own psychosocial development during their first year of college. More recently, a variety of campuses recognize the need for academic and student affairs to partner and offer the course jointly, utilizing the expertise of both groups. Often these courses are team taught by both a student affairs staff member and a faculty member. Courses try to combine goals from both models of first-year experience seminars, such as the purpose of a liberal arts education, general education and majors, career exploration, study skills, psychosocial development, and life skills in college, such as financial education.

Another example of a curricular partnership that is being institutionalized on many campuses is service learning. Similar to first-year experience programs, service-learning programs have evolved on some campuses exclusively within student affairs (usually taking more of a volunteerism approach) or academic affairs (tied more directly to the curriculum). However, on campuses that have recognized the power of collaboration, student affairs staff work directly with faculty members to offer service learning. Student affairs staff work with academic affairs providing training on reflection, helping establish relationships with community agencies, leading sessions in the residence halls connecting the service work to their life experiences, working on transportation and logistics, helping connect faculty members across campus who are conducting similar work, and bringing together faculty to share techniques. Faculty work with student affairs staff to amend their curricula, develop new syllabi, learn reflection and journaling activities, and connect students with other types of service activities beyond their specific class. These partnerships enhance the service learning experience for the student, as students have a better opportunity to connect the curricular experience with their co-curricular and life experiences. As a result, service becomes more prevalent throughout their learning experience.

Learning communities are another curricular innovation that student affairs is creating jointly with academic affairs. Learning communities take a variety of forms, but their essential feature is that they intentionally group students together (by matched schedules, living and learning environments, or linked courses with common themes) so that students have the opportunity to work with the same group over time and engage in out-of-classroom conversations and activities. Campuses that partner to offer learning communities often incorporate a residential component. Students enroll in a set of similar courses, and faculty encourage students to extend the conversation into the dining hall or residence hall to create a seamless intellectual experience. In addition, faculty often attend social events or dinners within the residence hall and connect with students outside of class time and in more informal settings. Residential staff become familiar with the content of the courses, offer programming within the residence halls that relates to class topics, and invite faculty to social and programmatic events. A synergy between the learning in and out of classroom creates an extremely powerful learning experience.

Another critical finding in the literature on partnerships is that recommendations are specific to the type of curricular program being developed. For example, developing a partnership in service learning will be slightly different from developing a partnership in learning communities (Kezar, 2001; Schuh & Whitt, 1999). Therefore, reading the literature on the specific type of partnership to be created is important. For information on creating a service-learning partnership, read Jacoby (1999).

After reading the specific literature, identify model programs or institutions and contact them for advice. As Westfall (1999) notes, "Talk with colleagues engaged in similar work at sister institutions. This helps identify potential landmines, provides practical examples of success and broadens the range of realistic options open to your campus" (p. 60).

The need to obtain information cannot be emphasized enough. Most campuses still coordinate service rather than collaborate because true partnerships require intensive planning and fail without careful coordination. So, conducting some background work can make the process much easier. There are now hundreds of models to examine. Senior administrators should take their staff on field trips to other campuses. Staff members should be encouraged to conduct Internet research and talk to people on other campuses. All staff and faculty should read about partnerships they are interested in creating. Knowing key areas of collaboration that have worked at hundreds of colleges and universities across the country to create seamless learning helps leaders to determine where to focus their efforts.

Action Steps

There are several action steps that will enable student affairs leaders to form rich partnerships with faculty and academic administrators on their campuses. Four of these are described in this section.

1. Start with a Problem and Success Area

Various scholars (Hirsch & Burack, 2001; Schroeder, 1999b) with experience working on collaboration or helping campuses to form partnerships, such as the New England Resource Center for Higher Education (NERCHE), have noted the importance of beginning the process of collaboration by identifying a problem to be solved that crosses traditional organizational boundaries. These problems become opportunities to bring people across campus to work together because they represent fundamentally different challenges that are difficult for an individual unit to resolve. Schroeder (1999b) describes his experience scouting for problems to be solved at his institution that became opportunities for collaboration: achieving general education outcomes, improving graduation rates, developing learning communities, responding to institutional accrediting agencies' mandates, fostering civic leadership, or enhancing the success of special populations. An identified problem can become a common reference point and help to create a shared vision for undergraduate education or addressing institutional problems (Schroeder, 1999a). Areas in which collaboration between academic affairs and student affairs might occur include recruitment and retention (Hirsch & Burack, 2001; Kezar, 2001; and Schroeder 1996b); understanding changes in the student body, student beliefs, and student behavior; and responding to the needs of students who are active duty military, reservists, or veterans (Moon & Schema, 2011).

Research also demonstrates that beginning with programs or activities in which there has been a history of some coordination, such as orientation or first-year programs, can be a very successful strategy (Kezar, 2001). Kezar's (2001) national survey found that campuses were most successful with partnerships when they began with an area that already had some coordination of service. The survey also found that areas of coordination differed by institutional type. Community college leaders are much more likely to coordinate on academic advising, while academics in private four-year institutions are working with student affairs on community service learning. Areas in which there is already some common work provide a platform for moving to more and deeper partnerships.

2. Leadership for Success, Top-Down and Bottom-Up

Over the past few decades, scholars and practitioners have put energy into providing a vision for what collaboration can look like. Recent research suggests a variety of proven principles for helping to initiate and sustain partnerships on campus (Kezar, 2001).

Not surprisingly, institutional leadership from both academic and student affairs is necessary to ensure that partnerships are successful (Kezar, 2001). Senior administrators provide resources, a sense of priority, staffing, capacity to hire new staff, and philosophical support. Leaders also help to initiate the various strategies (described in the next section) that initiate and sustain partnerships. Thus, developing senior administrative support is a first critical step. If calls for collaboration are not coming from the top, then staff members need to meet with and garner senior administrative support (usually the senior student affairs and academic affairs officers). Without this support, success can be very difficult. However, leadership does not just entail senior administrative support but also requires champions who will work to nurture and sustain the partnership over the years (Schroeder, 1999a and b). This means that leadership is not just limited to the senior administration. Research has identified strategies for grassroots leadership that can either initiate or complement efforts on campus (Kezar & Lester, 2011). In this section, we highlight both the top-down and bottom-up approaches to supporting collaboration.

Top-Down Leadership. What exactly do senior leaders do to effectively support partnerships and collaboration? First, it is important for leaders to examine their own assumptions about collaboration in order to develop a vision or philosophy related to collaborative work. If leaders have not thought through the advantages of collaboration and when collaboration works best, motivating others to work collaboratively can be difficult. As mentioned earlier, leaders who are in the process of developing a vision or philosophy related to collaborative work can employ ideas such as reading groups and key documents.

Collaboration often involves a shifting of resources and, at times, additional resources. Groups on campus can only get so far if they do not have the appropriate resources to initiate the partnership activities. On many campuses you hear stories about well-meaning senior administrators who talk about their support for the collaboration, but when it comes time for the budget process do not allocate appropriate funding. Leaders need to make sure that the resources exist for partnerships to succeed (Schroeder, 1999b).

Senior administrators can also establish rewards and incentives for staff to engage in partnerships and collaboration (Keeling, 2004). Many campuses that are successful at collaboration have modified their employee evaluation forms to include involvement in collaborative projects. In addition, bonuses and merit increases are tied to supporting new collaborative initiatives. Leaders also create motivation by signaling partnership as a priority. At campuswide and divisional meetings, senior administrators should discuss the importance of collaboration and partnerships to let people know they take this seriously. Last, motivation can be created through evaluation processes in which leaders set expectations about how roles and responsibilities are structured. In these meetings, they can stress the importance of collaborative work and help to brainstorm ways to be successful in this work.

Leadership also has the ability to hire new staff (Kezar, 2001). On many campuses with successful partnerships, one or two strategic hires were critical to help move the partnership forward. These new employees may come from a campus that has already been successful with partnerships or are individuals who have enthusiasm for collaborative work. Furthermore, senior administrators can be open to various restructuring plans that might emerge from staff that can better support collaborative endeavors (Keeling, 2004).

Senior administrators are also pivotal in making sure that partnerships and collaborative efforts are assessed. As many scholars have pointed out, if partnerships are not assessed and their value established, they will be subject to losing funding in times of tight resources (Bourassa & Kruger, 2001; Keeling, 2004; Kezar, 2001; Schroeder, 1999b; Schuh, 1999). Increasingly, campuses are examining their processes of measuring student outcomes. The good news is that many campuses are conducting outcomes assessment of academic and student affairs collaboration; in fact, 45 percent of the campuses polled nationally were conducting some form of outcomes assessment; most assessments focused on institutional effectiveness, but some also examined student learning and development (Kezar, 2001). We need more data on specifically how collaboration improves student learning and development to ensure that it will be supported in the future in light of funding constraints and accountability (see chapters 4 and 5 of this volume).

Bottom-Up Leadership. Grassroots leaders are individuals who do not have formal positions of authority, are operating from the bottom up, and are interested in and pursue organizational changes that often challenge the status quo of the institution (Kezar & Lester, 2011). New professionals in student affairs as well as midlevel staff are grassroots leaders, and on some campuses even those with titles of directors or associate directors may be grassroots leaders if they have limited formal authority on campus for hiring, budgets, and other strategies described in the previous section. The work of grassroots leaders differs considerably from that of individuals in formal positions of authority. As noted earlier, individuals who hold formal positions benefit from structures to enact leadership through rewards, established networks, committees, formal responsibilities, and delegating authority. Grassroots leaders typically create their own structures, networks, and support systems in order to garner change and make collaboration part of the fabric of their institutions. Grassroots leaders tend to work collectively, in informal ways, work to obtain buy-in from their colleagues, and often take longer to create changes because they lack the formal structures that can create a sense of priority and shift people's direction.

Several strategies can support grassroots leadership on campus to allow for greater collaboration among academic and student affairs practitioners (Kezar & Lester, 2009). First, not all staff and faculty recognize the benefits of collaboration, and based on the type of collaboration, grassroots leaders need to evoke the logic of why collaboration is important in order to educate their peers and often their superiors. The process of educating those in positions of authority is called "managing up." Grassroots leaders can send articles about collaboration and its benefits and ability to meet institutional goals and priorities to their supervisors. Also, pointing to successful collaborations from earlier can remind people of its value. Campus leaders might not know about a successful orientation or service-learning program jointly offered because it preceded their tenure. Again, grassroots leaders are well served by exploiting areas of success.

Second, it is important to identify supportive individuals on campus who can help break down barriers to collaboration across academic and student affairs. For student affairs practitioners, these are often supervisors who have the necessary social capital and networks on campus to connect staff with others across campus. This allows practitioners to learn from one another about strategies and best practices for pursuing collaboration on their own campus. Attending national conferences is another strategy to gain social capital, overcome barriers, and develop a network—albeit an external one. Ideally, staff would use both of these strategies to broaden their ability to create collaboration through an expanded knowledge base.

Student affairs grassroots leaders can also harness their work with students to support collaboration. Nothing is more compelling to administrators than having a major constituent group like students support an initiative. Working with students is a form of coalition building by aligning with a group that has power on many campuses. Students are likely to be supportive of sustainability, technology, diversity, and student success efforts, for example. Although the amount of power students have varies by campus, in our increasingly consumer-oriented world, students are more and more seen as a voice that cannot be ignored in planning the educational experience. Because student affairs staff typically have a close connection with students, mentoring them about the advantages of certain collaborative arrangements on campus will encourage students to support collaboration when they speak formally through student government or as representatives on campus task forces or committees, or informally as student leaders when meeting with administrators.

Staff can collect and use data to garner support for a collaborative initiative. For example, for a sustainability initiative, staff might garner data from the Association for the Advancement of Sustainability in Higher Education about the carbon footprint of comparable campuses and compare it to their own campus to provide a compelling case for the need to start an initiative. Data help raise consciousness about an issue's importance, mobilize action, and garner support. Finally, utilizing campus networks can contribute to academic and student affairs partnerships. Although a single office or department might have limited resources or personnel, the collective student affairs division can serve as a helpful venue to share resources and increase connections in order to connect with the academic affairs side of the institution. Making connections with other individuals and offices enhances grassroots leaders' abilities to activate a collaborative initiative. In general, building relationships facilitates collaboration. Leaders at any level can build relationships on an ongoing basis that can later serve to foster collaboration.

3. Attend to Culture, People, and Planning

In addition to identifying a problem or issue and providing leadership, there are a variety of strategies that can be used to initiate partnerships between academic and student affairs. Key strategies identified in the literature and research include encouraging cross-institutional dialogue, setting expectations, generating enthusiasm, creating a common vision, promoting staff development, hiring new people committed to collaboration, examining personalities, choosing the right people as partners, and planning (Kezar, 2001; Kuh, 1996). Underlying these various strategies are three main principles: attend to culture and values, get the right people, and be intentional in planning.

Culture and Values. Campuses that have successful collaborations between academic and student affairs create opportunities for cross-institutional dialogue (Hirsch & Burack, 2001; Kezar, 2001; Kuh, 1996; Schroeder, 1999a, 1999b). The cross-boundary work described earlier (in areas such as technology, changing student demographics, general education, and student retention) represents areas that interest individuals across campus and can be used as opportunities for cross-campus dialogue. In addition, the areas noted as benefits of collaboration (such as creating seamless learning or improved service) and research demonstrating the success of collaborations are issues that can be used to begin dialogue among groups that can result in collaboration. Dialogue leads directly into the next two strategies: creating a common vision and generating enthusiasm for collaboration. Cross-campus dialogue helps people to understand each other's values and work toward a shared vision of seamless learning. It can be helpful if someone writes a concept paper outlining the goals and benefits of a particular collaboration, helping people to see more concretely the direction to head. These dialogues also generate enthusiasm and create champions or change agents for the initiative that help to provide buy-in from others. More structured and formal collaborations (Streit et al., 2009) require even more attention to values and culture because the more formal collaborations require greater changes in and support from the culture to be successful.

People. After discussion, creation of a common vision, and the development of champions, the next step is to get the right people in place or to work with existing staff to develop the skills to collaborate effectively. As mentioned earlier, campuses successful in developing partnerships often hired new people who were committed to collaboration to lead one or more efforts. Although this strategy can be used by senior administrators, it can also be used at other levels of the organization to generate enthusiasm for a collaborative effort. Since the new staff already understand the importance of collaboration, they help other employees to develop a shared vision. However, the opportunity to hire is not always available, so staff development can be another option. Sending staff to NASPA, ACPA, American Association of Colleges and Universities (AAC&U), and other conferences that describe the importance of collaboration can open their eyes to new ways of doing work. In addition, human resources offices on campus sometimes offer leadership training that emphasizes collaboration.

Collaboration also requires committees that initiate the partnership. In creating these cross-functional committees, careful attention needs to be paid to the personalities and experiences of the people involved. A single individual can upset the best-laid plans. Therefore, composition of committees needs to be carefully considered: Does this person have experience with collaboration? Does this person share in the common vision of the project? Has the person been involved with cross-campus dialogues? Is this person likely to generate more enthusiasm and talk to others about the project? Are there any historical or political circumstances that would make the appointment of this person problematic?

Planning. Last, even with discussion, enthusiasm, and the right people on board, without intentional and careful planning and implementation, partnerships often fail (Kezar, 2001; Schroeder, 1999b; Schuh & Whitt, 1999). Members of the planning team need to move from a shared vision to specific goals, strategies, and an implementation plan. Habits are extremely hard to break, and a planning process reminds people on an ongoing basis that the nature of work is changing. Dialogues can assist people in reconsidering their values, but the hard work of changing day-to-day work and responsibilities is better enabled by a planning process (tied to evaluation and merit pay) that holds people accountable for new behaviors. Therefore, planning is only as effective as the accountability structures and expectations that are put in place to follow up on goals. Again, more structured or formal collaborations require even more planning to ensure that the right structures, roles, and accountability structures are in place to make it last over the long term (Streit et al., 2009).

4. Sustaining Partnerships

Once the collaboration is up and going, a leader's work is not complete; leaders (whether positional or grassroots) need to evaluate, provide feedback mechanisms, and be observant of group dynamics. Campuses need to make sure that they provide mechanisms to sustain and institutionalize the partnership. One of the key strategies for ensuring that partnerships are successful is to evaluate the effort (Schuh, 1999). Evaluation should examine both the process and outcomes. In terms of the process, evaluations should examine whether the right people are included, whether there are clear decision-making structures, whether there are appropriate feedback mechanisms and communication channels, whether they have the appropriate structures and resources (both financial and human), whether both student affairs and academic affairs are involved, and whether there is a balance in perspective between academic and student affairs. Through these evaluations, leaders and senior administrators can provide necessary resources and direction to continue the success of the partnership. An evaluation should examine student learning outcomes. In particular, questions should determine whether the students' learning process appeared seamless and whether the specific goals that were developed for the partnership were met. This approach to assessment can be intentionally included in any planning, especially in more structured forms of interaction and collaboration (Streit et al., 2009)

Evaluation is one form of obtaining feedback, but less formal processes can be used as well. Some examples include reflection on the work through online surveys or pulling aside a few members to obtain input on the process. As Fuller and Haugabrook (2001) note, "Much of the actual work of collaboration boils down to team building and attending to the individual relationships beyond the larger partnerships. A member of a collaborative team's unaddressed concerns can stall the whole project if not dealt with effectively. Mechanisms for feedback need to be part of the system and stakeholders should feel that they have opportunities to express their ideas or take the lead in aspects of the project for which they have particular expertise" (p. 85).

One of the major areas that can destroy collaborations and partnerships is dysfunctional group dynamics. Several resources on intergroup dynamics should be given to chairs or facilitators of partnerships to ensure that they have skills in mediating intergroup dynamics and conflict (Bensimon & Neumann, 1993; Parker, 1990). Evaluation, feedback, and attention to intergroup dynamics ensure that communication channels are open, helping to avoid collisions of culture between student and academic affairs. Also, if a staff member leaves a partnership, leaders may need to step in to attend meetings until the position is filled. Once the replacement is hired, leaders can also help the new person to transition onto the team. Many partnerships fall apart when key staff leave and interpersonal dynamics become strained, partly because trust is low when new people join the group. Trying to incorporate more unstructured means of interaction among key stakeholders could contribute to building these relationships, leading to more structured collaborations (Streit et al., 2009). Leaders need to be aware that these are key times to step in and be more involved.

Conclusion

Although Barr (1997) reminds us that collaboration has been part of the student affairs field since its origin, marked change in philosophy and practice has occurred in recent years. Student affairs sees itself as an equal partner in student learning and development. Thousands of individual partnerships exist, and models continue to be developed on campuses and replicated on other campuses. Partnerships between academic and student affairs are no longer a passing fad or hope; they are now an organizational reality with hundreds of different examples. However, many of the existing partnerships involve coordination rather than deeper forms of collaboration, which is still relatively rare. The models of deep partnerships, as highlighted in documents such as *Powerful Partnerships* (AAHE, ACPA, & NASPA, 1998), continue to evolve. These deep partnerships require careful leadership and attention; otherwise, they fail or do not manifest the anticipated benefits. Although coordination is helpful, true collaboration is transformative for students. We need more courageous leaders who will make collaboration a priority, knowing it is best for students.

The ideas we have discussed in this chapter are very applicable to existing models of higher education. However, we are on the precipice of potentially deep change in higher education. Christensen and Eyring (2011), in their book on disruptive innovation and higher education, point to trends that may fundamentally change the ways in which higher education institutions operate. These trends include the rise in online universities and programs, emerging new technologies to contribute to teaching and learning, and educational institutions created around competency-based frameworks. These trends hold the potential to change the ways in which higher education institutions operate and function. Although we do not fully know what the future holds, we acknowledge that higher education leaders need to adapt to these changes and be intentional in the ways in which academic and student affairs partnerships are formed and sustained. It is our hope that the reflections and strategies described in this chapter will provide guidance in this evolving landscape.

What we do know is that collaboration is not only transformative for students but also for student and academic affairs divisions. As academic and student affairs work together more closely, their values and philosophies will likely be changed. After working closely with student affairs, deans of academic units often start to question the "sink or swim" approach to education and "weeder" courses. They begin to set up peer-mentoring programs or faculty and student affairs social hours to create better relationships between the groups. And many deans of students, after working more closely with academic affairs, examine the learning outcomes of their co-curricular programs or incorporate ideas from the book assigned by academic affairs to all incoming students into leadership programs (Kezar, 2001). Both academic and student affairs can be transformed into units that are more aligned to the overall goal of supporting student success in learning.

References

American Association for Higher Education, American College Personnel Association, & National Association of Student Personnel Administrators. (1998). *Powerful partnerships: A shared responsibility for learning*. Washington, DC: Author.

American College Personnel Association. (1994). *The student learning imperative: Implications for student affairs*. Washington, DC: Author.

Barr, M. J. (1997). *Student affairs collaborations and partnerships: Our future challenges*. Greensboro, NC: ERIC Counseling and Student Services Clearinghouse.

Bensimon, E. M., & Neumann, A. (1993). *Redesigning collegiate leadership: Teams and teamwork in higher education*. Baltimore, MD: Johns Hopkins University Press.

Bloland, P. A. (1997). *Strengthening learning for students: Student affairs collaborations and partnerships*. Greensboro, NC: ERIC Counseling and Student Services Clearinghouse.

Bourassa, D. M., & Kruger, K. (2001). The national dialogue on academic and student affairs collaboration. In A. J. Kezar, D. J. Hirsch, & C. Burack (Eds.), *Understanding the role of academic and student affairs collaboration in creating a successful learning environment*. New Directions for Higher Education, no. 116. San Francisco, CA: Jossey-Bass.

Christensen, C. M., & Eyring, H. J. (2011). *The innovative university: Changing the DNA of higher education from the inside out*. San Francisco, CA: Jossey-Bass.

Diamond, R. M., Bronwyn, S., & Adam, E. (2004). Balancing institutional, disciplinary and faculty priorities with public and social needs: Defining scholarship for the 21st century. *Arts and Humanities in Higher Education, 3*(1), 29–40.

Eckel, P., Kezar, A., & Lieberman, D. (1999). Learning for organizing: Institutional reading groups as a strategy for change. *AAHE Bulletin, 25*(3), 6–8.

Engstrom, C. M., & Tinto, V. (2000). Developing partnerships with academic affairs to enhance student learning. In M. J. Barr, M. K. Desler, & Associates (Eds.), *The handbook of student affairs administration* (2nd ed., (pp. 425-452). San Francisco, CA: Jossey-Bass.

Ferren, A. S., & Stanton, W. W. (2004). *Leadership through collaboration: The role of the chief academic officer.* Westport, CT: American Council on Education/Praeger.

Fried, J. (2000). *Steps to creative campus collaboration.* Washington, DC: National Association of Student Personnel Administrators.

Fuller, T.M.A., & Haugabrook, A. K. (2001). Facilitative strategies in action. In A. J. Kezar, D. J. Hirsch, & C. Burack (Eds.), *Understanding the role of academic and student affairs collaboration in creating a successful learning environment.* New Directions for Higher Education, no. 116. San Francisco, CA: Jossey-Bass.

Guthrie, K. L. (2012). Coordinating services to seamless learning: Evolution of institutional partnerships. In K. M. Boyle, J. W. Lowery, & J. A. Mueller (Eds.), *Reflections on the 75th anniversary of the student personnel point of view* (pp. 57-61). Washington, DC: American College Personnel Association.

Hagadoorn, J. (1993). Understanding the rationale of strategic partnering: Interorganizational modes of cooperation and sectoral differences. *Strategic Management Journal, 14,* 371–385.

Hirsch, D. J., & Burack, C. (2001). Finding points of contact for collaborative work. In A. J. Kezar, D. J. Hirsch, & C. Burack (Eds.), *Understanding the role of academic and student affairs collaboration in creating a successful learning environment.* New Directions for Higher Education, no. 116. San Francisco, CA: Jossey-Bass.

Hyman, R. E. (1995). Creating campus partnerships for student success. *College and University, 72*(2), 2–8.

Jackson, B., Levine, J., & Patton, J. (2000). *Restructuring for urban student success: Essay collection.* Indianapolis, IN: Restructuring for Success.

Jacoby, B. (1996). *Service-learning in higher education: Concepts and practices.* San Francisco, CA: Jossey-Bass.

Jacoby, B. (1999). Partnerships for service learning. In J. H. Schuh & E. J. Whitt (Eds.), *Creating successful partnerships between academic and student affairs.* New Directions for Student Services, no. 87. San Francisco, CA: Jossey-Bass.

Keeling, R. P. (Ed.). (2004). *Learning reconsidered: A campus-wide focus on the student experience.* Washington, DC: National Association of Student Personnel Administrators & the American College Personnel Association.

Kezar, A. (Ed.). (1999). *Early intervention for college programs: A collection of research to inform policy and practice.* Advances in Education Research, no. 4. Washington DC: Government Printing Office for the National Library of Education.

Kezar, A. (2001). Organizational models and facilitators of change: Providing a framework for student and academic affairs collaboration. In A. J. Kezar, D. J. Hirsch, & C. Burack (Eds.), *Understanding the role of academic and student affairs collaboration in creating a successful learning environment.* New Directions for Higher Education, no. 116. San Francisco, CA: Jossey-Bass.

Kezar, A., Chambers, T., & Burkhardt, J. (Eds.). (2005). *Higher education for the public good: Emerging voices from a national movement.* San Francisco, CA: Jossey-Bass.

Kezar, A., Hirsch, D., & Burack, C. (Eds.). (2001). *Understanding the role of academic and student affairs collaboration in creating a successful learning environment.* New Directions for Higher Education, no. 116. San Francisco, CA: Jossey-Bass.

Kezar, A. J., & Lester, J. (2009). *Organizing higher education for collaboration: A guide for campus leaders.* San Francisco, CA: Jossey-Bass.

Kezar, A. J., & Lester, J. (2011). *Enhancing campus capacity for leadership: An examination of grassroots leaders in higher education.* San Francisco, CA: Jossey-Bass.

Knefelkamp, L. L. (1991). *The seamless curriculum: Is this good for our students?* Washington, DC: Council for Independent Colleges.

Kolins, C. A. (1999). *An appraisal of collaboration: Assessing perceptions of chief academic and student affairs officers at public two-year colleges. Unpublished doctoral dissertation.* University of Toledo.

Kuh, G. D. (1996). Guiding principles for creating seamless learning environments for undergraduates. *Journal of College Student Development, 37*(2), 135–148.

Kuh, G. D. (1999). Setting the bar high to promote student learning. In G. S. Blimling & E. J. Whitt (Eds.), *Good practice in student affairs* (pp. 67-89). San Francisco, CA: Jossey-Bass.

Kuh, G. D., Kinzie, J. Schuh, J. H., & Whitt, E. J. (2011). Fostering student success in hard times. *Change: The Magazine of Higher Learning, 43*(4), 13–19.

Kuh, G. D., Kinzie, J., Schuh. J. H., & Whitt, E. J. (2005). *Student success in college: Creating conditions that matter.* San Francisco, CA: Jossey-Bass.

Lockwood, A. T. (1996). *School-community collaboration.* Washington, DC: Office of Educational Research and Improvement.

Martin, J., & Murphy, S. (2000). *Building a better bridge: Creating effective partnerships between academic affairs and student affairs.* Washington, DC: National Association of Student Personnel Administrators.

Moon, T. L., & Schma, G. A. (2011). A proactive approach to serving military students. In J. B. Hodson, & B. W. Speck (Eds.), *Entrepreneurship in student services.* New Directions for Higher Education, no. 153. San Francisco, CA: Jossey-Bass.

Nesheim, B. E., Guentzel, M. J., Kellogg, A. H., McDonald, W. M., Wells, C. A., & Whitt, E. J. (2007). Outcomes for Students and student affairs-academic affairs partnership programs. *Journal of College Student Development, 48*(4), 435–454.

Oliff, P., Palacios, V., Johnson, I., & Leachman, M. (2013). *Recent deep state higher education cuts may harm students and the economy for years to come.* Washington, D.C: Center on Budget and Policy Priorities.

Parker, G. (1990). *Team players and teamwork.* San Francisco, CA: Jossey-Bass.

Potter, D. L. (1999). Where powerful partnerships begin. *About Campus, 4*(2), 11–16.

Schroeder, C. C. (1999a). Collaboration and partnerships. In C. S. Johnson, & H. E. Cheatham (Eds.), *Higher Education trends for the next century: A research agenda for student success* (pp. 43-50). Washington, DC: American College Personnel Association.

Schroeder, C. C. (1999b). Forging educational partnerships that advance student learning. In G. S. Blimling & E. J. Whitt (Eds.), *Good practice in student affairs* (pp. 133-157). San Francisco, CA: Jossey-Bass.

Schroeder, C. C. (1999c). Partnerships: An imperative for enhancing student learning and institutional effectiveness. In S. A. McDade & P. H. Lewis (Eds.), *Developing administrative excellence: Creating a culture of leadership.* New Directions for Higher Education, no. 87. San Francisco, CA: Jossey-Bass.

Schroeder, C. C., Minor, F. D., & Tarkow, T. A. (1999). Learning communities: Partnerships between academic and student affairs. In J.H. Levine (Ed.), *Learning communities: New structures, new partnerships for learning* (pp. 59-69). National Resource Center for the First-Year Experience and Students in Transition. Columbia, SC: University of South Carolina.

Schuh, J. H. (1999). Guiding principles for evaluating student and academic affairs partnerships. In J. H. Schuh, & E. J. Whitt (Eds.), Creating successful partnerships between academics and student affairs. *New Directions for Student Services, no. 87.* San Francisco, CA: Jossey-Bass.

Schuh, J. H., & Whitt, E. J. (Eds.). (1999). Creating successful partnerships between academics and student affairs. *New Directions for Student Services, no. 87.* San Francisco, CA: Jossey-Bass.

Smith, B. L., & McCann, J. (Eds.). (2001). *Reinventing ourselves: Interdisciplinary education, collaborative learning and experimentation in higher education.* Bolton, MA: Anker.

Smith, D. G. (1982). The next step beyond student development: Becoming partners within our institutions. *NASPA Journal, 19*(4), 53–62.

Streit, M. R., Dalton, J. C., & Crosby, P. C. (2009). A campus audit of student affairs–faculty collaborations: From contacts to compacts. *Journal of College and Character, 10*(5), 1–14.

Task Force on the Future of Student Affairs. (2010). *Envisioning the future of student affairs.* Washington, DC: American College Personnel Association & National Association of Student Personnel Administrators.

Westfall, S. B. (1999). Partnerships to connect in- and out-of-class experiences. In J. H. Schuh & E. J. Whitt (Eds.), *Creating successful partnerships between academic and student affairs* (pp. 51-61). San Francisco, CA: Jossey-Bass.

Williams, J., & Wilson, V. C. (1993). Project C.A.R.E.: A university's commitment to African-American student retention. *College Student Affairs Journal, 13*(1), 48–57.

Zumeta, W. (2010). The great recession: Implications for higher education. In H. Wechsler (Ed.), *The NEA 2010 almanac of higher education* (pp.29-42). Washington, DC: National Education Association.

CHAPTER TWENTY-TWO

THE POLITICAL DIMENSIONS OF DECISION MAKING

Shannon Ellis

Tip O'Neill, former speaker of the United States House of Representatives, once observed, "All politics is local" (O'Neill & Hymel, 1994, p. 16); so too is decision making. O'Neill used this phrase to make the point that a politician's success is directly tied to the ability to understand and influence the issues of their constituents. Good decisions, effective decisions, one's that are fair and reasoned, that move an agenda ahead, that take into consideration the issues that matter most to the staff, the students, the surrounding community, and to the institution as a whole are an administrative legacy all student affairs professionals should aspire to leave their colleges or universities. Politics *and* decision making lay the foundation for administrative success through such political concepts as cultivating organizational relationships (Birnbaum, 1988), the ability to listen and act (Capelo & Dias, 2009), use of power and authority (Baldridge, 1971), understanding and influencing process (Ellis, 2012), identifying context and culture (Amey, Jessup-Anger, & Tingson-Gatuz, 2009), and, at the very heart of all administrative actions, knowing how to use decisions to get things done. Peter Drucker (1990) adds, "It's in the decision that everything comes together. That is the make or break point of the organization" (p. 121).

It is important for student affairs professionals to take politics into consideration when making decisions because politics affect the institutions where they work, the communities where they live, current and future colleagues, and the lives of tens of thousands of students and their families. Lee Bolman and Terrence Deal warn that "a jaundiced view of politics constitutes a serious threat to individual and organizational effectiveness" (2003, p. 181). To dismiss or avoid political dimensions is a mistake. *Mastering the connection between politics and decisions is the key.* "Student affairs leaders can enhance their effectiveness by learning how to consider issues through a political framework" (Stringer, 2009, p. 429).

Business management literature is prolific on the topic of politics and decision making. Many of higher education's ideas on politics and decision making come from studies of the private sector (Cohen, March & Olsen, 1972; Dean & Sharfman, 1996; Mintzberg, Raisinghani & Theoret, 1976; Zeleny,1982) as well as the social sciences (Capelo & Dias, 2009; Eggert & Bogeholz, 2010; Schwenk, 1984). There is now emerging more on politics and decision-making in the field of higher education and student affairs (Levy & Kozoll, 1998; Amey et al., 2009).

It is important to understand politics and decision making in the context of the student affairs profession because colleges and universities differ in many ways from other organizations (Baldridge, Curtis, Ecker, & Riley, 1971; Corson, 1960; Whetton, 1984). This chapter recognizes higher education's unique characteristics, the most significant being its governance: "the structure and processes through which institutional participants interact with an ability to influence each other and communicate with the larger environment" (Birnbaum, 1988, p. 4).

Stringer (2009) states, "Student affairs administrators who want to operate effectively need to find ways of integrating political principles into their administrative skill sets" (pp. 425–426). Experienced professionals recognize the truth of this statement, but for new student affairs professionals it can seem bewildering at best or anxiety inducing at the worst. This is "because new professionals are more likely to see themselves as counselors, programmers, or hall directors rather than as administrators, they do not always have the context for understanding and dealing with institutional challenges" (Amey et al., 2009, p. 16). McClellan (2013), in "Things I Didn't Learn in Graduate School," observes, "It has not been uncommon over the years for me to hear from new professionals who seem surprised by how political our work settings can be. They feel under prepared or overwhelmed in trying to gain competence in, if not mastery of, internal politics" (p. 7).

The goal of this chapter is to better understand the political dynamics of decision making so they can be managed in achieving individual and organizational goals. The political dimensions of decision making in student affairs are discussed. Key higher education decision making models are presented along with political frameworks. A discussion on how institutions of higher education are governed lays the foundation for understanding the entities and processes that provide a variety of means for decision-making across campus and within student affairs. The most important concepts for effective decision making in a higher education political environment are elaborated upon and emerging political considerations for making organizational decisions are explored in the context of student affairs administrative work. At the conclusion of this chapter, the limitations of taking a political view on decision making are set forth for balanced consideration. By understanding decision making and politics, we hope that readers will have a better understanding of why decisions get made the way they do and how to use this knowledge in their own professional responsibilities throughout their student affairs careers.

Developing a Political Mind-Set in Student Affairs

Collegial is the word most often used to describe the higher education environment. It conjures up images of a professional community of scholars with a round-table type of decision making in a utopian prescription of how the educational process should operate (Baldridge, 1971). Colleges and universities are family, with a history of ritual and tradition, in which civil discourse and the discovery of new knowledge transcends power and authority, negotiation over resource allocation, salaries, and titles. If this were ever true, it is no longer the culture, climate, and context of higher education in the United States. J. Victor Baldridge (1971) introduced a new political interpretation of university governance, acknowledging campus power struggles in conflict, political dynamics of community power, and the influence of informal groups with special interests.

All colleges and universities are political organizations. They vary in how susceptible they are to political behavior and, therefore, how much new student affairs professionals might be affected (Hirt, 2006). Political organizations are systems of social actions that in any way influence the making of binding value allocations for all. A political system is a framework that defines acceptable political methods within a given society.

In an era of declining resources for higher education, competition for enrolling the best students and hiring the best faculty and staff, increased calls for accountability and performance-measure funding, higher education institutions in the United States are "becoming arenas for coalition-building, win-lose games, ambiguous goals, and uneven power distribution" (Amey et al., 2009, p. 17). Recognizing already established connections, prior collaborations, and previous relationships is useful in navigating organizational politics. Student affairs professionals who understand the political dimensions of their institutions, divisions, and units and use the tools available to them will not only survive but also thrive as effective practitioners (Kuh, Siegel, & Thomas, 2001).

What Does It Mean to Be Political?

When discussing student affairs and political dimensions of decision making, one should consider three definitions associated with the word *politics*. The first is from the Greek word, *politicos*. Using Aristotle's definition, "it is the art or science of influencing people on a civic or individual level, when there are two or more people involved" (trans. 2000, p. 1). A second definition refers to politics in the broadest sense, as the activity through which people make, preserve, and amend the general rules under which they live. "A political system is any persistent pattern of human relationships that involves power, rule, or authority" (Dahl, 1964, p. 6). A third meaning is succinctly defined by the title of political scientist Harold Lasswell's 1936 book, *Politics: Who Gets What, When, and How.*

The imagery of politics is very helpful in understanding the operation of a college or university. There are forces both inside and out with pressure to manage the shifting demands in a higher education environment. According to Baldridge (1971), these internal and external groups emerge from the complex fragmented social structure of higher education and its publics drawing on divergent concerns and lifestyles of hundreds of miniature subcultures. These groups articulate their interests in many different ways, bringing pressure on the decision-making process from any number of angles and using power and force whenever it is available and necessary.

Decision-Making Models for Student Affairs

A decision involves a choice between two or more alternatives: whether to allow pets in the residence halls, when to end a long-standing program, to whom you should delegate an important project, or what budget to reduce so that another can be increased. Making a choice implies a commitment to the chosen alternative. A general framework for what constitutes a decision involves a choice, which requires alternatives that could be chosen. Each alternative is associated with a set of beliefs about the outcomes that are potentially associated with each alternative. Every outcome is associated with a value or preference. These three characteristics—alternatives, beliefs about outcomes, and values associated with these outcomes—provide a general framework for any decision (Hastie, 1986).

Models from Other Fields

The field of student affairs has readily and effectively adopted decision-making models from the fields of medicine, the military, and business, The medical field has a number of decision-making models for triage, diagnosis, and treatment that can be applied in higher education and student affairs (Kitchner & Anderson, 2011; Sonnenberg & Beck, 2008). The Military Decision Making Process (MDMP) (US Department of the Army, 2010) offers a highly structured seven-step process linked closely to decisions that achieve the organizational mission. Business decision-making models often focus on decision premises based on information available (March & Simon,1958), behavioral theory (Cyert & March,1963), data analysis (McAfee & Brynjolfsson, 2012), intuition linking knowledge, experience and emotions (Matzler, Bailom, & Mooradian, 2007), and ethics (Callahan, 1988).

Nonlinear Decision Making in Higher Education

One of the most accurate models refuting careful and calculated decision making is referred to as "garbage can decision-making" (Cohen, March, & Olsen, 1972). Cohen et al. note that higher education decision making is not simplistic, nor does it follow a linear, rational process. "The garbage can process is one in which problems, solutions, and participants move from one choice opportunity to another in such a way that the nature of the choice, the time it takes, and the problem it solves all depend on a relatively complicated intermeshing of elements" (Cohen et al., 1972, p. 16). Gary Klein's research on how people make decisions under emergency conditions, something common in the work of student affairs, discovered a nonlinear approach involving intuition and less rational means than traditional decision-making models (Kouzes & Posner, 2002).

Baldridge (1971) proposed a political process model for decision making that took into account political forces such as interest groups and bureaucracies, some of whom will engage in political struggles, pinpointing the legitimacy of the decision maker or the decision network because it influences the outcome, and bringing decisions to an end in an environment in which decisions can be confusing, unmade, or forgotten. This is realistic but complex within the loosely coordinated, fragmented political system of higher education.

A Linear Decision-Making Model

Most of us were taught to make decisions on a logical, rational basis by following an orderly process. "The concept of rationality assumes that people make decisions in the context of clearly defined environments" (Vaccaro, McCoy, Champagne & Siegel, 2013, p. 4). Many scholars and practitioners argue that rationality accounts for the emotional and political complexities used in real-life decision making (Cohen et al., 1972; Knighton, 2004; Mintzberg, Raisinghani, & Theoret, 1976; Zeleny, 1982).

Vaccarro et al. (2013) share a decision-making framework (DMF) specifically designed for new student affairs professionals. It is composed of three components: (1) four decision-making phases, (2) tasks, and (3) key questions and considerations. The four phases in the first component serve to identify the problem, scan the options, implement and assess. "The most important part of the effective decision is to ask: what is the decision really about? Very rarely is a decision about what it seems to be about" (Drucker, 1990, p. 121).

An example of being clear about the decision you are trying to make is obvious in budget-cutting scenarios across the country. "What do we cut?" is the wrong decision. The decision to make is "What do we absolutely keep?" or, even better, "What will be our signature programs that keep us on the pathway to our preferred future as a student affairs division and as an institution of higher education?" The decision isn't about the budget. It is about the future. "A decision is a commitment to action" (Drucker, 1990, p. 127).

Governance in Higher Education

If politics involves the authoritative allocation of values (Easton, 1953), a decision-making structure must be in place. The intersection of politics and decision making involves individuals and groups who are either decision makers or stakeholders. Because few decisions are made in total isolation from others, a political perspective involves relationship- and coalition-building as well as alliances and partnerships. All institutions are made up of individuals, of course, but institutions also have their own particular governance structures—legislatures, regents, trustees, administrators and various committees—and ways—laws, traditions and standard operating procedures for gathering information, assessing public opinion and taking action.

Governance in higher education is the way in which colleges and universities are operated. It refers to the structures and organization established to manage the increasingly complex business of the higher education institution from within and outside. Governing structures vary greatly in purpose, scope of authority, power and relationships. Despite this, they are the formal mechanisms for institutional decision making. What we mean by governance in higher education often depends on the level of analysis: national, local, institutional, subunit, or discipline level. The dynamics within each level and between levels differ according to political context (Amaral, Jones, & Karseth, 2002).

The literature provides a number of different conceptual models of governance: collegial (Millett, 1978), bureaucratic (Stroup, 1966), political (Baldridge, 1971), organized anarchy (Cohen & March, 1974), and professional (Mintzberg, 1979). The more recent literature adds to this list: entrepreneurial (Clark, 1998), service (Tjeldvoll, 1998), enterprise (Marginson & Considine, 2000), and corporate/managerial (Deem, 1998).

In earlier times, governing boards exercised full authority. Governance was the will of the board. But as institutions became more complex, boards delegated de facto authority to presidents. Faculty took on authority for curriculum and academic matters. As a result, different campus constituencies now assert their claim areas as primary decision makers in areas over which boards retain legal obligations and responsibility (Birnbaum, 1988). Faculty and administrators fill different roles, encounter and are influenced by different backgrounds. "As a consequence, university executives and faculty form separated and isolated enclaves in which they are likely to communicate only with people similar to themselves" (Birnbaum, 1988, p. 7).

There is always a governing approval entity, a written policy to follow, an established vetting process, or a legislative directive to consider, follow, consult, or negotiate. Decision making is spread among trustees, presidents, and faculty. The collection of these entities in a political organization is what constitutes the government of that system (Dahl, 1964). In higher education these are specialized governing bodies with like-minded values and principles. Interaction with higher-level administrators, boards of regents, faculty senates, and legislators is less frequent for entry-level professionals, yet it is important to understand the context in which decisions affecting students are made. Most student affairs professionals likely interact with their institution's governing board through a student affairs committee of regents or trustees. Student affairs professionals and these committees share a common mission, which is "to support and enhance the institution's focus on student learning and success. It is the committee's responsibility to review and monitor policies and practices concerning students" (Ellis, 2012, p. 10). It is a professional's responsibility to instill confidence in the board committee that the institution's student affairs staff has adopted appropriate values, metrics, and measures of accountability against which to gauge success.

Today's colleges and universities live in complex contexts, compete in many different marketplaces, and perform an array of services for many different constituencies. The variety of organizational structures that govern higher education institutions ranges from a simple model that places the campus in a single, not-for-profit entity responsible to a board of trustees to the ornate configurations of state higher education systems with their overlapping boards of politically appointed regents and trustees with an obligation to report to legislatures, governors, and their higher education coordinating commissions that may limit the institutional board's authority and its multiple subsidiary foundations and other enterprises.

Despite this range of governance, each institution has a structured governance system that adapts to the challenges of the external environment, as well as to the academic, student services, physical plant and operational needs of the institutions they govern. Among private institutions, governance models may change little over the period of a century or more. For many public institutions, however, governance mechanisms that link the institution to the state that sponsors and owns them often change—sometimes dramatically. Kezar and Eckel (2004) suggest that governance is a multilevel concept including several different bodies and processes with different decision-making functions. In this way, governance at the macro-level and micro-level can disagree on issues related to the institution. Coordinating and governing bodies serve as both bridge and buffer to coordinate governance and management.

Public Versus Private Matters

Institutional type, size, culture, and climate should inform a student affairs professional's decision-making process. The same is true for the governance construct. In private institutions, the single governing board not only focuses exclusively on the success of an individual college or university but may also see its role as supporting rather than controlling the institution. Public institution boards, whether politically appointed or elected, usually serve to regulate the institution on behalf of public constituencies. This fundamental difference in orientation and focus is the primary difference between public and private governance.

The purpose and function of governance ensures delivery of services as asserted in an institution's mission and progress toward improvement as set forth in a strategic vision. Governance also serves as a means to monitor costs, sometimes restraining them, other times increasing them, and to ensure that those with responsibility for the higher education institution are carrying out their duties with integrity as well as efficiency and effectiveness. Measures of accountability accompany topics beyond budgetary matters, and include matters such as admissions, access, transferability, and economic development programs.

The Political Context

Every college and university is subject to the policy control of a board, and in the case of public institutions, to the control of the state legislature and often the policy objectives of the state's executive branch. Depending on the traditions and legal basis of an institution's charter, the form of intervention may vary, but the state's influence in higher education issues comes in large measure from the power to appropriate funds. When legal and administrative traditions place the institution directly in the legislative process, this authority over academic and student service matters can appear in explicit legislation specifying program content, graduation standards, and even detailed curricular and co-curricular matters (Lombardi, 2002).

On-Campus Governance

Most campuses have a faculty senate made up of academic representatives charged with advising the administration in such areas as developing curriculum, methods of instruction, degree requirements, and tenure appointments. Some campuses incorporate professional staff into the faculty senate, while others have a separate non-academic employee's council. The campus president or chancellor often presides over a council of vice presidents and other high-ranking administrators to deal with large issues such as budget decisions and reorganization plans. Various standing committees on a campus ensure continuity in allocating space, setting salaries, and the physical appearance of campus. Unions exist on an increasing number of campuses, and an awareness of their role in personnel matters and working conditions must be understood and considered by a higher education administrator. On some campuses the student government carries considerable influence, particularly when voicing opinion on tuition rates, admission criteria, and academic program reorganization or elimination.

An effective student affairs practitioner must continually survey the governance landscape to ensure alignment of the institution's agenda with student needs and support for student success. As student affairs practitioners take on more responsibility, they should expect more formal and informal interaction, not only with high-level administrators, but also with regents, trustees, legislators, and system administrators if they are part of a public coordinating body. The duty of student affairs is to articulate the impact of the policy, the reallocation, the process, or the action on current and future students.

Shared Governance

An affirmation of the importance of shared governance accompanied by common principles was set forth in the 1966 *Statement on Government of Colleges and Universities* that was issued jointly by the American Association of University Professors, the American Council on Education, and the Association of Governing Boards of Universities and Colleges. The concept of shared and participative governance at an institution of higher education is not a simple matter of committee approval or consultation with faculty. "Shared governance is more complex in that it is a delicate balance between faculty and staff participation in planning and decision-making processes, on the one hand, and administrative accountability on the other" (Olson, 2009, p. 2). Shared governance on college campuses came into existence in the 1960s, giving stakeholders representation in the decision-making process. Institutional governance is a collaborative venture, giving various groups a share in key decision-making processes and allowing certain groups to exercise primary responsibility for specific areas of decision making. *Shared* means everyone has a role, but it doesn't mean every stakeholder gets to participate at every stage. In fact, certain constituencies are given primary responsibility over decision making in certain areas such as student affairs and student conduct; students and student government issues; academics and curriculum development.

Moore (2005) believes that shared governance is not a cumbersome system of management, but is necessary given the organizational dynamics and complexities of university systems.

Olson (2009) reminds us that in truth, all legal authority in any public or private college or university originates from one place and one place only: its governing board. The board delegates the day-to-day operation of the campus to the president, who, in turn, delegates management authority to vice presidents, deans, and other administrative leaders. "Genuine shared governance gives voice (but not necessarily ultimate authority) to concerns common to all constituencies as well as issues unique to specific groups" (Olson, 2009, p. 5). The key is ongoing communication about a wide array of institutional issues.

Shared governance may not exist or may take a different shape at a private institution. To illustrate, there are twenty-eight Jesuit universities in the United States. In *Conversations on Jesuit Higher Education*, Quinn (2005) indicates that support for the values of shared governance in Catholic universities emerged in the 1960s. In Jesuit institutions, some Jesuit priests serve on each institution's governing board. When serving in the role of a board member, a Jesuit provides guidance on the philosophy of Jesuit education, while facilitating "the mutuality so essential for shared governance before the law and in reality, respecting Catholic traditions with a democratic spirit of institutional governance" (Quinn, 2005, pp. 30–31). Private institutions generally maintain autonomy from local, state, and federal governments.

The Changing Face of Governance

In 1997, Marvin Lazerson brought forth the politicization of public systems in his accounting of how governing boards increasingly are asserting their authority, often in conflict with institutional leaders. "At public institutions trustees, often speaking for governors and state legislators, claim their responsibility to taxpayers. On private campuses, trustees speak of representing the institution's 'investors'—alumni, students, philanthropists, even the public—asserting the institution is as much theirs as anyone's" (Lazerson, 1997, p. 11). This is a change from the majority of institutions in which trustees and administrators stand by one another and use their assertive alliance to increase fiscal resources and strengthen the institution. Lazerson warns us that in recent years the level of trustee activism has escalated and become more conflict ridden, with potentially long-term consequences for the governance of higher education. According to Lazerson, power in public institutions is shifting to the governing boards. A solution to this concern is "the resuscitation of shared governance" among trustees, administrators, and faculty" (Lazerson, 1997, p. 15). Shared governance recognizes that shared goals are more likely to result in productive actions, and that mutually strengthened parties bring greater strength to the institution as a whole.

The Intersection of Politics and Decision Making in Higher Education

Higher education institutions are political systems. Because of this, political activity and decision making are connected.

The Political Frame

Bolman and Deal (2003) describe four frames for effective management practice, one of which is political. The political frame is well suited to student affairs and higher education. It characterizes operations as a competitive environment with scarce resources, competing interests, and struggles for power and advantage. The model assumes that the power of members determines the outcome. Members of political systems interact with one another to influence the meeting of desires and objectives through decisions that allocate resources, give approvals or denials, move agendas forward or delay their progress.

Authority and Power

Bolman and Deal (2003) believe that the most important decisions in the political frame involve the allocation of scarce resources. In doing so, the distribution and exercise of power is the most important asset. *Authority* can be most simply defined as legitimate power, whereas *power* is "the potential ability to influence behavior, to change the course of events, to overt resistance, and to get people to do things they would not otherwise do" (Pfeffer, 1992, p. 188).

The face of power consists of conscious actions that influence decisions; the ability to prevent decisions from being made (nondecisions); and the ability to influence another by shaping what he or she thinks, wants, or needs. "It is the ability to produce intended change in others, to influence them so that they will be more likely to act in accordance with one's own preferences" (Birnbaum,1988, p. 12).

Bargaining and Negotiating

Negotiation is one of the most common approaches used to make decisions. It is the art and science of collaborative decision making (Raiffa, 2007) and a powerful political tool (Bolman & Deal, 2003). Negotiation is a dialogue between parties intended to reach an understanding, resolve a difference, or gain an advantage in the outcome. *Distributive negotiation* is used when a finite amount of a thing (for example, money or space) is being distributed among people. *Integrative negotiation* is a set of techniques that attempts to improve the quality and likelihood of negotiated agreement by providing an alternative through creative problem solving. *Bargaining* is a subset of negotiation. Good negotiating either gets things to the point at which bargaining can occur or no bargaining is needed (Shell, 2006).

Campus Culture and Context

Campus context matters in decision making (Vacarro et al., 2013). Be aware that each institution will vary in the political experience it offers a student affairs professional. Learn to scan the organizational landscape for stakeholders, influencers, decision-making processes, power holders, and authority figures, as well as principles and values. For example, the context for decision making at a community college varies from that of a research university or a private liberal arts college or a religiously affiliated school. A program on safer sex will likely evoke different rules and reactions at each of those institutions. Smaller institutions may have fewer administrative levels; this can streamline decisions, and news of a decision may spread quickly, which is both an asset and challenge. "To some degree, you have to be immersed in an organization in order to develop an appreciation for, and sensitivity to, the nature of relationships within it—to understand the hidden histories and dangerous discourses, and the ways in which you can (and can't) enter into political negotiations without harming you career aspirations" (McClellan, 2013, p. 2).

Values

Each decision made builds an organizational culture in which values are communicated through consistent action. Fairness is one of the most important values, but the exercising of this value may look like a lack of values to some because it requires making decisions without bias. Tierney emphasizes the importance of utilizing "deeply embedded patterns of organizational behavior and the shared values, assumptions, and beliefs, or ideologies that members have about their organization or work" (1990, p. 6) when making decisions.

Values are empowering. When values are clear, a professional need not rely upon direction from someone in authority (Kouzes & Posner, 2002). By knowing what is most important and by recognizing conflict or compatibility between our own values and the values of the organization, a student affairs administrator can make wise decisions.

Stakeholders and Constituencies

As higher education moves away from the power elite to a more democratic model, decision makers practice coalition building (Bolman & Deal, 2003). Coalition builders seek to clearly understand everyone's interests by providing opportunities for individuals and groups to make their interests known. This is because their decisions distribute and assign power among stakeholders. It is important to pay attention to all stakeholders and constituencies, both internal and external to the institution. Although students should be the center of all considerations in our work, there are other groups to consider when making decisions. Always ask, Who will care about this decision? Whose pocketbook, neighborhood, status, business, or reputation will benefit or be harmed? Local community groups and leaders, as well as parents, faculty, politicians, donors, alumni, and neighbors, are all important constituencies when making decisions.

Communication, Sharing, and Transparency

Leaders can enhance their political decision-making capacity by maintaining a free flow of information and access. Accessible information breaks down bureaucracy. In some institutions people hoard information, thinking it gives them power and prestige. Student affairs divisions carve out an important niche for themselves in their institutions by gathering ongoing data regarding their students from nationally normed surveys, such as the CIRP Freshman Survey (from the College Institutional Research Program at the University of California, Los Angeles) and the NSSE (the National Study of Student Engagement), in addition to demographic data and profiles of those who persist as well as drop out, and then sharing the data freely with faculty, students, administrators, legislators, regents, and trustees.

Emerging Considerations

This section presents several practical considerations for successful political practice in higher education. These are personal reflections based on the author's many years of experience.

Scan Your Landscape for Decision-Making Opportunities

A key to professional advancement and exemplary performance in each role is the wisdom and courage to make sound decisions. There are those who avoid them and others who make consistently poor decisions. These are opportunities for student affairs professionals to hone their decision-making skills and to shine. Look for decisions to be made! Cohen and March (1974, p. 82) call this seeking out "choice opportunities": "These are occasions when an organization is expected to produce behavior that can be called a decision. Opportunities arise regularly, and any organization has ways of declaring an occasion for choice. Contracts must be signed, people hired, promoted, or fired; money spent and responsibilities allocated" (Cohen & March, 1974).

Good Relationships Make Good Decisions

A political system is any persistent pattern of human relationships that involves power, rule, or authority (Dahl, 1964). Use of the power, rule, and authority in those relationships guides effective decisions and exemplary leadership. For this reason, Kouzes and Posner (2002) stress that "leadership *is* relationship" (p. 20). Existing networks of trust, familiarity, and shared values and objectives make for good decisions. Success at work and in life has been, is now, and will continue to be a function of how well people work and play together. Drucker points out that one of the most basic differences between nonprofit organizations and businesses is that the typical nonprofit has so many more relationships that are vitally important. "In all but the very biggest businesses, the key relationships are few—employees, customers and owners, and that's it. Every non-profit has a multitude of constituencies and has to work out the relationship with each of them" (1990, p. 157).

Embrace Conflict in Decision Making

In a political organization, divergent interests are an enduring fact of life (Birnbaum, 1988; Bolman & Deal, 2003). Politics is linked to the phenomena of conflict and cooperation. Conflict comes from competition between differing needs and interests and cooperation from working together, achieving goals through collective action. Do not work to prevent disagreement and conflict. Asking for disagreement openly gives people the chance to be heard, and effective leaders listen. In many cases a decision maker can integrate objectors' ideas and accommodate concerns in order to resolve conflict. Collaboration on a resolution can build common ground if not complete agreement.

Harness the Power of Data

Data-driven decisions are better decisions. It's as simple as that. Using data enables student affairs managers to decide on the basis of evidence rather than intuition. For that reason it has the potential to revolutionize decision making. Evidence-based decision making allows student affairs professionals to make better predictions (Who will persist? Who will graduate?) and thus, smarter decisions that can be defended, sold, and used to make a campus focused on student success. An effective political dimension to decision making is to get the data. Facts and figures inform thinking and make a powerful statement about what needs to happen and why.

Engage in Second Guessing

Once the decision has been made and sets things in motion, a student affairs professional is not finished. After implementation it is important to reflect on the success or failure and impact of actions. It is politically astute for leaders to question whether or not they made the right decision. Engage in analysis to derive lessons for the future. Ask evaluative questions on process and style. "Were the desired outcomes achieved? Were unintended outcomes realized?" "After they make the tough decisions, strong leaders build the habit of debriefing. When possible they identify learning points that may have been overlooked in the heat of the decision and its fallout" (O'Hara Devereaux, 2004, p. 111).

Practice Artful Procrastination

Leaders buy time. The politically astute among us never make an instantaneous decision. If someone pressures them to make a decision they say, "Well then, if you can't give me even an hour my answer is no." Leaders practice this over and over. "Let me think about this before I respond," says highly respected University of Southern California President Emeritus Steven Sample. He calls it "artful procrastination" (2003, p. 81). Sample uses President Harry Truman as an example by telling the story that whenever a staff member came to him with a problem or opportunity requiring a presidential decision, the first thing Truman would ask was, "How much time do I have?" Truman understood that the timing of a decision could be as important as the decision itself. "A long lead time opened the door for extensive consultation and discussion; a very short lead time meant the president could only look inside his soul, and then only briefly, for an answer that might affect millions of people" (Sample, 2003, p. 81). Once timing was determined, it was "the "how" that mattered politically. It is my hope that the many pages of this chapter leading up to this final point have provided direction and answers.

Limitations of the Political Dimension in Decision Making

Different models of organization, governance, and decision making exist, including the bureaucratic, the collegial, the organized anarchy, the structural, the human resource, and the symbolic (Baldridge 1979; Birnbaum,1988; Bolman & Deal, 2003). They all describe different ways of thinking, leading, deciding, and acting in an institution of higher education. They help users to understand the processes and operations of colleges and universities. Each model is "right," but each is incomplete (Birnbaum, 1988).

At any given time, one of these models fits a particular institution, but no college or university is consistently any one model. Limiting oneself to just the political dimensions of decision making while effectively managing one's organization would be a mistake. There are other strong and effective models to consider when confronting an issue, seeking to resolve a problem, making a decision. "Closure is elusive, systems come undone, solutions create new problems, no group is ever satisfied without another being dissatisfied, and criticisms about process can overwhelm substance" (Birnbaum,1988, p. 176).

One way to increase administrative effectiveness is to resolve these dilemmas by seeking more rational ways to make decisions, more structured methods to make a choice or exercise authority. "Appreciate the cybernetic nature of academic institutions" (Birnbaum, 1988, p. 176), which means each institution has its own patterns of behaviors, relationships, social norms, hierarchical structures, preferences, limitations, and biases, all with varying levels of influence and importance.

"Most capable leaders develop an ability to shift their focus to see other ways an issue might be considered" (Stringer, 2009, p. 429). Morgan (2006) warns, "When we analyze organizations in terms of the political metaphor it is almost always possible to see signs of political activity. This can lead to increased politicization of the organization, for when we understand organizations as political systems we are more likely to behave politically in relation to what we see. We begin to see politics everywhere and to look for hidden agendas even where there are none" (p. 205).

Conclusion

Viewing decision making as a political process is useful in keeping student affairs administrators focused on their increasingly important decision-making role in ensuring student success. To characterize the maneuverings and actions of decision making as a political process is to emphasize that there is a powerful common interest in reaching an outcome that is not enormously destructive to both sides.

Even if a student affairs administrator has no natural ability to build relationships, analyze stakeholder needs, or survey the organization's political landscape, she can be effective by gaining experience and practicing the political elements of decision making presented in this chapter. At some point in a long student affairs career, decisions become predictable, inevitable, and repetitive. Considering the political dimensions of decisions in student affairs work is part of the craft of an effective administrator. Use these lessons to think ahead and determine how you will make decisions, create some decision rules, and share them with the rest of the organization to follow. Adopt a resolute acceptance of the need for relationships, use of process, and data-influenced decisions. That is the virtue of politics. If, as Drucker says, "a decision is a commitment to action" (p. 127), then why do far too many decisions remain "pious intentions" (p. 127)? Every decision is a commitment of present resources to a future. Here, as Drucker points out, one can learn from the Japanese. They build the implementation in *before* they make the decision. Everyone who will be affected, especially those enlisted to carry it out, is asked to comment on the issue before the decision is made. Once made, everyone understands, everyone acts. Too frequently the Western concept is to decide and then sell the decision to stakeholders. Ponder that political framework the next time a decision must be made!

References

American Association of University Professors, American Council on Education, & Association of Governing Boards of Universities and Colleges. (1966). *Statement on government of colleges and universities, 1966.* http://www.aaup/org/AAUP/issuesed/governance/default.htm. 2013.

Amey, M. J., Jessup-Anger, E., & Tingson-Gatuz, C. R. (2009). Unwritten rules: Organizational and political realities of the job. In M. J. Amey & L. M. Reesor (Eds.), *Beginning Your Journey: A guide for new professionals in student affairs.* Washington, DC: National Association of Student Personnel Administrators.

Amaral, A., Jones, G. A., & Karseth, B. (Eds.). (2002). *Governing higher education: National perspectives on institutional governance.* Dordrecht, the Netherlands: Kluwer Academic.

Aristotle. (2000). *Politics, II, 2.* (B. Jowett, Trans.) Mineola, NY: Dover. (Originally published 350 BC).

Baldridge, J. V. (1971). *Power and conflict in the university.* New York, NY: John Wiley and Sons.

Baldridge, J. V., Curtis, D. V., Ecker, G., & Riley, G. L. (1971). *Policy making and effective: A national study of academic management.* San Francisco, CA: Jossey-Bass.

Birnbaum, R. (1988). *How colleges work.* San Francisco, CA: Jossey-Bass.

Bolman, L. G., & Deal, T. E. (2003). *Reframing organizations* (3rd ed.). San Francisco, CA: Jossey-Bass.

Callahan, J. C. (1988). *Ethical issues in professional life.* New York, NY: Oxford University Press.

Capelo, C., & Dias, J. (2009). Feedback learning model and mental models perspective on strategic decision making. *Educational Technology Research and Development, 57* (5), 629–644.

Clark, B. R. (1998). *Creating entrepreneurial universities: Organizational pathways of transformation.* Oxford, England: Pergamon.

Cohen, M. D., March, J. D., & Olsen, J. P. (1972). A Garbage can model of organizational choice. *Administrative Science Quarterly, 17* (1), 1–25.

Cohen, M. D., & March J. D. (1974). *Leadership and ambiguity.* New York, NY: McGraw-Hill.

Corson, J. J. *Governance of colleges & universities.* New York, NY: McGraw Hill, (1960). .

Cyert, R. M., & March J. G. (1963). *Behavioral theory of the firm.* Cambridge, MA: Blackwell.

Dahl, R. (1964). *Power, pluralism, and democracy: A modest proposal.* New Haven, CT: Yale University Press.

Dean J. W., Jr., & Sharfman, M. P. (1996). Does decision process matter? A study of strategic decision-making effectiveness. *Academy of Management Journal, 39* (2), 368–396.

Deem, R. (1998). New managerialism and higher education: The management of performances and cultures in the United Kingdom. *International Studies in Sociology of Education, 8*(1), 47–70.

Drucker, P. (1990). *Managing the non-profit organization.* New York, NY: Harper Collins.

Easton, D. (1953). *The political system: An inquiry into the state of political science.* New York, NY: Knopf.

Eggert, S., & Bogeholz, S. (2010). Students' use of decision making strategies with regard to socioscientific issues: An application of Rasch Partial Credit Model. *Science Education, 94*(2), 230–258.

Ellis, S. (2012). *The student affairs committee.* Washington, DC: Association of Governing Boards of Universities and Colleges Press.

Hastie, R. (1986). A primer of information-processing theory for the political scientist. In R. Lau & D. O. Sears (Eds.). *Political cognition: The 19th annual Carnegie symposium on cognition.* Hillsdale, NJ: Erlbaum.

Hirt, J. B. (2006). Where you work matters: Student affairs administrators at different types of institutions. Lanham, MD: University Press of America.

Kezar, A., & Eckel, P. D. (2004). Meeting today's governance challenges. *Journal of Higher Education, 75*(4), 371–398.

Kitchner, K. S., & Anderson, S. K. (2011). *Foundations of ethical practice, research, and teaching in psychology and counseling.* New York, NY: Taylor & Francis.

Knighton, R. J. 2004). The psychology of risk and its role in military decision making. *Defense Studies, 4*(3), 309–334.

Kouzes, J. M., & Posner, B. Z. (2002). *The leadership challenge.* San Francisco, CA: Jossey-Bass.

Kuh, G., Siegel, M. J., & Thomas, W.A.D. (2001). Higher education: Values and cultures. In R. B. Winston Jr., D. G. Creamer, & T. K. Miller (Eds.). *The professional student affairs administrator: Educator, leader, manager* (pp. 39-63). New York, NY: Brunner-Routledge.

Lasswell, H. (1936). *Politics: Who gets what, when, and how.* Gloucester, MA: Peter Smith.

Lazerson, M. (1997, March/April). Who owns higher education. *Change, 10–15.*

Levy, S. R., & Kozoll, E. E. (1998). *A Guide to decision making in student affairs: A case study approach.* Springfield, IL: Charles C Thomas.

Lombardi, J. V. (2002, August). *University organization, governance, and competitiveness.* The Lombardi Program on Measuring University Performance http://mup.asu .edu/UniversityOrganization.pdf

March, J. G., &, Simon, H. A. (1958). *Organizations.* New York, NY: Wiley.

Marginson, S., & Considine, M. (2000). *The enterprise university.* Melbourne, Australia: Cambridge University Press.

Matzler, K., Bailom, F., & Mooradian, T. Fall (2007). Intuitive decision making. *MIT Sloan Management Review.*

McAfee, A., & Brynjolfsson E. (2012, October). Big data: The management revolution. *Harvard Business Review, 60–68.*

McClellan, G. S. (2013, March 11). Things I didn't learn in graduate school. *Chronicle of Higher Education.* http://chronicle.Com/article/article-content/137807/.

Millett, J. D. (1978). *New structures of campus power: Success and failure of emerging forms of institutional governance.* San Francisco, CA: Jossey-Bass.

Mintzberg, H. (1979). *The structuring of organizations.* Englewood Cliffs, N.J.: Prentice Hall.

Mintzberg, H., Raisinghani, P., & Theoret, A. (1976). The structure of "unstructured" decision processes. *Administrative Science Quarterly, 21*(2), 246–275.

Moore, R., Jr. (2005). In shared governance, what role for the AAUP? *Conversations on Jesuit Higher Education, 28,* 26-28.

Morgan, G. (2006). *Images of organization.* Thousand Oaks, CA: Sage.

O'Hara Devereaux, M. (2004). *Navigating the badlands*. San Francisco, CA: Jossey-Bass.

Olson, G. A. (2009, July 23). Exactly what is "shared governance"? *Chronicle of Higher Education*. http://chroncile.com/article/Exactly-What-Is-Shared/47065/.

O'Neill, T., & Hymel G. (1994). *All politics is local and other rules of the game*. Holbrook, MA: Bob Adams.

Pfeffer, J. (1992). *Managing with power: Politics and influence in organizations*. Boston, MA: Harvard Business School Press.

Quinn, K. P. (2005). Shared governance: The elusive role of Jesuit as trustee. *Conversations on Jesuit Higher Education, 28*, 30-31.

Raiffa, H. (2007). *Negotiation analysis*. Cambridge, MA: Belknap Press of Harvard University Press.

Sample, S. (2003). *The contrarian's guide to leadership*. San Francisco, CA: Jossey-Bass.

Schwenk, C. R. (1984). Cognitive simplification processes in strategic decision making. *Strategic Management Journal, 5*(2), 111–128.

Shell, G. R. (2006). *Bargaining for advantage*. New York, NY: Penguin.

Sonnenberg, F. A., & Beck, J. R. (2008). Markov models in medical decision making: A practical guide. *Medical Decision Making, 13*(4), 322–338.

Stringer, J. (2009). The political environment of the student affairs administrator. In G. S. McClellan & J. Stringer (Eds.). *The handbook of student affairs administration* (3rd ed., pp. 425-446)). San Francisco, CA: Jossey-Bass.

Stroup, H. (1966). *Bureaucracy in higher education*. New York, NY: Free Press.

Tierney, W. G. (Ed.). (1990). Assessing academic climates and cultures. *New Directions for Institutional Research, no. 68*. San Francisco, CA: Jossey-Bass.

Tjeldvoll, A. 1998, Fall). The idea of the service university. *International Higher Education, 13*, 9–12.

US Department of the Army. (2010). *The operations process* (Field Manual 5–0). http://www.fas.org/irp/doddit/army/fm5-0.pdf.

Vaccaro, A., McCoy, B. Champagne, D., & Siegel, M. (2013). *Decisions matter*. Washington, DC: NASPA.

Whetton, D. A. (1984). Effective administrators: Good management on the college campus. *Change, 16*, 39–43.

Zeleny, M. (1982). *Multiple criteria decision making*. New York, NY: McGraw-Hill.

CHAPTER TWENTY-THREE

PARTNERSHIPS AND RELATIONSHIPS INTERNAL AND EXTERNAL TO THE COLLEGE

Penelope H. Wills

For many years higher education scholars have written about the value of collaboration between student affairs and their academic partners (Bourassa & Kruger, 2001; Dale & Drake, 2005; Ellis, 2009; Roper, 2002; Sandeen, 2000). Authors of such articles and books have focused on the critical characteristics of student and academic partnerships (Banta & Kuh, 1988; Schroeder as cited in Dale & Drake, 2005). "These writings identified the strategies needed to develop and maintain partnerships, described organizational models that support and enhance partnerships, and outlined skill sets for effectively navigating partnerships" (Dale & Drake, 2005, p. 51).

Chapter 21 in this volume presents some ideas and insights on collaborative partnerships between academic and student affairs colleagues. The current chapter offers a broader perspective than the relationship between student affairs and instruction. It focuses on the institutional level, which includes relationships with partners within a college such as faculty, finance and administration staff, and advancement, as well as essential partners external to the institution, such as legislators, economic developers, civic organizations, and governmental agencies. The value of such collaborations is discussed, as well as reasons for such partnerships and the benefits to both the college and the community. In addition, elements of successful alliances and characteristics of successful leaders in such programs are addressed. The scope of the chapter is from an institutional perspective but can apply to all levels within an institution. The chapter is more attitudinal for prospective partners and constituents than relationships between existing roles, such as advisor to advisee. Although the roles described focus on higher-level leaders, who are typically seasoned professionals, it is vital that new student services professionals develop these skills early in their careers. Roper may have stated it best: "Our success as student affairs professionals is more closely tied to our ability to construct and manage essential relationships during our careers than to any other activity" (Roper, 2002, p. 11).

It is important to recognize that the author of this chapter is a professional in student development and firmly believes that student success is contingent on an integration of student and academic affairs. If the reader is interested in learning more about this type of collaboration, in addition to reviewing chapter 21 in this volume, she or he might want to review the relevant chapters in the second and third editions of *The Handbook of Student Affairs Administration* (2000 and 2009). In his chapter entitled, "Developing Effective Campus and Community Relationships," Arthur Sandeen (2000) captured the essence of the requisite elements of good campus relations: being worthy and honest, being competent, listening and being involved, maintaining confidentiality, ensuring effective planning, and following up. As explained later in this chapter, all of these elements are applicable to the elements of successful leadership in institutional partnerships.

Sixteen years later, in the third edition of the same book, Shannon Ellis (2009) wrote an excellent chapter entitled "Developing Effective Relationships on Campus and in the Community." She focused on campus relationships by explaining the importance of such communication between the student affairs practitioner–students; advisor-advisee; teacher-learner; developer-enforcer; and mentor-mentee. Ellis also spoke to the value of finding common ground, creating a trustworthy system, sharing common values and a linked vision. Again, these elements are also critical to effective partnerships with groups outside the college community. In this chapter the author explains to readers the underpinnings of all successful partnerships for both internal and external relationships to the college.

Another possible bias (but also a matter of credibility) of the author is that she is currently a president of a community college. There is a vast array of types of colleges and universities in the United States (for example, technical institutes, community colleges, liberal arts colleges, state and regional colleges, research universities), yet not all have embraced collaboration across the institution nor the notion of college-community partnerships. As Bourassa and Kruger (2001) stated, "Without a doubt, the entire higher education community should keep track of factors with the community college sector that cultivate successful partnerships that are easily adapted by either community colleges or four-year colleges and universities" (p. 15). In their study of community engagement among research universities, Weerts and Sandmann (2010) found that "during the last decade, community engagement has emerged as an important priority among many colleges and universities" (p. 632). "Research universities have been slower to implement engagement compared to community and liberal arts colleges" (p. 633). It is this author's belief that community colleges, by their very mission, are more closely tied to the communities they serve. They are also known to readily blur the lines between college administrative divisions. Again, there are many aspects of this chapter that can be applied to all of higher education.

The Value of Partnerships

The phrase, "The days of going solo are over," is very pertinent to this discussion. "Partnerships are relevant to a number of issues confronting higher education. They extend far beyond local relations; they force us to think about the overall purpose of higher education" (Maurrasse, 2001, p. 2). Colleges' accountability to their communities is expected. This is more than a best practice concept; it is now borderline ethical. "The trend of university-community partnerships is part of the universities' response to the general sense that higher education institutions are socially detached and academically irrelevant to the greater social disease of the age" (Strier, 2011, p. 82). Kisker and Garducci (2003) found community colleges' partnerships with the private sector are very popular, not only because of the colleges' missions and values, but also because of the current economic slowdown. Essentially, these colleges must look for financial support to augment their low tuition and decreased public funded support. "Partnerships with the private sector are also influenced by the intense pressure community colleges continually face to provide innovative curriculum to their students, especially in the areas of technology and information systems" (p. 56). Close collaboration by community colleges with such public entities as workforce development boards, chambers of commerce, and economic development councils all strengthen the ties with their college districts (Van Wagoner, Bowman, & Spraggs, 2005).

Legislators view partnerships as "strategic ways of meeting the state's education and economic goals" (Amey, Eddy, & Ozaki, 2007, p. 5). Creating strong partnerships provides an opportunity for colleges to maximize their resources while responding to the needs in their communities and, as such, advances their institutional missions (Sink & Jackson, 2002). Quite simply, these relationships pay off in political clout and community support for the college (Van Wagoner et al., 2005).

"Partnerships are sometimes considered fringe activities that are risky, difficult to negotiate, political, and easily challenged by the institutional status quo" (Amey, Eddy, & Campbell, 2010, p. 14). Even with the many benefits of partnerships to both the college and the community, discussed later in this chapter, many academics do not view such community involvement as a priority (Buys & Burnsall, 2007). Faculty are reluctant for many reasons: (1) lack of respect for the knowledge base of people outside the academy; (2) the perception of academicians that community members are research objects rather than partners; and (3) poor understanding on their part about the benefits that partnerships may offer (Buys & Burnsall, 2007). Equally interesting is that fears also inhibit the community members from joining in such collaboration. Ahmed (as cited in Buys & Burnsall, 2007) suggested reasons for such hesitancy include: faculty are often perceived to exist in an ivory tower, and the research that may be produced is irrelevant to the community's needs. The truth is that such college–private sector partnerships are often challenging to develop and hard to sustain (Amey et al., 2007). It is the opinion of this author that the same hesitancy regarding college–private sector alliances can be said of interdivisional collaborations within a college. Although faculty and academic administrators understand the value of support services, do they fully understand the critical link to student development? Does the administrative services staff view student affairs as being solely responsible for students' recruitment and retention? Does the student development staff fully appreciate the special relationships between students and their instructors?

To better appreciate the value of partnerships, one should begin with the concept of engagement. *Community engagement* is defined as the "collaboration between institutions of higher education and their larger communities (local, regional/state, national, global) for the mutually beneficial exchange of knowledge and resources in a context of partnership and reciprocity" (Carnegie, as cited in Weerts & Sandman, 2010). As Weerts and Sandmann (2010) explain, engagement is not the same as public service outreach. "Specifically, service and outreach are typically conceived as *one-way* approaches to delivering knowledge and services to the public, whereas engagement emphasizes a *two-way* approach in which institutions and community partners collaborate to develop and apply knowledge to address social needs" (p. 632). The concept of community engagement is embedded in this broader notion of engagement, according to Buys and Burnsall (2007). "Essentially, the engagement provides the context in which partnerships can flourish, rather than there being a series of fragmented links with industry" (Coldstream, as cited in Buys & Burnsall, 2007).

A number of groups and educational associations have also affected the relatively recent increase in college-community engagement. For example, the Kellogg Commission called on public research universities to become more productively engaged with the communities they serve (Weerts & Sandman, 2010). Also, the American Association of State Colleges and Land-Grant Universities has urged its members to be better "stewards of place" (Weerts & Sandmann, 2010, p. 635). As Harkavy and Hartley (2009) stated, "Universities have increasingly come to recognize that their destinies are inextricably linked with the communities" (p. 9).

In summary, partnerships engender more ownership of education; that is, they help others appreciate its value. Likewise, such collaborations strengthen the internal college community as well.

Benefits for the College and the Community

Strier (2011) found in her study of university-community alliances "that solid partnerships with communities are vital sources for teaching, research, and practice" (p. 82). As mentioned earlier, government officials view partnerships as a key way of meeting the state's education and economic goals. "Institutions benefit from facilities and resource sharing and students gain access to additional instruction and a smoother transition to postsecondary education" (Amey et al., 2007, p. 5). When partnerships are successful, they are beneficial for all engaged parties because they maximize state and local resources as well as provide more opportunities for students' learning needs (Amey et al., 2010). Such partnerships are better for students because they can strengthen programs through applied learning as well as career development and job placement opportunities

(Buys & Burnsall, 2007). In addition, colleges benefit from enhanced public relations and the communities feel a stronger connection to the institution. These college-community relationships can have a significant impact with legislators, taxpayers, and donors because they allow the institution to better tell its story.

The private sector also gains many benefits from collaboration with the college community. Through joint efforts with civic leaders, these partnerships promote regional competitiveness and are very attractive to new businesses. Community colleges, in particular, provide a skilled workforce as well as many retraining opportunities (Kisker & Carducci, 2003).

Whether with internal college departments or with external entities, the process of collaborating offers opportunities for college departments to share a common vision. Through this experience, departments develop trust and a commitment to continuously strive for enhanced communication across the institution (Bracken, 2007). "This is demonstrated by a commitment to learning from each other and changing our own ideas as a result" (p. 41).

It is important that one appreciates that such alliances are process oriented and should be viewed as living organisms. Morgan (as cited in Amey et al., 2007) describes various aspects of a partnership. For example, who instigates the idea, how do members understand and interpret the relationships with the partnership, how does it change over time, and how do the members solve problems? Another important factor to consider is the development of the partnership itself. "How does the partnership move from an individual orientation to a group orientation to a collaborative one? Leadership shifts from being directive to facilitative and then to inclusive and servant-oriented" (Amey et al., 2007, p. 8). This process of collaboration itself can have a very positive effect on the morale and spirit for both parties. As Strier (2011) states, "Successful partnerships are characterized by mutuality, supportive leadership, university immersion, and asset building" (p. 82).

Essential Aspects of Successful Partnerships

The success of any collaborative effort depends on two major factors: the characteristics of the leaders and the formation process of the partnership. Many authors (Buys & Burnsall, 2007; Roper, 2002; Sandeen, 2000) have studied the personal traits of leaders. The key characteristics include trust, ability to communicate clearly, mutual respect, and integrity. The parties must share a strong commitment to a balanced alliance. The partnership will be much stronger if there is no ego involvement on the leadership's part. Leaders must be willing to bend their institutions' rules to make the vision happen. The key elements of a successful partnership include "shared goals; relations with partners; capacity for partnership work; governance and leadership; and trust and trustworthiness" (Billett, Ovens, Clemans, & Seddon, 2007, p. 637).

One critical aspect that is often overlooked is the buy-in by the larger bodies involved in the partnership. The leaders may be very aware of their own organizations' missions and strive to better understand the other's perspective and values. But they often do not take sufficient time to garner their own organizations' full support. Leaders not only lead but also frame the collaboration for others (Ozaki, Amey, & Watson, 2007). This is essential, because the partnership often has resource implications as well as political ramifications. In any partnership it is important to recognize that many potential barriers must be addressed. Dale and Drake (2005) list some of the significant challenges, which include differing cultures, values, lack of a common language, and differing organizational status.

The process of forming an alliance, whether internal to the college or with the private sector, is important. The first step is to identify the right partner(s). In this initiation phase, it is important to focus on the motivation of the interested parties (Buys & Burnsall, 2007). Leaders must be ever mindful of their missions and remember that the department and/or college cannot be all things to all entities. It is important for leaders initiating partnerships to know their institution's' or department's' strengths. Likewise, they must identify their own organizational weaknesses and search for organizational partners that can strengthen their mission and goals. As the partnership begins to form, it is important to remain open to learning from others and their ideas. Participants must be open to change, especially in an entrepreneurial partnership, but not lose sight of their institution's mission. This process does not occur quickly. The following steps in creating an effective alliance are described well by Kollie (2013): build the relationship; meet regularly; communicate goals and visions; develop trust; and believe in the intended benefits. These steps can be applied to both college-community collaborations and to interdivisional college programs.

An essential component of partnerships is the planned evaluation of any collaborative effort. Once it is decided to implement an alliance, the parties should plan how the partnership will be evaluated and set benchmarks for such activity. All too often the parties consider this activity only when concerns are voiced or if and when the project becomes stale.

Related to evaluation, the entities must also consider succession planning for the leadership team. Presidents, vice presidents, and deans, as well as chief executive officers of private sector organizations, change positions frequently. If the entities have not garnered the support of their organizations, it may quickly appear to others that such a partnership was a temporary matter and solely based on the former leaders' ownership or involvement.

Characteristics of Successful Leadership Teams

The role of the "champion" of partnerships has been studied and is consistent wherever the leader's position may be in the organization. For purposes of this section, the roles of president and vice presidents are used to illustrate the essential traits, but the principles are applicable to all levels of an organization. The president must remove barriers for the staff to create, maintain, and improve the partnership. Because presidents represent the essence of their colleges, they must be known for their values, which in turn should be consistent with those of the colleges they represent. At this level, the presidents' roles are both strategic and symbolic; they send a message to internal and external partners about the importance of engagement (Weerts & Sandmann, 2010). Leaders usually have to allocate more energy to "connect the dots" for the internal college community to fully understand the relationship to the mission. Because presidents must be mindful of the internal level of morale, they must also be ever vigilant of the level of respect that the college holds in the community. It is critical that these champions stay connected with the activities of the collaboration and the balance of influence by both parties (Weerts & Sandmann, 2010).

The vice presidential team is another critical aspect of leadership. Vice presidents must fully appreciate and support each other's divisions and possess a clear institutional vision. Members of effective leadership teams appreciate each other's professional perspectives and personal styles. It is important that vice presidents seek opportunities to build bridges and educate college employees, including the faculty, together as a team. As a team, they should share the commitment to continuous improvement of not only the partnership but also their own staff's professional development.

In closing, all members of the leadership team should adopt a genuine spirit of inquiry, always being mindful of the college's mission and always being open to ways to strengthen that mission. Some of the most successful partnerships have occurred because of the leaders' genuine openness and respect for others.

Conclusion

Although this chapter has expanded the scope of partnerships from the interinstitutional divisions of a college, it has explained the essence of all successful alliances. The concept of engagement is fundamental to any collaboration. Leadership teams must share a commitment to strengthen the mission of all parties in order to garner and maintain the resultant benefits of such collaboration. The intent of an effective partnership is to "get outside the structure of the two entities representing two separate things at the table, and get inside them representing one thing: a community moving forward" (Kollie, 2013, p. 18).

References

Amey, M. J., Eddy, P. L., & Campbell, T. G. (2010). Crossing boundaries: Creating community college partnerships to promote educational transitions. *Community College Review, 37*(4), 333–347.

Amey, M. J., Eddy, P. L., & Ozaki, C. C. (2007). Demands for partnership and collaboration in higher education: A model. In M. J. Amey (Ed.), *Collaborations across educational sectors.* New Directions for Community Colleges, no. 139. San Francisco, CA: Jossey-Bass.

Banta, T. W., & Kuh, G. D. (1988, March/April). A missing link in assessment: Collaboration between academic student affairs professionals. *Change*, 40–46.

Billett, S., Ovens, C., Clemans, A., & Seddon, T. (2007). Collaborative working and contested practices: Forming, developing and sustaining social partnerships in education. *Journal of Education Policy, 22*(6), 637–656.

Bourassa, D. M., & Kruger, K. (2001). The national dialogue on academic and student affairs collaboration. In A. Kezar, D. J. Hirsch, & C. Burack (Eds.), *Understanding the role of academic and student affairs collaboration in creating a successful learning environment.* New Directions for Higher Education, no. 116. San Francisco, CA: Jossey-Bass.

Bracken, S. J. (2007). The importance of language, context, and communication as components of successful partnership. In M. J. Amey (Ed.), *Collaborations across educational sectors.* New Directions for Community Colleges, no. 139. San Francisco, CA: Jossey-Bass.

Buys, N., & Bursnall, S. (2007). Establishing university-community partnerships: Processes and benefits. *Journal of Higher Education Policy and Management, 29*(1), 73–86.

Dale, P. A., & Drake T. M. (2005). Connecting academic and student affairs to enhance student learning and success. In S. R. Helfgot & M. M. Culp (Eds.), *Community college student affairs: What really matters.* New Directions for Community Colleges, no. 131. San Francisco, CA: Jossey-Bass.

Ellis, S. (2009). Developing effective relationships on campus and in the community. In G. S. McClellan & J. Stringer (Eds.), *The handbook of student affairs administration* (3rd ed., pp. 447-462). San Francisco, CA: Jossey-Bass.

Harkavy, I., & Hartley, M. (2009). *University-school-community partnerships for youth development and democratic renewal.* New Directions for Youth Development, no. 122. San Francisco, CA: Jossey-Bass.

Kisker, C. B., & Garducci, R. (2003). Community college partnerships with the private sector: Organizational contexts and models for successful collaboration. *Community College Review, 31*(3), 55–74.

Kollie, E. (2013). Creating a strong town-gown relationship. *College Planning and Management, 16*(8), 16–19.

Maurrasse, D. J. (2001). *Beyond the campus: How colleges and universities form partnerships with their communities.* New York, NY: Routledge.

Ozaki, C. C., Amey, M. J., & Watson, J. (2007). Strategies for the future. In M. J. Amey (Ed.), *Collaborations across educational sectors.* New Directions for Community Colleges, no. 139. San Francisco, CA: Jossey-Bass.

Roper, L. (2002). Relationships: The critical ties that bind professionals. In J. C. Dalton & M. Clinton (Eds.). *The art and practical wisdom of student affairs leadership.* New Directions for Student Services, no. 98. San Francisco, CA: Jossey-Bass.

Sandeen, A. (2000). Developing effective campus and community relationships. In M.J. Barr and M. K. Desler (Eds.), *The handbook of student affairs administration* (2nd ed., pp. 377-392). San Francisco, CA: Jossey-Bass.

Sink, D. W. Jr., & Jackson, K. L. (2002). Successful community college campus-based partnerships. *Community College Journal of Research and Practice, 26*(1), 35–46.

Strier, R. (2011). The construction of university-community partnerships: Entangled perspectives. *Higher Education, 62*(1), 81–97.

Van Wagoner, R. J., Bowman, L. S., & Spraggs, L. D. (2005). Editor's choice: The significant community college. *Community College Review, 33*(1), 38–50.

Weerts, D. J., & Sandmann, L. R. (2010). Community engagement and boundary-spanning roles at research universities. *Journal of Higher Education, 81*(6), 632–657.

CHAPTER TWENTY-FOUR

VALUING THE ROLE OF CONFLICT IN ORGANIZATION ENRICHMENT

Dale Nienow and Jeremy Stringer

Higher education institutions, as with any communities, experience conflict. In addition to interpersonal disputes, cultural conflict may occur among groups with varying religious, political, racial, and cultural traditions, perspectives, and lifestyles. Universities reflect the tensions that exist in society at large. There are people of diverse backgrounds, multiple perspectives on nearly every issue, and willing and engaged participants at varying developmental levels. Student affairs administrators at all stages of their careers need to understand and navigate through the many nuances of conflict. Sometimes student affairs administrators or their supervisors just want a conflict to go away. However, administrators who attempt to make this happen forcefully, such as by exercising positional power, may make the situation worse. Administrators at all levels need to develop the capacity to grow in their ability to respond to conflict in ways that will strengthen their organizations.

Suppose, for example, that a group of students is concerned about tuition increases and makes the decision to disrupt a meeting of the board of trustees on campus. Although the campus has clear procedures covering student protest, stipulating when, where, and how protests may be conducted, the students choose to ignore them because following the procedures would not allow them to protest in the manner they feel is best suited to communicating their strong concern about the cost of their education. How should administrators respond? Legally, they could call the police and have the students removed. But should they? This is a powerful teaching moment for the institution. But what is it the institution wants to teach, and what is the best way to teach it?

Because conflict in higher education is inevitable, student affairs professionals must understand themselves and their dispositions regarding conflict as well as how others typically choose to deal with it. They must also have an understanding of the value of positively dealing with conflict in order to develop and maintain healthy organizations. This chapter discusses varying approaches to conflict. It begins by discussing how administrators can prepare themselves to deal with conflict and reviews various types of conflict interventions. It then turns to a discussion of gracious space as a process for developing a healthy organization, and follows by reviewing processes that might utilize the opportunities presented by conflict to develop healthier individuals and organizations. In summary, we suggest a different perspective on conflict, one that allows individuals to interact with others with respect and appreciate the gifts offered by different perspectives. At the end of the chapter there is a short list of resources that may prove helpful to administrators preparing to face conflict.

Preparing to Deal with Conflict

Every individual has a predisposition to deal with conflict in accustomed ways. A first step in preparing to deal with conflict as a student affairs administrator is understanding one's own natural inclinations. Kenneth Thomas (1992) discusses various approaches to conflict, based on behavior across two dimensions: assertiveness and cooperativeness. Considering these two spheres together, Thomas (1992) defines five basic methods individuals use to deal with conflict. The five methods are competing, accommodating, avoiding, collaborating, and compromising.

The *competing* mode is assertive and uncooperative. This is a power-oriented mode, and the person utilizing it is unwavering in the attempt to "win" an argument or get her way. This mode produces clear winners and losers.

The opposite of the competing mode is *accommodating*. The person who employs this mode is unassertive and cooperative, and willingly accedes to the other person's arguments without attempting to compete. The person may exhibit a self-sacrificing demeanor by yielding when he would prefer not to.

Individuals may exhibit a pattern of *avoiding* conflict. This mode typically describes those who are unassertive and uncooperative. A person may postpone dealing with a conflict until a more opportune time, secretly hoping it will go away (it rarely does).

The opposite of avoiding is *collaborating*. Individuals demonstrating this approach are both assertive and cooperative. They search for a solution to a conflict that will satisfy both parties. It may mean creating a new alternative solution instead of the resolution both sides may have originally had in mind.

Finally, *compromising* individuals search for an intermediate solution that will at least partially satisfy both parties. Compromising individuals address conflict situations but may not spend as much time or energy searching for creative solutions. Compromise solutions may be reached more quickly than collaborative ones. This may be crucial when time is short to reach a resolution, but it may not be as satisfying as a truly collaborative agreement.

Administrators who understand their own proclivities regarding conflict are best prepared to positively deal with conflicts that arise in their work settings. A valuable instrument for assessing differing approaches to conflict in a work setting is the Thomas-Kilmann Conflict Mode Instrument (Thomas & Kilmann, 1974). This instrument can be administered within a given unit and scored very simply. It measures a person's behavior across the two dimensions of assertiveness and cooperativeness. Taking the Thomas-Kilmann Conflict Mode Instrument will help a leader identify her dominant modalities for dealing with conflict as well as those that are utilized infrequently.

Another tool available to help staffs understand approaches to conflict is the Myers-Briggs Type Indicator (MBTI) (Myers, 1998). This instrument can be interpreted to help understand the impact of preferences on conflict. Damien Killen and Danica Murphy (2003) provide a model for managing conflict based on the Myers-Briggs. Completing the MBTI as a staff, particularly before difficult conflicts arise, allows the staff to discuss the tendencies each person has when dealing with conflict and subsequently discuss as a team how team members can work together effectively when faced with tough situations.

Completing instruments to help understand one's own conflict predispositions and those of a staff who must work together when conflict arises is a staff development opportunity. But it is important to stress that there is no magic formula for dealing with conflict. There are times in organizational life when different conflict behavior modes are most appropriate.

The competing mode might be employed when an unpopular course of action, such as cutting the budget, has to be employed. Accommodation might be utilized when avoiding disruption is more important than the outcome of the issue being discussed, or when a party realizes he is wrong. Avoidance might be practiced in order to let people cool down, or when one might do more damage than good by confronting a situation. Collaboration might be sought when integrative solutions are required and all parties have the time to deal with differences in depth. And compromise might be the best option when the parties are intractable and there are immediate time pressures to reach a conclusion.

Types of Conflict Interventions

In addition to preparing in advance how they might by accustomed to resolving difficult problems, leaders in student affairs need to be skilled in a variety of conflict interventions. They will need to utilize various conflict-handling modes in their own relationships, and they may need to conduct or arrange for third-party interventions. Understanding different modes and discerning which is best in a given situation requires both knowledge of available options and skillful application. The four most common types of interventions student affairs professionals will need to understand are *facilitation, negotiation, mediation,* and *arbitration*.

Facilitation

Student affairs leaders are sometimes called upon to facilitate conversations between two parties (individuals as well as groups) who are at odds with each other. Facilitators provide an even playing field for the parties to discuss issues of immediate concern as well as long-term goals. It is usually helpful if the facilitator is a neutral party to whatever dispute is being discussed. Sandra Cheldelin and Ann Lucas (2004) describe several steps in a typical facilitation process. They include "ensuring all members have an equal opportunity to speak and to be heard; clarifying goals and agendas; keeping the group focused; helping them to accomplish their tasks; and 'walking the talk' in terms of demonstrating capacities to listen, paraphrase, reframe, and otherwise model nonconflictual ways of working together" (p. 81). The facilitator is the guardian of the process. Although supervisors may feel they are totally objective, they may not always be perceived as such by other parties. Because of this, it is useful to consider asking someone outside the organization with good group process skills to conduct the facilitation.

Negotiation

Negotiation is different from facilitation. Whereas facilitation tends to be process oriented, negotiation is outcomes orientated (Cheldelin & Lucas, 2004). Roger Fisher and William Ury (Fisher, Ury, & Patton, 1991) provide a useful framework for negotiated agreements. Drawing on the work of the Harvard Negotiation Project, they advocate a method called "principled negotiation" designed to produce agreements "efficiently and amicably" (p. 10). The four parts of principled negotiation are separate the people from the problem; focus on interests, not positions; invent options for mutual gain before deciding what to do; and insist that the result be based on some objective standard. Each of these aspects of principled negotiation is discussed in turn.

Separate the People from the Problem. Authorities on conflict resolution (Fisher et al., 1991; Rockquemore & Laszloffy, 2008) advocate structuring a negotiation so that solving difficult problems is separated from discussing the interpersonal relationships between the negotiators. They advise negotiators to "protect people's egos from getting involved in substantive discussions" (Fisher et al., 1991, p. 37). They suggest that building a solid working relationship makes a negotiation easier. Sitting side by side with an antagonist may help competing parties to think of themselves as partners in search of an equitable solution instead of adversaries out to defeat the other side.

Focus on interests, not positions. The second of Fisher and Ury's (Fisher et al., 1991) principles is to focus on interests instead of positions. While positions are concrete and out in the open, the underlying interests may be more unexpressed and difficult to discern. But a skillful negotiator realizes that figuring out the other side's interests is at least as important as expressing her own. The negotiator might use probing questions to better comprehend the other's interests. Part of a prayer of St. Francis of Assisi popularized by Stephen Covey (2004) is helpful to remember: "Seek first to understand, then to be understood" (p. 235).

In searching for a person's dominant interests, one might remember the power of basic human needs. A negotiation over money, for instance, might be more about respect or recognition than the dollar amount.

Fisher and Ury (Fisher et al., 1991) admonish negotiators to be specific about their interests and to articulate them to the other party. They warn that sometimes people fall into a pattern that resembles a negotiation, but it serves only to perpetuate disagreement. People go back and forth to score hurtful points or to confirm their preexisting biases. Hurt feelings can get in the way of reaching agreement. It is only when they are able to put past offences (real and imagined) behind them that they can focus on resolving their differences and moving forward. Fisher and Ury advise, "Be hard on the problem, soft on the people" (p. 54).

Invent options for mutual gain. Searching for a single right answer is often a barrier to reaching a decision that satisfies all parties. Identifying several solution options may pave the path to a creative solution, perhaps one even better than the parties had expected. Participants need to guard against premature criticism, as well as premature closure, in order to find meaningful solutions. They should look for opportunities to make each party gain from the exchange rather than forcing a situation in which one side wins and the other side loses.

Insist on using objective criteria. Fisher and Ury's final principle (Fisher et al., 1991) is that effective negotiators insist on using objective criteria. This requires preparation in order to identify what criteria exist and to apply them to the case at hand. For example, in a discussion about salary, one might propose that the salary be set by comparing the position's compensation to that at comparable colleges in the region, or to comparable positions whose mean salaries are available from the College and University Professional Association for Human Resources (CUPA-HR). Fisher and Ury suggest that participants "reason and be open to reason as to which standards are most appropriate and how they should be applied" (p. 88).

Mediation

Mediation is considered an extension of the negotiation process. It involves helping the parties reach an agreement by "problem solving, transforming the relationship, or some combination of the two" (Cheldelin & Lucas, 2004, p. 22). A mediator is not party to the dispute. A student affairs professional who serves as a mediator should help the parties "communicate more clearly with each other, identify misunderstandings or misconceptions, sort out multiple issues related to the conflict, and assist them to agree on which issues need attention" (Taylor, 2003, p. 532).

In a litigious society a party who perceives he has been wronged may be quick to file a lawsuit in order to seek justice. However, senior student affairs officers may want to see whether a dispute can be mediated instead of going to court. As Cheldelin and Lucas (2004) affirm, mediation is less costly than court settlements, takes less time, and has a higher rate of compliance with the outcomes. It allows a party to express his emotional hurt and to get a less costly impartial hearing of the grievance. Particularly when the threat of a lawsuit is present, student affairs administrators are wise to consider engaging a professional mediator to conduct the process.

Arbitration

Like mediation, arbitration is an alternative to a court hearing. It may be binding on the parties or nonbinding. More formal than many types of dispute resolution, an arbitrator hears evidence and issues rulings in the dispute. Student affairs professionals who work with unions might have occasion to deal with arbitration, but others in the field are unlikely to be involved with arbitration. Still, it is a type of dispute resolution that could be considered should the situation warrant it.

Gracious Space

Despite their best preparation, even experienced administrators can be challenged to find a way to work through conflict with others positively and productively. But doing so is critical to building a healthy student affairs organization. This can require stretching beyond personal comfort with closely managing the process to exploring processes that draw on deeper goodwill and the collective wisdom of members of the community, present even among those experiencing conflict. This is when belief in whole-person development and drawing on student development theory can be an asset.

Some administrators seem more adept at building trusting relationships and working through social dynamics. In their human development model, Chickering and Reisser (1991) include two components: managing emotions and developing interpersonal competence. Both are particularly relevant to working with conflict. Goleman (1995, 2006) highlights the importance of emotional and social intelligence. Emotional intelligence involves self-awareness and self-management, evidenced in being able to "persist in the face of frustrations, control impulse and delay gratification, regulate one's moods and keep distress from swamping the ability to think, to empathize and to hope" (1995, p. 34). Social intelligence is "being intelligent about relationships" (2006, p. 11). There are two main elements: social awareness, "what we sense about others," and social facility, "what we do with that awareness" (2006, p. 84).

Administrators who intentionally work on development of their own emotional and social intelligence create different possibilities for those involved in the conflict. They can know what to do with emotions that have been triggered and can choose wisely how to address the relationship messages sent. This can transform the spirit of the conflict. With less developed social and emotional intelligence, negative emotions and social interactions can be given back to the sender or transferred to others. As social and emotional intelligence increase, the administrator can transform negative interactions into something more helpful. This can better position the administrator to draw out the emotional and social intelligence of others in the conflict to tap into their best energy and ideas. This accumulated emotional and social intelligence creates greater likelihood of handling conflict productively and of building healthy student affairs organizations.

A positive and supportive organizational culture can make a critical difference in conflicts. People shape the cultures of their organizations. The culture we ultimately create will strongly influence the behavior of its members. Cultural development requires taking a long-term view versus one focused on a quick fix. Student affairs divisions need to develop norms and spirit over time by asking themselves key questions. "What values will guide our work together? What kinds of relationships does the group want to have? What culture will we create?" These conversations need to be shared by everyone in the group to avoid building the norms in separate informal conversations.

Think of the range of different work environments. An open and honest working environment helps people discuss and work through challenges. Contrast this with a hit-and-run culture in which it is okay to drop a bomb of disruption into the room and let others deal with the aftermath. Or consider a culture of gossip in which gossip is the fuel that reinforces conflicts and disruptive behavior. Or a student organization culture that allows or promotes bullying or hazing. Culture can be intentionally established or created by default—there is a choice. Whenever we are tempted to let it happen on its own we should ask whether our culture is as positive as it can be or whether it can be strengthened.

An innovative approach, developed by the Center for Ethical Leadership (Hughes & Grace, 2010; Hughes, Ruder, & Nienow, 2011), draws on the emotional and social intelligence of community members in building organizational cultures where individuals can address conflicts positively. It is called "creating gracious space," defined as a spirit and a setting in which we invite the stranger and learn in public. This method can help student affairs administrators change the way they interact, particularly around conflict. It is illustrated in the following vignette.

> At an advisory board meeting for a graduate program, the program director presents the dilemma of the cohort of students not getting along and behaving unprofessionally. He asks the board for suggestions. A number of thoughtful ideas are suggested: one is to confront the students behaving unprofessionally and give them notice of shaping up or leaving the program. Another is "tell the students they have to sit down and work it out." A third suggestion is to invite them to a day of creating gracious space and discussing what matters most to them.
>
> The director chooses the creating gracious space option. As students in the graduate program gather, they are invited to hold two questions throughout the day: What kind of professional do you want to be? What kind of professional do you want to inhabit? Students go through a core values exercise to identify the values that most centrally guide them in their lives. They are taught the concept of gracious space. After learning the concepts, they are invited to create an opening for a different relationship dynamic by assuming goodwill and suspending their judgments. Through storytelling and dialogue they get to know each other more fully and begin to have the difficult conversations they need in order to create their professional norms and begin acting in the way they want to engage professionally. The culture of the graduate program begins to shift.

As illustrated in the foregoing example, creating gracious space involves intentionally integrating the following elements into the group's interaction: spirit, setting, welcoming the stranger, and learning in public.

Spirit

Participants are encouraged to bring a positive spirit to their work. We all have conversations in our heads as we deal with others. What are you bringing into the work with others? Judgment? Fear that others' inadequacies will limit your own productivity? Preparing to bring positive spirit into the interaction requires changing an internal conversation that dreads the interaction to one that looks for the gifts the other can offer to the relationship.

Setting

It is important to create enough time and an inviting physical space to enable people to open up to relationship building and deeper dialogue. It usually does not work to schedule a difficult conversation in an uncomfortable setting squeezed into a busy day.

Welcoming the Stranger

The concept of welcoming the stranger means intentionally building into the interaction those factors that make others feel that they belong, that they matter, and that you want to get to know them. It can help to invite group members to remember a time when they were outsiders and made to feel welcome. As they tell their stories and identify together the conditions that made them feel welcome, the welcoming environment becomes more explicit. This may also include trying to understand the stranger within yourself.

Learning in Public

Learning in public means allowing others to provide feedback and receiving it as constructive, not being defensive and argumentative. It means being open to the ideas and perspectives of others, and not critical of the person offering comments. Can you make yourself vulnerable in a public setting? Exceptional educators are able to make their own behavior part of the learning of the group (Parks, 2005). Demonstrated vulnerability opens the space for greater learning. It creates room for the wisdom of others. Are you willing to be influenced by another? Are you willing to not be the expert, but to ask the question that draws out others?

Learning together can be a powerful tool for change. Peter Senge and his colleagues (Senge, Scharmer, Jaworski, & Flowers, 2004) have created *Theory U,* which describes the movement of letting go, opening up to collectively seeing the world, and creating new patterns together. It is important to "not impose preestablished frameworks" and "mental models" in this process (Senge and others, 2004, p. 88). They stress that it is important to determine what we need to unlearn together before we can open up to new ideas.

In the concept of social intelligence, "a mood can sweep through a group with great rapidity" (Goleman, 2006, p. 48). Intentionally building gracious space through these four elements helps create a safe, supportive, and open field of energy that can sweep through the group in a positive way. This can lead to conversations that are open, honest, and safe rather than open, honest, and destructive.

Gracious space does not stop at basic civility. It breaks through the limits of surface civility to create space in which conflict can be productively engaged in order to move people into deeper relationships of shared purpose. It transforms the violent energy that can sometimes come out in conflict. Parker Palmer (2004) defines this violence as "violating the identity and integrity of another person" (p. 169). Sometimes our instincts with conflict are to turn down the temperature or remove the tension as soon as possible. In reality it may be much more effective to act as the thermostat that turns up the heat and holds it there. Gracious space can allow the heat to be turned up long enough to help the group break through to the other side of superficial politeness, peaceful coexistence, or shallow support. It can offer an alternative to approaches that seek to fix others, remove the offender as though cutting out the cancer, or acting on righteous indignation. It allows participants to remember who they are at their core and to act on what they most care about and allow others the space to do the same.

Valuing the Opportunities Presented by Intergroup Conflict

Although the creation of gracious space facilitates the development of a healthy organization that can be strengthened through conflict, student affairs administrators will still be called on to deal with tensions, disruptions, and conflict between student groups and between students and the administration. The issues that can catalyze such conflicts are seemingly limitless. They include racial and cultural incidents in which an individual or group has been diminished, stereotyped, or harassed. Or students could be pressuring the board and administration to change a policy on a moral or social issue.

When passions mobilize groups of students, there are multiple issues to consider, such as keeping people safe and minimizing the likelihood of harm, whether physical or emotional. Administrators also need to determine what approach best aligns with the mission of the institution. There can sometimes be great pressure by senior administration to manage the situation and maintain order. But when groups of students are mobilizing, it can be difficult to resolve a situation by administrative mandate. In this type of situation it is important to ask, What kind of community do we want to create? Will we honor different community voices and frame the underlying moral values that are at work? Will we use our power to stifle or suppress others, or can we utilize it to create a stronger community that aligns with our institution's values?

If administrators choose to see through a community-building lens, they will endeavor to engage participants in processes that not only address issues but also help people understand each other better. There are a number of effective social technologies that they can utilize as resources to frame the social interaction of groups who have experienced conflict. The underlying assumption in briefly describing these in this chapter is that conflict, present in all organizations, can be channeled into opportunities to develop stronger higher education communities. Social technologies referenced here include the Art of Hosting, the National Coalition Building Institute Controversial Issue Process, and Restorative Circles.

Art of Hosting

The Art of Hosting (Berkana Institute, 2013) is a self-organized network of practitioners who engage groups around issues that matter most to them. The Art of Hosting approach combines a number of leading social engagement processes to create opportunities for people to address critical challenges. This approach is facilitated by leaders-as-hosts. Advocates for the Art of Hosting, Margaret Wheatley and Deborah Frieze (2013), describes the potential benefits of leaders-as-hosts this way:

> Leaders-as-hosts need to be skilled conveners. They realize that their organization or community is rich in resources, and that the easiest way to discover these is to bring diverse people together in conversations that matter. People who didn't like each other, people who discounted and ignored each other, people who felt invisible, neglected, left out—these are the people who can emerge from their boxes and labels to become interesting, engaged colleagues and citizens. (para. 16)

Art of Hosting practice offers multiple ways for people to express themselves, hear from others, and collect the wisdom of the group. The hosts-facilitators offer a thoughtful progression of approaches that prepare and open participants up to discussing challenging issues. For instance, when addressing a conflict or challenge, people could be invited to prepare themselves for the discussion by sharing their answer to a question with one other person. This utilizes aspects of Appreciative Inquiry (Cooperrider & Whitney, 2005), in that questions are posed that do not put other parties on the defensive, such as, What gives you strength when in challenging situations? Or, how do you stay open to what others are saying when you are angry or disagree with them?

National Coalition Building Institute Controversial Issue Process

Sometimes turning to an outside resource is the best approach to take in dealing with a campus conflict. One well-established group that can be called upon is the National Coalition Building Institute (NCBI) (National Coalition Building Institute, 2013c). NCBI is a nonprofit organization that has successfully worked on many campuses across the country. Probably best known for their diversity work, they offer organizational assessment and training. NCBI has a campus affiliate program that serves as a "pro-active response to discrimination, controversy, and intergroup conflict" (NCBI, 2013b).

A program NCBI offers that student affairs administrators may find particularly salient is the Controversial Issues Process. This training equips leaders to accurately define a controversy, listen to and repeat back another side's concerns, ask questions that elicit the concerns underlying another side's position, map out the concerns on each side of an issue, and reframe the issue in a way that produces action points that all sides can support (NCBI, 2013a).

Restorative Circles

Another process for addressing conflict is a Restorative Circle. This process, originally developed by Dominic Barter to address community violence and conflicts in Brazil, "brings together the people involved in and impacted by a conflict—including community members—to promote understanding, self-responsibility, and action" (Fien, 2012, para. 5). Restorative Circles have been utilized in schools, prisons, neighborhoods, and larger communities. They are designed to quickly resolve the conflict and restore the sense of community. They progress through three phases: identifying the key factors in the conflict, reaching agreements on next steps, and evaluating the results ("Restorative Circles," 2013). The process utilizes deep listening and paraphrasing what is heard in order to develop shared understanding.

Restorative Circles are an aspect of restorative justice. This concept has gained acceptance around the world as an alternative to traditional forms of incarceration. A review of the research on restorative justice (Sherman & Strang, 2007) found that restorative justice techniques, such as Restorative Circles, substantially reduced repeat offending for some, but not all, offenders; reduced crime victims' post-traumatic stress symptoms; and provided both victims and offenders with more satisfaction with justice than conventional criminal justice.

Student-conduct administrators in higher education have begun to apply restorative justice techniques (Lipka, 2007). Administrators can connect their application to college mission statements that emphasize holistic growth, or the development of the educational community. Restorative Circles result in customized agreements and some conduct administrators indicate there are "fewer repeat offenders" than customary sanctions (Lipka, para. 8).

What Makes These Processes Work?

The Art of Hosting, the National Coalition Building Institute Controversial Issue Process, and Restorative Circles give voice to people who have been affected by others. They focus on building trust and restoring community relationships while still addressing divisive issues. They foster shared understanding of multiple perspectives on challenges. They can hold both short-term and long-term views of building a strong community. They honor and work with the energy and passion of others rather than trying to manipulate or suppress the energy. These processes fundamentally trust the collective wisdom of the community.

Conclusion

Conflicts occur in higher education. Conflict management has long been regarded as a core skill of effective student affairs practitioners (Cooper & Boice-Pardee, 2011; Moore, 2000; Pope & Reynolds, 1997; and Sandeen, 1991). Poor conflict management can turn highly functioning organizations into toxic ones. Well-handled conflict can stimulate an organization's creativity and innovation (Kotter, 1985).

There are several different ways student affairs administrators can improve their individual abilities to manage conflict. They should begin with honest self-reflection about how they approach conflict. Such self-reflection can be accompanied by taking the Thomas-Kilmann Conflict Mode Instrument (Thomas & Kilmann, 1974) described earlier in this chapter. Taking this instrument as a staff allow staff members to understand and appreciate the different conflict resolution strengths represented on the staff.

Although we all have different preferences for dealing with conflict, each individual has a choice of how to behave in conflict situations. The action taken can continue the conflict, add to it, or move toward positive developments or resolution. It is easy to get locked into an unproductive impasse of egos and righteousness. It is harder to take a step that invites others to higher levels of behavior.

What risks and first steps are we willing to take in our organizations to create an opening for others to remember their highest and best behavior? It is easy to expect the other party in a conflict to change. It is harder to try to change ourselves. However, this may be the most important key to resolving a conflict.

Student affairs leaders may need to attempt to change the systems and structures that harbor unhealthy conflict. Systemic change may be required to provide support so individuals do not have to engage in heroic acts of courage just to do their jobs. When the conflict is personally threatening, or too big for an individual, we need to have supporting structures and processes. One such supporting structure is *gracious space,* a spirit and setting in which the stranger is welcome and learning in public is embraced. Student affairs administrators can establish this space as a way to create a positive working environment. Further information about gracious space training is included in this chapter's resources section.

When intergroup conflict erupts on campus, student affairs administrators are frequently called on to intervene and search for resolution. This could be seen as an educational opportunity to strengthen the community. Processes such as the Art of Hosting, the National Coalition Building Institute Controversial Issue Process, and Restorative Circles are available as potential resources.

Regularly denying and suppressing conflicts is a form of self-deception. Conflict is something to be respected, not feared. Bennis (1989) indicates that leaders should see conflict as an opportunity, indicating that once they embrace that perspective, conflict becomes a challenge, not a threat. He writes that true leaders "are not deterred by hard times. That is perhaps, finally, what makes them leaders" (p. 159).

References

Bennis, W. (1989). *Why leaders can't lead*. San Francisco, CA: Jossey-Bass.

Berkana Institute. (2013). *What is the Art of Hosting conversations that matter?* http://www.artofhosting.org/what-is-aoh/.

Cheldelin, S. I., & Lucas, A. F. (2004). *Academic administrator's guide to conflict resolution.* San Francisco, CA: Jossey-Bass.

Chickering, A. W., & Reisser, L. (1991). *Education and identity* (2nd ed.). San Francisco, CA: Jossey-Bass.

Cooper, M-B, & Boice-Pardee, H. (2011). Managing conflict from the middle. In L.D. Roper (Ed.), *Supporting and supervising mid-level professionals.* New Directions in Student Services, no. 136. San Francisco, CA: Jossey-Bass.

Cooperrider, D. L., & Whitney, D. (2005). *Appreciative Inquiry: A positive revolution in change.* San Francisco: Berrett-Koehler.

Covey, S. R. (2004). *The seven habits of highly effective people.* New York, NY: Free Press.

Fien, C. C. (2012, September 5).Rochester's underground justice system. *City Newspaper.* http://www.rochestercitynewspaper.com/rochester/rochesters-underground-justice-system/Content?oid=2136848.

Fisher, R., Ury, W., & Patton, B. (1991). *Getting to yes: Negotiating agreement without giving in* (2nd ed.). New York, NY: Penguin.

Goleman, D. (1995). *Emotional intelligence: Why it can matter more than IQ.* New York, NY: Bantam.

Goleman, D. (2006). *Social intelligence: The new science of human relationships.* New York, NY: Bantam.

Hughes, P., & Grace, B. (2010). *Gracious space: A practical guide for working better together* (2nd ed.). Seattle, WA: Center for Ethical Leadership.

Hughes, P., Ruder, K., & Nienow, D. (2011). *Radical collaboration with gracious space: From small opening to profound transformation.* Seattle, WA: Center for Ethical Leadership.

Killen, D., & Murphy, D. (2003). *Introduction to type and conflict.* Palo Alto, CA: Consulting Psychologists Press.

Kotter, J. P. (1985). *Power and influence: Beyond formal authority.* New York, NY: Free Press.

Lipka, S. (2009, April 17). With "'Restorative Justice,'" colleges strive to educate student offenders. *Chronicle of Higher Education,* pp. A26–A28. http://search.proquest.com.proxy.seattleu.edu/docview/214644578/fulltext/141E6F39E065B91C21/1?accountid=28598. Nov. 2013.

Moore, L. V. (2000). Managing conflict constructively. In M. J. Barr & M. K. Desler (Eds.), *The handbook of student affairs administration* (2nd ed., pp. 393-409). San Francisco, CA: Jossey-Bass.

Myers, I. B. (1998). *Introduction to type.* Palo Alto, CA: Consulting Psychologists Press.

National Coalition Building Institute. (2013a). *Controversial issues process.* .http://ncbi .org/workshop-training-descriptions/controversial-issues-process/.

National Coalition Building Institute. (2013b). *Higher education.* http://ncbi.org/ customized-programs/higher-education/.

National Coalition Building Institute. (2013c). *Overview.* http://ncbi.org/overview/.

Palmer, P. (2004). *A hidden wholeness: The Journey toward an undivided life.* San Francisco, CA: Jossey-Bass.

Parks, S. D. (2005). *Leadership can be taught.* Boston, MA: Harvard Business School Press.

Pope, R. C., & Reynolds, A. L. (1997). Student affairs core competencies: Integrating multicultural awareness, knowledge, and skills. *Journal of College Student Development, 38,* 266–277.

"Restorative Circles. (2013). http://www.restorativecircles.org/home.

Rockquemore, K. A., & Laszloffy, T. (2008). *The Black academic's guide to winning tenure—without losing your soul.* Boulder, CO: First Forum Press.

Sandeen, A. (1991). *The chief student affairs officer: Leader, manager, mediator, educator.* San Francisco, CA: Jossey-Bass.

Senge, P., Scharmer, C. O., Jaworski, J., & Flowers, B. S. (2004). *Presence: Human purpose and the field of the future.* Cambridge, MA: Society for Organizational Learning.

Sherman, L. W., & Strang. H. (2007). *Restorative Justice: The evidence.* London, England: Smith Institute.

Taylor, S. L. (2003). Conflict resolution. In S. R. Komives & D. B. Woodard Jr. (Eds.), *Student services: A handbook for the profession* (4th ed., pp. 525-538)). San Francisco, CA: Jossey-Bass.

Thomas, K. W. (1992). Conflict and negotiation processes in organizations. In M. D. Dunnette & L. M. Hough (Eds.), *Handbook of industrial and organizational psychology* (Vol. *3,* 2nd ed., pp. 652-717).. Palo Alto, CA: Consulting Psychologists Press.

Thomas, K. W., & Kilmann, R. H. (1974). *Thomas-Kilmann Conflict Mode Instrument.* Woods Road, NY: Xicom,

Wheatley, M., & Frieze, D. (2013). Leadership in the age of complexity. http:// berkana.org/berkana_articles/leadership-in-the-age-of-complexity/3/.

Resources

These resources will help the reader to gain an understanding of these processes and how they work. However, they may be insufficient to qualify readers to utilize them unless they go through more extensive training. If you are in a hurry to get a conflict resolved, you may wish to bring in a qualified expert.

Gracious Space Training http://ethicalleadership.org/programs/gracious-space

National Coalition Building Institute Training http://ncbi.org/workshop-training-descriptions/

Understanding Conflict Modes http://www.kilmanndiagnostics.com/catalog/ thomas-kilmann-conflict-mode-instrument

PART SIX

SKILLS AND COMPETENCIES OF PROFESSIONAL PRACTICE

Student affairs administration consists of a vast array of functional areas, each requiring unique qualifications. However, there are a number of skills and competencies that are common across all student affairs areas. This part addresses several of these. In chapter 25, Margaret Barr discusses budgeting, including sources of funds, the differences between budgets and financial management in public and private institutions, and practical ideas on how to maximize resources and deal with unexpected budget cuts. chapter 26, by John Wesley Lowery, addresses legal and risk management issues. Lowery covers the general legal landscape of higher education and details many specific laws and regulations affecting the practice of student affairs administration. Another responsibility common to all those in student affairs is assessment. In chapter 27, Marilee Bresciani Ludvik discusses the need for assessment, explores common approaches to assessment, and provides a brief explanation of how assessment may differ, yet complement, institutional research. Friend raising and fund raising are increasingly common to the practice of student affairs. David Wolf explores this topic in chapter 28. He introduces basic concepts of friend-raising fund raising and provides insights into both. Another topic with wide-ranging implications for student affairs practice is the impact of technology. In chapter 29, Kevin Guidry and Josie Ahlquist address the implications of computer-mediated communication and social media for student affairs professionals, including positive and negative impacts and the potential to utilize technology for community building and leadership development. The section concludes with Eugene Zdziarski's look at the management of campus crisis. In chapter 30 he provides a detailed and systematic look at the process of crisis management, and what administrators can do to prevent crises and protect their campus communities.

CHAPTER TWENTY-FIVE

BUDGETING AND FISCAL MANAGEMENT FOR STUDENT AFFAIRS

Margaret J. Barr

It does not sound very interesting or engaging, but acquiring skills in fiscal and budget management is an essential skill for any student affairs professional. Understanding budgets and fiscal management makes your job easier whether you are a new professional with responsibility for a relatively small budget or a seasoned student affairs professional with responsibility for many programs and services. In addition, being successful in fiscal management will aid you when you are presenting a new idea. If you are prepared, present a realistic budget, and have a good track record in budget management, your ideas are more likely to be supported. Adequate fiscal resources are critical for the success of student affairs programs and services. As competition for funding increases both within and without higher education, it is clear that student affairs administrators must be good fiscal managers and excellent stewards of financial resources.

Fiscal management skills are often learned on the job. This chapter seeks to accelerate that process by providing basic information on budgeting and fiscal management. The chapter provides a brief review of the larger fiscal environment of higher education (see chapter 4 for further discussion), identifies sources of funds to support the student affairs enterprise, and highlights concerns related to some sources of funds. The focus then shifts to the differences between budget and financial management in public and private institutions. The purposes of budgets are discussed, as is the budget cycle and the responsibilities of student affairs administrators within that cycle. The chapter concludes with a presentation of practical ideas on how to maximize resources and how to deal with unexpected budget cuts.

There are limitations, however, in the material that can be covered in a single chapter in an edited handbook. Readers wishing a more comprehensive discussion of budgets and budget management may find Barr and McClellan's *Budgets and Financial Management in Higher Education* (2011) to be a helpful resource.

The General Fiscal Environment for Student Affairs

Higher education institutions, whether public or independent, are experiencing great challenges in identifying and capturing the needed fiscal resources to support the work of the institution. A first step in sound fiscal management for student affairs professionals is to understand the broader fiscal context of higher education, because that context sets very real constraints on what can and cannot be accomplished at any college or university.

External Issues

There are a number of issues external to the institution that can influence the fiscal management of student affairs. These include increased competition for resources; increased concerns from legislative bodies and the general public regarding the costs of attending higher education; paying for unfunded legally required mandates; increased regulation from government at the state and federal level; the cost of technology; the rising costs for other goods and services; and the increase in competition for qualified students, faculty, and staff.

Of particular concern in public higher education are the diminishing levels of support from state and local governmental sources. The National Center for Higher Education Management Systems (2011) reports that the average support from state and local governments for full-time students was $7,106 in 2008 but only $6,290 in 2011. This reduction is not merely a reflection of the recession that occurred around that time. The American Council on Education (2012) notes that state support for public higher education as a function of overall state investment has decreased by just over 40 percent since 2008.

Internal Issues

Some of the internal issues arise from the private or public status of the institution. Resources for public institutions are often shaped by political forces that are sometimes not directly related to higher education. Private or independent institutions' budgets are shaped by the strength of their endowments and their ability to raise funds both for specific projects and for ongoing operations.

Internal competition. Student affairs units must compete with other parts of the institution for support for their programs and services. There are always more requests for budget support than there are funds to support such requests. Mayhew (1979) said in part that "budgets are really a statement of educational purpose phrased in fiscal terms" (p. 54). Some items seem not to be debatable on the surface but can be examined from a different perspective. Utilities provide one good example. They can either be assumed as a given cost of business or seen as an opportunity for conservation. Some items are genuinely not debatable such as a settlement in a lawsuit or an unfunded mandate from the federal government.

Competition for the available dollars from within the institution will continue to be a major issue for student affairs. Remember there are many other worthy programs requesting funding in the institution, and all cannot supported in the budget process. As the resource pool diminishes, the competition for available funds becomes more intense.

Failure to link student affairs to the mission of the institution. Success for the division of student affairs in securing adequate resources depends on the ability of managers within the division to directly link their programs and services to the educational purposes of the institution. It is easy for the English Department to link a budget request to the educational purpose of the institution. For student affairs to be successful in capturing financial resources, budget managers must be able to link unit programs and services, in a concrete way, to the educational mission of the institution. For example, how does the program concretely contribute to increasing retention of at-risk students? Or, how many graduates of the institution are employed in their chosen fields within a specified period of time after graduation? Both of these are examples of how to link a student affairs program to the mission of the institution.

Unwarranted optimism. In general, student affairs professionals are optimistic souls and look for the best in most situations. However, those with budget responsibility must learn to curb optimism and not make assumptions that, having made the case once, they will not have to make the case for support again in the future. The prudent budget manager learns to curb their enthusiasm and be prepared for any contingency.

Understanding the larger fiscal environment of higher education and the pressures within it is the first step in successful fiscal management. The next step is an increased understanding of the sources of funds to support the institution and any limitations that exist regarding the expenditure of those funds.

Sources of Funds

A number of funding sources support both public and independent institutions of higher education. The emphasis and dependence on a specific source of financial support varies among institutional types, but current trends seem to indicate that those distinctions are becoming more blurred in the changing fiscal environment of higher education.

State-Appropriated Funds

Funds from the state government are the primary source of income for most public colleges and universities, though, as suggested by the earlier information regarding state support for higher education, the proportion of revenue being derived from state appropriations is diminishing. At a community college such income may be supplemented by direct support from the county or municipality in which the institution is located.

Some states use formula funding based on the number of full-time or part-time, graduate and undergraduate students, with different funding formulas provided for each student category. In other states, formula funding is based on a rolling average of credit hours generated over the previous five years by the institution at the undergraduate and graduate levels. In many states, legislative review of each institutional budget is extensive and may even involve line item review of all budget items. Some states use a combination of formula funding (overseen by the higher education agency of the state) and extensive legislative review of new requests and capital budgets. Finally, a limited number of institutions are constitutionally autonomous (not subject to the regulation of other state agencies) and are treated in the budget process the same as any other state agency.

The role of state appropriations for private (independent) institutions is much narrower than for their public counterparts. State appropriations for private colleges and universities are usually limited to support for specific programs that meet state priorities or interests, such as working with the physically challenged or dental education. In addition, state support for private institutions may come in the form of capital budget support (see later section) or direct financial aid programs for state resident students.

Tuition

Undergraduate tuition is the financial engine that drives much of higher education in the private sector and is becoming more important in the public sector as state support for higher education diminishes. The cost of tuition can be calculated on the basis of each credit hour and the level of enrollment (undergraduate or graduate), or it can be calculated on a full-time enrollment basis defined by the state or the institution.

For private institutions, tuition is a critical component of the institutional budget. In smaller, struggling institutions, enrollment (and thus tuition dollars) can be the difference between making the budget and going into the red. Attracting and retaining students is critical to the sound fiscal base of all higher education institutions, and in most cases student affairs plays a central role in that task.

Public institutions often have statutory restrictions regarding the amount of tuition that may be charged to in-state residents. The rationale is based on the notion that because the state allocates money to the institution, state citizens should not have to pay high tuition in order to attend their state college or universities. Usually there are no such restrictions on out-of-state tuition rates or tuition rates for international students.

Graduate tuition, whatever the source of funds to pay it, does not begin to pay the cost of graduate education. Exceptions to this rule include specialized graduate degree programs usually offered on a full-time basis for full-tuition-paying students. Doctoral programs are very expensive, and tuition generated by such programs usually does not offset the cost associated with them. Professional school programs also provide similar budgetary challenges to the institution. Although graduate programs may be essential to expanding knowledge (a core function of higher education institutions), they are not money makers or contributors to the funding stream for any institution.

Mandatory Student Fees

At public institutions, and increasingly at private institutions, mandatory student fees have been used as one means to obtain needed revenue without raising tuition. In the politicized context of higher education, mandatory student fees are used as a way to avoid confrontations with the legislature or the public on the volatile issue of tuition. Such fees are usually charged on a term basis and are assessed from, at least, all undergraduate students. Examples include building use fees, technology fees, bond revenue fees, laboratory fees, breakage fees, student services fees, and student activity fees. Such fees are usually dedicated as support for a specific building or program and must be reserved for those uses. To illustrate, a steady stream of mandatory fees from all undergraduates provides the financial foundation for building many campus recreation centers.

The process of allocating general mandatory fees, such as a student service fee, is institutionally specific. In some institutions, mandatory fees are routinely allocated to support units as part of the general budget process. In others, a committee with student representation allocates the fees after holding budget hearings with departments and agencies. In most cases, mandatory student activity fees are allocated by student government groups under the general supervision of an office in student affairs. Working effectively with such allocation processes is clearly a key task for student affairs professionals.

Private institutions are much less likely to adopt the use of mandatory student fees as a strategy to generate money. Many of the programs supported by student fees (recreation, health services, disability services) at public institutions are funded by tuition income at private institutions. This is particularly true of programs that serve all students, such as student centers or recreation facilities. Mandatory student fees, in addition to high tuition, are not seen as a positive recruitment tool for expensive private institutions. However, as competition for resources becomes more intense, this practice may surface more often in private institutions.

Special Student Fees

Two types of special student fees are used as a means of budget support: one-time fees and fees for services. Such fee structures are present in both public and independent (private) institutions.

One-time fees are assessed for participation in a specific program or activity. Examples of one-time fees include study abroad fees, loan processing fees, and commencement fees. The income from the fee helps offset the cost of the program and reduces the dependence of the program on general revenue funds of the institution.

Fees for service are a growing phenomenon in higher education and are commonly linked to psychological services, health care, or the ability of students to attend popular intercollegiate athletic events. To illustrate, at some counseling centers students seeking help are provided a limited number of therapy sessions but must provide some copayment for continued therapy. The impact of this approach to funding services ought to be carefully evaluated. Will the charging of a fee discourage participation or make participation a privilege that only some students can afford? Reliance on special mandatory student fees for central services in student affairs also may make the unit particularly vulnerable to rapid changes in enrollments or higher demand for services.

Endowment Income

Income from the institutional endowment is a major source of budgetary support for private institutions. Overall fiduciary responsibility for managing the endowment rests with the institutional governing board although day-by-day management decisions are the responsibility of institutional staff or investment managers. Prudent institutions do not use all of the income generated by the investment of the endowment for current operations. Instead, spending rules are adopted by the governing board, regarding the percentage of the endowment income that may be spent on operations in any fiscal year. Such spending limits accomplish two goals: providing a relatively steady income stream to the institution and reinvesting a portion of the income in the endowment to help it grow.

Currently, most public institutions have much more modest endowments than their private counterparts. That is likely to change in the future as state support for public higher education erodes and alternate sources of income are needed. In private institutions the endowment is clearly under the control of the governing board in order to meet the fiduciary responsibilities of the institution. At some public institutions, independent foundations have been established to raise money and invest it for the support of the institution. Although any foundation must meet the requirements of state statutes and regulations of the state where the foundation is located, the organization and control of foundations at public institutions varies. For example, some have institutional representatives on the foundation governing board, some do not. Some are absolutely independent, and some receive office space, and clerical and accounting support from the institution.

Fund Raising

Acquiring private financial support for the institution is becoming increasingly important at both public and private institutions. Identifying potential donors, cultivating them, and providing opportunities for them to financially support the programs, services, and offerings of the institution is a major task. Two equally important types of fund raising are essential to higher education: annual giving and long-term campaigns for programs and facilities.

For most private institutions, annual giving is a critical revenue source for the operating budget of the institution. Revenue goals are set for the development office based on past performance and usually revenues from annual giving become a source of funds for the general budgeting process of the institution. Chapter 28 in this volume provides a comprehensive overview of issues in fund raising for student affairs, and readers should peruse that chapter for further information. The expectations, however, for student affairs to actively participate in fund raising are growing, and the ability to attract additional resources to support programs will become more important to student affairs in the future.

Grants and Contracts

The research enterprise at most institutions is primarily funded by grants from the federal government, state agencies, business and industry, and private foundations. In addition to providing direct support in terms of salaries and operating costs of the specific research activity, grants are also required to recapture some of the indirect costs related to the grant. Indirect costs include services provided by the institution such as payroll, accounting, purchasing, space renovation, maintenance, utilities, and administration. The federal government indirect cost rate is negotiated between the institution and the federal government and applies to all federal research grants.

Indirect costs are also assessed on grants from other sources. Charges for indirect costs do not accrue to the unit budget but are considered part of the general revenue stream of the institution.

Contracts are time-limited arrangements with business, industry, or the government whereby the institution provides a direct service in return for payment. Examples of contracts include providing training for a state agency, teaching an academic course for the employees of a specific company, or providing technical support for a computer project being completed by local government. Overhead rates are established for such contracts to cover some of the same costs previously noted in grants.

Foundations are a special case when writing grants for support. Some have well-defined missions and support proposals aligned only with those missions. Others may be more open to innovative programs and activities. Each foundation is different and should be carefully researched to determine whether the proposal is aligned with foundation goals and whether the institution is comfortable with the goals of the foundation.

Most institutions have a centralized approval process for grants and contracts to assure that appropriate charges are being made and that the proposed grant or contract is congruent with the institutional mission. Finally such offices supervise fund disbursement to the unit and assure that all reporting requirements of the grant are met.

Auxiliary Services

Auxiliary services usually do not receive any institutional support and are expected to generate sufficient income to cover all operating expenses (including maintenance) as well as long-term facility costs associated with the enterprise. Auxiliary services are, however, governed by the same institutional rules regarding compensation, purchasing, and human resources. Each institution defines what programs and activities will be designated as auxiliaries. Examples include student housing, food services, student unions, recreation buildings, and, on occasion, intercollegiate athletic programs. Auxiliary enterprises are, for many student affairs divisions, a major part of the total budget of the division.

Special Programs

Special programs may be one-time events such as a department-sponsored seminar for which entrance fees are charged to cover the cost of the event.

Or, special programs may be recurring ventures such as a sports camp offered every summer. In either case, the program must be self-supporting unless specific institutional permission has been given to have expenses exceed income. The revenue from the program is usually retained by the unit to offset expenses. The goal of the enterprise is to break even at the end of the fiscal year. Sometimes, if revenue exceeds expectations, modest reserve funds can be established to cover the unit for an unanticipated shortfall in revenue in future years.

Contracted Services

In both public and private institutions, functions such as food services, bookstores, and copying services are increasingly outsourced to private enterprise. Through competitive bidding processes, such contracts become a source of funds to support both operations and capital expenditures such as facility repair, renovations, new construction, and program enhancements. Negotiations for such contracts may include yearly lump sum payments for capital expenses in addition to a regular income stream from sales. In recent years, this concept has been expanded to include exclusive contracts for certain soft drinks, telephone service, washer and dryer services, and so on, whereby the institution receives a percentage of the gross sales in return for the exclusive privilege of providing services on campus.

Religious Support

Some private institutions of higher education also rely on financial support from religious groups. Such support usually carries with it the requirement for representation on the governing board of the institution and institutional support for the values of denomination or religious group.

State and Federal Capital Budgets

Most public institutions must go through a separate budgeting process in order to receive funds for new construction or massive facility renovation. That process is separate from the regular state budgeting process. At times, private institutions can access state capital funds if the project meets a pressing state priority such as medical research.

If the new facility is consistent with a federal priority and there is support for the facility in the federal appropriation process in Congress, then federal dollars may be available to both public and private institutions for facility construction. This avenue is long, complicated, and very political.

Other Sources of Income

There are a number of miscellaneous sources of income used to support programs and facilities in higher education. Facility rental fees or rental fees for specialized equipment are but two examples. The privilege of parking on campus generates revenue through a parking fee that helps support parking facilities. Although individually such sources of support are small, in the aggregate such income sources are essential to the financial health of the institution's various units.

Implications

Budgeting and financial management in student affairs requires understanding of the sources of funds that directly support the units under the auspices of student affairs. First, it is critical that the budget manager and directors of units understand where the money is coming from and what the restrictions are (if any) on the use of the money.

Second, if mandatory student fees are part of the budget support for the unit, then the responsible administrator must have a clear understanding of the annual and long-term processes used by the institution to access those funds. For example, must a budget be first submitted to a fee committee and receive approval from the committee before it can become a part of the overall division of student affairs budget?

Third, if a division of student affairs has auxiliary enterprises such as housing and food services, what are the bond obligations to support those units? What is the long-term plan for repair and replacement of existing buildings and equipment? How are new structures funded? What new regulations regarding health and safety need to be accounted for in the operating budget as well as the capital budget? These are but a few of the questions that must be asked by those responsible for building auxiliary budgets and reserve funds to operate those units.

Fourth, if supervision of any contracted institutional services such as housekeeping or food service are part of the responsibility of the division, is there a clear understanding of institutional responsibilities for enforcement of the contract? Who in the institution must be involved in contract review and who has authority to sign the contract on behalf of the institution?

Fifth, has the division of student affairs clearly defined the opportunities for fund raising that exist within the division and communicated those opportunities to those in development and elsewhere in the institution? Understanding the sources of funds supporting student affairs units and the implications related to those fund sources is an essential first step in sound financial management practices.

Public Versus Private Financial Issues

Distinctions between public and private institutions with regard to revenue and expenses have already been discussed. There are also differences in other areas, and several of those are discussed in this section.

Controls

Although both types of institution must conform to applicable state law, financial policies and investment strategies at private institutions are controlled either through the governing board or through other campus-based governance and administrative bodies. This provides greater degrees of freedom in using resources to meet unexpected needs. For example, rising energy costs can be met through campus-based reallocation at many private institutions, while their public counterparts often are required to seek permission to respond to such changes from the state coordinating board or other oversight body.

Fiscal policies at private institutions are likely to be less cumbersome, permitting transfers of funds for reasonable purposes without many approvals or other bureaucratic barriers. The budget manager is, however, held accountable for assuring that at the end of the fiscal year there is no deficit in the unit budget.

In public institutions, usually the institutional budget office must grant permission for line item transfers over a certain dollar amount. Sometimes for certain categories of expenditures the governing board or the supervising state agency must approve such transfers.

Purchasing

Both public and private institutions have regulations regarding the purchase of goods and services. For many public institutions, purchasing of goods and services is complicated by state regulations, required low bid acceptance and overarching state contracts for certain goods and services. When a state contract is in place for a certain product, the campus must provide a viable justification to not purchase the item through the state contact.

Usually at private institutions, purchasing requirements are less rigid and are not complicated by state contracts. In fact, at many private institutions purchasing for some items is highly decentralized with the unit budget manager taking responsibility to seek bids and then making the decision on the purchase. Whereas on the surface such freedom can be very attractive, it also requires that each budget manager exercise due diligence to assure the institution is getting the most for its purchasing dollar.

Audit Requirements

Audit requirements exist at both public and private institutions. An external audit provides an independent review of the financial and management decisions made by a unit. Both financial and management reports are issued at the conclusion of the audit and the budget manager and other administrative officials review the reports and agree to needed changes in policies and procedures. A regular follow-up is then conducted to assure that the needed changes have been made. Sometimes such audits are conducted by outside auditors and sometimes there is an internal audit office.

If the institution has an internal audit office that regularly conducts audits of all units, policies and procedures can be strengthened rather rapidly because less time is spent on bringing an outsider auditor up to date on institutional policies. New budget managers should also ask the internal audit office to conduct an initial audit of office accounts to identify problems or issues that could be improved.

Public institutions often have the added complication of audits from an independent state agency. State auditor general offices conduct such audits, and the outcomes are public records. A negative audit finding, though minor in nature, can result in negative publicity and institutional embarrassment.

Human Resources Issues

Both types of institutions have complex human resources issues, including compliance with state and federal law, unions, benefits, position classification, and the like. Although in some ways it may seem that human resource management is easier in the private institution, do not be misled. Personnel issues are a complicated area, and prudent administrators seek help early and often from those who know more about policies and procedures than they do.

The Purposes of a Budget

There are many purposes for a budget in higher education. Maddox (1999) defines five general purposes of a budget: putting business strategy into operation, allocating resources, providing incentives, providing control, and providing a means of communication both within and without the institution.

Putting Business Strategy into Operation

Although it is difficult for many student affairs professionals to think of higher education as a business enterprise, in a very real sense that is what it is. Like any business, income comes into the institutions for services rendered or promised, and invoices for goods and services must be paid. Higher education is usually a not-for-profit enterprise (the exception being proprietary schools). Any excess income over expenses at the end of the fiscal year is used to help finance the future of the institution, meet pressing operating costs, construction or infrastructure needs, or in some public institutions reverts to the state (Barr, 2002).

The institutional budget reflects the plans, priorities, goals, and aspirations that drive the institution. The budget is the fiscal blueprint of what is important. For example, if the institution has adopted the goal of having the number one business school in the country, the budget will reflect substantial investment over multiple years in that unit. Or if the institution is committed to keeping access open to low-income students, the student financial aid budget will rise in direct proportion to any increases in tuition, room and board, and fees. Each institution has unique and sometimes conflicting priorities and goals, and the astute budget manager understands those goals as requests are made for financial support.

Sometimes the budget is not goal directed but instead is focused on identifying resources to cover unexpected increases in costs such as utilities. In other words, the institution does not have a strategic goal of paying higher utility costs but must do so in order to provide basic educational services. Some institutional priorities simply involve keeping the doors open, the water flowing, and the heat and lights turned on. A careful examination of the budget of the unit and the institution can help student affairs budget managers understand both the problems faced by the institution and the priorities held by the board and the central administration. With this base of understanding it becomes much easier to present budget requests that comport with institutional priorities.

Allocating Resources

The reality is that no institution of higher education has unlimited resources and the ability to meet all the needs and wants of all budget units within the institution. Decision makers must make clear distinctions between the two. A *need* is an essential element of the service, program, or instructional unit that must be funded in order to meet institutional expectations and priorities. For example, if English is required for all entering freshmen and the freshman class is larger than expected, then the English Department may need additional instructors. Other alternatives should be explored prior to making such a commitment. Examples of alternatives might include increasing the size of each section of freshman English or rescheduling some sections into peak demand times for students; if an analysis reveals that such changes still will not provide English instruction for all freshmen, then the institution is faced with two choices: adjust the budget to increase the resources to the English department or modify the requirements regarding freshman English. Either decision has consequences (intended and unintended) that must be understood by decision makers.

A *want* is something desired by the unit or an individual member of the unit. A want may have the potential to move both the unit and the institution forward, but it is not essential to either the operation of the unit or the institution. For example, an administrator might want all staff members in the unit to have cell phones but does not have a compelling reason to support the request. At times, wants are simply amenities that might make life easier but are not essential to either the institution or the unit. An effective institutional budget assures that the general funds of the institution are used to support the highest priorities and the greatest needs of the entire institution.

Providing Incentives

Sometimes the institutional rules governing budgets are structured in ways that work against sound fiscal management. For example, at the end of the fiscal year there is a frenzy of spending. Supplies are ordered in bulk, computers are purchased, and so forth. This activity is usually caused by budgeting rules that require excess funds in a unit to revert back to the control of the central administration or the state. Sometimes end-of-year spending includes unnecessary purchases just to demonstrate that the unit needed all of its allocated resources. A better approach to budgeting might be to provide an incentive for budget managers to keep a tight rein on expenses. One method is to allow the unit to retain some (if not all) of the money left in the unit budget at the end of the year. This money then could be placed in a reserve account to support major equipment purchases or facility renovation or carried forward to fund some *wants* of the unit in the next fiscal year.

Control

The most traditional role of the budget is to exert fiscal control within the institution (Maddox, 1999). There are two basic approaches to budget control: highly centralized (institution centered) and highly decentralized (unit centered). In the highly centralized approach a central budget authority approves all changes and modifications to the approved budget and the planned expenditures therein. Under the decentralized model each unit budget manager is held responsible for using fiscal resources in a prudent and responsible manner. Most institutions have developed a hybrid approach incorporating elements of both the centralized and decentralized model. Routine decisions are made at the unit level, and central budget control is exercised for large fund expenditures. This combination approach seems to work quite well, providing some degree of institutional control yet permitting some degree of freedom for those who are closest to the problems and issues within the unit (Barr & McClellan, 2011).

Communication

Mayhew (1979) indicated that the budget was a tool for communication to a variety of publics about the goals, priorities, and aspirations of an institution of higher education. When a decision is made to allocate resources to a particular program or activity it signals the importance of that program or activity to the overall mission of the institution. For example, if retention of faculty is an important institutional goal, then the merit increment pool for faculty members may be larger than that for other members of the institutional workforce.

In public institutions, the budget is usually an open document and provides evidence to the legislature and state agencies of the priorities of the institution. Private institutions are more apt to consider budget documents private information, and no requirement exists that they be made public. Budget information does, however, need to be made available for review by foundations and agencies providing funding to the institution. Finally, the budget is the primary means for the institutional administration to convey to the governing board the priorities and needs of the institution.

Types of Budgets

Generally there are three major types of budgets on any campus: the operating budget, the capital budgets, and auxiliary budgets. In some cases, affiliated hospitals or other service providers may also have a separate budget. For purposes of this chapter the discussion is limited to the operating budget and the capital budget.

Operating Budget

The operating budget is the core budget of the institution for the fiscal year (Woodard & von Destinon, 2000). An operating budget reflects all income from all sources (including restricted funds) as well as all approved expenditures for the fiscal year (Meisinger & Dubeck, 1984). The fiscal year varies from institution to institution and is generally aligned with the academic calendar. Each institution has specific rules governing the movement of money within the operating budget; the astute student affairs administrator both understands and complies with those rules.

Capital Budgets

Capital budgets reflect the money set aside to improve the physical plant, finance new construction, purchase major pieces of equipment, replace vehicles, or for expenses that must be paid over several fiscal years. All capital expenses are not automatically funded by the capital budget. Replacement of personal computers in offices, for example, is often funded as part of the operating budget. Sometimes available funds in the capital budgets are not sufficient to meet construction needs. When that occurs, an institution sells bonds to potential investors and has a plan to pay the investors through the operating budget of the institution from one of the sources of funds previously discussed. The bond rating assigned to the institution at the time of selling the bonds reflects the general fiscal health of the institution.

Budget Models

There is more than one correct way to develop a budget. This section reviews some of the common budget models used in American higher education.

Incremental Budgets

An incremental budget is based on the assumption that both needs and costs vary only a small amount from year to year. It also assumes that the budget from the previous fiscal year is accurate and fairly reflects the yearly expenditures of the unit. Both of these assumptions may be false. The budget for the current year becomes the base budget for the next fiscal year. Under an incremental budget model, all units of the institution receive the same percentage increases for the same line items within the budget. Those increases are based both on the amount of money available and often reflect some index for inflation such as the *Higher Education Price Index* (Research Associates of Washington, 2005). There is no strategic examination of the expenditure patterns of the total institution or of individual budget units.

Incremental budgeting models minimize conflicts within the institution because every unit is treated in the same way. Such budget models also avoid examination of past commitments to determine whether or not they are meeting the current needs of the institution. Maddox (1999) indicates that "a unit that has a generous budget will only get better off relative to other units—its budget grows on that budget excess, whereas another unit treads water as essential funding is increased just (or not) enough to keep pace with cost increases" (p. 16). Formula budgeting is another version of incremental budgeting and is used by most states to allocate money to state supported institutions of higher education (see earlier discussion on sources of funds).

Redistribution

At times institutions will combine incremental budgets with a redistribution process. This approach provides a general budget increase for operations but permits the budget manager to redistribute the dollars within all budget line items. The new budget cannot be increased more than the allocation provided through the budget increment. Although an improvement, redistribution still does not address inequities between units. That problem can be partially addressed by providing the percentage increment to all budgets within an administrative unit such as a division of student affairs. The dean or vice president can then address within division inequities between units that have developed as a result of incremental budgeting.

Zero-Based Budgeting

The zero-based budgeting model requires that each item in the budget be justified and that nothing is assumed to be guaranteed in the budget. Incremental funds are not distributed to units; instead each budget manager must justify every expense in the budget request. A zero-based budgeting model has the advantage of enabling careful review of all institutional expenditures and requires that all expenditures be linked to the strategic goals of the unit and the institution. Although effective, zero-based budgeting is labor intensive and time consuming.

Some institutions have developed a modified version of zero-based and incremental funding. Incremental funding is provided for all but a few line items; those line items then must be justified using the zero-based budgeting model.

Cost- or Responsibility-Centered Models

Though slightly different, these two alternative budget models are grouped together for purposes of this discussion. Under a strict cost-centered approach, each part of the organization is responsible for generating revenue to meet its expenses and is expected to stand on its own. Although this works for auxiliary enterprises, the model does not adapt itself to instructional, academic support and student support units.

Responsibility-centered budgeting has been adopted by many institutions as a means to extend decision making for budgeting beyond the central administration (Woodard & von Destinon, 2000). Each unit is responsible for management of its enterprise, and if the unit incurs a deficit in any fiscal year, that deficit must be made up the following fiscal year from budget resources allocated to the unit. If the unit has excess income over expenditures, the unit is permitted to carry forward the surplus for reallocation or support of new projects. Responsibility-centered models in budgeting provide incentives and greater flexibility to meet changing priorities (Stocum & Rooney, 1997). It has the disadvantage of concentrating on unit goals to the exclusion of institutional goals and objectives.

The Budget Cycle

The two major elements of any budget are revenue and expenses. The key to successful budget management is being able to closely predict the revenue and to assure that expenses do not exceed available funds.

Identifying Revenue

The first step in budgeting is to identify all sources of funds that support the enterprise, including general revenue support; reimbursed costs for services provided; grant, contracts; fees for certain programs and activities; and, if the unit is lucky, income from a designated endowment to support the program. Each revenue source should be classified as to whether it is ongoing or a one-time source of funds.

Identifying Expenses

Expenses vary from year to year dependent on the activities of the unit. Some are *required* or *fixed costs* such as telephone and data service, postage, and the like. For auxiliary enterprises there are also costs set outside the unit for utilities and maintenance of facilities. Even though such costs are fixed, they should be examined to see if there is not a more cost-effective way to conduct business.

Discretionary costs include travel, registration fees, library acquisitions, publicity and program promotion, and so forth. Some discretionary costs are directly related to programs and should be budgeted so that expense does not exceed revenue.

Institutional Parameters

Development of institutional guidelines is not an easy process and requires financial staff to analyze past budgetary performance of the institution, including both fixed and discretionary costs and the influence of the greater environment on the financial health of the institution. Although the environmental scan may be rigorous in some institutions and less so in others, each institution seeks to understand the outside forces that impinge on the financial operation of the college or university.

Simultaneously, large variances in the prior year's budget are examined in detail. Problem units or line items are identified and must be accounted in any institutional rules. Budget guidelines and parameters reflect the assumptions of the planners regarding enrollment, demand for services, opportunities, and problems facing the institution. Each unit budget manager should understand the assumptions and beliefs that drive the budget parameters.

Timetables

Institutional budget instructions include the timetable(s) for the submission of all budget documents. Each unit budget manager then must establish earlier deadlines to make sure the unit can meet the required submission deadline. If there are problems meeting the deadline, then the unit budget managers should immediately discuss those issues with their administrative superiors. The important thing is not to ignore budget timelines, because such actions can adversely affect the budget of the unit.

Developing Unit Budget Requests

There are at least ten specific steps that can assist a unit budget manager in organizing and submitting the unit budget request. Some steps can occur simultaneously and others proceed in a sequential order.

1. Take the time to analyze previous unit budget performance and understand what happened and why.
2. Share information; budgeting should not be a secret process. Information regarding the parameters established by the institution should be shared widely within the unit.
3. Establish an internal process for development of the budget request. The process should be clear and unambiguous, and once it is established it

should be followed. As part of the unit budget process, additional internal guidelines may be set for all program areas.

4. Listen carefully, and listen to everyone. It is essential that the members of the organization have an opportunity to present their ideas and concerns as the budget is developed. Depending on the size and complexity of the unit, informal hearings or informal conversation can be held. It is important that members of the unit have an opportunity to share their goals and aspirations for their programs. Remember that the process of listening to aspirations does not have to wait until formal budget guidelines are issued.

5. Establish internal guidelines and timetables and provide an opportunity for those responsible for submitting budget requests understand those guidelines and timetables.

6. Review proposals for new or increased funding from programs or departments. Such proposals should be clearly linked to the plan and goals of the larger unit and the institution. The following questions are useful as proposals are reviewed at the unit level:

   a. What is the rationale for the proposal and can it easily be understood by others?
   b. What will change as the result if this funding request is granted?
   c. Are any anticipated savings in the proposal real?
   d. Does the proposal rely on off-loading a program or service to another unit or agency? Are they prepared to take it on?
   e. Is the basic arithmetic of the proposal correct? Arithmetical errors occur frequently and should be identified and corrected prior to budget submission.
   f. Finally, have the routine inflationary increases been examined to assure that they are really needed or whether savings could be realized?

7. Prior to submitting the budget proposal, all available options for funding should be reviewed and tested, including limiting or eliminating a current program in order to fund a new venture. The reader is referred to *Prioritizing Academic Programs and Services* (Dickenson, 1999) for a well-developed discussion on how to prioritize programs within the academy.

8. Feedback to those who developed budget requests should be provided both for those requests supported by the unit and those not forwarded as part of the budget process. Improvement in the quality of requests and the accuracy of budget documents will occur only if specific feedback is provided to the proposers.

9. Prepare the final budget submission for the unit. Be clear, concise, and accurate as budget documents are prepared. As part of the final budget

proposal to the central administration clearly identify the implications of the request beyond the current fiscal year that is being reviewed.

10. Approval of the budget request is an iterative process. The work is not done when the request is submitted. The budget manager or others in the unit must be prepared to answer questions and concerns. Once the budget is agreed upon by the institution, it is submitted to the governing board for approval. Final approval of the budget only occurs after the ongoing process of information sharing and decision making by the administration, the board, and the various committees of the governing board.

Monitoring Performance

After the budget is approved and the fiscal year begins, regular monitoring of the budget must occur. The diligent budget manager monitors budget performance each and every month. For budget monitoring to be productive, the budget manager must understand the ebb and flow of expenditures and the institutional rules governing accounting and charges, including encumbrances.

Adjusting Current Budget

If there is a revenue shortfall, then expenses, where possible, should be adjusted downward to cover at least part of the projected deficit. If there are uncontrollable costs being faced by the unit, those costs should be identified and clearly communicated to appropriate administrative and budget personnel.

Closing

When the current budget is closed, no more charges can be made against that budget year and no new revenue can be added. Invoices for goods and services not paid by the time of closing will be charged to the next fiscal year. This has the effect of starting the new fiscal year in debt. The budget manager must understand the closing dates used by the budget office and plan for those dates in their year-end fiscal planning.

Analyzing Results

When the budget cycle for the fiscal year is completed, the results must be analyzed. Earlier it was noted that the first step in the budget cycle was to analyze past performance. Such analysis is also the last step in the process of budget management. If variances from the budget plan occurred then the reasons why those variances occurred must be uncovered. Such information will assist in the planning process for the next fiscal year. The unit budget manager is always dealing with three budgets: understanding what happened in the prior fiscal year, monitoring the current fiscal year budget, and planning for the next fiscal year.

Dealing with Budget Cuts

Two levels of decisions govern the response to budget cuts: the response from the institution and the response from the unit. Both institutional strategies (which affect all departments) and unit reduction strategies are usually used to handle reductions in resources.

Institutional Strategies

There are four common strategies employed by an institution facing a budget cut: a freeze, across-the-board cuts, targeted reductions, and restructuring. A budget freeze is not really a budget cut, but it is perceived as one by faculty and staff members. Under a budget freeze new hires are postponed and major purchases are postponed. A budget freeze is a good way to get the attention of faculty and staff regarding the serious nature of the financial problem faced by the institution.

Across-the-board cuts are the easiest, most expedient way to manage a budget reduction. Funds captured from the budget reduction are used to offset income shortfalls.

Targeted reductions occur when selected line items are earmarked for savings. Travel, honoraria, and new equipment purchases are often the line items chosen in the initial phase of a budget reduction.

A more draconian measure involves restructuring the way the institution does business through combining programs, instituting new fiscal rules, and reorganizing reporting relationships to reduce overhead.

Unit Reduction Strategies

Rumors abound when the institution faces fiscal concerns, and the first step is to share information with those within the unit. Second, ask for suggestions on how to curtail costs; faculty and staff have a number of good ideas that could be considered. Third, use contingency funds as the first step in responding to a budget cuts—it may be labeled as a contingency line or could be an equipment replacement line—no matter what the label use those funds first.

Ask for voluntary cutbacks; some interesting ideas may surface. If members of the unit understand the dimensions of the problem they may come up with new ideas, such as a change in a position from twelve months to nine months, or even a solution as simple as charging for office coffee when it has been provided at no charge. A number of little steps can result in substantial savings.

Sometimes outsourcing is a valuable strategy because costs may be less expensive if an outside vendor is used for certain functions. This strategy may have implications beyond the unit and should be discussed with decision makers prior to seeking proposals from vendors. Finally, sharing resources is a viable strategy for units in close proximity to each other where shared equipment (fax, copy machine) or personnel (receptionists) may reduce costs.

A Final Word

The ability to translate information to those within a unit and to decision makers within the institution is a key factor in the success of budget managers. Four simple rules should guide your professional practice in budgeting and financial management:

1. *Be honest and trustworthy.* Do not try to cover up mistakes or be less than forthcoming with decision makers about problems and issues in the unit.
2. *Be consistent.* This rule is a corollary to rule #1. Consistency is a virtue in budget management.
3. *Be creative.* Within the rules and regulations of the institution, think creatively about possible solutions to problems.
4. *Be fair.* Treat all members of the organization with dignity and respect, and do not provide special budget benefits to one part of the organization without a rationale to support such a decision.

Conclusion

Sound fiscal management at all levels of the organization is necessary for an institution of higher education to succeed. The financial health of the institution is predicated on the aggregate financial health of all the units within the institution.

Good budgeting and financial management requires attention to detail, a curious mind, and a willingness to persist while seeking answers to questions. The art of budgeting and financial management can be mastered by investing time and energy.

References

American Council on Education. (2012, Winter). *State funding: A race to the bottom.* http://www.acenet.edu/the-presidency/columns-and-features/Pages/state-funding-a-race-to-the-bottom.aspx.

Barr, M. J. (2002). *Academic administrators guide to budgets and financial management.* San Francisco, CA: Jossey-Bass.

Barr, M. J., & McClellan, G. S. (2011). *Budgets and financial management in higher education.* San Francisco, CA: Jossey-Bass.

Dickenson, R.C. (1999). *Prioritizing academic programs and services: Reallocating resources to achieve strategic balance.* San Francisco, CA: Jossey-Bass.

Maddox, D. (1999). *Budgeting for not-for-profit organizations.* New York, NY: Wiley.

Mayhew, L. B. (1979). *Surviving the eighties: Strategies and procedures for solving fiscal and enrollment problems.* San Francisco, CA: Jossey-Bass.

Meisinger, R. J., & Dubeck, L.W. (1984). *College and university budgeting: An introduction for faculty and academic administrators.* Washington, DC: National Association of College and University Business Officers.

National Center for Higher Education Management Systems. (2011). *State and local public higher education support per full-time equivalent student.* http://www.higheredinfo.org/dbrowser/index.php?measure=36.

Research Associates of Washington. (2005). *Higher education price index.* Washington, DC: Author.

Stocum, D. L., & Rooney, P. M. (1997). Responding to resource constraints: A departmentally based system of responsibility centered management. *Change, 29*(5), pp. 50–57.

Woodard, D. B. Jr., & von Destinon, M. (2000). Budgeting and fiscal management. In M. J. Barr, M. K. Desler, & Associates (Eds.), *The handbook of student affairs administration* (2nd ed., pp. 327–346). San Francisco, CA: Jossey-Bass.

CHAPTER TWENTY-SIX

ADDRESSING LEGAL AND RISK MANAGEMENT ISSUES

John Wesley Lowery

Gehring (2000) observed, "The law has definitely arrived on campus. It permeates every program, policy, and practice of the institution" (p. 371). A decade and half later these words ring with even more truth. Kaplin and Lee (2009) noted that the relationship between the courts and colleges and universities has changed significantly over the past half-century, as the courts abandoned their deferential attitude toward higher education. During the same period, the government became more actively involved in the regulation of higher education (Kaplin & Lee, 2009).

In responding to the legal issues that arise on campus, student affairs professionals should not work in isolation, but instead, when appropriate, consult with the campus general counsel or attorney. This consultation can take both a reactive form when litigation is anticipated or imminent and a proactive form as policies and practices are developed. Because of their training to be risk-averse, attorneys often advise clients to avoid potentially litigious choices. As such, direct questions are often answered with a firm "no" (Lake, 2011). As a result, in many cases, a different question is more productive. Instead of asking should the institution do X, ask what are the potential legal consequences if the institution does X, and how can those be effectively managed?

When considering the legal and risk management issues that shape student affairs professional practice in the United States, one must consider the various sources of law. These include: federal and state constitutions, federal and state regulations, contracts, and negligence and tort liability. These include both external sources of the law such as constitutions and regulations, as well as internal sources of the law including contracts, and custom and usage. An understanding of this framework for higher education law will offer student affairs professionals an introduction to the legal landscape in which their work must be understood and practiced. This chapter frames these legal and risk management issues around the relationships that colleges and universities routinely have with our students and federal and state governments.

Legal Relationships with Students

There are several key types of documents that serve to define the legal relationship between higher education institutions and students. In public higher education, this analysis must begin with constitutions, both federal and state. Private colleges and universities are generally not bound by either federal or state constitutions, but instead these institutions' legal relationship with students is defined by their contracts. When private colleges promise students constitutional rights like free speech, the courts hold private institutions to those promises. Contracts are also important in public higher education because those documents serve to identify rights that public institutions have promised students beyond those minimum rights required by the US Constitution and by state constitutions.

Constitutions

Federal and state constitutions are the most important source of the law shaping higher education practice. Constitutions serve to both establish the limits of governmental powers as well as articulate individual rights. Although the federal Constitution does not speak directly to education, state constitutions often specifically address higher education either by establishing specific institutions or establishing state governing bodies for higher education. State constitutions can give more rights than are afforded by the federal Constitution. However, state constitutions cannot take away rights guaranteed by the US Constitution, which supersedes any conflicting provisions of state constitutions.

Private institutions are typically not required to follow the federal Constitution, unless engaged in state action. State action is a legal doctrine that examines the interaction between a private institution and a government entity that so entangles those activities as to make the private institution, or aspects of the institution, legally indistinguishable from the state. For example, Alfred University, a private institution in New York, administers the New York State School for Ceramics, a public entity. The court ruled in *Powe v. Miles* (1968) that when disciplining students in the School for Ceramics those students must be afforded all the rights described following, but students enrolled in other programs did not enjoy those constitutional rights.

The aspects of the federal Constitution that most commonly affect student affairs practice are the First Amendment; Second Amendment; Fourth Amendment (particularly search and seizure); and the Fourteenth Amendment's guarantee of due process. Each of these is briefly described next.

First Amendment

During the past half-century, the courts have considered a number of issues under the First Amendment that expanded or clarified student rights and shaped student affairs practice (Bird, Mackin, & Schuster, 2006). In the student affairs context, the rights of greatest significance include freedom of speech, free exercise of religion, and the implicit right of association. In *Tinker v. Des Moines* (1968), the Supreme Court observed, "It can hardly be argued that either students or teachers shed their constitutional rights to freedom of speech or expression at the schoolhouse gate" (p. 506). Student affairs administrators would be well advised to remember the Supreme Court's admonition in *West Virginia State Bd. of Educ. v. Barnette* (1943):

> Freedom to differ is not limited to things that do not matter much. That would be a mere shadow of freedom. The test of its substance is the right to differ as to things that touch the heart of the existing order. If there is any fixed star in our constitutional constellation, it is that no official, high or petty, can prescribe what shall be orthodox in politics, nationalism, religion, or other matters of opinion or force citizens to confess by word or act their faith therein. If there are any circumstances which permit an exception, they do not now occur to us. (p. 642)

When difficult disputes arise around issues of freedom of speech, student affairs professionals are well served by remembering the field's primary role as educators.

One area in which colleges have struggled to balance competing interests is the effort to create an inclusive campus environment. A number
of institutions adopted policies that sought to prohibit speech that was
regarded as racist, sexist, or homophobic, often described by institutions
as harassment policies. Many of these policies have been invalidated by
the courts as unconstitutional because they prohibited some speech protected by the First Amendment (see *Doe v. University of Michigan*, 1989; *Iota
Xi Chapter of Sigma Chi Fraternity v. George Mason University*, 1993; *McCauley
v. Univ. of the Virgin Islands*, 2010; and *UWM Post, Inc. v. Board of Regents of
the University of Wisconsin System*, 1991). The courts have commonly voided
these policies for vagueness or overbreadth—meaning they prohibit both
protected and unprotected speech. Justice Samuel Alito noted while serving on the US Court of Appeals for the Third Circuit that the free speech
clause protected a "wide variety of speech that listeners may consider deeply
offensive, including statements that impugn another's race or national
origin or that denigrate religious beliefs" (*Saxe v. State College Area School
District*, 2000, p. 206). In recent years, the courts have been increasingly
willing to consider student challenges to harassment policies even when
those policies have not been applied under the theory that the mere existence of the policy creates a chilling effect that limits student speech (*DeJohn
v. Temple Univ.*, 2008).

One of the areas within which First Amendment law remains relatively
unresolved is the extent to which students can be disciplined for speech on
Facebook or other social media sites. In those cases when the courts have
sided with institutions, there has been a clear link between the student's
academic major and the online speech, combined with clearly defined
policies (*Tatro v. University of Minnesota*, 2012; and *Yoder v. University of
Louisville*, 2013).

The First Amendment does not demand that public institutions
develop policies for the recognition of student organizations, but once
an institution creates such a system, a group cannot be excluded because
the institution disagrees with the group's beliefs (*Healy v. James*, 1972). This
is not limited to recognition itself, but also the benefits associated with
recognition (*Widmar v. Vincent*, 1981). These decisions have been based
upon the First Amendment's protection of the freedom of expression as
well as an implicit right to freedom of association (*Healy v. James*, 1972).
A number of these student organization cases have involved religious
student groups. In *Board of Regents of the Univ. Wis. System v. Southworth*
(2000), the Supreme Court ruled that mandatory student activities fees
that were used, in part, to fund student organizations were constitutional
as long as the funds were distributed in a manner that was viewpoint

neutral. This viewpoint neutrality extends to funding the programs of student religious groups when other groups are eligible for funding for similar activities (*Badger Catholic v. Walsh*, 2010; and *Rosenberger v. Rector and Board of Visitors of the University of Virginia*, 1995). However, the courts have allowed institution's to deny recognition to student religious groups that refused to comply with an all-comers policy (*Christian Legal Society v. Martinez*, 2010) or the institution's nondiscrimination policy (*Alpha Delta Chi-Delta Chapter v. Charles Reed*, 2011). These legal issues involving religious student groups are not yet fully resolved and litigation in this area continues.

Regarding students' right to protest on campus, Kaplin and Lee (2009) noted that the courts begin their analysis with a consideration of the forum, which includes both public and nonpublic forums. The courts have allowed public institutions some flexibility in limiting the locations and manner in which students can protest or by extension speak or distribute literature on campus. Taken together these referred to time, manner, and place restrictions. However, these restrictions must be narrowly tailored to serve substantial and content-neutral governmental interests (*Ward v. Rock Against Racism*, 1989). Institutions may also punish protests that materially disrupt the institution's operation (*Shamloo v. Mississippi State Board of Trustees*, 1980). Several institutions have sought to manage student speech and protests through the identification of free speech zones, but the courts have overturned those polices when the zones are too restrictive (*Roberts v. Haragan*, 2004; and *University of Cincinnati Chapter of Young Americans for Liberty v. Williams*, 2012). The courts have traditionally given public institutions greater latitude in establishing policies for off-campus speakers. In *ACLU v. Mote* (2005), the court noted that the university could "constitutionally exclude outsider speech as long as the exclusion is viewpoint neutral and reasonable" (p. 446). Over a series of recent cases, the courts have considered various elements of outside speaker policies for this reasonableness: different polices for outside speakers (*Gilles v. Blanchard*, 2007), requirements for advance notice, and limitation to specific parts of campus for assemblies (*Sonnier v. Crain*, 2010). However, those restrictions must be content neutral (*Orin v. Barclay*, 2001).

Second Amendment

In recent years, there have been multiple efforts, successful and unsuccessful, to expand the rights of concealed carry permit holders to legally carry firearms on public college campuses. State courts in Colorado (*Regents of the Univ. of Colo. v. Students for Concealed Carry on Campus*, 2012), Oregon

(*Oregon Firearms Education Foundation v. Board of Higher Education*, 2011), and Utah (*University of Utah v. Shurtleff*, 2006) have interpreted state laws in light of the Second Amendment's protection of the right to "keep and bear arms" to prevent campuses from banning concealed carry on campus. By contrast, the Virginia Supreme Court upheld George Mason's policy that prohibited concealed carry in buildings and at large outside events (*Digiacinto v. Rector and Visitors of George Mason University*, 2011). The efforts to expand concealed carry are not limited to the courts; state legislatures have passed legislation expanding the right to concealed carry on college campuses. For example, the legislatures in Arkansas, Idaho, Kansas, Mississippi, and Wisconsin have passed laws expanding the right to concealed carry on public college campuses (National Conference of State Legislatures, 2014). It is likely that both the courts and state legislatures will continue to address these issues.

Fourth Amendment

The Fourth Amendment protects individuals against unreasonable searches and seizures. Although primarily associated with searches of homes, the Fourth Amendment also applies to a variety of types of searches including residence halls, lockers, individuals, drug testing, and purses and backpacks. The courts have distinguished between searches by the police, campus or otherwise, for the purpose of law enforcement and searches by campus officials other than police to enforce campus rules without encouragement or involvement by the police. The courts have typically not required search warrants for searches by campus officials for the enforcement of campus rules, or in response to emergencies when acting independently of the police (*Commonwealth v. Neilson*, 1996; *New Hampshire v. Nemser*, 2002; *Piazzola v. Watkins*, 1971; and *State v. Hunter*, 1992). However, the courts still demand that these searches be reasonable when conducted by campus officials, even if the standard used to judge reasonableness is lower than that for law enforcement.

Fourteenth Amendment

The Fourteen Amendment prohibits the federal or state governments from depriving "any person of life, liberty, or property, without due process of law" (U.S. Const. amendment XIV, § 1). Relying primarily on the Fourteenth Amendment, in *Dixon v. Alabama State Board of Education* (1961) the

US Court of Appeals for the Fifth Circuit fundamentally redefined the relationship between colleges and their students. Prior courts had ruled that the constitution had no impact on how public institutions disciplined students, suggesting in *Gott v. Berea College* (1913) that a college had the same authority to punish students as a parent did, or stood *in loco parentis*. The court ruled that "due process requires notice and some opportunity for [a] hearing before students at a tax-supported college are expelled for misconduct" (*Dixon*, p. 151). However, the courts have not consistently established the exact standards of due process that must be met (Kaplin & Lee, 2009; Silverglate & Gewolb, 2003; and Stoner & Lowery, 2004). The Supreme Court in *Goss v. Lopez* (1975) required only that students "be given some kind of notice and afforded some kind of hearing" (p. 579) before lengthy suspensions. Although the *Goss* case involved K–12 students, these principles apply in higher education as well.

Regarding the institutions' rules themselves, the courts have required that rules not be vague and avoid violating the First Amendment rights described earlier in this chapter. Kaplin and Lee (2009) noted that seldom have the courts invalidated college rules for vagueness, citing *Soglin v. Kauffman* (1969) as one of the few cases to reach this result. In *Soglin*, the University of Wisconsin's rules simply prohibited "misconduct" (p. 167) without further elaboration, which denied students any guidance on the behavior the university expected them to avoid. Silverglate and Gewolb (2003) noted that the more obvious it would be to the average student that the behavior in question would be prohibited, the less likely the court would be to overturn a rule for vagueness.

The courts have also outlined a series of procedural protections for students facing suspension or expulsion for behavioral violations, including allegations of academic dishonesty. The Supreme Court in *Goss v. Lopez* (1975) required that a student be provided prior notice "of what he is accused of doing and what the basis of the accusation is" (p. 582). The lower courts have not consistently held that a specific number of days of notice must be provided—only that the notice be provided in advance (Kaplin & Lee, 2009; and Stoner & Lowery, 2004). The notice requirement has varied from as few as two days (*Nash v. Auburn University*, 1987) to as long as ten days (*Esteban v. Central Missouri State College*, 1969). Because these requirements vary by circuit, institutions should consult with legal counsel to determine the appropriate time frame in their jurisdiction.

Once the hearing begins, the fundamental right that students must be afforded is "an opportunity speak in their own defense and explain their side of the story" (Kaplin & Lee, 2009, p. 463). Students have raised additional due process claims regarding the conduct of hearings, on which the courts reached varying decisions. Students often claim that the hearing body or decision maker was biased against them, or complained that administrators played multiple roles, but the courts have proven unreceptive to these claims absent clear proof of bias (*Gorman v. University of Rhode Island*, 1988; and *Nash v. Auburn University*, 1987). A more complicated question is the circumstances under which a student should have a right to consult with an attorney during the hearing, and what role the attorney may play (*Osteen v. Henley*, 1993). The courts have "never recognized any absolute right to counsel in school disciplinary proceedings" (*Donohue v. Baker*, 1997, p. 146). The situation most likely to give rise to a right to seek the advice of legal counsel during a disciplinary hearing is when students are facing concurrent criminal charges. However, the attorney's role is quite limited. In *Osteen v. Henley* (1993), the court concluded:

> Even if a student has a constitutional right to consult counsel ... we don't think he is entitled to be represented in the sense of having a lawyer who is permitted to examine or cross-examine witnesses, to submit and object to documents, to address the tribunal, and otherwise to perform the traditional function of a trial lawyer. (p. 225)

Kaplin and Lee (2009) have noted that the right of cross-examination is also not generally acknowledged as a constitutional requirement. The US Court of Appeals for the Eleventh Circuit concluded, "There was no denial of appellants' constitutional rights to due process by their inability to question the adverse witnesses in the usual, adversarial manner" (*Nash v. Auburn*, 1987, p. 664). A related issue is the use of visual barriers between the accused student and a complainant or witness, which are most commonly used in sexual assault cases and are for the purpose of preventing direct visual contact rather than shielding the identity of the witness (Stoner & Lowery, 2004). Several courts have accepted these systems as constitutional (*Cloud v. Boston Univ.*, 1983; and *Gomes v. Univ. of Maine Sys.*, 2004).

The courts have not imposed any specific standard of proof that colleges and universities must use in reaching decisions at the hearing. The most commonly used standard of proof in a campus student conduct system is a preponderance of the evidence, or a more likely than not standard. However, the Office for Civil Rights in the US Department of Education has identified this standard as necessary under Title IX of the Education Amendments of 1972 (United States Department of Education, 2011a).

Once the hearing is concluded and a decision is reached, the courts expect that the accused student be notified in writing, at least in serious cases, of the decision. The courts have not generally required any content in that notice beyond some brief explanation of the reasons for its decision (*Jaksa v. University of Michigan*, 1984). The courts have not required that public institutions offer any form of appeal after the decision is reached (Kaplin & Lee, 2009; Silverglate & Gewolb, 2003). Although, many recommend that an appeal be offered to promote "an image of fairness" (Stoner & Lowery, 2004, p. 60). Furthermore, the Office for Civil Rights requires in sexual harassment cases that whatever appeal rights exist be offered to both sides (Dear Colleague Letter on Sexual Violence, 2011).

The requirements of due process briefly described here apply to cases in which students are facing suspension or expulsion. The courts have not carefully outlined the process required in less serious cases. In fact, the courts have even suggested that some cases are so minor as to require "very little or no process" (Silverglate & Gewolb, 2003, p. 22). Many institutions go well beyond the minimal procedural due process requirements established by the courts. Gehring (2001) warned institutions against "unnecessarily formalized ... procedures" (p. 477). Dannells (1997) concluded that this excessive focus on procedural rights had "undermined the informal and uniquely educational element of college student discipline" (p. 69). This is not to suggest that institutions should only provide with exacting precision the minimal due process rights outlined by the courts. In fact, Pavela and Pavela (2012) identified an ethical and educational imperative of procedural due process, especially in serious cases.

Contracts

Beyond those rights afforded to students at public universities by either federal or state constitutions, students at all universities have a contractual relationship with their institutions. A variety of institutional documents are likely to be seen by the courts as contracts, including the college catalog and student handbook. When disputes arise, the courts will look first to these written agreements, or express contracts, for guidance to their resolution (Kaplin & Lee, 2009). The courts have afforded colleges and universities considerable deference in amending their contracts while students are enrolled provided the students are informed of the changes (Kaplin & Lee, 2009; and *Mahavongsanan v. Hall*, 1976). When ambiguities in these express contracts exist, the courts are likely to interpret those ambiguities in favor of the student (Ledbetter, 2009), but even then not as strictly as commercial contracts (Kaplin & Lee, 2009).

The courts have also applied contract theory to an implied contractual relationship between the college and its students that can be traced back to *Carr v. St. John's University* (1962), although later cases applied this principle to public institutions as well (*Healy v. Larsson*, 1974; and Kaplin & Lee, 2009). Even more ambiguous is the concept of academic custom and usage, which Kaplin and Lee (2009) describe as the "campus common law" (p. 21) in which the courts examine common practices at the institution, not set forth in policies but commonly understood, to resolve disputes arising on campus (*Perry v. Sindermann*, 1972).

These contractual agreements have become a "source of meaningful rights for students, particularly when faculty or administrators either fail to follow institutional policies or apply those policies in an arbitrary way" (Kaplin & Lee, 2009, p. 247). Given the extent to which the courts hold institutions to their contractual obligations, it is vital that these documents are reviewed annually to ensure that they accurately describe the college's promises to its students and expectations for them (Ledbetter, 2009). As Kaplin and Lee (2009) advised, "Language suggestive of a commitment (or promise) to students should only be used when the institution is prepared to live up to that commitment" (p. 252).

Tort Liability and Risk Management

Another significant legal issue that student affairs professionals must confront is tort liability that arises from our various relationship with students, such as business-invitee, landlord-tenant, and less commonly a special (unique) relationship between a college and its students that some courts have recognized. Torts are civil wrongs rather than criminal or contractual violations for which lawsuits may be brought. The most common remedy in tort liability cases is damages to compensate the plaintiff for injuries, but they can include punitive damages punishing the defendants in the case for the harm caused (Ledbetter, 2009). There are several factors that may limit institutional liability. Sovereign immunity limits the ability of institutions, but not individual employees, from being sued in state or federal court. Many states have elected to allow tort liability lawsuits to proceed against the state in their courts but limit total liability by legislation (Kaplin & Lee, 2009). Institutional liability can be further limited by *contributory negligence* that considers the role that the plaintiff's action played in the injury, limiting or barring damages (Ledbetter, 2009).

Colleges and universities face "a growing array of negligence lawsuits, often related to students and others injured on campus or at off-campus functions" (Kaplin & Lee, 2009, p. 112). After the death of the concept of *in loco parentis* in 1960s, the courts grew increasingly unreceptive to student tort liability lawsuits during the next several decades, regarding institutions as bystanders (Bickel & Lake, 1999). However, during the past decade and half, that trend has largely been reversed (Kaplin & Lee, 2009; Lake, 2011). In assigning liability, the courts consider whether the harm was foreseeable and whether the risk of harm was unreasonable (Kaplin & Lee, 2009).

There are four basic elements of a tort liability claim, all of which must be proven in order for a lawsuit to be won:

1. Duty—A legal obligation that is owed or to another person
2. Breach—Failure to meet that obligation
3. Injury
4. The breach is the proximate cause of the injury (Ledbetter, 2009; and Prosser, 1971)

The most common relationship that institutions of higher education have that is a potential source of legal liability is its business-invitee relationship that gives rise to premise liability. *Peterson v. San Francisco Community College District* (1984) can help illustrate these principles. The college was found liable for the assault of a student by a third party because the college was aware that a dangerous situation (an area of untrimmed foliage) was being used by criminals to hide in several previous assaults, but the college took no action to correct this unseen risk. This duty to maintain premises in a safe condition also includes a more common category of injuries, slip-and-fall cases. When the dangerous condition is obvious, the duty to invitees is often removed (Kaplin & Lee, 2009).

Some courts have also found a special relationship between a college and its students that gives rise to additional duty to protect students from harm. However, those duties have been recognized by the courts in narrow situations that involve college students close to the age of eighteen and residing on campus. Beyond these relationships that give rise to duties, the law also demands that when the college voluntarily assumes a duty that the duty be carried out with reasonable care (Lake, 2011; and Ledbetter, 2009). The existence of duty alone does not assure that the institution is liable. Instead the question becomes whether the institution met the standard of care that accompanies that duty—did the college act reasonably given the circumstances or breach its duty (Lake, 2011).

Unlike the other legal issues addressed in this chapter, tort liability and risk management require a careful weighing of alternatives to make informed decisions that limit, but cannot eliminate, institutional risk. Although insurance and risk avoidance are dimensions that help to limit and mitigate liability, a risk management approach that does not go further is incomplete and likely to ultimately prove insufficient. It is vital that institutions engage actively in a risk management process. Sokolow (2004) identified a four-step process for considering and addressing potential risks: "Assess risk for the operations of the institution, prioritize the risks, address the risks, and evaluate the efficacy of the methods chosen to address the risks" (p. 86). It is important to understand risk management as an ongoing process rather than one-time event. Student affairs professionals should also carefully consider their own circumstances to determine whether they should purchase personal liability insurance that is available from several national organizations. As Lake (2011) noted, liability lawsuits naming student affairs professionals personally remain rare, but individual and institutional circumstances may lead one to conclude that the purchase of personal liability insurance is a wise investment.

Federal and State Regulation of Higher Education

Laws passed and regulations promulgated by the federal government and the state governments have been another primary source of the expansion of legal requirements that colleges and universities face since the late 1980s. In the case of the federal government, Congress passes laws, and departments and agencies within the executive branch are responsible for writing regulations and guidance to implement those laws. Those federal regulations are developed through a process that includes the opportunity for public commentary and have force of law. The guidance from federal agencies does not have force of law but offers additional information on the interpretation of statutes and regulations. At the state level, state legislatures and agencies also pass laws and issue regulations whose scope is limited to institutions that offer academic programs in that state and most often to public institutions (Ledbetter, 2009). The US government has increasingly used the power of the purse, whether through rewards or sanctions, as an instrument to implement its policy interests, along with legislative and administrative action.

The majority of federal laws with which college and universities are required to comply build upon Congress's constitutional authority to provide for the general welfare for the American people or the spending power. This includes both direct funding from the federal government to institutions and indirect funding through federal financial aid for students (*Bob Jones University v. Johnson*, 1975; and *Grove City v. Bell*, 1984). These laws apply with equal force to public and private institutions of higher education. The funding that institutions receive through federal financial aid are often referred to as Title IV funds, a reference to Title IV of the Higher Education Act that addresses the student financial system. Congress also has the power to regulate higher education through its constitutional authority to regulate interstate commerce, which is used less frequently to regulate higher education, most commonly with laws that also apply other aspects of society such as businesses (Ledbetter, 2009).

There are several means through which federal departments and agencies can enforce regulations. These regulations largely govern institutions themselves and agencies have enforcement powers that include the power to fine institutions for noncompliance, to order changes to policy or practice, and ultimately to declare an institution ineligible to participate in the federal financial system, which is the government's most significant enforcement power. Some laws also include a private right to action allowing individuals to sue institutions for violations of federal law, but that right of action must be clearly stated (*Gonzaga v. Doe*, 2002). This is most commonly seen with antidiscrimination laws. Some laws also allow for both fines and/or criminal sanctions against individuals (Ledbetter, 2009).

There are nearly two hundred federal laws that directly affect higher education practice (Hunter & Gehring, 2005). As a result, in recent years a number of large colleges and universities have established compliance offices to coordinate institutional efforts to meet the demands of this myriad of federal laws. However, as Ledbetter (2009) noted, although some coordination is necessary, compliance cannot be regarded as the job of one individual or one office. There are several laws that are so unique in their impact on student affairs practice that student affairs practitioners should have a working understanding of their requirements. These include federal antidiscrimination laws, Family Educational Rights and Privacy Act (FERPA), and the Jeanne Clery Disclosure of Campus Security Policy and Campus Crime Statistics Act (Clery Act). This is not to suggest that these are the only laws affecting student affairs practice. Other laws affecting student affairs policy and practice include the federal financial aid law, Drug-Free Schools and Communities Act Amendments, college costs, and voter registration (National Postsecondary Education Cooperative, 2009). In the context of student employees and professional staff, health care, fair labor, and workplace safety laws are also significant. However, the scope of this chapter makes it impossible to cover all of these additional laws.

Antidiscrimination Laws

Since 1964, Congress has passed a series of antidiscrimination laws that apply to all programs or activities that are recipients of federal financial assistance, including indirect funding through the student financial aid system. These antidiscrimination laws include:

1. Title VI of the Civil Rights Act of 1964 which prohibits discrimination on the basis of race, color, and national origin;
2. Title IX of the Education Amendments of 1972 which prohibits discrimination on the basis of sex; and
3. Section 504 of the Rehabilitation Act of 1973 as amended which prohibits discrimination against qualified individuals with a disability.
4. The Americans with Disabilities Act of 1990 also prohibits discrimination against qualified individuals with a disability, but is not directly tied to the receipt of the federal funding and instead applies to state and local governments, including public colleges (Title II) and public accommodations, including private colleges (Title III).
5. Enforcement of Title VI, Title IX, and Section 504 rests with the US Department of Education's Office for Civil Rights (OCR). OCR establishes regulations and guidelines for these laws and investigates allegations of non-compliance. In addition to withholding federal funds, OCR can also refer cases to the U. S. Department of Justice for enforcement. Individuals can also sue institutions for non-compliance. Primary enforcement of ADA rests with US Department of Justice, but enforcement can take place through both the OCR's complaint process as well the Justice Department's litigation. (Kaplin & Lee, 2009).

Title VI

Title VI of the Civil Rights Act prohibits discrimination on the basis of race, color, and national origin, but the majority of cases have been around claims of discrimination on the basis of race and ethnicity. Although the Supreme Court has continued to support the legality of affirmative action programs in college admissions (*Gratz v. Bollinger*, 2003; *Grutter v. Bollinger*, 2003; and *Regents of the University of California v. Bakke*, 1978), the standard by which those policies are judged has grown stricter in recent years (*Fisher v. Univ. of Tex. at Austin*, 2013). Taken together, the Supreme Court has established strict scrutiny as the test by which the consideration of race in public higher education will be judged. The first question is whether there is a compelling state interest that justifies the consideration of race, and the means by which race is considered is narrowly tailored to that interest. Those same standards and principles also apply to other programs that consider race and ethnicity as factors, such as academic enrichment programs, retention programs, and student services (Ledbetter, 2009).

Title IX

Title IX is primarily associated in minds of the public with gender equity in athletics at K–12 and college levels. Title IX requires that colleges "provide equal athletic opportunity for members of both sexes" (34 C.F.R. § 106.41(c)). Title IX also prohibits discrimination on the basis of sex in admissions and access to programs, including discrimination against pregnant and parenting students (Supporting the Academic Success of Pregnant and Parenting Students Under Title IX of the Education Amendments of 1972, 2013). However, in recent years, considerable attention has also been paid by both courts and the Office of Civil Rights to sexual harassment of students as a form of sexual discrimination prohibited under Title IX. The Supreme Court has addressed sexual harassment in educational settings in multiple cases involving harassment by both employees (*Franklin v. Gwinnett County Public Schools*, 1992; and *Gebser v. Lago Vista Independent School District*, 1998) and other students (*Davis v. Monroe County Board of Education*, 1999). Student on student sexual harassment is almost always a form of hostile environment sexual harassment. The Court ruled that students could be held legally liable for this form of sexual harassment when the institution has "substantial control over both the harasser and the context in which the known harassment occurs" (*Davis*, 1999, p. 645) and the harassment is "severe, pervasive, and objectively offensive that it effectively bars the victim's access to an educational opportunity or benefit" (*Davis*, 1999, p. 633). Institutional liability is further limited by the Court's ruling in *Gebser* (1998), which limited liability to those cases in which a school official who has authority to take corrective action has actual knowledge of the harassment and responds with "deliberate indifference" (p. 290). Kaplin and Lee (2009) warned that the law "provides scant opportunity for student victims of harassment to succeed with Title IX damages actions against educational institutions" (p. 543). However, the US Department of Education employs a different standard in determining institutional compliance with Title IX. OCR will find an institution in violation of Title IX "if the school knows or reasonably should know about the harassment, the school is responsible for taking immediate effective action to eliminate the hostile environment and prevent its recurrence" (United States Department of Education, 2001, p. 12).

In 2011, the US Department of Education issued a Dear Colleague Letter on Sexual Violence and Title IX that greatly amplified the OCR's expectations for how institutions would prevent and respond to allegations of sexual violence that create hostile environment. Among the most controversial requirements of the Dear Colleague Letter were a requirement that a preponderance of the evidence standard be employed in grievance procedures, as well as equal opportunities to appeal findings (including the code of student conduct if that was part of the institution's Title IX policy). In the years since the release of the 2011 Dear Colleague Letter, sexual violence on college campuses and institutional responses have been under a microscope by the White House, the US Department of Education, Congress, student activists, and the media. In 2014, President Barack Obama and Vice President Joe Biden announced the creation of the White House Task Force to Protect Students from Sexual Assault that released its first report, *Not Alone,* and launched an accompanying website in April 2014. As part of the work of the task force, the US Department of Education issued additional guidance, Questions and Answers on Title IX and Sexual Violence, responding to a number of questions raised by the higher education community in response to the 2011 Dear Colleague Letter. As part of the task force's work, the US Department of Education has become much more transparent in its investigations of colleges and universities for allegations of Title IX violations and a year later, there are approximately a hundred active Title IX investigations. Many of these investigations started based upon complaints filed by student activists. These student activists are supported and encouraged by several grassroots organizations, including KnowYourIX and End Rape on Campus. In both 2014 and 2015, multiple pieces of legislation were introduced in Congress, but have not yet passed, to expand the federal regulations surrounding sexual violence on college campuses.

Section 504 and ADA

Section 504 and ADA both prohibit discrimination against qualified individuals with disabilities, defining a qualified person as meeting "the academic and technical standards requisite to admission or participation in the recipient's educational program or activity" (34 C.F.R. § 104.3 (I) (3)). The Supreme Court addressed this issue in *Southeastern Community College v. Davis* (1979), upholding a hearing-impaired student's rejection from a nursing program, but Kaplin and Lee (2009) cautioned against over-reading this case because of the unique nature of the academic program in question. When considering access to other programs or facilities, the courts have proven more receptive to students' claims than this narrow ruling might suggest (Kaplin & Lee, 2009). During the past decade, there has been considerable attention paid to student mental health issues that have implications under both Section 504 and ADA. Students who may have a mental illness cannot be removed from the institution on the basis of that disability alone. Students can be removed for behavior that violates institutional rules, independent of their disability, and can also be removed after an analysis of the direct threat.

Family Educational Rights and Privacy Act (FERPA)

The Family Educational Rights and Privacy Act (FERPA) of 1974 governs how colleges and universities handle students' education records. Under the FERPA regulations from the US Department of Education, education records were defined as "those records, files, documents, and other materials which contain information directly related to a student; and are maintained by an educational agency or institution, or by a person acting for such agency or institution" (34 CFR § 99.1). Regarding those education records, FERPA affords college students three primary rights:

1. Right to inspect and review education records
2. Right to challenge the content of education records
3. Right to consent to the disclosure of education records

Since its passage in 1974, FERPA has been amended numerous times, and many of those amendments serve to create additional exceptions to the third of these rights.

Students have a right to inspect and review their education records. Their access to these records need not be immediate, and the regulations allow up to forty-five days for the institutions to comply with the student's request for access. There are also some records that rest beyond the definition of education records, including law enforcement records, medical treatment records, and parents' financial records. Although students have a right to inspect and review their education records, the regulations do not grant students a right to copies of their records, unless refusing to provide students with copies would effectively completely deny them access. One of the more confusing issues in recent years is the interaction between the Health Insurance Portability and Accountability Act (HIPAA) and FERPA. The regulations for HIPAA specifically exclude student health records, which are defined under FERPA as treatment records and instead require that FERPA's protections be afforded to these records (United States Department of Health and Human Services, 2008). However, state privacy laws may also govern access and disclosure of student's medical records (Ledbetter, 2009).

FERPA generally requires that information not be released from a student's education record without the student's written consent. However, there are numerous exceptions that allow for release without a student's consent. Many of the amendments to FERPA after its passage have created additional exceptions. One of the most commonly occurring situations is the exception that allows for the release of information from a student's education record to another school official who has legitimate educational interest in that information. Institutions are required to define these terms in their FERPA policy and have broad flexibility in determining the appropriate scope for both terms. School officials, for example, can include students serving on official college committees, student workers assisting school officials, board members, and outside parties who contract with the college to provide specific services. Legitimate educational interests are generally defined as information that a school official needs to carry out their job responsibilities. Other exceptions include lawfully issued subpoenas, releases to the parents of dependent students (as defined by the Internal Revenue Service), parental notification for alcohol and drug violations, release of the final results of disciplinary proceedings in specific circumstances (although disciplinary records are still generally considered education records), and release to authorized government agencies. Although FERPA allows the release of records under these exceptions, it does not require institutions to release the information.

After the shootings at Virginia Tech in 2007 and Northern Illinois University in 2008, there was considerable discussion about whether

FERPA should be amended to make it easier to release information from students' education records. Although the statute was not changed, the US Department of Education amended the regulations governing health and safety emergencies, making clear that institutions can release information from a student's education record when it determines that an emergency situation exists, to provide information to parties who are in a position to help mitigate the emergency, including local police and parents (Ledbetter, 2009).

Complaints of violations of FERPA are heard by the Family Policy Compliance Office (FPCO) in the US Department of Education. If a violation is found, FPCO works with institutions to change their policies or practices to correct the error. Although in theory an institution could lose its eligibility for federal funds as well, that process has never been initiated for a FERPA violation. Individuals do not possess a private right of action to sue institutions for violations of FERPA (*Gonzaga Univ. v. Doe*, 2002) but may raise claims under state laws.

Jeanne Clery Disclosure of Campus Security Policy and Campus Crime Statistics Act

The Jeanne Clery Disclosure of Campus Security Policy and Campus Crime Statistics Act was originally passed in 1990. Jeanne Clery was murdered by another student at Lehigh University in 1986. Her parents founded Security on Campus (now the Clery Center for Security on Campus), and were instrumental in the passage of the original legislation and subsequent amendments. The Clery Act has been significantly amended a number of times since its passage, including in 1992, 1998, 2008, and 2013.

The central feature of the Clery Act is the publication of the Annual Security Report (ASR), which must be distributed each year absolutely no later than October 1. Institutions have several options for meeting the reporting requirements with the ASR, including sending the report to every current student and employee or posting the report on the Internet and providing notice to all current students and employees that includes a summary of its contents. There are a number of campus policies that must be described in the Annual Security Report including:

Reporting crimes and other emergencies on campus

Security of campus facilities

Campus law enforcement policies

Information regarding crime prevention and awareness programs

Monitoring the off-campus locations of student organizations

Policies regarding possession, use, and sale of alcohol and other drugs

Statement that the final results of a disciplinary proceeding involving an allegation of a crime of violence will be provided to the victim or next of kin if requested in writing

Emergency response and evacuation

Sexual assault policies, which have been expanded to include domestic violence, dating violence, and stalking starting with the 2014 ASR

Advising the campus where information is available about sex offenders

Institutions with on-campus student housing are also required to have and disclose their missing student notification policy and provide information regarding fire safety and fires on campus (United States Department of Education, 2011b).

The ASR includes statistics for the three most recent calendar years for a host of crimes. Institutions must provide statistics for reports of the following crimes reported to campus security authorities and local law enforcement: murder/non-negligent manslaughter, negligent manslaughter, forcible sex offenses, nonforcible sex offenses (statutory rape and incest), robbery, aggravated assault, burglary, motor vehicle theft, and arson. Institutions must also provide statistics for arrests or referral for disciplinary action for liquor law violations, drug law violations, and illegal weapons possession. The final category of crime statistics information that must be reported are for hate crimes including those listed previously, as well as incidents of larceny/theft, simple assault, intimidation, and destruction/damage/vandalism of property. Hate crime statistics must be reported by category of prejudice, which include race, gender, sexual orientation, ethnicity/national origin, and disability. Beginning with the 2013 calendar year statistics reported in the 2014 ASR, the list of hate crime categories expanded to include national origin and gender identity. All of the statistics listed here must be reported by calendar year for the following geographic areas: on campus, of crimes on campus those in student housing facilities, noncampus buildings or property, and public property. Campus security authorities include campus police or security as well as any official who has "significant responsibility for student and campus activities" (34 CFR § 668.46 (a)).

The most recent changes to the Clery Act were made in 2013, with the reauthorization of the Violence Against Women Act. The majority of these changes are directly related to institutional responses to sexual assault, domestic violence, dating violence, and stalking. Under these changes, institutions are required to provide prevention and awareness programming for all new students and employees regarding sexual assault, domestic violence, dating violence, and stalking, as well as offering ongoing prevention and awareness campaigns for the campus community. Institutions are also required to greatly expand the information included in the Annual Security Report on institutional responses and policies regarding sexual assault, domestic violence, dating violence, and stalking. The law dictates specific aspects of institutional policies governing the adjudication of these cases. Beginning in 2014, institutions are required to include statistics for domestic violence, dating violence, and stalking in the ASR.

There are ongoing reporting obligations as well, including timely warning to the campus community of crimes that pose ongoing threat, emergency notifications to the campus community, and the creation of a daily crime log by institutions with campus police or security departments. Federal law requires institutions to maintain records to document their compliance with the Clery Act, and other federal laws, for at least three years. However, because crime statistics are reported for three years, records must be retained to document statistics for essentially seven years (The Handbook for Campus Safety and Security Reporting, 2011).

The Clery Act is enforced by the US Department of Education, which is authorized to fine institutions up to $35,000 for each violation of the law. In the past decade, the US Department of Education has fined several institutions more than $100,000 each for Clery Act violations (including Eastern Michigan University, Tarleton State University, and Yale University). There does not, however, exist a private right of action allowing individuals to sue for damages for Clery Act violations.

Conclusion

Not only is the breadth of legal and policies issues facing student affairs staggering, but those issues are ever evolving. Kaplin and Lee (2009) suggested that the way to keep pace with these evolving legal issues is to "understand and respond constructively to change and growth in the law while maintaining its focus on its multiple purposes and constituencies" (p. 9). Student affairs professionals must all be aware of the general legal and risk management issues set forth in this chapter and be more knowledgeable about those issues that most directly affect their functional area. This chapter has sought to provide an introduction to that landscape and both campus resources and programs from professional organizations are valuable sources of additional professional development opportunities and information.

For those readers interesting in expanding their knowledge in this area, there are a number of resources worth of consideration. William Kaplin and Barbara Lee's *The Law of Higher Education* (2013) remains an outstanding reference work. For a more student affairs–oriented consideration of the topic, there is Peter Lake's *Foundations of Higher Education Law and Policy: Basic Legal Rules, Concepts, and Principles for Student Affairs* (1991). There are also at least three national conferences that address student affairs legal issues: NASPA's Law and Policy Conference, Stetson University's National Conference on Law and Higher Education, and the University of Vermont's Legal Issues in Higher Education Conference.

References

Bickel, R., & Lake, P. (1999). *The rights and responsibilities of the modern university.* Durham, NC: Carolina Academic Press.

Bird, L. E., Mackin, M B., & Schuster, S. K. (2006). *The First Amendment on campus: A handbook for college and university administrators.* Washington, DC: NASPA.

Dannells, M. (1997). *From discipline to development: Rethinking student conduct in higher education* (ASHE-ERIC Higher Education Report, no. 25:2). San Francisco, CA: Jossey-Bass.

Gehring, D. D. (2000). Understanding the legal implications of student affairs practice. In M. J. Barr, M. K. Desler, & Associates, *The handbook of student affairs administration* (2nd ed., pp. 347–376). San Francisco, CA: Jossey-Bass.

Gehring, D. D. (2001). The objectives of student discipline and the process that's due: Are they compatible? *NASPA Journal, 38,* 466–481.

Hunter, B. & Gehring, G. D. (2005). The cost of federal legislation on higher education: The hidden tax on tuition. *NASPA Journal, 42,* 478–497.

Kaplin, W. A., & Lee, B. A. (2009). *A legal guide for student affairs professionals* (2nd ed.). San Francisco, CA: Jossey-Bass.

Kaplin. W. A. & & Lee, B. A. Barbara (2013). *The Law of Higher Education* (5th ed.). San Francisco: Jossey-Bass.

Lake, P. F. (2011). *Foundations of higher education law and policy: Basic legal rules, concepts, and principles for student affairs.* Washington, DC: NASPA.

Ledbetter, B. E. (2009). Legal issues in student affairs. In G. S. McClellan, J. Stringer, & Associates (Eds.), *The handbook of student affairs administration* (3rd ed., pp. 505–525).

National Conference of State Legislatures. (2014). *Guns on campus: Overview.* http://www.ncsl.org/research/education/guns-on-campus-overview.aspx.

National Postsecondary Education Cooperative. (2009). *Information required to be disclosed under the Higher Education Act of 1965: Suggestions for dissemination* (NPEC 2010–831), prepared by Carol Fuller & Carlo Salerno, Coffey Consulting. Washington, DC: Author.

Pavela, G., & Pavela, G. (2012). The ethical and educational imperative of due process. *Journal of College and University Law, 38,* 567–627.

Prosser, W. L. (1971). *The handbook of law on torts.* St. Pail, MN: West.

Silverglate, H. A., & Gewolb, J. (2003). *FIRE's guide to due process and fair procedure on campus.* Philadelphia, PA: Foundation for Individual Rights in Education.

Sokolow, B. S. (2004). Risk management in the community college setting. In R. C. Cloud (Ed.), *Legal issues in the community college* (pp. 85–94). San Francisco, CA: Jossey-Bass.

Stoner, E. N. II, & Lowery, J. W. (2004). Navigating past the "spirit of insubordination": A twenty-first century model student conduct code with a model hearing script. *Journal of College and University Law, 31,* 1–77.

United States Department of Education. (2011a). *Dear colleague letter.* Washington, D.C.: Office of Civil Rights, U.S. Department of Education. http://www2.ed.gov/about/offices/list/ocr/letters/colleague-201104.html.

United States Department of Education. (2011b). *The handbook for campus safety and security reporting.* Washington, D.C.: Office of Postsecondary Education, U.S. Department of Education. https://www2.ed.gov/admins/lead/safety/handbook.pdf.

United States Department of Education. (2001). *Revised sexual harassment guidance: Harassment of students by school employees, other students, or third parties.* Washington, D.C.: Office of Civil Rights, U.S. Department of Education. http://www2.ed.gov/about/offices/list/ocr/docs/shguide.html.

United States Department of Health and Human Services. (2008). *Joint guidance on the application of the Family Educational Rights and Privacy Act (FERPA) and the Health and Insurance Portability Act of 1996 (HIPAA) to student health records.* Washington, D.C.: U.S. Department of Health and Human Services. http://www2.ed.gov/policy/gen/guid/fpco/doc/ferpa-hipaa-guidance.pdf.

White House Task Force. (2014). *Not alone: The first report of the White House Task Force to protect students from sexual assault.* https://www.whitehouse.gov/sites/default/files/docs/report_0.pdf.

Cases

ACLU v. Mote, 423 F.3d 438 (4th Cir. 2005).

Alpha Delta Chi-Delta Chapter v. Charles Reed, 648 F.3d 790 (9th Cir., 2011).

Badger Catholic v. Walsh, 620 F.3d 775 (7th Cir., 2010).

Board of Regents of the Univ. Wis. System v. Southworth, 529 U.S. 217 (2000).

Bob Jones University v. Johnson, 396 F.Supp. 597 (D.S.C. 1974), affirmed, 529 F.2d 514 (4th Cir. 1975).

Carr v. St. John's University, 187 N.E.2d 18 (N.Y. 1962).

Christian Legal Society v. Martinez, 561 U. S. ___ (2010).

Cloud v. Boston Univ., 720 F.2d 721 (1st Cir. 1983).

Commonwealth v. Neilson, 666 N.E.2d 984 (Mass. 1996).

DeJohn v. Temple Univ., 537 F.3d 301 (3d Cir. 2008).

Dixon v. Alabama State Board of Education, 294 F.2d 150 (5th Cir. 1961).

Doe v. University of Michigan, 721 F. Supp. 852 (E.D. Mich. 1989).

Donohue v. Baker, 976 F. Supp. 136 (N.D. NY 1997).

Davis v. Monroe County Board of Education, 526 U.S. 629 (1999).

Digiacinto v. Rector & Visitors of George Mason Univ., 704 S.E.2d 365 (Virginia, 2011)

Esteban v. Central Missouri State College, 415 F.2d 1077 (1969).

Fisher v. Univ. of Tex. at Austin, 133 S. Ct. 2411 (2013).

Franklin v. Gwinnett County Public Schools, 503 U.S. 60 (1992)

Gebser v. Lago Vista Independent School District, 524 U.S. 274 (1998).

Gilles v. Blanchard, 477 F.3d 466 (7th Cir. 2007).

Gomes v. Univ. of Maine Sys., 304 F. Supp. 117 (D. Me. 2004).

Gonzaga Univ. v. Doe, 536 US 273 (2002).

Gorman v. University of Rhode Island, 837 F.2d 7 (1st Cir. 1988).

Goss v. Lopez, 419 U.S. 565 (1975).

Gott v. Berea College, 161 S.W. 204 (Kentucky, 1913).

Gratz v. Bollinger, 539 U.S. 244 (2003).

Grove City v. Bell, 465 U.S. 555 (1984).

Grutter v. Bollinger, 539 U.S. 306 (2003).

Healy v. James, 408 U.S. 169 (1972).

Healy v. Larsson, 323 N.Y.S.2d 625, affirmed, 318 N.E.2d 608 (N.Y. 1974).

Iota Xi Chapter of Sigma Chi Fraternity v. George Mason University, 993 F.2d 386 (4th Cir. 1993).

Jaska v. University of Michigan, 597 F. Supp. 1245 (E.D. Mich. 1984) aff'd 787 F.2d 590 (6th Cir. 1986).

Mahavongsanan v. Hall, 529 F.2d 448 (5th Cir. 1976).

McCauley v. Univ. of the Virgin Islands, 618 F.3d 232 (3d Cir. 2010).

Nash v. Auburn University, 812 F.2d 655 (11th Cir. 1987).

New Hampshire v. Nemser, 807 A.2d 1289 (N.H. 2002).

Or. Firearms Educ. Found. v. Bd. of Higher Educ., 264 P.3d 160 (Oregon, 2011).

Orin v. Barclay, 272 F.3d 1207 (9th Cir. 2001).

Osteen v. Henley, 13 F.3d 221 (7th Cir. 1993).

Ottgen v. Clover Park Technical College, 928 P.2d 1119 (Wash. Ct. App. 1996).

Perry v. Sindermann, 408 U.S. 593 (1972).

Peterson v. San Francisco Community College District, 205 Cal. Rptr. 842 (Cal. 1984).

Piazzola v. Watkins, 442 F 2d 285 (5th Cir. 1971).

Powe v. Miles, 407 F.2d 73 (2d Cir. 1968).

Regents of the University of California v. Bakke, 438 U.S. 265 (1978).

Regents of the Univ. of Colo. v. Students for Concealed Carry on Campus, LLC, 271 P.3d 496, (Colo., Mar. 5, 2012).

Roberts v. Haragan, 346 F. Supp. 2d 853 (N.D.Tex 2004).

Rosenberger v. Rector and Board of Visitors of the University of Virginia, 515 U.S. 819 (1995).

Saxe v. State College Area School District, 240 F.3d 200 (3d Cir. 2000).

Shamloo v. Mississippi State Board of Trustees, 620 F.2d 516 (5th Cir. 1980).

Soglin v. Kauffman, 418 F.2d 163 (1969).

Sonnier v. Crain, 613 F.3d 436 (5th Cir. 2010).

Southeastern Community College v. Davis, 442 U.S. 397 (1979)

State v. Hunter, 831 P.2d 1033 (Utah App. 1992).

Tatro v. University of Minnesota, 816 N.W.2d 509 (Minn. 2012).

Tinker v. Des Moines Independent Community School District, 393 U.S. 503 (1968).

University of Cincinnati Chapter of Young Americans for Liberty v. Williams, 2012 U.S. Dist. LEXIS 80967 (S.D. Ohio, 2012)

Univ. of Utah v. Shurtleff, 144 P.3d 1109 (Utah, 2006).

UWM Post, Inc. v. Board of Regents of the University of Wisconsin System, 774 F. Supp. 1163 (E.D. Wis. 1991).

Ward v. Rock Against Racism, 491 U.S. 781 (1989).

West Virginia State Bd. of Educ. v. Barnette, 319 U.S. 624 (1943).

Widmar v. Vincent, 454 U.S. 263 (1981).

Woodis v. Westark Community College, 160 F.3d 435 (8th Cir. 1998).

Yoder v. University of Louisville, 2013 U.S. App. LEXIS 9863 (6th Cir.2013).

Federal Laws, Regulations, and Guidance

Dear Colleague Letter on Sexual Violence. (2011, April 4). Office for Civil Rights, US Department of Education. http://www2.ed.gov/about/offices/list/ocr/letters/colleague-201104.html.

Drug-Free Schools and Communities Act, 20 U.S.C. 3181(a) (1989).

Family Educational Rights and Privacy Act, 20 U.S.C. §1232g (1974).

The handbook for campus safety and security reporting. (2011) Washington, DC: US Department of Education, Office of Postsecondary Education. http://www2.ed.gov/admins/lead/safety/handbook.pdf.

Jeanne Clery Disclosure of Campus Security Policy and Campus Crime Statistics Act, 20 U.S.C. §1092 (1990).

Joint guidance on the application of the Family Educational Rights and Privacy Act (FERPA) and the Health Insurance Portability and Accountability Act of 1996 (HIPAA) to student health records. (2008). Washington, DC: US Department of Health and Human Services and US Department of Education. http://www2.ed.gov/policy/gen/guid/fpco/doc/ferpa-hipaa-guidance.pdf.

Questions and answers on Title IX and sexual violence. (2014). Washington, DC: US Department of Education, Office for Civil Rights. http://www2.ed.gov/about/offices/list/ocr/docs/qa-201404-title-ix.pdf.

Revised sexual harassment guidance: Harassment of students by school employees, other students, or third parties. (2001). 66 Fed. Reg. 5512. http://www.ed.gov/about/offices/list/ocr/docs/shguide.html.

Section 504 of the Rehabilitation Act of 1973, 29 USC § 794.

Supporting the academic success of pregnant and parenting students under Title IX of the Education Amendments of 1972. (2013). Washington, DC: US Department of Education, Office for Civil Rights. http://www2.ed.gov/about/offices/list/ocr/docs/pregnancy.html.

Title VI of the Civil Rights Act of 1964, 41 USC § 2000d.

Title IX of the Educational Amendments of 1972, 20 U.S.C. § 1681 et seq.

U.S. Const. amend. I.

U.S. Const. amend. II.

U.S. Const. amend. IV.

U.S. Const. amend. V.

U.S. Const. amend. XIV.

Violence Against Women Reauthorization Act of 2013, Public Law 113–4.

Violence Against Women Act; Final Rule. (2014). 79 Fed. Reg. 62752.

CHAPTER TWENTY-SEVEN

IMPLEMENTING ASSESSMENT TO IMPROVE STUDENT LEARNING AND DEVELOPMENT

Marilee Bresciani Ludvik

Conversations about outcomes-based assessment are ubiquitous due to regional accreditors, state legislators, and federal government officials placing increased pressure on university leaders to become more transparent about what their students are learning and how they are developing (Ewell, 2009; Jankowski et al., 2012; and Jankowski & Provezis, 2011). Outcomes-based assessment is not a new idea, and yet, for some reason, university leaders have consistently failed to provide transparent information about the value of a higher education degree. If student affairs practitioners are confused about what is meant by outcomes-based assessment and how it may differ from previous self-reflection practices (Bresciani, Moore-Gardner, & Hickmott, 2010; Bresciani, Zelna, & Anderson, 2004; Maki, 2004; Schuh & Gansemer-Topf, 2010; Suskie, 2009; and Upcraft & Schuh, 1996), perhaps it is because outcomes-based assessment has existed for many years in various forms. It may be that the lack of readily available evidence of contributions to student learning and development from student affairs practitioners is not because of a lack of reflection, inquiry, and evaluation practice, but because of a lack of a shared conceptual framework and common language for a systematic reflective practice.

This chapter provides a brief historical overview, discusses the need for assessment, explores four common approaches to assessment, and provides a brief explanation of how assessment may differ, yet complement, institutional research.

In addition, this chapter illustrates the importance of student affairs practitioners' ability to evaluate their contributions to student learning and development through these varied approaches. The chapter concludes with some suggestions for implementing assessment so that it is systematic and consistent.

A Brief Historical Overview

Having at its core the inquiry-based notion of how well are we doing what we expect to accomplish, outcomes-based assessment has been around in various versions for some time (Baker, Jankowski, Provezis, & Kinzie, 2012; Bresciani et al., 2010; Bresciani, 2006; Ewell, 2002; Maki, 2004; Palomba & Banta, 1999; Suskie, 2009; and Upcraft & Schuh, 1996). In its earliest form and with regard to student learning, outcomes-based assessment dates back to AD 1063 at the University of Bologna, where outcomes-based assessment of student learning was known as juried reviews (Carroll, 2006).

Assessment or program evaluation has existed over time in various forms. Identified as total quality management (TQM), Six Sigma, continuous quality improvement (CQI), institutional effectiveness (IE), or other well-known acronyms, the notion of exploring whether what you are doing is working in the way you had intended remains a consistent theme in spite of what it is called or how it is systematically implemented (Bresciani, 2006; Bresciani et al., 2010; Ewell, 2002, 2009; Schuh & Gansemer-Topf, 2010; & Upcraft & Schuh, 1996). Regardless of its organizational model, the idea of investigating whether what we *expect* to accomplish is what we *are* accomplishing has historically been most often identifiable in the business community (Bresciani, 2006; Ewell, 2002; and Upcraft & Schuh, 1996). As such, those student affairs professionals attentive to business practices found themselves readily adapting such inquiry and evaluation processes as their own, particularly in the area of evaluating the effectiveness of their services. However, these same professionals may have still found it challenging to address their units' contributions to student learning and development (Moore-Gardner, Kline, & Bresciani, 2014; and Wellman, 2010).

Publication of several helpful how-to documents on implementing outcomes-based assessment (Baker et al., 2012; Banta, Griffin, Flateby, & Kahn, 2009; Bresciani et al., 2004; Bresciani et al., 2010; Moore-Gardner et al., 2014; Palomba & Banta, 1999; Schuh, 2008; Suskie, 2009; and

Upcraft & Schuh, 1996) have been instrumental in many co-curricular professionals' refining the evaluation of their services; however, legislators are still demanding more evidence as to how student affairs organizations are contributing to student learning and development. The following section illustrates the reasoning behind the increase in demand for evidence of student affairs' and services' contributions to student learning and development.

Documenting Contributions to Student Learning and Development

There are multiple pressures on colleges and universities to document student learning and development. These provide opportunities for student affairs organizations to demonstrate their contributions. Fortunately, there are resources available to assist practitioners in this process.

Increased Demand for More Evidence

Since 1985, several regional accrediting organizations, in response to increased pressure from the federal government, have steadily increased their demand for institutions to articulate and evaluate student learning outcomes. As a part of this requirement, many regional accreditors have articulated clear and rigorous expectations that student support services document their contributions to student learning and development. Such accreditation requirements have appeared to raise the awareness among many professionals that their role in learning and development is recognized; now all they need to do is to provide evidence of their contributions through outcomes-based assessment. There have been several calls for higher education administrators and faculty to establish good practices in the assessment of student learning and development. These include the Higher Education Re-authorization Act conversations of 2002, 2006, and 2013–2014, along with conversations among the Council of Regional Accrediting Commissions (CRAC) in 2003 and the Commission on the Future of Higher Education (DOE) in (US Department of Education, 2006). In all of these conversations, the demand for evidence of student learning and development cut across political party lines and across state and federal thresholds. At the time of publication of this volume, states are being asked to carry the burden of demanding evidence of student learning and development from all aspects of the academy and from all institutional types; regional accreditation is under scrutiny, and current drafts of the reauthorization act vary in degree as to the kinds of flexibility that institutional leadership will have in gathering evidence of student learning. The current conversation in Washington, D.C., has significant implications for student affairs practitioners who design and deliver their work informally.

Opportunities for Student Affairs

With the increasing inquiry into the value of a degree and growing demands to lower the cost of higher education, which include the need to identify alternative sources of funding, representatives of disciplines are being asked to demonstrate how they know students are learning and what they expect students to learn regardless of institutional organization. This is an opportunity for student affairs professionals to come together to articulate the contributions of their services. For example, the discipline, if you will, of career services could join with the discipline of electrical engineering to articulate shared learning and development outcomes for students they serve. The same could be developed for many of the student affairs disciplines such as residence life, academic advising, health and wellness, and financial aid. A coupling of what was once thought to simply be a service area or one that was accessed informally within higher education could join in a disciplinary conversation to articulate the value of any academic degree, particularly as it relates to the development of leadership skills, intra- and interpersonal skills, collaboration, creative problem solving, and becoming a responsible, civic-minded citizen. The ability to identify how student affairs work is contributing to these employer-desired outcomes (AAC&U, 2014b) could position student affairs organizations to use evidence to reallocate resources, make donor requests, draft grant proposals, and determine how to provide the learning outcomes that employers are demanding while offering ideas to decrease the cost of education and demonstrating the value of what these organizations provide.

Resources to Enhance Opportunity

The Student Learning Imperative (American College Personnel Association, 1996) is considered by many to be a pivotal piece in highlighting the role of student affairs in the support of student learning and development. The characteristics describing learning-oriented student affairs practitioners outlined in the preamble were designed to stimulate ideas and connections illustrating a variety of ways that student affairs professionals contribute directly and indirectly to student learning and development. The ideas presented in this document appear to be designed to generate discussion, planning, and action for many divisions. Although *The Student Learning Imperative* is packed with provocative ideas and challenges, it is not evident how many institutions have adopted *The Student Learning Imperative's* visionary thought and put those inventive ideas into practice.

Learning Reconsidered: A Campus-Wide Focus on the Student Experience (Keeling, 2004) seemed to command practitioners' attention more than the documents that preceded it, possibly because of increasing accreditation requirements. Timely in its publication, *Learning Reconsidered* (2004) highlighted much of the previous research in student development and learning and emphasized the importance of evaluating student learning and development within student affairs and in partnership with academic colleagues. It was a call back to the holistic student learning and development efforts imperative for promoting student success of any type, including increased persistence and degree attainment.

The National Survey of Student Engagement (NSSE) Documenting Effective Educational Practice (DEEP) Project (Kuh, Kinzie, Schuh, & Whitt, 2005a, 2005b) illustrates twenty colleges and universities that collaborate across division lines to identify how they are improving student learning and development, in addition to providing questions for any institution to adapt and investigate on their campuses. The intent of the NSSE DEEP Project (Kuh et al., 2005a, 2005b) is to provide guidelines for reflection and conversation across departmental and division lines, so that student learning-centeredness can be collaboratively planned, delivered, and jointly evaluated. Another recent report with similar purpose is the Council for the Advancement of Standards in Higher Education's *Frameworks for Assessing Learning and Development Outcomes* (2006).

The previously mentioned work, along with updates on American Association of Colleges & Universities' important work on LEAP (Liberal Education and America's Promise) (AAC&U, 2014a), is advanced and updated today through online publications offered free of charge by the National Institute for Learning Outcomes Assessment. Here, multiple research papers and briefs are published annually in an attempt to keep faculty and student affairs practitioners up to date on good practices in collaborative outcomes-based assessment. Through these manuscripts student affairs practitioners can stay in touch with emerging trends, demands, and practices in assessing holistic student learning and development.

The Varied Assessment Approaches

There are a variety of assessment approaches that could be employed to gather much-needed assessment data to address how student affairs programs and services contribute to student development and learning. The aforementioned resources, along with many others that are continually being published, are designed to assist academic and/or instructional services and student affairs professionals with the steps and guidelines to implement meaningful and manageable outcomes-based assessment.

The first step may be, however, to determine whether the institutional leadership has a specific research question that they want answered or whether they want to know how well one program is contributing to institutional learning outcomes, competencies, or key performance indicators (that is, retention rates). If the question addresses how well one program contributes to institutional learning outcomes, competencies, or key performance indicators, then outcomes-based assessment is a perfect avenue to pursue. If however, the institutional leadership has a question that requires a formal research study to be designed, then we recommend the exploration of Stage and Manning's (2003) book, *Research in the College Context.* Finally, if the institutional leadership would like to gather data that inform policy discussions, then it is likely a mixture of research and assessment may be helpful, yet it depends on the extent of the policy discussion (Ewell, Jankowski, & Provezis, 2010).

There are a number of approaches to implementing assessment, four of which are discussed following. Each may be different in its intent and purpose, all contributing to information that leads to various decisions or conversations about the quality and value of higher education. For simplicity, these approaches are categorized as follows:

1. Pre-assessment, student satisfaction, utilization data, and needs assessment
2. Outcomes-based assessment
3. Competency-based assessment
4. Astin's Inputs-Environment-Outcomes Model or value-added assessment

There are a number of resources provided that should be consulted, as they more fully illustrate the details of each approach.

Pre-assessment, Student Satisfaction, Utilization Data, and Needs Assessment

This group of assessment approaches produces helpful data that can inform the planning of services and educational support activities (Schuh, 2008; Upcraft & Schuh, 1996). Utilizing data gathered from these methods allows student affairs practitioners to more purposefully plan their programs, outreach, services, and activities with student attributes in mind.

Pre-assessment data are collected on students prior to their entering the collegiate experience, participating in a program, or utilizing a service. Using these data, programs can be intentionally designed with outcomes in mind, in order to ensure that the programs will meet the needs of the targeted students. For example, instruments such as Sedlacek's noncognitive variables (2004) can be instrumental in informing specific interventions to assist students to address noncognitive challenges—not readily identifiable in pre-assessment data found in transcripts—yet that are instrumental to students' academic success.

Although pre-assessment data are very helpful in informing the preparation of programs and services, they are not helpful in indicating whether a planned program has accomplished what it was intended to accomplish on its own. However, pre-assessment data, if used intentionally, may be very helpful in articulating outcomes and planning their delivery so that those outcomes can later be evaluated with outcomes-based assessment practices.

Student satisfaction instruments are useful when discussing how satisfied students are with services and programming (Bresciani et al., 2004; Bresciani et al., 2010; Palomba & Banta, 1999; Schuh, 2008; and Upcraft & Schuh, 1996). Many administrators and constituents simply want to know whether students are happy with services and programs. However, such data rarely provide information that can meaningfully identify what is *wrong* if a student is unsatisfied. For example, if 60 percent of the first-year students report that they are satisfied with financial aid front counter staff, what would the financial aid office do with that information? If they wanted to improve that 60 percent satisfaction rate, what would they do? This method of assessment does not provide the kind of detail needed to inform specific decisions.

Utilization data can be useful for understanding how often and at what frequency services are used, by whom, and when (Schuh, 2008; and Upcraft & Schuh, 1996). These data assist managers with staff scheduling, providing explanations to students as to when and why service response declined, and informing resource reallocations and budgeting. Utilization data is often used in outcomes-based assessment to supplement an understanding of why an outcome was met or not met. Take the following situation: If the quality of learning certain outcomes in systematic substance abuse peer-advising sessions declines, the decline may be attributed to the fact that peer advisors are shuffling through students quickly in order to ensure that the students do not wait longer than one hour. In moving students through so quickly, the peer advisors do not have time to teach students all they want them to know in their one-on-one appointments and have no time to check in to see if their students understand what they were taught. In this example, the office utilization data can support the interpretation for the decline of learning. Similarly, if students report low satisfaction with student health services during the time when there was increased utilization of student health services, the utilization data can support the interpretation and possibly the explanation of the low satisfaction findings.

Needs assessment data are collected so that students' needs can be identified empirically (Schuh, 2008; and Upcraft & Schuh, 1996). Program coordinators can gather needs assessment data to assist with planning activities and programs that students report they need. Outcomes-based assessment, however, can require that students draft their own outcomes for programs they request, thus asking them to clarify their needs in a manner whereby they identify the end results of a requested activity. Such an exercise allows the students to differentiate between requesting an activity for an activity's sake and desiring and then intentionally planning for the end result of the activity. In essence, student affairs professionals can discover students' needs through the students' articulation of outcomes generated from the students' desire for a particular activity or program.

Outcomes-Based Assessment

Outcomes-based assessment has many definitions (Palomba & Banta, 1999; and Suskie, 2009). Regardless of which scholar's definition is utilized, many definitions have in common the notion of continuous improvement (Allen, 2003; Banta, 2002; Bresciani 2011; Bresciani et al., 2004; Maki, 2004; Palomba & Banta, 1999; and Suskie, 2009). Continuous improvement means there is an assumption of purposeful planning for the delivery and evaluation of intended end results. In addition, the evaluation process is designed so the information gathered can be used to inform meaningful decisions about how the intended outcomes or end results can be met at a greater level of quality for the group that was included in the evaluation.

In outcomes-based assessment, the professional is intending to evaluate the end results of the "doing," in a manner that specifies what she wants to have accomplished and how she plans to deliver and evaluate it. She later reports on what she has learned about what she intended to accomplish in a manner that allows her to make decisions to specifically improve the "doing." In outcomes-based assessment, the professional is simply asking and answering the following questions:

What are we trying to do and why? *or*

What is my program supposed to accomplish? *or*

What do I want students to be able to do and/or know as a result of my workshop/orientation/service?

How well are we organized, structured, and/or resourced to deliver that which is expected of us?

How well are we accomplishing what is expected of us?

How do we know?

How do we use the information to improve the delivery of what is expected of us, reallocate resources, strengthen or build collaborations, or celebrate successes?

Do the improvements we make based on this evidence contribute to the improvement as we intended? (Bresciani et al., 2010)

Outcomes-based assessment is not used to *prove* that learning and development are occurring; rather it embraces Papert's (1991) epistemology of situational constructionist learning. That is, the notion of discovery and response to that discovery is paramount. Papert (1991) posits that the more we learn about how well we are delivering what we hope students will be able to know and do within a certain situation, the more we will refine our delivery so that we will see more evidence of student learning and development in that specific situation for those specific students.

This epistemology of situational constructivist learning highlights the iterative nature of outcomes-based assessment. The end result of outcomes-based assessment is not intended to be considered research or inform how practices should be done for all students. Rather, the intended end result of outcomes-based assessment is to engage in a systematic self-reflection process through which one uses the findings to inform refinements in how programs are delivered and evaluated, as well as to inform how resources are reallocated, policies improved, and organizational values clarified. The self-reflection process is necessary in an effort to improve the underperforming student and his situation that is specific to his current institution or program within that institution.

Practitioners commonly draw upon research to determine what proven interventions could address a concern that the professionals have for a certain group of students when planning to deliver their outcomes. Research may also help articulate what the end results of that activity should be and often assist the professional with interpretation of the outcomes-based assessment results. However, the results of most outcomes-based assessment cannot be considered research, for often the methodology used in the process is not one that would hold up to the rigor of many established research procedures. In addition, often the sample or population being evaluated is likely not generalizable to other populations. However, outcomes-based assessment can be used to formulate a specific research question.

Outcomes-based assessment is not intended to be research. Outcomes-based assessment is designed to be a systematic, self-reflection process that provides the practitioner with information on how to improve his planning and delivery processes. Although findings from this process are most likely not generalizable to other settings, the data gathered can be instrumental in demonstrating accountability. *Merriam-Webster* defines *accountability* as "the quality or state of being accountable; *especially*: an obligation or willingness to accept responsibility or to account for one's actions" ("Accountability," 2007). Used in this manner, outcomes-based assessment exemplifies accountability because it demonstrates responsibility for purposeful planning and the use of information derived from systematic evaluation to illustrate what is needed to improve student learning and development.

Competency-Based Assessment

Competency-based assessment is not a new concept; however, it is being introduced here as a direct response to the current national accountability conversation. In essence, competency-based assessment requires the focus of the assessment to be placed on the individual student rather than on the program (Klein-Collins, 2014). This is a helpful approach for those student affairs practitioners whose services are designed to serve individual needs, rather than the services that are systematically designed to serve groups of students needs. In essence, the intention of competency-based assessment is that students can progress through their academic degrees by demonstrating individual achievement of degree learning and development programs, without regard for where the learning and development was obtained. This may sound exciting to student affairs professionals who are comfortable in knowing how and when they interact with individual students and how they assist them with their mastering the learning and development required for their degree attainment.

The challenge with implementing competency-based assessment, however, is that many institutions don't provide a clear path for students to progress through the achievement of degree competencies (learning and development outcomes). In addition, the manner in which many institutions offer the path to achieve competencies (learning outcomes) may be via individual course learning outcomes, and the manner in which students weave individual course outcomes together to create competencies becomes less clear or less systematic, thus creating challenges for meaningful data collection about the effectiveness of the service that student affairs professionals offer. Think about this with regard to student affairs professionals being coaches of the learning and development process; the more successful the students are that you coach, the more effective of a coach you would be considered.

Perhaps the most powerful way to approach competency-based assessment is by requiring the use of individual student learning and development portfolios using outcomes-based assessment within Astin's Inputs-Environment-Outcomes (IEO) Model (1993). In a well-designed reflective learning portfolio, students upload evidence of their out-of-classroom learning and development experiences along with their reflections of what was learned and how it was learned. This method can provide rich direct evidence of the influence of individual student affairs professionals in students' overall learning and development experiences.

Astin's IEO Model

Astin's IEO model (1993) focuses on assessing the characteristics of incoming students, exploring their interactions with the institution, and evaluating their outcomes when departing. In this model "I" stands for Inputs, in that an institution would thoroughly evaluate what skills and attributes a student is bringing into a program. "E" indicates Environment, which is that which an institution can account for in delivering the learning and development that occurs while a student is at the institution. "O" illustrates outcomes, meaning the end results of student learning and development that the student possesses when leaving the institution.

In Astin's IEO model, more rigorous methods of research can be employed, because one is evaluating how well prepared, cognitively and affectively, the student is at entrance into the program. Then, the purposeful planning ensues to deliver the appropriate experience or intervention to heighten learning. Finally, the evaluation of the outcomes ensues, so it can be determined what was gained during the educational experience. Cause-and-effect research may still be elusive, because controlling for variables that may intervene from outside the learning environment is nearly impossible. However, with the Astin IEO model, the types of pre- and post-evaluation that informs value-added conversations are within reach and should be explored by those programs that have the resources to do so.

Inputs. Input indicators in higher education have traditionally been centered on those that are easy to measure, gather, compare, and report (Astin, 1993). Studies summarized by Pascarella and Terenzini (2005) indicate a multitude of inputs that may prove more illustrative of understanding how well prepared students are to enter college and therefore can inform the design of a more successful college experience (for example, Astin's Experience). Such input indicators include evaluating students' readiness to learn, such as understanding their motivation for learning, their commitment to taking responsibility for their own learning, and the support that they have in place to enhance their learning (Pascarella & Terenzini, 2005). Sedlacek (2004) adds to these variables positive self-concept or confidence, realistic self-appraisal, understanding of and agency for diversity, preference for long-term planning over short-term goals or immediate needs, availability of strong support persons, successful leadership experience, demonstrated community service, and knowledge acquired in a field.

Institutional leadership would evaluate these complex input variables prior to a student's matriculation into the institution. In so doing, the leadership would better understand how the student is prepared to succeed and gather additional information at the level of detail that could influence planning curriculum, programs, and interventions in order to contribute to the student's success. Keep in mind, however, that with inputs assessment, we are deconstructing the human experience into measurable variables, and that may not be the most effective way to design learning and development. Emerging neuroscience illustrates what the authors of *The Learning Imperative* already knew: learning and development are inextricably intertwined. Emerging neuroscience (Bresciani Ludvik, 2015) illustrates how intertwined emotion, development, and cognitive processes are; this emphasizes the importance of always seeing a whole human being in front of us when we are using pre-assessment data to design learning experiences.

Environment and Outputs. Pascarella and Terenzini (2005), along with Astin (1993) and others (Kuh et al., 2005a; Manning, Kinzie, & Schuh, 2006) emphasize that if it is understood how a student enters college, and a supportive educational experience is designed with intended learning outcomes, then that student should be able to be successful in her educational endeavors, given all foreseeable variables. There are many unforeseeable variables in life and in the life of the adult learner; however, the process of mindfully designing a student's learning experience seeks to work within what is known and therefore improve the student's ability to learn (Bresciani, 2006; Papert, 1991).

Therefore, it must be clearly understood how students enter into college, how the college is designed to specifically contribute to that student's success (using outcomes-based assessment), and how the college intends to evaluate the student's success— (using competency-based assessment). Given all this complexity, one can quickly see the need for collaboration and intentional planning that cuts across reporting lines or programs and departments.

As mentioned earlier, portfolio assessment is an example of the evaluation of such a comprehensive learning and development experience. The process of evaluating value-added learning requires a great deal of communication so that the collaborative ways in which students learn specific outcomes can be identified and agreed upon by all the players in the educational experience. In addition, the criteria for evaluating that learning across the demonstrated domains must also be discussed and agreed upon. Many institutional leaders may not have the time or the means to even host such collaborative discussions, as this can be a very time-consuming process. Models for establishing such collaborative, rich reflections of value-added student learning can be found in the research of Mentkowski (2000), the National Research Council (2001), Maki (2004), Huba and Freed (2000), Kuh et al. (2005a), Ewell, Paulson, and Kinzie (2011), Baker et al. (2012), and the Council for Adult and Experiential Learning (2014).

Moving Forward with Implementing Assessment

Because the need for engagement in outcomes-based assessment of student learning and development is real, and because there appears to be little chance that the need will dissipate, especially with the possibility of performance-based funding re-emerging and the continued debate about the value of a higher education degree, the challenges facing student affairs officials in preparing to competently engage in outcomes-based assessment and possibly competency-based assessment must be addressed.

ACPA/NASPA Professional Competency Areas for Student Affairs Practitioners (National Association of Student Personnel Administrators & American College Personnel Association, 2010) posits that assessment, research, and evaluation are expected competencies for student affairs professionals. Practitioners are encouraged to understand how what they do daily contributes to enhancing the learning and development of the students with whom they interact. The following considerations attempt to share some practical suggestions referenced in the research of Baker et al. (2012), Banta et al. (2009), Moore-Gardner et al. (2014), Bresciani et al. (2010), Bresciani (2006), and Schuh and Gansemer-Topf (2010) for addressing the concerns facing student affairs practitioners as they engage in outcomes-based assessment.

1. *Make reflective assessment a priority and reallocate the time to engage in it.* Take the time to reflect and plan for your program's contribution to student learning and development. It is often said that we spend time on what we value or what we are told to value. If leadership emphasizes the importance of setting aside time to plan for how each unit directly or indirectly contributes to student learning, each unit may be able to better articulate how it intends to support and contribute to student development and learning. As such, each unit would then be able to better plan for the evaluation of its contributions to learning and development. In addition, if the college or university states that it is committed to collaborating across departmental and division lines to improve student learning, then it would follow logic that leadership would provide opportunities for such collaborative dialogue, planning, and action to occur. If assessment is not made a priority or if leadership does not provide opportunities for learning to be improved, it simply will not occur (Allen, 2003; Banta, 2002; Bresciani, 2006; Maki, 2004; Palomba & Banta, 1999; Suskie, 2004). Furthermore, prioritization regarding what should be assessed and what should not be assessed is important, as is the prioritization of the resources needed to improve what evidence shows needs improved.

In considering the reallocation of time to implement assessment, consider reallocating time for each of the following steps (adapted from Bresciani et al., 2010):

A. *Identify the alignment of the program's values or goals* with the divisional, institutional, statewide, or systemwide goals and the professional standards, if applicable. Goals are broad, general statements derived from mission statements of (1) what the program wants students to be able to do and to know or (2) what the program will do to ensure what students will be able to do and to know.

B. *Articulate the primary outcomes for your program.* (You will not be able to evaluate everything you do, so select the outcomes that represent your theoretical or programmatic priorities.) Outcomes are detailed statements derived from each one of your goals, specifically addressing the intended end result of your efforts. They use action verbs that help you identify how well the student knows and can do that which you expect of them.

C. *Identify the ways in which you will provide students all of the opportunities to learn* that which you expect of them (for example, outcomes). It is important to ensure that you are actually providing students the opportunities to learn what you expect them to learn, and at the level that you expect them to learn (for example, Bloom's Taxonomy such as knowledge, comprehension, application, analysis, synthesis, and evaluation [Anderson, Krathwohl, & Bloom, 2001]). Literally mapping out the opportunities for students to learn that which you expect them to learn, albeit systematic or by systematically consulting individual coaches along the way, also provides an opportunity to identify embedded opportunities to evaluate the learning and development. Furthermore, it helps you understand whether you are organized and resourced in a manner where the outcomes can actually be met.

D. *Select evaluation methods, tools, and criteria* to assess each outcome. Begin with one tool or method for each outcome and, as you develop habits of reflection, you can add tools and methods to your repertoire.

E. *Analyze the results* utilizing any expert help available to you, if necessary.

F. *Interpret the findings,* using research, expert opinion, and community partner perspectives, if applicable. Involving your colleagues and students in the interpretation of the findings may also prove beneficial.

G. *Make decisions and/or recommendations* to improve the opportunities for student learning and development, and refine the assessment process, outcomes, or evaluations tools and criteria. Prioritize the decisions that the evidence informs and allocate resources toward those decisions.

H. *Follow up at the appropriate time* (for example, next semester or three years later) to determine whether the decisions made contributed to improved student learning and development. And determine how your results can be used in your strategic planning, budgeting, program, review, annual reports, institutional or program marketing materials, and any other communication pieces or decision-making processes that are evidence based.

2. *Learn the theoretical underpinnings of what you do and align theories to planning and the evaluation of the planning.* Many student affairs staff members have never had the opportunity to learn the theoretical underpinnings of what they do, such as the learning and developmental theories that inform their leadership development models or engagement theories that inform their intervention programming. Moreover, those who previously learned the theories may not have been provided opportunities to discover new identity development hypotheses and groundbreaking notions such as what we are discovering in neuroscience about the plasticity of the brain and how what a student focuses on literally changes the structure and function of her brain (Bresciani Ludvik, 2015).

3. *Consider whether you can soundly engage in Astin's IEO Model.* In this age of accountability, some practitioners get lost in thinking they need to prove that their program is accomplishing that which they say it is. Attempting to prove that one program can solely develop a student or be the one reason that learning was improved is simply not possible, unless you construct a randomized control trial. Thus, assessment is not trying to prove cause and effect; rather practitioners are engaging in systematic purposeful reflection during which they state what they intend to accomplish (outcomes), plan the program intended to meet those outcomes (planning), evaluate the extent the outcomes were achieved (assessment), and use the information to further improve the program (accountability). If your program is sophisticated enough and you are able to collaborate with others to design a rigorous Astin IEO model for evaluation along with a randomized control trial, then by all means do it.

If you employ the exemplar Astin's (1993) IEO model of assessment, consider evaluating the entire educational experience at your institution rather than evaluating just one program. The current competency-based assessment movement, driven by the concern for the value of a higher education degree, along with emerging findings in neuroscience, are inviting us to demonstrate individual student learning and development. This means that as student affairs professionals, we can ask the questions that identify the value that has emerged as a result of a student's engagement in the entire undergraduate or graduate experience, not just within one program. If we keep this broader goal in mind, it may further encourage us to engage in collaborative discussions about the very essence of our profession: exploring and improving the whole student learning and development experience through outcomes-based assessment.

4. *Involve the students.* Students themselves can be incredibly helpful in your realization that you are expecting too much learning from them, given the mechanisms you have to deliver the learning. For example, students can assist in illustrating to you that they cannot be expected to synthesize the wellness decision-making model in one one-hour workshop; rather, maybe all you can do with them is get them to identify the steps in a wellness decision making in a case study. Students are incredibly helpful in critiquing student learning and development outcomes, in identifying means to evaluate the outcomes, and in articulating criteria that will evaluate the outcomes. If you begin to illustrate for your staff how the student development and learning theories they learned in graduate school feed into the design and evaluation of their programs, they can better articulate this to students, allowing for students to better understand themselves and the role they play in their own learning. Likewise, students will be able to better facilitate the connection from their classroom learning to their co-curricular learning because you are facilitating their self-evaluation of their learning and development (Kuh et al., 2005a, 2005b, Mentkowski, 2000).

5. *Collaborate, prioritize, and collaborate.* Many student affairs practitioners make the mistake of articulating student development and learning outcomes in isolation from their student affairs colleagues and from their academic colleagues. We also make the mistake of not prioritizing all that we do. If we truly desire more connectedness in the total student learning and development experience, then we must make ourselves vulnerable to enter into conversations with our faculty colleagues about how their classroom work could be reinforced or emphasized in the out-of-classroom experience. Take the initiative to learn about what faculty are teaching so you can potentially prioritize your programs as opportunities for their learning laboratories. This kind of collaboration does take time, and it takes relationship and trust building.

Conclusion

Outcomes-based assessment in its name has been evolving for centuries and will likely continue to evolve; however the practice of systematically reflecting on how well we do what we intend to do and whether it contributes to identifiable student learning and development will continue to be a key concern for leaders within higher education and among those who fund its efforts. This chapter is intended to provide the reader with various ways to conceptualize the most meaningful approach for assessment work within student affairs. In addition, this chapter provides the reader with a few considerations as he moves forward with implementation. The resources cited in this chapter and in this book will, I hope, provide the reader with information to refine practices that currently exist or engage in practices that are needed in order to ensure institutional accountability for students' learning and development.

References

"Accountability." (2007). *Merriam-Webster on-line dictionary.* http://www.m-w.com/dictionary/accountability.

Allen, M. J. (2003). *Assessing academic programs in higher education.* Bolton, MA: Anker.

American College Personnel Association. (1996). *The student learning imperative: Implications for student affairs.* Washington, DC: Author.

Anderson, L. W., Krathwohl, D. R., & Bloom, B. S. (2001). *A taxonomy for learning, teaching, and assessing: A revision of Bloom's taxonomy of educational objectives.* Boston, MA: Allyn & Bacon.

Association of American Colleges & Universities (AAC&U). (2014a, March 23). *Liberal education and America's promise.* https://www.aacu.org/leap/.

Association of American Colleges & Universities (AAC&U). (2014b, March 23). *Public opinion research.* https://www.aacu.org/leap/public_opinion_research.cfm.

Astin, A. W. (1993). *Assessment for excellence: The philosophy and practice of assessment and evaluation in higher education.* Phoenix, AZ: Oryx Press.

Baker, G. R., Jankowski, N., Provezis, S., & Kinzie, J. (2012). *Using assessment results: Promising practices of institutions that do it well.* Urbana: University of Illinois and Indiana University, National Institute for Learning Outcomes Assessment.

Banta, T. W. (2002). *Building a scholarship of assessment.* San Francisco, CA: Jossey-Bass.

Banta, T. W., Griffin, M., Flateby, T. L., & Kahn, S. (2009, December). *Three promising alternatives for assessing college students' knowledge and skills* (NILOA Occasion Paper, no. 2). Urbana: University of Illinois and Indiana University, National Institute for Learning Outcomes Assessment.

Bresciani, M. J. (2006). *Outcomes-based academic and co-curricular program review: A compilation of institutional good practices.* Sterling, VA: Stylus.

Bresciani, M. J. (2006, October). *Expert driven assessment: Making it meaningful to decision makers.* (ECAR Research Bulletin, no 21). Boulder, CO: EDUCAUSE.

Bresciani, M. J. (2011, August). *Making assessment meaningful: What new student affairs professionals and those new to assessment need to know* (NILOA Assessment Brief: Student Affairs). Urbana: University for Illinois and Indiana University, National Institute for Learning Outcomes Assessment,

Bresciani, M. J., Moore-Gardner, M., & Hickmott, J. (2010). *Demonstrating student success: A practical guide to outcomes-based assessment of student learning and development in student affairs.* Sterling, VA: Stylus.

Bresciani, M. J., Zelna, C. L., & Anderson, J. A. (2004). *Techniques for assessing student learning and development: A handbook for practitioners.* Washington, DC: NASPA.

Bresciani Ludvik, M. J. (Ed.). (2015). *The neuroscience of student learning and development: Enhancing creativity, compassion, critical thinking, and peace in higher education.* Sterling, VA: Stylus.

Carroll, M. (2006). Keynote at the Association of Institutional Research National Conference. San Diego, CA, 2005. As cited in M. J. Bresciani, *Outcomes-based academic and co-curricular program review: A compilation of institutional good practices.* Sterling, VA: Stylus Publishing.

Council for Adult and Experiential Learning (CAEL). (2014). *Competency-based education.* http://www.cael.org/pdfs/CAEL_competency_based_education_2013.

Council for the Advancement of Standards in Higher Education (CAS). (2006). *Frameworks for assessing learning and development outcomes.* Washington, DC: Author.

Council of Regional Accrediting Commissions. (2003). *Regional accreditation and student learning: Principles of good practices.* Washington, DC: Author.

Ewell, P. T. (2002). An emerging scholarship: A brief history of assessment. In T. W. Banta (Ed.), *Building a scholarship of assessment*, pp. 3-25. San Francisco, CA: Jossey-Bass.

Ewell, P. T. (2009, November). *Assessment, accountability, and improvement: Revisiting the tension* (NILOA Occasional Paper, no. 1). Urbana: University of Illinois and Indiana University, National Institute for Learning Outcomes Assessment.

Ewell, P., Jankowski, N., & Provezis, S. (2010). *Connecting state policies on assessment with institutional assessment activity.* Urbana: University of Illinois and Indiana University, National Institute for Learning Outcomes Assessment (NILOA).

Ewell, P., Paulson, K., & Kinzie, J. (2011). *Down and in: Assessment practices at the program level.* Urbana: University of Illinois and Indiana University, National Institute for Learning Outcomes Assessment.

Huba, M. E., & Freed, J. E. (2000). *Learner-centered assessment on college campuses / Shifting the focus from teaching to learning.* Needham Heights, MA: Allyn & Bacon.

Jankowski, N. A., Ikenberry, S. O., Kinzie, J., Kuh, G. D., Shenoy, G. F., & Baker, G. R. (2012). *Transparency and accountability: An evaluation of the VSA college portrait pilot.* Urbana: University of Illinois and Indiana University, National Institute for Learning Outcomes Assessment.

Jankowski, N., & Provezis, S. (2011). *Making student learning evidence transparent: The state of the art.* Urbana: University of Illinois and Indiana University, National Institute for Learning Outcomes Assessment.

Keeling, R. P. (2004). *Learning reconsidered: A campus-wide focus on the student experience.* Washington, DC: American College Personnel Association & National Association of Student Personnel Administrators.

Klein-Collins, R. (2014). *Sharpening our focus on learning: The ride of competency-based approaches to degree completion.* National Institute for Learning Outcomes Assessment (CAEL). http://learningoutcomesassessment.org/documents/Occasional%20Paper%2020.pdf.

Kuh, G., Kinzie, J., Schuh, J. H., & Whitt, E. (2005a). *Student success in college: Creating conditions that matter.* San Francisco, CA: Jossey-Bass.

Kuh, G., Kinzie, J., Schuh, J. H., & Whitt, E. (2005b). *Assessing conditions to enhance educational effectiveness.* San Francisco, CA: Jossey-Bass.

Maki, P. (2004). *Assessing for student learning: Building a sustainable commitment across the institution*. Sterling, VA: Stylus.

Manning, K., Kinzie, J., & Schuh, J. H. (2006). *One size does not fit all: Traditional and innovative models in student affairs practice*. New York, NY: Routledge.

Mentkowski, M. (2000). *Learning that lasts: Integrating learning, development, and performance in college and beyond*. San Francisco, CA: Jossey-Bass.

Moore-Gardner, M., Kline, K. A., and Bresciani, M. J. (2014). *Assessing student learning in the community and two year colleges: Successful strategies and tools developed by practitioners in student and academic affairs*. Sterling, VA: Stylus.

National Association of Student Personnel Administrators (NASPA) & American College Personnel Association (ACPA). (2010). *ACPA/NAPSA professional competency areas for student affairs practitioners*. http://www.naspa.org/about/boarddocs/710/competencies.pdf.

National Research Council. (2001). *Knowing what students know*. Washington DC: National Academy Press.

Palomba, C. A., & Banta, T. W. (1999). *Assessment essentials: Planning, implementing, and improving assessment in higher education*. San Francisco, CA: Jossey-Bass.

Papert, S. (1991). Situating constructionism. In S. Papert & I. Harel (Eds.), *Constructionism*, pp. 1-11. Norwood, NJ: Ablex.

Pascarella, E. T., & Terenzini, P. T. (2005). *How college affects students, Vol. 2. A third decade of research*. San Francisco, CA: Jossey-Bass.

Sedlacek, W. E. (2004). *Beyond the big test: Noncognitive assessment in higher education*. San Francisco, CA: Jossey-Bass.

Schuh, J. H. (Ed.). (2008). *Assessment methods for student affairs*. San Francisco: Jossey Bass,

Schuh, J. H., & Gansemer-Topf, A. M. (2010, December). *The role of student affairs in student learning assessment* (NILOA Occasional Paper, no. 7). Urbana: University of Illinois and Indiana University, National Institute for Learning Outcomes Assessment.

Stage, F. K., & Manning, K. (Eds.). (2003). *Research in the college context: Approaches and methods*. New York, NY: Brunner/Routledge.

Suskie, L. (2009). *Assessing student learning: A common sense guide* (2nd ed.). San Francisco, CA: Jossey Bass.

US Department of Education (DOE). (2006, August 10). *The commission on the future of higher education draft Report of 8/9/2006*. http://www.ed.gov/about/bdscomm/list/hiedfuture/reports/0809-draft.pdf.

Upcraft, M. L., & Schuh, J. H. (1996). *Assessment in student affairs: A guide for practitioners*. San Francisco, CA: Jossey-Bass.

Wellman, J. V. (2010, January 10). *Connecting the dots between learning and resources* (NILOA Occasional Paper, no. 3). Urbana: University of Illinois and Indiana University, National Institute for Learning Outcomes Assessment,

CHAPTER TWENTY-EIGHT

RAISING FRIENDS AND RAISING FUNDS

David F. Wolf

Friend raising and fund raising are critically important in college student affairs programs. Though there may be slight variations, the underlying art and science of friend raising and fund raising is largely the same across various institutional types and sizes. This chapter provides and introduction to that art and science.

The chapter begins by introducing basic concepts of fund raising/friend raising and next moves into donor development. It then discusses integration of the university's central development organization into the departmental or student affairs divisional development operations. Next the chapter provides insight into the realities of campaigns and how a student affairs program can integrate and position itself into a university-wide comprehensive fund-raising initiative. The chapter concludes with discussion of the unique qualities of student affairs programs as they relate to external initiatives with their alumni and constituents and how these qualities play in the possibilities of resource development.

Basics of Raising Friends and Raising Funds

Universities, including their student affairs programs, are dependent on the availability of a variety of resources in order to function. Establishing friends and raising funds are among the most important of these resources. Friends of the university are individuals who can offer support in any number of ways—donating funds, providing political support on issues of concern to the institution, or facilitating innovative relationships with economic or cultural partners, for example. Raising friends and raising funds within the context of today's universities' financial constraints are becoming increasingly more vital. Whether developing alumni networks, community support, unrestricted gifts, or endowments, building a healthy pipeline of external support is very much a necessity for today's universities. There are limited avenues to develop new resources for academic, capital, and extracurricular activities. Countless speeches have been made by university presidents and chancellors over the years noting that the only opportunities for new significant revenue increases stem from tuition increases, research grants, and philanthropic support. Of these three sources of income, philanthropy can be the most rewarding and challenging to develop and maintain.

Developing and managing a friend-raising and fund-raising program should have clear objectives and a sense of reality in terms of what can be accomplished both short and long term. The purpose of a friend-raising enterprise should be to develop friends, alumni, and other stakeholders to invest emotionally and financially within a department or program. Friend raising creates loyalty and stewards long-term relationships. Fund raising is the mechanism by which we develop our friends into donors. One without the other is limiting and shortsighted. It seems unlikely there could be a quality fund-raising enterprise without friend-raising activities and concepts fully integrated into the core philosophy of the academic or student affairs program. Fund raising is the result of building loyalty and donor passion with friends. This portion of the chapter presents both basic and advanced concepts in developing a friend-raising and fund-raising program.

Raising Friends

Raising friends is typically seen as the process by which a department or program develops and maintains a strategic communications or public relations plan directly connected to its important stakeholders and community. The program of building and strengthening relationships with friends is often led by a university's alumni relations program in conjunction with other development operations at the institution.

Friend raising typically involves both events and communication, such as direct mail, websites, and electronic and social media, to engage and inspire alumni and friends of the university to keep connected. Electronic communication through e-mail, websites, blogs, and other social media outlets (Facebook, Twitter, LinkedIn) is increasingly being used to further connect with alumni and friends. These media are tempting outlets given that they are an inexpensive way of getting out the message. However, electronic and other social media outlets are passive by design and cannot take the place of personal visits and events. Developing personal relationships is the key to building long-term opportunities of deep engagement and philanthropic support.

Friend raising is the initial step toward developing meaningful relationships with external constituencies. Friend-raising activities can be illustrated as the large funnel that eventually provides a steady stream or output of loyal and generous patrons and donors. Specifically, within the context of a student affairs division, it is important to understand the unique position that student affairs is afforded through its connection to the entire universe of its university alumni base as well as the special relationships it has with such important constituencies as former student leaders, Greek and other social organizations, and parents.

Fund Raising

Fund-raising programs typically take one of three forms: annual giving, major giving, and planned giving. Each of these categories has unique purposes and requires unique approaches. It takes all three combined correctly to form a fully operable and vibrant fund-raising program.

Annual Giving. Annual giving is commonly understood as gifts that bring in small- to modest-sized amounts that help fund immediate needs or unrestricted purposes. In a business context, annual giving can be seen as a cash flow enterprise. It creates small- to modest-sized immediate infusions of cash, creating opportunities for academic or program needs. Annual gifts are typically unrestricted and allow immediate investment into programmatic needs by the department. Given the size of annual gifts, a very wide and broad net should be cast when soliciting.

Typically, annual gifts are solicited through direct mail, telemarketing, and e-mail or other electronic communications. The costs associated with annual gift solicitations can be high when correlated with return on investment. Thus, it is important to consider how an annual gift campaign fits into the long-range plan for friend-raising/fund-raising strategy.

Most professional fund raisers consider annual giving the foundation for an emerging fund-raising program. Specifically, through a healthy annual giving program, donor relationships and enthusiasm can begin to be captured and recorded, thus developing long-term relationships for larger future gifts. Healthy annual giving programs develop potential high-end annual gift relationships with individuals. High-end annual donors are those donors who provide larger annual gifts to one's program or department. It is important to recognize who these donors are and research their long-term capacity. Over time, these donors will be prime prospects for major gift investments.

Major Gifts. Major gifts can be of different sizes and scope depending on the type of department or organization. Typically, major gifts start at the $25,000 to $100,000 level, again depending on the fund-raising culture of the university and the department. Major gifts can be given immediately with cash or pledged over a specific period of time. Industry best practices (CASE, 2009) typically require that pledged gifts be paid over a period not longer than five years. It may be necessary on some occasions to lengthen the amount of time a major gift donor requires to pay a pledge. However, these types of arrangements should be carefully determined with the institution and university's chief development officer so that university policy is followed when accepting pledged or other unique gifts. The longer the payment period for pledged gifts is, the greater is the possibility that changes in a donor's personal and economic factors can affect the pledge fulfillment.

Major gift fund raising is where the art and science of fund raising converge. Good major gift operations include extensive amounts of research and donor visits to determine donor passion and donor capacity. Understanding and analyzing donor capacity is becoming easier through technology and Internet-driven information. Research and its impact on fund raising is discussed later in the chapter, but it is important to note here that good research can raise the ability to take a conversation and relationship with a donor to new levels.

Understanding donor motivation is a more artful enterprise. Through cultivation of major gift donor prospects, the art of listening and sharing donor and institutional passion is the opportunity to connect someone of financial means to one's department or program goals. As a major gift program develops, it becomes increasingly important to incorporate more complex and sustainable opportunities for major gifts.

Planned Giving. Planned giving or gift planning is the third, and possibly the most important, category for long-term and legacy-generating enterprises. Planned giving is really two fund-raising strategies rolled into one category: estate gifts and specialized gifts.

Most people know planned giving as the receiving of estate-related gifts. Estate- or bequest-driven fund raising is a vital component for sustained long-term fund raising. Specifically, estate-driven gifts are those gifts received through a will, trust, annuity, or life insurance vehicle. It is becoming more common for donors to notify charities of their intent to give through their estate. However, most gifts are received without prior notification before death.

Specialized giving is the intersection at which major gifts and planned gifts meet. Specialized gifts are those that are negotiated and solicited through the use of financial instruments such as charitable remainder trusts, gift annuities, real estate, gifts of stock or other securities, charitable lead trusts, life insurance, and other more complicated instruments. Success in using specialized giving in major gift negotiations typically involves working with a donor's financial planner, accountant, or attorney. Specialized giving is typically incorporated into planned giving because of the unique and more complicated finance structure that it brings. Good development operations have access to both staff who can consult on these types of gifts and attorneys who specialize in tax, finance, and estate planning (Ashton, 2004).

Planned and specialized giving is a vital component to moving donors toward making large gifts. It also allows for a more strategic plan to be created with relation to the donor's philanthropic interests and ability to pass their wealth to future generations as well as avoid some taxes. Although more complex and creative, more substantial major gift fund raising is accomplished through planned and specialized giving by utilizing these more sophisticated gift planning concepts. Specifically, gifts created through trusts, annuities, and testamentary pledge (a gift pledged through one's estate) can create enormous opportunities for both donors and organizations.

Utilizing planned giving is typically best accomplished through the university's central development office. Most universities employ planned giving professionals who either have the expertise or are connected to local experts such as estate and tax attorneys who can assist both the donor and university in utilizing this very impacting strategy. It is also important to partner with the university's planned giving department to begin to develop marketing and long-term strategies for realizing gifts through estates and other planned giving opportunities.

Art and Science of Fund Raising

Fund raising can be as complicated or as simple as one wants to make it. The realities of today's university-driven development operations are that they are continually becoming more sophisticated and technologically driven. Yet without a basic philosophy of what the department or institution wants to accomplish, and how much that vision costs, all the technology and research in the world will not aid much in building a quality and sustainable development operation. Like academic department fund raising, student affairs departments need to develop both a vision and goals for their needs.

Both fund raising and friend raising boil down to one very simple yet seemingly difficult to manage philosophy:—to develop lasting and meaningful relationships between the organization and the prospective donor. Though on the surface that seems easy, the difficulty lies within the context of how to effectively communicate and honestly build deep sustained relationships with the constituency.

Constituency

The first step toward understanding a constituency is to know how many people it includes. Most, if not all, modern universities and colleges maintain an alumni base in the thousands. Small liberal arts colleges might have less than a hundred thousand known alumni, whereas a large public institution will probably have an alumni base several hundred thousands strong. However, the alumni base is only part of one's constituency. Student affairs departments, by virtue of being programs within the university that touched students and their families outside of the classroom, maintain a large number of non-alumni contacts such as parents and community friends.

Donor Expectations

The reality of fund raising is that gifts are made through relationships with a specific cause or organization. Those relationships are created and sustained by individuals representing the organization. Donors want to know that those who represent their institution are honest and understand their intentions for their gift. More and more donors expect continued validation, reporting, and stewardship related to their charitable giving (Wolf, 2012). What this means is that donors want to know that the organization is using their gifts as agreed upon and that there is some articulation of the benefits that their gift is making within the organization and possibly within society. It is increasingly common for donors to treat a gift as if it were a personal investment, wanting to know how the gift will be used, invested, and the overall return on investment. The challenge is to articulate the return on investment in terms of both a financial and social impact.

A department should consider each of the previously discussed forms of fund raising (annual giving, major gifts, planned giving) and develop a friend-raising/fund-raising enterprise that captures and explores how relationships will be managed within each of these contexts. Also, connecting donors to their gifts through high-quality stewardship programming can create continued giving and new support. Consider what the donor's intent is with their gifts and regularly connect with them through correspondence or events intended to showcase how their support has made an impact within the department. Scholarship recipients, program outcomes, and capital expenditures or improvements are all excellent ways to showcase for donors how their support makes a difference.

Staff

The professional fund raiser, or development officer, is a key component to any gift program. Finding and retaining a quality development professional to focus on meeting with and engaging donors allows for the organization to have a face and conduit to the leadership of the department.

Development professionals should be measured mostly on activity instead of dollars generated. Development programs take significant time to realize a return on investment. Development professionals are only conduits; unless significant time and energy are devoted by departmental, school, college, and university leaders, development programs cannot be successful. Typically, development officers are measured on such activities as developing active donor prospect lists, making face-to-face visits, and soliciting or making proposals to cultivated persons or entities.

There are no exact industry-determined metrics or standards to gauge quality development officer activity, but it is typical for productive development officers to make anywhere between ten and twenty visits per month (see CASE Gift Officer Metrics and Reporting). Furthermore, once a healthy donor prospect list of approximately a hundred or more individuals is generated, it is reasonable for major gift-focused development officers to generate between one and four proposals per month. Annual gift-focused officers should generate ten or more gift proposals per month. Furthermore, utilization of school, department, or program leadership is an important part of the friend-raising/fund-raising enterprise. Leadership should consider taking a development officer approach to their day-to-day operations, whereby they commit to making personal calls and visits monthly to build relationships with key donors.

The Ask

Much of the work needed to have a successful solicitation, sometimes called "the ask," is done early in the donor relationship process. There is an old saying in fund raising that to be successful one must have the right person making the solicitation, for the right amount of money, at the right time for the donor (Smith, 2009). This concept alone will help generate successful gifts for a program. The solicitation is the proverbial icing on the cake—the cake itself is the process and work done to build strategic relationships with donors.

Once the relationship is built, the case for support is articulated over time. The person who likely will be doing the solicitation has a good idea whether the donor is motivated to give either through loyalty to the program or because he or she has emotional connectivity or passion for the program.

The solicitation should be conducted in a setting quiet enough to have an honest and candid conversation. Donor offices or home settings are always best. Restaurants or other public places can be troublesome because of interruptions and uneasiness of asking in a loud or busy setting.

When the solicitation occurs, allow the donor to process what has been asked. Often there is a period of uncomfortable silence after the solicitation is made. This is not a good time to reengage with small talk or further discussion about the solicitation. Allow the donor to make a decision and provide his or her answer. In short, the solicitation itself is the climax of bringing together the donor and the donor's relationship with the department. Most development professionals like to work donors up the scale of gifts over time, thus a large major gift donor could conceivably have been solicited ten to twenty or more times successfully before making the stretch or large notable gift.

The written proposal is a summary case for support that asks a donor for a specific amount to contribute to doing some sort of specific activity. The proposal, which should be left with the potential donor, ought to be concise, organized, and presented in an artful manner. There is no right or wrong way to create a donor proposal. However, there are some basic essential elements that must be included:

Explanation of how the gift will used, invested, and stewarded over time

Impact the gift will make over time

Exact amount that the donor can consider

University Development

Individuals who wish to plan a successful fund-raising and friend-raising enterprise in a student affairs setting need to become familiar with their institution's type of external affairs operations and culture. Most universities use either the term *advancement* or *development* when describing their externally focused engagement operations. Usually advancement is a more holistic approach in which fund raising, marketing, alumni affairs, university communications, and governmental relations all share a common executive line to the president. Development is typically defined as the actual fund-raising enterprise.

The university's central development operation is a critical partner in building a quality departmental-level fund-raising/friend-raising enterprise. The resources and expertise that the university can provide broadly determines the opportunities that can be achieved at the departmental level. Teaming up with the university's central development operations allows the department to move quickly into the major gift arena of fund raising. The challenge often is separating major gift prospects and working within the central development's prospect management system.

Prospect management is a key feature of any successful fund-raising program. Often there are major gift donors who reach multiple departments on a campus. For example, it is easy to see how a major gift donor could be an alumnus of a specific school on campus, and the spouse an alumnus of a different program; they support the arts, and also hold season tickets to multiple athletics teams. To whom do they belong? Are they prospects for the school or department from which they graduated? Are they prospects of the athletics department? Or are they defined as arts patrons? The answer is all of these. In reality, sometimes it comes down to a first-come-first-served basis—meaning that whichever of the entities establishes a relationship first tries to capture that donor as its own. Yet in a healthy and thriving development operation, the donor has a relationship with the entire university and in time will give more generously to all of the programs and ideas with which they share passion if all of the departments work together and solicit in an organized, unified manner. The key to good prospect management is not to capture donors, but instead develop them and build a relationship that benefits not only their interests but also the institution's goals.

Prospect management also relies on research and the capturing of good data. Nearly every university development office utilizes some sort of comprehensive database to capture information about donors and their giving interests. The key to a good data system is the information captured within it. Thus, having a repository of development officer contact reports, giving history, university affiliations, and many other attributes can allow a healthy development operation to build deeper understandings about donor interests and long-term relationships with the university and its programs.

Campaigns

A common occurrence in higher education is the news that one university or another is developing, announcing, and declaring success in some sort of capital or comprehensive campaign. What exactly does the term *campaign* mean? A campaign is a carefully planned, well-articulated, and suitably marketed strategy to connect donors to big ideas and targeted goals on a campus. It used to be that campaigns were special long-term goal-driven enterprises. Today, however, more and more institutions see the campaign as a cyclical necessity to generate or fuel new programs and building projects, and further develop the overall fund-raising enterprise. Regardless of the reason for having a campaign, most universities see themselves as needing to be either in the midst of a campaign or planning for the next campaign.

Campaigns are meant to create new levels of funding, bring new generations of donors, and drive new opportunities for excellence. How a university plans, develops, and executes a campaign can be unique to its culture and fund-raising sophistication. At the departmental level it is important to develop achievable fund-raising priorities and bring those into the framework of the university's campaign objectives. The financial goal for the campaign should be formulated by knowing the donor base, having a defined pipeline of major gift prospects, and articulating a case for support to constituencies.

The success of any campaign rests on the ability to cultivate and achieve major gifts. When planning for a campaign, understand that it is widely accepted that 90 percent or more of the gifts received will be given by 10 percent or less of the donors (Worth, 2002).

There are some key concepts for successful campaign planning and implementation. One very important planning strategy is to simply dream big but be realistic. Once the university has determined that it intends to develop a comprehensive campaign, it becomes the work of the department or program to conceptualize its needs and wants. Whereas it seems easy to dream big about where a program or department might want to go and achieve whether programmatically or in capital projects, the tougher issue is what is realistically achievable.

Connecting the program or department to the goals of the university is incredibly important. This concept alone will catapult big ideas into strategic ideas that can be articulated into the university's case for support. The process the university will take to approve departmental or programmatic strategies that can only be achieved through strategic fund raising can be lengthy and varying depending on the culture of the institution. However, the more a program does to plan and build its own case for support, the more likely the success of moving forward.

A very important concept in moving the strategic fund-raising goals forward is to test ideas on the best donors connected to the program. What a best donor is needs to be considered by the program's relationships with its donor base. Relating back the campaign reality that 90 percent of gifts will be given by only 10 percent of donors, it is necessary to test ideas, concepts, and goals with the program's best major gift prospects. However, it is folly to test concepts if no prior relationship exists. Thus, the strategic work done in developing relationships with the donor base will pay big dividends when moving forward in a campaign environment.

Suggestions for Startups

Starting a friend-raising and fund-raising program may seem daunting; however, as with anything, it always good to think big and start small. What this means is begin to develop the ideas and strategy for where the program is going and what resources and sustained help are required to continue its trajectory. Begin to build a donor base through annual giving programs while also developing and marketing a long-term base through planned giving concepts. Also, target influential and affluent donors through building personal relationships with them on behalf of the department or program. It is important to work closely with the university's central development office in order to utilize their resources and be a team player in helping the university build its more comprehensive development program. Last, remember that it takes time to develop friends and donors. Make it a weekly priority to spend time on activities that will bear fruit in time.

Uniqueness of Development Within Student Affairs

Student affairs departments have a unique connection with students. These outside-the-classroom impressions live long within the memories of alumni. This relationship creates incredible opportunities for alumni donor engagement by utilizing their connections to events, social networks, and campus traditions. As a leader within student affairs, it is important to research in detail your prospective donors' utilization of these clubs, events, and social climate on campus during their time on campus. Specific foci of interest should be concentrated on former student leaders, Greek fraternity or sorority members, and participants in social clubs, service clubs, and other activities in which students are engaged. The key to success is having the knowledge of who participated in these activities over the years. The older or more detailed the information about a former student's experience at the university the better.

Given their relationship with students, student affairs professionals (along with faculty colleagues who serve as advisors to student organizations) are sometimes afforded opportunities to support student learning through the areas of friend making, fund raising, and philanthropy. It is important to use these opportunities to advance learning in goal setting, marketing, salespersonship, and ethical conduct.

Another important aspect that gives student affairs an edge is its ability to connect alumni and friends through current on campus programming and events. Utilizing the many social, academic, and cultural events sponsored by student affairs departments is a powerful mechanism to engage alumni and friends. Working in concert with your campus partners to invite and market events to alumni and friends will create immediate opportunities to showcase the meaningful and amazing work a student affairs department creates. At these events, it is imperative to tactfully remind your guests that extramural connections and opportunities created by student affairs can only be enhanced through generosity and philanthropy.

Many student affairs departments also operate the college or university's enrollment management program. Enrollment management or admissions work is an opportunity to engage alumni in the process of recruiting worthy students to campus. The act of recruiting for one's alma mater is an immediate way of connecting the donors to the reasons they came to the college while providing them an opportunity to be both an expert and advocate. Alumni volunteers who engage in admissions-related work are excellent prospects for regional, merit, or other scholarship initiatives.

Last, a good student affairs friend-raising/fund-raising program works to deepen its connection with new and current parents. Parent giving is typically an annual fund activity. However, depending on the demographics of the campus, there are major gift prospects within the population of parents. Parent clubs or other parent and family programs are now, more than ever, effective in generating annual fund dollars. The key to raising funds with parents lies with reaching out to them very early in their child's college enrollment.

Conclusion

This chapter has offered information and advice regarding friend making and fund raising in the student affairs domain. Here are two final pieces of advice. First, be mindful of the axiom regarding avoiding a gift that eats. Hypothetically imagine that a friend offers to give your son or daughter the gift of a puppy. It is a thoughtful gesture, but it may not be one you can afford unless you already have a place to care for and keep the dog, the time to properly care for it, and the resources associated with feeding and maintaining a dog. Similarly, gifts with onerous restrictions, significant associated expenses moving forward, or that obligate the university in specific ways over very extended windows of time may best be politely passed by rather than accepted. Second, always showcase programs as worthy rather than needy. People give to excellence and programs that show promise. Be honest about the program or department, but always present its strengths and the vision for it. Doing that and building lasting relationships with friends and alumni will assure necessary and meaningful support.

References

Ashton, D. (2004). *The complete guide to planned giving: Everything you need to know to compete successfully for major gifts*. Quincy, MA: Aston.

Council for Advancement and Support of Education. (2009). *CASE reporting standards and management guidelines* (4th ed.). http://www.case.org.

Smith, J. F. (2009). *Fund raising: Rules of the road to success*. Auburn, AL: JF Smith Group.

Wolf, D. F. (2012). Managing friends and raising funds. In G. S. McClellan, C. King, & D. L. Rockey Jr., (Eds.), *The handbook of college athletics and recreation administration* (pp. 232–245). Francisco, CA: Jossey-Bass.

Worth, M. J. (Ed.). (2002). *New strategies for educational fundraising*. Westport, CT: Praeger/American Council on Education.

CHAPTER TWENTY-NINE

COMPUTER-MEDIATED COMMUNICATION AND SOCIAL MEDIA

Kevin R. Guidry and Josie Ahlquist

The pervasiveness of technology in the lives of most students and student affairs professionals demands that those professionals understand technology and its social impact. Student affairs has a long history with technology that has been largely unexplored. That history can serve as a valuable foundation as scholars and professionals begin to integrate student affairs' unique bodies of knowledge with findings from disciplines such as computer science, communications, and sociology.

This chapter opens with brief examples of how student affairs professionals have used technology throughout the history of the profession. Having provided this context, it then focuses more narrowly on computer-mediated communication (CMC) and student use of technology with a brief overview of relevant demographics and trends. The section that follows examines student use of social media and the interplay between CMC and student development. The chapter closes by presenting a few ways in which students and student affairs professionals can productively use CMC and social media.

Student Affairs' Historical Relationship with Technology

Student affairs and technology may seem like as unlikely a pair as "oil and water" (Barrett, 2000, p. 1), but student affairs professionals have made extensive use of technology throughout the profession's history.

Although there is often a tension between its high-touch roots and the increasingly high-tech world, student affairs professionals have kept pace with, experimented with, and worried about technology since their earliest days. Some brief examples from the historical record illustrate this relationship. Scholars who study human communication and technology have called for their work to be grounded in a deeper understanding of their long history of work in that area (Baym, 2009), and student affairs must follow suit.

In some of the earliest meetings of what would become the National Association of Student Personnel Administrators (NASPA), members of the National Association of Deans and Advisers of Men (NADAM) discussed concerns about the role of technology in US higher education. Many student affairs professionals can directly relate to a lament made at the 1928 NADAM meeting: "Today we have so surrounded ourselves with mechanical records that we may have ceased being personalities and become machines" (NADAM, 1929, p. 40). To cope with increasing enrollments and institutional complexity, student affairs professionals have routinely turned to the latest high-tech tools like punch cards to automate data collection and tabulation (Iffert, 1935), recorded lectures to preserve professional knowledge and facilitate professional development (NADAM, 1950), used mainframes to organize and manipulate data (for example. Hewes, 1963; Menke, 1966), and automated telephone systems to augment counseling (Johnson, 1976).

Even during the rapid growth of personal computers in the late 1970s and 1980s, student affairs professionals stayed abreast of the technology trends. As *Time* magazine was declaring the computer the 1982 Person of the Year (Friedrich, 1983), the American College Personnel Association (ACPA) and NASPA both made technology a formal theme of their conferences in 1983. The 1983 ACPA conference in Houston, Texas, for example, featured thirteen programs and one major address focused on technology and hosted the first meeting of the ACPA Task Force on Microcomputer Application to Student Affairs Work. Around the same time, a small number of campuses began installing computer networks and microcomputers in residence halls to enhance student learning and provide access to academic resources (Auguston, 1988; King, 1988). Within a decade, many campuses began installing these networks in response to market pressures and to entice students to live on campus (Futey & Bender, 2005). These networks quickly became mechanisms for entertainment, reaching a high point when a student in a Northeastern University residence hall created the music-sharing program Napster, overwhelming many computer networks and changing the economics and logistics of many of the world's largest corporations (Guidry, Anderer, Futey, & Pee, 2010).

Computer-Mediated Communication

The brief selection of historical examples previously presented demonstrates that technology is a very broad construct. Space limitations dictate a narrower focus in this chapter. Hence, the balance of the chapter focuses on computer-mediated communication. Although different types of CMC have different properties—synchronous versus asynchronous, message lengths, available privacy settings, and so on—this chapter addresses CMC with a specific focus on the social impacts and uses of CMC by students. The authors of this chapter are both US citizens working at US institutions, and much of the work in this field has focused on people in the United States. This chapter focuses primarily on students in the United States.

Student Internet Access and Computer Ownership

This section begins its overview of Internet access and computer ownership by challenging and problematizing common myths about student technology competence. First, it revisits what Dudley Woodard, Patrick Love, and Susan Komives (2000) called a heresy of student affairs: "the field of student affairs continues to focus almost solely on the 'traditional' undergraduate college student" (p. 35). This heresy persists, although most US college students are nontraditional; although only about a third of undergraduate students are twenty-five years or older and 37 percent attend school part time (US Department of Education, 2012), three-quarters of students are nontraditional when accounting for all of the factors typically associated with that label: for example, part-time enrollment, commute to campus, pay their own tuition and fees (Complete College America, 2011).

Second, there are significant differences in how different students access and use the Internet. Broadly speaking, it is true that nearly all students regularly access and use the Internet. The most current statistics available indicate that 85 percent of adults in the United States and 95 percent of teens in the United States use the Internet at least occasionally (Pew Internet & American Life Project, 2013a, 2013b). Among college students, nearly all (89 percent) own laptop computers or smartphones (76 percent) (Dahlstrom, Walker, & Dziuban, 2013).

These impressive numbers mask some important differences. In the broader US population, there are differences in Internet access among people of different races and ethnicities, age, education, income, and urbanity, with non-Hispanic, younger, more educated, richer, and urban or suburban dwellers more likely to use the Internet (Pew Internet & American Life Project, 2013a, 2013b). Those who are less likely to have Internet access are also those who are less likely to participate in higher education.

In the past ten years, researchers have begun exploring nuances that lie beyond the access/no access dichotomy of the digital divide. Most notably, media scholar Henry Jenkins has advanced the concept of the "participation gap," an idea that explicitly acknowledges that those who have had access to technology have had different experiences with it and have thus gained different skills, predilections, and comfort levels with different technologies (Jenkins, 2006a, 2006b). For example, American teens with computers and Internet access in their homes use tools such as Facebook and MySpace differently than teens who access the Internet from different locations, such as school or the public library (boyd, 2008; Weber & Mitchell, 2008), supporting the notion that mere access to technology is insufficient without "a supporting social and cultural world" (Ito et al., 2010, p. 17).

Together, these facts about Internet access and use undermine common beliefs that all of today's college students typically are "digital natives" (Prensky, 2001) who are highly skilled with technology. Students are not a homogenous group and have had different experiences that have shaped their technology skills and preferences. Empirical research has soundly demonstrated that students have a wide range of technology skills and preferences (see, for example, Palfrey & Gasser, 2008), and "schools and universities [are] perpetuating—rather than resisting—inequalities associated with the digital divide" (Goode, 2010, p. 497).

Mobile Internet Access

Trends related to the access to and use of the Internet on mobile devices such as smartphones and tablets are particularly interesting for student affairs professionals. First, in contrast with the historic trends of Internet access, non-White people in the United States are significantly more likely to use a smartphone to access the Internet than are people from other ethnic groups (Duggan & Smith, 2013). Unsurprisingly, however, among college students, younger students are more likely to own a smartphone

(Dahlstrom, et al., 2013). Second, these devices' omnipresence presents new and unique opportunities and challenges. Students frequently use mobile devices to seek emotional and physical support from others, including their parents, and believe that these devices make them safer (Chen & Katz, 2009; Nasar, Hecht, & Wener, 2007). However, students report that faculty often discourage or prohibit the use of these devices while in class, and some students believe they are distracting when other students use them in class (Dahlstrom et al., 2013).

College Students and Social Media

Social networking sites (SNSs) such as Facebook, Instagram, and Twitter are communication and community-building tools. Nicole Ellison, Charles Steinfield, and Cliff Lampe (2007) defined a SNS as: "a web based service that allows for individuals to (1) contrast a public or semi-public profile within a bounded system, (2) articulate a list of other users with whom they share a connection and (3) view and traverse their list of connections and those made by others in the system" (p. 211).

Social media, a term almost synonymous with social networking, expands that concept to embrace user-generated content (Kaplan & Haelien, 2010), including peer-to-peer communication (Constantinides & Zinck Stagno, 2011). Social media provides a means of interaction whereby individuals and communities can share, create, discuss, and exchange ideas and information, properties of a virtual community (Cheung, Chiu, & Lee, 2011). When used strategically, they can support educationally purposeful activities that contribute to student engagement and success. Much of the research literature uses *social media* and *social networking* interchangeably, a convention also followed in this chapter. Interactive media such as blogs, instant messaging, and podcasts are often classified as social media (Saee, Sinnappan, & Yang, 2009).

Much of the newer research on social media conducted has focused on two of the most popular SNSs: Facebook and Twitter. With more than a billion active users (Facebook, 2014) and more than 302 million active users (Twitter, 2014), respectively, these sites make for rich research sites. Researchers have specifically described Twitter as "a good case to understand how people integrate information and communication technologies to form new social connections, collaboration, and conversation" (Gruzd, Takheyev, & Wellman, 2011, p. 1313).

Frequency of Use

Nearly all college students in the United States use social media several times a day (Junco, 2011a; Junco, Heighberger, & Loken 2011; Pempek, Yermolayeva, & Calvert, 2009; and Steinfield, Ellison, & Lampe, 2008). In 2009, researchers observed students logging on to Facebook for at least thirty minutes daily, with more time spent on the weekend (Pempek, et al., 2009). Three years later, according to another study, students were averaging 1 hour and 40 minutes per day on Facebook (Junco, 2011a). First-year students tend to use Facebook more than others, with usage decreasing as they progress through school (Gemmill & Peterson, 2006; and Yang & Brown, 2013). First-year students are also the college student group most likely to post negative or inappropriate content (Lifer, Parsons, & Miller, 2010). These differences probably occur because students become more integrated into the campus and spend more time interacting with one another in person as they progress through college (Gemmill & Peterson, 2006).

Although some people may believe that online communication tools are replacing face-to-face communication for young people, widespread access to communication technologies facilitates offline interaction and does not replace face-to-face communication (Huang, Hood, & Yoo, 2013). In fact, college students prefer face-to-face interactions over Internet-aided communication (Sponcil & Gitimu, 2013) and blended learning environments over completely online ones (Dahlstrom et al., 2013). However, most teens and young adults prefer using social media through mobile devices (Dahlstrom, 2012).

Reasons for Using

In a recent study by Megan Sponcil and Priscilla Gitimu (2013), almost half of the students reported that social media has affected them positively. Students use Facebook primarily to build and maintain relationships (Mangao, Taylor, and Greenfield, 2012; Pempek et al., 2009; Sponcil & Gitimu, 2013; Tosun, 2012). Teens and young adults also use Facebook to express their identity (Pempek et al., 2009; Tosun, 2012) and gain attention (Mangao et al., 2012) through photos, status updates, or profile information. Active participation in Facebook that draws attention makes college students believe that it is "a useful tool for acquiring social resources" (Mangao et al., 2012, p. 377). Researchers are not unanimous, however, with others reporting that 78 percent of the respondents believed that they were not using social media to impress others (Sponcil & Gitimu, 2013).

There are, of course, negative reasons that students use social media. Students sometimes post content that they know is inappropriate (Lifer et al., 2010). Examples include using harsh language and pictures involving alcohol. This type of behavior was observed more from first-year students (Morgan et al., 2010). In addition, first-year students used social media when looking to fill free time and when they were bored (Jacobsen & Forste, 2011; Pempek et al., 2009; Sponcil & Gitimu, 2013). Many students—half of them in one study (Pempek et al., 2009)—lurk (read others' contributions without posting; for example, scrolling down the Facebook home page, observing posts and pictures, or looking at Facebook friends' profiles without commenting or contributing in any way) (Brandtzaeg, 2012; Sponcil & Gitimu, 2013).

Impact of Use

With nearly every college student using social media, researchers have explored ways in which social media affects students, including their social, personal, and cognitive dimensions. As the previous section described, students engage in positive and negative behaviors online. This is also true of the impact social media use has on students.

Positive results that can be attributed to college students being online include development of identity, increased self-esteem, decreased loneliness, increased social capital, and increased student engagement. Social media offers a vehicle for self-expression, allowing students to display and express their identities (DeAndréa, Ellison, LaRose, Steinfield, & Fiore, 2012; and Pempek et al., 2006). Students can increase their self-esteem or cope with high levels of introversion with social media by using it as a vehicle to find their voices even if they are internally struggling with self-confidence (Ellison, Steinfield & Lamp, 2007; Gonzales & Hancock, 2011; and Steinfield, Ellison, & Lampe, 2008). Facebook usage can have a positive impact on loneliness by being a useful social tool for students who are homesick, missing friends, or having trouble meeting new people (Brandtzaeg, 2012; and Lour, Yan, Nickerson, & McMorris, 2012). Facebook usage is also associated with students' formation and maintenance of social capital (Brandtzaeg, 2012; and Ellison et al., 2007), an important resource for college students, transitioning into university life, being successful in and out of the classroom, and going into the workforce. Social media use positively influences student engagement on campus; once a student becomes involved on campus, social media resources such as Facebook friends will expand in person and online (Gray, Vitak, Easton, & Ellison, 2013; Junco, 2011a; and Mangao et al., 2012).

Like the positive impacts, negative impacts are often closely related to how students use social media. For example, Chia-chen Yang and B. Bradford Brown (2013) found that students who post many negative statements on Facebook tended to experience loneliness and poor social adjustment. Other negative impacts of social media include disruptions and stress. Technology, including social media, is often disruptive for students when studying or attending class (Gemmill & Peterson, 2006; and Jacobsen & Forste, 2011). Stress is also related to the impact technology has on students (Gemmill & Peterson, 2006; and Pempek et al., 2009).

Computer-Mediated Communication and Student Development

It is important to understand the experiences of college students with CMC, including social media, from a student development perspective. A significant amount of development occurs for traditional-age college students who are teens and young adults. A variety of research, including theories and frameworks, provide reference throughout the entire developmental process.

Transition to College

The arrival and transition into campus life for a new student is significant, successfully occurring through adjustment into campus networks through social, emotional, and academic means (Gray, Vitak, Easton, & Ellison, 2013). Through Facebook, students can maintain relationships with people at their universities and people who are physically distant. Other social media sites can also be beneficial to college transition.

Social media—including social network sites (SNSs), personal blogs, and geographically bounded discussion forums—may ease students' transition from high school to college by providing them with information and social support, as well as, a way to find and connect with other students (Gray et al., 2013, p. 193).

The transition to college begins before and continues during matriculation. Facebook guides students through new territory and what it would mean to be a student at that particular university (DeAndréa et al., 2012), providing information and facilitating connections before they are even accepted to the university (DeAndréa et al., 2012). Social media continues to aid students transitioning into college and retaining them into their sophomore year (Gray et al., 2013; and Heiberger & Harper, 2008).

Campus Involvement

Student involvement theory posits students involved on campus are more successful with higher grades, higher rates of retention, and so on (for example, Astin, 1984; and Wolf-Wendel, Ward, & Kinzie, 2009). This theory can also be used to explore the impact of how students spend their time and energy through social media. The impact of student use on SNSs and student involvement is positively correlated (Junco, 2011a; Mangao et al., 2012). Rey Junco (2011a) persuasively explained that when students actively participated in social media they were more likely to show that same activity level on campus.

Student Engagement

Building on Alexander Astin's work, George Kuh (2009) gives insight into student engagement in and out of the classroom. Student engagement involves two factors, "what the student does and what the institution does" (Wolf-Wendel et al., 2009, p. 413). Several factors position universities to respond to student engagement research and meet students where they are, providing educational activities physically and virtually. For example, college students spend a great deal of time and energy on Facebook (Junco, 2011b), maybe even more than with their university portal or e-mail accounts (Heiberger & Harper, 2008). Greg Heiberger and Ruth Harper (2008) as well as Junco (2011a) have found positive correlations between Facebook and student engagement. Twitter can also be used as a tool to engage students and contribute to their academic and psychosocial development (Junco, Heighber, & Loken, 2011).

Identity Development

Identity exploration, experimentation, and commitment are necessary for human development. Identity is socially constructed and based upon the sense of self and beliefs (Torres, Jones, & Renn, 2009). Like the traditional college experience, social media allow identity experimentation away from parental oversight (Gray et al., 2013). Social media use also satisfies a number of psychosocial needs including aiding student development, success, and identity exploration through meeting emotional, cognitive, social, and habitual needs (Wang, Tcherneve, & Salloway, 2012). Although technology clearly has an impact on the college environment, specifically on student development, "more research is needed to understand how technology can influence identity" (Torres et al., 2009, p. 592).

Digital Identity Formation

Scholars are beginning to explore how long-standing student development theories align with twenty-first-century practices. Echoing seminal CMC research by Sherry Turkle (1995), Shanyang Zhao, Sherri Grasmuck, and Jason Martin (2008) assert that a technologically mediated environment can allow for a new mode of identity production to emerge. Online, students can try on different identities, sometimes even different than their real-life ones. Joanna Goode (2010) called this new identity their "technology identity," which describes how personal technology experiences and social (peer) expectations will lead to skills and perceptions of technology.

Zhao et al. (2008) explored identity on Facebook with sixty-three college students' Facebook profiles, follow-up interviews, and focus groups. They found a continuum of identity construction through specific identity strategies and frequencies for expression, including the visual self, cultural self, and narrative self. Identity expression on Facebook followed a "show rather than tell" (p. 1826) model, with students in the study mostly keeping their Facebook profiles open to the public. This study suggests that a social media platform such as Facebook can provide students with an ability to present themselves, go around psychological barriers, and explore the idea of a hoped-for possible self that may not be possible offline.

Student Self-Presentation. Many scholars who have studied CMC and online behaviors have focused on *self-presentation*, a concept related to identity development but more narrow in scope (Goffman, 1959). In an influential 2007 paper, danah boyd argued that online self-presentation is different than offline presentation with four specific differences: persistence (content online has a long life span), searchability (finding content online is easier than in print), replicability (one can multiply or change original works published online), and invisible audiences (one is not completely aware of who sees their activity). Considering mediated technologies, Don Slater (2002) declared, "You are what you type" (p. 536) because of users' ability to have a choice in creating, modifying, and even having multiple identities.

Zhao et al. (2008) called this phenomenon "digital selves," real identities that "serve to enhance the users' overall self-image and identity claims and possibly increase their chances to connect in the offline world" (pp. 1831–1832). Student development researchers have called for a congruence of digital selves with real-life selves, with the possibility that shifting expressions of identity can be observed by the changing and choice of photos, posting of quotes, and membership in online groups (Torres et al., 2009).

CMC Applications for Student Affairs

This section builds on the research presented thus far to discuss three concrete areas related to CMC that student affairs professionals can explore and impact: digital citizenship, digital leadership, and personal learning networks. The underlying ideas are not new or unique to CMC, but they are enabled or enhanced by the prevalence of social media.

Digital Citizenship

Students engage in CMC in and out of the classroom, usually for non-academic reasons and often in ways that can be understood using student development theories as lenses. Therefore student affairs professionals should play a role in educating students on the digital tools available to communicate and contribute online. One particularly useful idea that can be borrowed from K–12 research is "digital citizenship."

Digital citizenship includes norms of behavior and practice with an "ability to practice and advocate online behavior that demonstrates legal, ethical, safe, and responsible uses of information and communication technologies" (Greenhow & Robelia, 2009, p. 125). Ribble, Bailey, and Ross (2004) developed nine digital citizenship elements: etiquette, communication, access, literacy, commerce, law, rights and responsibilities, health and wellness, and security. Digital citizenship challenges student affairs professionals to engage in holistic development and awareness, including methods for decision making, ethical and legal activities, safety and security, and "becoming an effective member of digital communities" (2011, p. 38). Students' online actions not only affect themselves but also their families, universities or colleges, and possibly their future professions (Greysen, Kind, & Chretien, 2010).

Digital Leadership

Student affairs professionals should also develop student leaders who can be influential through digital means. Digital technology education does not focus merely on introducing tools but guiding students in using them in their roles as students on campus, active members of the global community, and future leaders in their chosen professions (Ahn, 2011). It requires the entire campus to build a community of learners empowered and equipped with knowledge and resources to become digital stewards of technology (Lewis & Rush, 2013).

Personal Learning Networks

This chapter now turns from how students use technology to how student affairs professionals can positively use social media in professional development. This section describes the emerging idea of a Personal Learning Network (PLN), a growth of the social networking that student affairs professionals have always conducted but expanded to include social media (Siemens, 2005). In a PLN, the user is central to creating his or her network and responsible for contributing and sharing.

Twitter. Twitter is a prime example of how a PLN can be fostered. The Twitter student affairs community is active, filled weekly with chats like #sachat, #sagrad, and #sadoc. The participants of #sachat, a community initially formed in 2009, are particularly active (Guidry & Pasquini, 2012). The Student Affairs Collective provides more information about #sachat at http://studentaffairscollective.org/sachat/. Inside Higher Ed (http://www.insidehighered.com/twitter_directory) provides a comprehensive directory that lists other education-related hashtags.

Collaborations. A valuable part of PLNs are collaborative student affairs websites, including blogs and videos. Created and managed by student affairs professionals, a collaborative spirit is fostered as these projects grow and take on additional contributors as guest contributors and new as comanagers. A few examples include:

- Student Affairs Collective http://studentaffairscollective.org/
- The Student Affairs Feature http://studentaffairsfeature.com/
- Student Affairs Women Talk Tech http://www.sawomentalktech.com/blog/
- Student Affairs Fitness http://studentaffairsfit.com/
- Higher Ed Live http://higheredlive.com/

Conclusion

Social media and CMC permeate the lives of many student affairs professionals and the lives of many—but not all—undergraduate students. Student affairs professionals have a rich history of technology usage, but they are not content to leave social media for students. Student affairs professionals are instead making innovative and rich use of social media to inform and enrich their professional practices. This active use and the rich links between research by student affairs scholars, particularly student development theories, and work done by scholars in other diverse disciplines paint a future as bright as the past for technology in student affairs.

References

American College Personnel Association. (1983). *Conquering our new frontiers: Creativity, technology, and untapped resources [*conference program*]*. Bowling Green, OH: Bowling Green State University Center for Archival Collections, National Student Affairs Archives, MS-319. American College Personnel Association (ACPA) Convention Files Box #2.

Ahn, J. (2011). Digital divides and social network sites: Which students participate in social media? *Journal of. Educational Computing Research, 45*(2), 147–163.

Astin, A. W. (1984). Student involvement: A developmental theory for higher education. *Journal of College Student Personnel, 25*, 297–307.

Auguston, J. G. (1988). The Pennsylvania State University. In C. Arms (Ed.), *Campus networking strategies*. Bedford, MA: Digital Press.

Barrett, W. (2000). Technology and student affairs: An unlikely pair. *Student Affairs On-Line, 1*(1). http://studentaffairs.com/ejournal/Spring_2000/article4.html

Baym, N. (2009). A Call for grounding in the face of blurred boundaries. *Journal of Computer-Mediated Communication, 14*, 720–723.

boyd, d. m. (2007). Why youth love social network sites: The role of networked publics in teenage social life. In D. Buckingham (Ed.), *Youth, identity and digital media* (pp. 119-142). The John D. and Catherine T. Mac Arthur Foundation series on digital media and learning: Cambridge: MIT Press.

boyd, d. m. (2008). *Taken out of context: American teen sociality in networked publics*. Unpublished doctoral dissertation, University of California, Berkeley.

Brandtzaeg, P. B. (2012). Social networking sites: Their users and social implications: A longitudinal study. *Journal of Computer-Mediated Communication, 17*, 467–488.

Chen, Y., & Katz, J. E. (2009). Extending family to school life: College students' use of the mobile phone. *International Journal of Human-Computer Studies, 67*, 179–191.

Cheung, C.M.K., Chiu, P., & Lee, M.K.O. (2011). Online social networks: Why do students use Facebook? *Computers in Human Behavior, 27*, 1337–1343.

Constantinides, E., & Zinck Stagno, M. C. (2011). Potential of the social media as instruments of higher education marketing: A segmentation study. *Journal of Marketing for Higher Education, 21*(1), 7–24.

Complete College America. (2011). *Time is the enemy.* Washington, DC: Author

Dahlstrom, E. (2012). *ECAR Study of Undergraduate Students and Information Technology.* Louisville, CO: EDUCAUSE Center for Applied Research.

Dahlstrom, E., Walker, J. D., & Dziuban, C. (2013). *ECAR Study of Undergraduate Students and Information Technology, 2013.* Boulder, CO: EDUCAUSE.

DeAndréa, D. C., Ellison, N. B., LaRose, R., Steinfield, C. & Fiore, A. (2012). Serious social media: On the use of social media for improving students' adjustment to college. *Internet and Higher Education, 15,* 15–23.

Duggan, M., & Smith, A. (2013). *Cell Internet use 2013.* Washington, DC: Pew Internet & American Life Project.

Ellison, N., Steinfield, C. & Lampe, C. (2007). The benefits of Facebook "friends": Social capital and the college students' use of online social network sites. *Journal of Computer-Medicated Communication, 12,* 1143–1168.

Facebook. (2014, January). Key facts. http://newsroom.fb.com/Key-Facts.

Friedrich, O. (1983, January 3). The computer moves in. *Time, pp. 14-29.*

Futey, D., & Bender, B. (2005). ResNet: At the crossroads of academe, residence life, and technology *(ECAR Research Bulletin, 2005, no. 11).* Boulder, CO: EDUCAUSE.

Gemmill, E., & Peterson, M. (2006). Technology use among college students: Implications for student affairs professionals. *NASPA Journal, 43*(2), 280–300.

Goffman, E. (1959). *The presentation of self in everyday life.* New York, NY: Anchor.

Goode, J. (2010). The digital identity divide: How technology knowledge impacts college students. *New Media and Society, 12*(3), 497–513.

Gonzales, A. L., & Hancock, J. T. (2011). Mirror, mirror on my Facebook wall: Effects of exposure to Facebook on self-esteem. *Cyberpsychology, Behavior, and Social Networking, 14,* 79–83.

Gray, R., Vitak, J., Easton, E. W. & Ellison, N. B. (2013). Examining social adjustment to college in the age of social media: Factors influencing successful transitions and persistence. *Computers and Education, 67,* 193–207.

Greenhow, C., & Robelia, B. (2009). Informal learning and identity formation in online social networks. *Learning, Media and Technology, 34*(2), 119–140.

Greysen, S. R., Kind, T., & Chretien, K. (2010). Online professionalism and the mirror of social media. *Journal of General Internal Medicine, 25*(11), 1227–1229.

Gruzd, A., Takheyev, Y., & Wellman, B. (2011). Imagining Twitter as an imagined community. *American Behavioral Scientist, 55*(10) 1294–1318.

Guidry, K. R., Anderer, C., Futey, D., & Pee, C. (2010). A perspective on residential computer networks: An analysis of ResNet symposium presentations, 1995–2006. *Journal of College and University Student Housing, 36*(2), 92–108.

Guidry, K. R., & Pasquini, L. A. (2012). Twitter chat as a non-formal learning tool: A case study using #sachat. In H. Yang & S. Wang (Eds.), *Cases on formal, non-formal, and informal online learning: opportunities and practices* (pp. 356-377). Hershey, PA: IGI Global.

Heiberger, G., & Harper, R. (2008). *Have you Facebooked Astin lately? Using technology to increase student engagement.* New Directions for Student Services, no. 124, 19–35.

Hewes, R. E. (1963). Some general thoughts on the use of a computer in the area of academic administration. *Journal of College Student Personnel, 5*(2), 73–76, 107.

Huang, W.H.D., Hood, D. W., & Yoo S. J. (2013). Gender divide and acceptance of collaborative Web 2.0 applications for learning in higher education. *Internet and Higher Education, 16,* 57–65.

Iffert, R. E. (1935). Fraternities. In G. W. Baehne (Ed.), *Practical applications of the punched card method in colleges and universities* (pp. 171–174). Morningside Heights, NY: Columbia University Press.

Ito, M., et al. (2010). *Hanging out, messing around, and geeking out: Kids living and learning with new media*. Cambridge: MIT Press.

Jacobsen, W. C., & Forste, R. (2011). The wired generation: Academic and social outcomes of electronic media use among university students. *Cyberpsychology, Behavior, and Social Networking, 14*(5), 275–280.

Jenkins, H. (2006a). *Convergence culture: Where old and new media collide*. New York, NY: New York University Press.

Jenkins, H. (2006b). *Confronting the challenges of participatory culture: Media education for the 21st century* (John D. and Catherine T. MacArthur Foundation Digital Media and Learning Initiative Occasional White Paper). Washington, DC: John D. and Catherine T. MacArthur Foundation.

Johnson, C. W. (1976). The effectiveness of a phone help line as indicated by student awareness and use. *Journal of College Student Personnel, 17*(5), 227–231.

Junco, R. (2011a). The relationship between frequency of Facebook use, participation in Facebook activities and student engagement. *Computers and Education, 58*, 162–171.

Junco, R. (2011b). Too much face and not enough books: The relationship between multiple indices of Facebook use and academic performance. *Computers in Human Behavior, 28*(1), 187–198.

Junco, R., Heiberger, G., & Loken, E. (2011). The effect of Twitter on college student engagement and grades. *Journal of Computer Assisted Learning, 27*(2), 119–132.

Kaplan, A. M., & Haenlein, M. (2010). Users of the world, unite! The challenges of Social Media. *Business Horizons, 53*, 59–68.

King, K. (1988). Cornell University. In C. Arms (Ed.), *Campus networking strategies* (pp. 162-164). Bedford, MA: Digital Press.

Kuh, G. (2009). *The National Survey of Student Engagement: Conceptual and empirical foundations*. New Directions for Institutional Research, no. 141. San Francisco: Jossey-Bass.

Lewis, B., & Rush, D. (2013). Experience of developing Twitter-based communities of practice in higher education. *Research in Learning Technology, 21*, 1–35.

Lifer, D., Parsons, K., & Miller, R. (2010). Students and social networking sites: The POSTING paradox. *Behavior and Information Technology, 29*(4), 377–382.

Lour, L. L., Yan, Z., Nickerson, A. & McMorris, R. (2012). An examination of the reciprocal relationship of loneliness and Facebook use among first-year students. *Journal of Educational Computing Research, 46*(1) 105–117.

Mangao, A. M., Taylor, T., & Greenfield, P. M. (2012). Me and my 400 friends: The anatomy of college students' Facebook networks, their communication patterns, and well-being. *Development Psychology, 48*(2), 369–380.

Menke, R. F. (1966). Electronic data in processing placement. *NASPA Journal, 3*(4), 10–12.

Morgan, E. M., Snelson, C., & Elison-Bowers, P. (2010). Image and video disclosure of substance use on social media websites. *Computers in Human Behavior, 26*, 1405–1411.

National Association of Deans and Advisers of Men. (1929). *Secretarial notes on the tenth annual conferences of Deans and Advisers of Men*. Lawrence, KS: Author.

National Association of Deans and Advisers of Men. (1950). *Proceedings of the thirty-second anniversary conference of the National Association of Deans and Advisers of Men.* Williamsburg, VA: Author.

Nasar, J., Hecht, P., & Wener, R. (2007). "Call if you have trouble": Mobile phones and safety among college students. *International Journal of Urban and Regional Research, 31*(4), 863–873.

National Association of Student Personnel Administrators. (1983). *NASPA '83 in Toronto: sixty-fifth annual national conference* [conference program]. Bowling Green, OH: Bowling Green State University Center for Archival Collections, National Student Affairs Archives, MS-391. NASPA Convention Files Box #5 (Programs).

Palfrey, J., & Gasser, U. (2008). *Born digital: Understanding the first generation of digital natives.* New York, NY: Basic Books.

Pempek, T. A., Yermolayeva, Y. A. & Calvert, S. L. (2009). College students' social networking experiences on Facebook. *Journal of Applied Developmental Psychology, 30,* 227–238.

Pew Internet & American Life Project. (2013a). *Who's online: Internet user demographics.* Washington, DC: Author.

Pew Internet & American Life Project. (2013b). *Teen Internet user demographics.* Washington, DC: Author.

Prensky, M. (2001). Digital natives, digital immigrants. *On the Horizon, 9*(5), 1–6.

Ribble, M. S., Bailey, G. D., & Ross, T. W. (2004). Digital citizenship: Focus questions for implementation. *Learning and Leading with Technology, 32* (2), 12–15.

Saeed, N., Yang, Y., & Sinnappan, S. (2009). Emerging web technologies: A case of incorporating blogs, podcasts and social bookmarks in a web programming course based on students' learning styles and technology preferences. *Educational Technology & Society, 12*(4), 98–109.

Siemens, G. (2005). Connectivism: A learning theory for the digital age. *Journal of Instructional Technology and Distance Learning, 1*(2), 3–10.

Slater, D. (2002). Social relationships and identity online and offline. In L. Lievrouw & S. Livingstone (Eds.), *Handbook of new media* (pp. 533-546), London, England: Sage.

Sponcil, M., & Gitimu, P. (2013). Use of social media by college students: Relationship to communication and self-concept. *Journal of Technology Research, 4,* 1–13.

Steinfield, C., Ellison, N. B., & Lampe, C. (2008). Social capital, self-esteem, and use of online social network sites: A longitudinal analysis. *Journal of Applied Developmental Psychology, 29,* 434–445.

Torres, V., Jones, S. R. & Renn, K. A. (2009). Identity development theories in student affairs: Origins, current status, and new approaches. *Journal of College Student Development, 50*(6), 577–596.

Tosun, L. P. (2012). Motives for Facebook use and expressing "true self" on the Internet. *Computers in Human Behavior, 28,* 1510–1517.

Turkle, S. (1995). *Life on the screen: Identity in the age of the Internet.* New York, NY: Simon & Schuster.

Twitter. (2014). About Twitter, Inc. https://about.twitter.com/company.

US Department of Education. (2012). *National Center for Education Statistics, Integrated Postsecondary Education Data System (IPEDS), Spring 2008, 2010, and 2012, Enrollment component.* Washington, DC: Author.

Wang, Z., Tcherneve, J. M., & Solloway, T. (2012). A dynamic longitundinal examination of social media use, needs, and gratifications among college students. *Computers in Human Behavior, 28*, 1829–1839.

Weber, S., & Mitchell, C. (2008). Imagining, keyboarding, and posting identities: Young people and new media technologies. In D. Buckingham (Ed.), *Youth, identity, and digital media* (pp. 25-47). Cambridge: MIT Press.

Wolf-Wendel, L., Ward, K., & Kinzie, J. (2009). A tangled web of terms: The overlap and unique contribution of involvement, engagement, and integration to understanding college student success. *Journal of College Student Development, 50*(4), 407–428.

Woodard, D. B., Love, P., & Komives, S. R. (2000). *Leadership and management issues for a new century.* New Directions for Student Services, no. 92. New York, NY: Wiley.

Yang, C., & Brown, B. B. (2013). Motives for using Facebook, patterns of Facebook activities, and late adolescents' social adjustment to college. *Journal of Youth and Adolescence, 42*, 403–416.

Zhao, S., Grasmuck, S., & Martin, J. (2008). Identity construction on Facebook: Digital empowerment in anchored relationships. *Computers in Human Behavior, 24* (5), 1816–1836.

CHAPTER THIRTY

CAMPUS CRISIS MANAGEMENT

Eugene L. Zdziarski II

The reality of campus crises and the role that student affairs administrators play in responding to and dealing with such incidents has been a subject of student affairs literature for a number of years. Indeed, the two previous editions of *The Handbook of Student Affairs Administration* (Duncan & Miser, 2000; and Miser & Cherrey, 2009) have each included a chapter devoted to campus crisis. Though the topic has been an ongoing area of discussion, our approach to campus crisis has shifted over time from simply dealing with it, or responding to it, to understanding the process of crisis management, and in particular what we can do to prevent crises and protect the campus community.

Campus crisis is inevitable. As student affairs administrators we deal with various types of crises on a regular basis, and if you are in the profession long enough, you will likely experience a major campus crisis. Though it is not necessarily something we seek out in our professional careers, it is also not something we should fear.

It is often noted that the Chinese ideogram for the word *crisis* contains symbols representing both *danger* and *opportunity* (Duncan & Miser, 2000; Fink, 1986; Lagadec, 1993; and Zdziarski, 2001). In the second edition of *The Handbook of Student Affairs Administration*, Duncan and Miser (2000) acknowledged the wisdom in this representation of crisis. Building on their original thoughts, and integrating a modern approach to the crisis management, it can be restated that "student affairs professionals can use the Chinese wisdom and see [opportunity in the process of crisis management] to create a better program, a stronger institution, more accurate and inclusive communication systems, and a more organized, close-knit staff" (p. 453).

This chapter is a significant departure from the discussion of campus crisis in previous editions of this volume, in which the topic was covered in a broader overview and identified a variety of issues for consideration. In this edition, campus crisis management is addressed in a more detailed and systematic manner both theoretically and practically. We begin by looking at the crisis management process and the five phases of the process that serve as frameworks for institutional planning. We then consider scalability, stakeholders, and crisis management teams. Finally, we discuss crisis management plans, including situational and functional protocols that are of particular importance to student affairs professionals.

Crisis Management: A Process Approach

In the past, crisis management was often interpreted as a set of actions college administrators implemented to deal with or respond to a crisis incident or event. Today we understand that crisis management is an ongoing process that involves a series of stages or phases that campus administrators should work through regularly.

There have been a number of crisis management models introduced over the years. One of the earliest models described crisis management in terms of three phases: pre-crisis, crisis and post-crisis (Coombs, 1999; Koovor-Misra, 1995; Mitchell, 1986; and Ogrizek & Guillery, 1999). Essentially this model guided crisis management efforts by directing activities before, during, and after a crisis. Later this model was revised to include mitigation, preparedness, response, and recovery (Federal Emergency Management Agency [FEMA], 1996).

Initially, organizations understood the importance of planning to respond appropriately during a crisis event or the crisis phase. After Hurricane Katrina in 2005 and the extended time it took to restore the region to some semblance of normalcy, significant attention was given to developing specific plans for recovery or the post-crisis phase. Still, little attention was given to the need for appropriate planning in the mitigation stage or pre-crisis phase. This was particularly true for higher education. In studies of institutional preparedness to respond to campus crises (Catullo,

2008; and Zdziarski, 2001), colleges and universities across the country demonstrated growing proficiency in crisis management planning, but most of this attention was directed toward the crisis and post-crisis phases. Little and sometimes no attention was directed to pre-crisis efforts. Then in April 2007, catastrophe struck Virginia Tech when thirty-two people were gunned down by another student. Less than a year later, a similar incident happened at Northern Illinois University, where an assailant killed five people and wounded twenty-one others. As a result of these incidents, questions were posed as to what higher education should do to prevent such incidents from happening, and what can we do to better protect the students, faculty, and staff within our campus communities. Crisis management efforts began to put a much greater focus on pre-crisis actions.

President Barack Obama signed a Presidential Policy Directive (PPD)-8 (US Department of Homeland Security, 2011) in March 2011 designed to strengthen national preparedness to threats that pose the greatest risk to the security of our nation. This directive redefined our national preparedness system into "a series of integrated planning frameworks covering prevention, protection, mitigation, response and recovery" (p. 3). Through the directive, government agencies were charged with providing businesses, communities, families, and individuals with recommendations and guidance to assist in their own preparedness planning.

Recommendations and guidance for higher education were provided in June 2013, when the *Guide for Developing High-Quality Emergency Operations Plans for Institutions of Higher Education* was issued by the US Department of Education (2013). This *Guide* defined the five planning frameworks for institutions of higher education (IHE) as follows:

1. *Prevention*: The capabilities necessary to avoid, deter, or stop an imminent crime or threatened or actual mass casualty incident. Prevention is the action IHEs take to prevent threatened or actual incident from occurring.
2. *Protection*: The capabilities to secure IHEs against acts of terrorism and man-made or natural disasters. Protection focuses on ongoing actions that protect students, teachers, staff visitors, networks, and property from a threat or hazard.
3. *Mitigation*: The capabilities necessary to eliminate or reduce the loss of life and property damage by lessening the impact of an event or emergency. Mitigation also means reducing the likelihood that threats and hazards will happen.

4. *Response:* The capabilities necessary to stabilize an emergency once it has already happened or is certain to happen in an unpreventable way; establish a safe and secure environment; save lives and property; and facilitate the transition to recovery.
5. *Recovery:* The capabilities necessary to assist IHEs affected by an event or emergency in restoring the learning environment (p. 3).

Crisis Levels and Scalability

In addition to addressing the various phases of the crisis management process, effective preparedness plans must also be able to adapt to the different crisis levels. With some crisis events the scope and size of the situation is apparent from the onset. Other crisis events can evolve over time or rapidly escalate. Preparedness plans need to be able to mobilize the appropriate personnel, systems, and resources necessary to manage the situation.

Emergency management is the term most often used by government agencies and local authorities and is typically associated with types of events that pose the threat of mass casualties or major damage to infrastructure or facilities. Such events include active shooter situations, fires, floods, hurricanes, earthquakes and pandemic influenza. This is the context in which the D.O.E. *Guide* was written. These large-scale events, or *disasters*, affect not only the institution but the surrounding community as well, and appropriate management of these events draws upon the resources of the local municipality, county, state, and sometimes the federal government in addition to the institution.

A campus *crisis* "is an event, which is often sudden or unexpected that disrupts the normal operations of the institution or its educational mission and threatens the well-being of its personnel, property, financial resources and/or reputation of the institution" (Zdziarski, 2006, p. 5). Such events significantly affect or disrupt the entire institution, but may have little or no direct effect on the surrounding community.

As student affairs professionals, however, we deal with crises on a regular basis. These smaller, more localized events, or *critical incidents*, significantly affect a subset of the campus population but do not affect the normal operations of the institution. Responding to these types of incidents is what we excel at, and often we develop a positive reputation across campus for managing these situations well. It is not uncommon, because of our prowess at managing these types of situations, that student affairs professionals are sometimes engaged as a campus crisis manager or crisis management team leader. Although smaller and limited in the scope of their impact, effectively managing these incidents is no less important than larger-scale campus crises or emergencies, because if not handled well, these incidents can spiral out of control and easily become campus crises or emergencies.

It is important for student affairs administrators to understand the crisis levels and ensure that preparedness plans are scalable to address the issues presented by each of these different levels of crisis, whether the event is a disaster, a campus crisis, or a critical incident.

Stakeholders

A variety of individuals, groups, and organizations can be affected by a crisis or affect an institution's ability to manage a crisis. These stakeholders may be both internal and external to the institution. The primary institutional stakeholders are students, faculty, staff, and visitors to the campus. A secondary set of institutional stakeholders includes parents, alumni, trustees, and donors. Tertiary stakeholders include local agencies (for example, police, fire, medical), government officials, media, and the general public. In order to effectively plan and prepare for a crisis, administrators must understand who these stakeholders are, how a crisis might affect them, and how they might be able to assist in managing a crisis event.

Though primary stakeholders are the most vulnerable to a crisis situation and the individuals we have a responsibility to protect, they can also play significant roles in preventing, responding, and recovering from crises. In particular, it is important not to overlook the role that students can play in preparedness planning. Students are often the most in tune with what is going on around campus and can be instrumental in identifying and detecting potential threats or problems. Students know best how they communicate and interact, and can provide useful insight in the most effective ways to alert the campus about potential crises or assist in locating individuals who may be unaccounted for. Student leaders are frequently called upon to serve as spokespersons for the institution in times of crisis, and have contributed significantly in recovery efforts by planning memorials and other events that can assist in the healing process after a crisis event. Recognizing the roles that students are often called upon to play during campus crisis events, administrators would be wise to regularly engage student leaders in appropriate crisis training. For example, residence hall staff, student government leaders, and Greek organization leaders are ideal groups of students to provide with specific emergency management training. It is in many ways an extension of bystander intervention training most campuses provide to the general student population. Such training should provide key student leaders with knowledge and understanding of institutional emergency plans and how to inform and access relevant institutional resources.

External stakeholders such as local emergency personnel can also play major roles in institutional preparedness plans. The services and support of police, fire, and medical personnel within the surrounding community are vital in many crisis situations, and their support greatly increases an institution's response capabilities. However, understanding how these agencies coordinate and interact with institutional units and personnel well before a crisis event occurs is essential. Including appropriate representatives from these agencies in the planning process is a critical step in preparedness planning and ensuring effective interagency operability.

It may be readily apparent how a crisis may affect some stakeholders, and how other stakeholders may be able to affect the management of a crisis situation, but well-developed preparedness plans should include an in-depth assessment of all potential stakeholders, and relevant stakeholders should be actively engaged in the planning process.

Crisis Management Teams

A crisis management team (CMT) is a multidisciplinary team of individuals that is created to perform three primary functions: (1) develop and maintain a crisis management plan; (2) implement the plan; and (3) deal with contingencies that may arise that are not specifically addressed by the plan. Individuals involved on the team are key stakeholders who have appropriate authority over significant functional areas internal and external to the institution, and are able to access information and resources that are necessary in times of crisis. Team members need not include the top administrator in a functional area. However, members need to be positioned at a significant enough organizational level to call upon and direct the resources of the areas they represent, and also must be able to devote adequate time to team training and exercises if the team is to operate effectively in crisis situations. In addition to function, authority, and time, team members should possess personal characteristics that allow them to work cooperatively, solve problems, and resolve conflict.

Specific functional areas represented within a CMT vary based on the culture and dynamics of the institution. Some of the most common functions represented on a CMT include campus police, public relations, senior student affairs officer or dean of students, residence life, counseling services, health services, physical plant, and environmental health and safety (Catullo, 2008; and Zdziarski, 2001). Other functional areas should include academic affairs, business office, food services, human resources, information technology, international student services, general counsel, transportation, and a representative from central administration.

As this list of potential functional representatives to include in a CMT is considered, it also raises the question of the appropriate size of the team. Team size is a function of the size of the institution and the crisis level at which an event is being managed. The larger the institution, the greater the number of potential stakeholders who need to be included in preparedness plans. This also means that a larger institution has a greater set of resources from which to draw. Similarly, as a crisis event moves from a critical incident, to a campus crisis, to a disaster, a larger set of resources will be required to appropriately respond to the event.

The crisis management team, like the crisis management plan, must be scalable in order to effectively manage crisis. Though the overall team may be extensive, not all team members may be initially engaged in the response. Instead, as a crisis event unfolds and escalates, additional team members are called upon to address the emerging issues and needs as they are identified. When crisis level moves from a campus crisis to a disaster, or when the crisis event requires an institution to engage external emergency services and resources, it is critical that the institutional crisis management team integrate smoothly with these agencies.

Under the Homeland Security Presidential Directive 5 (US Department of Homeland Security, 2003) all federal, state, tribal, and local organizations are required to coordinate interagency operations using the National Incident Command System (NIMS). Originally developed for fighting wildfires in the western United States, NIMS provides a comprehensive, nationwide, systematic approach to incident management. NIMS guides "departments and agencies at all levels of government, nongovernmental organizations, and the private sector to work seamlessly to prevent, protect against, respond to, recover from, and mitigate the effects of incidents, regardless of cause, size, location, or complexity" (US Department of Homeland Security, 2008, p. 1). A key component of NIMS is the Incident Command System that includes five operational components: command, planning, operations, logistics, and finance/administration. In consultation with local emergency management personnel, campus crisis management teams should align functional responsibilities of the various team members within the five operational components of the incident command structure. In addition, institutional team members should complete the appropriate online NIMS training courses as outlined by FEMA (see NIMS Implementation Activities for Schools and Higher Education Institutions). With an understanding of how to function in an Incident Command System, institutions are able to work more effectively with emergency responders in their communities and better address the needs of the campus community in a disaster.

Crisis Management Plans

It is important to recognize that there is no singular crisis management plan. There are plans at the national, state, county, local, institutional, divisional, departmental, and office levels. Each of these plans must be integrated with the plans above and below them. With this in mind, crisis management is not something that is limited to just senior administrators. Department heads, middle managers, and even new professionals all have a role in developing and maintaining campus crisis management plans.

Crisis Audit

Before beginning to develop a crisis plan it is necessary to first assess the institutional environment and its susceptibility to crisis. In conducting this kind of crisis audit it is important to understand the unique characteristics of the institution as well as the different types of crisis events that might occur.

As indicated earlier in this book (see, in particular, chapter 2), every institution is different and has unique characteristics. The size of the institution, its student profile, the location of the institution, the number and type of facilities, the academic programs offered, and the availability of community resources are all salient factors to consider in preparedness planning.

Given these characteristics, campus administrators need to consider what crisis events might occur and what would be the impact on the campus community if certain crisis events were to occur. Preparedness planning should be focused not only on crisis events that are most likely to occur, but also on those events that, although unlikely, could have a devastating effect on the campus community. For example, an active shooter situation is not likely to occur on most campuses; however, events within the past decade have clearly illustrated the need for all institutions to develop plans for such an event.

The crisis management literature (Clement & Rickard, 1992; Koovor-Misra, 1995; Meyers, 1986; and Mitroff, Pauchant, & Shrivastava, 1988) notes that the various crisis events group together in distinctive clusters or types of crises. Though institutional preparedness planning needs to take an "all-hazards" approach, the types of crises most common to higher education are environmental, facility, and human crises (Zdziarski, Dunkel, & Rollo, 2007). Environmental crises are crisis events that originate from the environment or nature and include such events as earthquakes, hurricanes, and floods. Facility crises are events that originate in a campus facility or structure, including fires, chemical leaks, and power outages. Human crises are events that are originated by human beings, whether by conscious act or error, and include criminal acts, accidents, and mental health situations.

Components of Crisis Management Plan

A crisis management or emergency preparedness plan has three key components: a basic plan, functional annexes, and situational annexes. A basic plan should outline the overall process and procedures for how the institution or unit will operate before, during, and after a crisis. The basic plan explains the purpose of the plan, how the plan is activated, who has authority to implement the plan, and defines the fundamental steps in the plans implementation and how the plan relates to other unit or agency plans (that is, local city or county emergency operations plans).

The annexes are protocols that extend the basic plan by providing more detailed action steps necessary to perform specific functions or address specific situations. These protocols should take the form of checklists, rather than extensive narratives, in order to trigger personnel to take essential actions that they have been trained to perform. Functional annexes outline key functions or operations the institution or unit must perform that are independent of a specific crisis event. Functional annexes may include communication and notification protocols, security protocols, early/rapid assessment protocols, evacuation protocols, shelter-in-place protocols, accounting for personnel protocols, medical and mental health protocols, continuity of operations, and recovery protocols.

Situational annexes are threat or hazard specific and outline detailed action steps related to a particular crisis event (for example, tornado, explosion, active shooter). Each of these situational protocols should address the unit's actions unique to that particular crisis event, and where appropriate, reference a functional annex that may apply to that situation. For example, an active shooter protocol may reference functional annexes for notification, and shelter-in-place, rather than repeat these action steps within the situational annex. At its foundation, a preparedness plan should have at least one solid situational protocol for a significant environmental, facility, and human crisis that may affect the campus. This could include protocols for a hurricane (depending on the geographic location), a building fire or explosion, and an active shooter. Additional protocols can be added as time and experience identify gaps or areas where there is a need to provide more specific guidance to crisis team members.

Through this combination of functional and situational annexes preparedness planning should focus on developing a solid portfolio of protocols that are best suited to address the types of crises an institution might experience. When developing a preparedness plan, it is easy to develop an expansive list of crisis events or situations that could potentially affect the campus community. Creating detailed plans and protocols for each of these situations, however, is not effective or practical. Each crisis event is unique, and rarely do detailed plans address every contingency campus administrators might face as a crisis event unfolds. Therefore, functional protocols that address key operations an institution or unit must perform allow crisis managers to adapt to the situation and address the situation as it develops. A good preparedness plan provides a solid portfolio of functional and situational protocols that are best suited to address the types of crises an institution might experience.

Protocols

The remainder of this chapter is devoted to discussing some functional protocols of significant relevance to student affairs professionals. These protocols are presented in relation to the five phases of the crisis management process: prevention, protection, mitigation, response, and recovery. These are by no means the only functional protocols that would exist in a preparedness plan. For example, evaluation is a very important protocol that should be incorporated into all crisis management plans. These five categories match the planning frameworks for institutions of higher education identified by the US Department of Education (2013). These examples are intended to illustrate the important functions that student affairs professionals participate in and the need for advance planning and consideration of how to carry out these functions in times of crisis.

Prevention

Occasionally we watch a television news story or read a news report about a violent incident that has recently occurred. Often these news reports provide accounts from individuals who either knew or had interactions with the violent perpetrator. These accounts typically provide information about previous conversations, observations, or behaviors that seem to foretell the violence that has just been witnessed. These reports often imply, and sometimes claim outright, that this person's violent acts could have easily been predicted, and someone should have done something to stop it.

Mental health professionals however, clearly state (Brown, 2013) that there is no reliable way to predict whether a person will commit a violent act. Instead we need to seek to identify individuals that exhibit distressing and disruptive behaviors, and intervene with support and assistance for these individuals to address their needs and attempt to resolve issues that could lead to potential violent outcomes. The overall goal is early intervention to ensure the health, safety, and success of the individual as well as the rest of the campus community.

Though many campuses have had informal approaches to providing this kind of care to members of the campus community, it is now an expectation and sometimes a legal requirement (for example, Virginia §23–9.2:10) that institutions of higher education develop and maintain formal systems for the identification and assessment of individuals whose behavior may present a threat, as well as policies and procedures for the intervention and resolution of that threat.

Most often a team of individuals is assembled to monitor the campus environment by collecting reports and information to identify and address situations in which the behavior of members of the campus community indicates that they are distressed or disruptive and may pose a threat to themselves or others. When the emphasis on creating such formalized teams first began, they were typically referred to as threat assessment teams. This name, however, conveyed to the campus community that the individuals reviewed by the team posed a specific threat to the campus. Instead, the real focus of such teams is on early intervention, support, and assistance to prevent the situation from escalating and becoming a real threat. For this reason, many institutions have adopted names such as behavioral intervention teams (BIT), care teams, or students of concern (SOC).

Like a crisis management team, a behavioral intervention team should be a multidisciplinary group of professionals who represent key functional units within the institution and often includes representatives from the following areas: campus law enforcement, dean of students, student conduct, residence life, counseling center, health services, disability services, academic affairs, human resources, and general counsel. Student affairs professionals frequently make up a large portion of most BITs. Because of this and the high volume of student cases on many campuses, BITs are often led and coordinated through the division of student affairs. Though the larger percentage of cases tends to be students, BITs should also address behavioral concerns associated with faculty and staff. In these situations, the role of representatives from human resources and academic affairs become even more prominent.

To be effective, a BIT needs information and reports on behavioral issues and concerns within the campus environment, and members of the campus community need to know and understand how to access the team and provide them with information. An important function of a BIT is to provide training to students, faculty, and staff on recognizing distressing and disruptive behavior and how to report such behaviors. A growing number of institutions are providing online reporting systems that allow members of the campus community to report specific incidents or general concerns about colleagues, coworkers, and friends, sometimes anonymously. Then, based on the nature, type and severity of the behavior those reports are automatically routed to appropriate members of the team for follow-up. Team actions however, should always be based on an individualized assessment that is grounded on factual information about specific conduct and behavior. Broad generalizations, unfounded fears, and prejudices should not be the basis for team actions.

The development and operation of a behavioral intervention team is an essential function of campus crisis management. Teams should be well trained, have broad awareness and acceptance within the campus community, and be utilized regularly. Documenting the purpose, composition, processes, and actions of your behavioral intervention team is a primary functional protocol to address the prevention phase of the crisis management process.

Protection

Effective communication is key in times of crisis, especially when trying to alert people of an impending threat or danger. An essential functional protocol for protecting a campus community is the emergency communications system.

In 1990, Congress enacted the Crime Awareness and Campus Security Act of 1990 (Title II of Public Law 101-542). It has been amended a number of times and in 1998 was renamed the Jeanne Clery Disclosure of Campus Security Policy and Campus Crime Statistics Act. Today, it is generally referred to as the Clery Act (see chapter 26).

Since the original act (1990), campus administrators have had a legal responsibility to provide timely warnings to the campus community. Amendments to the Clery Act in 2008 added an additional duty to provide emergency notifications. Understanding the differences between these two requirements and ensuring there are sound functional protocols in place for issuing both types of communications is essential to any preparedness plan.

Timely warnings are triggered when college administrators determine that a Clery Act–reportable crime presents a continuing threat to the safety of students or employees. Clery Act–reportable crimes are determined by two major characteristics: the type of crime and the location of the crime. Under the Clery Act, criminal homicide, sex offenses, robbery, aggravated assault, burglary, motor vehicle theft, and arson as defined by FBI Uniform Crime Reporting Program are the types of crimes all institutions must report. In addition to reporting crimes that occur on the campus, institutions are required to report crimes that occur on public property within or immediately adjacent to the campus, and in or on noncampus buildings or property that the institution owns or controls. The determination to issue a timely warning is made by one or more college officials who are identified in the institution's annual Clery Act report.

Emergency notifications are triggered when college administrators confirm that a "significant emergency or dangerous situation involving an immediate threat to the health or safety of students or employees" is occurring on the campus (US Department of Education, 2011, p. 97).

There are several key differences between emergency notifications and timely warnings. The scope of emergency notifications is much broader than timely warnings and covers crimes not reported under the Clery Act as well as noncriminal incidents. Emergency notifications are limited to incidents that occur on the campus and not property adjacent to the campus or other property owned by the institution. More significant, however, is that emergency notifications communicate situations that are currently occurring or imminent and must be issued immediately upon confirmation that the dangerous situation exists or threatens the campus. Timely warnings, in contrast, communicate situations that have occurred but pose an ongoing threat and should be issued as soon as valid information is available.

Whether an emergency notification or a timely warning, institutions must have the capacity to communicate this information to students, faculty, and staff in a rapid and comprehensive manner. Text messaging systems have gained significant attention and popularity for their ability to disseminate emergency communications. Yet, institutions should not rely on any one method for communicating emergency information. Institutions need to establish a multimodal system for distributing emergency communications to the campus community. Such systems should minimally include an outdoor audible device, weather radio, text messaging system, and internal mass telephone notification system (State of Florida, 2007). Campus e-mail messages, websites, message marquees, as well as institutional radio and television stations are also potential modes for emergency communications.

In addition to these traditional communication methods, it is also important to recognize the role that social media can play in emergency communications. Facebook, Twitter, Instagram, YouTube, and other social networking services commonly used by students has dramatically changed the way we respond to and manage crisis events. Social media applications provide an instantaneous and continuous stream of information, photos, and video from any individual user to the entire world across the Internet. Used by an institution, social media can be a very effective way to communicate with the campus community in times of crisis. However, social media posts can often preempt institutional alerts and notices and demand significant attention to manage misinformation or rumors that could rapidly spread. For these reasons, monitoring and managing social media during crisis events is an essential element of an emergency communications system.

In developing an emergency communications system, the strengths and limitations of the various modes of communication and how each of them can best be utilized needs to be acknowledged. For example, text messages and tweets provide the ability to send information to users in a very timely and rapid manner. Unfortunately, both have a limited number of characters that can be transmitted (generally 160 characters for text and 140 characters for tweets) making it difficult to provide detail and clarity to users. Thus, although text messages and tweets may be ideal methods for alerting members of the campus community that an emergency exists, they should direct the user to other sources (that is, e-mails and websites) for more detailed information.

Well-prepared institutions have developed emergency communications templates. These templates are designed for various types of emergency situations (for example, active shooter, weather emergency, power outage) and provide draft messages for the various modes of communication that will be utilized (for example, text message, e-mail, audio announcement). Developing such templates in advance can be extremely helpful in developing effective messages that meet the necessary parameters of the various modes of communication.

Another key consideration in an emergency communications system is determining who has authority and responsibility for issuing such communications. Though campus law enforcement officials play a primary role, it is not unusual for public relations personnel and student affairs administrators to be an integral part of the system. Individuals with this authority need to be trained on how to initiate emergency communications using the various modes of communication, and the system should be tested on a regular basis.

A well-defined emergency communications system is an important functional protocol for every campus crisis management plan. Student affairs administrators need to understand the system, know the different modes of communication used by the system, and be able to initiate messages when appropriate for the protection of the campus community.

Mitigation

The last thing anyone wants when dealing with a crisis is for individuals to unknowingly or inadvertently put themselves in harm's way. Ideally, people should stay put and allow the emergency personnel to do their work. The goal is to mitigate the situation and minimize or reduce any additional injury or damage from occurring.

When discussing crisis mitigation in an educational setting, a concept that is frequently advocated is a campus lockdown. In an elementary or secondary school setting where one is talking about locking down a single building, or a couple of closely situated facilities, a lockdown is a difficult but achievable strategy to protect and mitigate a crisis situation. College and university campuses, however, are acres, if not hundreds of acres, with educational facilities spread across vast expanses.

Aside from just the size of the campus and number of facilities, an elementary or secondary school environment consists of minor-age students who are on campus for a specific period of time. A college or university campus is made up of students who have the legal authority to make decisions for themselves and their own safety. Students move freely throughout the campus, accessing classrooms, offices, dining halls, libraries, gyms, and other facilities without a hall pass or record of their specific whereabouts at a given time. Access to these facilities is open from early morning hours till late in the evening. Many campuses, if not most, have residential facilities in which students, staff, and sometimes faculty live around the clock.

Given these key differences between elementary and secondary schools and institutions of higher education, a campuswide lockdown is not typically a practical or feasible alternative for many institutions of higher education. This is not to say that the strategy should be ignored or omitted altogether. Depending on the size and number of facilities an institution has, a lockdown might be a plausible action for some colleges and universities, assuming the adult characteristics of the student population and open nature of the campus are properly accounted for within the protocols. For others, although a campuswide lockdown may not be feasible, locking down specific buildings or portions or quadrants of the campus may be practical alternatives.

Campus law enforcement, in conjunction with local police, will most likely initiate such a protocol and establish a perimeter around the area designated for lockdown. Student affairs leaders need to establish procedures consistent with institutional protocols, yet appropriate to the buildings and facilities we have responsibility for operating, including residence halls, dining halls, recreational facilities, student unions, and administrative offices.

In conjunction with the lockdown protocol, an order to shelter in place is also often issued. This directive applies not only to the people in the area that is being locked down but is often issued to the entire campus. Doing so helps to mitigate the situation in several ways: (1) individuals are actively taking precautions to protect themselves; (2) it reduces the likelihood that individuals will inadvertently enter the area in which the specific threat exists; and (3) it clears access for emergency services and personnel to respond to the specific threat.

Though it is common for preparedness plans to include action steps that call for sheltering in place, carrying out this action step is an activity unique to each building and facility. Students, faculty, and staff throughout the campus need to be actively engaged in planning and training to shelter in place in the buildings and facilities they typically utilize. Student affairs professionals, regardless of their positions, should work with their colleagues to develop specific protocols to shelter in place within the buildings and facilities in which they work. Special care should be given to facilities in which guests and visitors to the campus might gather and how to inform and direct them to secure locations. The DHS Active Shooter Course Materials (US Department of Homeland Security, 2013) provide some general guidance in identifying locations to shelter in place and the actions that should be taken:

- Select a location that is out of direct view, and provides protection if shots are fired in your direction.
- Lock the door.
- Blockade the door with heavy furniture.
- Close, cover, and move away from windows.
- Silence your cell phone and/or pager. (Even the vibration setting can give away a hiding position.)
- Hide behind large items (that is, cabinets, desks).
- Remain quiet.

Consult with campus law enforcement concerning the locations identified for sheltering in specific buildings. Once protocols are developed, all staff and students within those facilities should be properly trained in these protocols to respond appropriately should a call go out to shelter in place.

Response

During a crisis situation the police, medical personnel, and other emergency responders will take many of the response actions. But a key role that student affairs staff often play in the response effort is to assist in accounting for students. Though different from other school settings, there remains a strong expectation and need of higher education to be able to account for our students' whereabouts. This is a challenge because our students are not minors and roam freely about the campus and off campus. As adults they attend class and participate in various activities as they please. So how do we go about accounting for students when an emergency arises?

In 1999, a tower of logs five stories high collapsed on a group of students who were building the annual bonfire at Texas A&M University. As rescue workers and emergency personnel poured onto the scene to render assistance, the primary question became how many more might be trapped under that pile of logs. There was no list of students who were working on site that night. Students from various living groups on campus came out to lend a hand as time and studies permitted. It was the student affairs staff on the scene that night who ultimately developed the list of students who were missing. Through their connections and relationships with student leaders, their interpersonal and counseling skills, they worked with the students who were on site when the collapse occurred and within the first two hours developed an initial list of fifteen students who were missing. After a variety of phone calls, resident assistants knocking on room doors, and other personal contacts, this list was refined to twelve. Twenty-two hours after the initial collapse the twelfth and final body was removed from the stack.

Every crisis event is different, and there is no single method to account for students involved in a crisis, but an early consideration for any student affairs professional when responding to a campus crisis is developing a method to account for our students. In many ways student affairs professionals are uniquely qualified for this role because they are used to interacting with students, understand the groups and affiliations they belong to, and have an established rapport with student leaders. A variety of resources might serve as an initial starting point. This could include a class roster, residence hall assignments, swipe-card access logs, or organizational membership rosters. From there it takes personal interactions with the students to determine who was there, who was not, and where they are now. These interactions could take place in person, digitally, or on the phone.

Recognizing that accounting for students is an important task during the response phase, student affairs administrators want to ensure that access to important resources, databases, and records are available in times of crisis. With advance planning, emergency protocols can be designed to facilitate the accounting process. For example, building evacuations could be designed so that individuals rally at certain locations to account for everyone. It is impossible to predict the different types of crisis events that might occur, and it is essential that student affairs staff consider the various possibilities and assemble some basic plans on how they might go about accounting for students if a crisis were to hit.

Recovery

After the danger has subsided and the immediate threat has passed, it is time to start picking up the pieces and bring the campus back to a semblance of normalcy. The recovery phase is when student affairs staff really shine. We are the caregivers of the community. We are there to help others and support them so that they can succeed. Caring for our students, faculty, and staff is an important function that must be performed during this phase of the process. There are several ways in which we go about this, each of which could be developed as a meaningful functional protocol.

One of the most common approaches taken to assist people in recovering from a crisis event or situation is to connect them with appropriate resources such as physical and mental health services. Having medical and counseling staff on scene is an obvious initial response, but it is important to recognize that there are significant limitations to the type of physical and mental assistance that can be provided to an individual on the scene. At best, this is a first-aid approach to the physical and emotional wounds that may occur from a crisis. Follow-up care and support need to be provided to assist those who may not experience the real impacts of the crisis until days or weeks after the incident. It is not uncommon to facilitate meetings with groups of individuals who may have been affected by a crisis (for example, floor meetings, chapter meetings, or department meetings). The purpose of these meetings is to acknowledge the trauma that participants have experienced, to normalize and clarify that everyone deals with the stress and grief from the situation in different ways, and to inform them of the various resources that are available to assist them. In these sessions, facilitators can identify negative coping behaviors and encourage members of that community to be conscious of these signs in each other and alert appropriate personnel so that these individuals can receive the support and assistance needed. How such meetings are coordinated, who should facilitate these meetings, and the general approach and content of such meetings are good functional protocols for any student affairs unit to develop.

When a death occurs in the campus community, it is sometimes helpful to conduct a memorial service. Such a service can help to heal the emotional pain after a tragic loss and begin to provide some closure for the community. On the surface it might seem appropriate to plan a memorial service whenever there is a death in the campus community, but some challenging issues can arise. Should you always conduct a memorial service? What if the deceased committed suicide or died while committing a violent crime? What if you plan a service and no one comes? Should you invite and include family in such a service? Who determines the content or program of the service? If the family wants a religious service, will individuals from other faiths be welcome or feel comfortable at such a service? Who pays for such a service? These are issues we often grapple with when planning memorial services. Some of us have worked through these issues and developed an understanding of how many of these things should be handled, but rarely are these things written down or communicated beyond the small circle of individuals who regularly deal with them. Having a functional protocol for conducting memorial services can be a useful tool when you and your campus are trying to recover from a major crisis. Discussing these issues in advance and reaching a consensus with relevant stakeholders about how the institution will respond to these types of circumstances without the immediate pressures of needing to act is a worthwhile exercise for any crisis management team.

Another frequent request that is often made is to create some type of memorial on campus. Such memorials can be trees that are planted in memory of the deceased, benches that are erected, or other artifacts that are installed. Though such memorials are well intentioned and serve as a mechanism for individuals to actively honor someone important to them, it is not practical to create a memorial for every request. Not only is there limited space on a campus for such memorials, but there is also the challenge of their ongoing upkeep and maintenance. Most campuses develop some type of criteria or process for creating such memorials, often requiring high-level approval from a committee or group. Alternatives are often the creation of a scholarship in honor of the deceased, but again challenges can be encountered in generating sufficient resources to endow the scholarship and sustain it over time. An alternative is to establish an account with your foundation to which gifts can be made in the honor of various individuals. Should gifts for any one individual be sufficient to endow the scholarship, then a named scholarship is created. Otherwise the collective funds are used to award a scholarship with a more general name or title. Memorializing those who have been lost is a common and helpful way for people to deal with grief. Having a clear understanding of the ways in which such memorials can be created and the processes necessary to create them, well in advance of a crisis situation, can be extremely helpful to the people we seek to support.

These are just a few examples of the types of functional protocols institutions might develop in regards to the recovery phase of the crisis management process. These functional protocols need not be elaborate and extensive documents, but rather checklists that provide a quick reference to the actions necessary to perform the functions. Some of these functions are things that individuals or groups of individuals have done repeatedly over the course of their careers, and it might not seem valuable to document or record them. However, personnel change over time, and it is important to retain the historical knowledge and experience of these individuals to ensure an effective response to a campus crisis.

Conclusion

Sooner or later, most student affairs professionals will be called upon to respond to a campus crisis. Effectively responding to a crisis and managing its many aspects, however, requires advance preparation and planning. Using the five phases of the crisis management process (prevention, protection, mitigation, response, and recovery) as a framework for institutional planning, campus communities can begin to develop plans and strategies not only to minimize the impact of a crisis event but also potentially prevent one from occurring. Such planning takes time, but is an ongoing and continuous process in a well-prepared organization. Understanding the different types of crisis situations your campus might face, the stakeholders who will be involved in such situations, and the functions each of those stakeholders will be required to perform are keys to effective campus crisis management.

References

Brown, D. (2013). Predicting violence is a work in progress. *Washington Post*. http://www.washingtonpost.com/national/health-science/predicting-violence-is-a-work-in-progress/2013/01/03/2e8955b8-5371-11e2-a613-ec8d394535c6_story.html.

Catullo, L. A. (2008). *Post-September 11, 2001, through pre-Virginia Tech massacre, April 16, 2007: The status of crisis management preparedness as perceived by university student affairs administrators in selected NASPA member institutions.* Boca Raton: Florida Atlantic University.

Clement, L. M., & Rickard, S. T. (1992). Managing crises. In L. M. Clement & S. T. Rickard (Eds.), *Effective leadership in student services: Voices from the field* (pp. 145–164). San Francisco, CA: Jossey-Bass.

Coombs, W. T. (1999). *Ongoing crisis communication: Planning, managing, and responding* (Vol. 2). Thousand Oaks, CA: Sage.

Duncan, M. A. & Miser, K. M. (2000). Dealing with campus crisis. In M. J. Barr, M. K. Desler, & Associates (Eds.), *The handbook of student affairs administration* (2nd ed., pp. 453–473). San Francisco, CA: Jossey-Bass.

Federal Emergency Management Agency. (1996). *Guide for All-hazard emergency operations planning.* (State and Local Guide SLG 101). http://www.fema.gov/pdf/plan/slg101.pdf.

Fink, S. (1986). *Crisis management: Planning for the inevitable.* New York: American Management Association.

Koovor-Misra, S. (1995). A multidimensional approach to crisis preparation for technical organizations: some critical factors. *Technology Forecasting and Social Change, 48,* 143–160.

Lagadec, P. (1993). *Preventing chaos in a crisis: Strategies for prevention, control and damage limitation.* London, England: McGraw Hill.

Meyers, G. C. (1986). *When it hits the fan: Managing the nine crises of business.* New York, NY: Mentor.

Mitchell, T. H. (1986). Coping with a corporate crisis. *Canadian Business Review, 13*(3), 17–20.

Miser, K.M., & Cherrey, C. (2009). Responding to campus crisis. In G.S. McClellan & J. Stringer (Eds.), *The handbook of student affairs administration* (3rd ed., pp. 602–622). San Francisco, CA: Jossey-Bass.

Mitroff, I. I., Pauchant, T. C., & Shrivastava, P. (1988). Forming a crisis portfolio. *Security Management, 33,* 101–108.

Ogrizek, M., & Guillery, J. M. (1999). *Communicating in crisis: A Theoretical and practical guide to crisis management* (H. Kimball-Brooke & R. Z. Brooke, Trans.). Hawthorne, NY: Aldine de Gruyter.

State of Florida. (2007). *Working group on domestic preparedness ad hoc committee on university and college campus emergency notification systems report.* http://www.fdle.state .fl.us/Content/getdoc/c2c4f5df-1fa5-4b26-adad-4d3e23665c43/ SWGUniversityCollegeEmergencyNotificationSystems.aspx.

US Department of Education, Office of Elementary and Secondary Education, Office of Safe and Healthy Students. (2013). *Guide for developing high-quality emergency operations plans for institutions of higher education.* Washington, DC: Author.

US Department of Education, Office of Postsecondary Education (2011). *The handbook for campus safety and security reporting.* Washington, DC: Author.

US Department of Homeland Security. (2003). *Homeland security presidential directive–5.* http://www.dhs.gov/publication/homeland-security-presidential-directive-5.

US Department of Homeland Security. (2008). *National incident management system.* FEMA Publication P-01, Catalog no. 08336–1.

US Department of Homeland Security. (2011). *National Preparedness.* Presidential policy directive/PPD-8. http://www.dhs.gov/presidential-policy-directive-8- national-preparedness.

US Department of Homeland Security, (2013). FEMA, Emergency Management Institute, IS-907: Active Shooter: What Can You Do. http://training.fema.gov/ EMIWeb/IS/courseOverview.aspx?code=is-907.

Zdziarski, E. L. (2001). *Institutional preparedness to respond to campus crises as perceived by student affairs administrators in selected NASPA member institutions.* College Station: Texas A&M University.

Zdziarski, E. L. (2006). Crisis in the context of higher education. In K.S. Harper, B.G. Paterson & E.L. Zdziarski (Eds.), *Crisis management: Responding from the heart* (pp. 3–24). Washington, DC: NASPA.

Zdziarski, E. L., Dunkel, N. W., & Rollo, J. M. (Eds.). (2007). *Campus crisis management: A comprehensive guide to planning, prevention, response, and recovery.* San Francisco, CA: Jossey-Bass.

PART SEVEN

LOOKING BACK AND LOOKING FORWARD IN PROFESSIONAL PRACTICE

The final section of the book contains both a look back at the practice of student affairs and a discussion of some challenges faced by the profession moving forward into the future. In chapter 31, Margaret Barr and Arthur Sandeen, two highly respected senior statespersons in student affairs, take a very personal look at the field as they have experienced it over the past five decades. They identify some of the major changes influencing those served by the profession, what programs are offered to students and others in the community, and how new programs and services have become part of student affairs. They articulate the need for student affairs leaders to be change agents, and provide practical wisdom useful to educators at all levels in the profession. The book concludes with chapter 32 in which George McClellan and Jeremy Stringer challenge professionals to consider new paradigms for practice as they continue to build on the profession's strong legacy of helping all of our students make the most of their precious opportunities to obtain a college education.

CHAPTER THIRTY-ONE

CAREER SPAN

Changing Roles, Responsibilities, and Opportunities

Margaret J. Barr and Arthur Sandeen

This chapter focuses on what has changed and what has remained the same for professionals in student affairs during the past five decades. In addition, it focuses on how responsibilities for professionals change as their roles within an institution of higher education expand or are refocused. The chapter reflects our experiences over the course of our service as student affairs professionals, and it is written with a sense of appreciation and obligation to the field that has provided us with many wonderful opportunities.

Change is a part of everyday life for professionals in student affairs. Students enter, leave, or graduate. Staff members are hired, stay, are promoted, or leave. Programs are tried; some fail and some are successful. Issues arise and are either resolved or linger for some time. Leadership within the institution changes, and new strategic plans are instituted. Support for higher education ebbs and surges. Some changes are fleeting, and some influence the landscape of higher education for decades. For all these reasons and many more, learning to deal effectively with change is essential for success in student affairs.

Despite all the changes in the assumptions and beliefs of the student affairs profession, professional values as outlined in *A Perspective on Student Affairs* (NASPA, 1987) effectively describe the core values of those who work in the field. Although significant growth and enhancement of student affairs programs and services has occurred in the past fifty years, the fundamental commitment to the education of students has remained unchanged. Student affairs professionals at all levels and in all kinds of institutions strive to help students. Thanks to the insights and efforts of thousands of staff, including new professionals, middle managers, and senior student affairs officers (SSAOs), the profession is now more inclusive, more on the cutting edge of needed programs and services, and better able to serve the educational and personal needs of students.

The authors both started graduate school in the early 1960s and then joined the professional ranks in student affairs. Both earned their doctorates. Both were highly involved in professional organizations at the local, regional, and national levels. Both have written professionally for some time and have taught while working full time as senior student affairs officers. It is from those shared experiences and personal perspectives, and from working in both public and private institutions, that this chapter is written.

We have identified some of the major changes that have influenced who we serve at our institutions, what programs are offered to students and others in the community, and how new programs and services have become part of what is now known as student affairs. Three perspectives are provided regarding how these major changes affected professionals at different stages and levels in their careers: one is focused on the new professionals, one on middle managers in student affairs, and one focused on the position of the senior student affairs officer (SSAO). The chapter closes with some of our personal thoughts and feelings regarding our shared profession.

How Change Influenced Student Affairs

The student affairs field expanded significantly during the past fifty years, and, of course, most of its growth was a function of the dramatic increases in enrollment in higher education across all sectors, including community colleges. In the decades of the 1960s and '70s, major changes occurred in the country as opposition to the war in Vietnam grew, the civil rights movement grew and changed laws, the women's movement became a cause for many, and the Watergate scandal made some citizens lose faith in their government. Technology came to higher education first with small steps, and then it profoundly changed the ways we communicated with students and others. As the authors began their careers in student affairs, every day seemed filled with challenges, and student protests regarding both institutional and global issues occurred on many campuses. All of these factors and more influenced higher education in deep and profound ways.

Changes in the Student Body

The college campus of today does not look like the campus of 1964. Women are now the majority of undergraduate enrollments on most campuses. Members of diverse minority groups, including African Americans, Hispanics, and Asian Americans represent more than half of the enrollment in many institutions. The number of Native American students remains small. The number of international students has increased. Older students are much more likely to be enrolled. GLBT (gay, lesbian, bisexual, transgender) students are visible, accepted, and involved on most campuses. Concern about political unrest has decreased. More students with both visible and unseen disabilities are enrolled. More students are enrolled part time. Mental health issues of students are of concern on most campuses. Many graduates are frustrated at not being able to find jobs in their fields. Technology has changed both social interaction and the ways students learn. These changes and many more have increased opportunities and challenges for student affairs professionals.

New Professionals. On many campuses, new professionals are closer in age to the changed student body and often understand them more clearly than anyone else in higher education. Often they have been the agents of change and innovation when addressing the needs of students who were either invisible or overlooked for many years. The best of these new professionals learned to deal with conflict and resistance to change within their institutions as they argued for more recognition, services, and compassion for special populations of students. For example, when the AIDS epidemic became known in the early 1980s, it was often the new professionals who understood this issue best, who knew the students affected by it, and pushed successfully for support for programs, education, and understanding. New professionals on many campuses took the initiative to challenge their institutions to take action. Moreover, in many cases, younger staff took risks for doing so, because their proposals were sometimes, not at first, popular with their SSAOs and their presidents. Their perspective and understanding of the changing student populations helped shape the responses of student affairs to these new students.

Middle Managers. Middle managers also took risks as they supported new professionals and helped them navigate the political waters of higher education. Without the support of their direct supervisors, the new professionals from the 1960s to the present would not have been able to be as effective as they were in bringing about change. Active supervision of new and eager professionals requires a great deal of time and energy by middle managers. As their departments grew, middle managers took on greater responsibility for management functions, including staff supervision and fiscal and facility issues. Their firsthand knowledge of students and their ability to translate that knowledge into programs to help students experiencing stress or needing support was very effective. For example, a health education support group, directed at graduate students experiencing serious personal stress, may be created by middle managers and new professionals because they know students who are experiencing those issues.

Middle managers also were inventive, and based on their knowledge of students and their knowledge of the campus were very effective in creating partnerships to help students flourish and expand their educational experiences. These middle managers became advocates for students with both seen and unseen disabilities and worked to make sure all educational options were available to them, including access to facilities. Becoming an advocate for students was sometimes uncomfortable but was necessary as the diversity of the student population grew.

Senior Student Affairs Officers. One of the most difficult roles for a SSAO is being an advocate for students, particularly in venues where they are not present or cannot speak for themselves. It is no accident that services focused on minority student populations, LGBT students, women, veterans, or a religious group new to the institution often start in student affairs. Seeking support for new programs within the academy is never easy because time must be spent in helping others within the institution understand why such services are needed and why resources should be spent on them.

Advocacy is also needed in policy discussions that can involve important issues such as freedom of speech. Annual reviews of policies regarding student demonstrations, controversial speakers, and other issues can assure that if revisions are needed because of changed conditions, new statutes, or recent judicial decisions, those revisions can be made prior to the time when such policies need to be followed.

Or advocacy can take a different form. At one private university, students expressed concern about the lack of transparency in the budget process. They believed students had no meaningful role in determining the budget priorities of the institution. In this case the SSAO and the vice president for business affairs collaborated and proposed to the institutional budget committee that students have a voice in the process through establishment of an Undergraduate Budget Priorities Committee. Students were appointed by the student government to the committee, surveyed student needs, and made an excellent presentation regarding their priorities. They were so successful that this approach has been in place for more than a decade and is seen by all concerned as a positive way to assure student input and involvement in setting funding priorities.

Finally, SSAOs must provide leadership to their staffs in times of crisis and help them understand their responsibilities when a tragedy such as a student death, fire, or a natural disaster comes to a campus. Translating general policy into understandable and supportable actions became and remains a key role for current and future SSAOs.

Specialization

As the field expanded, specialized offices focused on specific functions or groups of students were developed in student affairs. Examples include financial aid, admissions, career counseling, retention, judicial affairs, student activities, recreational sports, residential life, orientation, disability services, health education, and multicultural affairs. These new services brought opportunities for both new professionals and middle managers.

New Professionals. New professionals during this period of growth experienced unparalleled opportunities as both the number and variety of new positions within student affairs expanded rapidly. Moreover, the growth of institutions made advancement and promotion within the field quite common. The explosive growth of community colleges provided thousands of additional positions for new student affairs professionals, affording them the opportunity to assume more responsibility more quickly than they might have had in more traditional colleges. Movement from one institution to another was a typical way for new professionals to gain more responsibility more quickly, and it was not unusual for young professionals to move two or three times within a ten-year period. However, since 2007, and the economic recession, this movement from one institution to another has slowed considerably.

During this period, especially in the years 1965 to 1975, there was great social and political unrest in the nation and the world, and many new professionals struggled with where they should place the emphasis in their careers. With the new specialty services now so apparent, they had many choices. Although most remained in the field, significant numbers of new professionals decided to leave the field. Some may have felt trapped by the increased specialization of the field, while other simply found more attractive opportunities outside of higher education.

Middle Managers. The number and types of specialty units in student affairs grew rapidly during this period of expansion in higher education. The middle managers who were appointed to direct them often remained in their positions for their entire careers. Their positions assumed major fiscal, personnel, and programmatic responsibilities, and although they usually reported to the SSAO, many of them became visible, semi-autonomous managers on a campus.

Several studies of the roles of middle managers have appeared in the professional literature in recent years (Ackerman, 2007; Fey & Carpenter, 1996; Johnsrud, Heck, & Rosser, 2000; Roper, 2012; Rosser, 2004; Tull & Kick, 2012; and Young 1990). This increased attention to middle managers, their careers, conflicts, and opportunities has often resulted in better understanding and support for those in the bottleneck of the organization (Belch & Strange, 1995). Komives (1992) referred to middle managers as the "middles" and discussed the critical but sometimes underappreciated role they play in a student affairs division.

In many areas, middle managers formed or joined new professional associations in their specialty student affairs fields. Groups such as the National Orientation Directors Association were founded and grew during this period of expansion. Some middle managers aspired to become SSAOs and were pleased to find the path to the senior student affairs officer position now more accessible to leaders from diverse ethnic, racial, gender, academic, and experience backgrounds. Others, however, remained in their middle manager positions, assuming significant leadership roles on their campuses and within their specialized areas of student affairs.

Specialization also brought problems to those aspiring to be SSAOs. It became increasingly difficult to become a generalist in student affairs. For those with such aspirations, finding opportunities to expand their skills and knowledge in areas outside their specialties became a priority. In response, one public institution developed an internal fellowship program though which professionals interested in expanding their knowledge base were released from their home office for ten hours a week to work in another unit in student affairs. In addition, in order to broaden their perspective with regard to issues facing the institution, individuals chosen for these internal fellowships participated in a monthly seminar led by the SSAO and involving other institutional guest speakers. Experiences such as these assisted middle managers in planning their own career paths in a thoughtful way. Whatever the pathway middle mangers followed in their careers, their role has been critical to the growth and development of student affairs.

SSAOs. The addition of many specialized units to the student affairs organization required many SSAOs to expand their own knowledge about these diverse areas. Reading, attending professional conferences of specialized organizations, participating in webinars, and joining staff meetings in the specialty areas were among the many ways SAAOs learned about their new responsibilities.

No matter what the size and complexity of the institution, one of the primary roles of an effective SSAO is to be an excellent manager of the resources available. Use of those resources must be consistent with the strategic plan of the institution and the mission and goals of the college or university. Sandeen (1991) indicates that in order to be an effective manager the SSAO must have a plan and a "clear idea of what they want to accomplish" (p. 89). Although the SSAO may have a vision, it is imperative that staff at all levels become involved in developing the details of the plan, because those closest to services often have the most insight on what would help improve them. Any credible plan should be open to adjustments, but it should also provide a clear direction on how student affairs can and will contribute to the mission and goals of the institution.

One of the most important tasks of any SSAO involves supporting middle managers in their efforts to hire, supervise, and develop staff members. The skilled SSAO communicates the importance of understanding the mission of student affairs and how their specific roles contribute to the success of that mission. Developing and implementing useful and timely evaluation procedures for staff performance is important. Regular evaluation procedures help staff members focus on skills and competencies they need to master but also help the individual staff member assess her or his own performance. Keeping up to date on new theories, methods, and approaches regarding staff supervision and management is time well spent. Some resources include Kuk, Banning, and Amey (2010), Jackson, Moneta, and Nelson (2009), and Ignelzi (2011).

Growth in Professional Preparation Programs

During this fifty-year period, the impressive growth of graduate preparation programs in the field significantly advanced the quality of work by
new professionals and middle managers. Those working in such positions
were stimulated by the influx of well-prepared new professionals from a
growing number of institutional graduate programs. Student affairs staffs
became more diverse and less local in nature as a result.

New Professionals. These new professionals came well prepared in the
areas of student development, student cultures, and learning theory.
Their application of the theories they learned in graduate preparation
programs resulted in improved services and options for students.

Many new professionals took responsibility for their own continuing
education and helped create programs to advance their own knowledge
and that of their colleagues. As new skills and knowledge (for example,
technology) needed attention, it was often these staff who organized and
conducted professional development programs, both on their own campuses and in their specialized professional associations.

Reflecting on the expansion of professional preparation programs,
new student affairs staff who aspired to positions of more responsibility
recognized that earning a doctorate was often necessary for advancement.
Thus, many of them enrolled in graduate programs while they were still
working, and others left their jobs for several years to pursue the terminal
degree on a full-time basis.

Middle Managers. With the influx of well-prepared new professionals,
middle managers invested more time in supervision and staff development. They held prime responsibility for helping new professionals
understand the unique political and decision-making structures of their
new institutions.

Middle managers also sought advancement, and some returned to graduate school to earn the doctorate while working full time. Others returned
and studied full time to earn the degree and hone their research and assessment skills. This made them more marketable for new roles that were
developing in large and complex student affairs organizations involving
supervising not just one unit but several related units. Those experiences
made them better prepared if they aspired to the SSAO position.

SSAOs. A successful SSAO supports the academic mission of the institution (NASPA, 1987). Modeling behavior that demonstrates that support is

an important task for SSAOs. Many hold faculty rank themselves and regularly teach in graduate preparation programs in student affairs and higher education or in their specialized academic fields. In addition, divisions of student affairs under the leadership of a committed SSAO have partnered with preparation programs to provide internships, graduate assistantships, and research opportunities for students enrolled in those programs.

Staff Diversity

As graduate preparation programs grew and more well-prepared new professionals entered the job market, the result was a changed pool of candidates for positions. New professionals became more representative of the gender, disability, racial, sexual orientation, and ethnic composition of the students on their campuses.

New Professionals. In many cases, it was the diversity of these newer professionals that caused the entire student affairs profession to move away from more traditional approaches to students. Some of these new professionals faced special challenges as they came to campuses across the country. In some cases they felt isolated as the only minority person on a staff or the only woman in a department. Finding ways to deal with feelings of being "the other" (Madrid, 1988) became an important issue for many of these new professionals.

Middle Managers. Those in middle management positions carry the important responsibility of providing direct supervision for diverse new professionals. Simultaneously, many of them were new to their positions and learning how to supervise and help less experienced staff. The numbers of middle managers representing diverse backgrounds also grew. Many became pathfinders simultaneously helping new professionals deal with conflict and resistance to change within the institution at the same time they experienced difficult adjustments. The focus of many new middle managers was on serving diverse student populations. This was usually not an easy task, but their efforts paid off as they pushed for more recognition, services, and compassion for special populations of students.

SSAOs. The role of the SSAO also changed dramatically during these years. Individuals who shaped the early years of our shared profession came from the faculty and were chosen by their presidents because of their skill in working well with students. In addition to chapter 1 in this volume, the works of Knock (1985), Rhatigan (2009), and Sandeen (1991) all provide insight into the growth of student affairs from the early dean of men and dean of women positions into the broader role of senior student affairs officer.

There is not one clear academic pathway to become a SSAO. Unlike our colleagues in academic departments, where earned doctorates in specific fields are required for initial appointment and promotion, student affairs professionals can come from very different academic backgrounds and experiences. Whatever her background, the effective SSAO must have the ability to build strong relationships with students, faculty, alumni, members of the broader community, and other administrators at her institution.

As diversity came to the campus and to the staff the SSAO had to provide consistent leadership regarding the common goals and responsibilities of the division to students and to the institution. Within such a diverse community, providing a focus on the key values of our shared profession and our ethical and legal responsibilities to students is essential for the effective SSAO.

Emphasis on Financial Management

During the past twenty years, expectations have grown regarding the responsibility of all sectors of the institution to be better and more prudent financial managers. With the traditional emphasis in graduate preparation programs on student development, sometimes new professionals and middle managers entered their positions unprepared for their financial management responsibilities.

New Professionals. Although program budgets for which new professionals are responsible are often not very large, they provide excellent opportunities for less experienced staff members to learn the ins and outs of sound fiscal management. Uncovering hidden costs, figuring out what to eliminate to balance the budget, and involving students in decision making helps new professionals become a good stewards of fiscal resources. They can then transfer that learning to more complex budgets in the future.

Middle Managers. The budget responsibilities of middle managers can be large and complicated, because middle managers often have responsibilities for extensive facilities, staffs, and programs. Some of them discovered, to their dismay, they were not well prepared for these responsibilities. Astute managers sought help from both within and without the division of student affairs, read extensively and gradually acquired the skills to be effective financial managers. Those who acknowledged the importance of learning to be a good financial manager made themselves more valuable to their institutions and also made them better leaders.

SSAOs. Strong fiscal management is imperative for successful divisions of student affairs. "Budgets are really a statement of educational purposes phrased in fiscal terms" (Mayhew, 1979, p. 54). The wise SSAO understands the source of funds supporting divisional units and the restrictions, if any, on the use of those funds. If fiscal management is not a strength of the SSAO then she or he should be sure to have an excellent budget manager on their staff. Three roles are very important in matters concerning budgeting and accountability: being an effective advocate for needed resources to serve the increasingly diverse student body, being a prudent manager of the resources already allotted to student affairs, and being an active partner with the budget office.

Three fiscal issues have become more important during times of financial stress in higher education: funding essential student services on a fee-for-services model; moving additional student programs to the auxiliary services budget, and being able to offer competitive salaries, especially for specialized staff members in health services and counseling centers. Of greatest concern to student affairs is the fee-for-services model for essential student affairs units. Although it can be very successful in areas such as campus recreation, there are pitfalls associated with the model when it is the only way for students to get care for physical and psychological problems.

There are also ethical issues involved in moving some services available and used by all students to the auxiliary services budget. Auxiliaries are funded by the users through contracts for housing and food service or mandatory fees for users. If a unit previously funded in the revenue budget is moved to the auxiliary budget but continues to serve all students, what is the rationale? Is it really fair for one group of students to foot the bill for a service used by all students? It is clear that the effective management of fiscal resources is a key responsibility for the SSAO.

Collaboration and Cooperation

Good student affairs professionals have always recognized that to succeed there are few things that they can do entirely on their own. They need the support of faculty, other staff on their own campus, community leaders, alumni, students, and others.

New Professionals. Collaboration has sometimes been a difficult lesson to learn for some new professionals because they may be so focused on doing a good job in their first year or two that they do not look beyond themselves. Identifying opportunities for collaboration is also difficult in a new environment. Discussing with colleagues collaborations that were successful in the past is usually helpful, as is seeking their perspective on less successful collaborations. New professionals can learn a lot by asking and listening and by being inquisitive as they seek partnerships with others.

Middle Managers. The role of middle managers as mentors to new student affairs staff has become increasingly important during the past fifty years. Helping new professionals become confident and effective in working with others outside of student affairs has been a major contribution of middle managers. Middle managers who hold responsibility for facility management can also demonstrate how both collaboration and cooperation work. Identifying how management of the facility can be improved and clarifying responsibilities of multiple users becomes a key responsibility under such circumstances. Middle managers in student affairs who hold management responsibility for recreational facilities, residence halls, dining halls, student centers, health centers, and other facilities hold important roles. Exploring and implementing ways to make maximum use of those facilities to meet student needs has become a major priority for middle managers.

In addition, the involvement of middle managers and their staffs has been very important to the growth of service-learning opportunities for students. Not only do many campuses have volunteer centers, but student affairs often collaborates with faculty teaching courses with service-learning components. The student affairs professionals can provide support to these faculty efforts by identifying effective and sustainable opportunities for service in the broader community.

SSAOs. Whether the institution is small, medium-sized, or large, the SSAO must demonstrate leadership in reaching out and forming partnerships with individual faculty members, academic departments, and schools and colleges. The SSAO cannot expect staff members to engage in such activities if they do not lead by doing. For example, when James Rhatigan was the vice president for student affairs at Wichita State University, he and key members of his leadership team personally welcomed new faculty to the campus, forging relationships that lasted many years. Personal contact makes a difference and helps develop positive and productive relationships with others in the academic community. Many

SSAOs regularly attend faculty lectures and award ceremonies of their colleagues in academic affairs. Still others start their day by writing notes of praise to faculty who have received grants or honors or to students who have done outstanding service. Each of these approaches personalizes the relationship of the SSAO with the broader institutional community. SSAOs must reach out in ways that fit their personal styles, but they must demonstrate that collaboration and cooperation is an important value for them and for the division of student affairs.

Serving as an Educator

Those of us who work in student affairs teach in all that we do—our classrooms are just different than those of our academic colleagues. This notion is reflective of the work of Smith and Lloyd-Jones (1954) in their publication focused on student personnel work as deeper teaching. Peter Magolda and Tony Ribera provide an extensive and thoughtful discussion of this topic in chapter 8 in this volume. In addition to the information presented there, it is important to note that as professionals we can and should model ethical and responsible behaviors in our approach to dealing with crises situations, disciplinary issues, and student unrest both as a matter of good professional practice and as a matter of making use of the teaching opportunities afforded to us. How we do what we do is just as important as what we do.

New Professionals. Very often it is difficult for new professionals to see themselves as educators. But they can be very effective teachers to students through their everyday interactions as they meet with individual students and advise student organizations. Sharing their knowledge of theories and practices learned in graduate school can help students become more effective leaders. Developmental theories, for example, can provide a different lens to student leaders dealing with issues of inappropriate behavior by members of their group. Discussions involving how leadership theory can be applied to organizations in society can help student leaders see implications for their own leadership dilemmas. It is helpful for student leaders to know, for example, that fundamentally men and women approach issues of justice and fairness from different perspectives (Gilligan, 1982; and Kohlberg, 1984). Just as important, however, is demonstrating constructive responses to disappointment or anger with the behavior of students or student leaders. New professionals teach in all that they do.

Middle Managers. Those in middle management positions are teaching when they supervise younger and less experienced staff members. Helping staff members identify effective ways to work cooperatively is a key educational responsibility for middle managers. Taking the time to explain why their idea is not being supported or sharing the history of a relationship with another department or responding to questions about why a conflict is resolved in a certain way can all be effective teachable moments by a middle management professional.

SSAOs. Staff members in student affairs know a great deal about students and their experiences in college. Finding useful ways to share results of research and evaluation data with academic colleagues helps them gain greater understanding of the collegiate experiences from the perspective of the student. Providing information each year on whom to contact in student affairs if a faculty member or a staff member in another unit on campus has a concern about a student provides useful information to others concerned about students. Opening up staff development programs that might be of interest to faculty members or other administrative colleagues provides another opportunity to share information and data about contemporary college students.

In all of these ways and many more, SSAOs and their staff colleagues are educators in the best sense of the word. Modeling such behavior is among the key tasks for a SSAO now and will be in the future. With online learning opportunities growing for students, defining the role for student affairs services in that environment will continue to be an exciting challenge.

Adjusting to Changing Societal Issues and Norms

When we both started in student affairs expectations for the behavior of students were quite clear, especially for women. Curfew hours for women were the norm, coed housing occurred as separate wings in the same building, and male students were permitted much more freedom than women. All of those standards changed rapidly in the mid- to late '60s. With those changes came new expectations for student affairs professionals.

New Professionals. Some societal changes occurred in midstream for some new professionals. Rules for women students were changed on many campuses as a direct result of the nation's women's movement. The focus of their work changed from rule enforcement for women to instilling responsibility for building security; building keys were distributed and key code entries were installed in residences halls for women. Housing also changed in this period, with coed housing becoming much more common. By the end of the 1960s coed housing often meant alternate floors in a building or alternate rooms. Currently, student affairs staff members working in residence halls are faced with managing requests for coed rooms, housing for transgendered students, and other accommodations. For some new professionals, these changes were not unexpected; for others, adjusting to the changes was difficult.

Middle Managers. Those in middle management positions in housing faced some of the same questions and dilemmas as did new professionals. Often they were the first institutional officials confronted by parents who were upset with changes in living arrangements for their sons and daughters. Those middle managers who worked in other areas of student affairs also had facility issues to contend with in their daily work. Where could students nursing their children feed their babies? Could students in the process of a sex change use the locker rooms assigned for their new sexual identity? Those were not easy questions for an individual manager to answer, but middle managers in student affairs often provided the impetus for institutional-wide responses to such issues.

College campuses were not immune from protests regarding policies that were seen as discriminatory for women, for gays, lesbians, and transgendered students, and middle managers were often the first people to note the effects of societal changes on the policies and procedures for use of facilities. Finally, those working in health and psychological services had to assure that appropriate services were available to all students, including those with sexual identity issues.

SSAOs. The changes brought about by responding to concerns of members of the GLBT community simultaneously often raised concerns by parents, donors, and some religious groups. It was often the SSAO who was charged with responsibility for communicating the institutional policies and explaining why the changes were made. In addition, the SSAO often was called to explain changing institutional policies to governing board members, legislators, and others in the community. Simultaneously, the SSAO had a responsibility to staff to help them adjust to and support changes in regulations and operations to accommodate a changed student body.

Often staff members in student affairs were also the first to respond to requests for accommodations for students with disabilities, as more students with both hidden and visible disabilities came to campus. This required cooperation and consultation with academic colleagues to assure that all students received the services they were entitled to under both federal and state statues. The result was an expansion of student affairs, on many campuses, to include disability services offices and careful examination of standards for what constituted reasonable accommodations for disabilities under the law.

Growing Concerns About Psychological Health of Students

The number of students coming to college with long-term psychological issues has increased, and institutions have to expand psychological services to accommodate them. The demand for services increased and new resources were needed.

New Professionals. The growing demand for psychological services affected new professionals throughout the division of student affairs. All staff required clear explanations of the limits of service provision and, more important, needed to understand their own limits in dealing with student depression, eating disorders, and suicidal behaviors among students with whom they had regular contact. Learning how and when to make referrals for needed psychological help became an even more important skill for new professionals to master. Also, they needed to be alert to issues within groups or living units that came to the surface when a student who was a member demonstrated difficulty in coping and needed professional help. Feeling comfortable with their own limits and establishing strong working relationships with psychological staff became a key skill for new professionals to master.

Middle Managers. Helping new professionals both understand the campus resources that are available to them when dealing with students, and assisting them in honing their skills in making referrals, are key responsibilities for middle managers. Working cooperatively with the psychological services staff can help students get the appropriate help that they need in a timely manner. The important lesson is for both the new professional and the middle manager to listen carefully to students and seek help when the problem being presented seems too serious for their skill set.

SSAOs. Building a team that effectively works together to help students in great need is one of the most important responsibilities for a SSAO.

Consistent policies and meaningful staff development and training programs are essential, but perhaps most important is the attitude and involvement of the SSAO. Crisis situations involving students are part of the work of student affairs. This is another case in which the SSAO needs to speak up for students in need by advocating policy changes (if needed) for both withdrawal and reentry that support the continued mental health of students and those involved with them.

Conclusion

These certainly are not the only forces of change that have influenced student affairs over the past fifty years. They were highlighted because of their influence on the day-by-day work of professionals in student affairs at all levels. We both know from experience that involved supervision can make a difference in the growth and development of a professional in student affairs. Both of us were privileged to have such supervisors in our early years in the profession and are grateful for it.

We strongly believe that providing leadership for other changes to come will be a key role for student affairs in the future. Accepting the status quo is not an option for the active change agent who must look for opportunities to influence the underlying structure and culture of the organization or institution in positive ways. Sometimes it involves giving up something rather than holding on to it because it has always been a part of student affairs. At one institution, for example, an annual student-run musical production had been a part of student affairs for many years. In reality, the students involved would have been better served by being part of the theater department, but they feared they would lose their independence. Over a couple of years the SSAO facilitated an ongoing dialogue between the student leadership and the leadership in the theater department. They began to see a greater support system for what they wanted to accomplish; the move of the production to the theater department was made and was more than satisfactory to everyone involved.

Sometimes being a change agent requires the SSAO to have everyone stop and think about the newest campus crisis, be it excessive alcohol use or the introduction of a new drug into the campus community. Reminding those concerned that it is not a new crisis but is a continuing issue with new dimensions is important. By taking the time to review what has been successful and not successful in the past, using the literature and research, talking to colleagues in other institutions, and using the resources available to them, staff members can focus their efforts by using what they already know.

Being a change agent involves not just adopting what is new and trendy but taking the time to assess what fits the institution, the students, and the capabilities of the staff. Sometimes it involves confronting nonperformance by staff members and helping them understand new expectations. It may involve letting some people go or reassigning them to other duties. Change is never easy, but American higher education has learned to adjust to new expectations coming both from inside the institution and from outside forces.

Over the past fifty years a great deal has changed in student affairs. New services and programs have been instituted to respond to the needs of an ever-changing student body. Graduate preparation programs have expanded and new professionals are coming to our institutions better prepared than ever before. Diversity in all phases of life is evident both within the profession and the students we serve. With diversity has come a need for greater understanding of differences and also opportunities for misunderstanding and conflict to surface within our communities. As our students have changed so has the range and scope of services provided by student affairs, and that brings with it diversity in academic backgrounds and experiences of staff members providing specialized services.

There can no longer be an assumption that all staff hold a common understanding of the core values of our shared profession that are so essential for success in student affairs. Intentional efforts need to be made to share those core values with both new and experienced professionals and build a common base of understanding of the roles and functions of student affairs within institutions of higher education.

Challenges will still occur as we do our daily work. Conflicts will emerge on campus, policies will be questioned, demonstrations will occur, and tragedies will happen, but we are confident that the student affairs profession is ready to meet the challenges of the next fifty years in higher education.

We have been proud to be part of a profession that cares about people, is active in responding to needs, and consists of prudent managers who can make a difference in the success of students and others on the campus. Both of us have learned a great deal from our colleagues and our academic preparation, but we have learned the most from students who never cease to both confound and amaze us.

References

Ackerman, R. L. (2007). *Mid-level managers in student affairs: Strategies for success.* Washington: DC: National Association of Student Personnel Administrators.

Belch, H., & Strange, C. C. (1995). Views from the bottleneck: Middle managers in student affairs. *NASPA Journal, 32*(3) 208–222.

Fey, C., & Carpenter D. S. (1996). Mid-level student affairs management skills and professional development needs. *NASPA Journal, 33*(3), 218–231.

Gilligan C. (1982). *In a different voice: Psychological theory and women's development.* Cambridge, MA: Harvard University Press.

Ignelzi, M. G. (2011). The case for developmental supervision. In P. M. Magolda & M. B. Baxter Magolda (Eds.), *Contested issues in student affairs* (pp. 416–426) Sterling, VA: Stylus.

Jackson, M. L., Moneta, L., & Nelson, K. A. (2009). Effective management of human capital in student affairs. In G. S. McClellan & J. Stringer (Eds.), *The handbook of student affairs administration* (3rd ed., pp. 333–354). San Francisco, CA: Jossey-Bass.

Johnsrud, L. K., Heck, R H., & Rosser, V. J. (2000). Morale matters: Mid-level administrators and their intent to leave. *Journal of Higher Education, 71*(1), 34–59.

Knock, G .H. (1985). Development of student services in higher education. In M. J. Barr & L. A. Keating (Eds.), *Developing effective student services programs* (pp. 15-42). San Francisco, CA: Jossey-Bass.

Komives, S. (1992). The middles: Observation on professional competence and autonomy. *NASPA Journal, 29*(2), 83–90.

Kohlberg, L. (1984). *Essays on moral development. Vol 2. The Psychology of moral development.* San Francisco, CA: Harper Collins.

Kuk, L., Banning, J. H., & Amey, M. J. (2010). *Positioning student affairs for sustainable change.* Sterling, VA: Stylus,

Madrid, A., (1988 May–June). *Missing people and others: Joining together to expand the circle. Change,* 54–59.

Mayhew, L. B. (1979). *Surviving the eighties: Strategies and procedures for solving fiscal and enrollment problems.* San Francisco, CA: Jossey-Bass.

National Association of Student Personnel Administrators (NASPA). (1987). *A perspective on student affairs: A statement issued on the 50th anniversary of the student personnel point of view.* Washington, DC: Author.

Rhatigan, J. J. (2009). From the people up: A brief history of student affairs administration. In G. S. McClellan & J. Stringer (Eds.), *The handbook of student affairs administration* (3rd ed., pp. 3–18). San Francisco, CA: Jossey-Bass.

Roper, L. (Ed.). (2012). *Supporting and supervising mid-level professionals.* New Directions for Student Services, no. 136. San Francisco, CA: Jossey-Bass.

Rosser, V. (2004). A national study on midlevel leaders in higher education: The unsung professionals in the academy. *Higher Education, 48,* pp. 317–337.

Sandeen, A. (1991). *The chief student affairs officer.* San Francisco, CA: Jossey-Bass.

Smith, M., & Lloyd-Jones, E. (1954). *Student personnel work as deeper teaching.* New York, NY: Harper.

Tull, A., & Kick, L. (2012). *New realities in the management of student affairs: Emerging specialist roles and structures for changing times.* Sterling, VA: Stylus.

Young, R. B. (Ed.). (1990). *The invisible leaders: Student affairs middle managers.* Washington, DC: National Association of Student Personnel Administrators.

CHAPTER THIRTY-TWO

TOUGH QUESTIONS FOR GOOD FRIENDS

George S. McClellan and Jeremy Stringer

The typical practice in the final chapter of handbooks such as this one is to offer a synthesis of the information that has appeared in earlier chapters as well as some thoughtful comments about how the various identified themes or trends might play themselves out moving forward. The final chapter for this handbook is a marked departure from that tradition.

Our divergence from the norm is not an indication of any disinterest in or disrespect for the other chapters in this handbook, and neither is it meant to say that there are not important themes or trends that appear through those chapters. On the contrary, our choice for this chapter reflects confidence that the contributing authors have done well in providing an overview of the contexts, frameworks, purpose, and skills and competencies required for meaningful professional practice in student affairs. It also reflects our belief that the readers of this handbook do not need us to tell them what they have just read or why it is important. So, with those two ideas in mind, we feel free to take a different approach.

Peggy Barr and Art Sandeen, writing in the previous chapter, shared their thoughts on changes they have observed in student affairs and the roles of student affairs professionals over the span of their distinguished careers. In the current chapter the attention is turned to the future and in particular to what we feel are five critical questions for consideration.

It is not our intent in posing these questions to call into question the legitimacy of the field, as others have done in the past (Bloland, 1979; and Bloland, Stamatakos, & Rogers, 1994). It is our belief that student affairs as a professional field is well past this criticism, and we do not wish to revisit that discussion. We echo the sentiments of Tyrell and Fey (2011), who in their commentary on the future of student affairs, wrote, "Our critiques are … not per se dissatisfaction with the profession but a concern that the profession has failed to step back and truly be critical of itself" (p. 18). We believe that the questions we raise in this chapter relate to the future viability of the student affairs profession. The threats do not stem from challenges to legitimacy or importance but rather to matters of integrity, purpose, and vitality.

How Will We Respond to the Narrative of Efficiency?

Much of the prevailing public discourse regarding higher education is informed, if not driven, by what can be understood as a "narrative of efficiency." According to this perspective, students should start college before finishing high school. They should be steered to cost-efficient higher education options designed to minimize time to degree, and earning a degree is the one true measure of educational performance. Under considerable pressure from policymakers and the buying public, the higher education marketplace is responding with no frills and accelerated pathways to degrees (or badges, certificates, or other work-related credentials).

The implications of the narrative of efficiency for student affairs as we know it today are profound. Some students are opting to pursue the no-frills, low-cost options that offer very limited student affairs support. Although the majority of students are still attracted to more traditional college pathways, the number of months that students spend on campuses (either two-year or four-year) is decreasing for two reasons. First, increasing numbers of students earn a significant number of college credit hours, if not a full associate's degree, while in high school. Second, both state governments and the federal government are ratcheting up policy pressure designed to cap time-to-degree by placing limits on credit hours for degree programs or limits on the number of credit hours for which financial aid is available.

The pressures to reduce the cost of college attendance are strong. Accomplishing these reductions is complicated by an amenities arms race, especially affecting student services facilities. It is no secret that prospective students compare student unions, residence halls, and recreation facilities when making their college choices. The construction of new facilities has sometimes been criticized by a cost-conscious public. For instance, a new student union at the University of Wisconsin-Madison, featuring climbing walls, a wine and coffee bar, and bowling lanes was referred to as "opulent" and a "playground" in the local press (Carlson, 2011). Although some institutions look to eliminate or consolidate space on campus (Carlson, 2014), many other institutions see expenditures such as these as necessary to attract and retain students. Students themselves are sometimes willing to contribute to funding them, willingly saddling future generations of students with ongoing fees to offset their construction.

How will we respond to the narrative of efficiency? Will we seek to implement practices and policies that are effective in supporting the persistence of students from all backgrounds? Will we take it head on and challenge the premise that cheaper and faster are better or that graduation is the one and only measure of student success? There can be risks for both the individual practitioner and the institution they represent, but engaging in political discourse is essential in a public enterprise such as higher education (Tyrell & Fey, 2011). Will we reach into the high schools to work with students there in an effort to have time with them to learn who they are and how we can help them develop? Will we find ways to compress the learning and development processes that we have tried to facilitate for students during their four to six years on our campuses into the new two-year window of opportunity?

How Will We Respond to Continuing Inequality of Access and Attainment?

Thankfully, we live in a time when the law prohibits discrimination in college admissions based on gender, religion, ethnicity, disability, and other social identity factors. The facts on the ground, however, are that whether or not a person attends college (Aud et al., 2010), which college they attend (Wade, 2013), and their likelihood to attaining a degree regardless of academic achievement (Roy, 2005) still vary dramatically based on socioeconomic status.

Self-selection, social capital deficits, sticker shock, and stereotype threat are among the myriad factors cited to explain one simple unavoidable truth. Following more than five decades of government policy and public discourse in support of equal educational opportunity, the results do not provide evidence of sufficient progress toward the goal.

Although not a new challenge, the issue is of existential importance to student affairs given the profession's espoused commitment to social justice. Continuing to engage in efforts to help students from all economic backgrounds to enroll in college and to succeed in their educational pursuits will be even more challenging in light of the narrative of efficiency described in the previous section. How will we respond? Will we support new ideas regarding the funding of higher education? Will we adapt our professional practice to embrace liberation pedagogy? Or will we simply redouble our efforts using existing policies and programs?

How Will We Respond to Threats to Academic Freedom and Tenure?

Academic freedom is under threat from a variety of sources, including legislatures, court systems, corporate interests, and higher education institutions (Gerber, n.d.; Redden, 2008; and Salkin, 2014). So too is the system of tenure. Though a topic worthy of discussion in its own right, academic freedom and tenure do not apply directly to the professional practice of many student affairs professionals, certainly not those working in American higher education. It is perhaps understandable therefore that little attention has been given to either in the literature or conference programs of the profession. After all, why should we take up these matters when there is already so much on our plate?

An argument can be made that both academic freedom and tenure have contributed to the strength of American higher education. This is not to say that there are not times at which both have been subject to abuse, but on the whole our students have benefitted from faculty independence in matters of the curriculum, conduct of research, and analysis of social opportunities and problems. Beyond the benefit to students, professionals in student affairs ought to take heed of underlying effort to deskill the professoriate. Part of the narrative of efficiency, the argument goes that hiring adjuncts or non-tenure-track faculty helps control costs and therefore is desirable. Similar thinking can inform decisions regarding the necessary qualifications for filling student affairs positions.

How will we respond to threats to academic freedom and tenure? Will we purposefully educate ourselves about the history, contributions, and challenges of these two constructs? Will we actively ally ourselves with those who are interested in reinforcing both? Or will we stay focused on what most immediately affects our daily practice at the moment?

How Will We Respond to Charges of Administrative Bloat?

Benjamin Ginsburg's (2011) *The Fall of the Faculty: The Rise of the All-Administrative University and Why It Matters* and the American Institutes for Research's (2014) Delta Cost Project serve as twin pillars in the assault on administrative bloat in higher education. Although not the earliest voices in the discussion, taken together they offer a scathing indictment of the rise of administrative costs in higher education. Both Ginsburg and the Delta Cost Project make specific reference to student services or student affairs administrative costs as one area of expansive growth. For at least some of the proponents of the charge of administrative bloat, the argument extends to suggesting that increased spending in the area of student services or student affairs is particularly wasteful given that much of the programs in these areas are nonessential functions.

At a time when faculty members are feeling threatened by changes in the teaching labor force, critiques of liberal education and traditional teaching methods, and challenges to academic freedom and tenure, there is understandable interest from them on the issue of administrative bloat. The argument also resonates with students and family members concerned about the rising costs of higher education and with legislators and other policymakers for whom it is helpful to deflect the attention away from their own roles in contributing to those rising costs.

There are a number of common rejoinders to the charge of administrative bloat. These include challenges to accurate reporting bases on staff classification systems; increased staffing as a result of mandated activities or reporting; increased staffing as a response to consumer demand for goods and services; increased staffing to address changes in the needs of the student body (particularly as it relates to remediation or other student success issues); and increased staffing to take on duties and responsibilities that faculty are unable or unwilling to perform. With regard to student affairs, the assertion that the work is nonessential is sometimes challenged as well.

Summing the situation up, it appears there is a great deal of finger pointing going on around the issue of administrative bloat. Although lamentable, it is not all that surprising given the continuing economic and political pressures associated with higher education.

How will we in student affairs respond to the charges of administrative bloat as they relate to our field? Will we take a defensive posture? Will we allow the charge to go unchallenged? Will we take issue with the characterization of our work as nonessential, and will we provide evidence to support our argument? Will we take an honest and critical look at ourselves and accept any responsibility at all for taking advantage of situations (for example, responses to campus safety concerns) to expand our role and our numbers on campus?

Who Will Lead Us in the Future?

If it is not already clear from the information shared in this handbook, it is not easy being a student affairs professional. It requires considerable knowledge and skill as well as personal qualities such as empathy, integrity, resilience, and a willingness to be driven by intrinsic rewards more than extrinsic ones. The environment in which the profession is practiced is challenging. We serve a multitude of constituents, and their interests are not fully mutually complementary. In addition, as demonstrated in this chapter, there are important and difficult questions ahead of us for which the best answers are neither immediately obvious nor the solutions readily attainable.

Nearly half (48 percent) of new senior student affairs officers (SSAOs) obtained their positions through promotion from another position, usually at director level, at their current institution (Sponsler & Wesaw, 2014). This suggests a strong need for current SSAOs to provide well-organized and comprehensive staff development programs to enhance the preparation of administrators on their staffs to assume higher-level positions. Utilizing the ACPA-NASPA competency document (American College Personnel Association & National Association of Student Personnel Administrators, 2010) and the model iterated by Komives and Carpenter in chapter 20 are good starting points. However, the concern about who our future leaders will be extends well beyond individual campuses. It is the responsibility of the profession as a whole. Both NASPA and ACPA recognize the importance of preparing newly appointed SSAOs and provide seminars for new senior student affairs officers. However, we encourage more effort to identify SSAO candidates and nurture their development.

Given the opportunities and challenges ahead of us, it is important that we develop, select, and support leaders who can serve our profession and our students well. This is true on our campuses and in our professional associations. Who will we want those leaders to be? Sage veterans or fresh blood? Advocates, communicators, and salespersons? Great thinkers and visionaries? Pragmatists and the politically savvy? Students and scholars of the field? Local, regional, national, or international in their perspective?

Conclusion

The questions addressed in this chapter are profession-wide. They are especially applicable to institutions in the United States. Universities in other countries have other vexing issues, and colleges in some regions within the United States may have issues of equal or greater importance. For instance, in some geographical areas, student enrollments continue to rise, and some state institutions find themselves in the position of having to serve more students with less money. We might well ask the question in these circumstances, What is the role of student affairs leaders in articulating the case for increased funding to legislative bodies?

It is particularly fitting that Peggy and Art's chapter in this volume serves as partner to this one. Their book *Critical Issues for Student Affairs: Challenges and Opportunities* (Sandeen & Barr, 2006) in part informed our decision to use this final chapter to put these difficult questions on the table for consideration. They are tough questions about student affairs asked of good friends who share our love for the profession. We look forward to participating in the discussion.

References

American College Personnel Association & National Association of Student Personnel Administrators. (2010). *ACPA/NASPA professional competency areas for student affairs practitioners*. Washington, DC: Authors.

American Institutes for Research. (2014). *Delta Cost Project*. Washington, DC: Authors. http://www.deltacostproject.org/.

Aud, S., Hussar, W., Planty, M., Snyder, T., Bianco, K., Fox, M., Frohlich, L., … & Drake, L. (2010). The condition of education 2010 *(NCES 2010–028)*. Washington, DC: US Department of Education, National Center for Education Statistics, Institute of Education Sciences.

Bloland, P. A. (1979). Student personnel training for the chief student affairs officer: Essential or unnecessary? *NASPA Journal, 17*(2), 57–62.

Bloland, P., Stamatakos, L., & Rogers, R. (1994). *Reform in student affairs: A critique of student development*. Greensboro, NC: ERIC Clearinghouse on Counseling and Student Services. http://files.eric.ed.gov/fulltext/ED366862.pdf.

Carlson, S. (2011, April 7). New student union a "playground" at U. of Wisconsin at Madison. *Chronicle of Higher Education.* http://chronicle.com/blogs/buildings/new-student-union-a-playground-at-u-of-wisconsin-at-madison/29345.

Carlson, S. (2014, March 10). Less is more: Campus officials trim square feet to cut costs. *Chronicle of Higher Education.* http://chronicle.com/article/Less-Is-More-Campus-Officials/145229/.

Gerber, L. (n.d.). *Academic freedom under threat.* American Association of University Professors. http://www.aaup.org/node/342.

Ginsburg, B. (2011). *The fall of the faculty: The rise of the all-administrative university and why it matters.* New York, NY: Oxford University Press.

Redden, E. (2008, October 31). Academic freedom under many assaults. *InsideHigherEd.* https://www.insidehighered.com/news/2008/10/31/inquiry.

Roy, J. (2005). *Low income hinders college attainment for even the highest achieving students.* Washington, DC: Economic Policy Institute. www.epi.org/publication/webfeatures_snapshots_20051012/.

Salkin, G. (2014). Five issues that threaten academic freedom. *Education Dive.* http://www.educationdive.com/news/5-issues-that-threaten-academic-freedom/227738/.

Sandeen, A., & Barr, M. (2006). *Critical issues for student affairs: Challenges and opportunities.* San Francisco, CA: Jossey-Bass.

Sponsler, B. A., & Wesaw, A. J. (2014). *The chief student affairs officer: Responsibilities, opinions, and professional pathways of leaders in student affairs.* Washington, DC: National Association of Student Personnel Administrators.

Terrell, S., & Fey, C. (2011). The future of student affairs is dependent on choosing roads less traveled. *CSPA-NYS Journal of Student Affairs, 11*(1), pp. 17–36.

Wade, L. (2013, September 5). How socioeconomic class affects the college choices of even the best students. *Pacific Standard.* www.psmag.com/education/socioeconomic-class-affects-college-choices-even-best-students-65582/.

NAME INDEX

A

Abelman, R., 32, 39
Abes, E. S., 138, 140, 144, 152
Abney, R., 329, 331
Ackerman, R. L., 642
Adam, E., 440
Addelston, A., 293
Agbayani, A., 269
Agudo-Peregrina, A. F., 358
Ahlquist, J., 507, 595
Ahmed, 482
Ahn, J., 606
Ali, R., 217, 347
Alick, B., 144
Alito, S., 538
Allen, I. E. 344
Allen, K., 375
Allen, M. J., 568, 574
Alstete, J. W., 226, 227
Amaral, A., 463
Ambler, D., 369, 375, 381
Amelink, C., 36
Amey, M., 368, 381, 457, 458, 460, 482, 483, 484, 485, 643
Anderer, C., 597
Anderson, J., 269, 343, 561

Anderson, L. W., 575
Anderson, M. S., 31
Anderson, R. M., 212
Anderson, S. K., 461
Anfara, V. A., 138
Antonio, A. L., 292
Appleton, J. R., 16
Arcelus, V., 1, 49, 65, 66
Archibald, R. B., 73
Arellano, L., 61
Argyris, C., 138
Aristotle, 202, 460
Arminio, J., 104, 226, 227, 229, 233, 234, 236, 237, 402
Ashkenas, R., 380, 381
Ashton, D., 585
Asimou, H. M., 13
Aslanian, C. B., 345
Astin, A. W., 50, 52, 54, 138, 139, 145, 146, 177, 178, 277, 309, 311, 312, 334, 571, 572, 573, 576, 603
Astin, H. S., 309
Atwater, M. M., 144
Aud, S., 75, 76, 77, 78
Auguston, J. G., 596
Ausubel, D. P., 138
Avolio, B. J., 421

SUBJECT INDEX

A

Ability status and students, 275

Academic colleagues, partnerships with: action steps for, 444–452; conclusions on, 452–453; defining and framing, 434–435; four reflections on, 435–443; for seamless learning environments, 433–434; seven types of student-affairs-faculty interaction, 436

Academic freedom and tenure, threats to, 660–661

Access and attainment, continuing inequality of, 659–660

Accommodating mode, 490, 492

Accountability, institutional: conclusions on, 106–107; and Council for the Advancement of Standards in Higher Education (CAS), 103–104, 208–209; defined, 96–97; importance of, 99–100; relevant literature on, 97–99; resources on, 104–106; stakeholders for, 100–101; and student affairs, 101–102, 104

Accreditation organizations, six regional, 227, 228

Accreditation process, 102–103

Actual-to-Expected Graduation Rate Model, 182–183

Actual-to-Peer Graduation Rate Model, 183–184

Additive stage professional, 420

Administrative bloat, responding to charges of, 661–662

Alabama State Board of Education, Dixon v., 540–541

Alcohol policies and practices, 216

Alliances, university-community: benefits of, 483–484; conclusions on, 487; essential aspects of, 484–486; and leadership teams, 486–487; value of, 481–483

American College Personnel Association (ACPA), 17, 121, 209–210, 230, 231, 247, 249–250, 251, 257, 258, 259, 260, 407, 596

American Graduation Initiative, President Obama's, 179

American Indian Higher Education Consortium (AIHEC), 254

Americans with Disabilities Act (ADA), 77, 275, 548, 551

Annual giving, 516, 583–584

Annual Security Report (ASR), 553–555

Antidiscrimination laws, 548–551

Application stage professional, 420, 423

Arbitration, 492, 495

Art of Hosting, 500–501, 502

Artifact analysis, 63

Assessment: and Astin's IEO model, 566, 571–573; competency-based, 566, 570–571;